SCOTLAND
THE BEST!

Scotland the best!

THE ESSENTIAL GUIDE

Peter Irvine

MAINSTREAM
PUBLISHING

EDINBURGH AND LONDON

This edition 1994
Reprinted 1995

First published in Gread Britain in 1993 by
MAINSTREAM PUBLISHING COMPANY (EDINBURGH) LTD
7 Albany Street
Edinburgh EH1 3UG

ISBN 1 85158 622 9

A catalogue record for this book is available fom the British Library

Designed by James Hutcheson
Maps by Natalie Hunter
Edinburgh photographs by Kevin Maclean
Glasgow photographs by Kevin Low
All other photographs by Douglas Corrance
Illustrations by Glen McBeth

Typeset in 8 on 9 Stempel Garamond by Origination, Luton
Printed in Great Britain by Butler & Tanner Ltd, Frome

CONTENTS

NEW CATEGORIES IN THIS EDITION

ACKNOWLEDGMENTS

For this new edition I'd particularly like to thank all the people who wrote in with suggestions – an extraordinary and truly encouraging response to my first efforts. Most of these folk were, of course, unknown to me and although one must often rely on the kindness of strangers, it's very heartening that so many people seem to know what I'm on about. This edition is greatly enhanced by their correspondence. It would be impossible to name them all, but as before, and in addition, I would like to thank: Aly Bain, Susan Baird, Dave Belcher, Angus Bell, Gill Bellamy, Brian Burnett, Judy Clancy, Geraldine Coates, Craig Cockburn, Miles Cooney, David Cooper, Neil Dalgleish, Stevie Dunn, Stewart Grant, William Hardwick, Martin Hunt, Natalie Hunter, John Kerr, Kevin Low, Thomas Macinally, Glen McBeth, Mark Mackie, Kevin Maclean, Jim MacNiven, Della Matheson, Moira Pfusch, Eileen Rae, Marianne Ramsay, John Richardson, Marlene Ross, Billy Sloan, Billy Sloane, Fraser Smith, Robert Sneddon, Simon Sumner, Kim Tweedie, Fiona White, Philip Woika, Barry Wright, Tourist Offices up and down the land, and everyone at Mainstream.

INTRODUCTION

I'm delighted to be writing a new beginning to this Introduction so soon after the first one. It's not often, I'm sure, that it's possible to produce a completely new edition of a guide book in the same year. And there is a great advantage to this. *Scotland the Best!* took two years to write and research. By the time it was published a lot of the information was going out of date and we'd been through a recession which claimed many victims. This new edition has enabled me to bring the information up to date quickly with a much shorter time between collation and publication and to correct some of the gaffes.

It also allows me to include lots of new data and categories. I'm pleased that this has been a very interactive book and has generated a great deal of correspondence. This new edition incorporates ideas and suggestions from many people, all of whom understand what the book is on about; they have added to my own idiosyncractic impressions and have helped to draw attention to all the best things that Scotland has to offer.

Every item listed has been selected because it is better than the ordinary. Whether indoors or out, it has an atmosphere, a sense of history, individuality, class. If it's a business, the owners have an attitude to quality which sets it apart (and deserves recognition).

It will be obvious that I've described places subjectively, complete with prejudice and personal observation, but everywhere mentioned is superlative in some way and worth going to (assuming it's your sort of thing). The corollary is also true: if it's not in, it doesn't mean it's not been noticed, it just means it's not very good. This is not a 'list all the options' kind of guide and there are omissions, but I have not avoided the obvious, only the mediocre.

Scotland is full of places to find and call your own, and unpredictable moments can be the most memorable, so I hope that I've left enough space for that, and that after the big build-up and the detour, you aren't disappointed.

There is also the concern that when everybody knows about a place, its attraction is diminished and, in commending it, one is helping to spoil it, but I have to hope that everywhere that I've mentioned can cope with any increased numbers that the book may generate and that most people show respect. Scotland has become well organised in the last few years and most of the walks that I refer to, for instance, have set paths and carparking facilities. Scotland's great resource is its scenery and inevitably it has to be properly managed; that includes us.

I don't share the view that visitor centres are a blight on the landscape; they are helpful and useful. The existing infrastructure may point out much that is commonplace, but is still the easiest route to the best places once you know where they are.

In selecting the best from the rest, different criteria were used for each category, but factors like attitude and service, ambience and comfort, accessibility and (for walks or climbs) reward for effort, were commonly employed. Vast numbers of people – experts, connoisseurs, locals and regulars – were consulted.

I check out all the places that anyone suggests so that everywhere in this book, including all the new entries, has been visited and tried out. The Scottish Tourist Board local offices have been especially helpful. So although many others had a hand in the shortlist (and to them my great thanks), the final selection had to be made by a committee of one. Your disagreements and comments are welcome: please keep writing (see p.11).

As many folk know already, Scotland is one of the most beautiful and diverse countries in the entire wide world. In this book, I reckon, you'll find the best that it has to offer in these early 1990s. Go to it.

HOW TO USE THIS BOOK

There are three ways to find things in this book:

1. There's an index at the back. Towns are in bold type and may have a number of entries. If the first one is in bold type it means there is a whole page or section devoted to the town; the number listed is a page number.

2. The book can be used by category e.g. you can look up the best restaurants in the Borders or the best scenic routes in the whole of Scotland. Each entry has an item number in the outside margin. These are in numerical order and allow easy cross-referencing.

3. You can start with the maps and see how individual items are located, how they are grouped together and how much there is that's worth seeing or doing in any particular area. Just look up the item numbers.

    The maps correspond to the four city centres (of Edinburgh, Glasgow, Aberdeen and Dundee) and the 10 regions of Scotland. There's also an overall map to show how the regions fit together. The list of maps is on page 12 and the map section is at the back of the book.

    Entries for the cities have a map co-ordinate only, to enable you to locate the place to within a small area.

    All other items have a code which gives (1) the co-ordinate; (2) the map on which it can be found; and (3) the specific item number.

The Codes

1. The Item Code

At the outside margin of every item is a code which will enable you to find it on a map. Thus 625 should be read as follows:

> MAP 5
>
> xE4

625 is the item number, listed in simple consecutive order; MAP 5 refers to Fife – the map list is on p.12, and the map section is at the back of the book; xE4 is the map co-ordinate, to help pinpoint the item's location on the map grid. The 'x' indicates that the item can be reached by leaving the map at grid reference *E4*.

2. The Hotel Code

Below each hotel recommended is a band of codes as follows:

> 20RMS   JAN-DEC   T/T   PETS   CC   KIDS   TOS   LOTS

20RMS means the hotel has **20 bedrooms** in total. No differentiation is given as to type of rooms. Most hotels will offer twin rooms as singles or put extra beds in doubles. This code merely gives an impression of size.

JAN-DEC means the hotel is open all year round; apr-oct means approx from the beginning of April to the end of October.

T/T T/ means there are direct-dial phones in the bedrooms.

/T means there are TVs in the bedrooms.

PETS means the hotel accepts dogs and other pets probably under certain conditions (e.g. pets should be kept in the bedroom).

XPETS indicates that the hotel does not generally accept pets.

CC means the hotel accepts major credit cards (e.g. Access and Visa).

XCC means the hotel does not accept credit cards.

KIDS indicates children are welcome and special provisions and rates may be available.

XKIDS does not necessarily mean that children are not able to accompany their parents, only that special provisions and rates are not usually made. This should be checked by phone.

TOS means the hotel is part of the 'Taste of Scotland' scheme and has been selected for having a menu which features imaginative cooking using Scottish ingredients. The 'Taste of Scotland' scheme produce an annual guide of members.

LOTS Rooms cost more than £50 per night per person. The theory is that if you can afford over £100 a room, it doesn't matter too much if it's £105 or £150. Other price bands are:

EXP Expensive, £40-50 per person.

MED.EX Medium (expensive), £30-40.

MED.INX Medium (inexpensive), £25-30.

INX Inexpensive, £20-25.

CHP Cheap, less than £20.

Remember these rates are per person. They are worked out by halving the published average rate for a twin room in high season and should be used only to give an impression of cost. They are based on 1992 prices. Add between £2-5 per year, though the band should stay the same unless the hotel undergoes improvements.

3. The Restaurant Code

Found at the bottom right of all restaurant entries. It refers to the price of an average dinner per person with a starter, a main course and dessert. It doesn't include wine, coffee or extras.

EXP Expensive, more than £25.

MED Medium, £15-25.

INX Inexpensive, £10-15.

CHP Cheap, under £10.

Once again these are based on 1992 rates. With inflation, the relative price bands should stay about the same.

Where a hotel is notable also for its restaurant, there is a restaurant line below the hotel entry and a separate restaurant code in the corner.

4. The Walk Code

A great number of walks are described in the book, especially (but not solely) in section 8.

2-10KM CIRC BIKE 1-A-1

2-10KM means the walk(s) described may vary in length from 2 to 10km.

CIRC means the walk can be circular, while XCIRC shows the walk is not circular and you must return more or less the way you came.

BIKE indicates the walk has a path which is suitable for ordinary bikes.

XBIKE means the walk is not suitable for, or does not permit, cycling.

MTBIKE means the track is suitable for mountain or all-terrain bikes.

5. The 1-A-1 Code

First number (1, 2 or 3) indicates how easy the walk is.

1 the walk is easy.

2 medium difficulty e.g. standard hillwalking, not dangerous nor requiring special knowledge or equipment.

3 difficult, care and preparation and a map are needed.

The letters (A, B or C) indicate how easy it is to find the path.

A the route is easy to find. The way is either marked or otherwise obvious.

B the route is not very obvious, but you'll get there.

C you will need a map and preparation or a guide.

The last number (1, 2 or 3) indicates what to wear on your feet.

1 ordinary outdoor footwear including trainers are probably okay unless the ground is very wet.

2 you will need walking boots.

3 you will need serious walking or hiking boots.

Apart from designated walks, the 1-A-1 code is re-employed wherever there is more than a short stroll required to get to somewhere e.g. a waterfall or a monument. Found in bottom right corner of item.

The Abbreviations

As well as codes and because of obvious space limitations. A personal shorthand and ad hoc abbreviation system has had to be created. Some may be annoying especially 'restau' for restaurant, I'm the first to admit it, but it's a long word and it comes up often. The others are . . .

Aber	Aberdeen	Glas	Glasgow	pt	point/port
ADM	admission	hr	hour	r/bout	roundabout
Adj	adjacent	HS	Historic Scotland	rd	road
app	approach	incl	includes/including	restau	restaurant
Approx	approximately	jnct	junction	rt	right
AYR	all year round	L	Loch	Self/S	Self-service
betw	between	LO	last orders	S	South
Mins	minutes	poss	possible	stn	station
cl	closes/closed	N	north	TO	Tourist Office
E	East	nr	near	t/off	turn off
Edin	Edinburgh	NTS	National Trust	v	very
excl	excellent	no smk	no smoking	vis	visitor
esp	especially	o/look	overlooks/ing	w/end	weekend

The Celtic Crosses

Although everything listed in the book is notable and remarkable in some way, there are places that are outstanding even in this superlative company. Instead of marking them with a rosette or a star, they have been 'awarded' a Celtic Cross symbol, the traditional Scottish version of the cross.

✠ Amongst the very best in Scotland.

✠ ✠ Amongst the best (of its type) in the UK.

✠ ✠ ✠ Amongst the best (of its type) in the world or simply unique.

Listings generally are not in an order of merit although if there is one outstanding item it will always be at the top of the page and this obviously includes anything which has been given a cross.

Hotels and restaurants are also grouped according to price and this is why a cross-marked place may appear further down the page (crosses also indicate exceptional value for money).

NOTE ON CATEGORIES

The general rule is that there's one category per page, though some run over and a few, like 'Castles', of which Scotland has numerous fine examples, go to two or more pages.

Edinburgh and Glasgow, the destinations of most visitors and the nearest cities to more than half of the population, are covered in the substantial sections 1 and 2. Individual places in these sections are not marked on the maps but are given co-ordinates so that their general location can be found.

For the purposes of maps and particularly in section 3 (hotels and restaurants), I have used a subdivision of Scotland based on the current standard political regions, even though historical areas (e.g. Argyll, Perthshire, Aberdeenshire) are still commonly in use. It is expected that there will be a reorganisation of local government within the next few years. Strathclyde, a huge region covering a diverse area, has been further divided into north and south by the Clyde.

From section 4 to 12, categories are based on activities, interests and geography and refer to the whole of Scotland. Section 13 covers the islands with a page-by-page guide to the larger ones.

Section 14 is intended to give a comprehensive and compact guide to the best of the major Scottish towns in each area. Some of the recommended hotels and restaurants will be amongst the best in the region and will have been referred to in section 3, or even amongst the best in Scotland and referred to in sections 4 to 13, but otherwise they have been selected because they are the best there is in the town or the immediate area.

There are some categories like Bed and Breakfasts, Fishing Beats, Antique Shops that haven't been included because they are impracticable to assess (there are too many of them, they are too small, or they change hands too often). Fishing places would be spoiled if too many people knew about them, and for similar reasons I've declined to draw attention to (for example) Places to see Birds of Prey. There are some new nature categories in this edition, however, a list of which is given on p.5.

If there are other categories that you would like to see in future editions, please let us know (see below).

Your help needed (and win good whisky!)

As the vast correspondence generated by the first edition proved, the best way to improve and update the information is to hear from you, to know if you have found the information helpful and accurate and whether you agree or disagree with my selections. Have places lived up to your expectations and, in particular, are there any superlative places that ought to have been mentioned?

Please send your comments or suggestions to:

Peter Irvine/Scotland the Best!, c/o Mainstream Publishing, 7 Albany Street, Edinburgh EH1 3UG.

Once again, Mainstream have offered to supply a **bottle of good malt** (any from the list of suggestions on page 195) together with a **drum of Tobermory cheddar,** to the best three suggestions received by 30 September 1994. Recommendations can be for any category or for any number of categories, and anywhere that you recommend will be included next time, if it checks out. Please give reasons for your recommendation and specific directions if it might be difficult to find.

LIST OF MAPS

SECTION 1
Edinburgh

The telephone code for Edinburgh is 031

THE BEST HOTELS

1 THE BALMORAL: 556 2414. Princes St at E end above Waverley Station. ✝ ✝
D2 Meticulous refurbishment of familiar Edinburgh landmark refloated
from a recession sandbank by Trusthouse Forte. It has fine bars to meet in, a
business centre, the best hotel sports facilities in town (chlorine fug free), a palm
court for the taking of tea and luxurious and distinctive rooms with large
bathrooms and some ethereal views of the city. Informal brasserie and main
restau – The Grill (49/BEST RESTAUS) – are impressive. Parking is tricky.

189RMS   JAN-DEC   T/T   PETS   CC   KIDS   TOS   LOTS

2 THE CALEDONIAN: 225 2433. Princes St (West End). For a long time ✝ ✝
C3 Edinburgh's great city hotel. The individual rooms combine cosiness with
refinement; the suites are luxurious. Long corridors and spacious halls belie the
fact that it's a hive of activity. Quiet lounge for clients and/or afternoon tea. Many
regular visitors to Edinburgh wouldn't stay anywhere else. The Pompadour
Restaurant is very posh and very good (50/BEST RESTAUS).

239RMS   JAN-DEC   T/T   XPETS   CC   KIDS   TOS   LOTS

3 PRESTONFIELD HOUSE: 668 3346. Priestfield Rd (on S suburban edge of city), ✝
xE4 essential to book by phone (there are only 5 rooms) and to get directions.
Baronial mansion in own grounds, mainly known for its drawing-room restau
and 'upmarket' functions, but you could live in the bedrooms. The one single, the
Cupid Room, has no facilities but is probably the most charming single room in
town.

5RMS   JAN-DEC   T/X   PETS   CC   XKIDS   EXP

4 CHANNINGS: 315 2226. S Learmonth Gardens. Off and parallel to Queensferry ✝
B2 Rd after Dean Bridge. 5 Edwardian townhouses tastefully transformed for a
civilised withdrawal from uptown tourism. Well-balanced moods, shades and
furnishings. Views over the New Town rooftops from top-floor rooms. Rooms
vary. Cosy bar, large 'brasserie' and garden patio for those rare sunny days.

48RMS   JAN-DEC   T/T   XPETS   CC   KIDS   EXP

5 SCANDIC CROWN: 557 9797. 80 High St. Recently built, but well integrated into
D3 Edinburgh's ancient Royal Mile. Good centre for walkabouts and v calming to
return to. Comfy rooms have dream beds but thin walls and maybe not great
views. Gym and small pool. 238RMS   JAN-DEC   T/T   PETS   CC   KIDS   TOS   LOTS

6 ROYAL TERRACE: 557 3222. 18 Royal Terr off London Rd r/bout. With terraced
E2 gardens on to the private park on Calton Hill, this just off-centre townhouse
hotel is nice for the view. A trifle *nouveau* and a tad over-*riche* for some tastes.
Rooms vary in size but not in furnishings (attics cosy but costly). Good restau/
bar. 97RMS   JAN-DEC   T/T   XPETS   CC   KIDS   LOTS

6A THE SHERATON: 229 9131. Festival Square on Lothian Rd. Recent refurb has
C3 improved standards – esp the restau (The Grill) – in this city centre business
hotel which won no prizes for architecture when it opened at the end of the
1980s. Doing away with the escalators in favour of a 'grand staircase', adding a
few painting-by-numbers oils in heavy frames and generally tartanising the
bedrooms, has brought some cosiness to the concrete. Service is good. Some gr
Edinburgh views. The Terrace s/serv restau uninspired, The Grill menu under
Jean-Michel Gaufe is simple, elegant and Scottish.

261RMS   JAN-DEC   T/T   PETS   CC   KIDS   TOTS   LOTS

7 THE HOWARD: 557 3500. 36 Gt King St. Discreet, elegant hotel in a prized New
C2 Town street, which is cobbled and grand. The few rooms are all different but v
New Georgian. Coming here is like visiting smart friends. D/strs restau excl –
Gordon Inglis has his followers for dinner – and there's a splendid breakfast to
look forward to. 16RMS   JAN-DEC   T/T   XPETS   CC   XKIDS   TOS   LOTS

8 THE GEORGE: 225 1251. George St (betw Hanover St and St Andrew Sq). Room-
C2 wise a bit pricey for what you get (better on the top two floors which, at the
rear, have views over to Fife), but you pay for the very central location and the
Georgian niceties. Two restaus: a Carvery and a notable French, the Chambertin
(65/FRENCH RESTAUS). 195RMS   JAN-DEC   T/T   PETS   CC   KIDS   LOTS

9 THE ROYAL OVERSEAS LEAGUE: 225 1501. 100 Princes St. This is an unusual 'hotel'
C2 and by no means luxurious, but it has great character and is bang in the middle
of Princes St. The bedrooms have some of the best views in the city directly
across to the Castle. It's much cheaper than other city centre establishments,
which is why it's mentioned here. 17RMS   JAN-DEC   T/T   XPETS   CC   KIDS   MED.EX

THE BEST INEXPENSIVE HOTELS

BRUNTSFIELD HOTEL: 229 1393. **69 Bruntsfield Pl.** Convenient, refurbished hotel *10* between Tollcross and Morningside, 2km from centre. Brasserie (open till 10pm) *xC2* and conservatory. Rooms adequate and many look over park. Not so cheap, but more agreeable than many in this range.

50RMS JAN-DEC T/T PETS CC KIDS MED.EX

BRAID HILLS: 452 8888. **134 Braid Rd.** Southern edge of town, on A702, 8km from *11* centre (after you pass the sign, take first left then second left). Light, comfortable *xC4* rooms with open views.

68RMS JAN-DEC T/T PETS CC KIDS MED.EX

BANK HOTEL: 556 9043. **Corner of South Bridge and Royal Mile.** V central hotel in *11a* midst of tourist trail, small and convenient on a corner with 2 major hotels *D3* opposite. For half the price you get the same central location and more atmos. Former bank now converted into fashionable café-bar with bedrooms above, most have great urban views. Minimal room service. V European/capital city feel to the place.

9RMS JAN-DEC T/T X/PETS CC KIDS MED.EXP

THISTLE: 225 6144. **59 Manor Pl.** In the pristine streets behind the West End, a *12* small hotel just a modern cut above the rest. Big TVs (sic), if you're not going *B3* out. Short walk to Princes St. Bar.

10RMS JAN-DEC T/T PETS CC KIDS MED.INX

TEVIOTDALE HOUSE: 667 4376. **Grange Loan.** In quiet residential st beyond the *13* University area and 5km from centre. Fairly tasteful rooms and some individual *xD4* touches. One of the best and healthiest breakfasts in town, at any price. Kids made welcome.

7RMS JAN-DEC T/T XPETS CC KIDS MED.INX

AILSA CRAIG: 556 6055. **24 Royal Terr.** A couple of doors along from the plush *14* Royal Terrace Hotel and less than half the price (probably the best of several *E2* cheapies on this central residential st). Spacious, undivided rooms have views over the park.

18RMS JAN-DEC T/T XPETS CC KIDS MED.INX

STUART HOUSE: 557 9030. **12 E Claremont St.** Nr corner of main rd and pleasant *15* walk up to Princes St (1.5km). Residential New Town st and family house *D1* decorated with some taste and attention to detail. Best to book: people do know about this place already. Non-smk.

7RMS JAN-DEC T/T XPETS CC KIDS MED.INX

SIX ST MARY'S PLACE: 332 8965. **Address as is.** On main st of Stockbridge (St *15a* Mary's Pl is an extention of Raeburn Pl) and busy main rd out of town for Forth *B1* Rd Bridge and N, this is a tastefully converted Georgian townhouse on edge of New Town. Friendly, fashionable neighbourhood with interesting shops. More effort and efficiency than most GHs; and v congenial. B/fast in conservatory is mainly vegn.

8RMS JAN-DEC X/X CC KIDS INX

26 NORTHUMBERLAND ST: 556 1078. **28 NORTHUMBERLAND ST:** 557 8036. **2** classic *16* New Town houses adj but totally separate. Both intimate, elegant homes in *C2* which you will be made v welcome (if you can get in; unfortunately they're both booked well in advance). Do try.

EACH: 3RMS JAN-DEC X/T XPETS XCC KIDS INX

WEST END HOTEL: 225 3656. **35 Palmerston Pl.** The hotel in town where *17* Highlanders might feel at home. Gaelic is spoken and drams are drunk. Spacious *B3* rooms with furniture from better days look out on the elegant quiet streets that were built not long after Culloden.

8RMS JAN-DEC X/T XPETS CC KIDS INX

THE LINKS HOTEL: 223 3046. **3 Alvanley Terr.** On Bruntsfield Links, an open park. *18* Central and good value. Bar (tables outside in summer). *x D4*

7RMS JAN-DEC X/X PETS XCC KIDS INX

THE BEVERLEY: 337 1128. **40 Murrayfield Av.** Small hotel in quiet avenue in inner- *19* city suburb, off main Glasgow road. Centre 3km. Easy parking. Simple, basic *A3* accommodation at a very good price.

8RMS JAN-DEC X/X XPETS XCC KIDS CHP

TEMPLEHALL: 669 4264. **77 Promenade, Joppa.** Bondi Beach it is not, but Australians *20* may find this well-preserved pile of Victorian gothic oddly reminiscent of a *xE2* seaside hotel in Oz. Joppa is about 10km E of centre, even beyond the bright lights of Portobello, Edinburgh's 'resort', but a welcome awaits and there's a quiet strand to wander.

7RMS JAN-DEC T/T XPETS XCC KIDS CHP

ST BERNARD'S GUESTHOUSE: 332 2339. **22 St Bernard's Cres.** Like staying in *21* someone's flat in this quiet crescent in fashionable Stockbridge. Few frills but *B1* friendly. Pleasant walk through New Town to centre.

8RMS JAN-DEC X/T XPETS CC KIDS CHP

THE BEST HOSTELS

Edinburgh has some great hostels, and with many colleges and students who don't live at home, there are also lots of rooms available in the vacations.

22 **THE HIGH STREET HOSTEL:** 557 3984. 8 Blackfriars St. Just off the High St
D3 (the Royal Mile), close to Waverley Station. Excellent central location near pubs, tourist attractions and various action. Great buzz. You can stay for weeks and you might well want to! Single-sex bunk rooms hold 6+. No restricted access. S/C, but breakfast available. Understandably very popular, so phone first. Independently run (same people have one in Inverness, 665/HOSTELS).

23 **SYH, EGLINTON:** 337 1120. 18 Eglinton Cres. This must be one of the best
A3 YHA city hostels anywhere. Grand architecture, convenient location in quiet area and, most importantly, good attitude. Units for families and fours available, but mainly lofty Georgian rooms with bunks separated by partitions. Door open till 2am. S/C and cafeteria. Open all year except Dec. Can fax booking.

24 **MYLNE'S COURT:** 225 8400. Comprises Patrick Geddes Hall on Mound Pl and
C3 S/C flats at Sempill's Close, entering off Lawnmarket. Both part of a complex of university halls sympathetically converted from 17/18th-century closes and courts at the top of the Royal Mile, only 100m from Castle. For sightseeing you could not be better placed and the views from the rooms on Mound Pl are fab. Next door are some of the most sought-after flats in Edinburgh, as are these rooms for B&B. Phone first. Usual univ hostel facilities (no sports), shared showers etc. Vacs only.

25 **POLLOCK HALLS:** 667 1971. Off Dalkeith Rd. The main compound of
xE4 university halls, a village of modern low-rise blocks, situated 3km S of centre next to the huge Commonwealth Swimming Pool and in the shadow of Arthur's Seat on which to gaze or jog. Refectory and bar, squash courts. Shared kitchens and showers. Large number of rooms (850; all singles). Buses 21, 33. Vacs only. Not cheap.

26 **SYH BRUNTSFIELD:** 447 2994. 7 Bruntsfield Cres. S of Tollcross about 10 mins walk
xD4 from West End. Buses from Princes St (garden side) 11, 15, 16. Overlooks park (Bruntsfield Links) with Meadows walk to Old Town. Cycle hire nearby (Lochrin Pl 228 6333). Good Grade 1 hostel with late access, but only S/C. Open all year. Can fax.

27 **NAPIER UNIVERSITY:** 444 2266. Craiglockhart Campus off Colinton Rd. College
xC4 halls in high-rise blocks about 10km SW of centre. In grounds of imposing Craiglockhart Hospital where Siegfried Sassoon met Wilfred Owen. Too far out for some but buses 23, 27 from Mound. V good sports facs incl pool. Full meal service sometimes poss. Vacs only, avail may depend on conferences. B&B. Good value.

28 **QUEEN MARGARET COLLEGE:** 317 3000. Clerwood Terr. Way out, midway betw
xA2 main roads W to Glasgow and N to Forth Bridge; about 10km, so transport probably essential (or bus 26 from centre). Campus facilities e.g. refectory, laundrette, bank, good sports. Shared bathrooms etc and a bit dreary, so not exceptional value, but a private and well-equipped refuge from uptown hassles. Phone first. Also S/C flats. Vacs only.

29 **MORAY HOUSE COLLEGE:** 556 8455. Holyrood Rd. Another really well-situated and
E3 equipped complex off the bottom of the Royal Mile near Arthur's Seat. Over 400 rooms can be avail, mostly, but not all, singles. Excl sports incl pool (in another building). Cheaper than Pollock though without the campus village atmos. Vacs only.

The SYH(A) is the Scottish Youth Hostel Association of which you have to be a member (or an affiliated organisation from another country) to stay in their many hostels round Scotland. Phone 0786 51181 for details, or contact any YHA hostel.

THE BEST CAMPING AND CARAVAN PARKS

MORTONHALL PARK: 664 1533. 38 Mortonhall Gate. Off Frogston Rd, a kind of *30* inner-city ring-road. About 12km SW of centre. From South and City Bypass: *xC4* take Lothianburn junction into town and right at first lights for 4km. From centre: take A702 via Morningside to last left turn before bypass. Mortonhall marked, but enter via (and pass) Klondyke Garden Centre. 11 bus from town. Well-equipped park with 3 toilet and shower-blocks, shop, laundrette, lounge, play area and fully serviced pitches. Also bar/restaurant in converted stables/ courtyard serving food until 10pm. Coffee-shop with decent home-baking at the Garden Centre. 300 places.

MUIRHOUSE: 312 6874. West Marine Dr. 8km E of centre via Ferry Rd heading for *31* Cramond then right towards Leith; or Queensferry Rd turning right at Quality *xB1* St and follow signs. It's on the other side of Marine Dr from the foreshore but close to the sea (the Forth Estuary). Grassy. Not large and seems isolated, though not that far from town. No bar/restau but hotel bar etc 100m. Golf nearby. Open Apr-Oct. 250 pitches (100 tents).

LITTLE FRANCE: 666 2326. 219 Old Dalkeith Rd. 11km SE centre on A68 towards *32* Dalkeith, about 3km from the roundabout on the inner-city ring-route, which is *xE4* by the large Cameron Toll Shopping Centre. Not what you'd call picturesque and the busy road thunders in the backround, but an easy and convenient route into town (many buses). Near shops and Commonwealth Pool. 287 pitches.

FORDEL, DALKEITH: 660 3921. Lauder Rd. On A68 4km S of Dalkeith; 18km SE of *33* centre. Further out than Little France (above) but very well equipped and *xE4* serviced site secluded from the busy road. Behind a 24hr garage and pub/café which serves food till 7.30pm. Partly wooded landscape and fields give at least a sense of being in the country. Best to have a car; reasonable bus service to Dalkeith, but fewer go past gate. 110 pitches.

DRUM MOHR, MUSSELBURGH: 665 6867. Levenhall. 4km out of Musselburgh on the *34* coast rd to Prestonpans. 22km E of centre. Go through Musselburgh, signed off *xE2* bypass and take rd right at Mining Museum. Site is 400m up a country lane, within sight of the sea, quiet (apart from some traffic noise) and well maintained. You will be rather removed from Edinburgh, but within easy reach of the golf/beaches/walks and ice-cream of East Lothian. 120 pitches.

GOSFORD GARDENS, ABERLADY: 08757 487. Just off the A198, the coast road off the *35* A1 and about 35km E of Edinburgh. Caravan Club of GB site in former walled *xE2* garden 1km from the neat little East Lothian village of Aberlady. Attractive, secluded but perhaps too intimate for some. Perfect for golf/pony-trekking/ beach-combing but no good for nightclubbing in Edinburgh. 120 pitches. No tents.

17

THE BEST HOTELS OUTSIDE TOWN

See also BEST HOTELS AND RESTAURANTS IN LOTHIAN, *p. 88.*

36 **BORTHWICK CASTLE: North Middleton.** 0875 820514. On B6367 3km off the A7,
xD4 18km from bypass, 26km S of centre. The genuine article, a castle in Border
Country, centuries of history in the stone. With walls 100ft high this is an excl
example of a Scots tower house and is not ruined by refurbishment. Mary
Queen of Scots was blockaded here once and after the lights are out, you almost
expect to meet her swishing up the spiral stairs. Pure romance.

10RMS   JAN-DEC   T/X   PETS   CC   KIDS   LOTS

37 **JOHNSTOUNBURN HOUSE: Humbie.** 0875 833696. On B6457 2km from A68 and
xE4 25km S of centre. Bypass 22km. A 17th-century manor house in 18th-
century gardens and well-kept grounds on the edge of the Lammermuirs.
Comfy rather than grand, with wood-lined lounges and highly individual
rooms. Sports of the huntin'-shootin'-fishin' variety. Fine restau and altogether
a fine rest.

20RMS   JAN-DEC   T/T   PETS   CC   KIDS   TOS   LOTS

38 **DALHOUSIE CASTLE: Bonnyrigg.** 0875 820153. Just off A704 2km from the A7, 15km
xD4 from bypass and 23km S of centre. This imposing castle is an odd mix of the
authentic and the affected. Previous visitors incl King Edward I, Oliver
Cromwell, Queen Victoria and sundry rock 'n' roll stars. Some rooms cramped
but with fine open views. The restau is truly dungeonesque, cosy for dinner, but
perhaps a bit creepy for breakfast.

24RMS   JAN-DEC   T/T   PETS   CC   KIDS   LOTS

39 **HOUSTON HOUSE: Uphall,** 0506 853831. On A899 at end of Broxburn/Uphall Main
xA3 St, 8km from r/bout at the start of the M8 Edin-Glas m/way. Airport 10km,
18km W of centre. A tower house with modern annex betw the barren
hinterlands of two cities. Not the most scenic of settings but a hotel/restau of
some repute. The 7 rooms in the tower have the 4-poster beds that we're
supposed to like.

30RMS   JAN-DEC   T/T   PETS   CC   KIDS   TOS   LOTS

40 **DALMAHOY: Kirknewton, on A71 (Kilmarnock road)** 335 3203. On edge of town –
xA4 ring-road 5km, 15km W of centre, airport 6km. The elegant Georgian house has
only 8 (distinctive) bedrooms; others in incongruously modern but well-
appointed annex, housing sports complex and country club. Famous for golf,
great for tennis.

116RMS   JAN-DEC   T/T   XPETS   CC   KIDS   TOS   LOTS

41 **MEDWYN HOUSE: West Linton,** 0968 60542. 2km off main A702 through village (it
xC4 skirts the old conservation part) up Medwyn Rd following signs for Golf
Course. Small country and family house; tasteful, welcoming, great value.
Dinner for non-residents by arrangement only.

3RMS, COTTAGE   JAN-DEC   T/T   PETS   XCC   KIDS   MED.INX

42 **ORIGINAL ROSLIN HOTEL: 4 Main St Roslin.** 440 2384. 1km off A703. 4km bypass,
xC4 15km S of centre. Reasonably priced Main St hotel, comfortable and nr a pretty
special place. (241/WALKS; 982/CHURCHES).

6RMS   JAN-DEC   T/T   PETS   CC   KIDS INX

43 **HOTELS AT QUEENSFERRY:** Two v different hotels on the Forth and within easy
xA2 reach of city. Take rd N via Queensferry Rd heading for Forth Rd Bridge. **THE
HAWES INN, South Queensferry:** 331 1990. On front at Hawes Pier and literally
under the famous Rail Bridge (205/MAIN ATTRACTIONS). Brewery-owned and a
full-scale pub operation but rooms above facing sea or garden. Trades on
reputation – it does go back to the 15th century and was recommended by both
R. L. Stevenson (1028/LITERARY PLACES) and Walter Scott – but more setting
than atmos.

8RMS (NON EN-SUITE)   JAN-DEC   T/T   PETS   CC   KIDS   MED.EX

QUEENSFERRY LODGE HOTEL, nr North Queensferry: 0383 410000. At other end of
road bridge (so city is a toll away), but a good stopping-off place for all points
north. Dramatic setting with estuarine views. Restaus/bars/shop – a modern
purpose-built roadhouse. N Queensferry is less crowded than S (except for
Deep Sea World visitors)and has a nice bistro, the Smugglers (522/FIFE RESTAUS).

30RMS   JAN-DEC   T/T   PETS   CC   KIDS   MED.INX

44 **CASTLE INN: Dirleton.** 062085 221. On A198 coast rd off the A1, 35km SE of centre.
xE2 A charming village, a room above the pub on the Green and a very fine ruined
castle opposite.

8RMS   JAN-DEC   X/X   PETS   CC   KIDS   CHP

45 **THE OPEN ARMS: Dirleton.** 062085 241. Along the Green is v comfortable and is
xE2 often recommended, but is a good deal pricier, esp in season. It has 7 rms.   EXP

GREYWALLS: Gullane. 0260 842144. (504/LOTHIANS.)

THE BEST RESTAURANTS

† † **LA POTINIERE:** Main St, Gullane. 0620 843214. 36km W of city in delightful 46
(and notable golfing) village on A198 coast rd off A1. Very well worth *xE2*
the 45 min trip. David and Hilary Brown's tiny, much celebrated restau is where
you can reliably find simply excellent food. Outstanding wine-list. Set menu.
Dinner: Sats only (or groups by arrangement) so usually booked months in
advance. Lunch: (Tues-Sun) easier. However, there are often cancellations, so it
is worth trying. No smk.
MED

† **THE WITCHERY:** 225 5613. Castlehill. At the top of the Royal Mile within a 47
cackle of the Castle. Proximity may suggest that these atmospheric *C3*
chambers were designed with tourists in mind, but at lunch it's where you take
clients to impress them and at dinner it's often full of Edinburgh folk on a
special night out. In the 'Secret Garden' downstairs, converted from a school
playground, James Thompson has created an extraordinary ambience for the
mainly Scottish menu. Don't skip the pud. 7 days. Lunch and LO 11pm.
EXP

† **THE VINTNER'S ROOM:** 554 6767. 87 Giles St, Leith. Entering from a cobbled 48
courtyard to the wine bar, the long room with its long counter and open *xE1*
fire, these vaults, formerly used to store claret (Leith was an important wine
port), also include a restaurant with a memorable atmosphere (lit by candlelight)
and a mainly French menu using fresh Scottish produce – a good (Auld) alliance.
Same menu but less formal in bar. Excl cheeseboard and wine-list. Mon-Sat
lunch and 6.30-10pm. *Scottish Field* restau of the year '93.
MED

† **THE ATRIUM:** 228 8882. In foyer of new Traverse Theatre, behind the Usher 48a
Hall nr Lothian Rd. Celebrated chef Andrew Radford's new restau was long *C3*
awaited and is prob the most stylish place in town. Opening on to an airportish
atrium of interesting office block, it has a mellow contemporary ambiance, hand-
crafted lighting, railway sleeper tables etc. Menu equally urbane and though such
expectations of excellence must sometimes be hard to fulfil, dinner here always
has the feel-good factor. Lunch Mon-Fri, Dinner 6-11 pm.
EXP

† **THE GRILL, BALMORAL HOTEL:** 556 2414. 1 Princes St. Address with a certain ring 49
for the principal restau of the Balmoral (1/BEST HOTELS) entered thro lobby or *D2*
off st. Opulent subterranean salons with enough space even for the legions of
waiters who prepare or complete many of the dishes at your table. Emphasis on
Scottish produce esp anything that once swum, grazed or flew over Perthshire.
Tome of good wines. Vegn menu. Prices in large numbers of 'pounds'.
EXP

† **POMPADOUR CALEDONIAN HOTEL:** 225 2433. Princes St. The most expensive 50
nosh in town and not for the fainthearted or noisy eater. Dining-room hush *C3*
with reverence expected and often due for Tony Binks's gastronomic oblations
at astronomic prices. French cuisine with unwavering *haute* tone. Jacket and tie
and booking essential. Lunch: Mon-Fri; Dinner: 7 days, 7.30-10pm.
EXP

MARTINS: 225 3106. 70 Rose St North Lane. Quiet lane behind busy shopping 51
precinct nr Princes St, a stylish, discreet city centre restau with limited but *C2*
confident cuisine-marche menu. V personally run; superb cheeseboard. Excl for
business lunch and intimate supper. Tue-Fri lunch. Tue-Sat 7-10pm.
MED

KELLY'S: 668 3847. 46 W Richmond St. Unlikely location on S side and conversion 52
of tenement front room/bakery into small, but airy Scottish/French restau. *E4*
Neatly judged in every way esp Jacqui Kelly's blithe translations from modern
classic French like Bocuse (no flour sauces; cream has its place but mainly in the
puds) and in Mr Kelly's wine selection with lots of house choice for a tenner.
Their gallery adj supports new Scottish artists. Dinner: Tues-Sat, LO 10pm.
MED

CHAMPANY'S, nr LINLITHGOW: 0506 834532. On A904, Linlithgow to S Queensferry 53
road (3km LinL) close to M9 at jnct 3. Restau with many accolades and a 'Chop *xA2*
and Ale House' with budget version. Both heavily Surf 'n' Turf esp steaks.
Lobsters live on the premises. Some folk, e.g. vegetarians and *Guardian* readers
generally, may not be impressed. But American and European visitors may
appreciate the service and the helpings; bring plenty of dollars and ecus.
Chophouse: 7 days, Lunch and 6-10pm; Restau: Mon-Sat Lunch (not Sat) and 7-
10pm.
INX/EXP

MARINETTE: 555 0922. 52 Coburg St, Leith. I've run out of space but must 53a
recommend Marinette – a world away from the above, but fish 'n' chips doesn't *xD1*
come fresher or more befitting than this. Lunch, 6-9.30pm (11pm F/Sat). Cl
Sun/Mon.
MED

THE BEST BISTROS AND WINE BARS

All open for lunch unless otherwise stated. See also FRENCH RESTAUS, *opposite.*

54 **SKIPPERS:** 554 1018. 1A Dock Pl. In a corner of Leith off Commercial Rd by
xE1 the docks. Look for Waterfront (see below) and bear left into adjacent cul-
de-sac. The pioneer restaurant in the pre-yuppie Leith, it's still very much worth
finding. Very fishy, very quayside and quite French. Smells like Trouville.
Dinner: Mon-Sat LO 10pm.   MED

55 **THE WATERFRONT:** 554 7427. 1C Dock Pl. In a bistro cul-de-sac, the estimable
xE1 Waterfront sits with a conservatory on the backwater dock and is cosy in
winter, light in summer (you can sit outside). Long wine selection on blackboard
and bistro food which varies but can be excellent. Good vegetarian choices. 7
days.   MED

56 **THE SHORE:** 554 5080. 3 The Shore, Leith. Bar (often with live light jazz)
xE1 where you can eat from the same menu as the dining-room/restaurant. Real
fire and large windows looking out to the Water of Leith. Food, posted on a
blackboard, changes daily but is consistently good. Lots of fish, some meat,
some vegn. No smk restau/OK in bar. 7days, LO 10pm.   MED

57 **THE DORIC:** 225 1084. 15 Market St. Opposite the Fruitmarket Gallery and the
D3 back entrance to Waverley Station. Upstairs bistro (quite the best word to
describe it) with chequered cloths, awful paintings, an eclectic menu often with
organic veg and very reasonable wine. Very Edinburgh. Not so cheap anymore.
LO 10pm. Cl Sun lunch.   INX

58 **CELLAR NO.1:** 220 4298. 3 Chambers St. Basement wine bar at bottom end of
D3 Chambers St with reputation for being . . . well, a very good wine bar.
Great bistro food, excl wine (and ale) selection and buzzy but relaxed
atmosphere. We would go more often, but it always seems full. LO food
9.30pm, bar 12/1am. Cl Sun.   INX

Also **CELLAR NO.2:** 220 1208. at 110 Hanover St. Same menu, maybe serving later.
The essential Edinburgh wine bar of yore.   INX

59 **MAISON HECTOR:** 332 5328. Raeburn Pl. Busy corner of main st in Stockbridge
B1 which has been sort of trendy for years. Now this v designery bar/café/restau
has opened, as if it had blown in from Glasgow. But it works and the informal
food from pasta to poussin is a major plus. Clever snacky things and proper
meals. 132/SUNDAY BREAKFAST. Food all day, dinner 6-10/11pm.   INX

60 **BELL'S DINER:** 225 8116. 7 St Stephen St. Not really a bistro; in fact quite definitely
C1 a hamburger joint, but no Edinburgh Directory can be without it. Unchanged
since the halcyon days of Stockbridge, from the corn on the cob to the ice-cream
with chocolate sauce, it just never lets you down. Best to book! 7 days.   INX

61 **THE CRAMOND BISTRO:** 312 6555. 5 Riverside. Tucked away along the front at
xA2 Cramond opp passenger ferry (perfect stop after walk to Dalmeny; 218/CITY
WALKS). No microwave in sight in the tiny kitchen in which sound produce is
whisked into light meals and home-baking. Tables o/s in summer. BYOB. Cl
Sun evens and Mon/Tue in winter.   INX

62 **LE SEPT:** 225 5428. Old Fishmarket Close. The close or alley winds steeply off the
D3 High St below St Giles. Outside terrace in summer and narrow woody room
inside. Light French food like crepes and omelettes. Plats du jour. Cheerful,
busy rendezvous. LO 10.30pm (later in Festival).   INX

63 **HOWIE'S:** 668 2917. 75 St Leonard's St. Up on the south side, this small single room
E4 is always busy. BYOB keeps the cost down and the hubbub up. Unfussy,
French/Ecossais with one of the most wicked Banoffie pies you'll encounter. 7
days. LO 10/10.30pm. Cl Mon lunch.   INX
Also at 63 Dalry Rd. 313 3334. Same set-up and probably the best place to eat in
the neighbourhood. Only 100m up from Haymarket Station. Lunch and dinner.
LO 10/10.30pm. Cl Mon lunch.

64 **MAXIE'S:** 667 0845. 32 W Nicholson St. Basement wine bar with bistro section
D4 below busy pub in university area. Simple menu à la carte esp good selection for
vegns. Informal no-fuss food. 7 days, no Sun lunch. LO 10.30pm.   CHP

THE BEST FRENCH RESTAURANTS

Unless o/wise stated all are open for lunch and dinner 7 days.

L'AUBERGE: 556 5888. 58 St Mary's St. Set lunch good value, dinner is dear and 65
there is a bourgeois atmosphere and formality to this place which is v French C2
but, bit stiff. Nevertheless, it's one of Edinburgh's longest-standing premier
restaus and its style and service would not be out of place in e.g. Brussels.
Tending towards nouvelle cuisine. LO 9.30 pm, 7 days. Famed Sun lunch.   EXP

CHAMBERTIN AT THE GEORGE HOTEL: 225 1251. 21 George St. A discreet, v pro- 66
fessionally run hotel restau. The setting is opulent, the food is unmemorable but C2
dependable. Adj Carvery is much less formal.   EXP

LA BAGATELLE: 229 0869. 22A Brougham Pl. Unprepossessing frontage, intimate 67
though formal inside. A restau rather than a bistro but less exp than those that xD4
aim for food guides and expense accounts. Proprietor Thierry Menard aims for
down-to-earth cuisine marche; it's deliciously and delicately done.   MED

CAFE SAINT-HONORE: 226 2211. Thistle St Lane betw Frederick and Hanover St. A 68
corner of Paris reclaimed by Chris Colveson of Martins and Jerry Mallet and C2
much improved. V French (not much for veggies, and a bit cramped); dinner
more restau than bistro prices, but café-lunch is good value and excl grub. No
smk.

MARCHE NOIR: 558 1608. 2/4 Eyre Pl. Somewhere between a brasserie and a bistro 69
at the lower end of the New Town and not unlike the kind of neighbourhood C1
café you'd find in the older suburbs of Paris. Good on *poissons* and *tartes,*
specialising in regional dishes. Twice a month (last Thur and following Sun)
there's a *menu du region. Bon vin.* Cl other Sun   MED

LA VINOTHEQUE: 554 9113. Bonnington Rd Lane (off Bonnington Rd at Leith end). 70
Conscientiously French restau hidden away amongst wastelands and xD1
warehouses just before you get to Leith. Excellent wine-list (indeed, they supply
many other restaus) and table d'hôte more haute than nouvelle, with meat and
game and good cheeses. Cl Sun.   MED

LES PARTISANS: 225 5144. Royal Mile below Cathedral. When it appeared in 71
'92, it added a much-needed decent place to eat on the tourist route. D3
Although the decor in the long upstairs room with windows on to the busy
street may leave something (atmospheric) to be desired, the non-fussy
French/Scottish menu is consistently good (lunch an esp moderately priced
treat). Wines have been carefully selected and well priced. LO 10.30pm. Cl Sun.
JoJo and Andy's bar d/stairs is v cosy.   INX

PIERRE VICTOIRE: 225 1721. 10 Victoria St. This is where the Pierre Victoire 72
phenomenon began, the first of Pierre Levicky's chain of formulaic yet D3
individual and v French bistros which are now all over town (with several
offshoots) and all over Scotland (and in London). Others in Edinburgh are
Union St, 557 8451, Dock Pl in Leith, 555 6178 (the largest, some say the best),
Grassmarket, 226 2442, and S Queensferry main st, 331 5006. Elsewhere: Glasgow
(337/FRENCH RESTAUS); Aberdeen (608/BEST RESTAUS); Inverness (1385/CENTRES);
Ayr (1380/CENTRES); Perth (1387/CENTRES) . . . and more as we speak. Lunches
and vino famously cheap.   INX

CAFE D'ODILE: 225 5366. 13 Randolph Cres. A secret garden and small cafeteria 73
downstairs at the French Institute. Lunch only but can be booked for D3
parties at night. Great views over the New Town and simple French home-
cooking. Mon-Fri. Cl July. Not licensed.   CHP

CHEZ JULES: 225 7007. Craig's Close, off Cockburn St. In a narrow wynd, a 74
hole in the wall where simple French fare is remarkably cheap. With D3
complimentary *hors d'oeuvre* and bowl of salad you can perhaps forgive the
occasional lapse in the *plats du jour.* Quite potable plonk comes in jugs; white,
red or pink. Yet again part of the Pierre Victoire histoire. LO 10.30pm. Also at
61 Frederick St. 225 7007. Same simple stuff.
A good city centre nosh doesn't come cheaper and more relaxed than this.   CHP 75

LA POTINIERE: 0620 843214. Main St, Gullane. 46/BEST RESTAUS.   D3

POMPADOUR: 225 2433. Caledonian Hotel, Princes St. 50/BEST RESTAUS.

THE BEST ITALIAN RESTAURANTS

76 **TINELLI:** 652 1392 **139 Easter Rd.** Feels like it's been here for years; and it has. †
E1 Air-dried beef, polenta with gorgonzola; from the pastas to the zabaglione –
we are talking the real macaroni. Fine selection of cheeses. Intimate. LO
10.30pm.   MED

77 **PELLICANO:** 661 6914. **110 Easter Rd.** Nothing outside or in would suggest that †
E2 this was a damned good place to eat. You can see into the kitchen and you
could be sitting in their living-room. Somehow they always have asparagus
(parmigiana) and wild mushrooms; maybe they do get the stuff sent over from
home like they say. You have to start with that Bruschetta! But be choosy on the
wines – the house can be rough; the good ones are pricey. LO 11 pm.   MED

*Opinions are divided as to which of the two restaurants (above) on an
unpromising street off London Rd serve the best authentic Italian home cooking
in town, but they're both worth the detour from the West End.*

78 **COSMO:** 226 6743. **58 North Castle St.** Very much in the old, discreet style for †
C2 those of a certain constellation or expense account. The lighting and the
music are soft, Pavarotti stares from the bar; the food invites that kind of appetite.
Excellent Italian wine-list and cheese-board. Allow time. Cl Sun/Mon.   EXP

79 **UMBERTO'S CANTINA:** 556 2231. **33 Dublin St.** You might not drop into these cellars
D2 for a quick bite of pasta, but it's the right atmosphere for an occasion or a secret
affair. An extensive menu encourages you to eat rather a lot. Prop Richard
Coulthard and his largely non-Cosa Nostra staff nevertheless manage to weave
wonders with the spaghetti. Some rarish reds. LO 10.30pm. Cl Sun   MED

80 **DUNCAN'S LAND:** 225 1037. **8 Gloucester St.** Former coffee house, a conversion of
B2 an 18th-century country-house, tucked away nr the end of St Stephen St in
Stockbridge area and still with that cosy ambience. Imaginative variations of
mainly southern Italian cooking. Lunch: Tue-Fri, Dinner: Tue-Sat.   MED

80a **SILVIO'S:** 553 3557. **The Shore.** Recent arrival on the waterfront in Leith and
xE1 somewhere for the advertising arrivistes to linger over lunch. They're perhaps
amongst those who can easily afford it for this place ain't cheap, but neither does
it compromise over a menu of urbane Italian cuisine that's more than just sexier
sauces for pasta. BYO and wine-list. Mon-Sat lunch and LO 10.30pm.

81 **RAFFAELLI:** 225 6060. **10 Randolph Pl.** Back of the West End, a restau and wine bar.
B3 The latter is small but v good value with a simple blackboard menu and often
interesting wines. Quiet and discreet. Dining-room decidedly upmarket with
excellent service. LO Mon-Fri 9.30pm; Sat 10pm. Cl Sun.   INX.MED

82 **PEPE'S TAVERNA:** 337 9774. **96 Dalry Rd.** Taverna is right, it's a neighbourhood café
A4 on a busy road, deep in the urban vineyards of Dalry. Some people wouldn't pick
anywhere else. Often packed esp late. Usual menu; the decent wines (ask for the
big glasses for the red) aren't cheap. LO midnight or whenever.   INX

83 **CAPRICE:** 554 1279. **Leith Walk.** This place was here long before there were pizza
E1 parlours coming out of our ears, over 20 years, in fact, and of course they still do
it better. Huge pizzas, crisp and light, are the speciality (19 varieties) but all the
old Italian carbohydrates are here (though not the fashionable versions like pasta
pesto). LO 11pm. Cl Sun lunch.   INX

84 **GIULIANO'S:** 556 6590. **18 Union Pl** which is at the top of Leith Walk nr the main
D2 r/bout, opp and handy for the Playhouse Theatre. You couldn't tell from the
outside or even the inside but something about this place sets it apart from the
rest. Busy at lunchtime, packed every night, it's only pasta and pizza but it's
what we like. They have regulars and we do mean regulars: some folk eat there
practically every day. It just works! Lunch till late. Also 'on the shore' in Leith
(554 5272) which is esp good for kids (115/PLACE FOR KIDS).   INX

GORDON'S TRATTORIA: 225 7992. **231 High St** (128/LATE RESTAUS).

LAZIO'S: 229 7788. **95 Lothian Rd** (129/LATE RESTAUS).

BAR ROMA: 226 2977. **39A Queensferry St** (130/LATE RESTAUS).

THE BEST ETHNIC RESTAURANTS

✝ **SHAMIANA:** 228 2265. 14 Brougham Pl. Edinburgh is well served with good 85
Indian restaurants and though selecting the best few is a v debatable business, *C4*
Shamiana has to be one of them. They were the first with the calm damask interior
and non-repeating curries. Though you can tuck into spice-cured quail etc, their
vegetarian stuff is almost as good as Kalpna (see below). LO 11pm. Cl Sun. MED

✝ **KALPNA:** 667 9890. 2 St Patrick Sq. **ANA PURNA:** (99/99A VEGN RESTAUS). 86
B1

LANCERS: 332 3444. 5 Hamilton Pl. Bengali/N Indian, off busy Hamilton Pl, a fave
spot in smart Stockbridge/New Town area. One of the Great Days of the Raj-
type 'images' much favoured by Indian restaus since the 1970s, which can mean
over-unctuous service, but here allows a smooth curry to speak for itself. LO
11pm. INX

KUSHI'S: 16 Drummond St. The legendary Punjabi café (in the university area) 87
frequented by students and India Hands over the years. Very basic: no yoghurt *D3*
in the sauce, no linen, no change. Stripped-down curries, dahls, etc, all very
cheap and as they say . . . real! Lunch: 12.30-3pm. Dinner 5-9pm. Cl Sun CHP

✝ **KWEILIN:** 557 1875. 19 Dundas St. Large New Town place with imaginative 88
Cantonese cooking (real chefs) esp good seafood in pleasant but somewhat *C2*
uninspired setting. People do swear this is the place to go Chinese. LO 11pm
(week), midnight (w/ends). Open Sun. Must book. MED

✝ **CHINESE HOME COOKING:** 229 4404. 21 Argyle Pl. 100m up from Middle 88a
Meadow Walk on the S side. Nr University and the bed-sit land of *C4*
Marchmont, so this simple authentic Chinese has been a cherished secret for
years. Smoky kitchen, cheerful folk, great for kids, happy banquets. BYOB. 6-
11.30pm. INX

LOON FUNG: 556 1781. 2 Warriston Pl, Canonmills, on the left at the v bottom of 89
Dundas St. Upstairs (and down when it's crowded), their famous lemon chicken *C1*
and crispy ducks go round for ever. The seaweed's pretty snappy. LO 11pm
(week), midnight (w/ends). INX

LOON FUNG: 229 5757. 32 Grindlay St. No relation, and some say better. INX 90

LUNETOWN: 220 1688. 38 William St. A shade (or Venetian blind) upmarket and 91
often crowded (don't get stuck downstairs). Easier on the MSG than most; good *B3*
dim sum makes for lighter lunch. LO 11pm-midnight. MED

DRAGON'S WAY: 668 1328. 74 S Clerk St on S side. Running water effects, blood- 92
red, tassled and laquered, the decor here is fairly over the top in a dragon way. *E4*
The menu also leans to the exotic though all the Peking faves are here. A galazy
of prawns and prob the best in town for seafood generally. Till 11.30pm.

NEW EDINBURGH RENDEZVOUS: 225 2023. 10A Queensferry St. Let's just say it ain't 93
so new any more, but it still seems more like Chinatown than anywhere else in *B3*
town. On first floor (below the Anti-vivisection Society!), serving trad Pekinese.
An '83 Margaux hides nervously in the wine-list. The Toffee Banana is rather
yum yum. LO 11pm-midnight. INX

YEE KIANG: 554 5833. 42 Dalmeny St. Known by the cognos as . . . 'the Dalmeny St 94
Place', this is like eating in somebody's front room (there are only 8 tables). *E1*
They know about Peking food and kids (who are welcomed) but not so much
about wine. Cl Mon. INX

VIVA MEXICO: 226 5145. Anchor Close on Cockburn St. Reasonably authentic 95
Mexican cantina and still the best of a burgeoning bunch. Spicy, of course, and *D3*
OK for veggies. Cl Sun. LO 10pm. INX

SIAM ERAWAN: 226 3675. 48 Howe St. Popular Thai restau on corner of 96
Stockbridge area by folk who know their lemon grass. Authentic cuisine with all *C2*
the right flavours. Well-selected wine-list. The smiley, spaced-out waiters seem
to have gone back to Ko Samui. 7 days, lunch and dinner 7-11pm. INX

PARADOR: 225 2973. 26 William St. Through the back and down below at the 97
Bistro Bar, a place that's been through several incarnations seems finally to have *B3*
found one that works. The wide range of tapas is the best bet (available upstairs
as well as down in the restau). With generous helpings it's surprisingly easy to
pig-out. Reasonable riojas. LO 10pm. Cl Sun. INX

THE BEST VEGETARIAN RESTAURANTS

98 **HELIOS FOUNTAIN:** 229 7884. **7 Grassmarket.** A coffee house/bookshop with
C3 more than a shade of anthroposophy (i.e. Rudolph Steiner), but some very
conscientious cooking. Organic where possible and properly vegan. Soups, live
salads, hot food and the best bread. Self/S. No smk. 10-6pm. Cl Sun. CHP

99 **KALPNA:** 667 9890. **2 St Patrick Sq.** A vegetarian restau which is also something
D4 else – a good Indian place – so not the standard fare. Dry and creamed
dishes; lots of nutty things and okra, aubergine and coriander. Thali with a bit of
everything is a good bet. Wines unexciting. No smk. Cl Sun. LO 10pm. INX

99a **ANA PURNA:** 662 1807. **45 St Patrick Sq.** New at press-time but already highly
D4 regarded. Excl S Indian vegn nr University. Lunch (not Sat) and LO 11pm. Cl
Sun. INX

100 **HENDERSON'S:** 225 2131. **94 Hanover St.** One of the most famous and long-
C2 established vegetarian restaurants in the UK. Locals may find the hot dishes
and desserts a bit predictable, but you always go back after a while. Buzzy kind
of Euro-atmosphere in the side room. Good cheese and jolly vino. Self/S. Cl
Sun. LO 10pm. CHP

101 **BLACK BO'S:** 557 6136. **57 Blackfriars St.** Innovative vegetarian restau nr the bottom
D3 of a quiet st off the Royal Mile. Some vegan dishes and definitely more than
your average nut cutlet. A restau to take quite seriously and one that Edinburgh,
with its many vegetarian options, is pretty lucky to have. INX

102 **PIERRE LAPIN:** 668 4332. **32 W Nicolson St.** Upstairs in a spacious atelier formerly a
D4 comedy/cabaret room and now the vegn outpost of the Pierre Victoire empire
(72/FRENCH RESTAUS). French cuisine is usually not flexible enough for those
unenamoured by goose livers or steak tartare, but here the formula of decent
inexpensive *plats du jour* works to advantage and the menu is not so different
from the other PVs. It's far from mere rabbit food though quality can vary.
Lunch for less than a fiver. Dinner 6pm-11pm, LO 10pm. Cl Sun. INX

103 **NATURE'S GATE:** 668 2067. **83 Clerk St.** Another restau (or rather café) where the
E4 ethnic food happens to incl good vegn so it's not in the quiche niche. Persian
home-cooking in a light room below a 'health food' store; run by friendly Iranian
family. Some dishes strictly vegan. Self/S. No smk. 10am-8pm. Cl Sun. CHP

104 **SEEDS:** 667 8673. **58 W Nicholson St.** Small, old-style (i.e. 1960s) veggie place
D4 popular with students and people with causes and consciences. It's run on co-
operative lines and you'd need to get on with one another to produce the soups,
hot dishes, salads and home-baking in that tiny kitchen, the counter of which
you order your food from. Self/S. 10am-8pm. Cl Sun. CHP

105 **CORNERSTONE CAFE:** 229 0212. **Underneath St John's Church** at the corner of
C3 Princes St and Lothian Rd. V central and 'worthy' self-service coffee shop in
vaults below the church. Home-baking and hot dishes at lunchtime. Some seats
(in the graveyard!) outside in summer and market stalls during the Festival. The
One World shop adj, is full of Third World-type crafts and v good for presents.
A welcome respite from the fast-food frenzy of Princes St. Open 10am-6pm. Cl
Sun. CHP

106 **ENGINE SHED CAFE:** 662 0040. **19 St Leonard's Lane.** Tucked away in the 'South
E4 Side' off St Leonard's St by the modern-looking police station and on the second
floor of a workshop complex in a cobbled courtyard, this small café is not easy to
find, but has a loyal clientele who come for the friendly atmosphere and home-
cooked vegetarian food. Self/S. Mon-Fri 10.30am-3pm. CHP

Restaus serving good vegn food (but not exclusively vegn) include:

THE WATERFRONT and **THE DORIC** (55/57/BISTROS).

THE QUEEN ST CAFE (120/COFFEE SHOPS).

SHAMIANA (85/ETHNIC RESTAUS).

THE QUEEN'S HALL 668 3456. **87 Clerk St.** Self/S, Open 11am-5pm. Cl Sun.

107 **CHANS:** 556 7118. **1 Forth St.** A neighbourhood Chinese restau with Cantonese/
D2 Peking/Szechuan cooking and incl a page of choices for vegetarians. Lots of tofu
and deep-fried this and that but some welcome variations. Basic wines. Lunch,
5.30pm-midnight. Cl Tue. CHP

GREAT CAFES AND GREASY SPOONS

CANASTA: 554 5190. 10 Bonnington Rd. At end of busy rd for crosstown traffic, 108
just before Gt Junction St. Excellent home-cooked food for under a fiver and esp *xD1*
fine omelettes, bulging sandwiches that would put most sandwich bars to shame
and steaming mugs of coffee. Take-away also available. 8.30am-5pm. Cl Sun.

VITTORIA: 556 6171. 113 Brunswick St. On a corner halfway down Leith Walk, a 109
neighbourhood Italian café which is cheap, cheerful and open late. Fry-ups and *E1*
pasta and ice-cream concoctions. Even open late on Sun. Forget Burgerland.
10am-11.30pm.

BLUE MOON CAFE: 556 2788. 60 Broughton St. A back-room café beside the offices 110
of the Scottish Minorities Group, where gay people (and everybody else) come *D2*
for coffee and conversation and a range of home-made food of the soup/
quiche/cakes variety. Always busy and buzzy, the sort of place you meet rather
nice ordinary people. Open every day 11am-11pm (Sun from noon).

THE NOOK: 366 Morningside Rd. 'Nook' is right; this sliver of a café at the far 111
end of a busy shopping st is probably the nearest thing in town to an American *xC4*
coffee stop, where you drop in even for breakfast, or a fast-order snack. Stools
along the counter and friendly service, there should be one of these open 24
hours on every corner – like in a real city. 7.30am-6pm (Sun 10am.-5.30pm).

WAYFARERS: 667 6116. 53 Clerk St. Handy café in student-land but often bypassed. 112
Stools along the counter and booths. Home-made pasta for less than the tratt *E4*
price, and frys. 10am-8.30pm.

BONITAS: Trafalgar St, off Ferry Rd 200m Gt Junction St, Leith. Now we are 113
really getting out of the way, a neighbourhood café which even people in the *xD1*
neighbourhood don't know about; or don't know that it's one of the best-value
lunches in town. Breakfast also a steal. Just the job before work or after an all-
nighter. Mon-Fri 7am-2.30pm; Sat 8.30am-noon.

THE PALACE TEAROOM: Corner of Constitution St and Gt Junction St in Leith. V 114
visible site but easily passed over until you know that everything from the mince *xE1*
and tatties to the apple pie is home-made and very good. Licensed. OAP
specials. 8am-5pm. Cl Sun.

PLACES TO TAKE KIDS

GIULIANO'S ON THE SHORE: 554 5272. 1 Commercial St. Dockside outpost of 115
Giuliano's on the Walk (84/ITALIAN RESTAUS) (by the bridge over the Water of *xE1*
Leith) where kids are welcome to make their own pizzas (they get a hat and a
badge) and where there's enough going on to absorb any tantrums or
restlessness amongst the parents.7 days. Noon-10.30/11pm.

FAT SAM'S: 228 3111. 56 Fountainbridge. Another fun Italian place, this time on a 116
fairly lavish scale for kids of all ages including tablefuls of teachers and other *B3*
office outings. Big, brash, noisy, sometimes live music. A slice of life as well as
pizza. Noon-12/1am.

YE OLDE PEACOCK INN: 552 8707. Newhaven Rd nr Newhaven Harbour and opp 117
Harry Ramsden's Fish 'n' Chips (which is the more obvious place perhaps to *xC1*
take kids), but The Peacock, one of Edinburgh's unsung all-round good family
restaus for yrs, deserves wider recognition. The fish here really is fresh, the
menu is v varied with lots that wee kids and we kids like. High tea's a real treat.
Lunch, 4.30-6.30 and till 9pm, 7 days (1198/FISH 'N' CHIPS).

✝ **BRIDGE INN, RATHO:** 333 1320. Canal Centre, Ratho, West Lothian. 14km W 118
of centre via A71, turning right opp Dalmahoy Golf Club. Well worth the *xA4*
drive for an afternoon on, or by, the Union Canal. The 'Pop Inn Restaurant' has
special menus for kids, play areas and numerous distractions. Sailings and walks.
(180/PUB FOOD). Noon-11pm.

THE BEST TEA-ROOMS AND
COFFEE SHOPS

119 **LAIGH KITCHEN:** 225 1552. 117A Hanover St. There's been a Laigh coffee house
C2 in Edinburgh since yon times and this stone-flagged basement (underneath
Neil Grant hairdressers) evokes a more civilised age. Cosy in winter (you can sit
round the range) and cool in summer, there would be an outcry if they ever had
to close. Salads, rolls, baked potatos, home-baking; the chocolate and coffee
cakes and the hazelnut meringue are legendary. 10am-5pm. Cl Sun.

120 **QUEEN ST CAFE:** National Portrait Gallery, Queen St betw Hanover and St
D2 Andrew Sq (207/LESS OBV ATTRACTIONS). The coffee shop in the back of the
gallery (through the best atrium in town) is where delicious and imaginative hot
food and cakes are partaken of amongst well-chosen paintings and a bit of chat.
Good vegn. Mon-Sat 10am-4.30pm, Sun 2-4.30pm.

121 **GALLERY OF MODERN ART COFFEE SHOP:** Belford Rd (208/LESS OBV
xA2 ATTRACTIONS). Free entry to gallery. Self-service cafeteria opening out to
garden at the back of this 'country house' just beyond the New Town. The
home-baking and lunchtime cooking really is worth the trek, never mind the art
upstairs. Daily 10am-5pm; Sun afternoons.

122 **KINNELLS:** 220 1150. 36 Victoria St. Upstairs and a few tables at ground level in
D3 the shop which purveys coffees, teas, chocolates and Scottish goodies.
Soups, hot dishes, salads, croissants and cruel puddings. Some microwaving, but
the food's too good to bother about that. From the window seats you can watch
the traffic wardens going about their wretched business in Victoria St below.
Late open during the Festival, o/wise 9am-6pm. 7 days.

123 **CLARINDA'S:** 557 1888. 69 Canongate. Near bottom of the Royal Mile close to the
E3 Palace. Mainly frequented by tourists and you'd feel out of place in your Doc
Martens, but these cakes would win prizes at the WRI. The lentil soup is as good
as Mum's. 10am-4.45pm.

124 **CAFE FLORENTIN:** 225 6267. 8 St Giles St. The genuine *pâtisserie française* in two
D3 oddly connecting small rooms with enormous windows just off the High St by
St Giles. Has the particular kind of shabby chic that Edinburgh folk, from
lawyers to layabouts, adore. The cakes look too good to eat and there are
savoury quiche things that only the French can make properly. At Festival-time
it's open 24 hours which is a really good idea (134/SUN BREAKFAST). 8am-8pm.

125 **THE LOWER AISLE:** Underneath St Giles Cathedral (210/ATTRACTIONS), enter
D3 round back. Nr the courts. Harmonious conversion of the crypts below the
great Cathedral into a long, narrow coffee shop where people like lawyers and
their clients (you know . . . the rest of us) meet. Good coffee, baking and light
meals at lunchtime, served from a hatch. Mon-Fri 10am-4.30pm, Sat (Festival
only), Sun 10am-1.30pm.

126 **ROYAL SCOTTISH MUSEUM TEA-SHOP:** Chambers St (201/ATTRACTIONS). In the
D3 heart of the museum past aeons and aeons and habitats of stuffed animals, is this
watering hole amongst 'the birds'; glass cabinets of British birds to be precise.
This is certainly the most educational repast in town. And not at all . . . stuffy.
Gallery free. 10am-5pm, Sun 2-5pm.

127 **BOTANIC GARDENS CAFETERIA:** By 'the House' (where there are occasional
B1 exhibitions), within the gardens (206/LESS OBV ATTRACTIONS). For café only,
best to enter by Arboretum Pl. Self/S inexpensive home-made food with light
meals at lunchtime. The main attraction is to sit outside and look over the
gardens and the city from a sheltered and sunny spot. The squirrels will expect
some shortbread. 10am-5pm, 7 days.

127a **THE HAMLET TEAROOM, BLACKNESS:** 0506 834251. Out of town, a pleasant drive
Map 7 along from the Forth bridges (app via A904 off Forth Rd Bridge r/bout or jnct 2
B1 off M9 – 25km Edin centre). Blackness is 4km from main road on Forth estuary
opp Rosyth, with coast walks and a castle where once they filmed *Hamlet* –
hence this tea-room by the post office. Traditional, welcoming, surprisingly
large-scale operation, with all-day menu from home-baked scones to full meals
and pots of paraphernalia on sale around you. Your mum would love it! 7 days
till 8pm.

THE BEST LATE-NIGHT RESTAURANTS

GORDON'S TRATTORIA: 225 7992. 231 High St. Occasional footballers, local pop | 128
stars and other people with nowhere to go after the show are amongst the | *D3*
clientele of this central carbohydrate haven. It may be leaden to sleep on, but
Gordon's pasta and garlic bread are fine at any time of the day and you'll just
have to order another basket of chianti to get you through the night. Until
2.30am (Sun/Thu) or 3am (w/ends), 11.45pm. (Tue/Wed). Cl Mon.. | CHP

LAZIO: 229 7788. 95 Lothian Rd. The best of the bunch on Lothian Rd, a street | 129
where the flotsam of the night drifts from the clubs and bars in the wild West | *C3*
End (and of course Filmhouse across the road). This Italian place is better than it
probably needs to be. Till 2am (week), 3am (w/ends). | CHP

BAR ROMA: 226 2977. 39A Queensferry St. 2 mins from the Caledonian Hotel at the | 130
West End of Princes St and busy day and night. Big selection of the predictable | *B3*
pastas and pizzas and the wines aren't bad. Some of the most entertaining/rude
waiters in town. Delicious Luca's ice-cream in your knickerbocker glory. Till
2am (week), 3am (w/ends). | CHP

EFES: 229 7833. 42 Leven St. Turkish restau nr Kings Theatre and Cameo Cinema | 131
which stays open late and provides an alternative to pasta (and a solution to the | *C4*
perennial Edinburgh problem of where to eat after the flicks). Esp good for
vegn. Humus, tsatsiki and many unpronounceable things best partaken within a
selection of starters and main courses. Wash it all down with Buzbag, the
estimable Turkish plonk. Till 1/2am. Cl Mon. | CHP

*Many other places are open after midnight at weekends or during the Edinburgh
Festival period; the good ones include:*

LOON FUNG, LUNETOWN, YEE KIANG, KWEILIN: (see ETHNIC RESTAUS, p. 23) and
PEPE'S: (82/ITALIAN RESTAUS).

GOOD PLACES FOR SUNDAY BREAKFAST

MAISON HECTOR: Raeburn Pl. Brunch from 11am-4pm. Eggs Benedict and | 132
Finnan Haddies as well as the usual fry-up in designery surroundings. Sunday | *B1*
papers provided (59/BISTROS).

CAFE ROYAL: W Register St. Brunch in the Oyster Bar, prob the most stylish in | 133
town; dark wood and white linen. Buck's Fizz isn't out of place here and you | *D2*
can choose from Louisiana Beef Hash to Omelettes Key Largo. Nearest to traditional fare is poached egg with smoked salmon (139/GREAT PUBS). 12.30-2pm.

CAFE FLORENTIN: St Giles St off Royal Mile at George IV Bridge. The civilised | 134
and authentically French coffee shop with savouries (those little quiches), | *D3*
croissants and cakes you may not be able to resist. Papers provided. Open
8.30am (somewhere to go after the all-nighter). (124/COFFEE SHOPS.)

THE BRIDGE BAR: George IV Bridge opp Library. A good all-round pub | 135
(150/PUBS) that serves a good Sunday breakfast. From midday till 'they run out'. | *D3*
Papers provided.

BANNERMAN'S: Cowgate. A pub with a great atmosphere that serves a Sunday | 136
breakfast that becomes a habit. Esp good in winter and university term-time. | *D3*
Vegetarian alternative. 11am-2pm. Papers provided. (163/REAL ALE.)

NEGOCIANTS: Bristo Pl nr University. Open at the unusually early hour of 9am. | 137
Breakfast from 9.30am. Tables outside in summer. Excellent coffee. | *D3*

A SELECTION OF GREAT PUBS

Pubs notable for other specific reasons are on the following pages. Unless o/wise stated these pubs are open 7 days, 11am-11pm (Fri/Sat midnight).

139 **CAFE ROYAL:** Behind Burger King at the east end of Princes St is one of
D2 Edinburgh's longest celebrated pubs. Unrelated to the London version though there is a similar Victorian elegance. Through the glass partition is the Oyster Bar/French restau. Central counter and usually standing-room only. If you're going out on the tiles, the tiles here are a very good place to start.

140 **PORT O'LEITH:** Constitution St. An atmosphere you could never design in,
xE1 though breweries do try. Like all the best pubs it's down to the genial host(ess), Mary Moriarty, who makes Leithers, up-town voyeurs and Russian sailors alike, all welcome. Bridge (Mon nights), occ country and western combo, good crack. This place will always make you feel better. Sometimes till 1am.

141 **BENNETS:** 8 Leven St, by King's Theatre. Same era as Café Royal and similar
C4 ambience. Good food at lunch (173/PUB FOOD), altogether a pub of character and no pretence.

142 **BARONY BAR:** 81 Broughton St. A woody kind of Irish pub (draught Murphys
D1 and Guinness), a real fire and tables spread around the spacious room. Food at lunchtime of variable quality.

143 **THE PEAR TREE:** 36 W Nicolson St. Dark and woody inside, the main distinction
D4 is that it's one of the few places in Edinburgh where you can sit outside. There's a large yard/beer garden which rollicks on a summer evening. Near the university; young crowd.

144 **THE BAILIE:** 2 St Stephen St. On the corner literally and metaphorically of
C2 Stockbridge, this is the 'local' for the more interesting survivors (and some of the casualties) from the 1960s and its various progeny. Different cliques throughout the evening, but stick around and you'll leave with somebody.

145 **OLD CHAIN PIER:** 1 Trinity Cres. This pub was here forever then tarted up.
xC1 Mainly notable, as it always was, for its position on the seafront betw Newhaven and Granton. Built on the seawall so you can sit inside and look straight into the water. Pity about the expensive refit and the music, but the bar food isn't bad and the sunset and the site make up for everything.

146 **CITY CAFE:** 19 Blair St. Down the steep street from the Tron Kirk, the City Caff
D3 sprang up in the late 1980s and was immediately the hippest bar in town. The designer baby of Sam Piacentini, it sold sweeties as well as spritzers. Recently, it's changed hands and the crowd have changed haircuts, but if you're looking for club action or coolish people, it's not a bad place to try. City 2 downstairs.

147 **L'ATTACHE:** Rutland St. Underneath and very much in the basement of the
B3 Rutland Hotel. Dungeonesque (with stone alcoves and stone floors), you'd want to be upwardly mobile. Live music from folk to pub rock. The **RUTLAND** upstairs, on the corner, also teems with teams. Both good for meeting the opposite (for) sex.

148 **ODDFELLOWS:** 14 Forrest Rd. Big bar that gives it big licks. Up a narrow corridor
D3 in Forrest Rd near the university and into a crowded house with loud, happening music, MTV and teen spirit.

149 **PELICAN:** 209 Cowgate. Carved out of The Cowgate at the bottom of Blair St. A
D3 bit dark, but a good place to soujourn late at night. Sometimes live music; always lively (youngish) crowd.

150 **BRIDGE BAR:** George IV Bridge. Nr university and Central Library. A pub with
D3 youngish clientele and all-round good service. Several ales (167/REAL ALES), games, TV sports, Sunday breakfast (135/SUNDAY BREAK), good coffee, many lagers. Open 7 days till 1am.

THE BEST OLD 'UNSPOILT' PUBS

Of course it's not necessarily the case that when a pub's done up, it's spoiled, or that all old pubs are worth preserving, but some have resisted change and that's part of their appeal. Money and effort are often spent to oldify bars and contrive an atmosphere. The following places don't have to try.

Unless o/wise stated, these bars are open 11am-11pm (midnight at w/ends).

THE DIGGERS: 1 Angle Park Terr. Officially known as the Athletic Arms though we're actually talking football – and it's deep in the Hearts half. Long thought to be a very good pint, the pint they mean is McEwans 80/-. Also featuring the estimable Andersons pies, stovies and other health-freak horrors. Till 10.30pm. *151 A4*

THE CENTRAL BAR: 7 Leith Walk. At the bottom (or, as they say, 'the Fit') of the Walk, a grand old place that it would be a crime to 'improve'. Priceless tiling, mosaics and mirrors. Leithers and the odd ex-MP disport themselves around the bar and the banquettes. *152 xE1*

FIDDLER'S ARMS: 9 Grassmarket. On a corner at the W end of the Grassmarket and about the only pub in the area that hasn't been 'brought up to date'. McEwans 80/- again, dispensed from old fonts. Real fiddle music on Monday nights. Real folk at all times. *153 C3*

CLARK'S: 142 Dundas St. The sort of place where designers and advertising people drink: none of them have had a hand in it, it makes no statement and they don't have to live with what they've done. Side rooms for private arguments and assignations. McEwans 80/-, Theakstons, Deuchars. *154 C1*

OXFORD BAR: 8 Young St, corner of Young St South Lane in the westerly extension of Thistle St. Poky and at first glance undistinguished; then you notice it's full. Usually at least three ales incl Belhaven. Don't ask for the latest lager or snacks or a half pint of anything. For some reason, a lot of off-duty policemen hang out here – who'd have thought they'd have such good taste? *155 C2*

STEWART'S: 14 Drummond St on the 'South Side' and just off South Bridge. Narrow bar with a room through the back. Old soaks and young student soaks and anyone who prefers conversation to canned music (or going home). *156 D3*

THE GREEN TREE: 184 Cowgate. How old it is we don't know, but it long predates the trendification around it. Big attraction in summer is *al fresco* drinking in a strange concrete clearing of the surrounding concrete jungle. Live music (and clientele) of the various variety. *157 D3*

MATHER'S: 1 Queensferry St. Time stands still in this 'real' pub in the West End, where real men drown real sorrows. There's not a lot of real ale to do it with but maybe that's just a fashion too. Decades could go by in here while the crowd rushes by and the street changes hands and appearance outside. There's another pub called Mather's, but I won't talk about that; that's where we drink. *158 B2*

SANDY BELL'S: aka the Forrest Hill Bar. 25 Forrest Rd nr Greyfriars Church and the university. Small corner bar and noted folk music centre (1333/FOLK MUSIC). McEwans 80/-, Youngers No 3. *159 D3*

THE BEST REAL ALE PUBS

Pubs on other pages may have or feature real ale, but the following are the ones where they take it seriously and/or have a good choice.

Unless o/wise stated, these bars are open 11am-11pm, midnight at w/ends.

160
xE1
TOD'S TAP: 42 Bernard St, Leith. A small front bar on the narrow part of a busy street for traffic and a bigger, more comfortable room at the back with a fire. Usually 7 ales but with changing pedigrees. Atmosphere just right for quaffing them. And there's decent food. ✝

161
C1
THE CUMBERLAND BAR: Cumberland St, corner of Dundonald St. Opened by owner of Bow Bar (see below) after meticulous conversion of a former New Town pub into an immediately popular watering hole for ale drinkers and folk who like civilised surroundings, a good pub lunch and conversation. A dozen well-kept ales. Cl Sun. ✝

162
D3
THE BOW BAR: 80 West Bow (halfway down Victoria St). A row of fonts as long as your drinking arm and more malts than you could mention. Probably and properly in every beer guide. Beamish as well as Guinness. The connoisseur's choice. ✝

163
D3
BANNERMAN'S: 212 Cowgate, in the shadow of a high overhead bridge (South Bridge). Good, not lavish selection of beers (Caledonian, Theakstons etc). Busy with a youngish crowd who appreciate them and the live music in one of the side cellars, but mainly just loaf around the refectory-type tables and benches; bon bonhomie. (136/SUNDAY BREAKFAST.)

164
xC1
STARBANK INN: 64 Laverockbank Rd, Newhaven. On the sea-front road between Newhaven and Leith. Up to 9 different ales on offer incl Harviestoun, Courage Director's, Timothy Taylor and Golden Promise, the organic one. Also good for food (177/PUB FOOD).

165
B2
KAY'S: 39 Jamaica St (off India St in the New Town). Lawyers, architects and their ilk while away long lunch hours (and your money) here amongst the old barrels and the new ones, with about 6 ales to choose from. Food of the chilli and pie and beans variety. Smoky fire, snug back room. A very Edinburgh pub.

166
C3
MAGGIE DICKSON'S: 92 Grassmarket. One of the new upstart and themed kind of pubs, but better worked out than most. Ansells, Tetley and Edinburgh's own Caledonian, along with newspapers, games, video juke box, whatever. Usually kicking late on. Till 1am.

167
D3
THE BRIDGE BAR: George IV Bridge. Sometimes seems betw zones on the connecting route between the High St area and the university, but good selection of beers and okay for coffee and conversation. Near the Central and the National Libraries. (135/SUNDAY BREAKFAST; 150/BEST PUBS.) Till 1am.

168
xC4
THE CANNY MAN'S: 237 Morningside Rd. Officially known as the Volunteer Arms, but everybody calls it the Canny Man's. Good food at lunchtime (174/PUB FOOD), and wide range of ales incl IPA and all the Scottish ones e.g. Greenmantle, Caledonian, Belhaven. Management have a particular attitude.

169
D2
THE GUILDFORD ARMS: 1 W Register St. Just behind Burger King at E end of Princes St (opp Balmoral Hotel) and on the opp corner of the block from the Café Royal (139/PUBS). Lofty Victorian hostelry with 10 ales incl Harviestoun, Orkney Dark Island, Timothy Taylor. Pub grub on 'gallery' floor as well as bar. 11pm/midnight.

170
CALEDONIAN BEER FESTIVAL: An annual Beer Fest/Ale Fest held in early June at Edinburgh's own Caledonian Brewery, a red-brick Victorian brewery in Slateford Rd (on right-hand side going out of town). It's a great site, and ales (around 30), food and music esp jazz are partaken on the Thu even/Fri and Sat noon-11pm in a converted bottling plant and outside in the courtyard and bowling green. See local press for details or call (031) 337 1286.

THE PUBS WITH GOOD FOOD

Most of these pubs are also notable for other reasons.

THE GOLF TAVERN: 31 Wright's Houses. Off Bruntsfield Pl facing on to the Links. An Englishy, almost clubby ambience and what many think is the best pub lunch in town. A la carte and daily specials all home-made. Not just industrial desserts. Newspapers and leather sofas make for a civilised repast. Hot food is served all day till 7pm; does tend towards restaurant prices. |7|
C4

SHEEP'S HEID: Causeway, Duddingston Village. An 18th-century coaching inn 10km from centre behind Arthur's Seat and reached most easily through the Queen's Park. Restaurant upstairs and decent pub food down, including *al fresco* dining in summer. The village and the nearby wild-fowl loch should be strolled around if you have time. |72|
xE4

BENNET'S: 8 Leven St, next to the Kings Theatre. An Edinburgh stalwart, it could be listed for several reasons, not least for its honest-to-goodness (and cheap) pub lunch. A la carte and daily specials under the enormous mirrors. Lunch only: midday-2pm. (141/GREAT PUBS.) |73|
C4

THE CANNY MAN'S: 257 Morningside Rd. Not downtown (A702 via Tollcross, 7km from centre) but a well-managed pub that's been in guide-books for years. Budding publicans should come here and see how it's done. Complimentary hard-boiled eggs are free range (but then there is veal on the menu); the coffee's as good as the beer. Lunch only: midday-2pm. (168/REAL ALE PUBS.) |74|
xC4

KING'S WARK: 36 The Shore, on the corner of Bernard St. Quite simply the best pub fish 'n' chips (in beer batter) in town. Bistro-style layout. Lunch: till 2.30pm. Evenings, LO 10pm. |75|
xE1

THE ABBOTSFORD: 3 Rose St. A doughty remnant of Rose St drinking days of yore and still the best pub lunch nr Princes St. Nothing fancy in the à la carte of grills and mainly meaty entrées. Huge portions. Restau upstairs serves food in evening too; LO 9.30pm. |76|
D2

STARBANK INN: 64 Laverockbank Rd. On seafront betw Newhaven and Leith. Food lunchtime and evening and superior ales served in the bar or the new conservatory thro the back (164/REAL ALE PUBS). Lunch and evenings 6.30-8.30pm. |77|
xC1

SHORE BAR: 3 The Shore. A bistro/restau but the same (blackboard) menu faster and friendlier in the bar (where you can also smoke). Light meat dishes, lots of fish and always vegn. Open for lunch and till 10pm (56/BISTROS). |78|
xE1

Outside Town

THE SUN INN: Lothianburn, 663 2456. On a bend of the A7 near t/off for Newtongrange, beneath a towering viaduct, **18km S of city centre**. A family pub with adventurous yet homely menu from tsatsiki to Desperate Dan's Pie. Groaning cabinet of puds. Lunch till 2.30pm (all day at w/ends), evenings till 9.30pm. Also accom. |79|
xE4
MED.INX

THE BRIDGE INN/THE POP INN, RATHO: Canal Centre, Ratho, W. Lothian. 333 1320. **16km W of centre via A71,** turning right opp Dalmahoy Golf Club. Huge menu for all variations of comforting food in canal-side setting. This place wins awards for all kinds of things including their menu for kids. Restau as well as bar food; also canal cruises with full menu. Lunch: midday-2.30pm (all day w/ends). Evenings: 6-10pm. (118/PLACES TO TAKE KIDS.) |80|
xA4

DROVER'S INN: 5 Bridge St, East Linton, 0620 860298. Off the A1, **35km S of city**. Fair way to go for lunch (or dinner); but don't think about the A1, think about the food. A classic village pub with cosy warmth and delicious meals in bistro beside bar or restau up top. Big on seafood and traditional puddings. Lots of nice places nearby to walk off a blowout. Lunch till 2pm (Suns 3pm). Dinner: 5-10pm. 7days. |8|
xE2

PUBS AND CLUBS WITH GOOD LIVE MUSIC

Many other places have live music but programmes and policies can vary quickly. Best to look out for posters or consult The List *magazine. The following are the most likely bets.*

182 **THE MUSIC BOX:** At the top of Victoria St. Enter at street level and descend
D3 to what's probably the best place in town to see contemporary bands before they go on to greater things. Clubby, not too claustrophobic. Not open every night, so consult *The List* or phone 225 2564. Times vary. Different clubs on w/ends (10pm-3am).

183 **THE OYSTER BARS: ST JAMES,** 557 2925. Calton Rd opp St James Centre and off
D2 the top of Leith Walk. One of 4 'Oyster Bars' (all with live music at times), this is the one where many of the Edinburgh musos hang out and play, in their various hybrid forms. Sometimes it can be cookin', and bar snacks can be partaken (often late, which is handy). Other Oyster Bars which are all worth a visit if you like live music and live people are at The Shore (Leith), the West End Bar (W Maitland St) and the Queen St Oyster Bar (basement on the corner of Queen St and Hanover). The latter, though small, has wee bands most nights (226 2530). All are open past midnight (191/LATE BARS).

183a **THE VENUE:** 557 3073. Calton Rd behind the Main Post Office and Waverley Stn.
D2 Major live music venue with dance clubs on Fri/Sat (see p.41, CLUBS) and occ Thur (at time of writing, the estimable Tribal Funktion). On the UK club circuit, so often notable bands and the best of the Scottish scene. Tickets in advance 557 6969 and on the door. Watch for posters and flyers.

184 **PRESERVATION HALL:** 226 3816. 9 Victoria St. This large, long-established 'room',
D3 has live music as its main function and though it varies night by night, it's where to go for reasonable pub rock (or jazz, contemporary pop and esp, blues). Open 6pm-midnight, w/ends 1am. Bands usually on at 10.30pm. Free or small adm.

185 **NEGOCIANTS:** 225 6313. 45 Lothian St. Basement rock 'n' roll, loud and variable,
D3 occasionally 'happening'. Upstairs is a café-bar, serving Indonesian (*sic*) and other interesting food; bustling all day with studentish crowd. Open 9.30am-3am, 7 days. Food till 10pm. Music (free) usually from 10.30pm.

186 **THE CAS ROCK CAFE:** 229 4341. 104 West Port. Nr the Art college and the Broo
C3 office which may supply some of the clientele of this indie-attitude pub rock venue. In any case, you get close to the bands. Pool tables. Thu-Sat.

186a **LA BELLE ANGELE:** 225 2774. 11 Hasties Close behind the Pelican pub in the
D3 Cowgate. At time of writing, the hippest spot for a new band to tread the (bare) boards. If this was New York, we'd all know about it. Consult ads.

187 **PLATFORM ONE:** 225 4433. Side of Caledonian Hotel in Rutland St. Large room,
B3 long bar, stage at one end – this could be a music pub in Sydney (where pub rock rules). Music of a certain caste, for peopl without the E. Free.

188 **L'ATTACHE:** Rutland St. In the West End opp Platform One. Loud and standard
B3 rock 'n' roll in cellar bar where you shout, rather than chat, somebody up. Till 1am. Free.

189 **THE TRON CEILIDH HOUSE:** 220 1550. Hunter Sq, behind the Tron Church at the
D3 corner of the High St and 'The Bridges'. Spacious downstairs bodega for folk who like folk and occ jazz. Jam sessions, featured bands and ceilidhs. Most nights from around 9pm. Free. (1333/FOLK MUSIC.)

EDINBURGH FOLK FESTIVAL: April/May all over the city in selected pubs and with major performances in larger halls, particularly the Queen's Hall. Info: 220 1464.

EDINBURGH JAZZ FESTIVAL: Late August during the first two weeks of the International Festival. Mainly traditional jazz in participating pubs and larger halls. Info: 557 1642.

THE BEST LATE BARS

At time of writing Edinburgh's liberal licensing laws, whereby many pubs can stay open till the wee sma' hours, are under threat. If earlier closures are introduced they will apply to all the pubs below.

In addition to these, there are many other bars which currently stay open till midnight during the week/1am on Fridays.

BERTIE'S: Merchant St. At the very end of this overlooked alley at the Forrest Rd end of the Grassmarket. George IV Bridge goes overhead and the bar is tucked underneath. Inside, it opens into a vast cavernous space which gets loud and busy with studentish crowd later on. Live music Sun-Thur. Till 3am, 7 days. *190 D3*

ST JAMES OYSTER BAR: Calton St off top of Leith Walk.

WEST END OYSTER BAR: 28 Maitland St, beyond Princes St at Haymarket.

LEITH OYSTER BAR: 10 Burgess St, on the shore of Water of Leith.

QUEEN ST OYSTER BAR: 16a Queen St nr corner of Hanover St.

The Oyster Bars, run by the Brothers Donkin, are as solidly 'Edinburgh' as Arthur's Seat. All have live music at various times (183/PUBS WITH MUSIC) and all have a laid-back, friendly atmosphere. It is also possible to partake of oysters (and other light food). They're all open till 1am (Sun midnight). *191*

THE PELICAN: 235 The Cowgate at the bottom of Blair St. Cellar-like place (though it's on the ground floor). Good atmosphere. Packed to the gunnels at w/ends. Open 2/2.30am. W/ends till 3am. *192 D3*

NEGOCIANTS: 45 Lothian St by the University Union buildings. Civilised café/restau/bar and basement with live music that's open till 3am every night. (185/PUBS WITH MUSIC; 137/SUNDAY BREAKFAST.) *193 D3*

MADOGS: 38A George St betw Hanover and Frederick St. It's a while since the heyday of Madogs, once the most fashionable bar/diner in town. Some of that crowd, however, are still propping up the bar and staring into the tequila sunset. So it's an older crowd, but they could tell you a thing or two. Mon/Tue 1am, Wed/Thu/Sun 2am, Fri/Sat till 3am. *194 C2*

THE ANTIQUARY: 72 St Stephen St. Middle of Stockbridge watering-hole or basement, where the lowlife episodes of the St Stephen St soap opera are enacted often for the enjoyment of the rest of the bar. 'The Antick' may attract a motley crew, but hang out and you'll be written into the script. 12.30/1am w/ends. *195 C1*

THE COOLER: Calton St underneath The Venue (250/ROCK AND POP). A dive bar behind the station and below the live music club (at w/ends it's one of the most successful rave-ish clubs) and where you go when all else fails, or closes. Open till 4am, 7 nights. *196 D2*

THE BOUNDARY BAR: 379 Leith Walk. Not so much a late pub as an early pub: it opens at 5am. Nevertheless, once you've done the rounds, this pub halfway down Leith Walk on the ancient boundary of the city is open for the last or the first dram of the day. *197 E1*

THE MAIN ATTRACTIONS

198 **EDINBURGH CASTLE:** You can hardly miss it. Outside London, the
C3 most popular historical attraction in the UK. It does not disappoint.
Ancient, authentic, well-maintained and presented, there can be few places in the
world that are as much the real McCoy. Incomparable views all round. St
Margaret's Chapel, the Great Hall, the Crown Jewels, the National War
Memorial, Mons Meg – this is history that speaks above the clamour and
clambering of your fellow tourists. Apr-Sept 9.30-6pm, Oct-Mar 9.30am-5pm.
(905/CASTLES; 1031/SPOOKY PLACES.)   HS

199 **HOLYROOD PALACE:** Foot of the Royal Mile. The Queen's Hoose, open for
E2 guided tours only, which leave almost continuously and last 35 mins. That's
quite a lot of history in half an hour, but apart from the Mary Queen of Scots
story (better than any soap opera, the highlight being the room where Rizzio
was murdered), it's all a bit dreich. You can only gaze up at the Queen's
apartments, but it's hard to imagine anybody wanting to live in the sterile rooms
lined with gloomy portraits that the tour whisks you through. The Abbey ruins
are worth a meander as you're leaving. Apr-Oct 9.30am-5.15pm (Sun 10.30am-
4.30pm). Nov-Dec 9.30am-3.45pm (cl Sun).   HS

200 **THE ROYAL MILE:** The High St, the medieval main thoroughfare of
D3 Edinburgh. It follows the trail from the volcanic crag of the Castle rock
and connects the two landmarks above. There are innumerable distractions and
interesting corners down wynds and closes (e.g. Dunbar's Close, Whitehorse
Close, the secret garden opp Huntly House), and lots of tacky tartan shops.
During the Festival it's full on, but at night during the winter it can be almost
deserted and magical. One of the best ways to see it is on a Murder and Mystery
Tour leaving every evening from outside the Witchery Restau (225 6745).

201 **ROYAL SCOTTISH MUSEUM:** Chambers St. Imposing exterior with one of
D3 the most impressive light and lofty atriums you'll find anywhere.
Opened in 1866, it houses in its galleries and salons a diverse collection of
Industrial and Natural History both huge and minute and all quaintly
fascinating. 10am-5pm, Sun noon-5pm, Interesting coffee shop. 126/TEA-ROOMS.

202 **THE NATIONAL GALLERY AND ROYAL ACADEMY:** The Mound. The
C2 **National** is the rear one of the 2 neo-classical buildings on Princes St
and houses a superb collection of Old Masters in a series of hushed but
handleable salons. Many are world-famous, but you don't emerge goggle-eyed
as you do from the National in London. 10am-5pm. Sun 2-5pm. The Playfair
'temple' on Princes St itself is the **Royal Academy,** with changing exhibitions
which in early summer and midwinter show selected work from contemporary
Scottish artists. 10am-5pm. Sun 2-5pm.   ADM

203 **EDINBURGH ZOO:** 334 9171. Corstorphine Rd. 4km W of Princes St. Many
xA3 buses from the Princes Steet Gardens side. Whatever you might think of
zoos in general, this one is highly respected and its serious zoology is still fun for
kids. The penguins perform and the monkeys do vulgar things. And if you don't
catch their melancholy, accusative eyes, you can leave without imagining that one
day those wolves will have their revenge. 740/KIDS PLACES.   ADM

204 **ROYAL COMMONWEALTH POOL:** 667 7211. Dalkeith Rd. Hugely successful
xE4 pool complex which includes a 50m main pool, a gym, sauna/steam
room/suntan suites and a jungle of aquaslides. Goes like a fair, morning to night.
Some people find the water over-treated and over-noisy, but Edinburgh has
many good pools to choose from; this is the one that young folk prefer. Some
lane swimming. 9am-9pm. Sun 10am-4pm. Buses 21, 33.

205 **THE FORTH BRIDGE:** S. Queensferry, 20km W of Edinburgh via A90.
xA2 First turning for S Q from dual-carriageway, don't confuse with
signs for Road Bridge. Or train from Waverley to Dalmeny, and walk 1km. Or
bus 40. The engineering triumph of the Victorian world, it celebrated its
centenary in 1990 and was festooned with unflattering lights which attract
people by night as well as day. But the bridge is above all that and is still a
wonder to behold.

THE SLIGHTLY LESS OBVIOUS
ATTRACTIONS

✝ ✝ **THE ROYAL BOTANIC GARDENS:** Inverleith, 3km from Princes St. Buses 206
✝ ✝ 23, 27. Enter from Inverleith Row or Aboretum Pl. 70 acres of *B1*
ornamental gardens, trees and walkways; a joy in every season. Tropical plant
houses, the best rock and heath garden you'll see anywhere and enough space
just to wander. The squirrels are precocious and everywhere. Gallery with
occasional exhibs and café with outdoor terrace for serene afternoon teas
(127/TEA-ROOMS).

✝ ✝ **NATIONAL PORTRAIT GALLERY:** 556 8921. 1 Queen St. More a palace than a 207
✝ ✝ gallery. Marvellous Victorian gothic atrium, first-floor gallery and star- *D2*
studded ceiling (sic). Portraiture and mementos of the nobility and, on the
ground floor, their instruments for keeping down the rabble. Also houses the
Museum of Antiquity and its meticulous archaeology. Great café (120/TEA-
ROOMS).

✝ **GALLERY OF MODERN ART:** 556 8921. Belford Rd. Bus 13. Between 208
✝ Queensferry Rd and the Dean Village (nice to walk through). Best to start *xA2*
from Palmerston Pl and keep left. Country house/former school with permanent
collection from Impressionism to Hockney and the Scottish painters alongside.
An intimate gallery where you can fall in love with the paintings. Some
important temporary exhibs. Good café (121/TEA-ROOMS).

✝ ✝ **MUSEUM OF CHILDHOOD:** 225 2424. 42 High St. Fantastic collection of toys 209
✝ ✝ and kids' stuff which would enchant even bored adolescents and *D3*
certainly grown-ups. You can't play with any of it, but you could always try and
get locked in overnight. First class.

The above galleries all open 10am-5pm Mon-Sat and 2-5pm on Sundays.

✝ **ST GILES CATHEDRAL:** Royal Mile. A prominent site; less obvious as an 210
✝ attraction perhaps and often missed out on the well-worn path from the *D3*
Castle to the Palace. But here you can feel the deep pulse of history, the High
Kirk having been at the heart of the city since the 9th century. The building is
mainly medieval with Norman fragments and all encased in Georgian exterior.
Lorimer's Thistle chapel and the very latest addition, the 'big new organ', are
impressive. Good coffee shop in the crypt (125/TEA-ROOMS).

THE GEORGIAN HOUSE: 226 5922. 7 Charlotte Sq. A townhouse on magnificent 211
Charlotte Sq designed by Robert Adam and providing a stop-the-clock insight *B2*
into the life and the times of the leisured classes in the reign of George III (and
the aspirations of the New Georgians in the reign of Margaret Thatcher). Apr-
Oct 10am-5pm, Sun 2-5pm.   NT

LAURISTON CASTLE: 336 2060. 2 Cramond Road South. 9km E of centre by A90, 212
turning rt for Cramond. Bus 41. Elegant architecture and gracious living from *xA2*
Edwardian times. A largely Jacobean tower house set in tranquil grounds
o/looking the Forth. The liveability of the house and the preoccupations of the
Reid family make you wish you could poke around for yourself but there are
valuable and exquisite decorative pieces and furniture and it's guided tours only
(cont in July/Aug and at set times Apr-Oct). You could always continue to
Cramond for the air (218/CITY WALKS). Open 11am-5pm Apr-Oct and 2-6pm
(Sat/Sun only) Nov-Mar. Tour times 336 2060.

ARTHUR'S SEAT: 217/CITY WALKS.

THE PENTLANDS: 222/WALKS OUTSIDE THE CITY.

THE SCOTT MONUMENT/CALTON HILL: 215/213/VIEWS.

THE BEST VIEWS OF THE CITY AND BEYOND

213 **CALTON HILL:** Great view of the city easily gained by walking up from
E2 the east end of Princes St by Waterloo Pl, to the end of the buildings
and then up stairs on the left. The City Observatory and the Greek-style folly
lend an elegant backdrop to a panorama (unfolding as you walk round) where
the view up Princes St and the sweep of the Forth estuary are particularly fine.
At night, the city does twinkle but mainly for the CB fanatics up there looking
for reception and lonesome chaps looking for each other.

Calton Hill, Edinburgh (213)

214 **ARTHUR'S SEAT:** West of city centre. Best approached through the
E3 Queen's Park from the bottom of the Canongate by Holyrood Palace.
The igneous core of an extinct volcano with the precipitous sill of Salisbury
Crags presiding over the city and offering fine views for the fit. Top is 251m and
on a clear day you can see 100km. Surprisingly wild considering proximity to
city. 3 lochs incl Duddingston (follow road to right from Palace for 6km), a
birdlife sanctuary. Various climbs (less than an hour). 'Volunteers Walk' starts
opposite the carpark on macadam and continues on grass through 'Hunters Bog'
to the 'Pipers Walk' and the top. For other specific walks, see page opposite.

215 **THE SCOTT MONUMENT:** Princes St. The gothic steeple rising 200ft above Princes
D2 St Gardens, beneath which sit Sir Walter and his faithful dug carved from a 30-
ton chunk of marble. Recently the subject of some controversy over whether
and how the stonework should be cleaned. For a year it was encased in plastic
and looked like an elongated pagoda; and that was just the feasibility survey!
However, now it can be climbed again and it is worth the effort if you're fit; 4
flights of 287 stairs in a narrow spiral staircase take you that bit closer to heaven.
Apr-Sept 9am-6pm, Oct-Mar 9am-3pm.

216 **CAMERA OBSCURA:** Castlehill, Royal Mile. At v top of street nr the Castle
C3 entrance, a tourist attraction that, surprisingly, has been there for over a century.
You ascend through a bookshop and various exhibits of photography and
holograms to the viewing area where small continuous groups are shown the
wondrous effect of the giant revolving periscope. What you see depends on the
light, so it deteriorates towards dusk. Up top there's also an outdoor platform
for a real close-up view of the Old Town rooftops.

THE PENTLAND HILLS: 222/WALKS OUTSIDE THE CITY.

BLACKFORD HILL/THE BRAIDS: 221/WALKS OUTSIDE THE CITY.

CASTLE RAMPARTS: 198/MAIN ATTRACTIONS.

NORTH BERWICK LAW/TRAPRAIN LAW: 1040/FAVOURITE HILLS.

THE BEST WALKS IN THE CITY

Areas of these walks are not covered in the city centre map. See p.9 for walk codes.

ARTHUR'S SEAT: Of many walks (see previous page), a good circular one taking 217 in the wilder bits, the lochs and great views starts from St Margaret's Loch at the *E3* far end of the park from the Palace. Leaving the carpark, skirt the loch and head for the ruined chapel. Pass it on your right and, after 250m in a dry valley, the buttress of the main summit rears above you on the rt. Keeping it to the rt, ascend over a saddle joining the main route from Dunsapie Loch which appears below on the left. Crow Hill is the other peak crowned by a triangular cairn. Both peaks can be slithery in damp weather. From Arthur's Seat head for and traverse the long steep incline of the Crags. Paths parallel to the edge lead back to the chapel.

START: Enter park at Palace at foot of the High St and turn left on main road for 1km; the loch is on the right.

PARK: There are carparks beside the Loch and in front of the Palace (paths start here too, across the road). 5-8KM CIRC MTBIKE (RESTRICTED ACCESS) 2-B-2

CRAMOND: This is the charming village (not the suburb) on the Forth at the 218 mouth of the R Almond with a variety of great walks. **A)** To the right along the *xA2* 'prom'; the traditional seaside stroll. **B)** Across the causeway at low tide to Cramond Island (1km). Best to follow the tide out; this allows 4 hrs (tides are posted). People have been known to stay the night in summer but this is discouraged. **C)** Cross the mouth of the Almond River in the tiny passenger ferry which comes on demand (summer 9am-7pm, winter 10am-4pm) then follow coastal path to Dalmeny House which is open to the public in the afternoons (May-Sept, Sun-Thur); or walk all the way to S Queensferry (8km). **D)** Past the boathouse and up the R Almond Heritage Trail which goes eventually to the Cramond Brig Hotel on the A90 and thence to the old airport (3-8km). Though it goes through suburbs and seems to be on the flightpath of the London shuttle, the Almond is a real river with a charm and ecosystem of its own. The Cramond Bistro awaits your return (61/BISTROS).

START: Leave centre by Queensferry Rd (A90), then rt following signs for Cramond. Cramond Rd North leads to Cramond Glebe Rd; go to end.

PARK: Large carpark off Cramond Glebe Rd to right. Walk 100m to sea. 1/3/8KM XCIRC BIKE BUS 41 1-A-1

CORSTORPHINE HILL: W of centre, a knobbly hilly area of birch, beech and oak, 219 criss-crossed by trails. A perfect place for the contemplation of life's little *xA2* mysteries and mistakes. Or walking the dog. It has a radio mast, a ruined tower, a boundary with the Wild Plains of Africa (at the zoo) and a vast redundant nuclear shelter that nobody's supposed to know about. See how many you can spot. If it had a tea-room in an old pavilion, it would be perfect.

START: Leave centre by Queensferry Rd and 8km out turn left at lights, signed Clermiston. The hill is on your left for the next 2km.

PARK: Park where safe, on or near this road (Clermiston Rd). 1-7KM CIRC XBIKE BUS 26,85 1-A-1

WATER OF LEITH: The indefatigable wee river that runs from the Pentlands 220 through the city and into the docks at Leith can be walked for most of its length, though obviously not by any circular route. **A)** The longest section from Balerno 12km o/side the city, through Colinton Dell to the Tickled Trout pub carpark on Lanark Rd (4km from city centre). The 'Dell' itself is a popular glen walk (1-2km).

START: A70 to Currie, Juniper Green, Balerno; park by High School. **B)** Dean Village to Stockbridge: enter through a marked gate opp Hilton Hotel on Belford Rd (combine with a visit to Modern Art Gallery). **C)** Warriston, through the spooky old graveyard (994/GRAVEYARDS), to The Shore in Leith (plenty pubs to repair to). Enter by going to the end of the cul-de-sac at Warriston Cres in Canonmills; climb up the bank and turn left.

Most of the Water of Leith Walkway (A,B and C) is cinder track. 8KM (OR LESS) XCIRC BIKE BUS 43,44 1-A-1

EASY WALKS OUTSIDE THE CITY

Buses to starting places mostly from St Andrew Sq. Info: 556 8464. *See p. 9 for walk codes.*

221 **HERMITAGE OF BRAID:** Strictly speaking, this is still in town, but there's a real
xD4 sense of being in a country glen and from the windy tops of the Braid hills there are some marvellous views back over the city. Main track along the burn is easy to follow and you eventually come to Hermitage House info centre; any paths ascending to the rt take to the ridge of Blackford Hill. In winter, there's a great sledging place over the first bridge up to the left and across the main road.

START: Blackford Glen Rd. Go S on Mayfield to main T jnct with Liberton Rd, turn rt (signed Penicuik) then hard right immediately.

1-4KM   CAN BE CIRC   BIKE   BUS 7   1-A-1

222 **THE PENTLANDS:** Alan Jackson, poet of this parish, once wrote, 'Look wifie,
xC4 behind you, the wild Pentlands'. And wild they are: a serious range of hills rising to almost 2000ft, remote in parts and offering some fine walking. There are many paths up the various tops and round the lochs and reservoirs.

A) A good start in town is made by going off the bypass at Colinton, foll signs for Colinton Vill, then the left fork up Woodhall Rd. Second left up Bonaly Rd (signed Bonaly Scout Camp). Drive/walk as far as you can (2km) and park by the gate leading to the hill proper where there is a map showing routes. The path to Glencorse is one of the classic Pentland walks.

B) Most walks start from signposted gateways on the A702 Biggar Rd. There are starts at Boghall (5km after Hillend ski slope); on the long straight stretch before Silverburn (a 10km path to Balerno); from Habbie's Howe (43/HOTELS O/S TOWN), a fine inn 1km off the rd about 18km from town; and from the vill of Carlops, 22km from town.

C) The most popular start is prob from the visitor centre behind the Flotterstone Inn, also on the A702, 14km from town; trailboard. The remoter tops around Loganlea reservoir are worth the extra mile.

1-20KM   CAN BE CIRC   MTBIKE   BUS 4 OR ST ANDR SQ   2-B-2

223 **ROSLIN GLEN:** One of those special places, spiritual, historical and enchanting;
xC4 with a chapel (982/CHURCHES), a ruined castle on the bluff and woody walks along the R Esk.

START: A701 from Mayfield or Newington (or bypass, t/off Penicuik, A702 then fork left on A703 to Roslin). Walk from bend in Main St to chapel (500m) or follow B7003 to Rosewell (also marked Rosslynlee Hosp) and 1km from village the carpark is to left.

1-8KM   xCIRC   BIKE   BUS ST ANDR SQ   1-A-1

224 **ALMONDELL:** A country park to W of city (18km) near (and one of the best
xA4 things about) Livingston. A deep, peaceful woody cleft with easy paths and riverine meadows. Fine for kids, lovers and dog walkers. Visitor centre with tea-shop. Trails marked. 773/COUNTRY PARKS.

START: Best approach from Edinburgh by A71 via Sighthill. After Wilkieston, turn rt for Camp (B7015). 7km on – park on rt, just inside E Calder village. From carpark walk straight, not to the rt.

2-8KM   xCIRC   BIKE   BUS ST ANDR SQ   1-A-1

225 **BEECRAIGS AND COCKLEROY HILL:** Another country park W of Linlithgow with
xA3 trails and clearings in mixed woods, a deer farm and a fishing loch. Great adventure playground for kids. Best is the climb and extraordinary view from Cockleroy Hill, far better than you'd expect for the effort. From Ben Lomond to the Bass Rock; and the gunge of Grangemouth in the sky to the east.

START: M90 to Linlithgow (26km), through town and left on Preston Rd. Go on 4km, park is signed, but for hill you don't need to take the left turn. The hill (and nearest carpark to it), are on rt.

2-8KM   CIRC   MTBIKE   BUS ST ANDR SQ   1-A-1

226 **BORTHWICK AND CRICHTON CASTLE:** Takes in 2 impressive castles, the first a
posh hotel (36/HOTELS OUTSIDE TOWN) and the other an imposing ruin (929/RUINS) on a ridge o/looking the R Tyne. A walk thro' dramatic Border Country steeped in lore. Path signed at start peters out but castle in view.

START: A7 S for 16km, past Gorebridge, left at N Middleton; signed.

7KM   xCIRC   xBIKE   BUS ST ANDR SQ   1-B-2

SPORTS FACILITIES

SWIMMING AND INDOOR SPORTS CENTRES
COMMONWEALTH POOL: Dalkeith Rd. 667 7211. (204/ATTRACTIONS.) The biggest, 227 but Edinburgh has many others. Same phone number for all. Bus 21, 33. Particularly recommended are **INFIRMARY ST** off the Bridges, the most central, **WARRENDER** at Thirlestane Rd 500m beyond the Meadows S of centre. **THE LEITH POOL** in Junction Pl off the main st in Leith is a hidden gem (though closed at time of going to press); bus 12. All these pools are old and tiled, 25yd long, seldom crowded and excellent for lane swimming (at certain times). They are open Mon-Fri (last session 7pm) and Sat (last sess 3pm) but check. Few cities are as well served with such great swimming pools.

PORTOBELLO BATHS: On the Esplanade (see BEACHES below) similar to others (though gets busier) and wonderfully atmospheric Turkish Baths (Mon/Wed/Fri/Sat men; Tue/Thur/Sun women. 9am-7.30pm; till 3pm w/ends). Bus 26.

AINSLIE PARK: Trinity, 551 2400 to N of centre, 5km Princes St and **LEITH WATERWORLD:** foot of Leith Walk, 555 6000. Both new leisure centres with water thrills for kids. Buses: Ainslie Park – 27, 19, 29; Leith Waterworld – 7, 10, 17.

PORT SETON: 0875 811709 and **NORTH BERWICK:** 0620 2083 (1144/BEST SWIMMING POOLS). Both open air, down the coast, open in summer.

MEADOWBANK: London Rd. 661 5351. City athletics stadium with gym and courts for squash and badminton. Often booked. No pool.

MARCO'S: 51 Grove St. 228 2141. Commercial centre on labyrinthine scale with aerobic classes, gym, squash and snooker. No pool.

UNIVERSITY GYM: The Pleasance. 650 2585. No-nonsense complex, v. cheap. The best in town for weight training (Nautilus and Universal) and circuit training. Squash, badminton, indoor tennis. Not busy in vacs, membership not reqd. Fake sun *infra dig*. No pool.

EDINBURGH CLUB: 2 Hillside Cres. 556 8845. Probably the most civilised of non-hotel-type health clubs, but usually members only. Longer-stay visitors may be able to negotiate a rate. Good weights room (mainly Universal), sauna/steam/sun, bistro. Good aerobics classes.

GOLF COURSES
There are several municipal courses (see phone directory under Edin District Council) and nearby, esp down the coast, some famous names that aren't open to non-members. But three of the best available are:

BRAID HILLS: Braid Hills Rd. 447 6666. 2 x 18 holes. Thought to be the best in 228 town. Never boring; exhilarating views. Booking usually not essential. Women welcome (and that ain't true everywhere).

GULLANE NO.1: 0620 842147. The best of 3 courses around this pretty, twee village 229 (35km down the coast) that was built for golf. Now you are really golfing! (though not on Sats). 1100/GOLF.

NORTH BERWICK EAST LINKS: 0620 2726. Some say West is best, but most say East 230 and few would argue that N Berwick on a fair day was worth the drive (36km, A1 then A198) from Edinburgh. That's the Bass Rock out there and Fidra. Open to women. 1101/GOLF.

OTHER ACTIVITIES
TENNIS: There are lots of private clubs though only the **GRANGE** (332 2148) has lawn 231 tennis and you won't get on there easily. There are places you can slip on (best *B1* not to talk about that), but the municipal centres (Edin residents/longer-stay visitors should get a Leisure Access card – 661 5351 – allowing advance reservation) are:
SAUGHTON: 440 0422. 8km W of city centre. 2 astroturf courts and one other. Also *xA4* used for football, so phone to check. Bus 3, 33.
CRAIGLOCKHART: 443 0101. 8km SW of centre via Morningside and Colinton Rd. *xC4* Some lawn courts which you have as much chance of getting on as at Wimbledon, and up to 8 other all-weather courts, which are best to check/book by phone. Centre open Mon-Fri 9am-10.30pm, Sat/Sun 9am-10pm. Bus 23, 27.

232 **SKIING:** Artificial slopes at **HILLEND** on A702, 10km S of centre. 445 4433. Excellent
xC4 facility with various runs. The matting can be bloody rough when you fall and
the chairlift is a bit of a dread for beginners, but once you can ski here, St
Anton's all yours. Tuition every evening (not Thur) and w/ends. Open till 10pm
in winter, 9pm in summer. Bus 4.

233 **PONY-TREKKING: LASSWADE RIDING SCHOOL:** 663 7676. Loanhead exit from City
D4 Bypass then A768, rt to Loanhead exit from City Bypass then A768, rt to
Loanhead 1km and left to end of Kevock Rd. Full hacking and trekking facilities
and courses for all standards and ages. Bus 87.

xA4 **PENTLAND HILLS TREKKING CENTRE:** 0968 60579. At Carlops on A702 (25km from
town) has sturdy, footsure Icelandic horses who will bear you good-naturedly
into the hills. Exhilarating stuff. Bus from St Andrew Sq.

234 **ICE-SKATING: MURRAYFIELD ICERINK:** Riversdale Cres just off main Glasgow Rd
xA3 near zoo. 337 6933. Cheap, cheerful and chilly. It has been here forever and feels
like a great 1950s' B-movie . . . go round! Bus 26, 31.

GALLERIES

*Apart from those listed previously (LESS OBVIOUS ATTRACTIONS, p.35),
the following galleries are always worth looking into. The Edinburgh Gallery
Guide, free from any gallery, lists all the current exhibs.*

235 **THE CITY ART CENTRE:** 225 2424. Market St. Mounts major popular exhibitions
D3 often on the international circuit as well as those more locally relevant. Recent
full-scale refurbishment.

236 **THE FRUITMARKET GALLERY:** Across the road in Market St, a smaller, more
D3 warehousey space for collections, retrospectives, installations. Recent roof
raising and refurb has been a great improvement. Good café. Cl Mon.

237 **369:** 225 3013. 233 Cowgate. A small but vital private gallery often used for
D3 performances and interesting goings-on. Studios upstairs. A hub of activity
whenever Andrew Brown is about. Champions new Scottish art.

238 **THE COLLECTIVE GALLERY:** 220 1260. 22 Cockburn St. Newish premises for
D3 innovative gallery specialising in installations of Scottish and other young
contemporary trailblazers.

238a **FLYING COLOURS GALLERY:** 225 6776. 35 William St in W End. Tiny, influential and
B3 usually with well-chosen, accessible exhibs. 11am-6pm (Sat 10am-1pm); Cl Mon.

239 **THE PRINTMAKERS' WORKSHOP AND GALLERY:** 23 Union St off Leith Walk nr
D1 London Rd roundabout. Workshops that you can look over. Exhibs of work by
contemporary printmakers and shop where prints from many of the notable
names in Scotland are on sale at reasonable prices. Tue-Sat 10am-6pm.

BEACHES

240 **PORTOBELLO:** The town beach of Edinburgh, 8km from centre by London Rd. A
xE3 long promenade and the melancholy echo of pre-Benidorm hols. Bus 26, 85.

241 **YELLOWCRAIGS:** The nearest decent beach (35km). A1 or bypass, then A198 coast
xE2 rd. Left outside Dirleton for 2km, park and walk 100m across Links to fairly
clean strand and sea. Gets crowded, but big enough to share. Hardly anyone
swims but you can. Scenic.

242 **SEACLIFF:** The best beach, least crowded/littered; ideal for picnics, beach-
xE2 combing, dreaming and gazing into rockpools. There is a harbour, still in
use, which is also good for swimming. 50km from town, Seacliff is off the A198
out of N Berwick, 3km after Tantallon Castle. At a bend in the rd and a farm
(Auldhame) there is an unsigned rd off to left. 2km on there's a barrier, costing 2
x 50p to get car through. Carpark 1km then walk. From A1, take E Linton t/off,
go through Whitekirk towards N Berwick, then same.

GOOD NIGHTLIFE

For the current programmes of the places recommended below and all others venues, consult The List *magazine, on sale at most newsagents.*

MOVIES
Multiplex chains apart, these ones take movies seriously:

THE CAMEO: Home St in Tollcross 228 4141. 3 screens showing important new films and cult classics. Some late movies at weekends. Good bar.   243   C4

FILMHOUSE: Lothian Rd opp Usher Hall. 228 2688. 2 screens, Cinema 1 showing mainly first-run art-house movies of the kind 'you must see' and Cinema 2 for more minority tastes, retros etc. Large, busy bar/café open to non-viewers.   244   C3

THE DOMINION: Newbattle Terr. off Morningside Rd. 447 2660. Friendly, family-run cinema with 3 screens (one of them's like sitting on a plane), showing selected new films and those you missed first time round.   245   xC4

THEATRE
The main city theatres are **THE KINGS:** Leven St, Tollcross, 229 1201 and   246

THE LYCEUM: Grindlay St. 229 9697. Both are ornate and recently refurbished theatres with widely ranging popular programmes. Also: 247   C4 / C3

THE TRAVERSE: Small, but very influential theatre, dedicated to new work, moved in 1992 to these v architectural 2-theatre premises in Cambridge St (behind Lyceum). Good rendezvous bar (till 1am) and restau adj (open 10am-8pm). Box office 228 1404. Closed Mon.   248   C3

THEATRE WORKSHOP: 34 Hamilton Pl. 226 5425. A small neighbourhood theatre in Stockbridge with a growing reputation. Café-bar.   249   B1

CLASSICAL MUSIC
Usually from one of Scotland's national orchestras at regular concerts in the **USHER HALL**, Lothian Rd. 228 1155. Smaller ensembles more occasionally at **THE REID, ST CECILIA'S** or **THE QUEEN'S HALL**. See *The List* or Saturday's *Scotsman* newspaper.   250

JAZZ
There's a constant improvement in the jazz scene in Edinburgh not least due to the efforts of Mike Hart of The Jazz Festival and Roger Spence (such persistence and dedication deserves namechecks). Festival apart, the best venues are:

PLATFORM ONE: Rutland Sq behind the Caledonian Hotel. 225 2433.

THE QUEENS HALL: Clerk St. 668 3456. Occ 'concerts', see press.

NOBLES: 44A Constitution St. 554 2024. Definitely on the up. Th-Sat, Sun aft.

PULLMAN PLATFORM: Haymarket Bar by Haymarket Stn. 337 1006. Most nights.

FOLK
1333/FOLK MUSIC and PUBS WITH MUSIC, p.32. Best bets are: **SANDY BELLS** aka **THE FORREST HILL BAR:** Forrest Hill. **WEST END HOTEL:** Palmerston Pl. **THE TRON BAR** and **CEILIDH HOUSE:** Hunter Sq.

ROCK AND POP
See PUBS WITH MUSIC, p.32 and 1337/ROCK AND POP.
Major concerts are held at the Playhouse and less often at the Usher Hall. Smaller names at the Queen's Hall.

Current concert info from Regular Music, the major promoters, 556 1212. Or TOCTA, the major ticket agency, 557 6969.

CLUBS
Edinburgh doesn't have really great nightclubs and still none at time of writing that I'd heavily recommend. Recently, new local licensing decisions have restricted club openings to 3am, but this may change. The most interesting clubs are only on one night a week and come and go quickly. Ripping Records (226 7010) can tell you where.   251

Safe but sure is **BUSTER BROWN'S**, Market St, 226 4224. It's been there forever playing mainstream music. Much more funky is the **MAMBO CLUB**, West Tollcross, upstairs at the Network; Fri and Sat (on 2 floors) African/reggae/generally good vibes music. Younger ravers go to the **CITRUS CLUB**, Grindlay St, 229 6697. **PURE** is the longest running 'dance' one-nighter with a solid up-front reputation. It's on Fridays at the Venue, Calton St. **WAVE** at the same place on Sat is not so hardcore. The only club with club-edge and a mixed ménage of night animals (though not braying as far into the night as before) is **THE STORE**, formerly **MILLIES** (556 6050), in Niddrie St off the High St at the Bridges. Wed-Sat 11pm-3am. Wed is gay. This club is a long way from uptown Barcelona or even Tenerife, but it's real.

See GAY SCOTLAND THE BEST (p.244) for gay nightlife.

SHOPPING FOR ESSENTIALS

These are the shops that get it right. South means S of a central area bisected by Princes St, east is east of the city centre, etc.

Butchers
MACSWEENS, 130 Bruntsfield Pl. 229 1216. SOUTH
> *Free Range:* GEORGE BOWER, 75 Raeburn Place. 332 3469. NORTH

Bakers
PREACHERS, 88 Raeburn Pl. NORTH
> *Bread:* BREADWINNER, 20 Bruntsfield Pl. 229 7247. SOUTH
> *Patisserie:* FLORENTIN, 8 St Giles St. 225 6267. CENTRAL
> DELICATESSEN FRANCAIS, 123 Bruntsfield Rd. 229 2099. SOUTH

Fishmonger
GEORGE ARMSTRONG, 80 Raeburn Pl. 315 2033. NORTH
> *Seafood:* TSE'S FISH MARKET, 2 Warrender Park Rd. 662 4207. SOUTH
> *Seafood and Salmon:* CHARLES SCOTT, 4 William St. 225 5522. CENTRAL

Fruit & Veg
FARMER JACK'S, 5 Graham St. 553 6090. EAST
> *Organic:* REAL FOODS, 37 Broughton St. 557 1911. CENTRAL

Delicatessen
VALVONA AND CROLLA, 19 Elm Row. 556 6066. EAST
> *Cheese:* HERBY'S DELICATESSEN, 66 Raeburn Pl. 332 9888. NORTH
> IAIN MELLIS, 30A Victoria St. 226 6215. CENTRAL

Wholefoods
REAL FOODS, 37 Broughton St. 557 1911. CENTRAL; 8 Brougham St. 228 1201. SOUTH

Pasta
GOURMET PASTA, 52 Morningside Rd. 447 4750. SOUTH

Sandwiches etc.
WILSON'S, 27 Dublin St. 556 2157. CENTRAL
THE GLOBE, 42 Broughton St. 558 3837. CENTRAL
NIKKI'S SANDWICH BAR, 5A William St. 226 6715. CENTRAL
LE SANDWICH, Hanover St (above Henderson's). 225 2737. CENTRAL (and Gyle Centre)
THE FOREST, George IV Bridge. 225 4560. CENTRAL

Take-away
ROWLANDS, 42 Howe St. 225 3711. CENTRAL
EASTERN SPICES, 2 Canonmills Bridge. 558 3609. CENTRAL

Wine
J. E. HOGG, 61 Cumberland St. 556 4025. NORTH

Tobacco
THE PIPE SHOP, 92 Leith Walk. 553 3561. EAST

Department Store
JENNERS, Princes St/South St David's St. 225 2442. CENTRAL
> *General:* JOHN LEWIS, St James Centre. 556 9121. CENTRAL
> *Ironmongers:* GRAYS, 89 George St. 225 7381. CENTRAL

Flowers
RAEBURN GROCERS, 23 Comely Bank Rd. 332 5166. NORTH
> *Dried:* INSCAPE, 26 Dublin St. 557 5582. CENTRAL

Newspapers
INTERNATIONAL NEWSAGENTS, 367 High St. 225 4827. CENTRAL

Late-night
> *General:* Many to choose from, but none past 10pm
> *Chemists:* BOOTS, 48 Shandwick Pl. 225 6757 CENTRAL
> SOUTHSIDE PHARMACY, 79 Nicolson St. 667 4032. SOUTH

Shoes

Shoes That Last: **BARNETS,** 7 High St. 556 3577. CENTRAL.
Modish: **SCHUH,** 32 N Bridge. 225 6552. CENTRAL.

Men's clothes

New Labels: **CRUISE,** 14 St Mary's St. 556 2532. CENTRAL
SMITHS, 124 High St. 225 5927. CENTRAL
Establshed Labels: **AUSTIN REED,** 124 Princes St. 225 6864. CENTRAL

Women's clothes

Designer: **CORNICHE,** 2 Jeffrey St. 556 3707. CENTRAL
Second-Hand Chic: **HAND IN HAND,** 3 N W Circus Pl. 226 3598. NORTH
Cheap & Cheerful: **WHAT EVERY WOMAN WANTS,** South Bridge. SOUTH

Hairdressers

CHEYNES, various branches. 225 2234. CENTRAL
CHARLIE MILLER, 13 Stafford St. 226 5550 CENTRAL
PETER KOZUB, 20 Victoria St. 226 6745. SOUTH

Barbers

WOODS, 12 Drummond St. 556 6716. SOUTH

THE MOST INTERESTING SHOPS

Antiques

General: Grassmarket, Victoria St; Thistle St, St Stephen St, NW Circus Pl.
Bric-à-Brac: **BYZANTIUM,** 9 Victoria St. 225 1768. CENTRAL.
UNICORN, 65 Dundas St. 556 7176. NORTH
Jewellery: **JOE BONNAR,** 72 Thistle St. 226 2811. CENTRAL
Clothes: **HAND IN HAND,** 3 NW Circus Pl. 226 3598. NORTH

Comics

DEAD HEAD COMICS, 44 Victoria St. 226 2774. CENTRAL

Cards

General: **SWALK,** 14 Teviot Pl. 225 3027. SOUTH
PAPER TIGER, Stafford St. 226 5812. CENTRAL
Playing/Tarot: **SOMERVILLES,** 82 Canongate. 556 5225. CENTRAL

Ceramics

WARE ON EARTH, 15 Howe St. 558 1276. NORTH
AZTECA, 5 Grassmarket. 229 9368. CENTRAL

Clothes

General: See Shopping For Essentials
MACKENZIE, 2 Hunter Sq. 225 9359. CENTRAL
Old: **PADDIE BARRASS,** 15 Grassmarket. 226 3087 CENTRAL
ELAINE'S, 53 St Stephen St. NORTH
FLIP, 60 South Bridge. 556 4966. SOUTH
Outdoor: **GRAHAM TISO,** 13 Wellington Pl. 554 0804. EAST
COUNTRY STYLE, 14 Victoria St. 225 5714 CENTRAL

Furniture

Modern: **INHOUSE,** 28 Howe St. 225 2888. NORTH
Traditional: **SHAPES,** 33 West Mill Rd. 441 7936. SOUTH

Games

MAC'S MODELS, 168 Canongate. 557 5551. EAST

Ice-cream

LUCA'S, 34 High St. Musselburgh. 665 2237. EAST 20km

Jokes
SCORE COMMOTIONS, 99 West Bow. 225 2034. CENTRAL

Junk
JUST JUNK, Broughton St. NORTH

SAM BURNS' YARD, Main road to Prestonpans. EAST 25km

UTILITIES (bit more upmarket), Broughton St. CENTRAL

Presents
ROUND THE WORLD, 82 West Bow. 225 7086. CENTRAL

MARK ROWLEY, Royal Mile. SOUTH

IMAGES OF NEPAL, 10 Grassmarket. 220 4208. CENTRAL

STUDIO ONE, 10 Stafford St. 226 5812.

WRAP, 17 Stafford St. 220 2328. CENTRAL

QUERCUS, 16 Howe St. 220 0147. CENTRAL

GALERIE MIRAGES, 46a Raeburn Pl. 315 2603. NORTH

SCOTTISH GEMS, 126 Morningside Rd. SOUTH

Rugs
MIHRAB GALLERY, 297 Canongate. 556 6952. CENTRAL

WHYTOCK AND REID, Belford Mews. 226 4911. WEST

Sci-fi
FORBIDDEN PLANET, 3 Teviot Pl. SOUTH

Sports
MACKENZIE'S, 17 Nicolson St. 667 2288. SOUTH

Sweets
CASEY'S, 52 St Mary's St. SOUTH

Souvenirs
See below and **ANYWHERE ON THE HIGH ST.**
Tartan, Serious: **KINLOCH ANDERSON,** Commercial St. 555 1371. EAST
HECTOR RUSSELL, Princes St./High St.
Tartan and tacky: Not hard to find.

Video Rental
ALPHABET VIDEO, 22 Marchmont Rd. 229 5136. SOUTH

C & A VIDEO, 93 Broughton St. 556 1866. CENTRAL

Woollies
JUDITH GLUE, 64 High St 556 5443. CENTRAL

NUMBER TWO, St Stephen Pl. 225 6257. NORTH

HYNE AND EAMES, 299 Canongate. 557 4056. CENTRAL

BILL BABER, 66 Grassmarket. 225 3249. CENTRAL

THE CASHMERE STORE, 2 St Giles St. 225 4055. CENTRAL

HILLARY ROHDE, 332 4147. (exclusive cashmere, appointment only)

SECTION 2
Glasgow

The telephone code for Glasgow is 041

THE BEST HOTELS

253　**ONE DEVONSHIRE GARDENS:** 339 2001. 1 Devonshire Gardens. Off Gt ✝ ✝
xA1　Western Rd (the A82 W to Dumbarton) past the Botanics and some
distance from the youthsome and toothsome delights of Byres Rd. Festooned
with rosettes since it opened in late 1980s, this v civilised retreat composed of 3
separate terrace houses is a sophisticated designer product of its time and was
long overdue in Glasgow. Each bedroom presents a different colour-co-ordinated
concept and you will be cocooned in comfort. You may have to come out of no 3
to go to breakfast in no 1, but food and service are still the most perfectionist in
town. And you certainly don't need to go out to eat (293/BEST RESTAUS). UK
hotel of the Year '93. See why!　27RMS　JAN-DEC　T/T　PETS　CC　KIDS　LOTS

254　**THE DEVONSHIRE HOTEL:** 339 7878. 5 Devonshire Gardens. Confirming the ✝
xA1　theory that the best place to launch a new hotel or restau is next to one that
works, the Devonshire opened at the other end of the short terrace in 1991 and
is at first sight very similar though the managements are not connected. Though
not so perfectly serviced, it's less expensive and does stand out on its own as a
comfortable and relaxing refuge in the city. Friendly Glasgow folk in attendance.
24hr room service.　16RMS　JAN-DEC　T/T　PETS　CC　KIDS　LOTS

254a　**THE GLASGOW HILTON:** 204 5555. 1 William St, reached via Bothwell St ✝ ✝
C2　from centre. Glasgow's 5-star hotel opened in 1993, designed and ✝
managed to international standard of convenience and excellence. Although it
may lack atmosphere and the ground-floor restaus are v thematic (Raffles club-
bar/Minsky's eaterie), there's no question that for executive travellers they've
thought of just about everything (if you're Japanese, you have your own floor),
and it all helps to make life easier. (See 292/BEST RESTAUS.) Underground
parking.　319RMS　JAN-DEC　T/T　PETS　CC　KIDS　LOTS

255　**THE MARRIOTT:** 226 5577. Argyle St nr m/way. A modern and recently refurbished
C3　high-rise, until 1992 one of the flagship Holiday Inns and as a 'business' hotel,
hard to fault. Whether it is holding its corner now the Hilton has opened next
door remains to be seen, but the discreet, calm efficiency is very stress-relieving,
as may be watching the soundless traffic on the expressway outside your
window, or people lapping the pool while you're having breakfast. There are
'No smoking' floors. The Marriott promise individual service.
298RMS　JAN-DEC　T/T　PETS　CC　KIDS　LOTS

256　**THE TOWN HOUSE HOTEL:** 332 3320. Nelson Mandela Pl, W George St. Lavish and
D2　modish refurb of grand building opp a church and nr George Sq. Plush to
palatial, fulsome on the fabrics. Extravagantly lofty public rooms. As The Town
House, it is well named.　34RMS　JAN-DEC　T/T　XPETS　CC　KIDS　LOTS

257　**THE COPTHORNE:** 332 6711. George Sq. Situated on the square which is the
D2　municipal heart of the city and next to Queen St Station (trains to Edin and
points NE), Glasgow will be going on all about you and there's a conservatory
terrace, serving breakfast and afternoon tea, from which to watch. Bedrooms
vary greatly; some perhaps overfurnished.　121RMS　JAN-DEC　T/T　PETS　CC　KIDS　LOTS

258　**THE MOAT HOUSE:** 204 0733. Congress Rd. Along the river, next to the SECC
A2　(exhibition centre), away from city centre (though only 3km). A reflecting glass
monument to the 1980s which inside seems curiously dated already. Presides
over acres of carparks but most rooms have a spectacular view of the mighty
Clyde.　284RMS　JAN-DEC　T/T　PETS　CC　KIDS　LOTS

259　**THE CENTRAL HOTEL:** 221 9680. Gordon St. The old and happily somewhat old-
D2　fashioned railway hotel which sits astride the impressive Central Stn. Once had a
celebrated restau and urbane image, now standard/impersonal though some atmos
remains. Rooms are individual and you're at the hub of a great city. Taxis easy to
find, parking less so. New leisure centre.　221RMS　JAN-DEC　T/T　PETS　CC　KIDS　EXP

260　**KELVIN PARK LORNE:** 334 4891. 923 Sauchiehall St. By no means in the superluxe
A1　league, but included because many of the rooms, esp the suites, are individual-
istic, often rather grand. Location is handy for the West End (galleries/restaus/
Kelvingrove Park).　98RMS　JAN-DEC　T/T　PETS　CC　KIDS　EXP

THE BEST INEXPENSIVE HOTELS

✠ **CATHEDRAL HOUSE:** 552 3519. Cathedral Sq/John Knox St. Next to the Cathedral (some rooms o/look) and close to the Merchant City, this detached old building has been tastefully refurbished and converted into a café/bar (with occ live music), a separate and decent restaurant, and comfortable bedrooms above. Discreet and informal hospitality for the traveller; much as it always has been here, in the ancient heart of the city. 7RMS JAN-DEC T/T PETS CC KIDS MED.EX
262 E2

✠ **BOSWELL HOTEL:** 632 9812. 27 Mansionhouse Rd, Langside. Deep in Southside nr Queens Park. Go via Pollokshaws Rd, left up Langside Av then follow signs for Hospital, but do go! This hotel is a real haven (esp if . . . well, 389/REAL ALE PUBS), intimate and v friendly and yet good on service and room facilities. 3 bars and food all day till 9.45pm. Edinburgh could use a place like this. 13RMS JAN-DEC T/T PETS CC KIDS MED.INX
263 xC4

✠ **BABBITY BOWSTER:** 552 5055. 16 Blackfriars St. One of the pivotal and early innovative ventures in the redevelopment of what is now called the Merchant City (the commercial district behind George Sq), a bar (392/REAL ALE PUBS; 402/PUB FOOD) with basic accommodation above. Bed, book and breakfast when you like (in the bar). All very friendly, if a bit full-on at times; you won't have to leave the premises to get completely Glasgowed. Gets booked up. Don't forget that there's also a good restau upstairs – the Scottische (like Babbity Bowster, also a dance). LO11pm. Cl Sun. 6RMS JAN-DEC X/X XPETS CC XKIDS MED.INX
264 E3

✠ **THE TOWN HOUSE:** 357 0862. 4 Hughenden Terr. Quiet st off Gt Western Rd via Hyndland Rd; beyond Botanics but near West End nightlife. A tasteful home from home in listed terrace. Nice books, people and garden. Their limited but scrupulous supper menu seems a model of its kind for the small hotel that does care about its guests. 10RMS JAN-DEC T/T XPETS CC KIDS MED.INX
264a xA1

CLIFTON HOTEL: 334 8080. 26 Buckingham Terr. Sits above busy Great Western Rd nr Botanic Gardens and the mecca of Byres Rd. Slightly OTT 'stylish' refurb in 1992 and if they don't hike the rates, it will remain good value. Suspend your tastebuds. 23RMS JAN-DEC T/T XPETS CC KIDS MED.INX
265 B1

KIRKLEE: 354 5555. 11 Kensington Gate. The Stevens keep a tidy house and most notably a tidy garden (geraniums, lobelia, hydrangea etc) in this leafy suburb near the Botanics and the less botanical jungle of Byres Rd. They bother. 9RMS JAN-DEC T/T XPETS CC KIDS MED.INX
266 xA1

NUMBER 52 CHARLOTTE ST: 553 1941. Not a hotel but self-catering apartments in superb conversion of the one remaining Georgian townhouse in historic (now decimated) st betw the Barrows Market and Glasgow Green. V good rates for bedroom/lounge/kitchen; everything but breakfast. 6RMS JAN-DEC X/T XPETS CC KIDS MED.INX
267 E3

BUCHANAN HOTEL: 332 7284. 185 Buchanan St. Main advantage is central location nr Concert Hall. Rooms vary; first floor can be noisy till 11pm. Moderate mod cons; 24hr bar from night porter. 60RMS JAN-DEC T/T PETS CC KIDS MED.INX
268 D2

THE VICTORIAN HOUSE: 332 0129. 214 Renfrew St. Expansive guest house which has swallowed up a row of adj houses in this hilltop terr behind Sauchiehall St along from the Art School (434/MACKINTOSH). Basic, very clean accom. Rooms without facilities cheaper but bathrooms can be a floor away. Chuck out (sic) at 10.30am. 36RMS JAN-DEC X/T PETS CC KIDS INX
269 C1

THE WILLOW HOTEL: 332 2332. 228 Renfrew St. Next door to above, smaller and possibly friendlier. Once again standard, commercial, clean etc, but not a lot of atmos. Derek Jarman was there when I was; now that makes it more interesting. Art School along street. 17RMS JAN-DEC X/T XPETS CC KIDS INX ·
270 C1

AMBASSADOR: 946 1018. 7 Kelvin Dr. Nr Botanic Gardens and adj a bridge over the Kelvin, this terrace hotel has a pleasing location in the West End and fairly okay rooms and furnishings. 14RMS JAN-DEC T/T XPETS CC KIDS INX
270a xA1

THE GEORGE: 332 6622. 235 Buchanan St. Top of Buchanan St nr to Concert Hall (and a world away from it). Despite location and real estate value, this discreet commercial hotel seems to resist all expectations to upmarket itself and consequently it's devoid of all niceties and funky as hell. The Chelsea East. It should be legendary. 50RMS JAN-DEC X/X XPETS XCC XKIDS CHP
271 D2

THE BEST HOSTELS

272 **SYHA HOSTEL:** 332 3004. 7 Park Terrace. Close to where the old Glasgow
B1 hostel used to be in Woodlands Terr in the same area of the West End nr
the University and Kelvingrove Park. This building was converted in 1992 from
the Beacons Hotel, which was where rock 'n' roll bands used to stay in the
1980s. Now the bedrooms are converted into dorms for 4-6 (some larger) and
the public rooms are common rooms with TV/games/café etc. Still feels more
like a hotel than a hostel and is a great place to stay. You do need to be a
member of the YHA. Phone for info.

273 **BAIRD HALL, STRATHCLYDE UNIV:** 332 6415. 460 Sauchiehall St. The landmark
C2 Grade A listed art deco building nr the art school and the West End. Orig the
Beresford Hotel, built 1937 and once Glasgow's finest (very Miami Beach). 194
rms in vacs and 11 avail all year round. Spartan, almost drab, though the rooms
are fine, like an American Y. Reeks of nostalgia as well as disinfectant. Dining-
room, TV and reading room. Lots of groovy places nearby such as Nico's,
Canton Express, Variety Bar, Baby Grand and the Griffin. All are listed.

274 **CLYDE HALL, STRATHCLYDE UNIV:** 221 1219. 318 Clyde St. A very central block,
D3 off-campus at the bottom of Union/W Renfield St and almost o/looking the
river. 165 single and twin rooms mainly in summer vac (though 6 are avail
AYR). Refectory and TV room. Some smaller rooms on lower floor avail
cheaply as self-catering and specifically for backpackers, are a v good deal.

275 **MURRAY HALL, STRATHCLYDE UNIV:** 552 4400 (ext 3560). Collins St. Modern, but not
E2 sterile block of single rooms on edge of main campus and facing towards
Cathedral. Part of large complex (also some student flats avail by the week) with
bar/shop/laundrette. Relatively central, close Merchant City bars etc. Vacs only.

276 **HORSLETHILL HOUSE, GLASGOW UNIV:** 339 9943. 7 Horslethill Rd. Another off-
xA1 campus 'hall', a converted suburban mansion house with annexes in a quiet and
rather posh area v close to the delights (i.e. the bars, restaus etc) of famous Byres
Rd. Rooms vary. Vacs only.

277 **QUEEN MARGARET HALL, GLASGOW UNIV:** 334 2192. 55 Bellshaugh Rd. Off-campus
xA1 (in fact, rather a long way off from anything) but a big high-rise block of
comfortable rooms where there's a good chance of accom when more central
halls are full. Get a bike. Vacs only.

278 **REITH HALL, GLASGOW UNIV:** 945 1636. 10 Botanic Cres. Labyrinthine hostel
xA1 converted from several houses in quiet st behind the serenely beautiful Botanic
Gardens which you can walk through to Byres Rd where the action is. Good
location and a good student lair. Vacs only.

278a **CAIRNCROSS HOUSE, GLASGOW UNIV:** 221 9334. Kelvinhaugh St off Argyle at
A2 Murphy's Pakora. Nr Kelvingrove Park, Byres Rd and some good pubs and esp
Indian restaus, a recently built student hall complex not brickful of ambiance,
but well appointed and convenient. Vacs only.

*The SYH(A) is the Scottish Youth Hostel Association of which you have to be a
member (or an affiliated organisation from another country) to stay in their
many hostels round Scotland. Phone 0786 51181 for details or contact any YHA
hostel.*

*Note: Both Strathclyde and Glasgow Universities have several halls of residence
available for short-term accommodation in the summer months. For those above
(the best of them) and others, you may also phone:*

GLASGOW: 339 8481 or 339 5271

STRATHCLYDE: 555 4148 (central booking)

THE BEST CAMPING AND CARAVAN PARKS

STRATHCLYDE PARK: 0698 66155. **20km SE Glasgow.** M74 at junc 6 or M8/A725. *279* On the edge of a large popular country park (774/COUNTRY PARKS; *xE1* 882/BIRDWATCHING; 1134/WATERSPORTS) and easily reached by motorway system. Go left just after park entrance. Check in until 10.45pm. Stay up to 2 weeks. Usual but good standard facs on site and many others nearby e.g. café, windsurfing, gym (open till 8.30pm, 500m away). M/way close, so traffic noise, but no visual intrusion on this well-managed, parkland site. Caravans and tents separate. Glasgow's most accessible caravan park by car. 150 pitches. Open Apr-Oct.

BARNBROCK, LOCHWINNOCH: 0550 690133. **40km SW Glasgow** via M8/A8 Port *280* Glasgow then Kilmacolm rd A761, then B786; or via Johnstone A737, A760 to *xA4* Lochwinnoch. Let's face it, it's not exactly convenient but this beautiful, remote site (camping only) is on the edge of the wild and wonderful Muirshiel Country Park (776/CO PARKS) and Lochwinnoch Nature Reserve (890/WILDLIFE RESERVES) and it's not far to go to leave the city behind completely. 15 tents.

CLOCH CARAVAN PARK, GOUROCK: 0475 32675. **45km W of Glasgow** along the *281* coast. Take M8 then A8 through Greenock and Gourock; continue for 6km. *xA4* This is a residential caravan park (no tents) with only a few touring pitches. Vast terraced caravanland with shop etc. Best feature is that it o/looks the historical Cloch Point Lighthouse and the glittering Clyde. 10 places only.

TULLICHEWAN, BALLOCH: 0389 59475. **40km NW of Glasgow.** Once again a fair *282* distance from the city, but fast roads from this direction via A82 (dual c/way all *xA1* the way), or via Erskine Br and then M8. Best to leave the car here and take frequent train service from Balloch Stn nearby; 30mins to Glasgow Central Stn. This park is nicely situated nr Loch Lomond and tourist centres and is well managed and good fun for kids. Shop, laundrette, games room, TV, sauna, sunbeds etc. Probably the best park for holidaymaking hereabouts. 140 places.

The author had difficulties finding any other sites to recommend. Any suggestions will be gratefully received for possible inclusion in future editions. See page 11.

THE BEST HOTELS OUTSIDE TOWN

See also HOTELS IN STRATHCLYDE NORTH, *p.82, and South, p.83.*

283 **GLEDDOCH HOUSE, LANGBANK nr GREENOCK:** 0475 54711. M8/A8 to Greenock ✝
xA4 then B789 signposted Langbank/Houston, then 2km – hotel is signed.
30km W of centre by fast rd. A château-like country house hotel, formerly the
home of the Lithgow Shipping family. High above the Clyde estuary, there are
spectacular views across to Dumbarton Rock and the Kilpatrick Hills. Rooms
not lavish but comfortable, not all with view. Reputable dining-room with Brian
Graham's well-judged dishes from fresh Scottish ingredients. 18-hole golf course
and health club, though pool is v small.
33RMS JAN-DEC T/T PETS CC KIDS TOS LOTS

284 **CAMERON HOUSE, nr BALLOCH, LOCH LOMOND:** 0389 55565. A82 dual c/way into
xA4 West End or via Erskine Br and M8. **45km NW of centre.** Mansion with annexe
and large leisure complex in open grounds on the bonny banks of the loch. Excellent sports facs incl 9-hole golf, pool, tennis, busy marina for sailing/windsurfing
etc. Notable restau (The Georgian Room) and all-day brasserie. *Nouveau* and
riche; the good (and glitzy) life, Pavarotti stayed here – as did Runrig when they
played across the loch at Balloch Country Park. And U2 – I was there.
68RMS JAN-DEC T/T XPETS CC KIDS TOS LOTS

285 **BOWFIELD COUNTRY CLUB, HOWWOOD:** 05057 5225. Jnct 29 off M8 for Howwood
xA4 then 3km from Main St via steep Z-bend. **32km SW of centre.** Farmhouse-like
retreat in gentle hill country just beyond the conurbation. Rooms in modern
annexe are comfortable and with the club facs (squash, gym, saunas etc) and a
large pool (open till 10pm), represent good value. Less earnest than usual health
clubs.
12RMS JAN-DEC T/T XPETS CC KIDS EXP

286 **BOTHWELL BRIDGE HOTEL, BOTHWELL:** 0698 852246. Uddingston t/off from M74
xE1 **15km SE.** Main St. Nr Castle and good pub (924/RUINS; 382/UNSPOILT PUBS).
Not cheap or especially notable but well appointed.
8ORMS JAN-DEC T/T XPETS CC KIDS EXP

287 **CULCREUCH CASTLE HOTEL, FINTRY:** 036086 228. Off B818 in Campsie Fells **32km**
xE1 **N of centre** via A81 Milngavie rd from Glasgow. Fintry is well-kept and
pastoral in valley betw the Fells and the Fintry Hills. Some fine walking (445/
WALKS OUTSIDE CITY); a far cry from walking the West End though it's only 50
mins away. An ancestral home (of the Galbraiths) with slightly off-peak
elegance giving it character and intimacy. Quite Scottish and a good find.
8RMS JAN-DEC T/T PETS CC KIDS MED.INX

288 **THE BALLOCH HOTEL, BALLOCH, LOCH LOMOND:** 0389 52579. **40km NW** by fast
xA1 roads (see Cameron House, above) or frequent and convenient train. Busy hotel
(beer garden and local bar) in tourist centre by lochside moorings. Goes like a
Glasgow fair in summer.
14RMS JAN-DEC T/T PETS CC KIDS MED.INX

289 **BIRD IN THE HAND, QUARRELTON, JOHNSTONE:** 0505 29222. Jnct 29 off M8, A740
xA4 then Linwood rd A761 and rt at T-junction on the A737, the Beith Rd (for
5km). **30km SW of centre.** Look out for church on rt with weird steeple; hotel is
on other side, 100m. Cheap and cheerful old coaching inn only 15km from
airport.
4RMS JAN-DEC · X/T PETS CC KIDS INX

290 **THE INVERKIP HOTEL, INVERKIP:** 0475 521478. M8 from Glasgow then A8 and A78
xA4 from Port Glasgow heading S for Largs. **50km W centre.** Inverkip is a now
bypassed village now dominated from the other side of the main rd by Kip
Marina (1138/WATERSPORTS). Hotel is in Main St; a family-run coaching inn with
pub downstairs. The most reasonable place to stay on this part of the Clyde
coast.
6RMS JAN-DEC X/T PETS CC KIDS INX

THE BEST RESTAURANTS

† † **THE BUTTERY:** 221 8188. 652 Argyle St. In an area blitzed by the 291 motorway system, the Buttery and its little brother downstairs, the *B2* Belfry, occupy the one remaining tenement block. Best reached via the westerly extension of St Vincent St then Elderslie St, at the bottom of which is a distinctive conical church. Turn left to end. For many years, Glasgow's premier eatery and though there are now serious contenders, the sumptuous epicurean ambience and Stephen Johnson's clever, but no-nonsense menu are hard to beat. *Très écossais*. Mon-Fri lunch and 7-10pm. Sat 7-10pm only. EXP

† **CAMERON'S AT THE GLASGOW HILTON:** 204 5555. The flagship restau in the 292 corner of the Hilton's huge foyer with an elegant but Och Aye theme to *C2* food and decor. Ferrier Richardson, generally regarded as one of Scotland's star chefs, presides over all the Hilton menus but this is where you sense the master's spoon in the sauce. Scottish menu mainly of the hunted/shot/fished variety; also vegn. Didn't dare try the puds. Wine-list from all over incl most of the good places, and the Golan Heights. Good 1 hr lunch (or it's free) idea. EXP

† **ONE DEVONSHIRE GARDENS:** 339 2001. Same address. Glasgow's most stylish 293 hotel (253/BEST HOTELS) has a restau which has won accolades in its own *xA1* right. Like the sumptuous surroundings, dishes on the fixed-price menu are rich, voguish and seductive. Everything from the cutlery to the coulis is perfectly arranged; sometimes it just looks too good to eat. Staff are young and friendly. Right-on wine-list with biggies, organics, lots of halves and New World interest. All in all, a good food experience. EXP

† **THE UBIQUITOUS CHIP:** 334 5007. 12 Ashton Lane. The inimitable 'Chip' is a 294 restau with wine bar above and a wine shop in a bustling lane behind Byres *A1* Rd. Firm reputation founded on traditional and original menu using fresh Scottish ingredients; lots of West Highland seafood, Oban-landed fish, game from good suppliers and a fine cranachan for pud. Ask for table in main room, a lofty, vineclad conservatory, warm even in winter. Outstanding wine-list. Daily lunch and 6.30-11pm. 312/BISTROS. EXP

ROGANO: 248 4055. 11 Exchange Place. Just off pedestrian part of Buchanan St 295 leading to Queen St. An institution in Glasgow since the 1930s. Decor replicates *D3* a Cunard ship, the *Queen Mary*, and is the major attraction (recent attempts of 1980s' wine bars to impart a similar ambience cannot compare). Fish/seafood are specialities. Downstairs the supper and luncheon room has a lighter/cheaper menu. Decor here is less authentic but the picture captions still keep regulars amused. Restaurant: daily lunch and 6-10.30pm; Café Rogano: daily lunch and 6-11pm (Fri/Sat till midnight, Sun till 10pm). MED/EXP

55BC: 942 7272. 128 Drymen Rd, Bearsden. Fairly far-flung (18km centre) in 296 couthie N suburb and occupying the same space as one of Glasgow's great '80s *xC1* restaus (October), a completely new set-up (more a café-bar and more eclectic) that seems to work well. The restau in the rear with a simple menu based on good fresh ingredients has a growing rep. Bar-meals out front (the noise may intrude at weekends) and light decor with well-chosen pictures make this an informal but smart place to eat. Lunch (not Sun) and 7-10pm. MED

† **GINGERHILL, MILNGAVIE:** 956 6515. Hillhead St. At the end of the 297 pedestrianised centre of Milngavie (15km N of centre), an intimate, friendly *xC1* upstairs parlour. Coffee shop/restau during the day and in the evening specialising in seafood with excl fresh produce (Gigha-landed fish etc), thoughtfully prepared. Carol Thomson and Heather Andrew create a warm and highly individual atmosphere. Tables are yours for the night from 7pm. Only 20 mins by train from centre. BYOB (and 10% off booze if you buy at Oddbins nearby). Mon-Sat 11am-5pm. Thur-Sat 7pm onwards. INX

PEKING COURT: 353 1003. 285 Sauchiehall St. 323/ETHNIC RESTAUS.

HO WONG: 221 3550. 82 York St. 323A/ETHNIC RESTAUS.

TWO FAT LADIES: 339 1944. 88 Dumbarton Rd.. 1172/SEAFOOD RESTAUS.

KILLERMONT POLO CLUB: 946 5412. 2002 Maryhill Rd. 329/INDIAN RESTAUS.

THE BEST BISTROS AND CAFE-BARS

298 **BABY GRAND:** 248 4942. 3/7 Elmbank Gardens. An inviting haven amongst
C2 high-rise office blocks opp Charing Cross Station; a downtown-USA
location. (Go behind the King's Theatre down Elmbank St, rt at gas station and
look for train stn.) A busy and urban atmos. Narrow room with bar stools and
banquettes often with background music from the eponymous piano. Light,
eclectic menu from tapas to full meals materialise in the tiny gantry. Food till
11.45pm/12.45 incl Suns. Only real cities have places like this.   CHP

Baby Grand, Glasgow (298)

299 **CHADFIELDS/CHADI:** 331 1206. 158 Bath St. Spacious and stylish basement with
C2 rare restraint; a metropolitan atmos. Bar meals and light dining-room
through back. From interesting club sandwiches to full meals (meat/game/fish).
No potato skins in sight. Cool, calm and collected. Food noon-10.30pm, bar till
midnight. Cl Sun.   INX/MED

300 **MITCHELLS:** 204 4312. 157 North St. The left bank of the M8 at the Mitchell
B2 Library and next to the real ale Accord Bar. Ales here too (Belhaven),
Murphy's and designer lagers, but mainly a place for informal food with a genuine
(and for Glasgow, rare) bistro atmosphere. New west-end version upstairs at
Ashton Lane (off Byres Rd) is even better (339 2220). Both have food till 11pm, bar
till midnight. Cl Sun.   INX

301 **TRON CAFE-BAR:** 552 4267. 63 Trongate. Attached to the esteemed Tron
E3 Theatre (455/NIGHTLIFE). Café at the front for coffee and chat and a
bar/bistro at the back with a congenial atmosphere, decent house wines and a
simple menu offering imaginative variations in obliging large or smaller snackier
portions. Good Gaggia. Food till 10.30/11pm. Cl Mon evening.   CHP

THE CABIN: 954 7102. **996 Dumbarton Rd, Whiteinch, beyond the flyover.** 302 xA1
Unquestionably one of the best 'night's out' going, a restau/bistro with 4-
course dinner from 7.30 followed by singing – yes, singing (with prizes)!
Seafood spec and, of course, Wilma. Can BYOB. Legendary already. Lunch and
LO 9.30pm
MED

COTTIER'S: 357 5827. **93 Hyndland Rd.** (See 412/MUSIC PUBS for directions, it's not 302a
easy to find.) Converted church, great atmos; wine-bar/pub and restau upstairs xA1
serving regional US (but non-burger) fare, eg. creole. Fashionable
neighbourhood hang-out. 368/SUNDAY BREAKFAST for many reasons. 7 days.

CITY MERCHANT: 553 1577. **97 Candleriggs.** Upstairs is a café/restau while 303
downstairs is more a wine bar with food. Hugely varied menus (à la carte/lunch E3
and dinner/Taste of Scotland specials) of fish, seafood, game, meat and veggie
fare; the enormously wide choice must and does affect the quality. Continental
café atmos. Wines are well chosen. Food till 10.30pm, bar till midnight. Cl Sun.
INX

WAREHOUSE CAFE: 552 4181. **61 Glassford St.** The top floor of one of Glasgow's 304
premier designer clothes shops. Airy and well-lit; and the menu similarly lite, so D3
the pricey clothes you pass on the way up might still look okay on. Beverages
range from camomile to Irn-Bru; food eclectic and, of course, fashionable. Faves
at time of writing: Pastrami, ratatouille, rhubarb pie. Till 5.45pm. Cl Sun.
CHP

JUNKANOO: 248 7102. **11 Hope St.** Opp Central Stn and hotel. Not *muy Español* 305
but a goodly selection of tapas; you can choose to snack or make a meal of D2
several. Some things, as they say, are better than others. Best at night. Mon-Sat
noon-11pm, Sun 7-11pm.
CHP

PAPINGO: 332 6678. **104 Bath St.** Light basement café/restau with mildly adven- 306
turous menu along with safer bets. You'll find the likes of feta and fusilli in there C2
somewhere, and guinea fowl. Try hard to please everybody. Daily till
10.30/11pm.
INX

NICO'S: 332 5736. **375 Sauchiehall St.** Difficult to enthuse about the bar meals and 307
there's no bistro about it, but Nico's just has to be included somewhere. A fine C2
example of the French café-bar abroad, it serves a credible croissant and has
spawned innumerable imitators who never got it quite as right. Mon-Sat 8.30am-
midnight, Sun noon-midnight.
CHP

THE BELFRY: 221 0630. **652 Argyle St.** Approach via west extension of St Vincent 308
St, Elderslie St and left at the conical church. The basement of the Buttery, one B2
of Glasgow's finest restaus (291/BEST RESTAUS) in the one remaining tenement of
an area savaged by the M8. Bistro version of the Scot/French cuisine served up
top, in study-like cellar rooms with dark wood and books. Mon-Sat lunch and
6-11pm.
INX

CAFE ROYAL at the Theatre Royal: 332 3321 (theatre admin no.). Top of Hope St. 309
This recent café-bar is right on the corner. Same management as Baby Grand. A D1
light Euro kind of eaterie (or snackerie) perfect for pre/après suppers for this or
any theatre. STV types grab the odd lunch. LO 10pm, Cl Sun.
INX

BACK ALLEY: 334 7165. **8 Ruthven Lane, off Byres Rd nr Hillhead station.** More an 310
American burger joint than a café-bar or bistro but a good one. Part of the A1
Crolla empire (which is otherwise Italian), they've borrowed all the diner faves
that work the world over. Surf 'n' Turf, deep-fried zucchini, mushroom and
veggie burgers all leaven the junk-food load. American beers, el plonko vino.
Daily till 11.30pm, w/ends till 12.30am.
INX

THE CUL DE SAC: 334 8899. **44 Ashton Lane, the main lane off Byres Rd with the** 311
Grosvenor Cinema and The Ubiquitous Chip. Perenially fashionable A1
créperie/diner on a similar circuit to The Rock Garden (377/BEST PUBS) and Nico's
(see above). It was 'right' from the day it opened and seems to survive all the ebb
and flow and Versace variations. Good burgers. Bar upstairs has many kent
Glasgow faces. Daily noon-11pm (Fri/Sat midnight). 369/SUNDAY BREAKFAST.
CHP

UPSTAIRS AT THE CHIP: 334 5007. **12 Ashton Lane.** At other end of lane from Cul 312
de Sac (above) and upstairs from The Chip (294/BEST RESTAUS), this is the wine A1
bar and cheap seats version of the celebrated restau. Some tables are around the
gallery of the court-yard below. There's a scaled-down menu with some of the
same seafood and puds as well as bar-type salads and soups etc. The bill will
come to about a third of the restau; the atmosphere's more cheerful too.
INX

THE BEST ITALIAN RESTAURANTS

313 **LA FIORENTINA:** 420 1585. 2 Paisley Rd West. Not far from river and
B3 motorway over Kingston Br, but approach from Eglinton St (A77
Kilmarnock Rd). It's at the Y-junction with Govan Rd, in an imposing listed
building. Considered by many to be Glasgow's best truly Italian restau, you will
probably have to book. Great atmos, great Italian wine-list; long menu, long
meals. Mon-Sat noon-2.30pm and 5.30-11pm (LO 9.30pm). Cl Sun.   MED

314 **LA PARMIGIANA:** 334 0686. 447 Gt Western Rd. A ristorante with confident
B1 contemporary Italian cuisine, miles from the usual pasta/pizza land.
Carefully chosen dishes and wine-list, and solicitous service. Milano rather than
Napoli. Expect to find Italians. Mon-Sat lunch and 6-11pm. Cl Sun.   MED

315 **FAZZI'S:** 332 0941. 95 Cambridge St. Opp Hospitality Inn in a modern office-
D1 block, the café outpost of the famous Fazzi empire. There's a deli here too
and the unmistakeable authenticity the Fazzi Brothers were renowned for. It's
been 'taken over' but feels no different; a modern Italian café and not a tarted up
tratt. Tables and barstools; sometimes a small wait; the food (meals or snacks) is
generally stupendo. 8am-10.30pm, Sun 11am-7pm (366/SUN BREAKFASTS).   INX

315a **FRATELLI SARTI:** 248 2228. 133 Wellington St. A restau and a deli bursting
D1 with food, smells and atmosphere and a gr place just to drop-in. This is
where the Fazzis (see above) went. For full report see 353/COFFEE SHOPS.   CHP

316 **O'SOLE MIO:** 331 1397. 32 Bath St. Part of the Crolla empire. Nothing fancy or
D2 extraordinary about this restau nr the Concert Hall and the Pavilion Theatre,
but for years it's done the business in the trad tratt way and it always feels fine.
Daily till midnight.   INX

317 **RISTORANTE CAPRESE:** 332 3070. 217 Buchanan St. Basement café nr the Concert
D2 Hall. People swear (some in Italian) by this place and the masses of pics of
happy customers round the walls demonstrate how many miles of pasta must
have passed thro those grinning lips. Basic, intimate and reliable. LO 10/11pm.
Book at w/ends.   INX

318 **CAFE QUI:** 552 6099. The Italian Centre (betw Cochrane and Ingram St) in the
E3 Merchant City. Café upstairs going all day with cappuccino and cakes and
snacks (pizzas a good bet). D/stairs there's a cavernous space with alcoves all
round and a full menu. Decent food. Betwixt and below Armani and Versace, so
to speak. Mon-Sat lunch and 6-11pm. Sun 7-10pm.   INX

319 **THE NORTH ROTUNDA:** 223 4264. 28 Tunnel St. Beyond the city centre on the Clyde
A2 in the no-man's-land surrounding the Scottish Exhib Centre. A unique listed
building, completely circular, one of a pair on either side of the river which used
to be the access shafts to a tunnel underneath; converted in 1989 into bars and
two restaus of which the Pizzeria is the more recommendable and well priced.
LO 11pm/midnight.   INX

320 **IL PESCATORE:** 333 9239. 148 Woodlands Rd. Small restau in West End towards
B1 univ, with loyal following for home cooking. Specialises in seafood with the
likes of scampi and sole in many modes, but best just to ask what's on. Lunch a
good deal. Book at w/ends. Mon-Sat lunch and 6.30-10.30/11pm. Cl Sun.   INX

321 **SCOOZI:** 616 0088. Newton Mearns shopping plaza. Unlikely yes, but this
xC4 café/restau/deli is in the middle of a shopping mall opp Boots Health and
Beauty. We go there following Fausteo Mascia, the real Italian chef who presides
over this average suburban eaterie and makes it seem like a genuine Italian
suburban eaterie. The mall is empty at night, but open. Great! Look for Asda on
rt going out of town for Kilmarnock (10km centre). Mon-Sat LO10.30pm.   INX

322 **TREVI:** 334 3262. 526 Gt Western Rd. May look like an ordinary tratt in the midst
B1 of many, but folk who know go and there's a lot of them – it's often full. Worth
persevering though, as I did; usual pasta variations, but go for the daily specials.
You don't have to like football, but they do. Mon-Fri lunch and 6-11pm,
Sat/Sun 6-11pm.   INX

THE BEST ETHNIC RESTAURANTS

✝ **PEKING COURT:** 353 1003. **285 Sauchiehall St.** For years there was only the 323
Peking Inn (see below). Now Gerry Wan has gone off to start this serious C2
contender for the best authentic Peking Chinese food in town. In a section of the
West End strewn with ethnic restaus, go downstairs to a calm, sophisticated
lounge where the food is so reliable, well thought-out and prepared that you can
dispense with the menu and allow them to choose. You'll be indulged with a
sequence of exquisite dishes. Don't demur if offered the jellyfish and ginger to
start or the toffeed fruits to finish. Mon-Thu lunch and 6-11.30pm, Fri/Sat lunch
and 6-12.30am. Cl Sun. Sometimes special 'offers' Mon-Fri. MED

✝ **HO WONG:** 221 3550. **82 York St** in city centre nr river, betw Clyde St and 323a
Argyle St. A long-time favourite (particularly of newspaper men) and C3
mistakenly excluded from the first editon of *Scotland the Best!* Discreet, urbane
Pekinese/Cantonese restau which relies on its reputation and makes few
compromises. Notable for seafood and duck. Also best Szechuan in town (cool
down with a sorbet). Lunch (not Sun) and 6pm-late, LO11.30pm. MED

✝ **PEKING INN:** 332 8971. **191 Hope St.** The first proper Peking Chinese place in 324
town and, some would argue, still the best. Long à la carte, spicy Szechuan D2
specials, and any combination you ask for will be whipped out the wok and
brought in perfect order to your table by polite and sweetly coy waitresses.
Stylish lacquer in black, red and gold, and low light create a cool ambience in
which to try their hotter stuff. Mon-Sat noon-11.30 pm. MED

LOON FUNG: 332 1240. **417 Sauchiehall St.** On the face of it (at the W end of 325
Sauchiehall St) and in the plain interior of it, nothing would suggest that this was C2
one of Glasgow's most respected Cantonese restaus. But go on a Sunday
lunchtime or a Mon/Tues and you'll see this is where the Chinese community
choose. Genuine cookery using first-class ingredients is their simple formula. A
chef brought from Hong Kong freshly prepares the Dim Sum. Everybody uses
chopsticks. Daily noon-midnight. MED

CANTON EXPRESS: 332 0145. **407 Sauchiehall St.** A genuine Hong Kong fast-food 326
take-away and diner where you're v likely to see the staff from other Chinese C2
restaus eating. The limited menu (chow meins, lemon chicken etc) is sizzled up
before your eyes. Self/S, chopsticks in the tray. From the outside it could be just
another Chinese café, but it's the real downtown thing. Daily till 2am. CHP

ATHENA TAVERNA: 424 0858. **778 Pollokshaws Rd.** On the South Side about 2km 327
from the river. A Greek Cypriot restau and wine bar with snacks. Usual xC4
klefticos etc, many chicken dishes, rabbit, feta and olives, plus the salads you get
sick of on holiday then hanker for when you get home. Unlike the tavernas in
Athens, there are vegn options. Indifferent wine-list includes the inevitable
Demestica. Mon-Sat 11am-2.30pm and 5-11pm (LO 10.45pm). Cl Sun. INX

CAFE SERGHEI: 429 1547. **67 Bridge St** on south side but just over the Jamaica St (or 327a
Glasgow) Bridge. Greek restau in interesting conversion of former bank with D3
upstairs balcony beneath impressive cupola; tiles and woodwork. Friendly,
talkative waiters advise and dispense excl Greek grub incl vegn. Better moussaka
than you'll find easily in Athens and better everything than you'll find in Corfu.
A dancefloor is available. Lunch and 6-11pm, 7 days. INX

MATA HARI: 332 9789. **17 W Princes St.** Authentic Indonesian/Malaysian cuisine in 328
unusually colourful basement restau, designed by artist Hock Aun Teh, nr St C1
George's Cross and not far from the end of Sauchiehall St/Charing Cross.
Family recipes of a nyonya nature (i.e. some Chinese influence), also rendangs/
sati/nasi goreng and seasonal specials. Birds serenade from the trees. Mon-Fri
noon-2pm and 6-11pm, Sat 6-11pm. Cl Sun. INX

XO: 552 3519. At Cathedral House Hotel and bar nr Cathedral Sq on John Knox 328a
St. Cool name for a restau and interesting idea, viz Icelandic food. What it means E2
in practice is that it's a surf 'n' turf place with food cooked at your table on 'hot
rocks'. Different but not at all strange. Well-selected meat and fish that sizzles
while you nibble. Some views of the Cathedral from this woody room above the
bar (262/INX HOTELS). LO 9.45pm. Cl Sun. MED

THE BEST INDIAN RESTAURANTS

Since there's a tradition of Indian restaurants in Glasgow and a lot to choose from, a separate category (cf Edinburgh) has been created. All are open for lunch and at night, until the times shown.

329 **KILLERMONT POLO CLUB:** 946 5412. 2022 Maryhill Rd. A hill station up the
xC1 Maryhill Rd, almost in Bearsden in fact (whence comes a large proportion of the somewhat pukka clientele). You will need a car or a trishaw to get there. Unobtrusively located behind a gas stn, inside, cool opulence and a clubby atmosphere (they do actually run a polo team). The food is light, spicy and not overly exp. They take Indian cuisine seriously and experiment in their Sun/Mon buffet-dinner. Daily lunch (not Sun) and 5pm-midnight (LO 10.30pm). MED

330 **INDIA DINER:** 221 0354. 1191 Argyle St. Unassuming addition to the long list of
A1 eastern restaurants out west. Usual mesmerising regional menu but also some new imaginative combinations. A bit cramped but food-wise this family-run Indian diner can produce a better dish of dall than most. LO midnight, sometimes later at w/ends. INX

331 **CAFE INDIA:** 248 4074. 171 North St. When it opened in 1988, it instantly became
B2 the best of the new-style Indian restaus. Now there are other contenders, but the scale of this place gives it a good, bustling brasserie atmosphere. The extensive menu is busy with herbs and spices and is not merely hot. Sun-Thu 6pm-midnight, Fri/Sat till 1am. INX

332 **CREME DE LA CREME:** 221 3222. 1071 Argyle St. This grand statement of Glasgow's
B2 appetite for Indian food opened in 1991 (the biggest Indian restaurant in the universe etc) and was immediately packed. It still is sometimes and waiters rush about, but perhaps these days it's more popular for the hurry than the curry – mine was average but tablefuls of office outings were tucking in with gusto in the airport-lounge chic with a far-away ceiling. Wine-list better than most, with lots of celebratory sparklies (incl Dom Perignon '83). Lunch (not Sun) and till LO midnight, 7 days. MED

333 **SHISH MAHAL:** 334 1057. 68 Park Rd. Still a longish temporary station for this
B1 legendary Indian restau which has been plying Glasgow with curries for 26 years. They had to move on from the original Gibson St premises and at time of writing had still not settled on a new site. Ali Ahmed Aslam has committed the recipes already immortalised by Billy Connolly (yes, those curries!) to a cookbook. They stay with you a while! Long ago Glasgow took this first generation Indo-pak cuisine to its heart. Try it on yours. Till 11pm/midnight. INX

334 **BALBIR'S BRASSERIE:** 221 1452. 149 Elderslie St. In the West End area beyond the
B2 motorway where there are several Indian places to choose from, this is the one that many people swear by and where the name 'Brasserie' is correctly applied; a large bustling room with very good service. A regional menu (Kashmir/Punjabi/Parsee etc) doesn't offer much for vegns (though the thali selection may suffice). The wine-list is above average. Daily till midnight. INX

335 **ASHOKA WEST END:** 339 0936. 1284 Argyle St. It's all a bit confusing fusing with
B2 the various Ashokas, esp when the chefs move about; you don't know where you are. This Ashoka is in the curry quarter up Argyle St and not in the West End quarter where the other Ashokas are. However, provided the taxi takes you to the right place, you're in a restau which, in the 'where's the best curry' debate, gets lots of people hotly effusive. Daily till 12.30/1am. INX

335a **BALTI BAR:** 331 1980. 51 W Regent St. Below the Regent Sahib is Glasgow's first
D2 restau featuring this Brummie variation of Punjabi-style food. 'Balti' means bucket or rather a small wok, a hot wokful of curry etc, plentiful and cheap. Sauces tend to seem samey, but the price is right and at least it's a bit different. These extensive basement lounges are usually busy. Lunch (not Sun) and till LO 11.30pm, 7 days. CHP

ASHOKA VEGETARIAN: 248 4407. 139 Elderslie St. 340/VEGN RESTAUS.

THE BEST FRENCH RESTAURANTS

There are many Scottish/French menus in Glasgow, but hardly any properly French restaus with French chefs and/or proprietors. Enter Pierre Victoire!

FROGGIE'S: 332 8790. **53 W Regent St.** Adj Victorian Village, an antique market 336 during the day. Recently expanded café/bistro with French owners and French *D2* home cooking. From light snacks like crêpes or quiches to more elaborate meals. Bustling brasserie atmos. V reasonable wines. Open every day, best to book at w/ends. Mon-Sat 9am-midnight; Sun 5pm-midnight.   INX

PIERRE VICTOIRE: 221 7565. **91 Miller St.** and in the W end at **16 Byres Rd** (339 2544). 337 Since the first edition of *Scotland the Best!*, these two extensions along the M8, *D3/A1* of the empire that started in Edinburgh (72/EDIN FRENCH RESTAUS) have quickly become established and doubtless by the time you read this there will be several more. They're cheap, always cheerful and remarkably French. Who'd have thought that Edinburgh could ever have been first with anything consumer-wise that's even vaguely fashionable! Famously good-value lunch and 6-11pm.   INX

THE BEST VEGETARIAN RESTAURANTS

Since the last edition, one of Glasgow's few exclusively vegetarian restaus has closed. It leaves a big gap – Edinburgh has several, but at time of writing Glasgow had only these. Not enough wimps, I suppose!

BAY TREE: 334 5898. **403 Gt Western Rd.** A workers' co-op with high standards. 338 It's small and busy, the windows steam up and you might not get a table to *B1* yourself, but the food always has interest and integrity. Vegan options. Good vegeburgers and onions, soup, daily specials and lively salads. Some discounts (e.g. OAPs). 367/SUN BREAKFAST.   CHP

VEGVILLE DINER: 331 2220. **93 St Georges Rd** nr Charing Cross. A new (autumn 339 1993) vegn restau (diner is an accurate description) helping to fill the gap and the *B1* veggie appetite in Glasgow. Started by wholesalers of veggieburgers etc and in an airy room forming part of a studio complex. Some vegan. 7 days 10am-10pm. BYOB

ASHOKA VEGETARIAN: 248 4407. **137 Elderslie St.** A widely respected Indian restau 340 which happens to be vegetarian. No problem here with what animal is actually *B2* in the curry (that old joke still gets the odd airing in Glasgow). Small and popular, so best to book. Famously light pooris. Not No Smk. Daily 5-11pm.   INX

THE GRANARY: 226 3770. **82 Howard St.** Behind St Enoch Centre towards river, 341 but tucked away on a corner. Vegetarian food like your mother might make and *D3* home baking *par excellence* (354/TEA-ROOMS). Nothing fancy, nothing 'alternative', just good grub without the gristle. Self/S. Mon-Sat 8.30am-8pm, and may open later '94 (you should – Glasgow needs you!) Sun noon-5pm.   CHP

Restaurants that serve good vegetarian food but are not exclusively vegetarian include:

THE UBIQUITOUS CHIP and **ROGANO** (294/295/BEST RESTAUS)

BABY GRAND, THE TRON CAFE, CHADFIELDS (298/301/ 299/BISTROS)

MATA HARI (328/ETHNIC RESTAUS)

INDIA DINER (330/INDIAN RESTAUS)

CAFE GANDOLFI (352/COFFEE SHOPS)

GREAT CAFES AND GREASY SPOONS

342 **UNIVERSITY CAFE:** 87 Byres Rd. Ask almost anyone, café-wise this one is it. ✝
A1 It has been around as long as anyone incl the Verecchia family (who run it) can remember. It now has a take-away made in its own image which purists ignore; the place for pie and chips and bacon rolls is in the cramped confines of the ice-cream and sweetie shop next door where you fight for a hard seat and shove up. Daily till 10pm (w/ends till 10.30pm). Cl Tues.

343 **GROSVENOR CAFE:** 35 Ashton Lane, behind Byres Rd nr Hillhead Stn. This is the
A1 cheap café alternative in a busy lane for eats. Unaltered (now pointedly so) in 30 years. Rows of tight tables, friendly waitress service and the sort of snacks that don't come with chips. Crisp pizzas, good vegeburgers. There's a more suppery menu after 7pm. Always buzzing. Mon-Sat 9am-11pm.

344 **EQUI:** 449 Sauchiehall St. Long may this narrow café at the west end of the
C2 shopping part of Sauchiehall St serve the bacon rolls, frothy coffee and ice-cream for which it is renowned. Few tables, erratic service; quite indispensable. Mon-Sat 10am-8pm. Cl Sun.

344a **THE JEELIE PIECE:** 337 1852. 517A Gt Western Rd. There's no jam sandwich about
B1 it, and this tiny café/restau is certainly not a greasy spoon (or even a silver one) but an intimate and stylish addition to the cooler places to gobble, nibble or just hang-out up on the west side. All day b/fast. BYOB. 10am-9pm, Sun till 5pm. INX

345 **ALLAN'S SNACK BAR:** 6 Storie St, Paisley. Off the High St, a chip shop and café
xA4 adjacent. A chips-with-everything menu and very good they are too. Happy waitresses. Mon-Thu 11am-7pm, Fri/Sat 11am-8pm. Cl Sun.

346 **THE UNIQUE:** 223 Allison St. Quite the best high tea/fish 'n' chips. All the
xD4 traditional trimmings. 1197/FISH 'N' CHIP SHOPS.

347 **LORETO'S:** 285 Byres Rd. Narrow and typical 'high st' Glasgow café with
A1 waitress service. Spag bol/omelette and chips and the grub we Scots were brought up on. Mon-Sat 9am-10pm, Sun 9am-7pm.

PLACES TO TAKE KIDS

348 **TRADING POST:** 429 3445. 60 Carlton Pl. A country and western themed American
D4 eating house (and not part of a chain) big on steaks etc. Betw 6-8pm kids eat free (one per adult). A kids' menu has all the predictable stuff they like. Mon-Sat lunch and 6-11pm. Cl Sun.

349 **CHICAGO MEATPACKERS:** 248 4466. 50 Hope St beside Central Station. The
D3 Glasgow branch of a national chain and a huge emporium of a place, but kids love it not least because model train runs through the restau overhead and because there's a sensible 'cubs menu' with a burger/ribs/chicken choice and an ice-cream thing. Kids (one per adult) eat free on Sun. 7 days.

349a **HARRY RAMSDEN'S:** Paisley Rd West beside m/way flyover. Another branch of a
C3 national chain that caters well for kids. Greasy but good (1198/FISH 'N'CHIPS)

350 **FIRE STATION:** 552 2929. 33 Ingram St. Like the other restaus above, this is not
E3 merely a café that kids might like; it's esp popular with students, but kids are made welcome and they have their own section of the extensive menu. A converted fire station, roomy and informal. Daily noon-11pm.

351 **DI MAGGIO'S:** 334 8560. 61 Ruthven Lane off Byres Rd, West End and 632 4194 at
A1 1038 Pollokshaws Rd on a busy corner S of the river. Two bustling, friendly pizza joints with good Italian attitude to bairns. There's a choice to defy the most finicky kid. Wines for mum/dad are not so irresistible. Daily noon-11pm. Delivery service in area.

University Café, Glasgow (342)

THE BEST TEA-ROOMS AND COFFEE SHOPS

352 **CAFE GANDOLFI:** 552 6813. 64 Albion St, Merchant City nr City Hall. Very ✚
E3   Glasgow and very European, a coffee shop/bistro with all the right
     atmosphere and attitude. Woody interior, stunning stained glass and Tim Stead's
     distinctive furniture. Light menu – pastrami, dauphinoise, gravadlax, French
     apple tart – served all day Mon-Sat 9am-11.30pm. Sundays till 5pm.

353 **FRATELLI SARTI:** 248 2228. 133 Wellington St. Opened 1992 as an offshoot of ✚
D2   Fazzis at the time the Fazzi delis and café were taken over (315/ITALIAN
     RESTAUS). This downtown location has all the Fazzi hallmarks and ambience. A
     deli/takeaway and coffee shop/restau with sandwich/salad/pasta and pizza menu,
     authentic ingredients and excellent Costa coffee. Open 8am-10pm. Cl Sun.

354 **THE GRANARY:** 82 Howard St. Beside/behind the glass-domed St Enoch ✚
D3   Centre towards river. Difficult to know where to list (341/VEGETARIAN
     RESTAUS) because although it's open all day (till 8pm) for hot meals, it's the
     home baking that really does it. Mainly vegetarian hot dishes come with 2 simple
     salads. Serves the best apple pie in Glasgow as well as other WRI prizewinners.
     Cottagey inside; you'd never believe that BHS was a (glass-breaking) stone's
     throw away. Mon-Sat 8.30am-8pm (maybe later). Sun noon-5pm.

355 **UNDERGROUND CAFE:** Cresswell Lane, off Byres Rd nr Hillhead Station. Below
A1   stairs in back alley of craft shops and studios. Self/S hot dishes, salads and
     (bought-in) cakes. Does capture the atmosphere of the quarter, but after waiting
     a while in the perpetual queue you might not feel quite as laid-back as they are.
     Daily 9am-6pm.

356 **WILLOW TEAROOM:** 217 Sauchiehall St. Reputation precedes the famous
C2   Mackintosh Tearoom but it may disappoint. Firstly it's upstairs through a
     jewellery and ceramic shop so customers must follow a winding route past every
     kind of repro to get to his fabulous doors. These and the stained glass are
     actually about all that remains of the original; this version was opened in 1983.
     The fare is only fair and it's a bit fussy and very purple. These moans apart, it's
     still a must on the Mackintosh Trail (438/MACK). Mon-Sat 9.30am-4.30pm.

357 **BRADFORDS:** 245 Sauchiehall St. Coffee shop/restau upstairs from the flagship
C2   shop of this local and estimable bakery chain (1209/BAKERS). Very busy and
     bright and recent, but the hot dishes (e.g. potato scone with melted cheese and
     ham) are fine and the cakes and pies from downstairs represent Scottish bakery
     at its best. Also home-made chutneys and conserves. Mon-Sat 9am-5.30pm.

358 **PICKERING AND INGLIS, THE CHAPTERHOUSE:** 26 Bothwell St. A Self/S coffee
C3   shop at the back of a bookshop. Wholesome and home-baked; gets busy. The
     Christian vibe is not overbearing. Mon-Sat 8.30am-4.30pm.

359 **THE JENNY TRADITIONAL TEAROOMS:** 20 Royal Exchange Sq. Traditional they are,
D3   and inside a chintzy parlour just as you would imagine it though not perhaps off
     a main st in Glasgow. Sombrely lit and low-voiced for the serious business of
     making tea (several varieties) with excellent scones, cakes etc and their famous
     fudge. Open for dinner Thu-Sat, LO 9pm (those traditional puds!).

360 **CAFE ALBA:** 61 Otago St. Neighbourhood place off the beaten track but nr
B1   Gibson St and the University (and on quintessential Glasgow st walking through
     from Great Western Rd). Hot dishes and truly home-made cakes. Mon-Sat
     10am-5.30pm.

361 **TASHA BLANKITT:** 423 5172. 378 Cathcart Rd. An out-of-the-way and unusual gift
xD4 shop/coffee shop/bistro south of the river with a loyal following. Home cooking
     that's truthful and often imaginative. Mon-Sat 8.30am-5.30pm, w/ends 6.30-
     10pm for dinner.

362 **POLLOK HOUSE TEAROOM, POLLOK PARK:** The 'other' attraction in the park
xC4 (416/MAIN ATTRACTNS) – the big house. It has an Edwardian tea-room in the old
     kitchens in the basement. Big in 'Downstairs' atmosphere, tho' some of cook's
     baking may come out of a van rather than an oven. Can sit outside in summer.
     Mon-Sat 10am-5pm, Sun 2-5pm.

THE BEST LATE-NIGHT RESTAURANTS

See also INDIAN RESTAUS (page 56) for good places that are open to midnight and even 1am at weekends.

✠ **CHANGE AT JAMAICA:** 429 4422. Clyde Pl under railway bridge on S side of 363 Jamaica Bridge. Owned by the folk who run Peckham's (1226/DELIS), a *D3* café/restau which really comes into its own after midnight on Fri/Sat. 'Breakfast' (anything from porridge to pizza) served till 5am to night owls and more exotic party animals – an essential slice of Glasgow nightlife. You may have to wait for a table, but service is snappy. Good music, good puds. Drinks only till 1am, but pots and pots of tea. Also lunch and 7pm-midnight. Cl Sun.

THE PANCAKE PLACE: 91 Union St. Nr Central Stn and up from the fast-food 364 crossroads of Union St/Argyle St. This is another franchise chain, but more congenial than the big names down the street. Burgers, brunch and crêpes *ad infinitum*. House wine for less than 6 quid. Sun-Thu till 1am; Fri/Sat all the way till 5am.

CANTON EXPRESS: 332 0145. 407 Sauchiehall St (326/ETHNIC RESTAUS).

O' SOLE MIO and **THE NORTH ROTUNDA** both usually open till midnight. 316/319/ITALIAN RESTAUS.

Some selected late night take-aways across the city:

CASPIAN, 52 Renfield St. Mon/Tue till 1am; Wed-Sun till 4am. CENTRAL

CAFE ORIENTAL, 223 High St. Sun-Wed till 1am; Thu-Sat till 4am. EAST

KOSMOS, 194 Pitt St. Till 4am every night. CENTRAL

3 IN 1, 69 Elmbank St. Sun-Thu till 3am; Fri/Sat till 4am. WEST

727, 727 Gt Western Rd. Sun-Thu till midnight; Fri/Sat till 2am. WEST

GOOD PLACES FOR SUNDAY BREAKFAST

THE LOUNGE: W Nile St (378/GREAT PUBS). The latest venture of Colin Barr, this 365 is the first of a series of anti-style – but of course stylish – bars, and this one is *C2* chic and cheap for breakfast. Kelly Barr herself slaves over the hot stove (well, sometimes) and if you're bored with the *Sunday Times* there's always the *LA Times* to be seen with. Cool music. Noon onwards.

FAZZI'S: 95 Cambridge St. The fabuloso Fazzis (315/ITALIAN RESTAUS) is open 366 on Sunday mornings (11am and until 7pm) for the non-greasy alternative; *D1* croissants, toasties and usual menu. The coffee is to crave. Paper shop on next block.

BAY TREE: 403 Gt Western Rd. This excellent caff (338/VEGETARIAN RESTAUS) 367 provides another antidote to the toxins of Sat night. A hearty vegan or *B1* vegetarian breakfast is served all day. From 11am.

COTTIER'S: 93 Hyndland St off Hyndland Rd (302A/CAFE-BARS). Deep in the 368 hefty mortgage belt of fashionable Hyndland, this converted church probably *A1* gets more of a congregation now than it ever did. Mirroring the Southern US flavour of the menu in the upstairs restau, there's cajun kedgeree for breakfast along with your bacon and mushrooms and maybe a little gospel music? Noon-4pm.

369

CUL DE SAC: 44 Ashton Lane, off Byres Rd. (311/BISTROS). A smart relaxed place to phase into Sunday. The fry-up includes potato scones and comes in a *A1* vegetarian version, and there are better than average burgers and exotic crêpes. Brunch noon-4pm.

370

THE GLASGOW BUTTERY: 734 Dumbarton Rd. At the very end where the flyover starts can be found this unpretentious coffee shop with big windows and big *xA1* breakfasts (served all day). There may be a home-cooking atmosphere, but it's a pity the cakes ain't. Newspapers. Sun 10am-5pm. Also Mon-Thu 10am-3pm, Fri/Sat 10am-11pm.

A SELECTION OF GREAT PUBS

Pubs that are notable for other specific reasons are on the following pages. Pubs in Glasgow usually close at 11pm or midnight.

371 **VICTORIA:** 157 Bridgegate. 'The Vicky' is in the east end nr the Victoria
D3 Bridge over the Clyde close to Paddy's Market and the Barrows. Once a pub for the fishmarket and open odd hours, now it's a howff for all those who like an atmosphere that's old, friendly and uncontrived. Small interior; you can close the door on all that new Glasgow. Maclays, Theakstons and Greenmantle ales. Mon-Sat till midnight, Sun till 11pm.

372 **SCOTIA BAR:** 112 Stockwell St. Nr The Victoria betw the river and the
D3 consumer greenhouses of the St Enoch Centre. Another old, real Glasgow pub that hasn't visibly changed in years and was in fact a centre of resistance to the Culture pogroms of Glasgow 1990. Long the haunt of folk musicians, writers and raconteurs, you might well meet anyone in the affray. Maclays. Daily till midnight.

373 **BLACKFRIARS:** 36 Bell St. Unlike above, this is refurb à la Merchant City,
E3 covering all the contemporary bases. But it has been done well; the real ales are well chosen and cared for, the food (all day till 9pm, 403/PUB FOOD) is fine and there's a regular programme of live music and a comedy room downstairs (409/PUB MUSIC). A v civilised rendezvous. Mon-Sat till midnight, Sun till 11pm.

374 **THE HORSE SHOE:** 17 Drury St. A mighty pub since 1888 in the small st betw
D2 Mitchell and Renfrew nr the station. Island rather than horseshoe bar and an upstairs lounge where they serve high tea. The food is amazing value (399/PUB FOOD). It is said that you will meet everyone you have ever known if you stay in here long enough. Caledonian and Maclays. Daily till midnight.

375 **THE HALT BAR:** 160 Woodlands Rd. On the main route from the West End to the
B1 University. An ancient and unpretentious bar with great live music (380/OLD PUBS; 411/PUB MUSIC) and the difficult-to-define 'great pubs of our time' factor. The Halt is handily close to:

376 **UISGE BEATHA:** 246 Woodlands Rd. 'Oo-i-skay Bay' (or something like that)
B1 means 'the water of life' and is a recent Highland incursion. Shooting-lodge chic and cosy; more than a mere draught of the Gael. Good grub at lunchtime and Thu-Sat 6-9pm. Related to one of the great Highland bars (at the top of Loch Lomond), The Drover's Inn, Inverarnan (701/PUBS WITH ATMOS). Sun-Thu till 11pm, Fri/Sat till midnight.

377 **ROCK GARDEN:** 73 Queen St. Although it may seem similar to countless other
D3 'café-bars' in Glasgow, the Rock Garden is still a cool place to hang after all these years and will probably see off most of its imitators. Food noon-3pm, live bands sometimes but mainly just people drinking this month's lagers and shouting above this month's music. Daily till midnight.

378 **THE LOUNGE, THE LIVING ROOM:** W Nile St and 5-9 Byres Rd. 2 bars related in
C2/A1 theme and style (and to be followed after going to press by a more ambitious project). The latest manifestation of Colin Barr's here and now vision. The Lounge is a beach-bar basement with football TV and a big Sunday Breakfast (365/SUN BFAST). The L Room at the bottom of Byres Rd is a 2-room see-and-be-seen scenario with a Brazilian chef (food noon-8pm, Sun till 7pm) and smooth music. Both with rough decor circa 1994 are just ahead of the brewery pack. Wonder if he'll make it to the bathroom! 7 days till midnight.

379 **LOCK 27:** 1100 Crow Rd. At the very N end of Crow Rd beyond Anniesland, an
xA1 unusual boozer for Glasgow – a canalside pub on a lock of the Forth and Clyde Canal (442/CITY WALKS), a touch English (a very wee touch) where of a summer's day you can sit outside. Excl bar food, always busy. 7 days.

379a **THE DRUM AND MONKEY:** Corner of Renfield and St Vincent St in city centre,
D2 and recent well thought-out example of the downtown bar. Has the loungy and gentelemen's clubby look that makes the ambience of the more fashionable '90s bars with a sombre but comfortable interior. Food, ales, vino, champagne. Busy folk go to layabout. Bar snacks till 11pm. 7 days.

BABBITY BOWSTER: 16 Blackfriars St. Full report 392/ALES, 402/FOOD.

THE BEST OLD 'UNSPOILT' PUBS

Of course it's not necessarily the case that when a pub's done up it's spoiled, or that all old pubs are worth preserving but some have resisted change and that's part of their appeal. Money and effort are often spent to oldify bars and contrive an atmosphere. The following places don't have to try. Glasgow pubs close no later than midnight.

THE HALT BAR: 160 Woodlands Rd. Nr University with legendary status for generations of students. Oddly, it hasn't been so big on real ale since passing from the hands of Whitbreads, the major brewer, but it does have that kind of atmosphere of integrity and no froth. Varied (free) live music thro the back (411/PUB MUSIC). Sun-Thu till 11pm, Fri/Sat till midnight. Music usually from 9pm. *380 B1*

THE GRIFFIN: 266 Bath St. Corner of Elmbank St nr Kings Theatre. Best pub in this part of town for a jar and a jaw. Outstandingly good value lunches (398/PUB FOOD). Sun-Thu till 11pm, Fri/Sat till midnight. *381 C2*

THE ROWAN TREE, UDDINGSTON: 12km SE of centre via M74. In Old Mill Rd off Main St where sign points (in opp direction) for Bothwell Castle. A cottagey pub in the shadow of the world-famous Tunnock's Caramel Wafers factory and long frequented by the wafer makers. Food at lunchtime, coal fire in winter, folk music on Fridays. Maclays. Mon-Sat till 11.45pm, Sun till 11pm. *382 xE2*

THE SARACEN HEAD: Gallowgate, nr Barrowlands. A pub which can truly claim to be untouched or unimpressed by 'improvement'. To enter the dark, stained interior is to go back far beyond 'Glasgow – City of Culture' (to the 18th century, in fact). The 'Sarry Heid', however, does not trade in its history or its celebrity, and Boswell and Johnson can probably go and get stuffed. No real ale or recent lagers but plenty of real characters, some of them straight out of paintings by Ken Currie or Peter Howson who have studios nearby. If tonic wine is your tipple (and they've got quite a range as well as dynamite cider), you won't be there just to imbibe the atmosphere. Open early to late. *383 E3*

THE VARIETY: 401 Sauchiehall St. Not as old as you might think from the art deco/nicotine-stained look of the place, the Variety lives up to its name with an eclectic clientele of world-weary yet vibrant people. Few poseurs but plenty of disillusioned ex-trendsetters only too glad to have left the teen scene behind. Gets very busy at the weekend. *384 C2*

M. J. HERAGHTY: 708 Pollokshaws Rd. More than a touch of the Irish about this pub which is on a busy st that could be somewhere off St Stephen's Green. A local with loyal regulars who'll make you welcome; you won't want to go anywhere else on this side of the river. Sun-Thu till 11pm, Fri/Sat till midnight. *385 xC4*

BRECHIN'S: 803 Govan Rd. Nr jnct with Paisley Rd West and m/way overpass. Est 1798 and, as they say, always in the same family. A former shipyard pub which despite the proximity to Rangers FC is not partisan. It's behind a statue which is why it's known as the 'Black Man' and there's a cat on the roof which makes it a listed building. Unaffected neighbourhood atmos. Mon-Sat till 11pm, Sun till 6.30pm. *386 B3*

OLD EMPIRE BAR: 68 Saltmarket. In this ancient part of the city nr the Tron, a pub that was established underneath a railway arch in 1886 and hasn't changed much since. It's seen the East Enders come and go and now has the Merchant City galleries and recording studios on its doorstep – Costello's lounge through the back gets a fairly mixed bunch around the tables. Daily till midnight. *387 E3*

THE HORSE SHOE: 17 Drury St. The celebrated City Centre bar with the famous longest bar in the world and an assortment of Old and New Glaswegians arranged along it (374/GREAT PUBS; 399/PUB FOOD). *388 D2*

BAIRDS BAR and THE DISTRICT: 2 bars from opposite sides of the great divide. **BAIRDS** in the Gallowgate adj **BARROWLANDS** (456/GLASGOW MUSIC) is a Catholic stronghold green to the gills where, on days when Celtic play at home up the road at Parkhead, you'd have to be in by 11am to get a drink. **THE DISTRICT**, 252 Paisley Rd West, Govan nr Ibrox Park, is where Rangers supporters gather and rule in their own blue heaven. Both pubs give an extraordinary insight into what makes the Glasgow timebomb tick. Provided you aren't wearing the wrong colour (or say something daft), you'll be very welcome in either. *388a E3/xA3*

THE BEST REAL ALE PUBS

Pubs on other pages may purvey real ale, but the following are the ones where they take it seriously and/or have a good choice.

389 **BOSWELL HOTEL:** 27 Mansionhouse Rd. Southside via Pollokshaws Rd,
xC4 Langside Av and rt just before the Battlefield Monument at the edge of
Queen's Park. 3 busy bars where you can eat, drink and be mesmerised by an
outstanding collection of ales. Usually 3 or 4 regulars and 8 guests all well
looked after, as are the guests in the rooms upstairs (263/INEXP HOTELS). Fine,
unpretentious grub till 10pm. Kids and all non-believers welcome. Sun-Thu till
11pm, Fri/Sat till midnight.

390 **BON ACCORD:** 153 North St. On a slip rd of the m/way swathe nr the Mitchell
B2 Library, is this real ale oasis of long standing. Pub and quieter lounge at back.
Over 100 malts as well as up to a dozen beers; always Youngers 3, McEwan 80,
Theakston and Marsden and many guests on handpump. Food at lunchtime.
Mon-Sat till midnight, Sun till 11.30.

391 **TENNENTS:** 191 Byres Rd. Nr the always-red traffic lights at University Av, a
A1 big, booming watering-hole of a place where you're never far away from the
horseshoe bar and its several excellent handpumped ales incl Maclays,
Caledonian and Theakston. Unquestionably one of the best bars in an area that's
heaving with them.

392 **BABBITY BOWSTER:** 16 Blackfriars St. In a pedestrianised part of the Merchant
E3 City and just off the High St, a highly successful pub/restau/hotel; but the pub
comes first. Maclays is heavily featured, but there are guest beers and selected
malts. Food all day (402/PUB FOOD), occ folk music (esp Sun), outside patio and
exhibitions. Proprietor Fraser Laurie has thought of everything.

393 **SLOANE'S:** 63 Argyle Arcade at 108 Argyle St. Best to walk here since the arcade
D3 runs betw a busy part of Argyle St nr the Tron and pedestrianised Buchanan St
(this entrance closed at night). Odd location, though back in 1797 it was a
coaching inn on the edge of the city. Great 'period' bar with food from the
restau upstairs (404/PUB FOOD) and ales such as Labatts and Tetley.

394 **THE POT STILL:** 154 Hope St. There are ales (Youngers 3 and McEwans 80), but
D2 mainly noted for its mindboggling range of malts. They say they've got 301,
which makes them No 2 in Scotland (I reckon) for range of malts (WHISKY,
p. 194.) Mon-Sat till 11pm/midnight. Cl Sun.

395 **THE BREWERY TAP:** 1055 Sauchiehall St, nr Kelvingrove Park. Same management
A1 as Blackfriars (373/GREAT PUBS) and similar though perhaps more studentish
clientele. Handy for refreshment after those work-outs at the Kelvin Hall Sports
Centre, which is nearby (450/SPORTS FACILITIES). Bar area gets v busy but has
large lounge. Belhaven, Caledonian, Arrols, Tetleys and guests.

396 **THE HORSE SHOE:** 17 Drury St. Great for lots of reasons (374/BEST PUBS) not the
D2 least of which is its range of beers: Caledonian, Greenmantle, Maclays and Bass
on handpump.

397 **VICTORIA BAR:** 157 Bridgegate. Another pub mentioned before (371/BEST PUBS)
D3 where Greenmantle, Maclays and Theakstons can be drunk in a dark woody
atmosphere enlivened by occasional traditional music.

PUBS WITH GOOD FOOD

Most of these pubs are also notable for other reasons. Glasgow bars usually close no later than midnight.

✠ **THE GRIFFIN:** 266 Bath St. On corner of Elmbank St nr Kings Theatre at the West End. The Griffin! Always there on that prominent corner – how many people have passed it for years not knowing what a fine pub it is and how ridiculously cheap and good are its lunches. The basic pie and chips/macaroni cheese etc will not be bettered at this price (except see below). Food: noon-2.30pm. Pub till midnight/1am. 398 C2

✠ **THE HORSE SHOE:** 17 Drury St. Except maybe at the Horse Shoe. The great all-round pub crops up again. The food is a particularly good deal with lunches less than 2 quid and old favourites on the menu like jelly and fruit. Lunch noon-2.30pm and high tea served upstairs (which doesn't have quite the same atmosphere). Pub open daily till midnight. 399 D2

✠ **MURPHY'S PAKORA:** 1287 Argyle St. A good idea which solves the problem of what to drink with spicy Indian food (Murphy's Irish Stout). Pakora (best in mixed selections of 'thalis' or platters where you can choose any 3) are served all day; gram flour batter wrapped round anything you can think of, dipped in 3 sauces. Moist bits like aubergines and seafood work best. Table service and bar. Sun-Thu noon-12.30am, Fri/Sat noon-1am. 400 A2

CHIMMY CHUNGA'S: 499 Gt Western Rd. Some might see it as part of the Glasgow/Mexi-con: overloud, overthemed and over there they are eating burgers . . . natcho. But still a buzzy and reliable bar/diner in student-land. No sunset yet over the tequila. Mon-Thu till 11pm, Fri-Sun till midnight. 401 B1

BABBITY BOWSTER: 16 Blackfriars St. Already listed as a pub for real ale and as a hotel (there are rooms upstairs), it's necessary also to mention the food, mainly for its variety and all-day availability. Breakfast is served from 8am, there's Scottishy grub (incl 3 kinds of stovies as well as haggis and nut loaf) and daily specials esp at lunch and 9-11pm. The service when the bar's busy can be pretty slow (392/ALES; 264/INEXP HOTELS). 402 E3

BLACKFRIARS: 36 Bell St. Listed separately as one of the great Glasgow pubs due to all-round ambience, provision of real ale, comedy and music, there's also food which is available all day until around 9pm (or when it becomes too crowded). Menu changes slightly for evenings, but it's mainly pub grub favourites incl the ubiquitous potato skins and Death by Chocolate. Well-made omelettes and friendly salads show that they do care about food (373/GREAT PUBS; 409/PUB MUSIC). 403 E3

SLOANE'S: Argyle Arcade nr entrance on to Argyle St (nr and opp St Enoch's). Probably the best meal in this entire high st area of shops and a civilised backwater from the tide of shopping. Restau dining-room upstairs with quaint Edwardian elegance, bar below has simpler, more accessible menu and real ales (393/ALES). Mon-Sat, food till 11pm. 404 D3

FOX AND HOUNDS, HOUSTON: On B790 village main st in Renfrewshire, 30km W of centre by M8 jnct 29 (A726), then cross back under m/way on B790. Village pub with real fire and dining-room upstairs for family meals and suppers. Folk come from miles around. Sunday roasts. Great example of Couthie cuisine. Food available daily at lunchtime and from 6-10pm. 405 xA4

PUBS AND CLUBS WITH GOOD LIVE MUSIC

Many other places have live music but programmes and policies can vary quickly. Best to look out for posters or consult The List *magazine, on sale fortnightly from most city centre newsagents. The following places are the most likely bets:*

406 **KING TUT'S WAH WAH HUT:** 221 5279. 272a St Vincent's St. On the national
C2 touring circuit so the place to see new bands along with the best of the local crop. Live music most nights. Programme extensively advertised incl flyposting in the streets (which is where to look for most of the live music announcements in Glasgow). Music is taken seriously here; a musos' bar. Doors open 8.30pm. Tickets on sale at bar or Virgin Records, Union St.

407 **NICE 'N' SLEAZY:** 333 9637. 421 Sauchiehall St at the West End. Not especially
C2 sleazy and a mixed programme of rock and pop though biased slightly to the heavier end if only because there is a very rock 'n' roll atmosphere to the place. Music upstairs in main bar and also down on a nightly basis (esp Thu-Sun) with a nominal entrance charge. Usually commences 9pm. Daily till midnight.

408 **THE CATHOUSE:** 248 6606. Brown St at Broomielaw on the river. Live rock club
C3 with mixed programme on various nights depending on availability of touring bands (other 'clubs' on other nights). Tickets often sold in advance, as for King Tut's (above).

409 **BLACKFRIARS:** 552 5924. 36 Bell St. Merchant city pub with everything (373/BEST
E3 PUBS) which incl all kinds of live music though mainly the more subdued 30-something variety (e.g. some jazz, some folk). Great little comedy room downstairs for w/end sessions. Music: Thu-Sat 9.30pm. Admission free. Phone to check programme.

410 **SCOTIA BAR:** 552 8681. Stockwell St. Integral part of the Glasgow folk scene for
D3 years. Music: Wed 9pm, Sat/Sun 3.30pm. Free. 372/BEST PUBS; 456/FOLK MUSIC for other main Glasgow folk listings.

411 **HALT BAR:** 332 1210. Woodlands Rd. Mixed programme of music in great pub rock
B1 atmosphere. Usually Sun/Tue (Jazz: the estimable Bobby Wishart), Wed/Thu and Sat. Music starts around 9pm and admission is free.

412 **COTTIER'S:** 357 5825. 93 Hyndland St. Not easy to find unless you know the area
xA1 (the densely populated quadrant betw Dumbarton Rd and Byres Rd). There is a neighbourhood atmosphere to this converted church (not in, but off the top of, Hyndland St nr Highburgh Rd); it has the same management as the Baby Grand (298/BISTROS) and Cathedral House (262/HOTELS) which has similar music policy. Restau upstairs and bar/wine bar with live music of the good pub-entertainment variety, various nights esp Fri/Sat at 8/9pm. Free. See also 320A/CAFE-BARS.

413 **FIXX II:** 221 1568. 86 Miller St. Through several changes of image the Fixx is still a
D3 fairly funky bar/diner/good place for a gig (esp for up-and-coming bands). Live nights have varied over the years (Wednesdays at time of writing); check first. Otherwise there's a wide range of lagers and the sort of crowd that likes them and live music. Daily till 11pm/midnight. Food till 5pm.

414 **SOCIETY OF MUSICIANS:** 221 6112. 73 Berkeley St. Where to go for . . . the society of
B2 musicians. Seriously good music in a light and appreciative atmosphere with good, specifically constructed acoustics. Non-members pay at door (usually £1). Nightclub seating and bar till 11.30pm. Music (folk or jazz) every night except Tue and Fri. Phone for programme or consult *The List*.

THE MAIN ATTRACTIONS

† † **KELVINGROVE ART GALLERY AND MUSEUM:** At westerly extension of 415
Argyle St and Sauchiehall St by Kelvingrove Park. Huge Victorian A1
sandstone edifice with awesome atrium. On the ground floor is a natural
history/Scottish history museum. The upper salons contain the city's superb
British and European art collection. (Pity the Dali Crucifixion has gone elsewhere
– see 417A below.) There are strong contemporary exhibitions as well as the
permanent collection. Tea-room. The Museum of Transport (420/LESS OBV
ATTRACTS) is across the rd. Mon-Sat 10am-5pm, Sun from 11am.   FREE

† † **THE BURRELL COLLECTION AND POLLOK PARK:** South of river via A77 416
Kilmarnock Rd (over Jamaica St Bridge) about 5km, following signs xC4
from Pollokshaws Rd. Buses 45, 48, 57. Set in rural parkland, Glasgow's
foremost attraction is the award-winning modern gallery which was built to
house the eclectic acquisitions of Sir William Burrell. Showing a preference for
medieval works, amongst the 8,500 items the magpie magnate donated to the
city in 1944, are artefacts from the Roman empire to Rodin. The building itself
integrates old doorways and whole rooms reconstructed from Hutton Castle.
Pollok House and Gardens further into the park is worth a detour and has
(below stairs) the better coffee shop (362/TEA-ROOMS). Both open Mon-Sat
10am-5pm, Sun from 11am.   FREE

† **GLASGOW CATHEDRAL/PROVAND'S LORDSHIP:** High St. Across the road from 417
one another they represent what remains of the oldest part of the city which xE2
(as can be seen in the People's Palace below) was, in the early 18th century,
merely a ribbon of streets from here to the river. The present Cathedral, though
established by St Mungo in 543AD, dates from the 12th century and is a fine
example of the very real, if gloomy, Gothic. The House, built in 1471, is a
museum which strives to convey a sense of medieval life. Watch you don't get
run over when you re-emerge into the 20th century and try to cross the street.
In the background, the Necropolis piled on the hill invites inspection though it
was closed at time of writing (991/GRAVEYARDS).

† **ST MUNGO MUSEUM OF RELIGIOUS LIFE AND ART:** In the Cathedral precinct or 417a
square, Glasgow's latest 'cultural' attraction. Opened with some gnashing of xE2
teeth and wringing of hands in 1993, it houses art and artefacts representing the
world's six major religions arranged tactfully in an attractive stone building with
a zen garden in the courtyard. The dramatic Dali Crucifixion seems somehow
lost, and the assemblage seems like a good and worthwhile vision not quite
realised, but if you like your spirituality shuffled but not stirred this is for you.
The punters' comments board is always enlightening. Mon-Sat 10-5pm, Sun
from 11am.

† **THE PEOPLE'S PALACE:** Glasgow Green, the large park in the 'East End'. The 418
museum best approached via the Tron and London Rd, then turn right. xE4
This is a folk museum *par excellence* wherein, since 1898, the history, folklore
and artefacts of a proud city have been gathered, cherished and displayed. But
this is much more than a mere museum; it is the heart and soul of the city and
together with the Winter Gardens adjacent shouldn't be missed if you want to
know what Glasgow's about. Tea-room in the Tropics, amongst the palms and
ferns of the Winter Garden is wholefoodish but not faddish. Mon-Sat 10am-
5pm, Sun from 11am.   FREE

HUNTERIAN MUSEUM AND GALLERY: University Av. On one side of the st, 419
Glasgow's oldest museum with geological, archaeological and social history A1
displayed in a venerable building. The cloisters outside and the **UNIVERSITY
CHAPEL** should not be missed. Across the street and campus, a modern block
contains part of Glasgow's exceptional civic collection – Rembrandt to the
Colourists and the Glasgow Boys, as well as one of the most complete collections
of an artist's work and personal effects to be found anywhere, viz that of
Whistler. It's fascinating stuff even if you're not a fan. There's also a print gallery
and the amazing Mackintosh House (436/MACKINTOSH). Mon-Sat 9.30am-5pm.
FREE

THE SLIGHTLY LESS OBVIOUS ATTRACTIONS

420 **MUSEUM OF TRANSPORT:** Off Argyle St behind the Kelvin Hall and opp ††
A1 the Kelvingrove Art Gallery. May sound boring to all but train enthusiasts and not an obvious attraction to visitors, but Glaswegians know better and this is amazingly popular. Has something for everybody, especially kids. The reconstruction of a cobbled Glasgow street *circa* 1938 is an inspired evocation. There are trains, trams and fascinating collections of cars, motorbikes and bicycles under the one huge roof. And there are model ships in the Clyde room. Mon-Sat 10am-5pm, Sun 11am-5pm. FREE

Museum of Transport, Glasgow (420)

421 **BOTANIC GARDENS AND KIBBLE PALACE:** Gt Western Rd. Smallish park † †
xA1 close to River Kelvin (with riverside walks (441/CITY WALKS), and pretty much 'the dear green place'. Kibble Palace (built 1873) is the distinctive domed glasshouse with statues set amongst lush ferns and shrubbery from around the (mostly temperate) world. A wonderful place to muse and wander. Gardens open till dusk, 'Palace' 10am-4.45pm.

422 **THE BARROWS:** (pron 'Barras'.) The sprawling street and indoor market † †
E3 area in the East End of the city around Gallowgate (via Argyle St and the Tron). An experience, an institution, a slice of pure Glasgow. If you're only in town for one weekend, it's a must, and like no other market anywhere. Sat and Sun only. 1272/MARKETS.

423 **THE TENEMENT HOUSE:** 145 Buccleuch St. Nr Charing Cross but can approach
C1 from nr the end of Sauchiehall St and over the hill. The typical 'respectable' Glasgow tenement kept under a bell-jar since Our Agnes moved out in 1965. She had lived there with her mother since 1911 and wasn't one for new-fangled things. It's a touch claustrophobic, with hordes of visitors, and is distinctly voyeuristic, but if it was on the market you'd have an offer in tomorrow. Daily 2-5pm (Nov-Mar: 2-4pm Sat/Sun only). Ground-floor flat now open too. ADM

424 **ST ENOCH ICE-RINK:** In the glass-domed shopping centre off Argyle St (and quite
D3 the best thing about it), an ice-rink that's not quite the Rockefeller Center but because it's Glasgow, a friendly and fun alternative to going round and round the shops. Sessions daily within 10am-4.30pm and 7-10pm, Sun 1-4.30pm. Skates 50p.

POLLOK LEISURE CENTRE: 881 3313. Cowglen Rd. Adj Pollok Shopping Centre in South Side. From city centre take Pollokshaws Rd, then rt fork (after 3km) to Pollok Park and rt (after 1km) at r/bout along Barrhead Rd. Centre is 2km along on left at next r/bout. A place to take kids for water immersion thrills; slides etc in modern, safe leisurama. Mon-Fri 9.30am-9pm, Sat/Sun 10am-4pm. *425 xC4*

GREENBANK GARDENS: 10km SW of centre via Kilmarnock Rd, Eastwood Toll, Clarkston Toll and Mearns Rd. Then signposted (3km). A spacious oasis in the suburbs; formal gardens, parterre and woodland walks around elegant, still lived-in Georgian house. Very Scottish. Open all year, 9.30am-sunset. *426 xC4 NTS*

MITCHELL LIBRARY: North St. West End. On a slip road and o/looking the canyon of the M8, the landmark domed edifice of Glasgow's main library. Named after Stephen Mitchell, tobacco lord (1789-1874), who wanted to leave a building 'worthy of the city', it opened in 1911. Interesting just to wander through the vast halls or upstairs to the quieter reading rooms; the dome itself is astonishing. Theatre next door has a mixed theatre/music prog. Café till 4.30pm. Library: Mon-Fri 9.30am-9pm, Sat till 5pm. Cl Sun. *427 B2*

THE CITY CHAMBERS: George Sq. The hugely impressive building along the whole E end of Glasgow's municipal centre. Let's face it, it's not often that one could seriously recommend a visit to the District Council offices, but this is a wonderfully over-the-top monument to the days when Glasgow was the second city of the empire, a cross between an Italian Renaissance palace and an Escher marble maze. Guided tours Mon-Wed and Fri, 10.30am and 2.30pm. *427a D2*

FINLAYSTONE ESTATE: 30km W of city centre via fast M8/A8 signed off dual-carr just before Pt Glasgow. Delightful gardens and woods around mansion house with many pottering places and longer trails (and ranger service). Various 'attractions' incl Victorian laundry and kitchen (at certain times), Smelly Garden etc. Visitor centre and conservatory tea-room. Good for Granny and the kids' outings. AYR 10am-5pm, 7 days. *427b xA4*

THE McLELLAN GALLERIES: 270 Sauchiehall St. Purpose-built in 1854, these lofty salons were refurbished in 1992 and now house one of the most extensive galleries for temporary/contemporary exhibitions in Britain. Always worth stopping shopping for. Mon-Sat 10am-noon and 1pm-5pm. *427c C2*

PAISLEY ABBEY: Paisley town centre (15km from Glasgow). (972/ABBEYS.)

BOTHWELL CASTLE, UDDINGSTON: 15km E of centre via M74. (924/RUINS.)

FORMAKIN ESTATE, BISHOPTON: 30km W of centre via M8 W. (775/COUNTRY PARKS.)

Kibble Palace, Glasgow (421)

THE BEST VIEWS OF THE CITY AND BEYOND

428 **CATHKIN BRAES, QUEEN MARY'S SEAT:** The southern ridge of the city on the B759
xC4 from Carmunnock to Cambuslang, about 12km from centre. Go south of river
by Albert Bridge to Aitkenhead Rd which continues south as Carmunnock Rd.
Follow to Carmunnock, a delightfully rural village, and pick up the Cathkin Rd.
2km along on the right is the Cathkin Braes Golf Club and 100m further on the
left is the park. Marvellous views to north, the Campsies, Kilpatrick Hills, Ben
Lomond and as far as Ben Ledi. Walks on the Braes on both sides of the road.

429 **QUEEN'S VIEW, AUCHINDEN:** Not so much a view of the city, more a perspective
xC1 on Glasgow's Highland hinterland, this short walk and sweeping vista to the
north has been a Glaswegian pilgrimage for generations. On A809 N from
Bearsden about 8km after last r/bout and 2km after the Carbeth Inn which is a v
decent pub to repair to. Busy carpark attests to popularity. Walk, along path cut
into ridgeside, takes 40-50mins to cairn at 634ft from which you can see The
Cobbler (that other Glasgow favourite, 1038/HILLS), Ben Ledi and sometimes as
far as Ben Chonzie 50km away. The fine views of Loch Lomond are what
Queen Victoria came for. 1-A-1

430 **RUCHILL PARK:** A surprising and rewarding panorama from this overlooked park
xC1 to the north of the city nr the infamous Possilpark housing estate. Go to top of
Firhill Rd (past Partick Thistle football ground) over Forth and Clyde Canal
(442/WALKS) off Garscube Rd where it becomes Maryhill Rd. Best view is from
around the flagpole; the whole city and its surrounding hills from the Campsies
to Gleniffer and Cathkin Braes come into focus.

431 **BAR HILL at TWECHAR, nr KIRKINTILLOCH:** 22km N of city, taking A803
xE1 Kirkintilloch t/off from M8, then the 'low' rd to Kilsyth, the B8023 and bearing
left at the 'black and white bridge'. Next to Twechar Quarry Inn, a path is
signed for Bar Hill and the Antonine Wall. Steepish climb for 2km, ignore the
strange dome of grass, this isn't it. Over to left in copse of trees is the remains of
one of the forts on the wall which stretched across Scotland in the first two
centuries AD. Ground plan only explained on a board. This is a special place with
strong history vibes and airy views over the plain to the city which came a long
time after. 1-A-2

432 **BLACKHILL, nr LESMAHAGOW:** 28km S of city. Another marvellous outlook, but
xE1 in the opp direction from above. Take Jct 10/11 on M74, then off the B7078
signed Lanark, take the B7018. 4km along past Clarkston Farm, head uphill for
1km and park by Water Board mound. Walk uphill through fields to rt for about
1km. Unprepossessing hill which unexpectedly reveals a vast vista of most of
East Central Scotland. 1-A-2

433 **PAISLEY ABBEY:** About one Saturday a month between May and Oct (1-5pm) on
xA4 Abbey 'open days', the tower of this amazing edifice (972/ABBEYS) can be
climbed. The tower (restored 1926) is 150ft high and from the top there's a grand
view of the Clyde. Obviously this is a rare experience, but phone 889 7654 or 889
0711 for details; next Sat could be your lucky day. M8 to Paisley; frequent trains
from Central Stn.

CAMPSIE FELLS, GLENNIFFER BRAES, KILPATRICK HILLS: 445/447/449/WALKS
OUTSIDE THE CITY.

THE MACKINTOSH TRAIL

The great Scottish architect and designer Charles Rennie Mackintosh (1868-1928), had a complete vision which has had an extraordinary influence on contemporary design. His work is accessible and satisfying and Glasgow is the best place to see it. Here's where:

✝ ✝ **GLASGOW SCHOOL OF ART:** 167 Renfrew St. Mackintosh's supreme 434
architectural triumph. It's enough almost to admire it from the street C2
(and maybe better, since this is very much a working college) but there are
guided tours at 11am and 2pm (Sat 10.30am) of the sombre yet light interior, the
halls and library. You might wonder if the building itself could be partly
responsible for the remarkable output of acclaimed painters from this college.
'The Tenement House' (423/LESS OBVIOUS ATTRACTIONS) is nearby.

✝ ✝ **QUEEN'S CROSS CHURCH:** 870 Garscube Rd where it becomes Maryhill 435
Rd (corner of Springbank St). Built 1888-90. Calm and simple, the xC1
antithesis of Victorian Gothic. If all churches had been built like this, we'd go
more often. The HQ of the Charles Rennie Mackintosh Society which was
founded in 1973 (phone 946 6600). Open Tue/Thu/Fri noon-5.30pm, Sun 2.30-
5pm. 981/ CHURCHES.   FREE

✝ **MACKINTOSH HOUSE:** University Av. Opp and part of the Hunterian 436
Museum (419/ATTRACTIONS) within the university campus. The Master's A1
house has been transplanted and methodically reconstructed from the next st
(they say even the light is the same). If you ever wondered what the fuss was
about, go and see how innovative and complete an artist, designer and architect
he was, in this inspiring yet habitable set of rooms. Mon-Sat, 9.30-5pm.   FREE

✝ **SCOTLAND STREET SCHOOL:** 225 Scotland St. Opp Shields Underground and 437
best approached by car from Eglinton St (A77 Kilmarnock Rd over Jamaica C4
St Bridge). Entire school (from 1906) preserved as museum of education thro
Victorian/Edwardian and war times. Original, exquisite Mackintosh features esp
tiling, and powerfully redolent of happy schooldays. This is a uniquely evocative
time capsule. Café and temporary exhibs. Mon-Sat 10am-5pm, Sun 2-5pm.   FREE

WILLOW TEAROOM: Sauchiehall St. The café he designed or what's left of it; 438
certainly where to go for a teabreak on the trail. 356/TEA-ROOMS.   C2

THE ART LOVER'S HOUSE: Bellahouston Park. Closed at time of writing. Phone 439
CRM Society at Queen's Cross (see above) for details.

✝ **THE HILL HOUSE, HELENSBURGH:** Upper Colquhoun St. Take Sinclair St off 440
main Esplanade (at Romanesque tower and tourist office) and go 2km xA1
uphill, taking left on bend and follow signs. A complete house incorporating
Mackintosh's typical total unity of design, built for Walter Blackie in 1902/4.
Much to marvel over and wish that everybody else would go away and you
could stay there for the night. There's a library full of books to keep you
occupied. Tea-room; gardens. Open Apr-Dec, 1-5pm. Helensburgh is 45km
NW of city centre via Dumbarton (A82) and A814 up N Clyde coast.   ADM

THE BEST CITY WALKS

Areas of these walks are not covered in city centre maps. See p. 9 for walk codes.

441 **KELVIN WALKWAY:** A path along the banks of Glasgow's other river, the Kelvin,
xA1 which enters the Clyde unobtrusively at Yorkhill but first meanders through some of the most interesting parts and parks of the NW city. Walk starts at Kelvingrove Park through the University and Hillhead district under Kelvin Br and on to the wonderful Botanic Gardens (421/LESS OBVIOUS ATTRACTS). The river then flows N, under the Forth and Clyde Canal (see below) to the Arcadian fields of Dawsholm Park (5km), Killermont (the posh golf course) and Kirkintilloch (13km from start). Since the river and the canal shadow each other for much of their routes, it's possible, with a map, to go out one waterway and return by the other (e.g. start at Gt Western Rd, return Maryhill Rd).
START: Usual start at the Eldon St (off Woodlands Rd) gate of Kelvingrove Park or Kelvin Br. Only street parking. 2-13+KM XCIRC BIKE 1-A-1

442 **FORTH AND CLYDE CANAL TOWPATH:** The canal, opened in 1790 and once a
xA1/ major short-cut for fishing boats and trade betw Europe and America, provides
C1/D1 a fascinating look round the back of the city from a pathway that stretches on a spur from Port Dundas just N of the M8 to the main canal at the top of Lochburn Rd off Maryhill Rd and then E all the way to Kirkintilloch and Falkirk, and W through Maryhill and Drumchapel to Bowling and the Clyde (60km). Much of the route is through the forsaken or resuscitated industrial heart of the city, betw wastegrounds, warehouses and high flats, but there are open stretches and odd corners and by Bishopbriggs, it's a rural waterway.
START: (1) Top of Firhill Rd (great view of city from Ruchill Park, 100m further on, 430/VIEWS). (2) Lochburn Rd (see above) at the confluence from which to go E or W to the Clyde. (3) Top of Crow Rd, Anniesland where there is a canalside pub, 'Lock 27' with tables outside, real ale and food (noon-7/8pm). (4) Bishopbriggs Sports Centre, Balmuildy Rd. From here it is 6km to Maryhill and 1km to the 'country churchyard' of Cadder or 3km to Kirkintilloch. All starts have some parking. ANY KM XCIRC BIKE 1-A-1

443 **POLLOK COUNTRY PARK:** The park that (apart from the area around the Gallery
xC4 and the House, 416/MAIN ATTRACTIONS) most feels like a real country park. Numerous trails through woods and meadows. The leisurely Sunday guided walks with the Park Rangers can be educative and more fun than you would think (632 9299). Burrell Collection and Pollok House and Gardens are obvious highlights. There's an 'old-fashioned' tea-room in the basement of the latter (362/TEA-ROOMS). Enter by Haggs Rd or by Haggs Castle Golf Course. By car you are directed to the entry rd off Pollokshaws Rd and then to the carpark in front of the Burrell. Train to Shawlands or Pollokshaws W from Glasgow Central Stn.

CATHKIN BRAES: On S edge of city with impressive views. 428/VIEWS.

444 **MUGDOCK COUNTRY PARK:** Not perhaps within the city, but one of the nearest
xC1 and easiest escapes. Park which includes Mugdock Moor, Mugdock Woods (an SSSI) and 2 castles is NW of Milngavie. Regular train from Central Stn takes 20mins, then follow route of West Highland Way (1079/LONG WALKS) for 4km across Drumclog Moor to S edge of park. Or take Mugdock Bank bus from stn (not Sat) to end. By car to Milngavie by A81 from Maryhill Rd and left after Black Bull Hotel (on left) and before Railway Stn (over to rt) up Ellengowan Rd. Continue past reservoir then pick up signs for Park. 3 carparks, visitor centre is at second one. Many trails marked out and further afield rambles. This is a godsent place betw Glasgow and the Highland hills. 5-20KM CAN BE CIRC BIKE 1-A-2

EASY WALKS OUTSIDE THE CITY

For bus information, phone (041) 226 4826. *See p. 9 for walk codes.*

THE CAMPSIE FELLS: Range of hills 25km N of city best reached via Kirkintilloch 445 or Cumbernauld/Kilsyth. Encompasses area that includes the Kilsyth Hills, Fintry Hills and Carron Valley betw. (1) Good app from A803, Kilsyth main st up the Tak-me-Doon (sic) rd. Park by the golf club and follow path by the burn. It's possible to take in the two hills to left as well as Tomtain (453m), the most easterly of the tops, in a good afternoon; views to the east. (2) Drive on to the junction (9km) of the B818 rd to Fintry and go left, following Carron Valley reservoir to the far corner where there is a forestry rd to the left. Park here and follow track to ascend Meikle Bin (570m) to the rt, the highest peak in the central Campsies. (3) The bonny village of Fintry (287/HOTELS OUTSIDE TOWN) is a good start/base for the Fintry Hills and Earls' Seat (578m).

10KM+ · CAN BE CIRC · XBIKE · 2-B-2

CHATEAUHERAULT nr HAMILTON: Jct 6 off M74, well signposted into Hamilton, 446 follow rd into centre, then bear left away from main rd where it's signed for A723. The gates to the 'château' are about 3km outside town. A drive leads to the William Adam-designed hunting-lodge of the Dukes of Hamilton, set amidst ornamental gardens with a notable parterre and extensive grounds. Tracks along the deep, wooded glen of the Avon (ruins of Cadzow Castle) lead to distant glades. Ranger service and good guided walks (0698 426213). Unimpressive teashop in garden centre at estate gates. 20km SE of city centre. House open 10.30am-5.30pm, walks at all times.

2-7KM · CIRC · BIKE · 1-A-2

GLENIFFER BRAES, PAISLEY: Ridge to the S of Paisley (15km from Glasgow) has 447 been a favourite walking place for centuries. M8 or Paisley Rd West to town centre (many buses from Anderston/trains from Central) then: (1) S via B775/A736 towards Irvine or (2) B774 (Causewayside then Neilston Rd) and sharp rt after 3km to Glenfield Rd (Bus: Clydeside 24). For (1) go 2km after last houses, winding up ridge and park/start at Robertson Park (signed). Here there are superb views and walks marked to E and W. (2) 500m along Glenfield Rd is a carpark/ranger centre. Walk up through gardens and formal parkland and then W along marked paths and trails. Eventually, after 5km, this route joins (1).

2-10KM · CAN BE CIRC · MTBIKE · 1-A-2

GREENOCK CUT: 45km W of Glasgow. Can approach via Port Glasgow but 448 simplest route is from A78 rd to Largs. Travelling S from Pt Glasgow take first left after IBM, signed Loch Thom. Lochside 5km up winding rd. Park at Cornalees Bridge Centre. Walk left along lochside rd to Overton (5km) then path is signed. The Cut, an aqueduct built in 1827 to supply water to Greenock and its 31 mills, is now an ancient monument. Gt views from the Mast, over the Clyde. Another route to the rt from Cornlees leads through a glen of birch, rowan and oak to the Kelly Cut. Both trails described on board at the carpark.

15/16KM · CIRC · MTBIKE · 1-B-2

KILPATRICK HILLS: 25km NW; hills betw Loch Lomond and the Clyde. From W: 449 (1) Take A82 almost to Dumbarton, past Bowling. In Milton at gas stn and opp Little Chef, cross c/way and turn rt up Milton Brae Rd for 3km. Before low white house on rt and a loch, take unmarked rt-hand rd going uphill at Y-junction. Park 500m then walk 1.5km past quarry and farm and TV mast to left. Go through gate then over ford to forestry. Past small pond and through trees you come to reservoir. Go to end, along dam then path to hilltops. From E: (2) Go thro Bearsden on A81 Drymen rd and left at r/bout on A810 for Hardgate. After Electricity Stn turn rt, past entrance to Cochno Town Farm. Follow rd for 3km to Cochno Farm marked 'private'. Park here and walk along farm track for 100m, turning rt after woodland through gate and on to track. This route leads uphill to the Jaw and Cochno Reservoirs, Cochno Hill and great views. Limited space here doesn't allow much more than a description of the way on to these splendid hills, but various paths present themselves. (3) Queen's View, 429/VIEWS.

5-20KM · CAN BE CIRC · XBIKE · 2-B-2

SPORTS FACILITIES

450 SWIMMING AND INDOOR SPORTS CENTRES
The best two remaining municipal pools – Arlington Baths (332 6021) *and the Western Baths* (339 1127) *– have both become private members-only clubs. It may be possible to arrange temporary membership, but otherwise . . .*

xE3 **WHITEHILL POOL:** 551 9969. Onslow Dr parallel to Duke St at Meadowpark St in the East End nr Alexandra Park (Alexandra Parade Stn, buses: Strathclyde 1, 8, 6). Phone for times but usually Mon-Fri till 8.30pm and Sat/Sun till 3.30pm. 25m pool with sauna/multigym (Universal).

C1 **NORTHWOODSIDE LEISURE CENTRE:** 332 8102. Braid Sq. Not far from St George's Cross nr Charing Cross at the bottom of Gt Western Rd. In a rebuilt area; follow AA signs. Modern pool (25yds) and sauna/steam/sun centre. Open Mon-Fri 8/9am-7/8pm (Sat/Sun 10am-3pm). Buses: Strathclyde 18, 21, 21a.

xC4 **THE POLLOK POOL:** 632 2220. Ashtree Rd. Not to be confused with the Pollok Leisure Centre (425/LESS OBVIOUS ATTRACTS). It's not easy to find (phone for directions), but it's an old-fashioned pool with great atmos. Turkish baths: men/women different days. Times vary. Stn: Pollokshaws E or W. Buses: Strathclyde 21, 23.

A1 **KELVINHALL:** 357 2525. Argyle St by Kelvingrove Park and opp Art Gallery. Major Glasgow venue for international indoor sports comps, but open o/wise for weights/badminton/tennis/athletics. Book hour-long sessions. No squash.

xA4 **BELLAHOUSTON:** 427 5454. Bellahouston Dr on edge of Park via Paisley Rd West (no convenient stn, bus: 54, 54a, 54b). Multigym and various trainings. Good park to jog with extension to Pollok Park. Only a few squash courts; must book.

E3 **MARCO'S:** 554 7184. Templeton Business Centre (beside the hugely impressive Templeton Carpet Factory), 62 Templeton St by Glasgow Green in the East End. Like the Edinburgh one, a labyrinthine and massively successful complex with squash/snooker/gym (Universal and First Class)/indoor jogging track (even though it is next to the Green). Non-members OK. Daily 10am-11pm (Sat till 8pm). No pool.

xC1 **ALLANDER SPORTS CENTRE:** 942 2233. Milngavie Rd, Bearsden 16km N of centre via Maryhill Rd. Best by car. Squash (2 courts) badminton/snooker and swimming pool (open late, Mon/Wed/Sat/Sun till 9pm, Tue/Thu/Fri: 10.30pm.) No gym at time of writing but one on the way. Till 9/10.30pm.

451 GOLF COURSES
Glasgow has a vast number of parks and golf courses. The following clubs are the best of the ones that are open to non-members.

xC4 **CATHKIN BRAES:** 634 0650. Cathkin Rd SE via Aikenhead Rd/Carmunnock Rd to Carmunnock village, then 3km. Best by car. Civilised, hilltop course on the very southern edge of the city. Non-members Mon-Fri (though probably not Fri morning).

xC4 **HAGGS CASTLE:** 427 1157. Dumbreck Rd nr jnct 22 of the M8, go straight on to Clubhouse at first r/bout. Part of the grounds of Pollok Park, a convenient course, perhaps overplayed, but not difficult to get on.

xC4 **POLLOK GOLF CLUB:** 632 1080. On the other side of the White Cart Water and Pollok House and rather more upmarket. Well-wooded parkland course, flat and well-kept but not cheap. Women not permitted to play.

xC4 **TROON:** Just over 50km away is some of the best golfing to be had by visitors to Scotland. By car on the A77 via Kilmarnock or train hourly from Central Station. Glasgow Gailes, Western Gailes and the Portand Course are all possible and eminently playable links courses (Royal Troon is v dificult to get on). 3 other courses in and around Troon. Portland: 0292 311555. Gailes courses (via Irvine and requiring car to get there): 0294 311347 (1094/1996/GOLF).

OTHER ACTIVITIES

TENNIS: Public courts (Apr-Sept) where membership is not required at: 452

KELVINGROVE PARK, 6 courts, bus: Strathclyde 6, 9, 16, 42. A1
QUEEN'S PARK, 6 courts, bus: Strathclyde 45, 47, 48. xC4
VICTORIA PARK 6 courts, bus: Strathclyde 9, 42, 64, 62. Courts open noon-8pm. xA2
For information on coaching, phone 556 1266.

PONY TREKKING: HAZELDEN, NEWTON MEARNS: 639 3011. On A77 15km SW of centre. **GLEDDOCH FARM, LANGBANK nr GREENOCK:** 047554 350. Fast rd W of Glasgow (30km from centre) via M8 and dual c/way A8. **BUSBY EQUITATION CENTRE, BUSBY:** 644 1347. Wester Farm on 12km on A726, 200m Busby Stn.

ICE-SKATING: ST ENOCH (424/LESS OBVIOUS ATTRACTIONS).

SNOOKER: Q CLUB, 333 9035. 101 St Georges Rd nr Charing Cross heading for St C1 George's Cross. 22 tables. Every day 11am-11pm/midnight. **POTTER'S POOL,** 6 D2 W Regent St. Lounge with music and several tables in centre nr Odeon Cinema. Mon-Thu till 10.15pm, Fri/Sat till 11.15pm.

GALLERIES

Apart from those listed previously (see ATTRACTIONS/LESS OBVIOUS)*, the* 453 *following galleries are always worth looking into. The Glasgow Gallery Guide, free from any gallery, lists all the current exhibitions.*

† † **GLASGOW PRINT STUDIOS:** 552 0704. 22 King St. Influential and accessible D3 upstairs gallery with print work on view and for sale from many of Scotland's leading and rising artists. Cl Sun. Print shop over road. And combine with . . .

TRANSMISSION GALLERY: 552 4813. 28 King St. Front-line and often off-the-wall D3 work from contemporary Scottish and international artists. Conceptual, provocative, multi-media; streets ahead. Cl Sun/Mon.

COLLINS GALLERY: 552 4400 ext 2682. 22 Richmond St. Part of Strathclyde Univ E2 campus (betw George St and Cathedral St). Varied, often important exhibitions. Cl Sun.

COMPASS GALLERY: 221 6370. 178 W Regent St. Glasgow's oldest established C2 commercial contemp art gallery. Cl Sun. Their 'New Generation' exhibition in July/Aug shows work from new graduates of the art colleges and has heralded many a career. Combine with . . .
CYRIL GERBER FINE ART: 148 W Regent St. British paintings and esp the Scottish C2 Colourists and 'name' contemporaries.
Both these commercial galleries have Christmas exhibitions where small accessible paintings can be bought for reasonable prices. Cl Sun.

WILLIAM HARDIE GALLERY: 221 6780. 141 W Regent St. Another basement gallery across st from the 2 above with alternating contemporary one-person shows (incl Bellany, Howson etc) with Scottish and European modernists. Major coup in '93 was first European exhib of Hockney's new work. Cl Sun.

90's GALLERY: 339 3158. 12 Otago St off Kilvinbridge. Changing exhibs of interesting and often v affordable contemp Scottish art. An essential place to start looking if you've a wall to fill. Open 7 days.

BEACHES

*None near enough or good enough to recommend. For other watery pursuits the traditional and popular spots are Loch Lomond (45km via A82 or train to Balloch), up the Clyde to Helensburgh or Rhu, or 'doon the watter' to Rothesay via Wemyss Bay (1396/*JOURNEYS)*, Millport on the island of Cumbrae in the Clyde Estuary and Largs have nostalgia and Nardini's (1189/*CAFES) *and that seaside air.*

GOOD NIGHTLIFE

For the current programmes of the places below and all other venues, consult The List *magazine, on sale fortnightly at most newsagents.*

454 CINEMA
There are all the usual multiplexes, but the better cinemas are:

A1 **SALON:** 339 4256. Vinicombe St off Byres Rd nr university. A funky old movie palace closed at time of going to press to be absorbed by the Sports Complex through the wall – but not without a fight.

C2 **GLASGOW FILM THEATRE:** 332 6535. Rose St at downtown end of Sauchiehall St. Known affectionately as GFT, has bar and 2 screens for essential art-house flicks.

A1 **GROSVENOR:** 339 4928. Ashton Lane, off Byres Rd behind Hillhead Stn. Busy lane for eats and nightlife incl this old cinema with 2 screens and a selected programme with no compulsion to show Bergman retros.

455 THEATRE
The traditional theatres are the **KINGS,** 227 5511, *Bath St, with popular shows like pantos, Gilbert and Sullivan and other musicals; and the* **THEATRE ROYAL,** 332 9000, *Hope St, home of Scottish Opera and with mainly high-brow diet of opera, dance and drama. There are several other very notable places. Look out for:*

D3 **THE CITIZENS':** 429 0022. Gorbals St just over the river. Fabulous main auditorium and two small studios. Drama at its very best. One of Britain's most influential theatres esp for design. Still possible to see stimulating and highly professional theatre cheaply (with concessions, for a pound).

xC4 **THE TRAMWAY:** 227 5511. 25 Albert Dr on south side. A theatre and vast performance space. Dynamic and influential with an innovative and varied programme, the Tramway is undoubtedly a world stage.

C2 **CCA:** Centre for Contemporary Arts, 332 7521. 350 Sauchiehall St. Formerly the Third Eye Centre, this central arts-lab complex is mainly notable as a theatre for modern dance (esp in spring with its New Moves programme), but also has gallery and other performance space and a good café. Cl Sun/Mon.

D1 **THE ARCHES THEATRE:** 221 9736. Midland St betw Jamaica St and Oswald St. Experimental and vital theatre on a tight budget in the railway arches under the tracks of Central Stn.

D2 **RSAMD:** 332 5057. 100 Renfrew St. The Royal Scottish Academy of Music and Drama. Part and wholly student productions often with guest directors. Eclectic, often powerful mix.

E3 **THE TRON THEATRE:** 552 4267. 63 Trongate. Contemporary Scottish theatre and other interesting performance esp music. Great café-bar with food before and après (301/BISTROS).

456 CLASSICAL MUSIC
National and International orchestras at the **THEATRE ROYAL** and the **ROYAL CONCERT HALL,** top of Buchanan St, 227 5511. Smaller events and ensembles at the **CITY HALL** Candleriggs, 227 5511, **HUTCHESONS' HALL.** 2 John St and **RSAMD,** 100 Renfrew St, 332 5057.

JAZZ
For residencies and one-offs, see *The List,* but most consistent prog for jazz buffs is at the **SOCIETY OF MUSICIANS,** 73 Berkeley St. 221 6112. Sunday aft Jazz upstairs at the **PAISLEY ARTS CENTRE,** New St 887 1010. Occ concerts at **MITCHELL THEATRE,** 227 5511.

FOLK
Also at the aforementioned **SOCIETY OF MUSICIANS** and more pub-like at the **SCOTIA BAR,** Stockwell St, 552 8681 (372/BEST PUBS), and **BABBITY BOWSTERS,** Blackfriars St (Sun), **VICTORIA BAR,** Stockwell St (Fri and Sat). Some of the best fun can be had at the **RIVERSIDE,** Fox St off Clyde St, upstairs – ceilidh dance every Fri/Sat at 8pm, 248 3144. Don't be late. More details, see 1334/FOLK MUSIC.

ROCK AND POP
See also ROCK 'N' POP, p. 211.

† † † **BARROWLAND BALLROOM:** Gallowgate. When its lights are on, you *E3* can't miss it. The Barrowland is world famous and for many bands one of their favourite gigs. It's tacky and a bit run-down, but distinctly venerable; perfect for rock 'n' roll. The Glasgow audience is also one of the best in the world. Go and be part of it. (Then buy a t-shirt.)

SECC: 248 3000. Finnieston Quay beyond the city centre and, for many, beyond the *A3* pale as far as concerts are concerned (big shed, not big on atmosphere) but there are 3 diff size halls for mainly arena-sized acts.

Neither of these venues has its own box office. For tickets and information check with 'Just the Ticket', Virgin Mega Store, Union St, 226 4679. Regular Music, the major promoters in Scotland, also give individual (i.e. not taped) concert information on 031-556 1212.

Concerts also take place regularly at the **PAVILION THEATRE,** Renfield St, 332 1846, *D2* which is a very civilised place to watch a band, and more occasionally at the **MITCHELL THEATRE** behind the Mitchell Library. For live music in smaller *B2* venues, see p. 66 for PUBS AND CLUBS WITH LIVE MUSIC.

CLUBS   457
Glasgow is a club city – well, it was once – now it's a curfew city. At time of writing a city edict requires almost all central clubs to refuse admission after midnight. This has been vigorously opposed and may change. Those mentioned below are the club-culture places. To find out about the more transient one-night-a-week clubs, hang out at Bar 10 in Mitchell Lane, the Lounge or the Living Room (376/PUBS). *Or consult* The List.

THE TUNNEL: 204 1000. 84 Mitchell St. Quickly established as Numero Uno when it *D3* opened its designer doors in 1991. The famous toilets are in Starck (sic) contrast to club lavs of yore. Management and music formula has changed but it's still interesting enough to merit a visit. Mondays are gay nights.

VOLCANO: 337 1100. 15 Benalder St. The guys who opened the Tunnel then took *xA1* on another place, a cheaper, friendlier club up west nr the univ. Students and the likes of me feel happier here. It doesn't matter about your haircut and the drink is cheaper. Wed-Sat 11pm-2.30am. (It's not in the city centre so it opens later than 2am.) On Sun Bobby Bluebell's night is always a full house.

THE SUB CLUB: 248 4600. 22 Jamaica St. The Sub has been where to be seen if *D3* you're on the scene, for years. It's not big or flash but it has the *je ne sais quoi*. Nobody goes till 11.30, 5 minutes later it's packed. Impossible to prophesy what kind of music they'll be playing by the time you get there, but it will be the right stuff. Fri/Sat only.

REDS: 331 1635. 375 Sauchiehall St above Nico's. Different music on different *C2* nights. Generally a mellower atmos though crowded none the less like those above. Small upstairs room, lit low. Wed-Sun.

LOCO: At the Arches Theatre, Midland St (455/THEATRES) on Fri (young crowd, *D3* bit like the Sub) and Sat (probably the most interesting club in town, with 'cabaret', a bit of camp and music from dance to soul). Loco is still unique.

VICTORIAS: 332 1444. Sauchiehall St by the Savoy Centre. This place has such *D2* pretensions and is so tacky and dated, it's a slice of sticky Glasgow nightlife that might be worth smoothing out your shoulder pads for. At time of writing it was the only city centre place you can enter after midnight and stay after 2am – so it must be good, mustn't it?

For Gay Clubs and Bars, see GAY SCOTLAND THE BEST p244.

SHOPPING FOR ESSENTIALS

This is a selection of useful shops that get it right. South is S of a central area bisected by the river. E/W axis taken as Renfield St.

Butchers

GILLESPIE'S, 1623 Gt Western Rd, Anniesland. 959 2015. WEST

MURRAY'S, 117 Royston Rd. 552 2738. EAST

Bakers

BRADFORDS, 245 Sauchiehall St and branches. 332 2057. CENTRAL
Bread: **DASBROT,** 51 Hyndland St. 334 8234. WEST
Patisserie: **PATISSERIE FRANCOISE,** 138 Byres Rd. 334 1882. WEST

Fish shops

ALAN BEVERIDGE, 306 Byres Rd/1121 Pollokshaws Rd. WEST/SOUTH

FISH PLAICE, alley off Saltmarket by St Andrews St. EAST

Fruit & Veg

ROOTS AND FRUITS, 457 Gt Western Rd. 334 3530. WEST

NO. 1 FOR VALUE, 61 Candleriggs by City Hall. CENTRAL
Organic: as above and Grass Roots, see below.

Delicatessen

PECKHAMS, 100 Byres Rd/Central Stn/43 Clarence Dr. WEST/CENTRAL/SOUTH

COOKERY BOOK, 20 Kilmarnock Rd. 632 9807. SOUTH

TOSCANA, 44 Station Rd, Milngavie. 956 4020. NORTH
Kosher: **MORRISONS,** Sinclair Drive. 632 0998. SOUTH
Cheese: as above and Fazzis, see below.

Wholefoods

GRASS ROOTS, 48 Woodlands Rd. 353 3278. WEST

QUALITY DELI, 123 Douglas St. 331 2984. CENTRAL

Pasta

FAZZI BROTHERS, 67 Cambridge St/230 Clyde St. 332 0941. CENTRAL

Fish 'n' Chips

UNIQUE, 223 Allison St. 423 3366. SOUTH

PHILADELPHIA, 445 Gt Western Rd. 339 2372. WEST

CHIP CHIC INN, 31 Clarence Drive. 334 8834. WEST

Sandwiches

NO 1 SANDWICH ST, 9 Waterloo St. and branches. 204 4171. CENTRAL

Wine

UBIQUITOUS CHIP WINES, 12 Ashton Lane. 334 5007. WEST

PECKHAM AND RYE, 21 Clarence Drive (1226/DELIS). 334 4312. WEST

Tobacco

TOBACCO HOUSE, 9 St Vincent's Pl. 226 4586. CENTRAL

Department Store

FRASERS, 45 Buchanan St. 221 3880. CENTRAL
General: **DEBENHAMS,** 97 Argyle St. 221 9820. CENTRAL
Ironmongers: **CROCKETS,** 136 W Nile St. 332 1041. CENTRAL

Flowers

ROOTS AND FRUITS, 451 Gt Western Rd. 334 3530. WEST
Dried: **FLOWER POWER,** Tobago St. 551 0971. EAST

Newspapers

NEWSPAPER KIOSK, Buchanan St. 332 7355. CENTRAL

WM PORTEOUS, 9 Royal Exchange Sq. 221 8623. CENTRAL

Late night

General: **BEZALEEL**, 601 Gt Western Rd. 334 8224. WEST
GOODIES, 645 Gt Western Rd. 334 8848. WEST
Chemist: **SINCLAIRS**, 693 Gt Western Rd. 339 0012. WEST
C and M MACKIE, 1067 Pollokshaws Rd. 649 8915. SOUTH

Shoes

Shoes That Last: **ALLAN JAMES**, 388 Sauchiehall St. 332 3194. CENTRAL
Modish: **SCHUH**, 45 Union St 248 7319. CENTRAL

Men's Clothes

New Labels: **WAREHOUSE**, 61 Glassford St. 552 4181. CENTRAL
CRUISE, 47 Renfield St. 248 2476. CENTRAL
ITALIAN CENTRE, John St (Armani, Versace etc). CENTRAL
Established Labels: **HENRY BURTON**, 111 Buchanan St. 221 7380. CENTRAL

Women's Clothes

New Labels: **WAREHOUSE**, as above
ITALIAN CENTRE, as above (also Mondi).
Non-Labels: **FRASERS**, 45 Buchanan St. 221 3880. CENTRAL
Non-Labels: **WHAT EVERY WOMAN WANTS**, Argyle St

Hairdressers

RITA RUSK, 49 W Nile St. 221 1472. CENTRAL

RAINBOW ROOM, 15 Royal Exchange Sq. 226 3451. CENTRAL

DLC, Mitchell Lane. 204 2020. CENTRAL

SCRIMSHAWS, Wilson Court, 71 Wilson St. 552 7963. CENTRAL

Barbers

CITY BARBERS, 99 W Nile St. 332 7114. CENTRAL

THE MOST INTERESTING SHOPS

One shopping precinct in Glasgow is referred to many times below, namely
PRINCES SQUARE which is an indoor shopping mall off the middle of Buchanan
St (Argyle St end) and probably the single best concentration of high-quality,
interesting shops in town. These include **KATHERINE HAMNETT**, **BUTLER AND
WILSON**, **NANCY SMILLIE**, **NICE HOUSE**, **ANDRONICAS** and **JUMPERS**. For a coffee
break or snack, **D'ARCY'S** or **IL PAVONE** on the basement floor are excellent.

Antiques

General: **HERITAGE HOUSE**, 73 James St. 550 2221. WEST
LANSDOWNE ANTIQUES 334 8469 and **RETRO**, Otago St. WEST
Bric-à-Brac: **ALL OUR YESTERDAYS**, 6 Park Rd. 334 7788. WEST
TEMPTATIONS UNLIMITED, 127 Douglas St. 332 4402. WEST
Jewellery: **VICTORIAN VILLAGE**, 57 W Regent St. 332 0808. CENTRAL (also for
bric-à-brac, clothes etc; 1281/MARKETS)
Clothes: **STARRY STARRY NIGHT**, 19 Downside Lane. WEST

Art Supplies

MILLERS, 11 Clarendon Pl. 331 3203. WEST

ART STORE, 94 Queen St. 221 0266. CENTRAL

Comics

FUTERESHOCK, 88 Byres Rd. 339 8184. WEST

Cards

PAPYRUS, 374 Byres Rd. 334 6514. WEST (also 296 Sauchiehall St, CENTRAL)

Ceramics

NANCY SMILLIE, Princes Sq. 248 3874. CENTRAL; and Cresswell Lane. WEST

WARE ON EARTH, Italian Centre, Ingram St. CENTRAL; and Gt Western Rd.

Ceramics

NANCY SMILLIE, Princes Sq. 248 3874. CENTRAL; and Cresswell Lane. WEST

WARE ON EARTH, Italian Centre, Ingram St. CENTRAL; and Gt Western Rd.

Clothes

General: See Shopping For Essentials and Princes Sq (above).

Hip: **ICHI-NI-SAN,** 26 Bell St. 552 2545. CENTRAL

   McKENZIE, 128 Buchanan St. 221 1013. CENTRAL

   MUJI, 63 Queen St. 248 7455. CENTRAL

Old: **FLIP,** 68 Queen St. 221 2041.

   THE SQUARE YARD, Stevenson St West at the BARRAS (1272/MARKETS). EAST

Outdoor: **BLACK'S,** 254 Sauchiehall St. 353 2344. CENTRAL

   TISO'S, 129 Buchanan St. 248 4877. CENTRAL

Furniture

Modern: **INHOUSE,** 26 Wilson St. 552 5902. CENTRAL

   TONY WALKER, Charing Cross. 332 2662. WEST

Traditional: **ADRIENNE'S,** 28 Otago St. WEST

Games

GAMES WORKSHOP, 66 Queen St. 226 3762. CENTRAL

Hats

THE HATSHOP, Corner Wilson/Brunswick St. CENTRAL

Ice-cream

UNIVERSITY CAFE, Byres Rd. WEST

Jewellery

ARGYLE ST ARCADE. Vast selection of different shops.

Jokes

TAM SHEPHERD'S, 33 Queen St. 221 2310. CENTRAL

Junk

THE BARRAS, 1272/MARKETS. EAST

Presents

HARBINGERS, 417 Gt Western Rd. 339 9999. WEST

GREAT NORTHERN WOOD, St Enoch Centre. CENTRAL

NICE HOUSE, Princes Sq (see above). CENTRAL

Sci-fi

FUTURE SHOCK, 200 Woodlands Rd. 333 0784. WEST

Sports

NEVIS SPORT, 261 Sauchiehall St. 332 4814. CENTRAL

Tartan

Serious: **HECTOR RUSSELL,** 85 Renfield St. 332 4102. CENTRAL

   GEOFFREY'S, 309 Sauchiehall St. 331 2388. CENTRAL

Tacky: **ROBIN HOOD GIFT HOUSE,** 11 St Vincent St. CENTRAL

Theatrical costumes etc

THEATRICAL HIRE, 152 Park Rd. 334 4900. WEST

Woollies

ALISON GODWIN KNITWEAR, Cresswell St Market. WEST

JUMPERS, Princes Sq. 248 5775. CENTRAL

SECTION 3
Regional Hotels and Restaurants, including Aberdeen and Dundee

THE BEST HOTELS AND RESTAURANTS IN STRATHCLYDE NORTH

*Refer to Map 1. See also 1386/*CENTRES: OBAN, *p. 234.*

459 **AIRDS HOTEL, PORT APPIN:** 063173 236. 40km N of Oban. Exalted by many a † †
B1 guide-book esp for food; an excellent off-the-road (A828) hotel. Perhaps
pricey and a touch precious; however, this is more to do with the veneration of
food which you are famously enjoined to do. Lismore (1344/MAGIC ISLANDS) is the
place to walk or bike it off. (Passenger ferry 2km away at P Appin.)

14RMS   MAR-DEC   T/T   XPETS   XCC   KIDS   LOTS

One of the best meals you'll have in Scotland. Report: 565/HIGHLANDS.   EXP

460 **KILFINAN HOTEL, KILFINAN; TIGHNABRUAICH (13km):** 070082 201. On B8000 which
C3 7km further north joins Loch Fyne at Otter Ferry and continues to Strachur. A
coaching inn and friendly local; pleasant rooms above a terraced garden with a
burn at the bottom to follow down to the beach. Chocs in the bedrooms, apples
in the hall; not, alas, 'rooms above the pub' prices. Bar meals, LO 7.30 pm.

11RMS   JAN-DEC   T/T   PETS   CC   KIDS   TOS   MED.EX

Restau cosy and conscientious; quite the best in area, so book.   MED

461 **TAYCHREGGAN, KILCHRENAN; TAYNUILT (16km):** 08663 211. Signed off A85 just
C2 before Taynuilt, about 30km from Oban and nestling on a bluff by L Awe, in
imposing countryside. The quay for the old ferry to Portsonachan is nearby and
there are 2 boats available. The central courtyard would be nice for breakfast in
the sun. Rooms vary and some are particularly cosy. Much improved menu. The
loch is always there outside.   15RMS   JAN-DEC   T/X   PETS   CC   KIDS   TOS   MED.INX

462 **STONEFIELD CASTLE HOTEL, TARBERT (ARGYLL):** 0880 820836. Just outside town on
B3 the A83, a castle which evokes the 1970s more than preceding centuries.
Splendid gardens leading down to Loch Fyne. Unlikely open-air swimming pool
surrounded by luxuriant vegetation is a real plus. Dining-room with crazy
carpet and staggering views, flock wallpaper and friendly, flexible staff; overall it
seems quintessentially Scottish and rather ok esp for families.

33RMS   JAN-DEC   T/T   PETS   CC   KIDS   MED.INX

463 **ARDENTINNY HOTEL, DUNOON:** 36981 209. 20km N via A880/A885. A traditional,
C2 Clydeside inn by the Glen Finart forest and on a rise o/looking L Long. Nice in
summer to sit out in the garden and esp to arrive by boat! Pub meals and full
restau. Rooms vary.   11RMS   MAR-NOV   T/X   PETS   CC   KIDS   TOS   MED.INX

464 **BARRIEMORE, OBAN:** 0631 66356. Corran Esplanade. A decent hotel that doesn't
B1 cost the earth, the very last one in this street full of hotels and guest houses along
the coast to Ganavan. Rooms at front have excl views of Kerrera and Lorne.

13RMS   MAR-JAN   X/X   PETS   XCC   KIDS   INX

465 **CREGGANS INN, STRACHUR:** 036986 279. 2km N Strachur on A815 to Cairndow, †
C2 a busy rd in summer along L Fyne. Roadhouse bar/restau and more formal
dining-room in a v successful combination of the popular and the more
particular. From burgers in the bar to Arran queenies eaten off crisp linen, to
cream teas in a coffee shop where you can sit outside. The fiefdom of Sir Fitzroy
and Lady Maclean, the coffee shop sells their considerable canon of books.
Clutch of Les Routiers awards in '93. Something for everybody.   CHP/MED/EXP
Rooms overlooking loch are fine, but not cheap. Fishing nearby.

21RMS   JAN-DEC   T/T   PETS   CC   KIDS   TOS   EXP

ARDANAISEIG, LOCH AWE: 08663 333. (645/COUNTRY-HOUSE HOTELS.)

ISLE OF ERISKA nr OBAN: (22km) 063172 371. (648/COUNTRY-HOUSE HOTELS.)

466 **THE KILBERRY INN:** 08803 223. Superlative home cooking in roadside pub † †
B3 betw Tarbert and Lochgilphead by the coastal route (B8024). Better
than many more high falutin restaus. 726/PUB FOOD.   INX

THE BEST HOTELS AND RESTAURANTS IN STRATHCLYDE SOUTH

See also 1380/CENTRES: AYR, *p.228. Refer to Map 1.*

✝ ✝ **TURNBERRY HOTEL, TURNBERRY:** 0655 31000. Not so much a hotel, more a way of life centred on golf, a town in itself on the slopes above the 2 courses which are difficult (but not impossible) to get on unless you're a guest (1098/GOLF). Everything one would expect from a world-class hotel except cosmopolitan buzz; during the day it can feel almost abandoned. Leisure centre adj and linked by tunnel provides state-of-the-art 'treatments' and even exercise. The menu in the restau here is 'lighter'. Treat your mum to a Hydrotherapy Bath Massage and Sunday lunch in the grand dining-room looking out over the courses to Ailsa Craig beyond. *467 C4* 132RMS JAN-DEC T/T PETS CC KIDS TOS LOTS

✝ **GLEDDOCH HOUSE, LANGBANK nr GREENOCK:** 0475 54711. 35km from Glasgow by fast rd – M8/A8 t/off marked Langbank/Houston after last m/way jnct (31), then follow signs. Former home of Lithgow shipping family in extensive grounds (incl 18-hole golf course), with commanding view of Clyde by Dumbarton Rock (but not from all rooms). Small leisure club adj. Probably the most civilised place to stay within reasonable distance of Glasgow. Notable chef. Fine Scottish cuisine marche esp fish and game. Book. *468 D3* 33RMS JAN-DEC T/T PETS CC KIDS TOS LOTS EXP

CHAPELTOUN HOUSE HOTEL, STEWARTON: 0560 82696. 12km Kilmarnock, 12km Irvine, 32km Central Glasgow via A77/B778. An oak-lined mansion-house in rolling green Ayrshire, run by the McKenzie brothers (their parents have Culloden House, Inverness). A welcome alternative for business folk to standard hotels in the area. Of mixed taste, but the oak exonerates all. Still pricy but there's nothing this good anywhere nearby. Good menu. *469 D3* 8RMS JAN-DEC T/T PETS CC KIDS TOS LOTS

PIERSLAND HOTEL, TROON: 0292 314747. Craig End Rd opp Portland Golf Course which is next to Royal Troon (1095/GOLF). As they say in the brochure, this is 'a unique and historic house' with great character and ambience. Wood-panelling, open fires, lovely gardens only a 'drive' away from the courses (no preferential booking on Royal, but Portland usually poss) and lots of great golf nearby. *470 C3* 19RMS JAN-DEC T/T PETS CC KIDS TOS EXP

BURNS MONUMENT HOTEL, ALLOWAY nr AYR: 0292 442466. On the banks and by the rd bridge over the Doon, and gardens. A great setting and one which is visited by trillions of tourists, since in this corner are also situated the old Brig o' Doon (at the end of the garden), the Auld Alloway Kirk and the eponymous Monument (1023/LITERARY PLACES). However, don't let that put you off; it's a well-run inn with decent pub and restau. You get one of his poems above the bed. *471 D4* 9RMS JAN-DEC T/T PETS CC KIDS TOS MED.EX

LOCHGREEN HOUSE, TROON: 0292 313343. 1380/AYR.

✝ **FOUTERS, AYR:** 0292 261391. 2A Academy St. Situated in a small street off Sandgate, this has long been the best restau in town and now Laurie Black's oasis is appearing in lots of the national foodie charts. Clever but simple decor makes light work of the converted vaults. Some ambitious concoctions on the menu as well as staples for the more stolid citizens who know a good steak when they see one. The cheaper bistro menu has decent food (and still the same good cheeseboard) for less. Tue-Sat lunch and 6.30-10.30pm, Sun 7-10pm. *472 D4* INX/MED

WILDINGS, GIRVAN: 0465 3481. 56 Montgomery St, off rd into Girvan from Ayr. Five days before this book went to press, Brian Sage – who built a reputation at the Bruce Hotel in Maidens – opened this colourful, cosy restau in an area where you travel a long way for decent nosh. In the spirit of encouragement, though I haven't tried it, I'd say this place looks promising. Lunch and LO 9 pm. Cl Sun/Mon. *472a MAP 1 C5* MED

THE BEST HOTELS AND RESTAURANTS
IN SOUTH-WEST SCOTLAND

See also 1382/CENTRES: DUMFRIES, *p. 230. Refer to Map 9.*

473 KNOCKINAAM LODGE, PORTPATRICK: 077681 471. Over the cliffs from the
A4 village, and far away. Take A77 S of Stranraer about 12km and follow signs.
Victorian granite house on its own bay; family-run with a rep that transcends its
remoteness. Chef Daniel Galmiche makes each meal an occasion. A relaxed
atmos with lived-in furnishings. Clifftop and rock-pool rambles and, nearby, the
S Upland Way.

10RMS MAR-DEC T/T PETS CC KIDS LOTS

The best meal for miles. Prob book well ahead. Jacket/tie.

EXP

474 CREEBRIDGE HOUSE, NEWTON STEWART: 0671 2121. Uphill from the centre of
B3 town, a small mansion-house in own grounds. Fairly basic facilities but a
friendly place used by locals esp for the good bar meals (6-9pm) and real ale
(Boddingtons and Belhaven 80). Cosy public rooms o/look gardens.

18RMS JAN-DEC T/T PETS CC KIDS MED.EX

475 BALCARY BAY, AUCHENCAIRN, nr CASTLE DOUGLAS: 055664 311. 20km S of Castle
C4 Douglas and Dalbeattie at end of rd from bridge in the village. On the shore
with dreamy views, birdwatching and clifftop walks nearby. Basic food and
facilities but a good hideaway to know.

17RMS MAR-DEC T/T PETS CC KIDS TOS MED.EX

476 CALLY PALACE, GATEHOUSE OF FLEET: 0557 814341. 2km from A75 Dumfries-
C4 Stranraer rd. Imposing mansion in 100 leafy acres. Elegant public rooms and
every indoor and outdoor facility, from trouser presses and jacuzzi to tennis and
croquet. Pool. Good centre for walks and excursions. Gatehouse is a charming
village.

55RMS MAR-JAN T/T PETS CC KIDS TOS MED.EX

477 HILL OF BURNS, CREETOWN nr NEWTON STEWART: 067182 487. Above town on
B4 main A75. Elegant small town mansion in 3.5 acres of well-kept grounds incl
croquet lawn. Relaxing, light rooms with fires, books and no kids. Billiard room.
Discreet, but mind Ps and Qs.

8RMS JAN-DEC T/T PETS CC XKIDS MED.EX

478 COMLONGON CASTLE, CLARENCEFIELD nr DUMFRIES: 038787 283. Period house
D3 abutting 15th-century castle (open to public and well worth seeing) at end of
tree-lined avenue from village, 14km S Dumfries. V atmospheric, panelled
rooms, armour and weaponry, v credible ghost. Dinner preceded by tour of
castle and torturing times.

11RMS MAR-DEC T/T XPETS CC KIDS MED.EX

479 CORSEMALZIE HOUSE, PORT WILLIAM nr WIGTOWN/NEWTON STEWART: 098886 254.
B4 A714 from main A75 S of Newton Stewart then B7005 through Bladnoch,
follow signs after bridge (8km). Granite country house in woods in bucolic
Wigtownshire. Fishing on R Bladnoch. Peacocks and many paintings. Comfort
rather than luxury.

15RMS MAR-JAN T/T PETS CC KIDS TOS MED.INX

480 CLONYARD HOUSE, COLVEND nr ROCKCLIFFE nr DALBEATTIE: 055663 372. On main
C4 Solway Coast rd nr Rockcliffe and Kippford (793/COASTAL VILLAGES;
1070/WALKS) though not on the sea. House in wooded grounds with birds
everywhere (incl a parrot). Good value rooms, some in annex with private patios
for sitting out on and listening to the woods. Food good.

15RMS JAN-DEC T/T PETS CC KIDS TOS MED.INX

481 CRIFFEL INN, NEW ABBEY nr DUMFRIES: 038785 244. Roadside inn in village with
D3 Sweetheart Abbey and Criffel above (1036/HILLS), 12 km from Dumfries.
Rooms above; real ale and friendly natives below. Excellent pub food.

5RMS JAN-DEC X /T PETS CC KIDS CHP

482 RIVERSIDE INN, CANONBIE nr LANGOLM: 03873 71512. 2km from border,
E3 the last/ first great meal in Scotland. In almost every guide for restau
and bar meals (728/PUB FOOD). Go and find out why! Also 8 rooms (MED.EX).
Open Mon-Sat. Bar food 7 days till 9 pm (restau 8.30 pm). Cl Sun lunch. INX/MED

482a HOTELS IN KIRKCUDBRIGHT: Got to mention this town because it's such a must
C4 place to visit; concidentally it has 3 fine INX hotels. GLADSTONE HOUSE, 0557 31734,
a small GH with gardens, is superb; GORDON HOUSE HOTEL, 30670 (12 rms, esp
good value), and THE SELKIRK ARMS 30402 (15 rms), are both gr pub/hotels with
gardens. And eat at THE AULD ALLIANCE, 0557 30569 (Solway scallops, salmon etc),
7 nights.

THE BEST HOTELS AND RESTAURANTS IN THE BORDERS

See also 1384/CENTRES: HAWICK AND GALASHIELS, *p. 232. Refer to Map 8.*

† † **PHILIPBURN HOUSE, SELKIRK:** 0750 20747. Once they were Olympic **483**
swimmers, now Jim and Anne Hill are up there with the gold medals for *C3*
running one of the most relaxing country-house hotels in the UK. They've
thought of everything in their rambling house on the edge of Selkirk, well
positioned for Border touring. And they have the light touch that makes you feel
at home, with enough going on to make you feel on holiday. The food's great,
kids run free, there is an outdoor pool, an enormous wine-list and friendly staff. It
all works. 655/KIDS' HOTELS; 650/COUNTRY-HOUSE HOTELS.

16RMS JAN-DEC T/T PETS CC KIDS TOS EXP

Eat in bar or dining-room lightly or lavishly. Wide choice incl vegn.

MED

† † **SUNLAWS HOUSE, nr KELSO:** 0573 450331. Country-house hotel in rolling **484**
border farmland and the Tweed swishing nearby. 5km from Kelso on *D3*
the A698 Jedburgh rd at Heiton. Owned by the Duke of Roxburgh who has that
other place nearby – Floors Castle (940/COUNTRY HOUSES) – it's like a tasteful
and comfy country seat. They've found the magic balance – sumptuous yet
homely (chefs David Bates and Allen Hunter impart the same elegant simplicity
to dinner). Suppose it must be the effortless grace of the aristocracy! Can I have
that room back sometime?

22RMS JAN-DEC T/T PETS CC KIDS TOS EXP

Lunch exceptional value; dinner, game/fish exquisite. Eclectic wine-list.

MED

DRYBURGH ABBEY HOTEL, nr ST BOSWELLS: 0835 22261. On a bend of the Tweed **484a**
and in the grounds of the Abbey (974/ABBEYS), the setting is all. Hotel is *C3*
adequate, not lavish for the price. Rooms have river/abbey/garden views. 28 rms.
AYR.

EXP

THE LEY nr INNERLEITHEN: 0896 830240. 3km from village up Leithen Water thro' **484b**
golf course. Comfortable small mansion in wooded grounds and well-kept *B2*
gardens. An excl retreat with well-judged menu and wine-list.

4RMS FEB-OCT XCC MED.EX

BURTS, MELROSE: 089682 2285. In Market Sq/main st, some (double glazed) rooms **485**
overlook. Busy bars esp for food. Traditional but comfortably modernised *C3*
Border town hotel. Convenient location in interesting and mellow town.
977/ABBEYS; 1048/HILL WALKS; 768/GARDENS.

21RMS JAN-DEC T/T PETS CC KIDS TOS MED.EX

EDNAM HOUSE, KELSO: 0573 24168. Off main square on one side and sitting **486**
spectacularly on banks of Tweed on other. Georgian mansion; grandeur faded *D3*
into something more friendly. Fishing tricky on Tweed but see 1384/CENTRES:
HAWICK AND GALA. Fine dining-room o/looking river.

32RMS JAN-DEC T/T PETS CC KIDS MED.INX

CRINGLETIE HOUSE, PEEBLES: 07213 233. Country house 5km from town just off **487**
A703 Edinburgh rd (35km). Late 19th-century Scottish baronial; conservative *B2*
rather than cosy. Very personally run by the Maguire family. Good, discreet
service.

13RMS MAR-DEC T/T PETS CC KIDS TOS MED.EX

People come from Edinburgh for gracious dining in 2 formal rms.

MED

THE CROOK INN, TWEEDSMUIR: 08997 272. Historic, country inn on A701 Moffat- **488**
Edin rd in the hill country nr head of the Tweed, 32km S of Peebles. Warm, *A3*
welcoming. Unlikely and superb '30s features. Nr Dawyck Gardens
(764/GARDENS) and Tweed Sheepdog Centre (746/PLACES TO TAKE KIDS).

8RMS JAN-DEC X/X PETS CC KIDS MED.INX

GORDON ARMS, YARROW VALLEY: 0750 82232. Another historic inn in the famous **489**
hill country of the Ettrick Shepherd, James Hogg (1026/LITERARY PLACES). At *B3*
junction of A708/B709 nr St Mary's Loch and Grey Mare's Tail (832/WATER-
FALLS). Bunkhouse as well as rms.

6RMS JAN-DEC X/X PETS CC KIDS CHP

MARMIONS, MELROSE: 089682 2245. Buccleuch St nr the Abbey. Probably the best **490**
place in the Borders for an informal lunch and esp for supper. Bustling bistro *C3*
atmos and choices. Ok wines. Cl Sun.

INX

THE OLD FORGE, nr HAWICK: 0450 85298. 8km S on A7. Once a culinary oasis. New **491**
owners, so more reports please. 7 days incl high tea on Sun. Cl Mon lunch.

MED *C4*

THE BEST HOTELS AND RESTAURANTS IN 'CENTRAL' SCOTLAND

See also 1388/CENTRES: STIRLING, *p. 237, and* 1394/CALLANDER *p. 242. Refer to Map 6.*

Note: Some of Scotland's best hotels and restaurants are in this region.

492 GEAN HOUSE, ALLOA: 0259 219275. On edge of town on B9096 to Tullibody. † †
D4 Untypical Scottish manor-house, Edwardian and reminiscent of Lutyens' Greywalls at Gullane, rescued by John Taylor and Anthony Mifsud and turned into a hotel which is the epitome of stylish comfort. Warm, wood-panelled and furnished in simple good taste, with outstanding floral displays everywhere. When you go for dinner, you want to stay the night; when you stay the night, you want to stay full stop. Terraced gardens; Ochils not far away.

9RMS   JAN-DEC   T/T   PETS   TOS   LOTS

Always a memorable meal; the food is both simple and elegant.   EXP

493 THE ROMAN CAMP, CALLANDER: 0877 30003. Behind the main st (at E or † †
C3 Stirling end), away from the tourist throngs and with extensive gardens on the river; another world, really. There are supposedly Roman ruins nearby, but the house was built for the Dukes of Perth and has been a hotel since the war. Rooms are low-ceilinged and snug; amidst the elegance you can relax. Even the corridors have character. The drawing-room and the conservatory look on to the river. There's a library of readable books and a private chapel if you want to get married. Bedrooms vary, of course. Rods for fishing.

14RMS   JAN-DEC   T/T   PETS   CC   KIDS   TOS   LOTS

Dining-room is less romantic, but Simon Burns' menu is v sound.   EXP

494 STIRLING HIGHLAND, STIRLING: 0786 475444. Reasonably sympathetic conversion of
D4 former school (with modern accom block) in the historic section of town on rd up to Castle. Excellent location and service for both tourists and business people. Owned by Highland Hotel chain (they also have Carlton Highland in Edinburgh), this is their best. Both restaus are worth taking seriously. The leisure club is light and well equipped and has a 17m pool.

76RMS   JAN-DEC   T/T   PETS   CC   KIDS   MED.EX/EXP

Scholars (up top in a lofty, elegant room) may be the best restau in town. Rizzios (on the street) is a v acceptable Italian.   MED.INX

495 BLAIRLOGIE HOUSE, STIRLING: 0259 61441. 7km E of town centre on A91. A
D3 Victorian house which can truly be said to nestle at the foot of the hills, in this case the splendid Ochils (1049/HILL WALKS). Well-kept gardens (with azaleas and bluebells in spring) tumble to the rd. The family house is cosy and accommodating and much better value than many self-conscious country-house hotels. Views over Forth flood plain. Wallace Monument is nearby.

7RMS   JAN-DEC   T/T   PETS   CC   KIDS   MED.INX

496 LAKE HOTEL, PORT OF MENTEITH: 0877 5258. A very lake-side hotel on the Lake of
C3 Menteith in the purple heart of the Trossachs. Good centre for touring and walking. The Ichmahome ferry leaves from nearby (1011/MARY, CHARLIE AND BOB). The conservatory makes for a pretty nice start to the day, but only 2 bedrooms face the lake. The bistro/bar adj is not so peaceful. Good off-season rates.

13RMS   JAN-DEC   T/T   PETS   CC   KIDS   TOS   MED.EX

497 DUNBLANE HYDRO, DUNBLANE: 0786 822551. One of the huge hydro hotels left over
D3 from the last health boom, this one is part of the Stakis Org. Nice views for some and a long walk down corridors for most. Exercise also in the gym and the pool. Fade that grandeur!

219RMS   JAN-DEC   T/T   PETS   KIDS   TOS   EXP

498 INVERARNAN HOTEL/THE DROVER'S INN, INVERARNAN: N of Ardlui on L † †
A2 Lomond and 12km S of Crianlarich on the A82. A traveller's inn much as it always was (since 1705) i.e. not for those who need trouser presses and jacuzzis (or even private bathrooms). Bare floors, open fires, serious drinking in the bar (701/GREAT PUBS) and real Highland hospitality – which means they'll make you welcome but won't 'serve' you. Stuffed with atmosphere, old furniture and, undoubtedly, ghosts. Hogmanay nights are booked 7 years ahead. Many other nights are just as wild, outside and in. The sort of place that's easily romanticised; I guess I have.

20RMS   JAN-DEC   X/X   PETS   CC   KIDS   CHP

† † **BRAEVAL OLD MILL, ABERFOYLE:** 0877 2711. Just E of Aberfoyle on A873 **499**
for Port of Menteith and Stirling. Small, converted 'mill' on edge of golf **B3**
course. Nick and Fiona Nairn's restau has won many awards and you sit down,
perhaps with high expectations. I can only say that mine were fully realised and
the food was faultless. From the crudités and good old-fashioned crusty bread
through to the tablet at the end, all made with first-class ingredients and
consummate artistry, it is demonstrated that very good food needs little
elaboration. Galloping gourmets and your Auntie Flo will both agree, this is
how it should be. There are 7 decent house reds and whites and another 300,
including many half-bottles. Dinner Tue-Sat and Sun lunch. Must book.
EXP

† **CROMLIX HOUSE, DUNBLANE:** 0786 822125. 3km from A9 and 4km from town **500**
on B8033, first follow signs for Perth, and then Kinbuck. A long drive **D3**
through the estate that's been in the Eden family for 500yrs leads to a Victorian
house full, but not overfull, of family heirlooms, fine furniture and paintings.
Even if you're only there for dinner, try and see the chapel. Cromlix has won
many accolades and I'm sure there were good reasons why dinner was not quite
up to scratch on the night I was there. I've only been once (an omission I intend
to rectify before making any further comment) but it retains a star-rating here
because many, many people recommend it highly.
EXP

CREAGAN HOUSE, STRATHYRE: 0877 4638. End of the village on main A84 for **501**
Crianlarich. With the Big Two above making all the running in this neck of the **C2**
scenic woods, little Creagan House could easily be overlooked by the Food
Hawks. With hard-won rosettes now in place, the Gunns imaginative and
authentic cooking (e.g. their Smoky in a Poky is a genuine original, the banoffi is
from the first Hungry Monk recipe and other traditional puds are well
established) seem even better value. The dining-room is a touch too mock
baronial, but there's a friendly welcome and an incredibly large dog. 5 rooms
above are also inx. Book. Cl Feb.
INX

HARVIESTON INN, TILLICOULTRY: 0259 752522. On main A91 to St Andrews on edge **502**
of town. A roadside restau/inn complex renovated around a semi courtyard and **E3**
a field in front that might benefit from some landscaping. The bar is open for
lunch and dinner, the restau upstairs till 9.30 pm, 7 days. A new, more Scottish,
menu has come with new chef Robert Pew and a new owner, so at time of going
to press things remain to be seen. They augur well, however, and this place will
continue to be a better reason for coming to Tillicoultry than that damned
furniture warehouse they advertise so much on the telly.
MED

KIPLINGS, BRIDGE OF ALLAN: 0786 833617. Mine Rd off the main st and up the hill **503**
towards Sherriffmuir in a suburban area of Stirling/Bridge of Allan. Chef Peter **D3**
Bannister's reputation precedes him and this large, airy and modern restau seems
congenial enough, but I have to admit that I still haven't had the chance to eat
here. A lot of people say it's good and that's why it's in. More reports, please.
Tue-Sat lunch and dinner, Sun lunch.
EXP

THE BEST HOTELS AND RESTAURANTS IN THE LOTHIANS

See Section 1 for Edinburgh. Refer to Map 7.

504 **GREYWALLS, GULLANE:** 0260 842144. Along the coast, 36km E of Edinburgh ✝ ✝
D1 off the A198 and just beyond the golfer's paradise of Gullane. Overlooks
Muirfield, the championship course (hotel has some tee allocations; handicap
certs reqd) and nr Gullane's 3 courses and N Berwick's 2 (1100/GOLF). Lutyens-
designed manor of warm stone, gardens laid out by his partner, Gertrude Jekyll.
Edwardian furnishings and feel. A nice place to go even if only for tea.

22RMS APR-OCT T/T PETS CC KIDS TOS LOTS

Gracious, elegant dining but not stuffy. Paul Baron still excels.   EXP

505 **OPEN ARMS, DIRLETON:** 0620 85241. Dirleton is 4km from Gullane towards N
D1 Berwick, so all golfing advantages possible. Comfortable inn/hotel in centre of
village, opposite notable ruin of Dirleton Castle. A quiet place less than 45 mins
from Edinburgh (45/EDIN HOTELS OUTSIDE TOWN).

7RMS JAN-DEC T/T PETS CC KIDS TOS EXP

506 **TWEEDDALE ARMS, GIFFORD:** 0620 81240. One of two inns in this heart of E Lothian
D2 village 9km from the A1 at Haddington and within easy reach of Edinburgh. Set
among rich farming country, Gifford is conservative and cosy. Rooms look out
to green; the Green is nearby. Nice pictures.

16RMS JAN-DEC T/T PETS CC KIDS MED.INX

507 **THE COURTYARD, DUNBAR:** 0368 64169. Woodbush Brae nr end of town on seafront.
E1 Interesting conversion of seaside cottages looking directly on to foreshore. A
former 'resort', Dunbar has a fine old harbour and a new pool (757/LEISURE
CENTRES).

6RMS JAN-DEC X/T PETS CC KIDS TOS CHP

JOHNSTOUNBURN HOUSE: 0875 33696. (37/EDIN HOTELS OUTSIDE TOWN).

HOUSTON HOUSE, UPHALL: 0506 853831. (39/EDIN HOTELS OUTSIDE TOWN).

508 **BROWNS, HADDINGTON:** 0620 822254. 1 West Rd on way into Haddington from
D1 Edin. Elegant Georgian townhouse. And er . . . temper, temper, chaps!   MED

509 **HARDINGS, NORTH BERWICK:** 0620 4737. 2 Station Rd nr Stn and opp Royal Hotel.
D1 Informal, small with uncomplicated food you can see being prepared and excl
Australian wine-list (Chris Harding, formerly at Greywalls, is from Australia).
Open for coffee, home-made lemonade, cakes and lunch daily. Dinner Wed-Sat
7.30-9pm. No smoking, no credit cards.   MED

510 **THE WATERSIDE, HADDINGTON:** 0620 825674. Not so easy to find, but on the
D1 riverside nr pedestrian bridge. Best to ask, everyone knows. Enormously popular
E Coast bistro. Vast menu in labyrinthine bar downstairs; restau upstairs is also
informal. Great ambience, great idea and goes like a fair. Daily lunch and supper,
LO 10pm.   INX

511 **THE CREEL, DUNBAR:** 0368 63279. On corner nr Harbour. Modern bistro ✝
E1 specialising in seafood. Kitchen open to restau so you can see the honest,
unfussy cuisine marche being prepared. Sensible number and range of choices.
Just right! Tue-Sun lunch, Thu-Sat 6.30-9pm.   INX

512 **THE OLD CLUBHOUSE, GULLANE:** 0620 842008. East Links Rd behind main st, on
D1 corner of Green. Large woody clubhouse; a bar/bistro serving food all day till
10pm. Great clubby atmos. Good wine selection.   INX

512a **TANTALLON INN, NORTH BERWICK:** 0620 2238. On 'the front' past the putting green
D2 at the east end. Where the locals go for honest-to-goodness pub dining-room
food. And that pavlova!   INX

LA POTINIERE, GULLANE: 0620 843214. (46/EDIN BEST RESTAUS; 1232/WINE-LISTS). A
gem in the crown of the Auld Alliance.   MED

DROVER'S INN, EAST LINTON: 0620 860298. Nr A1. (181/EDIN PUB FOOD).   INX

CHAMPANY'S, nr LINLITHGOW: 0506 834532. (53/EDIN RESTAUS.)   INX/EXP

THE BEST HOTELS AND RESTAURANTS IN FIFE

See also 1381/CENTRES: DUNFERMLINE AND KIRKALDY, *p. 229, and* 1393/ HOLIDAY CENTRES: ST ANDREWS, *p. 241. Refer to Map 5.*

✝ ✝ **OLD COURSE, ST ANDREWS:** 0334 74371. The hotel you come to first on the 513 A91 from N or W. It sits on the Old Course and overlooks the others. D2 From a distance it looks rather like a Spanish Condo development, but inside all is tasteful opulence and relaxed ambience. In this lap of luxury there are many soothing places to wait – the conservatory, the pool, or just the bathrooms – to see whether you have come up in 'the ballot' (1108/GOLF).

125RMS JAN-DEC T/T PETS CC KIDS LOTS

RUFFLETS, ST ANDREWS: 0334 72594. 4km from centre via Argyle St opp the West 514 Port and out along Strathkinness Low Rd past univ playing fields. English feel to D2 mansion on the edge of town. The celebrated gardens are a joy to walk in after dinner or after getting married. Rooms may seem average for the money, but have rare features like firm beds, blackout curtains, windows that open (to garden).

20RMS JAN-DEC T/T PETS CC KIDS TOS EXP

BALBIRNIE HOUSE, MARKINCH: 0592 610066. Grecian-style mansion in Elysian fields 515 of Balbirnie Country Park. Signed from the road system around Glenrothes New C3 Town (3km). 'Elegance' is the word being striven for – and some of the rooms really make it. Golf in the park and craft studios in the stables.

36RMS JAN-DEC T/T PETS CC KIDS TOS LOTS

WOODSIDE HOTEL, ABERDOUR: 0383 860328. Attractive inn in main st of pleasant 516 village with prize-winning railway stn, castle and church (986/CHURCHES), coastal B4 walk and nearby beach. This is where to come from Edinburgh (by train) with your affair.

21RMS JAN-DEC T/T PETS CC KIDS MED.INX

FORTH VIEW, ABERDOUR: 0383 860402. What this small hotel may lack in fancy 517 trimmings it more than makes up for in atmos and setting, the best on the Forth. B4 Out there on the point beneath a cliff of airy walks (and famed for rock-climbing), reached by path from harbour or by car from the corner of the carpark for Silver Sands (a popular beach) and thence by a v steep track. The garden meets the shore and there's a jagged jetty. Somebody should write a novel here. You wake up with Edinburgh over the sea.

6RMS APR-OCT X/X PETS CC KIDS CHP

NIVINGSTON HOUSE: 05775 216. 7km Kinross. 651/COUNTRY-HOUSE HOTELS.

SANDFORD COUNTRY HOUSE HOTEL: 0382 541802. 7km S of Tay Bridge via A92/914. 652A/COUNTRY-HOUSE HOTELS.

✝ ✝ **THE PEAT INN nr CUPAR:** 033484 206. At the crossrds of the hamlet called 518 Peat Inn, which is signed from all over, this restau with 8 fall-upstairs D3 rooms, is in every other guide and needs no recommendation from me. David Wilson is a Chef Laureate of the Gastronomic Academy and also rather a good cook. Very French/very Scottish/very good. Have the cheese, the Petits Fours are a dessert in themselves. Also 1239/WINE-LISTS. Tue-Sat 1-3pm and 7-9.30pm. EXP

✝ **OSTLER'S CLOSE, CUPAR:** 0334 55574. Down a close(y) at the narrow part of the 519 main st, Amanda and Jimmy Graham run a bistro/restau that puts Cupar on D2 the gastronomic map. But no pretence here about 'fine cuisine'; this is honest and real. Lots of thought and flair. Tue-Sat 1-3pm and 7-9.30pm. MED

✝ **THE CELLAR, ANSTRUTHER:** 0333 310378. Behind the Fisheries Museum in this 520 most visited of East Neuk towns (795/COASTAL VILLS). Down an alley, E3 round the back, you step into a seafood bistro that's somewhere else in Europe. Never mind Peter Jukes' excl cooking and the freshness of the fish from the sea round the corner; you could sup the atmosphere. Tue-Sat 7-9pm, lunch Fri/Sat only. 1173/SEAFOOD RESTAUS. MED

BOUQUET GARNI, ELIE: 0333 330374. High St of genteel town (1109/GOLF; 521 1142/WINDSURFING) a formal restau and lighter lunches in lounge bar. Fish, game D3 and chocolate pudding. Building a reputation. Lunch and 7-9pm. Cl Sun. MED

THE SMUGGLERS BISTRO, N QUEENSFERRY: 0383 412567. Main st on the way to 522 harbour; the famous bridge . . . just is. The underwater world is round the corner. B5 Friendly, informal out of town bistro. Thu-Sat only. 7-10pm. INX

THE BEST HOTELS AND RESTAURANTS IN TAYSIDE

See also DUNDEE HOTELS AND RESTAURANTS, *pp. 101-2;* 1387/CENTRES: PERTH, *p. 236; and* 1391/HOLIDAY CENTRES: PITLOCHRY, *p. 241. Refer to Map 4.*

523 **FARLEYER HOUSE, WEEM nr ABERFELDY:** 0887 820332. 4km town on B846 to
B3 Tummel Bridge. V civilised country house in grounds with 6-hole golf course, nr Castle Menzies. Excl dining-room and bistro. Library for whiling away the afternoon. Well used to accolades.   11RMS   JAN-DEC   T/T   PETS   CC   KIDS   TOS   LOTS
ATKINS BISTRO: Daily menu cheaper, less formal than above. Open all day for coffee; lunch and dinner (LO 9.30pm). Not a v bistro-like atmosphere, but the blackboard menu meets every expectation.   INX

524 **DUNKELD HOUSE, DUNKELD:** 0350 727771. Former home of Duke of Atholl, a v
C3 large impressive country-house on banks of R Tay just outside Dunkeld. Leisure complex with pool etc and many other activities laid on. V decent menu. Fine for kids. Not cheap but often good deals available. Managed by Stakis Organisation.   92RMS   JAN-DEC   T/T   PETS   CC   KIDS   LOTS

525 **KINLOCH HOUSE, nr BLAIRGOWRIE:** 0250 84237. 5km W on A923 to Dunkeld. A
C3 country house with open views to Sidlaw Hills. Panelled and galleried, and rather formally attired and run. One would have to fit in, but if one does, it is a good centre for touring.   21RMS   JAN-DEC   T/T   PETS   CC   KIDS   EXP

526 **CASTLETON HOUSE, EASSIE nr GLAMIS:** 030784 340. 13km W of Forfar, 25km N of
D3 Dundee. App from Glamis, 5km SW on A94. Family-run country-house hotel with good restau. Not over-pricey or stuffy; bar meals as well as dining-rooms/conservatory. Popular Sunday lunch.   6RMS   JAN-DEC   T/T   PETS   CC   KIDS   TOS   EXP

526a **PINE TREES HOTEL, PITLOCHRY:** 0796 472121. A safe haven in visitor-ville – it's
C2 above the town and above all that. There are many grand mansions here; this is the real Strathblair. Take Larchwood Rd off W end of main st (signed golf course). Woody gardens, woody interior. It takes you back!   20RMS   FEB-DEC   T/T   T/T   XPETS   CC   KIDS   MED.EX

527 **KENMORE HOTEL, KENMORE:** 0887 830205. Ancient (they say the oldest in Scotland)
B3 inn in this charming, quaint conservation village. Great for golfing (Taymouth Castle, 1120/GOLF), fishing (the Tay's at the foot of the garden) and walking. 835/WATERFALLS; 815/GLENS. Original poem by Burns over fireplace (though it ain't one of his best); funky Boar's Head Bar in the yard; comfy, individual rooms; good bar meals. Perfectly Perthshire.   35RMS   JAN-DEC   T/T   PETS   CC   KIDS   TOS   MED.EX

528 **KILLIECRANKIE HOTEL, KILLIECRANKIE:** 0796 473220. 5km N of Pitlochry. Village
C2 inn ambience with cosy rooms of individual character. Carefully run. Great walks round about.   11RMS   MAR-DEC   T/T   PETS   CC   KIDS   TOS   MED.EX
V fine home-cooking in restau and bar (LO 9.30pm). No portion control at breakfast etc. *Menu du jour.* Pop over from Pitlochry.   INX

529 **KYNACHAN LODGE, nr TUMMEL BRIDGE:** 0882 634214. 2km S on B846 to Aberfeldy.
B3 Excellent value small country-house with simple but scrumptious dinner-party cooking. Pleasant outlook (once you're past the electricity station) in God's country where Schiehallion presides (1084/MUNROS).   6RMS   APR-OCT   T/T   PETS   CC   KIDS   INX

530 **CLOVA HOTEL, GLEN CLOVA:** 05755 222. Nr end of Glen Clova, one of the great
D2 Angus Glens (818/GLENS), on B955 25km N of Kirriemuir. A walkers'/climbers'/country retreat hotel of great character. Hot soup, warm stove, warm welcome. Superb walking nearby.   7RMS   JAN-DEC   T/T   PETS   CC   KIDS   INX

531 **THE OLD BANK HOUSE, BLAIRGOWRIE:** 0250 2902. Solid town-house top of (Brown)
C3 st off main st at Queens Hotel. Family-run, friendly.   9RMS   JAN-DEC   T/T   PETS   CC   KIDS   TOS   MED.INX

532 **HOTEL COLL EARN, AUCHTERARDER:** 0764 463553. Off main st. Extravagant
C4 Victorian mansion with exceptional stained glass. Comfy rooms.
    8RMS   JAN-DEC   T/T   XPETS   CC   KIDS   MED.EX

CROFTBANK HOUSE, KINROSS: 0577 863819. Small mansion-house hotel and restau 532a with great local reputation, on main rd into Kinross from M90, junct 6 2km. Bill *C4* Kerr's kitchen turns out inspired variations on the chicken/fish/steak theme and there's a small but satisfactory wine-list. Best to book dinner. LO 9pm.

5RMS JAN-DEC X/T PETS CC KIDS INX

CRIEFF HYDRO: 0764 655555. Good for loads of reasons, quintessentially Scottish (also 657/HOTELS THAT WELCOME CHILDREN). MED.EX

GLENEAGLES: 0764 662231. 647/COUNTRY-HOUSE HOTELS. LOTS

KINNAIRD HOUSE nr DUNKELD: 0796 482440. 641/COUNTRY-HOUSE HOTELS. LOTS

AUCHTERARDER HOUSE, AUCHTERARDER: 0764 663646. 646/COUNTRY-HOUSE HOTELS. LOTS

OLD MANSION HOUSE, AUCHTERHOUSE: 082626 366. 15km Dundee. (621/DUNDEE.) EXP

BALLATHIE HOUSE, nr PERTH: 025083 268. 20km N Perth. (1387/PERTH.) LOTS

THE BUT 'N' BEN, AUCHMITHIE nr ARBROATH: 0241 77223. 2km off A92 N from 533 Arbroath, 8km to town or 4km by clifftop walk. Village perched on clifftop *E3* where ravine leads to small cove and quay. Adj cottages converted into cosy restau open noon-3pm for lunch, 4-5.30pm for high tea, 7-10pm for dinner. Menus vary but all v Scottish and informal with emphasis on fish/seafood. You could take anyone here – kids, Auntie Maisie, your boss. Couthie cuisine at MacBistro best.

INX

CARLIN MAGGIE'S, KINROSS: 0577 63652. At 191 High St, through this small town 533a from the M90, 4km. An oasis of decent home-cooking conscientiously prepared *C4* in Helena Thomson's kitchen. With no red meat (though chicken and fish), the menu is especially good for vegetarians. See 1159/1159 VEGN RESTAUS. Monthly variations. Wed-Sat lunch/dinner (7-10pm).

INX

THE LOFT, BLAIR ATHOLL: 0796 481377. 50m off main st as you come in from A9 or 533b B rd south (Pitlochry 12km). Upstairs bistro in corner of caravan/chalet park *B2* where a real chef (Martin Hollis) presides over a (slightly chlorinated from pool downstairs) culinary oasis. The best meal for miles. Mar-Oct. lunch/dinner 7 days. No credit cards.

INX

THE BEST HOTELS AND RESTAURANTS
IN THE GRAMPIAN REGION

Excludes Aberdeen, but see also 1395/HOLIDAY CENTRES: BALLATER, *p. 243. Refer to Map 3.*

534 **INVERY HOUSE, BANCHORY:** 03302 4782. 2km from town along B974 to Ballater
D4 amidst 40 acres of woodland on the banks of the Feugh. Of the many good hotels on Deeside, this seems the most relaxed in its excellence. Fishing on the Feugh, billiards in a dark den downstairs and golf wherever you like, even Royal Aberdeen (patron Stewart Spence v well connected in this department). Civilised dining with excl wine-list, port, brandy etc.
14RMS JAN-DEC T/T PETS CC KIDS TOS LOTS

535 **PITTODRIE HOUSE, PITCAPLE:** 0467 681444. Large 'family' mansion house on estate
C3 in one of the nicest parts of Aberdeenshire with Bennachie above. 40km Aberdeen but 'only 30mins from airport' via A96. Follow signs off B9002. Tennis courts, croquet lawn, billiards and lots of comfortable rms. Fine menu based on local produce.
27RMS JAN-DEC T/T PETS CC KIDS TOS LOTS

536 **THE MANSION HOUSE, ELGIN:** 0343 548811. In town but not easy to find; it's beneath
B2 the left hand of the statue on the hill! Comfortable and elegant townhouse in a comfortable town with new 'leisure facilities' incl pool/gym and poolside snack bar.
24RMS JAN-DEC T/T XPETS CC KIDS TOS LOTS

537 **THE ROYAL HOTEL, ELGIN:** 0343 542320. A hotel in Elgin that hardly advertises its
B2 presence though it's just across the rd from the station. A well-kept secret; you may need to book.
MED.INX

538 **BANCHORY LODGE HOTEL, BANCHORY:** 03302 2625. A sporting lodge hotel nr town
D4 centre, but superbly situated on the banks of the Dee. They have the rights to the half-mile stretch but fishing must be booked well in advance. Public rms and many bedrms o/look the river. Sporty rather than stuffy atmos. People come back again and again.
12RMS FEB-DEC T/T XPETS CC KIDS TOS EXP

539 **CRAIGENDARROCH, BALLATER:** 03397 55858. On the Braemar rd (the A93). Part of a
B4 country club/time-share operation with elegant dining and leisure facilities (others include Cameron House at Loch Lomond). Though the elegance is contrived, there's no question that facilities and service are excl. 3 restaus, one by pool (more chlorine than cuisine); the Lochnagar and the upmarket Oak are both v good.
50RMS JAN-DEC T/T XPETS CC KIDS TOS LOTS

Oak Room is rated. A la carte (game, fish usually coated/masked/fenced/finished/sauced in some way) with Scottish and Gastronomic Evenings. Good service.
EXP

540 **WATERSIDE INN, PETERHEAD:** 0779 71121. Edge of town on A952 to Fraserburgh
E2 and, though you'd hardly notice, on banks of tidal R Ugie. Standard, well-run modern hotel, recommended for its service and convenience rather than ambience, and because it's the best option around. Food is better and less frozen than you might expect. Well-thought-out for kids (662/HOTELS THAT WELCOME KIDS).
110RMS JAN-DEC T/T PETS CC KIDS TOS MED.EX

541 **MINMORE HOUSE, GLENLIVET:** 08073 378. Adj to the famous distillery (1248/
B3 WHISKY TRAIL) and formerly the house of its founder George Smith, now a small, comfy country house with excl dining.
10RMS MAY-OCT T/X PETS CC KIDS TOS EXP

542 **OLD MELDRUM HOUSE:** 06512 2294. *In absentia*; much loved and once, very good
D3 value. Maybe that's why it's closed at time of writing; hopefully not for long. In village 30km N Aberdeen.

543 **THE OLD MANSE OF MARNOCH:** 0466 780873. 1km from A97, the Huntly to Banff rd.
C2 Exactly as you might imagine it, a charming old manse nr the banks of the R Deveron in bucolic surroundings.
5RMS JAN-DEC X/X PETS XCC KIDS TOS MED.EX

Everything home-made (incl the after-dinner mints), not wholefood but certainly wholesome. Dinner on Wedgwood, breakfast on Doulton. May seat round the one table, like a dinner-party. Must book.
MED

CRAIGELLACHIE HOTEL, CRAIGELLACHIE: 0340 881204. The quintessential Speyside 544 hotel, off A941 Elgin to Perth and Aberdeen rd by the bridge over Spey. Esp *B2* good for fishing, but well placed for walking (Speyside Way runs along bottom of garden, 1081/LONG WALKS) and distillery visits (WHISKY TRAIL, p.193). Informal.
30RMS JAN-DEC T/X XPETS CC KIDS TOS MED.EX

CASTLE HOTEL, HUNTLY: 0466 792696. Just behind ruin of Huntly Castle; approach 545 from town through Castle entrance and then over R Deveron up impressive *C2* drive. Large but family-scale lodge-house, not over-gentrified or country house-ified and consequently excl value. Rooms have character and green countryside views. Fishing arranged.
30RMS JAN-DEC X/T PETS CC KIDS MED.INX

DELNASHAUGH INN, BALLINDALOCH nr GRANTOWN ON SPEY: 08072 255. Roadside 546 and Speyside (actually it's the Avon, pron 'Arn') inn, comfy, tasteful; a pleasant *B2* surprise. On a bend of the A95 betw Craigellachie and Grantown nr the confluence of main roads and the rivers. Fishing arranged.
9RMS DEC-OCT T/T PETS CC KIDS EXP

UDNY ARMS, NEWBURGH: 03586 89444. Village pub with great food and character. 547 Rooms tasteful and individually furnished. Choice of dining-rooms and food *D3* in bar. Folk come from Aberdeen (28km) to eat here. Golf course adj; Cruden Bay (1105/GOLF) 16km N. Newburgh is on coast rd A975 just off main A92 Aberdeen-Peterhead.
26RMS JAN-DEC T/T XPETS CC KIDS TOS MED INX
Same à la carte menu, bar or dining-room with seafood/vegn/steak/salmon; great starters and puds. Daily lunch and till 9pm.
MED

BAYVIEW HOTEL, CULLEN: 0542 41031. 50m off main A98 Banff to Elgin rd, on a 548 corner overlooking the harbour. From most rms there really is a great view of *C1* the broad sandy sweep of Cullen Bay (811/BEACHES). Good pub food incl of course the local smoked fish soup known on many a Scottish menu as Cullen Skink. Food 6.30-9pm.
6RMS JAN-DEC T/X PETS CC KIDS MED.INX

GRANT ARMS, MONYMUSK: 0467 226. The village inn in delightful rural 549 Aberdeenshire, a good centre for walking (1045/HILLS), close to the 'Castle Trail' *C3* (917/CASTLES; 946/COUNTRY HOUSES) and with fishing rights on the Don.
10RMS JAN-DEC X/T PETS CC KIDS MED.INX
Best pub food for miles, and dining. Daily lunch and 6.30-9pm.
INX

THE OLD MONASTERY nr BUCKIE: 0542 32660. Most reliable place to eat in this long 550 stretch of the coast. Off main A98; instead of going into Buckie, follow small rd *C2* opp marked for Drybridge. The converted church is 5km on the left with great views of the distant Moray coastline. Lunch in the Cloisters Bar (with views) and dinner in the church itself. Fairly simple menu using fresh local ingredients and careful attention. Often booked. Tue-Sat.
EXP

FAGINS, WHITEHILLS nr BANFF: 02617 321. In Loch St which is off to right as you 551 enter this coastal village 3km W of Banff off the B9139. Good local reputation *C1* for surf 'n' turf suppers cooked in tiny kitchen in corner of dining-room. Restau situated unpromisingly above a rather ordinary-looking pub (The Cutty Sark), but serves honest-to-goodness fare with some flair. Fri-Sun lunch, Wed-Sat dinner 7-10pm.
INX

THE GREEN INN, BALLATER: 03397 55701. On the green in touring centre of Royal 551a Deeside, a restau with integrity and conscientious cuisine, and 3 rooms above so *B4* you get a healthy breakfast as well. No fry policy, heather honey instead of sugar etc; a generally good attitude towards diners and guests makes this quite the best nosh hereabouts, whatever your poison.
MED

THE BALLATER GUEST HOUSE, BALLATER: 03397 55346. At 34 Victoria Rd in this 551b Royal Deeside centre where there are a fair few hotels to choose from, an *B4* exceptionally good value GH with a warm welcome, warm home-made bread etc. Thanks to Ms Dyker for the tip-off.
10RMS JAN-DEC X/T XPETS CC KIDS CHP

FARADAYS, CULTS: 0224 869666. 8km W Aberdeen on A93. (599/ABERDEEN.)

BORSALINO, PETERCULTER: 0224 732902. 15km W Aberdeen on A93. (600/ ABERDEEN.)

THE BEST HOTELS AND
RESTAURANTS IN THE HIGHLANDS

Refer to Map 2. See also FORT WILLIAM, *p. 231,* ULLAPOOL, *p. 239,* SKYE, *p. 223, and* LEWIS, *p. 221.*

552 GLENBORRODALE CASTLE, ARDNAMURCHAN: 09724 266. On B8007 betw
B4 Kilchoan (Tobermory ferry) and Salen/Strontian. Ft William 65km. A tower-house castle in the splendid seclusion of the Ardnamurchan Peninsula, refurbished to an extraordinary standard in contemporary good taste. Everything discreetly 'laid on' incl loch and river fishing, croquet, a gym (in the stable block) and *en tous cas* tennis. Small dining-room, unfussy menu. Missed by many guides – but they're wrong. It costs a lot, but this is luxury; Peter de Savery (who owns it) should know. 16RMS APR-OCT T/T PETS CC KIDS LOTS

553 INVERLOCHY CASTLE, FORT WILLIAM: 0397 702177. 5km from town on A82
C4 Inverness rd, Scotland's flagship Highland (Relais and Chateaux) hotel. Amidst gardens and big scenery (Ben Nevis is visible from rd and the nearby golf course). The £200 per room doesn't incl dinner; it includes Inverlochy Castle. Very Victorian experience and hospitality. Reservations essential; I have my own. 16RMS MAR-NOV T/T PETS CC KIDS LOTS

554 CLIFTON HOUSE, NAIRN: 0667 53119. Seafield St off A96 to Inverness. A
D3 suburban mansion surprisingly capacious and full of J. Gordon MacIntyre's eccentric and camp good taste. A thespian haven (with occasional musical and theatrical evenings), this has been one of the most distinctly individual hotels in the Highlands for over 50 yrs. Mr Mac presides and cooks with fastidious attention. Every room is a different experience and dinner much more than a meal. Join the house party and live. 16RMS JAN-DEC X/X PETS CC KIDS EXP

555 DOWER HOUSE, nr MUIR OF ORD: 0463 870090. On A862 betw Beauly and
D3 Dingwall 18km NW of Inverness and 2km N of village. Charming personal place; you feel like a house guest. Cottage/country house, with Smallbone/Osbourne-type decor, cast-iron baths and comfy public rooms. Dinner intimate, simple but sophisticated. 5RMS APR-OCT T/T PETS CC KIDS EXP

556 BUNCHREW HOUSE, nr INVERNESS: 0463 234917. On A862 Beauly rd only 5km
D3 from Inverness yet completely removed from town; on the wooded shore of the Beauly Firth. Rooms look across water and you might see Ben Wyvis. Alan and Patsy Wilson run a very hospitable Highland lodge (kilts and fires in the evening). Fishing on estate. 11RMS JAN-DEC T/T PETS CC KIDS TOS EXP

557 CULLODEN HOUSE, INVERNESS: 0463 790461. 5km E of town nr A9, follow
D3 signs for Culloden village not the Battlefield. Elegant, Georgian mansion on edge of suburbia and of course history, and the most conscientiously *de luxe* hotel hereabouts. Standards one would expect. New garden suites. Excl chef. 24RMS JAN-DEC T/T PETS CC KIDS TOS LOTS

558 POLMAILY HOUSE, DRUMNADROCHIT, LOCH NESS: 0456 2343. On A831 (5km) from
D3 Drumnadrochit to Cannich in Glen Urquhart and nr awesome Glen Affric (814/GLENS). Good country house centre for walks etc and with tennis and small outdoor pool. Small, comfy public rooms, airy bedrooms. Sensible dinner and wine-list. Many guests return. 9RMS APR-OCT T/T XPETS CC KIDS EXP

559 DUNAIN PARK, INVERNESS: 0463 230512. 6km SW town on A82 Ft William rd.
D3 Mansion-house just off the rd, a quiet and more civilised alternative to hotels in town esp for those on business. Interesting books in bedrooms (one of mine was *Tropic of Cancer*). Particularly friendly and solicitous staff. Small pool in garden outhouse. Notable restau/dining-room. 1385/CENTRES: INVERNESS. 14RMS JAN-DEC T/T PETS CC KIDS TOS EXP

560 THE SUMMER ISLES HOTEL, ACHILTIBUIE: 085482 282. 40km from Ullapool on
C2 the famously remote peninsula, with the Isles scattered in the bays and Stac Polly and Suilven nearby. A walking guide has been compiled by Mark Irvine, the patron (Lucy's brother). Rooms fairly basic, dining exceptional. The 'village pub' is adjacent. 13RMS APR-OCT X/X PETS XCC XKIDS TOS MED.EX Fairly formal dining, but awfully good. All would-be restaurateurs should be shown this cheese-board. Must book. MED

HOLLY TREE HOTEL, KENTALLEN: 063174 292. 44km S of Ft William on A828. Shore 561 of L Linnhe, in a former railway station with decor based on Glasgow (Art) *C5* Nouveau. A friendly stopover.   12RMS JAN-DEC T/T PETS CC KIDS MED.EX

LODGE ON THE LOCH, ONICH: 08553 237. Ft William 15km. One of 3 good lochside 562 hotels in this village on L Linnhe on the main A82, the best place in the Ft *C4* William area for medium-priced hotels. The Lodge almost feels like a city hotel, but standardisation has been achieved without losing the 'place'. Soft Rudolph Steiner colour schemes. Vegetarian food not altogether brilliant (though mentioned in vegn guides), but most of menu adequate. Other decent hotels in Onich are the Alt-Nan-Ros and the Onich.
                18RMS MAR-OCT T/T PETS CC KIDS TOS MED.EX

KINLOCHBERVIE HOTEL, KINLOCHBERVIE: 097182 275. This is the village hotel, up the 563 hill from the main business of the area – the port and the fishmarket. Well- *C1* run/good service/all mod cons. 'Bistro' and dining-room. Pub with many malts and many fishermen.   14RMS JAN-DEC T/T PETS CC KIDS TOS MED.EX

SUTHERLAND ARMS HOTEL, LAIRG: 0549 2291. Town hotel overlooking L Shin. 564 Changing hands at time of writing, so some things may alter, but the great setting *D2* won't. All facilities you'd expect for price and Lairg is geographical centre for Sutherland pursuits, esp fishing.   27RMS APR-OCT T/T PETS CC KIDS MED.EX

KNOCKIE LODGE, LOCH NESS: 04563 276. 642/COUNTRY-HOUSE HOTELS.

ARISAIG HOUSE, ARISAIG: 06875 622. 652/COUNTRY-HOUSE HOTELS.

✝ ✝ **AIRDS HOTEL, PORT APPIN:** 063173 236. 40km N of Oban on A828 to Ft 565
William via Connel. Side rd to Port Appin (and the passenger ferry to *C5* Lismore, 1344/MAGIC ISLANDS). Airds is actually in Strathclyde but close to the boundary and feels 'Highland' (459/STRATH NORTH). This is one of the best restaus in the north. The dining-room annexed to the front of the hotel is small, and both the linen and the waiters seem a bit overstarched, but the food is faultless. No big deal about 'local produce', they use just whatever is very good and available. Betty Allen's menu here sets a standard by which I have measured other restaus in this book.   EXP

✝ **ARD-NA-COILLE HOTEL, KINGUSSIE:** 0540 673214. 3km S on A86. Another hotel 565a
and agreeable place to stay that is mainly notable for its dining-room and *D4* exceptional wine-list (1241/WINE-LISTS). Barry Cottam's artfully balanced 5-course (fixed) meal is a real find. 7.45pm nightly.   EXP

THISTLES, CROMARTY: 0381 7471. Church St. This bistro/restau in delightful village 566 (790/COASTAL VILLAGES) has recently changed hands. New reports, please.   *D3*

✝ **THE CROSS, KINGUSSIE:** 0540 661166. Off main st at traffic lights, head 200m 567
uphill then left into glen. Perfect setting for the best restau in the ski zone, *D4* part of simple, tasteful hotel in converted tweed mill. Extraordinary that there are two such excl chefs so close together in the wilderness S of Inverness (and so close to the A9). Here Ruth Hadley works wonders in the kitchen and Tony talks you through the wine and exemplary cheese. Mar-Nov. Cl Tue.   EXP

GOOD INEXPENSIVE HOTELS IN THE HIGHLANDS

Refer to Map 2.

✝ ✝ **THE CEILIDH PLACE, ULLAPOOL:** 0854 612103. A place with real individuality 568
(not to say conviviality) in the centre of town, away from the port (ferry *C2* to Lewis) area. Though the hubbub may be disturbing for early retirers, the guest lounge upstairs is uniquely comfortable and sociable. Pictures everywhere and a bookshop; a celebration really of all the good things in life. Separate 'clubhouse' offers cheap bunk accom incl family rooms. Events programme.
                24RMS MAR-OCT X/X PETS CC KIDS MED.INX
Self/S café/bistro day and night with great atmosphere plus a v decent restau in the evening. Good fish and vegn. All v laid back.   INX

569 LOCH MAREE HOTEL, TALLADALE: 044584 288. On A832 15km from
C3 Kinlochewe and right by the lochside. A classic Highland fishing hotel
catering for discriminating tourists (incl Queen Victoria) since 1872. All fishing
arrangements made incl ghillies. A good base for walking in Torridon. Nr
Inverewe (760/GARDENS) and Gairloch. Unpretentious comfort and great value.
839/LOCHS; 1091/WALKING AREAS. 18RMS MAR-NOV T/T PETS CC KIDS MED.INX

570 AUCHENDEAN LODGE, DULNAIN BRIDGE nr GRANTOWN ON SPEY: 047 985 347.
E3 A real Highland retreat in area of stunning scenery nr Aviemore skiing and
Whisky Trail. Tastefully and cosily furnished Edwardian lodge with log fires,
good malts and cellar, and books. Food with flair and imaginative use of local
ingredients. 7RMS JAN-DEC X/T PETS CC KIDS TOS INX

571 TIGH-AN-EILEAN, SHIELDAIG: 05205 251. On waterfront of this wee village looking
C3 out on Loch Shieldaig, an inlet of the mighty sealoch, Torridon. An island
completely covered in original Scots pine sits just offshore. Unfussy food and
furnishings. Is also the village pub. An excl base for walking (1091/WALKING
AREAS). 12RMS APR-OCT X/X PETS CC KIDS MED.INX

572 EDDRACHILLES HOTEL, nr SCOURIE: 0971 2080. I didn't find this hotel too friendly,
C2 but the rooms are nice and the setting is exceptional. Handy for Handa Island
(873/BIRDS). S of Scourie on A894. 11RMS MAR-OCT T/T XPETS CC XKIDS MED.INX

573 SUTHERLAND ARMS HOTEL, GOLSPIE: 0408 633234. Roadside inn at N end of town
D2 nr Dunrobin Castle and Big Burn Walk (1055/GLEN WALKS). First coaching inn
in Scotland and still a hospitable and cosy place to stop. Food fresh and local.
  16RMS JAN-DEC T/T PETS CC KIDS MED.INX

574 DORNOCH CASTLE HOTEL, DORNOCH: 0862 810216. A real castle that doesn't cost the
D2 earth. Some original, some Victorian and a new bedroom wing. Spiral upstairs to
reception, down to the dungeons for dinner. Town and countryside beyond.
The great golf is over there. 19RMS APR-OCT T/T PETS CC KIDS TOS MED.INX

575 LOVAT ARMS, BEAULY: 0463 782313. Hotel in the main st of this small town 20km
D3 from Inverness. A recent refurb has brought it up in the world. The family have
their own farm. Relaxed and welcoming. 22RMS JAN-DEC T/T PETS CC KIDS INX

576 TOMICH HOTEL, TOMICH nr DRUMNADROCHIT: 04565 399. The inn of a quiet
C3 conservation village, part of an old estate and on the edge of Guisachan Forest.
Nr Plodda Falls (824/WATERFALLS) and Glen Affric (814/GLENS). Basic facilities
but use of pool nearby in farm steading (9am-9pm) and esp good for fishing
hols. Also self-catering chalets. 9RMS MAR-OCT X/T PETS CC KIDS MED.INX

577 HEATHBANK HOUSE, BOAT OF GARTEN: 0479 83234. Quirky taste in wall
D4 decorations, lots of fans and odd pictures; but individual. Colonial-type house in
neat village nr skiing and famous osprey reserve (879/BIRDS). They care about
what they collect, incl you. 8RMS DEC-OCT X/X XPETS XCC KIDS TOS CHP

578 ACHANY HOUSE, LAIRG: 0549 2172. Small family mansion in grounds off the B864 to
D2 Shin Falls. More guest house than hotel, but an exceptional one & v good
value. Lots of books and space. 3RMS APR-NOV X/X PETS CC KIDS MED.INX

579 GLENGARRY CASTLE, INVERGARRY: 08093 254. Impressive castle for an impressive
D4 price and extensive grounds o/looking L Oich. Historical link with the infamous
15th Earl of Glengarry, one of the most oft-seen pictures of a Clan chief (an
incorrigible poseur) who squandered and betrayed his inheritance. See the ruin.
Hotel in the family for 34 yrs. Tennis, fishing. 26RMS APR-OCT T/T PETS CC KIDS MED.INX

580 GLENFINNAN HOUSE HOTEL, GLENFINNAN: 039783 235. A v Scottish hotel in a v
C4 Scottish place. Victorian mansion with lawns down to L Shiel and the
Glenfinnan monument over the water. Heady atmosphere.
  20RMS APR-OCT X/X PETS CC KIDS MED.INX

580a THE LOVAT ARMS, FT AUGUSTUS: 0887 830367. Old-fashioned gem (original features,
D4 great furnishings) in mansion above town at end of L Ness. No refurbs please!
  21RMS JAN-DEC T/T PETS CC KIDS MED.INX

THE CROSS, KINGUSSIE: Inx but elegant hotel in converted tweed mill by river.
Restau not cheap, but superb (567/HIGHL RESTAUS). To stay, you're expected to
eat – do! 9RMS MAR-NOV T/X XPETS CC XKIDS MED.INX

GOOD INEXPENSIVE RESTAURANTS
IN THE HIGHLANDS

Refer to Map 2.

✝ **BIADH MATH, KYLE OF LOCHALSH:** 0599 4813. This restau is in the railway 581
station so it's not hard to find. Nr port and ferry to Skye (or the bridge). A C3
brief and worthwhile encounter with good food in a trains-gone-by atmosphere.
Seafood from just over there and more than token vegn selection. Homebaking
and a breakfast worth missing the ferry for. Apr-Oct lunch/6.30-9pm (pron
'bee-ach ma').

✝ **LA MIRAGE, HELMSDALE:** 04312 615. Dunrobin St nr the Bridge Hotel. Pure 582
Brighton Beach on a barren coast, this place may come as a surprise. It's not E2
so much the food (plain and wholesome family fare), but the decor of both the
parlour and the proprietrix that creates a lasting impression. Suffice to say that
Nancy Sinclair and Barbara Cartland (who has a house nearby) seem to be a
mutual appreciation society. There's a salon through the back if you fancy a
rinse. Daily noon-8.45pm (Dec-Apr, noon-7pm). INX

THE BOATHOUSE, KINCRAIG: 0540 4272. 2km from vill towards Feshiebridge along 582a
Loch Insh. Part of L Insh Watersports (1139/WATERSPORTS), a balcony restau D4
o/looking beach and loch. Fine setting and ambience and good self/s food.
Friendly, young staff. Good vegn. Snacks and home baking till 6.30pm; supper
menu till 9/10pm. Apr-Oct. CHP

LIBRARY LODGE, ARISAIG: 06875 651. On 'the front' of village which gets busy in 583
summer. Seats outside to watch what's going on and the sunset over the islands. C4
Quay/beach for boats to Eigg/Rum nearby. Blackboard choices for inexp lunch
and *table d'hôte* dinner. Local seafood and usually several vegn options. Dinner
not cheap, lunch a good deal. Daily lunch and till 9.30pm. INX/MED

OLD SCHOOL, RHICONICH nr KINLOCHBERVIE: 097182 383. Halfway betw the 584
scattering of houses on the A894 rd from the N coast to Scourie and Lochinver, C1
and the port of Kinlochbervie on the scenic B801. Victorian schoolhouse with
home cooking; trad food suggestive of v good school dinners. Though there are
now several school rooms converted into restaus in Scotland, this one does
retain some atmos; an echo of chalk scratching in the long afternoon. Menu for
kids and vegetarians. We'll all eat the treacle sponge. Daily lunch and 6-8pm.
Also accom. INX

RIVERSIDE BISTRO, LOCHINVER: 05714 356. On way into town on A837, a deli and 585
restau overlooking the Inver as it tumbles into the sea after a journey (the river C2
and you) through some of Scotland's most engaging scenery. Sensible menu of
local fish, steaks and chicken with interesting sauces. Vegn. Home-made puds.
Daily lunch and 6-9pm. INX

MORANGIE HOUSE, TAIN: 0862 892281. On way into/out of Tain from A9, a hotel 586
with 11 rooms, but notable mainly as the 'place to eat' in this far-flung wedge of D3
Easter Ross. Dining-room and good value bar/coffee shop meals. May have to
book. Lunch and 6-9.30pm. MED/INX

THE DUNNET HEAD TEA-ROOM, DUNNET HEAD nr THURSO: 084785 774. 15km N of 587
Thurso on the coast rd via Castletown. Mainland Britain's most northerly place E1
to eat, and decent it is too. A roadside 'tea-room' with bistro atmos and tables
outside in summer. An 'anything, anytime' kind of menu incl vegn, pasta and
Bird's Eye Fishfingers. 3km from the famous Head, an essential stop. Daily
noon-9pm (Apr-Oct). INX

THE BEST PLACES TO STAY IN AND AROUND ABERDEEN

In oil city, hotels are expensive. They tend to be full during the week, but may offer reasonable deals at the weekend. It's difficult to find any cheaper hotels to recommend. Here's what there is:

588 ARDOE HOUSE, BLAIRS: 0224 867355. 12km SW of centre on the S Deeside (it's poss to turn off the A92 from Stonehaven and the south at the first bridge and get to the hotel avoiding the city). The Dee is on other side of rd from hotel, but nearby. A goodly chunk of Scottish baronial with a new annex which has tripled capacity (rooms here are standard but high standard); the older part is more individual. A good business hotel. Can do good weekend rates.
MAP 3
D4

71RMS JAN-DEC T/T XPETS CC KIDS TOS LOTS

589 MARYCULTER HOUSE HOTEL, MARYCULTER: 0224 732124. Another out-of-town hotel, in the same direction as above (and same owners) but 3km further on. Excl situation on banks of R Dee with riverside walks and an old graveyard and ruined chapel. New annex; most rooms o/look river. The Carvery and dining-room and Cocktail Bar are impressive. Friendly and comfortable and really in the country though only 20mins to town. Weekend deals.
MAP 3
D4

23RMS JAN-DEC T/T XPETS CC KIDS EXP

590 CALEDONIAN THISTLE HOTEL: 0224 640233. For the best of the city centre hotels, I'd probably plump for this Victorian edifice reminiscent of an old station hotel on Union Terr just off the middle part of Union (the main) St. All the usual facilities and trouser presses and a calming atmosphere.
MAP C
B3

80RMS JAN-DEC T/T PETS CC KIDS TOS LOTS

591 HOLIDAY INN CROWN PLAZA: 0224 713911. This modern hotel on the periphery seems to change hands a lot. On Old Meldrum Rd nr the airport about 5km from city centre. Standard stuff but a good business hotel, and more attractive than others in similar suburban locations. Leisure centre has pool etc.
MAP C
xA1

143RMS JAN-DEC T/T PETS CC KIDS LOTS

592 THE BRENTWOOD HOTEL: 0224 595440. 101 Crown St. In an area of many hotels and guest houses to the S of Union St, this one is a better prospect than most. Not over exp considering services provided and a perfectly adequate business hotel on a budget. Close to Union St and bars/restaus. Remember: during week, it gets full.
MAP C
B4

67RMS JAN-DEC T/T PETS CC KIDS MED.INX

593 THE CULTS HOTEL, CULTS: 0224 867632. 10km from centre on A93 Deeside rd so well placed for touring/Castle Trail etc. Recent refurb has transformed this roadside pub/hotel into good value accommodation. Fairly plush for the price with good bathrooms and big beds.
MAP C
D4

6RMS JAN-DEC T/T PETS CC KIDS MED.INX

594 THE BIELDSIDE INN, BIELDSIDE: 0224 867891. On main A93 N Deeside Rd betw Cults and Peterculter, 10km SW of centre. Literally on the roadside, but with pastoral views out the back. Basic rooms above the pub with shared facilities; perfectly serviceable and not exp. But even here you may need to book during the week. Pub food.
MAP 3
D4

7RMS JAN-DEC X/X PETS CC KIDS INX

595 HOSTELS: SYH at 8 Queen's Rd, an arterial rd to the west. Grade 1 hostel 2km from centre (plenty buses). No café. Rooms mainly for 4 to 6 people. You can stay out till 2am. Other hostels at Univ of which the best is probably the **CROMBIE-JOHNSTON HALLS**, off the main rd in Old Aberdeen, the most interesting part of the city but about 3km from centre. Sports and dining facilities to hand and more like a village than a campus. For student hall details (vacs only) phone 0224 273301/273305.
MAP C
xA4

596 CAMPING AND CARAVAN PARK: Only one to recommend is at **HAZELHEAD**, 8km W of centre. Follow signs from ring-rd. Swimming pool nearby. Grassy.
MAP C
xA4

THE BEST RESTAURANTS IN ABERDEEN

Though short on interesting hotels, Aberdeen has a lot of decent restaurants, some very good. Refer to Map C.

†† ✝ SILVER DARLINGS: 0224 576229. Outstanding restau both for location and **597** food. Not easy to find – head for the docks and then to the the the harbour *xD3* mouth (Pocra Quay). The harbour lights wink and boats glide past all the time. Inside, the room is simple and the seafood superb. Mostly chargrilled; the smell pleasantly pervades. Different menu for lunch and dinner, changes seasonally. Apposite wines, wicked desserts. Stroll it off and take the sea breeze. Mon-Fri lunch and Mon-Sun dinner 7-9pm. EXP

†† ✝ ASHVALE: 0224 596981. A 'seafood' place of a different sort altogether, the **598** famous Ashvale Fish 'n' Chip Shop. Nevertheless, you can sit-in; they *xA4* take up to 300 diners at a time. Long, varied menu, though you'd be daft not to settle for fresh fish (1196/FISH 'N' CHIPS). INX

✝ FARADAYS: 0224 869666. Kirkbrae, Cults. 8km W on A93, turning uphill opp **599** Kelly's. Imaginative cooking and unusual combinations in Victorian parlour *xA4* created from a former hydro-electricity stn. Fresh herbs/fish; other impeccable ingredients. Tue-Sat lunch, Mon-Sat 7-9pm. EXP

✝ BORSALINO: 0224 732902. Peterculter on main A93 (after Rob Roy Br), 15km **600** W of city centre but famously worth the drive out which is almost part of *xA4* the enjoyment of the meal. An unlikely roadside cottage situation for traditional Italian restau. Pasta, veal, zabaglione and all. Dinner only, 6-10.30pm. MED

✝ THE LEMON TREE: 0224 642230. 5 W North St. From E end of Union St **601** heading for beach, W North is off King St. Theatre upstairs and café- *C2* bar/restau downstairs with home-made food all day from noon and various cabaret-type entertainments as advertised. Mon-Sat, and Sun evenings. INX

POLDINO'S: 0224 647777. 7 Little Belmont St. The other favourite Italian haunt of **602** the Aberdonians. Good Italian home cooking incl puddings. City centre, always *B3* buzzy. Mon-Sat lunch and 6-10.45pm. Cl Sun. INX

THE ROYAL THAI: 0224 212922. Crown Terr (off Crown St which is off Union St). **603** Enormously popular. Reasonably authentic Thai food, ingredients, they say, *B3* from Bangkok. Not much on menu for vegns. 'Banquets' with sample dishes are a good idea. Good service, moody blue lighting. Daily lunch and 7-11pm. MED

JASMINE: 0224 572362. Crown Terr as above. Highly regarded restau serving Peking **604** cuisine in discreet, subtly-lit basement. Good service. Daily LO 10.30pm. EXP *B3*

YU: 0224 580138. 347 Union St. Stylish, airy, relaxed and central Peking Chinese. **605** Good on fish and light imaginative sauces. Designery but not unbearably so. *B3* Daily lunch and 7-11pm. MED

TAI PAN: 0224 596442. 124 Holburn St. Recent arriviste blown in from the east **605a** (Hong Kong in fact) with ambitious menu: Korea/Japanese/Malaysia/various *xA4* Chinese. Not surprisingly, some of it works, some not. Best to know your stuff. 7 days.

THE FORTUNE: 02s4 242456. 11 Dee St. Still the antithesis of the Asian restau above **606** even though it's moved uptown. Home-cooking, relaxed, nice room. LO 11.30. *B3*

GERARDS: 0224 639500. 50 Chapel St. The longest-established major restau in city. **607** Traditional French and *très* exp (set meal a good idea). Good ambience and the *A3* discreet charm of the bourgeoisie. Open 7 days. EXP

PIERRE VICTOIRE: 0224 640340. 3 Golden Sq. Here's Pierre again (72/EDIN FRENCH) **608** and as if to defy those who think *peut-être* his empire must outreach itself, the *B3* Aberdeen outpost is as funky, French and good value as any of them. Here the miracle is truly realised. Magnifique! Mon-Sat, lunch and LO 11pm. MED

OWLIES: 0224 649267. Littlejohn St. All-day brasserie and balcony restau (open **609** Fri/Sat only) owned by same people that have Silver Darlings (see above). *C2* Warehouse setting, plain French fare (with provincial and other variations e.g. gado gado). Mon-Sat till 10.45pm. INX

THE WILD BOAR: 0224 624216. 19 Belmont St. Narrow, intimate and usually **610** buzzing café-bistro. From cakes to steaks in gallery setting with changing *B3* exhibs. Brewery-owned. Mon-Sat 10am-midnight, Sun 6-11pm. LO 9.30pm. INX

THE BEST PUBS AND CLUBS IN ABERDEEN

Refer to Map C.

PUBS

611 **THE PRINCE OF WALES:** 7 St Nicholas Lane, just off Union St at George St. ✝
C3 An all-round great pub always mentioned in guides and one of the best places in the city for real ale; Bass, Theakston's Old Peculiar, Caledonian 80/- and guest beers. V cheap self-service food at lunchtime. Lots of wood, flagstones, booths. Large area but gets v crowded. 7 days 11am-11pm.

612 **FERRYHILL HOUSE HOTEL BAR:** Bon Accord St. Central hotel in own grounds
B4 (though not extensive, big enough for outside drinking in summer and for kids' play area). Ales aplenty like Greenmantle, McEwan 80/-, Orkney Dark Island, Taylor Landlord and guests. Huge malt whisky collection. Open 11am-11pm, later at weekend.

613 **THE BLUE LAMP:** Gallowgate. Pub with nice ambience and older student
B2 clientele. Small dark pub and large stone-floored lounge (the Blue Lampie). Ales: McEwan 80/-, Orkney Raven, Taylor Landlord, Theakston. Good juke box. 11am-midnight.

614 **MA CAMERON'S INN:** Little Belmont St. The 'oldest pub in the city' though the
B3 old bit is actually a small portion of the sprawling whole – but there's a good snug. Food: lunch and early evening. Cl Sun.

615 **THE GLOBE:** 13 N Silver St. Urban and urbane bar in single room – a place to
A3 drink coffee as well as lager, but without self-conscious, pretentious 'Café-Bar' atmos. Known for its food at lunch and 5-7.45pm. Bar open 11am-11pm.

616 **THE LEMON TREE:** 5 W North St. A theatre (upstairs) and a spacious bar/restau
C2 on street level where there's food all day (601/ABERDEEN RESTAUS) and a mixed programme of entertainment. Phone for details (0224 642230) or watch for fliers, but performances will include comedy, jazz, folk, pop and cabaret. No membership reqd.

617 **UNDER THE HAMMER:** 11 N Silver St. It was a long night and it was one of those
A3 nights, but at some point we passed through this bar in a basement along from the Globe which had a friendly, easy atmosphere with good conversation and music. I'm sure this is where I'd often drink if I lived in Aberdeen.

618 **HENRY J. BEANS,** Windmill Brae; **CHARLIES,** Bon Accord Terr; **SODA FOUNTAIN,**
Union St; **COCKY HUNTERS** Union St (at Holborn Jnct). At time of writing these 4 bar/diners are the most happening places for 18-20-somethings (Cockys not quite so terribly trendy) and the main 'feeder-bars' (as they're known in the trade), for the clubs (see below). Most nights they're packed to the gunnels and they've all got wide selections of current lagers and music. By the time you read this, their moment may have passed. Till 11pm/midnight/1am.

CLUBS *Aberdeen has some of the best clubs in Scotland (maybe they've just got more disposable income)*

619 **MINISTRY OF SIN:** 16 Dee St off Union St. You never forget you're in a ✝
B3 coverted church and it is a bit of a cheeky name (given the Presbyterian gravitas that often seems to permeate from the granite in Aberdeen), but this recent conversion from Christianity is a damned good club. Mixed crowd, oldies don't feel out of place. No jeans w/ends. Every night at press-time, but check 0224 211611.

B3 **THE HOOCHI COOCHI CLUB:** Windmill Brae. Owned by European Leisure, a club (at time of writing) mainly for young ravers. Thu-Sun 9pm-2am.

C3 **THE PELICAN at the METRO HOTEL:** Market St. A black beatbox in the basement with good indie attitude and live bands. Often notable names. Thu-Sun, live music depending on what's doing the rounds but esp Sun.

A3 **MR G'S:** Chapel St. The others above might not care to be in the same paragraph as this middle-of-the-road disco, but this is where you go if you can remember life before Ecstasy or if you're going to the rigs in the morning. Snooker
B3 Room/Lounge Bar. Wed-Sun, 10am-2am. Also . . . **O'HENRYS:** Adelphi Close off Union St. Bit of everything for everybody (incl students in term time). Open 7 days, 9pm-2am.

GAY BARS/CLUBS: see p.244.

THE BEST HOTELS IN AND AROUND DUNDEE

✠ **THE OLD MANSION HOUSE, AUCHTERHOUSE:** 082626 366. 15km NW of centre on B954 to Alyth (take Coupar Angus rd from ring route). A consoling, green distance from town and probably the nicest hotel in the entire area. 'Rambling' is the other word to add to the title to fully describe it. Loads of character in rooms tucked up and down stairs, along corridors. Outdoor pool; grounds with ruins and woods and a trickling burn, tennis; everything really. V reputable restau. **621** / MAP 4 / D3

6RMS JAN-DEC T/T PETS CC KIDS TOS EXP

ANGUS THISTLE HOTEL: 0382 26874. Marketgait. Dead central landmark, high-rise (6 floors) hotel. Not a pile of charm but, curiously, it does have a certain atmosphere – sort of '60s/'70s urban regeneration. Has all facilities expected of decent business hotel; was built before the leisure boom so, as yet, no token sauna etc. **622** / MAP D / B3

53RMS JAN-DEC T/T PETS CC KIDS LOTS

THE QUEENS HOTEL: 0382 22515. Nethergate/Perth Rd. There are a few modern block hotels in Dundee, but to my mind this older edifice v centrally situated (parking ok) is the most congenial. Rather like an old station hotel, grand staircase and a drawing room that looks down Nethergate. Rooms adequate, some with views (over Tesco's) to the Tay. Good, friendly service. **623** / MAP D / B4

47RMS JAN-DEC T/T PETS CC KIDS MED.EX

WOODLANDS, BROUGHTY FERRY: 0382 480033. Not exactly downtown – in fact in a back st of Broughty Ferry, the douce, seasidey suburb where many of the good restaus/pubs are. From B. Ferry main st, take left after 1.5km into Abercromby St, second left into Panmure Terr. V 'done-up' townhouse with much ruching of curtains and moody lighting. Leisure facilities include small pool and tiny gym. Popular with weddings. Dundee-wise, this is a cut above the rest. **624** / MAP 4 / D3

19RMS JAN-DEC T/T PETS CC KIDS MED.EX

THE SHAFTESBURY: 0382 67216. 1 Hyndford St just off Perth Rd (about 3km from city centre). A suburban (jute baron's) mansion converted into a comfortable hotel and rather good restau (Rachel's). All rooms different; loungeable lounge. Decent value. **624a** / MAP D / xA4

12RMS JAN-DEC T/T PETS CC KIDS MED.INX

FORT HOTEL, BROUGHTY FERRY: 0382 737999. 58 Fort St. The 'Ferry' is easily reached by bus/train or Arbroath A92, then A930. About 8km along Tayside and a pleasant, less urban place with good pubs and restaus. This recently modernised rooming-house is in main area, above the Fort Bar. Basic and adequate. **625** / MAP 4 / D3

7RMS JAN-DEC X/T PETS CC KIDS INX

HOTEL BROUGHTY FERRY, BROUGHTY FERRY: 0382 480027. 16 W Queen St. On main rd into the 'Ferry' (see above), another recent conversion with a touch of designerism, muted pink/green colour co-ords. On busy corner, but calm enough inside. Bar/restau. **626** / MAP 4 / D3

11RMS JAN-DEC T/T XPETS CC KIDS MED.INX

SANDFORD COUNTRY-HOUSE HOTEL: 0382 541802. Excellent rural retreat over the water 7km S of Tay Bridge via A92/914. 652A/COUNTRY-HOUSE HOTELS.

HOSTELS: There is no SYH in the area, although in summer months there may be temp accom available off Lochee Rd, 1.5 km N of centre. Info from Tourist Office, 0382 27723. Best bet is Univ Accom, especially:

CHALMERS HALL: 0382 23181 ex 4040. On High St, corner of Castle St above Halfords. V central, right on the High St amongst the shops. Next door is the best shop in town, Braithwaites at 6 Castle St – amazing coffees, teas and honey and also the best bakers, Fisher and Donaldson (1211/BAKERS). There are other halls at the Univ and Art College (23261). Tourist Office has all info 27723. **627** / MAP D / C3

CAMPING AND CARAVANNING: Town park is **RIVERVIEW,** which has great views of the Tay. It's in Monifieth, beyond Broughty Ferry. A92 Arbroath rd, B962 to Monifieth and off High St (the main st) at Union St towards sea. 1km down under railway bridge. 12km centre. 180 pitches on flat grassy site. 0382 532837. Good site also at: **TAYPORT,** across Tay Bridge, 8km SE of centre. 100 pitches on sandy/grassy site nr Tentsmuir (892/WILDLIFE RESERVES), 0382 552334. **628** / MAP 4 / E3

THE BEST PLACES TO EAT AND DRINK IN DUNDEE

628a THE AGACAN: 0382 644227. 113 Perth Rd. Zeki's fabled, atmospheric bistro
MAP D with Turkish eats/wines and beers. Where art is not dead. Say no more.
A4

629 RAFFLES: 0382 26344. 18 Perth Rd. For years, some would say, the 'only' place to
MAP D eat in Dundee. Not big on atmosphere, but always busy. An eclectic menu
B4 neither ambitious nor pretentious, sound on ingredients and with no-frills
presentation. Good value. Small, appropriate wine-list. Daily menu and delicious
bread. Tue-Sun noon-2pm and 6-9pm (Fri/Sat till 10.30pm). Cl Mon. INX

630 L'AUBERGE: 0382 730890. 594 Brook St, Broughty Ferry. In the seaside suburb, this
MAP 4 long-established corner restau is found at the end of the long st which leads from
D3 'town' to the Esplanade. Ray Parkinson, who also runs the café/restau at
Dundee Rep, keeps to fairly simple French cuisine in formal bistro setting.
Menu changes every 3 weeks. Wines fine. Tue-Sat lunch and 7-9pm. INX

631 JAHANGIR: 0382 202022. 1 Session St. In the West Port area behind University, a
MAP D *nouvelle indiane* emporium of low light, muted colours and bewildered fish in a
B4 turbulent illuminated pool. Fastidious service from a legion of costumed flunkies
and Dundee lassies in saris. Food inconsistent, but often good. Not too exp
despite appearances. Lunch and 6pm-midnight (Fri/Sat till 1am). /INX

632 FRANCO'S CANTINA: 0382 533143. 10 Maule St, Monifieth. On main rd into
MAP 4 Monifieth, next suburb along from Broughty Ferry. Approach via A92 Arbroath
E3 rd, then B962. The only decent Italian restau (though see below); a fair way from
town, but good home cooking is served up in Franco's parlour. Small wine-
list/BYOB. Mon-Sat lunch and 6-10pm. MED

633 VISOCCHI'S: 0382 79297. 40 Gray St. Broughty Ferry (also and originally in
MAP 4 Kirriemuir). While they've been making excl ice-cream since the 1930s
D3 (1222/ICE-CREAM), the downtown Ferry branch has branched out. Now it's a
proper Italian café for snacks and home-made pasta as well as the ice-cream
creations. Open every day 10am-9pm. CHP

634 THE RIVERSIDE: 0382 25108. 40 S Tay St. Stylish Chinese restau in West Port. No
MAP D English translation on the neon sign, no advertising, not even Yellow Pages and
B4 nowhere near the river – strange! But designed on clean lines and same approach
to mainly Cantonese cuisine. Seafood. LO 10pm (11 w/ends). Cl Sun. MED

635 THE PARROT CAFE: 0382 24813. 91 Perth Rd. A coffee shop rather than a restau; a
MAP D drop-in kind of place with home baking, cakes, daily specials etc. No smk.
A4 Tue-Fri 9am-6pm; Sat 9am-5pm. Cl Sun/Mon.

635a ROYAL OAK: 0382 29440. 167 Brook St beyond West Port. Undistinguished
MAP D exterior, but inside excellent pubfood. The unusual tapas/Indian mix to Jacob
B2 Chako's menu all works. Bar and dining-room. Lunch and LO 8pm (bar) and
9pm.

636 THE SHIP INN: 0382 79176. On 'front' in Broughty Ferry at 121 Fisher St round
MAP 4 corner from bottom of Fort St which is off Queen St, the main st of B. Ferry.
D3 Pub lounge downstairs, but food for which it is renowned more usually upstairs
at the back or best at the front, in a small dining-room with a picture window
looking out over the Tay estuary. Scottish menu with a fine clootie dumpling.
Lunch and 5.30-9.30pm (Sun 5-9pm). Book Fri/Sat. CHP

637 THE FISHERMAN'S TAVERN: 12 Fort St. Broughty Ferry. Good pub lunches here
MAP 4 too, but notable for real ales: Theakston's, Director's, Bateman's, Maclays. Snug
D3 portside atmosphere. Open till 11pm.

638 PUBS AT THE WEST PORT: THE GLOBE, TALLY HO, MC's, SESSIONS: All are large
MAP D pubs, newish with oldish interiors and a young crowd who, at weekends, roam
B4 between them. In West Port (at end of S Tay St and off Marketgait; behind
University) you can hang out. All have their moments, fashionable beers and
indistinguishable variations. Sessions, across the main st in Session St, has occ
live music. The WEST PORT bar across the way has good vegn food.

639 TAYBRIDGE BAR: 129 Perth Rd. Legendary drinking place. Est 1867: a man's pub,
MAP D tho women do venture in, esp to 'The Walnut Lounge'.
A4

SECTION 4
Particular Places to Eat and Stay throughout Scotland

SUPERLATIVE COUNTRY-HOUSE HOTELS

A selection of houses (both large and small, grand and intimate) in rural settings that have been turned into hotels and which are usually family-run or owner-occupied, with a relaxing away-from-it-all atmosphere.

640 ALTNAHARRIE INN, ULLAPOOL: 085483 230. 2km from town, but other side
MAP 2 of L Broom. They come in a launch to get you at certain times, or by
C2 arrangement; intimacy immediately established with one's fellow travellers. Hotel unique in every sense and now in every guide-book (except the STB directory). The food is to adore, though not to choose (there's a set menu); Gunn Eriksen does it like nobody else. Wester Ross is behind you.

8RMS APR-OCT X/X PETS XCC XKIDS LOTS

641 KINNAIRD HOUSE, DUNKELD: 0796 482440. 12km N Dunkeld (Perth 35km)
MAP 4 via A9 and B898 for Dalguise. In bucolic setting beneath woody ridge of
C3 Tay Valley, a country house which just envelops you with good taste and comfort. There's a teddy bear to take to bed or hang outside your door as a 'do not disturb' sign. Relaxing lounges, elegant dining-rooms, *en tous cas* tennis. Rosettes aplenty already, but John Webber's finely judged cuisine goes from strength to strength.

9RMS JAN-DEC T/T PETS CC KIDS LOTS

642 KNOCKIE LODGE nr FORT AUGUSTUS, LOCH NESS: 0456 486276. 3km down
MAP 2 rd/track from B862, the quiet E bank rd round L Ness (857/SCENIC
D4 ROUTES); 15km Ft Augustus. Rambling mansion on bluff overlooking loch, set amongst farmland with wide open views. Civilised yet relaxed, a fine Highland retreat. Had a small setback with a fire in 1993 but fully open for '94 season. Snooker room. Rooms vary in size, view and price. Vegn and special diets advise; it's a long way to go to eat out and once you're there, you're there.

10RMS MAY-SEPT T/X PETS CC KIDS LOTS

643 TIRORAN HOUSE, MULL: 06815 232. S of island 5km from B8035 Salen to
MAP 1 Fionnphort (the port for Iona) rd. Follow sign for Tiroran, but in any case
B1 get directions when you book (which you must). A sporting lodge in sweeping seaward grounds with a superb dining-room. Gentility somewhat enforced; best not to quiver the upper lip, even if you do see the otters on the shore. Packed lunches *par excellence* for island forays and there's soft-towelled civilisation to return to. Devotees do, often.

9RMS JUN-OCT X/X PETS XCC XKIDS TOS LOTS

644 KILDRUMMY CASTLE HOTEL, nr ALFORD, ABERDEENSHIRE: 09755 71288. 60km
MAP 6 W of Aberdeen via A944, through some fine bucolic scenery and the
D4 green Don valley to this spectacular location with the real aura of the Highlands. Well placed if you're on the 'Castle Trail' (*see p.142/145*), this comfortable chunk of Scottish baronial has the redolent ruins of Kildrummy Castle on the opposite bluff and a gorgeful of gardens between. Some rooms small, but all v Scottish.

16RMS FEB-DEC T/T PETS CC EXP

645 ARDANAISEIG, LOCH AWE: 08663 333. 16km from Taynuilt signed from main
MAP 1 A85 to Oban and 7km down single track from Kilchrenan. In sheltered
C2 landscaped gardens (nice to wander in even if you're not a guest; you can take afternoon tea) on a promontory of the loch – a particularly fine setting. Discreet, comfortable, expensive; a good balance of intimacy and formality. In short, a splendid retreat.

14RMS APR-OCT T/T PETS CC XKIDS TOS LOTS

646 AUCHTERARDER HOUSE, AUCHTERARDER: 0764 663646. Off B8062 Crieff rd
MAP 4 3km from this village more commonly associated with Gleneagles. In
C4 contrast, it is intimate, sumptuous and relaxing. The only activities in evidence are croquet and pitch 'n' putt, but leisure aplenty. Splendid conservatory and some bedrooms are v grand; grand enough for the Reagans (yes, those Reagans) when they paid an unobtrusive visit in 1991 (visitor book generally is a Who's Who). Luxurious but not at all stuffy. Chef David Hunt is excl.

15RMS JAN-DEC T/T PETS CC KIDS TOS LOTS

647 GLENEAGLES, AUCHTERARDER: 0764 62231. On A824 and rather difficult to
MAP 4 miss. There's the golf, there's the shooting school, there's the riding school
C4 and there's this huge hotel whose name is known and marketed around the world. Inside there's an arcade with other 'names' like Harvey Nichols, Mappin & Webb and Champneys. Service and facilities are all you'd expect.

Marvellous sense of space; everything on grand scale. But the name's the game.

✠ **ISLE OF ERISKA, LEDAIG:** 063172 371. **20km N of Oban.** The isle is a real island, essentially the hotel and its grounds joined by a bridge. They call it an island sanctuary and there's no doubt that (if you're in the bracket) you can pick up the racquet (rod, mallet etc) and very easily subside into this world of gracious living. It's a dream world but it's a very pleasant dream. Mind Ps and Qs. 648 MAP 1 B1

✠ **ARDSHEAL HOUSE, KENTALLEN:** 063174 227. **27km S of Fort William.** Interesting house with wooded policies stretching to shores of L Linnhe (2km drive from A828). Oak-panelled reception hall has curious barrel window; other lounges are dark and woody but you dine in the conservatory. Food is local, garden-grown, home-baked; the breakfast eggs are a perfect start. Exemplary wine-list. The single room is a superb bachelor retreat. Ps/Qs. 649 MAP 2 C5

✠ **PHILIPBURN HOUSE, SELKIRK:** 0750 20747. Informal and easy-going with lots to do and lots for kids. Outdoor pool with some rooms round it. Meals merge into one another and are invariably very good. Too many plus factors to mention, but see 483/BORDERS BEST HOTELS; 655/HOTELS THAT WELCOME KIDS. 650 MAP 8 C3

✠ **NIVINGSTON HOUSE nr KINROSS:** 05775 216. **7km Kinross and 5km M90 jnct 5.** Elegant mansion/extended farmhouse in lee of Cleish Hills which are popular with Fife and Edinburgh walkers. Loch Glow in these hills has a melancholy air but the hotel is quite the opposite; welcoming and comfortable. Looks out over a croquet lawn to rural Fife; Dollar Glen is nearby (1053/GLENS). Good restau with separate vegetarian menu and fine wine-list. 651 MAP 4 C4

✠ **ARISAIG HOUSE, ARISAIG:** 06875 622. On A830 the road to the Isles from Ft William to Mallaig. 2km before Arisaig and 18km from Mallaig in stunning countryside and on one of Scotland's most romantic coasts. One of Bonnie Prince Charlie's caves is at the bottom of the garden and this is the bay where he landed and left. Genuine courtesy, comfort and cosseting, and delicious food and exquisite afternoon tea. The gardens are a joy. Rum and Eigg are a v civilised excursion away. 652 MAP 2 C4

SANDFORD HILL, nr WORMIT (nr DUNDEE and ST ANDREWS): 0382 541802. About 7km S of Tay Bridge via A92 and A914 then 1km on B946 to Wormit. A very civilised withdrawal from the jams of Dundee or the bunkers of St Andrews. An inaustere mansion with unusual internal layout and mullioned windows looking out to well-kept gardens. Patio, wild but romantic tennis court, a 'jazz-gallery' and friendly pub-lunches. 652a MAP 5 D2

✠ **FLODIGARRY COUNTRY HOUSE, SKYE:** 047052 203. Near Staffin, 32km N of Portree. Although this is indeed a castle in a superb setting, commanding dreamy views of Staffin Bay and with the 'Quirang' behind, it is not a grand manor in the grand manner, and is remarkably good value. Rooms (esp at front) are spacious, the menu is imaginative, service is informal and the bar is a local for all kinds of folk. Breakfast when you like. Then walk. 653 MAP 2 B3

CORROUR HOUSE, AVIEMORE: 0479 810220. Small country house 3km from the concrete moor of Aviemore, handy for the ski slopes. Also close to Rothiemurchus and Glenmore Forests. (1078/SERIOUS WALKS). Without airs but not without graces, this family-run hotel is extremely good value and I should really keep it to myself. 654 MAP 2 D4

HOTELS THAT WELCOME KIDS

655 PHILIPBURN HOUSE, SELKIRK: 0750 20747. On the edge of Selkirk and in the
MAP 8 middle of the Borders, an excellent country-house hotel that has
C3 everything that adults, romantic couples, even singles could want (e.g. great food
and wine, walks, books, privacy) but which understands the *en famille*
requirement perfectly. 11 (out of 16) family rooms (some out of the main house,
round the outdoor pool). Grounds with play areas, trampoline, tree houses. Kids'
high tea at 5.30pm with wider than usual choice. (650/COUNTRY-HOUSE HOTELS.)

16RMS   JAN-DEC   T/T   PETS   CC   KIDS   TOS   EXP

656 BAILE-NA CILLE, TIMSGARRY, UIG, HARRIS: 085175 242. 58km W of Stornoway,
MAP 2 a long way to go perhaps, and although this isolation might be more usually
B2 sought by adults, the beach here is one that kids will remember all their lives –
wide, safe, untouched. Kids eat earlier and they will be tired. General air of
anything goes (except smoking). And it feels non-polluted.

12RMS   APR-OCT   X/X   PETS   CC   KIDS   MED.INX

657 CRIEFF HYDRO, CRIEFF: 0764 655555. When they claim this is Scotland's
MAP 4 favourite family hotel, they may not be far wrong. Approach via High St,
B4 turning off at Drummond Arms Hotel uphill then follow signs. Vast Victorian
pile with activities for everybody from bowlers to babies, and all v couthie and
Scottish. Still run by the Leckies after all these yrs, there's now a table licence
but still no bar. Winter Gardens café/lounge is simply fabulous. Great tennis
courts, ok pool (till 8.30pm). Tiny cinema showing only smut-free movies
(Thu/Sun after dinner); nature talks, donkey rides. You could stay for weeks,
some folk do stay for years. Beyond are the Trossachs.

192RMS   JAN-DEC   T/T   PETS   CC   KIDS   MED.EX

658 DRIMSYNIE: 03013 247. Lochgoilhead, Argyll. A hotel/chalet/caravan/leisure
MAP 1 complex – a holiday village, in fact, on the loch and on the rd to Carrick Castle.
C2 Every activity you could poss want (pool, ponies, golf and boating) to divert
attention from the scenery. Chalets best for larger families – then you don't have
to eat in the restau. The delights of the Sheep and Wool Centre may not detain
you long.

8RMS+CHALS   JAN-DEC   X/X   PETS   CC   KIDS   MED.INX

658a PEEBLES HYDRO, PEEBLES: 0721 720602. Innerleithen Rd. Huge hotel from the days
MAP 8 of hydrotherapy when people used go on health cures – things haven't changed
B2 much, and nor has this hotel. Grounds, corridors and floors of rooms where
kids can run around. Water fun downstairs in small pool. Entertainment and
baby-sitting services. Very trad and refreshingly untrendy. Rooms vary.

137RMS   JAN-DEC   T/T   PETS   CC   KIDS   TOS   MED.INX/EXP

659 STONEFIELD CASTLE HOTEL, TARBERT: 0880 820836. Outside Tarbert on A83 on
MAP 1 slopes of Loch Fyne with wonderful views. A real castle with (for older kids) 60-
B3 acres of woody grounds to explore and a great open-air pool. 462/HOTELS:
STRATHCLYDE NORTH.

660 ISLES OF GLENCOE HOTEL, BALLACHULISH: 08552 603. On edge of town and other
MAP 2 side of main rd, the A82 from Ft William to Crianlarich, a brand new hotel and
C5 leisure centre that's fine for kids in an area which is mainly fine for adults.
Glencoe and 2 ski areas nearby. It's somewhere to relax after the scenery.

39RMS   JAN-DEC   T/T   PETS   CC   KIDS   MED.INX

661 COYLUMBRIDGE HOTEL nr AVIEMORE: 0479 810661. 8km from Aviemore Centre on
MAP 2 B970 rd to ski slopes and nearest hotel to them. The best of the oft-criticised
D4 Aviemore hotels and the most facilities. 2 pools of decent size, sauna etc. Kids'
play park, video games, some organised kids' activities. Plenty to do in summer
as well as winter season. 1058/FOREST WALKS. Aviemore itself probably better
for kids than for adults who feel more trapped in the timewarp.

175(MOSTLY FAMILY)RMS   JAN-DEC   T/T   PETS   CC   KIDS   MED.EX

662 WATERSIDE INN, PETERHEAD: 0779 71121. Edge of town on A952 to Fraserburgh.
MAP 3 Modern hotel with pool etc and some activities for kids. Aden Country Park
E2 nearby (751/PLACES TO TAKE KIDS). Kids' menu and family rooms. Sometimes
special family weekends.

110(30 FAMILY)RMS   JAN-DEC   T/T   PETS   CC   KIDS   TOS   MED.EX

GLENCRIPESDALE HOUSE, L SUNART: 096785 263. In contrast to the leisuramas
above, this is where to get them away from it all (688/REMOTE HOTELS).

THE BEST HOSTELS

For Hostels in Edinburgh, see p.16; for Glasgow, see p. 48. SYHA Info: 0786 451181

† † † **CARBISDALE CASTLE, CULRAIN nr BONAR BRIDGE:** 054982 232. The 663 flagship hostel of the SYH, an Edwardian Castle in terraced grounds MAP 2 o/looking the flood plain of a river on the edge of the Highlands. Once the home D2 of the exiled King of Norway, it still contains original works of art (though nothing of great value, the sculptures are elegant). The library, ballroom, lounges are all in use and it's only a few quid a night. Shared dorms as usual but no chores. Kitchens and café. Bike hire in summer. Station (from Inverness) 1km. Buses: Inverness/ Thurso/Lairg. 80km from Inverness, 330km from Edinburgh. 226 beds.

THE BORDERS: There are some ideal *wee* hostels in this hillwalking tract of 664 Scotland (where it all began) and one major one: MAP 8

† **MELROSE:** 089682 2521. Grade 1, 90 beds, v popular. Well-appointed mansion C3 looking across to the Abbey; student hall standard.

† **BROADMEADOWS:** 075076 262. 8km from Selkirk off A7, the first hostel in C3 Scotland (1931) is a cosy howff with a stove and a view.

† **SNOOT:** 0450 88259. 10km S of Hawick, Snoot is cute; a country church by the C4 Borthwick Water converted into bunkrooms. Pastoral.
The 3 hostels above are all within an easy day's walk of one another.

ABBEY ST BATHANS: 03615:217. A farm cottage in an attractive village; a C4 refuge on the Southern Upland Way. Close to the river and the kirk.

† **INVERNESS STUDENT HOSTEL:** 0463 236556. Independent hostel opp the SYH at 665 8 Culduthel Rd, uphill from town centre (some dorms have views). Run by MAP 2 same folk who have the great Edinburgh one (22/EDIN HOSTELS), with similar D3 laid-back atmos and camaraderie.

† **STIRLING:** 0786 473442. Recent, superb conversion. Great part of town, close to 666 Castle, adj ancient graveyard and with fine views from some rooms. One of MAP 6 the new hotel-like hostels with student hall standard and facilities. Café (open 8- D4 8.30am and 6-6.30pm) or self-catering. Access till 2am.

ROWARDENNAN, LOCH LOMOND: 036087 259. The hostel at the end of the rd up the 667 E (less touristy) side of L Lomond from Balmaha and Drymen. Large, well MAP 6 managed and modernised and on a waterside site. Wind-surfing facilities. On W A3 High Way and obvious base for climbing Ben Lomond (1083/MUNROS). Good all-round activity centre.

TOBERMORY, MULL: 0688 2481. Looks out to Tobermory Bay. Central but simple 668 island hostel (grade 3), the only hassle, as usual, being that it's closed during the MAP 1 day. Members' kitchen. Near ferry to Ardnamurchan, but main Oban ferry is B1 35km away (791/COASTAL VILLAGES).

GLENCOE: 08552 219. Deep in the glen itself, 3km off A82/ 4km by back rd from 669 Glencoe village and 33km from Ft William. Modern timber house o/looking MAP 2 river; esp handy for climbers and walkers. Clachaig pub, 2km for good food and C5 crack. Also 848/SCENIC ROUTES; 1029/SPOOKY PLACES; 1004/BATTLEGROUNDS; 704/PUBS; 1129/SKIING; 1075/WALKS.

RATAGAN: 059981 243. 29km from Kyle of Lochalsh, 3km Shiel Br (on A87) A 670 much-loved Highland hostel on the shore of Loch Duich and well situated for MAP 2 walking and exploring some of Scotland's most celebrated scenery e.g. 5 Sisters C4 of Kintail (1077/SERIOUS WALKS), Glenelg (849/SCENIC ROUTES; 951/PREHISTORIC SITES), Falls of Glomach (823/FALLS). From Glenelg there's the short and dramatic crossing to Skye (continuous, summer only), quite the best way to go.

INDEPENDENT HOSTELS IN SKYE: DUN FLODIGARRY, nr STAFFIN: 047052 212. In far 671 N 32km from Portree beside Flodigarry Country-House Hotel, whose pub is MAP 2 one of the best on the island and has gr ceilidhs (1339/CEILIDHS), and amidst big B3/C3 scenery. O/looks sea. Bunkrms for 2-6 (holds 66) and gr refectory. AYR.

SKYE BACKPACKERS GUEST HOUSE, KYLEAKIN: 0599 4510. Convenient GH with mainly 4-bunk rooms and smallish gantry/lounge nr ferry/bridge for last/first stop. AYR.

GLEN FESHIE nr AVIEMORE: 05404 323. Privately run hostel in farmhouse by 672 roadside in Glen Feshie, signed Achlean from Feshiebridge on B970. Walkers' MAP 2 refuge and genuine, friendly atmosphere. Store sells basics; free porridge. Good D4 base for Cairngorm walking etc (1078/WALKS).

Glen Affric (671)

THE BEST ROADSIDE AND COUNTRYSIDE INNS

In the first edition this page was THE BEST CAMPING AND CARAVAN SITES. *It had to go: while researching and updating this book, I've spent more time behind caravans than I can bear to think about. I know we should be patient, but you get to the point where you just want them banned from the roads altogether (or restricted to moving between say, 4 and 7am). Why do they never pull over? So I can't in all honesty recommend anywhere for them to go except perhaps off the end of that great pier at Tighnabruaich. Consequently, this page now (hopefully) satisfies another need. All these inns are friendly, distinctive and inexpensive (good inexpensive hotels in Scotland are hard to find – I know). You will need a car but leave that bloody caravan in the drive!*

673 PREMNAY HOTEL, AUCHLEVEN, NR INSCH, ABERDEENSHIRE: 0464 20380. 4km S
MAP 1 of Insch, 40km NW of Aberdeen via main A96. At quiet crossroads in
B1 deepest Aberdeenshire, where quietly flows the Don etc, a log fire, a decent
dining-room, a welcome from the storm. More than a dream of Italy in the
menu, the OTT decor and, indeed, the proprietor; this place should be in more
guide-books.　　　　　　　　　　5RMS JAN-DEC T/T PETS CC KIDS MED.INX

674 CLUANIE INN, GLENMORISTON: 0320 40238. On main rd to Skye 15km before
MAP 6 Shiel Bridge, a traditional inn – and they do mean traditional: walkers and
B4 travellers have been coming here for aeons. Recent refurb to unusually good
standard (well, for a climbers' pub). The Kintail Ridge and the 5 Sisters await
you in the morning, but the porridge is good.
　　　　　　　　　　13RMS JAN-DEC T/X PETS CC KIDS MED.EX

GLENMORISTON ARMS HOTEL, INVERMORISTON, LOCH NESS: 0320 51206. On main 675
A82 betw Inverness (45km) and Ft Augustus (10km) at the Glen Moriston MAP 2
corner, and quite the best corner of this famous lochside to explore. Busy local C4
bar, fisherman's tales and window-boxes on your window-sill. Stop here and
you're in the calendar (June would be nice). 8RMS JAN-DEC T/T PETS CC KIDS INX

THE APPLECROSS HOTEL, APPLECROSS: 05204 262. The 'faraway' inn mentioned in 676
850/SCENIC ROUTES at the end of rd from Tornapress (W of Strathcarron betw MAP 1
Kyle of Lochalsh and Gairloch, but way out west), the legendary Pass of the C2
Cattle. Classic Highland inn on water, views to Skye over Raasay (all rooms
have seaviews). Peat fire, lively local, everything home made, and v good, fresh
seafood. 5RMS JAN-DEC X/X PETS CC KIDS CHP

KILDRUMMY INN, KILDRUMMY, nr BALLATER: 09755 71227. 30km N of Ballater via 677
A97 off main A93 Deeside Rd. Nr Kildrummy Castle and Kildrummy Castle MAP 2
Hotel and gardens. Roadside inn with nice walks around. Basic but basically B3
fine; and a bit Scottish. 5RMS JAN-DEC X/X PETS CC KIDS CHP

GLENISLA HOTEL, KIRKTON OF GLENISLA: 057582 223. 20km NW of Kirriemuir via 678
B951 at head of Glenisla, one of the God's-own Angus Glens (818/GLENS). MAP 2
Nothing much here except superb walking, air, scenery, quiet . . . and this C4
friendly, well-appointed inn to come home to. Pub meals; rather nice dining-
room. 6RMS JAN-DEC X/X PETS CC KIDS INX

GLENELG INN, GLENELG: 059982 273. At the end of that great rd over the hill from 679
Shiel Bridge on the A87 (849/SCENIC ROUTES) . . . well, not quite the end because MAP 4
you can drive further round to ethereal L Hourn, but this halt is a hostelry of B2
fame and infamy. Rms in annex are basic, but you probably won't be hanging
about in them. Decent food, good drinking, real people. From Glenelg, take the
best route to Skye (see p.223). 10RMS APR-OCT X/X PETS CC KIDS MED.INX

TOMDOUN HOTEL, nr INVERGARRY: 08092 218. 20km from Invergarry, 12km off the 680
A87 to Kyle of Lochalsh. A 19th-century coaching inn that replaced a much MAP 2
older one; off the beaten track but perfect (and we do mean perfect) for fishing, D4
walking (L Quoich and Knoydart have been waiting a long time for you) and
naturalising. Superb views over Glengarry and Bonnie Prince Charlie's country. 10RMS MAR-OCT X/X PETS CC KIDS CHP

ST MICHAEL'S INN, nr ST ANDREWS: 0334 839220. On A919 towards Dundee, 10km 681
from St Andrews. At cross-roads, a 200-year-old inn, v English, v fully MAP 3
functioning. Plenty golf and galivanting within reach. Well appointed. A2
7RMS JAN-DEC X/T PETS CC KIDS INX

TRAQUAIR ARMS, INNERLEITHEN: 0896 830229. 100m from the A72 Gala-Peebles rd 682
towards Traquair, a popular village and country inn that caters for all kinds of MAP 7
folk (and, at w/ends esp, large numbers of them). Notable for bar-meals, real ale B1
and family facilities. Rooms vary. 10RMS JAN-DEC T/T PETS CC KIDS INX

THE KAMES HOTEL, TIGHNABRUAICH: 0700 811354. An (end of the) roadside pub 683
that's mainly notable as a seaside inn, with only a grassy terrace betw the porch MAP 2
and the shore. A yachty haven with many bobbing in the bay, their crews ashore D4
for water and stronger stuff. Good pub grub and excl whisky selection.
10RMS JAN-DEC X/T PETS CC KIDS MED.INX

BRIDGE OF CALLY HOTEL, BRIDGE OF CALLY: 0250 886231. Exemplary roadside pub 683a
on a bend of the rd betw Blairgowrie and Glenshee/Braemar (the ski zone and MAP 4
Royal Deeside). Cosy and inexpensive betw gentle Perthshire and the wilder C3
Grampians. 9RMS DEC-OCT X/T PETS CC KIDS INX

CLACHAIG INN, GLENCOE: 08552 252. Basic accom but you will sleep well, esp after 683b
walking/climbing/drinking which is what most people are doing here. Great MAP 2
atmosphere both inside and out. 19RMS JAN-DEC X/X XPETS XCC KIDS CHP C5

SOME HIGHLAND AND ISLAND PLACES TO CAMP

KINTRA, ISLAY: 0496 2051. 8km from Pt Ellen, turning left at Maltings, then rt after 684
2km, following signs. Restau and bar at end of rd with long beach one way, wild MAP 1
coastal walk the other. Camping (room for few caravans only) on the grassy A3
strand looking out to sea; not a formal site but facilities avail. Also bunkhouse.

LOCHAILORT: A 12km stretch S from Lochailort on the A861, along the southern 685
shore of the sealoch itself. A flat, rocky and grassy foreshore with a splendid MAP 2
seascape and backed by brooding mountains. Nearby is Loch nan Uamh where C4
Bonnie Prince Charlie landed (1016/MARY, CHARLIE AND BOB). Once past the

salmon farm laboratories, you're in calendar scenery; the Glenuig Inn at the
southern end is a fine pub to repair to. No facilities except the sea.   FREE

686 **MULL:** Best official campsite is at Fishnish, nr ferry. In woodland with facilities
MAP 1 and a tea-shop in summer. 2 less organised sites particularly for camping are at
B1 Calgary Beach 10km from Dervaig, where there are toilets, and S of Kilchronan
on the gentle shore of Loch Na Keal where there is nothing but the sky and the
sea. Ben More's in the background (1085/MUNROS).   FREE

687 **GLEN ETIVE nr BALLACHULISH and GLENCOE:** One of Scotland's great unofficial
MAP 2 camp-grounds. Along the road/riverside in a classic glen (817/GLENS) guarded
C5 where it joins the pass into Glencoe by the awesome Buachaille Etive Mor and
with steep slopes on either side. Along the narrow bottom there are innumerable
grassy terraces and small meadows on which climbers and walkers have camped
for generations. The famous Kingshouse Pub is 2km from the foot of the glen
for sustenance, malt whisky and comparing midge bites.   FREE

GREAT HOTELS IN REMOTE PLACES

688 **GLENCRIPESDALE HOUSE, LOCH SUNART:** 096785 263. This civilised and
MAP 2 modernised 18th-century farmhouse on the S bank of L Sunart, is a long
C4 way from anywhere; Strontian the nearest village. Down a 12km forestry track
you don't go anywhere from here except on foot (or out in Bill's boat).
Beachcombing, hiking, fishing, reading and delicious eating are about all there is
to do (plus windsurfing for the energetic). Deer graze the lawn and there are
otters out there. Tariff incl all meals. The Hemmings collect you from Ft
William if you come by train. Quiet nights in Ardnamurchan don't come quieter
or more cosy than this. Despite lack of consumer stimulants, older kids might
find much to amuse them.   4RMS MAR-OCT X/X PETS XCC KIDS MED.EX

689 **KINLOCH CASTLE, ISLE OF RUM:** 0687 2037. Rum is wild and remote though not
MAP 2 that far from the mainland and full of outdoor possibilities (1350/MAGIC
B4 ISLANDS). This, the only hotel, is experience in itself. Two-tier accommodation,
the merely lavish and the basic bunk. Ferries not exactly convenient.
1360/ISLAND HOTELS.

690 **COZAC LODGE, nr CANNICH nr DRUMNADROCHIT:** 04565 263. Leaving L Ness at
MAP 2 Drumnadrochit up Glen Urquhart to Cannich (20km), then follow R Cannich
D3 to head of glen (12km) where it's blocked by the mighty Mullerdoch Dam. This
Edwardian shooting-lodge lies below the dam surrounded by hills. Only herds
of red deer wander here. Fixed menu but simple good food (advise vegn and
special diets). An inexpensive get-away-from-it-all.
7RMS JAN-DEC T/T PETS CC KIDS MED.INX

691 **CAPE WRATH HOTEL nr DURNESS:** 097181 274. 3km S Durness just off A838 on rd
MAP 2 to Cape Wrath Ferry (1068/COASTAL WALKS) which takes you to Britain's
D1 farthest flung corner and the Cliffs of Clo Mor. Hotel is cosy and congenial, esp
if you enjoy the company of fishermen. Fishing on 3 rivers including the
celebrated Dionard. Durness Golf Course is nearby (1125/GOLF) and there's
some of Britain's most spectacular and undisturbed coastline to wander.
17RMS APR-OCT X/T PETS CC KIDS MED.INX

692 **ETTRICKSHAWS, ETTRICKBRIDGE nr SELKIRK:** 0750 52229. Beyond village on B7009
MAP 8 and overlooking Ettrick water, a Victorian mansion (pebbledashed outside,
B3 somewhat eccentrically furnished in), which feels remoter than it is, being only
an hour's drive from Edinburgh. Deer wander into the garden from the wild
hills. Good fishing. No frills, but books and games and very decent food.
6RMS FEB-NOV T/T PETS CC KIDS MED.EX

692a **THE PIER HOUSE, INVERIE, KNOYDART:** 0687 2347. This is a place I haven't been, but
MAP 2 will do, will do. On the pier with wild Knapdale behind you, you can arrive
C4 only on foot from Kinlochhourn (25km) or on Bruce Watt's boat from Mallaig
(Mon, Wed, Fri). The Marriotts' GH seems v civilised despite its isolation, with
a tearoom, mt bikes for hire and fish/shellfish that couldn't be fresher if it tried.
Inverie even has a pub! If you're reading this on a tube, get out, phone them, get
there by the weekend!   4RMS JAN-DEC X/X PETS XCC KIDS CHP

KNOCKINAAM LODGE nr PORTPATRICK: 077681 471 (473/SOUTH-WEST BEST HOTELS).

CORSEMALZIE HOUSE nr WIGTOWN: 098886 254 (479/SOUTH-WEST BEST HOTELS).

REAL RETREATS

✝ ✝ **SAMYE LING, ESKDALEMUIR nr LOCKERBIE/DUMFRIES:** 03873 73232. Bus or 693
train to Lockerbie/Carlisle then bus to Boreland (halfway, walk 11km) MAP 9
or taxi (05762 2479). Lifts sometimes arranged. 2km from village, community E2
consists of an extraordinary and inspiring temple, main house (with some
accom), a dorm block, a café (open w/ends for visitors) and shop. On the hill
and out of bounds the area where people really retreat. Much of Samye Ling, a
world centre for Tibetan Buddhism, is still under construction, but they offer
daily stays (£12-16) and many w/ends and much longer courses in all aspects of
Buddhism, meditation, tai chi, Alexander Technique etc, even hillwalking. Daily
timetable, from prayers at 6am and work period. Breakfast/lunch and soup etc
for supper at 6pm; all vegn. Busy, thriving commune atmosphere; some space
cases and holier-than-thous, but rewarding and unique.

PLUSCARDEN betw FORRES and ELGIN: 034389 257. Signed from main A96 (11km 694
from Elgin) in a sheltered glen S facing with a background of wooded hillside, MAP 3
this is the only medieval monastry in the UK still inhabited by monks. It's a B2
deeply calming place. The (Benedictine) community keep walled gardens and
bees. There are 7 services a day in the glorious chapel (971/ABBEYS) which
visitors can attend. Retreat for men (15 places) and women (separate and
self/catering) with no time limit and no obligatory charge. Men eat with monks
(mainly vegn). Restoration and building work always in progress (of the Abbey
and of the spirit).

FINDHORN COMMUNITY, FINDHORN nr FORRES: 0309 690311. The world-famous 695
spiritual community (now a foundation) begun by Peter Caddy and Dorothy MAP 3
Maclean in 1962, a village of mainly caravans and wooden houses on the way A2
into Findhorn on the B9011. Open as an ordinary caravan park (681/CAMPING),
visitors can join the community as 'short-term guests' eating and working on-
site but probably staying at recomm B&Bs. Also full programme of courses and
residential workshops in spiritual growth/dance/healing etc. Accom mainly at
Cluny Hill College in Forres. Many other aspects and facilities available in this
cosmopolitan and organised New Age township.

**COLLEGE OF THE HOLY SPIRIT, adj CATHEDRAL OF THE ISLES, MILLPORT on the 696
island of CUMBRAE:** 0475 530353. Continuous ferry service from Largs (hourly in MAP 1
winter), then 6km bus journey to Millport. Off main st through gate in the wall, C3
into grounds of the Cathedral (983/CHURCHES) and another more peaceful
world. A retreat for the Episcopal Church since 1884, there are 25 simple but
comfortable rms in the college adj the church with B&B or full board (£14-24).
No set schedule but Matins/Eucharist/Evensong each day and occ concerts in
summer. Fine library. Bike hire. Phone 'the Provost'.

HOLY MANNA RETREAT, LARGS: 0475 687220. A small Benedictine convent and 697
retreat set rather incongruously on 'the front' in this busy seaside town. Small MAP 1
public chapel and 15 rms for holiday and respite. V basic accom in modern C3
building; views over to Cumbrae. Sitting-room and dining-room (lunch after
mass and supper at 6.30pm) and hagiography library. 8 nuns in residence, priests
come for retreat. No courses or schedule. Board around £15.

CARBERRY TOWERS, MUSSELBURGH nr EDINBURGH: 031 665 3135. Fine old house in 698
extensive well-kept grounds, converted into retreat and conference centre for MAP 7
Church of Scotland. Most retreat accom in new block 50m away; student hall C1
standard. No schedule but counselling from wardens possible. Cont courses for
church workers/group w/ends which visitors may sometimes join. Not a quiet
retreat but inexp for a break; a country-house ho(s)tel in a 'caring' atmos.

NUNRAW ABBEY, GARVALD nr HADDINGTON: 0620 83228. Cistercian community in 699
1300 acres of parkland and farmed E Lothian countryside near the MAP 7
Lammermuirs. Visitors stay in the 'guest house', a 15th-century manor 1km D1
walk from the monastery, a modern complex built in trad Cistercian pattern
around a cloister. Chapel open to visitors; 7 services daily, Vigils – Compline.
Facilities in house basic; meals are taken together (not vegn). Doors closed 8pm.
Mostly shared accom, some singles. Max stay 7days. Payment by donation.

SALISBURY CENTRE, EDINBURGH: 031 667 5438. 2 Salisbury Rd. A 'community and 700
creative resource centre' in a Georgian house in the South Side of the city. Est in MAP A
1973 by Dr Winifred Rushforth, a psychotherapist and dream specialist. Not a xE4
retreat in the isolated-away sense, although 'weekend retreats' are possible.
Mainly weekly and w/end classes/workshops in meditation, healing, aroma-
therapy, massage, yoga, shiatzu, tai chi and pottery. Some v basic accom.

UNIQUE PUBS

Pubs in Edinburgh, Glasgow, Aberdeen, Dundee are listed in their own sections.

701 DROVER'S INN, INVERARNAN: A famously Scottish drinking den/hotel on
MAP 6 the edge of the Highlands just N of Ardlui at the head of Loch Lomond
A2 and 12km S of Crianlarich on the A82. Smoky, low-ceilinged rooms, open
ranges, whisky in the jar, stuffed animals in the hall and kilted barmen; this is
nevertheless the antithesis of the contrived Scottish tourist pub. Very Gaelic and
possibly not where you'd take your Auntie Ada for a babycham.

702 CLUANIE INN: 0320 40257. On A87 at head of L Cluanie 15km before Shiel
MAP 2 Bridge on the long rd to Kyle of Lochalsh. A traditional wayside inn with
C4 good pub food, a restau and MED.INX fairly tasteful accom. Perfect base for
climbing/ walking (esp The Five Sisters of Kintail, 1077/SERIOUS WALKS). A cosy
refuge.

703 TIGH-AN-TRUISH, CLACHAN, ISLE OF SEIL: 085 23 242. Beside the much
MAP 1 photographed 'bridge over the Atlantic' which links the 'Isle' of Seil with
B2 the 'mainland'. On B884, 8km from B816 and 22km S of Oban. Country pub
with rooms/apartments above (with views of bridge), good home-made food
(nutburgers and hamburgers); lively at night. Early closing Mon-Thur, open all
day Fri-Sun. Music.

704 CLACHAIG INN, GLENCOE: Deep in the glen itself down the rd signed off the
MAP 2 A82, 8km from Glencoe Village. Both the pub with its wood-burning stove
C5 and the lounge are woody and welcoming. Real ale and real climbers and
walkers. Handy for hostel 2km down rd. Decent food and good, cheap accom.

705 TIGH OSDA ARMADAIL, ARMADALE HOTEL, SKYE: (Pron 'Tie osta Ar amadil'.) S of
MAP 2 Skye on Sleat next to Mallaig ferry. A sugar shack (formerly a doctor's surgery)
B4 beside the hotel with a somewhat untended beer garden – pubs don't get much
funkier than this. Music on Sat.

706 PIER HOTEL BAR, SKYE: (aka Harry Dick's). On the harbour front, this
MAP 2 unprepossessing pub is Portree's famous watering hole. At w/ends you hear the
B3 racket from the top of the Harbour Steps.

707 WHEELHOUSE, LOCHINVER: No real ale or fake nostalgia. A fisherman's pub and
MAP 2 pool room with no frills; often loud jukebox, Friday disco, some snacks (but no
C2 fish from over the quay). Outside: the busy fishmarket, the new harbour
development and the night.

708 POLLACHAR INN, S UIST: Southern tip; on the shore looking over to Barra.
MAP 2 Untouched by the late 20th century and not quaintified. It's a long way from
A4 Brighton. Sunsets can last for hours.

709 CASTLEBAY BAR, BARRA: Adj Castlebay Hotel. Unpromising exterior, but inside
MAP 2 the nearest thing you'll get to an Irish bar in exile outside of New York. In
A4 Glasgow this place would be legendary. Eclectic clientele from as far away
as . . . Vatersay.

710 PHOENIX, INVERNESS: 108 Academy St. Trad horseshoe bar, sawdust on the bare
MAP 2 boards, dominoes smacking on the tables; no fake atmos. Always lively. Back
D3 lounge more 1990s. Open Thu/Fri till 12.30am.

711 CAWDOR TAVERN, CAWDOR nr NAIRN: Trad village pub/coaching inn, in estate
MAP 2 village beside the mighty Cawdor Castle. Cosy and woody inside and with patio
D3 for *al fresco* drinking/snacking. Food 7 days in Summer.

711a LOCH INN, FT AUGUSTUS: Busy canalside (Caledonian Canal which joins L Ness
MAP 2 in the distance) pub for locals and visitors. Good grub, LO 9pm. Some live
D4 music.

712 SETTLE INN, STIRLING: St Mary's Wynd off Broad St which leads up to the
MAP 6 Castle. Interesting 18th-century pub (up and downstairs) with great atmos and
D4 good mix of drinkers. Occasional music; not big on food.

713 TIBBY SHIELS INN: Off A708 Moffat-Selkirk rd. Occupies its own particular
MAP 8 place in Scottish culture esp literature (1026/LITERARY PLACES) and in the Border
B3 hills SW of Selkirk where it nestles betw 2 romantic lochs. On S Upland Way.
832/FALLS. Food unremarkable but probably v welcome.

713a THE MURRAY ARMS and THE MASONIC, GATEHOUSE OF FLEET: 2 adj, unrelated
MAP pubs that just fit perfectly into the life of this gr wee town. Murray has OK food
C4 & accom.

GREAT PUBS FOR REAL ALE

THE STATION TAP, TAYNUILT: 20km Oban on A85. A pub and next door a tiny brewery converted from the waiting-rooms of the station where trains still leave for Oban and Glasgow. Sit round the stove drinking the Highland Ale and get caught up in the atmosphere of the place no matter how brief the encounter. 100m, main crossroads. Open till 11pm+. Occasional live music. 714 MAP 1 C1

THE BOW BAR, EDINBURGH: West Bow/Victoria St. A pub which became immediately pre-eminent when it opened with a barrage of fonts and a non-fussy attitude, to serve the more discriminating palate of the 1990s' beer drinker. Edinburgh's Caledonian 70 and 80/- and a pack of well-cared-for pedigrees. And many malts. 162/REAL ALE. 715 MAP A D3

THE CUMBERLAND BAR, EDINBURGH: Cumberland St. At time of going to press, Edinburgh's newest addition in the serious real ale stakes and like the above (opened by the same people having moved on from Victoria St), an instantly popular pub with innumerable ales and decent daily lunch menu. 716 MAP A C1

BOSWELL HOTEL, GLASGOW: Mansionhouse Rd on S Side via Pollokshaws Rd. An outstanding hostelry on many counts but esp for the range and respect given to ales. Reg Belhaven/Caledonian and ever changing guest-list. Busy country club atmos. Food/coffee/kids. 389/GLAS REAL ALE; 263/INEXP HOTELS. 717 MAP B xC4

FERRYHILL HOUSE HOTEL, ABERDEEN: Bon Accord St, 1km from Union St. Large busy hotel lounge with outside seating in summer and fine for the whole family. Several regs, Broughton/OrkneyRaven/Taylor/Theakston and guests. Other main pub in Aberdeen is Prince of Wales in city centre. 611/ABERDEEN PUBS. 718 MAP C B4

FISHERMAN'S TAVERN, DUNDEE: In Broughty Ferry, but not too far to go for great atmosphere and the best collection of ales in the area. In Fort St nr the seafront. Belhaven/Maclays/Theakston and guests. Low-ceilinged and friendly. 637/DUNDEE PUBS. 719 MAP 4 D3

THE PHEASANT, HADDINGTON: On corner where main st divides. They say they've got the best ales in E Lothian. Always 5 on, incl Belhaven (brewed up the road in Dunbar), Tetleys, Youngers and a guest or two. Busy market town atmos; snooker. 720 MAP 7 D1

ROYAL HOTEL, KINGUSSIE: Main St. Busy local with all sorts of folk, juke box, snooker; great lively atmos. Amazing range of malts packed along the shelves and about 8 ales on hand-pump. Makes you wonder who drinks them all in this small town. 721 MAP 2 D4

THE FOUR MARYS, LINLITHGOW: Main St near rd up to Palace. Mentioned in most beer guides. Usually 9 ales on hand-pump with various guests. Notable malt whisky collection and v popular locally for lunches and evening meals (6.30-8.30pm). Open 7 days. 722 MAP 7 B1

MARINE HOTEL, STONEHAVEN: Popular local on the harbour front with seats outside and pool/juke box/bar meals inside. Youngish crowd. 4 or 5 ales incl McEwans 80/-, Taylor's Landlord. Open all day. 723 MAP 3 D4

GREYFRIARS, PERTH: 15 South St nr the river. Snug and friendly (the landlord took me behind the tiny bar packed with fonts and through the trapdoor to the basement to see how he looks after the beers). Burton/Orkney Raven and guests; often unusual choices. 724 MAP 4 C4

CROOK INN, TWEEDSMUIR: On A701 Edin-Moffat rd, 32km S of Peebles. Off the beaten track, but a fine wayside inn and v close to the Broughton Brewery so the Greenmantle is fresh off the back of a lorry. Good place to stop the night. 488/BORDERS BEST HOTELS. 725 MAP 8 A3

PUBS THAT SERVE THE BEST FOOD

Pubs in Edinburgh, Glasgow, Aberdeen and Dundee are listed in their own sections.

726 KILBERRY INN, KILBERRY nr TARBERT: 08803 223. On B8024 from W Loch
MAP 1 Tarbert, the coast rd of Knapdale, 22km Tarbert/32km Lochgilphead. If
B3 it's a detour, it's one that's most certainly worth it. People have been known to
come from Glasgow just for lunch. Unpretentious menu, superbly done. The
pastry of the traditional pies and puds melts in the mouth. You eat in the parlour
of a roadside inn; you'll wish you lived nearby. Home-made jams and chutneys
to take away. Open noon-2pm and 6.30-9pm. Cl Sun.

727 THE WHEATSHEAF, SWINTON betw KELSO and BERWICK: 0890 86257. A
MAP 8 hotel pub in an undistinguished village about halfway betw the 2 towns
D2 (18km) on the B6461. In deepest, flattest Berwickshire, with an
incomprehensible number of Jim Clark boy-racer bends between you and the
best pub grub you've had in ages. Open noon-2pm and 6-9pm. Cl Mon.

728 RIVERSIDE INN, CANONBIE: 03873 71512. 2km from Border off A7 S of
MAP 9 Langholm. Superlative pub food (with restau/accom) in this calendar
E3 pub o/looking meadows of the Esk. The first/last great pub meal in Scotland.
Impeccable. Mon-Sat, lunch and 6-9pm.

728a THE GRANGE INN, nr ST ANDREWS: 0334 72670. 4km from E end of town off
MAP 5 Anstruther rd, a charming rural pub with 3 dining-rooms (one non-smk), a
D2 cosy fire in winter, dreamy views in summer and most excellent food all year
round. LO 9pm.

729 SHIP INN, ELIE: Pub on the bay at Elie, a douce wee toon in the picturesque
MAP 5 East Neuk of Fife (795/COASTAL VILLS). Small bar and room through back,
D3 but food mainly in recently refurbished boathouse next door and bistro above.
Blackboard menu of unpretentious good grub. Belhaven 80/-, Courage
Directors. Patio o/looks shore and gets v busy in summer. Food: lunch and
6-9pm.

730 PITSCOTTIE INN, nr CUPAR: 0334 82244. At a country crossroads in NE Fife, an
MAP 5 immensely popular roadside inn with family favourites like prawn cocktail or
D2 turkey nuggets and a daily changing selection of chef's specials. Lunch 7 days,
supper 6-9pm (9.30 w/ends), high tea on Sta/Sun.

731 WHEATSHEAF INN, SYMINGTON nr AYR: 0563 830307. 2km A77. Cute village (but
MAP 1 don't look round the corner) with this coaching inn opposite church. Folk come
D4 from miles around to eat (book w/ends) honest-to-goodness pub fare. Menu on
boards. Not wild about the wine. LO 10pm.

732 GOBLIN HA' HOTEL, GIFFORD. 0620 81244. Twee village in farming country; one of 2
MAP 7 hotels (506/LOTHIAN: BEST HOTELS). This, the one with the great name, serves a
D2 decent pub lunch and supper (6-9pm; 9.30pm weekends) in lounge and more
basic version in the pub.

733 TORMAUKIN INN, GLENDEVON: 0259 781252. On A823 through wooded Glen to
MAP 4 Auchterarder, 36km E of Stirling, 16km W of M90 at jnct 6/7. Roadside inn with
C4 v pleasant accom (10rms/MED.INX/0259 781252), restau and fine pub meals. A la
carte and daily specials with vegn. Lunch and 6-9.30pm.

734 THE BYRE, BRIG O' TURK: 0877 76292. On A821 from Callander at end of the village
MAP 6 adj the Dundarroch Hotel. Arrols/Burtons and blackboard *table d'hôte* in
B3 country inn in the deepest Trossachs. Lunch and 6-8pm. Cl Tue.

735 KYLESCU HOTEL, KYLESCU: Off A894 the main rd betw Scourie and Lochinver in
MAP 2 Sutherland. A hotel and pub with a great quayside location on L Glencoul where
C2 boats leave for trips to see the highest waterfall in Europe (826/FALLS). A
friendly local with mainly home-made grub, local fish and seafood. Lunch and
6-8.45pm.

735a OLD BRIDGE INN, AVIEMORE: Off Coylumbridge rd at S end of Aviemore as you
MAP 2 come in from A9 or Kincraig. 100m main st but sits in hollow. An old inn like it
D4 says with basic à la carte and more interesting blackboard specials. Kids' menu,
ski-bums welcome. Lunch and 6-8.30pm.

DROVER'S INN, EAST LINTON: 0620 860298. A village off A1, 35km from Edinburgh.
An E Lothian eatery within reach of city. 181/EDIN PUB FOOD.

OLD CLUBHOUSE, GULLANE: 0620 842008 (512/LOTHIANS BEST RESTAUS).

SECTION 5
The Main Attractions

THE GREAT ATTRACTIONS

Amongst the 'top ten visitor attractions' (paid admission) and the 'top ten' (free admission), the following are really worth seeing:

KELVINGROVE ART GALLERY, GLASGOW; THE BURRELL COLLECTION: 415/416/ GLASGOW: MAIN ATTRACTIONS.

THE MUSEUM OF TRANSPORT, GLASGOW; THE GLASGOW BOTANICS: 420/421/ GLASGOW: LESS OBVIOUS ATTRACTIONS.

THE PEOPLE'S PALACE, GLASGOW: 418/GLASGOW: MAIN ATTRACTIONS.

EDINBURGH CASTLE; HOLYROOD PALACE; EDINBURGH ZOO; THE NATIONAL MUSEUM: 198/199/203/201/EDINBURGH: MAIN ATTRACTIONS.

THE EDINBURGH BOTANICS: 206/EDINBURGH: LESS OBVIOUS ATTRACTIONS.

CULZEAN CASTLE; STIRLING CASTLE: 903/904/CASTLES.

ABERDEEN ART GALLERY: 1304/GALLERIES.

SOME OTHER MAJOR ATTRACTIONS ARE:

736 LOCH LOMOND: Approach via Stirling and A811 to Drymen or from Glasgow,
MAP 1 the A82 Dumbarton rd to Balloch. Britain's largest inland waterway and a
D2 traditional playground esp for Glaswegians.

W bank Balloch-Tarbert is most developed: marinas, cruises, ferry to Inchmurrin Island. Luss is tweeville, like a movie set (it's used for the Scottish TV soap, *Take the High Road*) and a good place to buy that souvenir tea-towel. Rd more picturesque beyond Tarbert to Ardlui and see 701/PUBS for the non-tourist/real Scots experience of the Drover's Inn at Inverarnan.

E bank more natural, wooded; good lochside and hill walks (1083/HILLS/ MUNROS). Rd winding but picturesque beyond Balmaha towards Ben Lomond. 667/HOSTELS.

737 THE CUILLINS, SKYE: This hugely impressive mt range in the S of Skye, often
MAP 2 shrouded in cloud or rain, is the romantic heartland of the Islands. The Red
B3 Cuillins are smoother and nearer the Portree-Broadford rd; the Black Cuillins gather behind and are best approached from Glen Brittle (1074/SERIOUS WALKS; 677/CAMPSITES; 829/FALLS). This classic, untameable mountain scenery has attracted walkers, climbers and artists for centuries. It still claims many lives every year. For best views apart from Glen Brittle, see 852/SCENIC ROUTES; 866/CLASSIC VIEWS. Vast range of walks and scrambles.

738 THE DISCOVERY, DUNDEE: The main 'attraction' in Dundee. New central location
MAP D at Discovery Point and state-of-the-art visitor centre. This tall masted ship built
C4 in Dundee for the 1901 Antarctica expedition with Scott and Shackleton lies permanently at anchor. A research vessel built to withstand the ice, using local shipbuilders' long experience from whaling (for whalecraft history, see the Broughty Ferry Museum in the Castle on the Esplanade). Go below decks to see a surprisingly comfortable abode. 'Marvel' at the officers' mess, the penguin in the oven (!), the thickness of the hull. 10am-5pm (till 4pm Nov-Mar), opens 11am on Sun. And don't miss the frigate *Unicorn,* further along in dockland, the oldest British warship afloat. ADM

739 LOCH NESS: Most visits start from Inverness (1385/CENTRES: INVERNESS) at the N
MAP 2 end via the R Ness. Ft Augustus is at the other 56km S. L Ness is part of the
D3 still-navigable Caledonian Canal linking the E and W coast at Ft William; many small boats line the shores of the R Ness and one of the best ways to see the loch is on a cruise from Inverness (Jacobite Cruises 0463 233999 or Scott II 0463 232955) or Drumnadrochit (L Ness Cruises 04562 395). Most tourist traffic uses the main A82 N bank rd converging on Drumnadrochit where the L Ness Monster industry gobbles up your money. If you must, the 'Official' L Ness Monster Exhibition is the one to choose. On the A82 you can't miss Urquhart Castle (932/RUINS); see also Dochfour (1297/GARDEN CENTRES). But the two best things about L Ness are: the south rd (B862) from Ft Augustus back to Inverness (857/SCENIC ROUTES; 837/FALLS); and the detour from Drumnadrochit to Cannich to Glen Affric (20-30km). 814/GLENS; 1052/WALKS; 823/FALLS.

GOOD PLACES TO TAKE KIDS

EDINBURGH ZOO: 334 9171. Corstorphine Rd. 4km W of Princes St. A large and long-established zoo, where the natural world from the Poles to the Plains of Africa is ranged around Corstorphine Hill. Enough huge/exotic/ghastly creatures and friendly, amusing ones to fill an over-stimulated day. The penguins and the seals do their stuff at set times. More familiar creatures hang out at the 'farm'. Café and shop stocked with environmentally ok toys and souvenirs. Open 7 days, 9.30am-6pm (till dusk in winter).
740
MAP A
xA3

KIDS' FESTIVAL, EDINBURGH: Annual event held around last week of May in tented village at Inverleith Park. Dozens of shows from around the world in continuous week-long programme. Adm to site free, then tickets. See local press for details.
741

BUTTERFLY FARM nr DALKEITH and EDINBURGH: 031 663 4932. On A7, signed Eskbank/Galashiels from ring road (1km). Part of vast garden centre complex which includes the Bird of Prey Centre (those long-suffering owls!), these butterfly (and insect) greenhouses – the first are probably still the best – have hatched many imitators. Myriads of butterflies flit noiselessly around you but the more horrid insects hide in their glass cases. A relentless army of ants goes about its business above you on a rope; well, it all makes you wonder. 7 days, mid-Mar – Mid-Jan, 10am-5.30pm.
742
MAP 7
C2

MUSEUM OF CHILDHOOD, EDINBURGH: 42 High St. An Aladdin's cave of toys through and for all ages. Much more fascinating than computer games. 209/LESS OBV ATTRACTS.
743
MAP A
D3

ARGYLL WILDLIFE PARK, INVERARAY: 4km W of town on A83. Another zoo-type place, but with many native animals in more or less their natural habitat. Lots of them just wander and waddle about. Set amongst pinewoods on the braes of L Fyne, there are probably even a few animals (e.g. mink and foxes), trying to get in. Of the many badgers, wildcats, deer and multifarious wildfowl, only one old boar has so far escaped. He swam across the loch and lived in Strachur. Apr-Oct, 9.30am-6pm, 7days. Similar is:
744
MAP 1
C2

THE HIGHLAND WILDLIFE PARK, KINCRAIG: On B9152 between Aviemore and Kingussie. Large drive through 'reserve' with wandering herds of deer, bison etc and pens of other animals, as above.
745
MAP 2
D4

THE TWEEDHOPE SHEEPDOG CENTRE nr TWEEDSMUIR: On A701, 14km N of Moffat/25km S of Biggar and 8km from Tweedsmuir; pretty much in the middle of nowhere though it is beside the main rd. A small farm where the Billinghams train Border Collies. From Apr-Oct there are 3 demonstrations a day (11am/2pm/3pm) of their uncanny ability to control sheep. It's done out in the field by the trickling Tweed with the hills all around. There's a tea-room and the 'smallest sheepdog in the world', in use till the 1930s. But don't even think about buying a puppy.
746
MAP 8
A3

THE RARE BREEDS FARM, OBAN: 4km from town via Argyll Sq, then south (A816), bearing left at church and on past golf course. A weird and wonderful collection of animals in hillside pens and runs, who seem all the more peculiar because they're versions of familiar ones – but are they sheep or dogs or goats or what? Leaving the caging questions aside, it's a funny farm for kids and the creatures seem keen enough for the attention and the far too many crumbs from the tea-room table. Open 7 days in season.
747
MAP 1
B1

SEALIFE CENTRE, OBAN: 16km N on the A828. Another zoo/aquarium attraction with quasi-scientific research cred; part of a national chain (also in St Andrews and soon L Ness). They claim to rescue marine life, esp seal pups, who gaze plaintively at you from their smooth-walled pool, while in the distance the cove and the sea glisten. We sigh and eat our crisps. Multi-level tanks get you eye-to-eye with some of the freakier (albeit common) fish and the silver darlings go round and round in a mesmerising way. This sealife is almost art. Café/shop/adv playground. Open Feb-Nov, 9am- 6pm.
748
MAP 1
C1

KELBURNE COUNTRY CENTRE, LARGS: 2km S of Largs on A78. Riding school, gardens, woodland walks up the Kel Burn and a central visitor/consumer section with shops/exhibits/cafés. Wooden stockade for clambering kids; commando assault course for exhibitionist adults and less doddering dads. 11am-5pm, 10am-6pm in high season.
749
MAP 1
C3

750 **LANDMARK CENTRE, CARRBRIDGE:** A purpose-built tourist centre with AV
MAP 2 displays and a great deal of shopping. Great for kids messing about in the woods
D3 on slides, in a 'maze' etc, in a large adventure playground. The Tower may be
too much for Granny but there are fine forest views. 7days, 10am-6pm.

751 **ADEN, MINTLAW nr PETERHEAD:** (pron A as in 'ark'). Country park just beyond
MAP 3 Mintlaw on A950 16km from Peterhead. Former grounds of mansion with walks
D2 and many organised activities and events. Farm buildings converted into
Heritage Centre (kids free), café etc. Adventure playground, 'working farm'.
AYR.

751a **STORYBOOK GLEN, nr ABERDEEN:** Fibreglass fantasyland in verdent glen 16km S
MAP 3 of Aberdeen via B9077, the south Deeside rd, which is a nice drive. Characters
D4 from every fairytale and nursery story (who made it even without TV) are
dotted around 20-acre park. Their fixed manic stares give them a spooky
resemblance to people you may know, but kids presumably don't find them so
real. Older kids may find it tame – no guns or big technology. Mar-Oct 10-6pm.

751b **AUCHINGARRICH WLDLIFE CENTRE, nr COMRIE:** 4km from main st turning off at
MAP 4 bridge then signed. Recent coralling in picturesque Perthshire Hills that's
B4 especially good fun for kids mainly because of its easy-going atmos. Lots of
baby fluffy things, some of which you can hold. Don't ask what happens to
them when they grow up! Good place to start sex education. AYR 10-dusk.
Coffee shop till 5pm.

EAST KILBRIDE: When you're out of ideas, take them to the mall. Seriously!

DRUMLANRIG CASTLE nr DUMFRIES: (772/COUNTRY PARKS)

THE BEST LEISURE CENTRES

See also SWIMMING POOLS, *p. 182.*

752 **MAGNUM CENTRE, IRVINE:** 0294 78381. From Irvine's throughway system, follow
MAP 1 signs for Harbourside, then Magnum. In an unalluring 'big shed', this
C4 phenomenally successful pleasuredrome provides every conceivable diversion
from the monotony of my namesake outside. From soothing bowls to frenetic
skating, pools, cinema, cafés, courses, you name it . . . Kids will not get bored,
everyone can get exhausted. All day, every day.

753 **PERTH LEISURE POOL:** 0738 30535. Another hugely successful water-based leisure-
MAP 4 land; makes you wonder where everyone went before. Large, shaped pool with
C4 outside section (open even in winter, when it's even more of a novelty); 2 flumes,
'wild water channel', whirlpools etc. 25m 'training' pool for lengths (check
sessions). Outdoor kids' play area. Daily 10am-10pm.

754 **THE TIME CAPSULE, MONKLANDS:** 0236 449572. They say Monklands, but where
MAP 1 you are going is downtown Coatbridge about 15km from Glasgow via M8.
D3 Essentially a leisure (rather than swimming) pool and ice-rink lavishly fitted out
on the prehistoric monster theme. Very *Jurassic Park* and noisy, but that's due to
excitement. Even if you haven't been swimming for years, this is the sort of
place you force the flab into the swimsuit. Cafés and spectator areas. Sports facs
of the clean-up-your-act variety (e.g. squash, sauna, sun, steam, gym). Many
'courses'. 10am-10pm (last adm 7pm).

755 **EAST SANDS LEISURE CENTRE:** 0334 76506. From South St take rd for Crail then
MAP 5 follow signs. About 2km from centre. Recently built 'bright and colourful'
D2 centre o/looking the East Sands, the less celebrated beach of St Andrews. Mainly
a fairly conventional pool with 25m lane area as well as 50m water slide,
toddlers' pool etc. Also 2 squash courts, gym with Pulsestar machines, 'remedial
suite', bar and café. Open daily till 7.30/8.30pm; Sat/Sun till 4.30pm.

756 **BEACH LEISURE CENTRE, ABERDEEN:** 0224 647647. Beach Esplanade across rd from
MAP c beach itself. Multisports facility with bars and cafés. 'Leisure' Pool isn't much
xD2 use for swimming (but Aberdeen has 4 others, 1152/POOLS) but it's fun for kids
with flumes etc. Linx Ice Arena is adj for skating, curling, ice hockey. Multigym
in foyer area has Universal Stations. Sessions vary.

757 **DUNBAR POOL:** 0368 65456. Spanking new, o/looking the old harbour (where folks
MAP 7 used to swim on a summer's day) and Castle ruins. Cool, modern design amidst
E1 the warm red sandstone. Flumes and wave machine that mimics the sea outside;
lengths just poss in between (though it's often v crowded). Daily 10am-8pm.

SECTION 6
Outdoor Places

THE BEST GARDENS

758 THE YOUNGER BOTANIC GARDEN, BENMORE: 12km Dunoon on the A815
MAP 1 to Strachur. An 'outstation' of the Royal Botanics in Edinburgh, gifted to
C3 the nation by Harry Younger in 1928 but the first plantations dating from 1820.
Walks clearly marked through formal gardens, woody grounds and the 'pinetum'
where the air is often so sweet and spicy it can seem like the very elixir of life.
Redwood avenue, terraced hillsides, views; a garden of different moods and fine
proportions. Café. Apr-Oct 10-6pm.
ADM

759 CRARAE, INVERARAY: 16km SE on A83 to Lochgilphead. The famous
MAP 1 gardens on the wooded banks of Loch Fyne were landscaped long ago
C2 around the gushing glen, and now seem as vast and lush as Borneo. 3 routes are
marked (easiest takes 45mins). Riotous rhodies in May, gigantic hogweed in
August and arbour after arbour in every season. Open all year: summer 9am-6pm,
winter daylight hours.
ADM

760 INVEREWE, POOLEWE: on A832, 80km S of Ullapool. The world-famous
MAP 2 gardens on a promontory of L Ewe. Osgood Mackenzie's concept in 1883
C3 (though the garden was first started in 1862) was a good one, and trillions of
visitors would attest to the abiding success of his life's work (and the ameliorating
effect of the Gulf Stream). The 'wild' garden became the model for many others.
Large area to amble but not much chance of quiet contemplation. Planned
'improvements' will probably do away with their classic cafeteria. No hogweed in
these immaculate acres. Open all year.
ADM

761 CRATHES nr BANCHORY, ROYAL DEESIDE: 25km W of Aberdeen and just
MAP 3 off A93. One of the most interesting tower houses (946/COUNTRY
D4 HOUSES) surrounded by exceptional topiary and walled gardens of inspired design
and tranquil atmosphere. Keen gardeners will be in their scented heaven. The
Golden Garden is a recent addition that works particularly well and there's a wild
garden beyond the old wall that many people miss. All in all, a v *House and
Gardens* experience. Grounds open all yr, 9.30am-sunset.
NTS ADM

762 DRUMMOND CASTLE GARDENS, MUTHILL nr CRIEFF: Signed from A822
MAP 4 2km from Muthill and then up a long avenue, the most exquisite formal
B4 gardens viewed first from the terrace by the house. A boxwood parterre of a vast
St Andrews Cross in yellow and red (esp antirrhinums and roses), the
Drummond colours, with extraordinary sundial centrepiece; 5 gardeners keep
every leaf in place. Best seen in July/Aug, but impressive at any time. Open
7days May-Sept 2-5pm. Grounds only; the house is not open to public.
ADM

763 ACHAMORE GARDENS, ISLE OF GIGHA: 1km from ferry. 1342/MAGIC ISLANDS. Walk
MAP 1 or cycle (hire at post office at top of slip road); an easy daytrip. In a kindly climate
B3 and already mature parkland, Sir James Horlicks pursued his passion for
rhododendrons and exotic shrubs, when he bought the island in 1944. Now,
despite recent uncertainties about the island as a whole and the Big House, the
gardens are commodious, diverse and peaceful. 2 marked paths, 40mins/2hrs.
There's a classic island vista from the viewpt above the house on the 'green' tour.
Malcolm Allen Garden, commemorating the dedication of an old gardener, is as
tranquil a glade as you could hope to find. Open all year.
ADM

764 DAWYCK, STOBO nr PEEBLES: On B712 Moffat rd off the A72 Biggar rd
MAP 8 from Peebles, 2km from Stobo. Another out-station of the Edinburgh
A2 Botanics; a recent acquisition, though tree-planting here goes back 300yrs.
Sloping grounds around the gurgling Scrape burn which trickles into the Tweed,
with landscaped woody pathways for meditative walks. A serene spot. The
chapel, however, has been closed due to vandalism. Mar-Oct 9am-6pm.
ADM

765 ANGUS' GARDEN, TAYNUILT: 7km from village (which is 12km from Oban
MAP 1 on the A85) along the Glen Lonan rd. Take first rt after Barguillen Garden
C1 Centre. A garden laid out by the family who own the centre in memory of their
son Angus, on the slopes around a small loch brimful of lilies and ducks. An
informal mix of the tended and the uncultivated, a more poignant remembrance
is hard to imagine as you while an hour away in this peaceful place. Open all
year.
Honesty box

766 STRONE WOODLAND, CAIRNDOW: Off the A83 L Lomond to Inveraray rd.
MAP 1 Through village to signed carpark and these mature woodlands in the grounds of
C2 Strone House on the southern bank near the head of L Fyne. Fine pines include
the 'tallest tree in Britain'. Magical at dawn or dusk.
Honesty box

Royal Botanics, Edinburgh (206)

LOGAN BOTANICAL GARDENS nr SANDHEAD, S of STRANRAER: 16km S of Stranraer by A77/A716 and 2km on from Sandhead. Remarkable out-station of the Edinburgh Botanics amongst sheltering woodland in the mild SW. Compact and full of pleasant surprises. Less crowded than other 'exotic' gardens. The Gunnera Bog is quite extra-terrestrial. Mar-Oct 10am-6pm. 767 MAP 9 A4
ADM

PRIORWOOD, MELROSE: Next to Melrose Abbey, a tranquil secret garden behind high walls which specialises in growing flowers and plants for drying. Picking, drying and arranging is continuously in progress. Samples for sale. Run by enthusiasts on behalf of the NTS, they're always willing to talk stamens with you. Also includes an historical apple orchard with trees through the ages. Heavenly jelly is on sale. Mon-Sat 10am-5.30pm. Sun 1-5.30pm. 768 MAP 8 C3
NTS ADM

KAILZIE GARDENS, PEEBLES: On B7062 Traquair rd. Informal woodland gardens just out of town; not extensive but eminently strollable. Old-fashioned roses and wilder bits. Some poor birds in cages and the odd peacock. Excellent courtyard tea-shop (1177/TEA-ROOMS). Kids' corner. Apr-Oct. 769 MAP 8 B2
ADM

PITMEDDEN GARDEN, nr ELLON: 35km N of Aberdeen and 10km W of the main A92. Formal French gardens recreated in 1950s on site of Sir Alex Seaton's 17th-century ones. The 4 great parterres, 3 based on designs for gardens at Holyrood Palace, are best viewed from the terrace. Charming farmhouse 'museum' has also been somewhat transplanted. For lovers of symmetry and an orderly universe only. May-Sept 10am-6pm. 770 MAP 3 D3
NTS ADM

DAMSIDE GARDEN, nr LAURENCEKIRK, S of STONEHAVEN: Signed off A92 15km N Montrose and 5km from rd. Also off A94 N of Laurencekirk; take Johnshaven t/off (also 5km). A herb garden still in its infancy but on an ambitious and expanding scale, and a Pinetum (acres) of mixed native and exotic species. A private botanical dream garden laid out as a series of themed 'rooms' e.g. Egyptian/Roman/Celtic/Monastic/a Camomile lawn etc. Tue-Sun. 10am-5pm (4.30pm wint). Self/S restau. 771 MAP 3 D5
ADM
There's another place specialising in Herbs at Brin School Fields at Flichity S of Inverness, 1298/GARDEN CENTRES.

ARDUAINE GARDEN, nr KIMELFORD: 28km S of Oban on A816, one of Argyll's undiscovered arcadias recently gifted to the NT and brought to wider attention. Creation of the micro-climate in which the rich, diverse vegetation has flourished, influenced by Osgood Mackenzie of Inverewe and its restoration a testimony to 20yrs hard labour by the Wright brothers. Fabulous rhododendrons. Enter/park by Loch Melfort hotel, gate 100m. Until dusk. Cl Th/Fri. 771a MAP 1 B2

THE HYDROPONICUM, ACHILTIBUIE: The 'Garden of the Future'. A strange fabrication in the far NW. Indoor watergardens and micro-climates (Hampshire, Bordeaux, the Canaries!). Here's the all-year-round strawb. Mr-Oct. Tours: 10am/12/2/5pm. 771b MAP 2 C2

ROYAL BOTANICS, EDINBURGH: 206/EDIN ATTRACTIONS.

BOTANIC GARDENS AND THE KIBBLE PALACE, GLASGOW: 421/GLAS ATTRACTIONS.

THE BEST COUNTRY PARKS

772 DRUMLANRIG CASTLE, THORNHILL nr DUMFRIES: Not that near Dumfries
MAP 9 (30km N, off A76) nor the central Borders in whose romance and history
C2 it's steeped, and it's a great deal more than just a Country Park, but included
here because it's the sort of place you could spend a good day, both inside the
castle and in the grounds. Apart from the art collection (Rembrandts, Leonardo,
Holbeins) and the Craft Courtyard (1264/CRAFTS), the outdoor delights include:
woodland and riverside walks, an adventure playground, the Falconry with
flying demonstrations (11.15am/2pm/4pm) and bike hire for further afield
explorations along the Nith etc. Castle open May-Aug, grounds till Sept. Mon-
Sat 11am-5pm, Sun 1-5pm. Castle Cl Thu.

773 ALMONDELL nr EAST CALDER: 12km from Edin city bypass. A well-managed
MAP 7 park in the valley of the R Almond, nestling amongst an area of redundant
B2 industrial sprawl and nr Livingston New Town. Nevertheless a peaceful and
verdant oasis with many intersecting walks through woods and meadows and
along cinder tracks. Picnic sites. Visitor centre with refreshments. Kids' areas.
River meadows. A71 from bypass (Kilmarnock), then B7015 (Camp) for 7km.
Park on rt just into E Calder village. Walk ahead into woods, not to rt.

774 STRATHCLYDE PARK betw HAMILTON AND MOTHERWELL: 15km SE of Glasgow.
MAP 1 Take M8/A725 interchange or M74/junct 5 or 6. Enormously popular park, a
E3 breathing space in the conurbation. Less notable for walking (though
Baronshaugh – see 882/BIRDWATCHING – and Dalzell Park are nearby), than
watersports, esp windsurfing and canoeing (1134/WATERSPORTS). But it's a great
place for just getting oot o' the hoose. 279/GLASGOW CARAVAN SITES; 965/
SPOOKY PLACES.

775 FORMAKIN ESTATE, BISHOPTON: 30km W of Glasgow via M8 jnct 31 signed just
MAP 1 before village and 3km further on. The estate of eccentric art connoisseur John
D3 Holms, who commissioned Robert Lorimer to restore and build a mansion and
lodges to house his collection. Between 1903-13 Lorimer produced what is
regarded as his most 'Scottish' work. The humorous and harmonious
architecture is a joy to behold and there are fine walks in the extensive grounds
which are open all year 11am-6pm. The Monkey House Restau is open for lunch
and dinner (7.30-9pm, best to book, it's v popular) in a conservatory setting and
there's also a café, shops and exhibits.

776 MUIRSHEIL nr LOCHWINNOCH: via Largs (A760) or Glasgow (M8, jnct 29 A737
MAP 1 then A760 5km S of Johnstone). N from village on Kilmacolm rd for 3km then
C3 signed. Park begins 6km on rd along the Calder valley. Despite proximity of
conurbation (Port Glasgow is over the hill), this is a wild and enchanting place
for walking/picnics etc. Trails marked to waterfall and summit views. Escape!
280/GLASGOW CAMPING.

777 MUGDOCK COUNTRY PARK nr MILNGAVIE: Another marvellous park v close to
MAP 1 Glasgow reached by train to Milngavie then bus, or by car to either of 3 carparks
D3 around the vast site. Highly recommended. For more info and directions see
444/GLASGOW CITY WALKS (pushing it a bit).

778 JOHN MUIR CO PARK nr DUNBAR, EAST LOTHIAN: Named after the 19th-century
MAP 7 conservationist who founded America's National Parks (and the Sierra Club)
E1 and who was born in Dunbar. This swathe of coastline to the W of the town
(known locally as Tyninghame) is an important estuarine nature reserve but is
good for family walks and beachcombing. 889/WILDLIFE RESERVES.

TENTSMUIR nr TAYPORT: Similar to above on the Tay Estuary. 892/RESERVES.

ADEN, MINTLAW nr PETERHEAD: 751/GOOD PLACES TO TAKE KIDS.

KELBURNE COUNTRY CENTRE, LARGS: 749/GOOD PLACES TO TAKE KIDS.

THE BEST TOWN PARKS

✝ ✝ **PRINCES ST GARDENS, EDINBURGH:** N side of Princes St. The world-   779
famous gardens between the Old and New towns, in the glacial trough   MAP A
beneath the Castle crags, once the town loch. In two sections with the National   C3
Gallery between (190/EDIN ATTRCTS). The Scott Monument (215/EDIN VIEWS)
dominates the eastern part and the Ross Bandstand the other; there's a wide-
ranging musical programme in summer. But the park is worth celebrating
mainly for its timeless, traditional features: the floral clock, the pitch and putt,
the open-air café. It's always been a great place to eat your lunch, lie on the grass
and watch the world go by. It's one of the few places where tourists and
townsfolk truly mingle in a relaxed way.

✝ **DUTHIE PARK, ABERDEEN:** Riverside Dr along R Dee from the bridge   780
carrying main A92 rd from/to Stonehaven. Large well-kept park with   MAP C
duckpond, bandstand, impressive and extensive rose gardens, carved sculptures   xB5
and, most famously, the large Winter Garden of subtropical palms/ferns etc
(10am-almost dusk). Park open all year.

✝ **PITTENCRIEFF PARK, DUNFERMLINE:** Large park alongside Abbey and Palace   781
ruins. Open areas, glasshouses, pavilion (more a function room) but most   MAP 5
notably a deep verdant glen criss-crossed with pathways. It's lush, full of birds,   B4
good after rain.

BEVERIDGE PARK, KIRKCALDY: Also in Fife area, another big municipal park with   782
a duckpond, wide-open spaces and many amusements e.g. bowling, tennis,   MAP 5
putting, paddling. A fine playground for kids.   C4

WILTON LODGE PARK, HAWICK: Hawick is perhaps not overfull of visitor   783
attractions, but it does have a pretty nice park with facilities and diversions   MAP 8
enough for everyone e.g. the civic gallery, rugby pitches (they quite like rugby in   C3
Hawick), a large kids' playground, a café and lots of riverside walks by the
Teviot. Lots of my schoolfriends lost their virginity in this park. It's a kind of all
round open-air recreation centre. At S end of town by A7.

ROUKEN GLEN AND LINN PARK, GLASGOW: Both on southside of river. Rouken   784
Glen via Pollokshaws/Kilmarnock rd to Eastwood Toll then rt. Good place to   MAP B
park is second left, Davieland Rd beside pond. Across park from here (or beside   xC4
main Rouken Glen rd) is main visitor area with garden centre (1295/GARDEN
CENTRES), a Chinese restau and 'Butterfly Kingdom'. Linn Park via Aikenhead
and Carmunock rd. After Kings Park on left, take rt to Simshill Rd and park at
golf course beyond houses. A long route there, but worth it; this is one of the
undiscovered Elysiums of a city which boasts 60 parks. Ranger Centre. Buses:
Rouken Glen 44, 66. Linn Park 38.

VICTORIA PARK, GLASGOW: Just N of the Clyde at Whiteinch on the Clydeside   785
Expressway, another of Glasgow's lesser known but notable parks. In its SW   MAP B
corner there's a surprising gem of a rock garden enclosing a 'Fossil Grove',   A2
Glasgow's 'oldest attraction': 300 million-yr-old tree trunks discovered during
excavations of the walkways. Pavilion open every day. Cl noon-1pm and dusk in
winter.

CAMPERDOWN PARK, DUNDEE: Calling itself a country park, Camperdown is the   786
main recreational breathing space for the city and hosts a plethora of distractions   MAP D
(a golf course, a wildlife complex, mansion house etc). Situated beyond   xA2
Kingsway, the ring-route; go via Coupar Angus rd/turn-off. Best walks across
the A923 in the Templeton Woods. Cycle hire, Nicholson's 0382 461212.

GRANT PARK, FORRES: Forres, rather proudly, is a frequent winner of the   787
Britain/Scotland in Bloom competitions. Grant Park, with its balance of   MAP 3
ornamental gardens, open parkland and woody hillside, is the carefully tended   A2
rose in its crown. Good municipal facilities like pitch and putt, kids' playground.
Through woods at top of Cluny Hill, a tower affords fabulous views of the
Moray and Cromarty Firths and surrounding forest from which the town takes
its name.

THE MOST INTERESTING COASTAL VILLAGES

788 PLOCKTON, nr KYLE OF LOCHALSH: A Highland gem of a place 8km over the
MAP 2 hill from Kyle, clustered around inlets of a wooded bay on L Carron. On
C3 the front, there's a grassy sward, cottage gardens down to the bay and palm
trees! Some great walks (1069/COASTAL WALKS). Haven Hotel is in many guides.
It's the best place to eat but the Plockton Hotel (good pub) or Creag nan Darach
(059984 222) beside the Haven are better value and you'll be more connected with
the village. Both CHP/INX 1255/CRAFT SHOPS.

789 STROMNESS, ORKNEY MAINLAND: 24km from Kirkwall and a different kettle
MAP 10 of fish. Hugging the shore and with narrow streets and wynds, it has a
unique atmosphere, both maritime and European. Some of the most singular
shops you'll see anywhere and the Orkney folk going about their business. The
Stromness hotel is funky and central and you might eat at the Hamnavoe.
1378/ORKNEY; 1305/GALLERIES.

79(CROMARTY nr INVERNESS: At end of rd across Black Isle from Inverness
MAP 2 (45km NE), but worth the trip. There are oil platforms marching up the
D3 Firth, but the village has a dreamy times-gone-by atmos, without being twee.
Lots of kids running about and a pink strand of beach. Delights to discover incl:
the Kirk, plain and aesthetic with countryside through the windows behind the
altar; Hugh (the geologist) Miller's house/museum; Florence's (1185/TEA
ROOMS); Thistle's (567/HIGHL/BEST RESTAUS); the shore and cliff walk
(1072/COASTAL WALKS). Royal Hotel has atmos and is inexp.

791 TOBERMORY, MULL: Not so much a village, rather the main town of Mull,
MAP 1 set around a hill on superb Tobermory Bay. Ferry port for Ardnamurchan,
B1 but main Oban ferry is 35km away at Craignure. Usually a bustling harbour
front with quieter streets behind; a quintessential island atmosphere. Some good
inexp hotels (and quayside hostel) well situated to explore the whole island.
1376/MULL; 1354/ISLAND HOTELS; 668/BEST HOSTELS.

792 PORT CHARLOTTE, ISLAY: A township on the 'Rinns of Islay', the western
MAP 1 peninsula. By A846 from the ports, Askaig and Ellen via Bridgend. Rows of
A3 whitewashed, well-kept cottages along and back from shoreline. On road in,
there's a creamery, an island museum and a coffee/bookshop. Also a 'town'
beach where you can bathe. Quiet and charming without being quaint. 1374/
ISLAY.

793 ROCKCLIFFE nr DUMFRIES: 25km S on Solway Coast rd, A710. On the 'Scottish
MAP 9 Riviera', the rocky part of the coast around to Kippford (1070/COASTAL WALKS).
C4 A good rock-scrambling foreshore and a village with few houses and a large
hotel set back; with great views (the Baron's Craig). Good pub at Kippford (the
Anchor).

794 CULROSS nr DUNFERMLINE: By A994 from Dunfermline or jnct 1 of M90 just over
MAP 5 Forth Rd Bridge (15km). Old centre conserved and still being restored by
A4 National Trust. Mainly residential and not awash with craft and coffee shops.
More historical than merely quaint; a community of careful custodians lives in the
white, red pantiled houses. Footsteps echo in the cobbled wynds. Some buildings
open. The 'Palace' closed at time of going to press. Eat at the Dundonald Arms or
Dawn Till Dusk coffee shop. Grangemouth fumes in the distance.

795 EAST NEUK VILLAGES: The quintessential quaint wee fishing villages along the bit
MAP 5 of Fife that forms the mouth of the Firth of Forth, CRAIL, ANSTRUTHER,
D3/E3 PITTENWEEM, ST MONANCE and ELIE all have different characters and attractions.
Crail esp its harbour; Anstruther as main centre and home of Fisheries Museum
(and see 1205/FISH 'N' CHIPS; 520/FIFE BEST RESTAUS; 876/BIRDS); Elie: 810/
BEACHES; 1142/WINDSURFING; 521/FIFE BEST RESTAUS; 729/PUB FOOD; 1109/
GOLF. Or just walk around – traffic can be awful.

796 ABERDOUR: Betw Dunfermline and Kirkcaldy and nr Forth Rd Bridge (10km E
MAP 5 from jnct 1 of M90) or better still go by train from Edinburgh (frequent service:
B4 Dundee or Kirkcaldy); it has the 'best-kept station'). Walks round harbour and
to headland, Silver Sands beach 1km, Castle ruins. 986/CHURCHES; 516/517/ FIFE
HOTELS.

MORAY COAST FISHING VILLAGES: From Speybay (where the Spey slips into the 797
sea) along to Fraserburgh, some of Scotland's best coastal scenery and many MAP 3
interesting villages in cliff/cove and beach settings. Esp notable are PORTSOY C1/D1
with 17th-century harbour (1153/SWIMMING POOLS); SANDEND with its own
popular beach and a fabulous one nearby (811/BEACHES); PENNAN made famous
by the film *Local Hero* (the hotel/pub is cosy and inexp: 03466 201);
GARDENSTOWN with a walk along the water's edge to CROVIE (pron 'Crivee') the
epitome of a coast-clinging community; and CULLEN which is more of a town
and has a great beach. 548/GRAMPIAN HOTELS.

DIABEG, WESTER ROSS: On N shore of L Torridon at the end of the unclassified 798
rd from Torridon on one of Scotland's most inaccessible peninsulas. Diabeg MAP 2
(pron 'Jee-a-beg') is simply beautiful. Fantastic road there and then walk! C3

DUNURE, AYR: 15km S of Ayr on A719, the coast rd past the Heads of Ayr (cliff 799
walks) 10km from Culzean (903/CASTLES). Only a couple of rows of cottages, a MAP 1
pub, 'The Anchorage' (with decent grub), an old harbour and, above, the C4
dramatic ruins of Dunure Castle, once the scene of horrific torture, now a kids'
playground.

ISLE OF WHITHORN: Strange faraway vill at end of the rd, 35km S Newton 799A
Stewart, 6km Whithorn (960A/PREHIS SITES). Mystical harbour where low tide MAP 1
does mean low, saintly shoreline, a sea angler's pub (Steam Packet) and B4
McDonald's amazing leaning stores. Ninian's chapel less uplifting, but you can
see why he landed.

FANTASTIC BEACHES AND BAYS

KILORAN BEACH, COLONSAY: 4km from quay (and hotel) past shop and on 800
to Colonsay House. Follow rd right, behind farm buildings for another MAP 1
1km. The main track leads to a corner of the beach. Has been described as the finest A2
beach in the Hebrides and it does not disappoint. Craggy cliffs on one side, negoti-
able rocks on the other and in between, tiers of grassy dunes. The island of Colonsay was once bought as a picnic spot. This beach was probably the reason why.

MACHRIHANISH: At the bottom of the Kintyre peninsula 10km from 801
Campbeltown. Walk N from Machrihanish village, or from the carpark MAP 1
on the main A83 to Tayinloan and Tarbert at point where it hits/leaves the coast. B4
A joyously long strand (8km) of unspoiled orange-pink sand backed by dunes and
facing the 'steepe Atlantic Stream' all the way to Newfoundland (1114/GOLF).

OSTAL BEACH/KILBRIDE BAY, MILLHOUSE nr TIGHNABRUAICH: Down rd 802
from 'Millhouse corner' on B8000, a track to rt at a white house (there's a MAP 1
church on the left) marked 'Private Road, No Cars' (often with a chain across to C3
restrict access). Park and walk 1km. turning rt after lochan. You arrive on a perfect
white sandy crescent known locally as Ostal and, apart from stranded jellyfish and
the odd swatch of sewage, in certain conditions, a mystical secret place to swim
and picnic. The north coast of Arran is like a Greek island in the bay.

SANDWOOD BAY, KINLOCHBERVIE: This mile-long sandy strand with its 803
old 'Stack', is legendary, but therein lies the problem since now too many MAP 2
people know about it and you may have to share in its glorious isolation. C1
Inaccessibility is its saving grace, a 7km walk from the sign off the rd at Balchrick
(nr the cattle grid), 6km from Kinlochbervie; allow 3hrs return plus time there.
More venturesome is the walk from the N and Cape Wrath (1068/COAST WALKS).

OLDSHOREMORE: The beach you pass on the rd to Balchrick, only 3km from 804
Kinlochbervie. It's easy to reach and a beautiful spot: the water is clear and MAP 2
perfect for swimming, and there are rocky walks and quiet places. POLIN, 500m C1
N, is a cove you might have to yourself.

ISLAY: SALIGO, MACHIR BAY AND THE BIG STRAND: The first two are 805
bays on NW of island via A847 rd to Port Charlotte, then B8018 past L MAP 1
Gorm. Wide beaches; remains of war fortifications in deep dunes. They say 'no A3
swimming'. At the Big Strand on Laggan Bay, 8km Port Ellen (to Kintra by rd
to left at Maltings, then right following signs) there's a bar/restau, accom,
camping and great walks in either direction, 8km of glorious sand and dunes
(contains the Machrie Golf Course). An airy amble under a wide sky.
684/CAMPING; 1113/GOLF; 1066/COASTAL WALKS.

806 SOUTH UIST: Deserted but for birds, an almost unbroken strand of beach
MAP 2 running for miles down the west coast and the machair at its best (esp early
A3 summer). Take any rd off the spinal A865; usually less than 2km. Good spot to
try is turn-off at Tobha Mor where you pass black houses and a chapel on the
way to the sea.

807 JURA, LOWLANDMAN'S BAY: Not strictly a beach (there is a sandy strand before
MAP 1 the headland) but a rocky foreshore with ethereal atmosphere; great light and
B3 space. Only seals break the spell. Go right at 3-arch bridge to first group of
houses (Knockdrome), thro yard on left and right around cottages to track to
Ardmenish. After deer fences, bay is visible on your rt, 1km walk away.

808 VATERSAY, OUTER HEBRIDES: The tiny island now joined by a causeway to Barra.
MAP 2 Twin crescent beaches on either side of the isthmus, one shallow and sheltered
A4 visible from Castlebay, the other an ocean beach with rollers. Dunes/machair;
safe swimming.

809 BARRA, SEAL BAY: 5km Castlebay on west coast, 2km after Isle of Barra Hotel
MAP 2 through gate across machair where rd rt is signed Taobh a Deas Allathasdal. A
A4 flat, rocky Hebridean shore and skerries where seals flop into the water and eye
you with intense curiosity.

810 WEST SANDS, ST ANDREWS: As a town beach, this is hard to beat and it dom-
MAP 5 inates the view to W. Wide swathe not too unclean and sea swimmable. Golf
D2 courses behind. Beach buffs may prefer Kinshaldy (892/WILDLIFE RESERVES),
Kingsbarns (10km S), or Elie (28km S).

811 MORAY COAST: Many great beaches along coast from Spey Bay to Fraserburgh,
MAP 3 notably **CULLEN** and **LOSSIEMOUTH** (town beaches) and **NEW ABERDOUR** (1km
C1/D1 from New Aberdour village on B9031, 15km W of Fraserburgh) and
ROSEHEARTY (8km W of Fraserburgh) both quieter places for walks and picnics.
One of the best-kept secrets is the beach at **SUNNYSIDE** where you walk past the
incredible ruins of Findlater Castle on the clifftop (how did they build it? And
what a place, on its grassed-over roof, for a picnic) and down to a cove which on
my sunny day was quite simply perfect. Take a left going into Sandend 16km W
of Banff and follow rd for 2km, turning right and park in the farmyard. Walk
from here past dovecote, 1km to cliff.

812 NORTH COAST: To the W of Thurso, along the N coast, are some of Britain's
MAP 2 most unspoiled and unsung beaches. No beach bums, no Beach Boys. There are
D1 so many great little coves, you can have one to yourself even on a hot day, but
those to mention are: **ARMADALE** (40km W Thurso), **FARR** and **TORRISDALE**
(48km) and **COLDBACKIE** (65km). My own favourite is further along where
L Eriboll comes out to the sea and the rd hits the coast again 7km E of Durness.
It's a small 100m cove flanked by walls of oyster-pink rock and shallow
turquoise sea. My footprints may still be there on the sand.

813 SANDS OF MORAR nr MALLAIG: 70km W of Ft William and 6km from Mallaig,
MAP 2 these easily accessible beaches may seem overpopulated on summer days and the
C4 S stretch nearest to Arisaig may have one too many caravan parks, but they go
on for miles and there's enough space for everybody. The sand's supposed to be
silver but in fact it's a very pleasing pink. Lots of rocky bits for exploration. One
of the best beachy bits is (coming from Mallaig) the next bay after the estuary;
park on the rd.

SOME GREAT GLENS

✝ ✝ ✝ **GLEN AFFRIC:** Starts at Cannich at the end of Glen Urquhart A831, 814
20km from Drumnadrochit on L Ness. A beautiful, dramatic gorge MAP 2
that strikes westwards into the wild heart of Scotland. Superb for rambles C3
(1052/GLEN WALKS), expeditions, Munro-bagging (further in, beyond L Affric)
and even just tootling through in the car. Shaped by the Hydro Board, L
Benevean nevertheless adds to the drama. Biking through the glen is an excl idea
as is the detour to Tomich and the Plodda Falls (824/FALLS).

✝ ✝ ✝ **GLEN LYON nr ABERFELDY:** One of Scotland's crucial places both 815
historically and geographically, much favoured by MAP 4
fishers/walkers/Munro-baggers. Wordsworth and Tennyson, Gladstone and B3
Baden Powell all sang its praises. The Lyon is a classic Highland river tumbling
through corries, gorges and riverine meadows. Several Munros are within its
watershed and rise gloriously on either side. Rd all the way to the lochside
(30km). Eagles soar over the remoter tops at the head of the glen. Fishing
permits from Fortingall Hotel on the way there (0887 830367). The 'oldest tree' in
Europe, a rather scraggy yew, is in the churchyard next to the hotel.

✝ ✝ **STRATHCARRON nr BONAR BRIDGE:** You drive up the N bank of this 816
Highland river from the bridge outside Ardgay (pron 'Ordguy') which MAP 2
is 3km over the bridge from Bonar Bridge. Rd goes 15km to Croick and its D2
remarkable church (990/CHURCHES). The river gurgles and gushes along its
rocky course to the Dornoch Firth and there are innumerable places to picnic,
swim and stroll. On a warm day there are few riversides as heavenly as this.

GLEN ETIVE: Off from more exalted Glencoe (and the A82) at Kingshouse, as 817
anyone hiking there will tell you, this truly is a glen of glens. And needs no more MAP 2
advertisement. C5

THE ANGUS GLENS: Glen Clova/Glen Prosen/Glen Isla. All via Kirriemuir. Isla 818
to W is a woody, approachable glen with a deep gorge, on B954 nr Alyth MAP 4
(834/FALLS). Others via B955, to Dykehead then rd bifurcates. Both glens stab D2
into the heart of the Grampians. 'Minister's Walk' goes between them from
behind the kirk at Prosen village over the hill to B955 before Clova village
(7km). Glen Clova is walkers' paradise esp from Glendoll 24km from Dykehead;
limit of rd. Viewpt. 'Jock's Rd' to Braemar and the Capel Mounth to Ballater
(both 24km). Campsite and SYH. Also great hotel at Clova (530/TAYSIDE
HOTELS) and famous 'Loops of Brandy' walk (2hrs, 2-B-2); stark and beautiful.

GLENDARUEL: The Cowal Peninsula on the A886 betw Colintraive (and ferry to 819
Rothesay) and Strachur on L Fyne. The humble but perfectly formed glen of the MAP 1
R Ruel, from Clachan in the S (a kirk and an inn) through gentle deciduous C3
meadowland to a more rugged grandeur 10km N. Easy walking and cycling. W
rd best. Fine views of L Fyne and Argyll from paths on the west ridge. 2-B-2

GLEN LONAN nr TAYNUILT: Betw Taynuilt on A85 and A816 S of Oban. Another 820
quiet wee glen, but all the right elements for walking, picnics, cycling and fishing MAP 1
or just a run in the car. Varying scenery, a bubbling burn (the R Lonan), some C1
standing stones and not many folk. Angus' Garden at the Taynuilt end should
not be missed (765/GARDENS). No marked walks; now get lost! 2-B-2

GLEN TROOL nr NEWTON STEWART: 26km N by A714 via Bargrennan which is 821
on the S Upland Way (1080/LONG WALKS). A gentle wooded glen of a place MAP 9
around Loch Trool. One of the most charming, accessible parts of the Galloway B3
Forest Park. 1018/MARY, CHARLIE, BOB.

THE SMA' GLEN nr CRIEFF: Off the A85 to Perth, the A822 to Amulree and 822
Aberfeldy. Sma' meaning small, this is the valley of the R Almond where the MAP 4
Mealls (lumpish, shapeless hills) fall steeply down to the rd. Where the rd turns B3
away from the river, the long distance path to L Tay begins (28km). Sma' Glen
8km, has good picnic spots, but they get busy and midgy in summer.

STRATHFARRAR, nr BEAULY or DRUMNADROCHIT: Rare unspoiled glen that is 822a
easily accessed from A831 leaving Drumnadrochit on L Ness via Cannich MAP 2
(30km) or S from Beauly (15km). Signed from Struy. Arrive at gatekeeper's D3
house. Access restricted to 12-20 cars per day (Cl Tues) and you must be out by
7pm. 22km to head of glen past lochs. Good climbing, walking, fishing. Peace!

THE MOST SPECTACULAR WATERFALLS

One aspect of Scotland that really is improved by rain. All the walks to these falls are graded 1-A-1 unless otherwise stated (see p. 9 for walk codes).

823 **FALLS OF GLOMACH:** 25km Kyle of Lochalsh. Off A87 nr Shiel Bridge,
MAP 2 past Kintail Centre at Morvich then 2km further up Glen Croe to bridge.
C3 Walk starts other side; there are other ways, (e.g. from the SY Hostel in Glen Affric), but this is most straightforward. Allow 5/7 hrs for the pilgrimage to one of Britain's highest falls. Path is steep but well trod. Glomach means gloomy and you might feel so, peering into the ravine; from precipice to pool, it's 200m. But to pay tribute, go down carefully into the gorge. Vertigo factor and sense of achievement both fairly high. 671/HOSTELS (Ratagan and Glen Affric). 2·C·3

824 **PLODDA FALLS nr TOMICH nr DRUMNADROCHIT:** A831 from L Ness to
MAP 2 Cannich (20km), then 4km to Tomich and a further 5km up mainly
C3 woodland track to carpark. 200m walk down through woods of Scots Pine and ancient Douglas Fir to one of the most enchanting woodland sites in Britain and the Victorian iron bridge over the brink of the 150m fall into the churning river below. The dawn chorus here must be amazing. This is a supernatural place. Good hotel in village (576/HIGHLAND INEXP HOTELS).

825 **FALLS OF BRUAR nr BLAIR ATHOLL:** Close to the main A9 Perth-Inverness
MAP 4 rd, 12km N of B Atholl. 'Gorgeous' is a word that springs to mind as you
B2 walk the 250m to the lower falls from the carpark and the lichen-covered walls of the gorge below the upper falls (1km) are even more dramatic. Circular path is well marked but steep and rocky in places. Some pools are tempting (896/SWIMMING HOLES).

826 **EAS A' CHUAL ALUINN, KYLESCU:** Britain's highest waterfall nr the head of
MAP 2 Glencoul, is not easy to reach. Kylescu is between Scourie and Lochinver
C2 off the main A894, 20km S of Scourie. There are boat trips at 11am/2pm/4pm May-Sept from beside the hotel that sail up the loch for 2hrs. You can see the falls 500m away, but the boat will not usually let you alight. Sea Wildlife Holidays (0971 2003) take smaller parties and will drop you at the beach and show you the way (3hr walk return to base of falls). They can also direct you along the trickier path to the top of the falls from 5km N of the Skiag Br on the main rd (4hrs return). The water freefalls for 200m, which is 4 times further than Niagara. There's a spectacular pulpit view down the cliff, 100m to rt. Take extreme care. 2·C·3

827 **EAS FORS, MULL:** On the Dervaig to Fionnphort rd 3km from Ulva Ferry; a series
MAP 1 of cataracts tumbling down on either side of the road. Easily accessible. There's a
B1 path down the side to the brink where the river plunges into the sea. On a warm day swimming in the sea below the fall is a rare exhilaration.

828 **GLENASHDALE FALLS, ARRAN:** 5km walk from Glenashdale Bridge on main rd
MAP 1 at Whiting Bay. Signed up the burn side, but uphill and further on than you
C4 think, so allow 2hrs (return). Short series of falls in a rocky gorge in the woods with paths so you get right down to the brim and the pools. Swimming. 1·B·1

829 **EAS MOR, SKYE:** Glen Brittle nr end of rd. 24km from Sligachan. A mountain
MAP 2 waterfall with the wild Cuillins behind and views to the sea. Approach as part of
B3 a serious scramble or merely a 30min Cuillin sampler. Start at the Memorial Hut, cross the rd, bear rt, cross burn and then follow path uphill. 2·C·2

Another impressive fall (I'm told) is the Lealt Falls about 20km N of Portree on the A855. They're off to the right there somewhere, but, to be honest, I couldn't find them.

830 **THE STEALL FALLS, GLEN NEVIS, FT WILLIAM:** Take Glen Nevis rd at r/about
MAP 2 outside town centre and drive 'to end' (16km) through glen. Start from the
C4 second carpark you come to, following path marked 'Corrour', uphill through the woody gorge with R Ness thrashing below. Glen eventually and quite dramatically opens out and there are great views of the long veils of the Falls. Cross to them, past Mt Rescue bothy by tricky 3-wire bridge. 2·A·2

831 **CORRIESHALLOCH GORGE/FALLS OF MEASACH:** Jnctn of A832 and A835,
MAP 2 20km S of Ullapool; poss to walk down into the gorge from both rds. Most
C3 dramatic approach is from the carpark on the A832 Gairloch rd. Staircase to swing bridge from whence to consider how such a wee burn could make such a deep gash. Very impressive.

Plodda Falls (824)

832 THE GREY MARE'S TAIL: On the wildly scenic rd betw Moffat and Selkirk, the
MAP 9 A708. About halfway, a carpark and signs for w'fall. The lower track takes
E2 10/15mins to a viewing place still 500m from falls; the higher, on the other side
of the Tail burn, threads betw the austere hills and up to Loch Skene from which
the falls overflow (45/60mins). Mountain goats cast a wary eye.

833 THE FALLS OF CLYDE, NEW LANARK nr LANARK: Dramatic falls in a long gorge
MAP 1 of the Clyde. New Lanark, the conservation village of Robert Owen the
E3 social reformer, is signed from Lanark. It's hard to avoid the tourist bazaar, but
I'd recommend getting out of the village and along the riverbank ASAP. The path
to the Power Station is about 3km, but the route doesn't get interesting till after it,
a 1km climb to the first fall (Cora Linn) and another 1km to the next (Bonnington
Linn). Swimming above or below them is not advised (but it's great). Certainly
don't swim on an 'open day', when they close the stn and divert all the water back
down the river in a mighty surge (about once a month in summer on Sundays;
details 0555 65262).

834 REEKIE LINN, ALYTH: 8km N of town on back rds to Kirriemuir on B951 betw
MAP 4 Br of Craigisla and Br of Lintrathen. A picnic site and carpark on bend of rd
D3 leads by 200m to the wooded gorge of Glen Isla with precipitous viewpts of
defile where Isla is squeezed and falls in tiers for 100ft. Can walk further along
the glen from here.

835 FALLS OF ACHARN nr KENMORE, LOCH TAY: 5km along S side of loch on unclass
MAP 4 rd. Walk from opp engineering plant in township of Acharn; falls are signed.
B3 Steepish climb for 1km up side of gorge; Falls on other side. Viewing platform
would make a great place to camp – waking up with that view out the end of
your tent.

836 FALLS OF ROGIE nr STRATHPEFFER: Carpark on A835 Inverness-Ullapool rd,
MAP 2 5km Contin/10km Strathpeffer. Accessibility makes short walk (250m) quite
D3 popular to these hurtling falls on the Blackwater River. Bridge (built by T
Army) and salmon ladder (they leap up in summer). Woodland trails marked,
allow circular route.

837 FOYERS, LOCH NESS: On southern route from Ft Augustus to Inverness, the
MAP 2 B852 (857/SCENIC ROUTES) at the village of Foyers (35km from Inverness). Park
D4 next to shops and cross rd, go through fence and down steep track to viewing
places (slither-proof shoes advised). R Foyers falls 150m into foaming gorge
below and then into L Ness throwing clouds of spray into the trees (you may
get drenched). Occasionally the Hydro 'turn the water off' and it just stops.

838 FALLS OF SHIN nr LAIRG, SUTHERLAND: 6km E of town on signed rd, carpark and
MAP 2 falls nearby are easily accessible. Not quite up to the splendours of others on this
D2 page, but an excl place to see salmon battling upstream (best June-Aug).
Café/souvenir teatowels.

GREAT (ACCESSIBLE) LOCHS LARGE AND SMALL

☩ ☩ **LOCH MAREE:** A832 betw Kinlochewe and Gairloch. An old favourite 839 (Osgood Mackenzie, Queen Victoria *et al*); the lambent sliver of water MAP 2 easily viewed from the rd which follows its length for 15km. Bienn Eighe rises C3 behind you and, on the other side, the omniscient presence of Slioch. Vis Centre at Aultroy (5km Kinlochewe), fine walks from carpark further on and excl accom at L Maree Hotel (569/HIGHLAND HOTELS; 1091/WALKING AREAS).

☩ ☩ **LOCH AN EILEAN:** An enchanted loch in the heart of the Rothiemurchus 840 Forest. 1058/WOODLAND WALKS for directions. There's a good Visitor MAP 2 Centre. You can walk right round the loch (5km, allow 1.5hrs). This is classic D4 Highland scenery, a landscape of magnificent Scots Pine. It was one of Wainwright's favourites.

☩ **LOCH ARKAIG:** 25km Ft William. An enigmatic loch long renowned for its 841 fishing. From the A82 beyond Spean Bridge (at the Commando Monument) MAP 2 cross the Caledonian Canal, then on by single track rd thro the Clune Forest and C4 the 'Dark Mile' past the 'Witches Pool' (a cauldron of dark water below cataracts), to the loch. Bonnie Prince Charlie came this way before and after Culloden; one of his refuge caves is marked on a trail.

LOCH LUBHAIR nr CRIANLARICH: The loch you pass (on the rt) on the A85 to 842 Crianlarich (4km), in Glen Dochart, the upper reaches of the Tay water system. MAP 6 Small, perfect with bare hills surrounding and fringed with pines and woody B2 islets. Beautiful scenery that most people just go past in the car heading for Oban or Ft William. Kayaks can be hired at lochside from Glen Dochart Water Sport (08383 315).

LOCH ACHRAY nr BRIG O' TURK: The small loch at the centre of the Trossachs 843 between L Katrine (on which the SS *Sir Walter Scott* makes thrice-daily cruises: MAP 6 041 355 5333) and L Venachar. The A821 from Callander skirts both Venachar B3 and Achray and there are numerous picnic sites. Ben Venue and Ben A'An rise above and offer great walks (1039/HILLS) and views. A one-way forest rd goes round the other side of L Achray and through the Achray Forest (enter and leave from the Duke's Pass rd betw Aberfoyle and Brig O' Turk). Details of all trails from Forest Vis Centre 3km N Aberfoyle.

LOCH MUICK nr BALLATER: At head of rd off B976, the S Dee rd at Ballater. 844 14km up Glen Muick (pron 'Mick') to carpark, Vis Centre and 100m to lochside. MAP 3 Lochnagar rises above (1087/MUNROS) and walk also begins here for Capel B4 Mounth and Glen Clova (818/GLENS). 3hr walk around loch and any number of ambles. Open aspect with grazing deer and without too much forestry.

LOCH ERIBOLL, NORTH COAST: 90km W of Thurso. The long sealoch that indents 845 into the N coast for 15km and which you drive right round on the main A838. MAP 2 The deepest natural anchorage in the UK, it exhibits every aspect of lochside D1 scenery incl, alas, fishcages. Ben Hope stands nr the head of the loch and there is a perfect beach on the coast (812/BEACHES). Walks from Hope.

LOCH MORAR nr MALLAIG: 70km W of Ft William by the A850 (a wildly scenic 846 route). Morar village is 6km from Mallaig and a single track rd leads away from MAP 2 the coast to the loch (only 500m but out of sight) then along it for 5km to C4 Bracora. It's the prettiest part with wooded islets, small beaches, lochside meadows and bobbing boats. The rd stops at a turning place but a track continues to Tarbet and it's possible to connect with a post boat and sail back to Mallaig on L Nevis. L Morar, joined to the coast by the shortest river in Britain, also has the deepest water. There is a spookiness about it, if not a monster.

LOCH LOMOND: The biggest, not quite the bonniest. 736/ATTRACTIONS.

LOCH NESS: The longest, not quite the least discovered. 739/ATTRACTIONS.

THE SCENIC ROUTES

847 ROTHESAY-TIGHNABRUAICH: A886/A8003. The most celebrated part
MAP 1 of this route is the latter, the A8003 down the side of L Riddon to
C3 Tighnabruaich along the hillsides which give the breathtaking views of Bute and
the Kyles, but the whole way, with its diverse aspects of lochside, riverine and
rocky scenery is supernatural. Includes short crossing betw Rhubodach and
Colintraive.

848 GLENCOE: The A82 from Crianlarich to Ballachulish is a fine drive,
MAP 2 but from the extra-terrestrial Loch Ba onwards, there can be few
C5 roads anywhere that have direct contact with such imposing scenery. After
Kinghouse and Buachaille Etive Mor on the left, the mountains and ridges rising
on either side of Glencoe proper are truly awesome. The Vis Centre, well
signposted 8km from Glencoe village, sets the topographical and historical
scene. 704/PUBS; 1075/SERIOUS WALKS; 1004/BATTLEGROUNDS; 1029/SPOOKY
PLACES; 669/HOSTELS.

849 SHIEL BRIDGE-GLENELG: The switchback rd that climbs from the A87
MAP 2 (Ft William 96km) at Shiel Br over the 'hill' and down to the coast
C4 opposite the Sleat Peninsula in Skye (short ferry to Kylerhea). As you climb
you're almost as high as the surrounding summits and there's the classic view
across L Duich to the 5 Sisters of Kintail. Coming back you think you're going
straight into the loch! It's really worth driving beyond Glenelg to Arnisdale and
ethereal L Hourn (16km).

850 APPLECROSS: 120km Inverness. From Tornapress nr Lochcarron for
MAP 2 18km. Leaving the A896 seems like leaving civilisation; the winding
C3 ribbon heads into monstrous mountains and the high plateau at the top is
another planet. All the better to arrive in the green fields of Applecross (though
it's often cut off in winter) where there is a campsite/coffee shop and a friendly
faraway inn.

851 THE GOLDEN ROAD, SOUTH HARRIS: The main rd in Harris follows the E
MAP 2 coast, notable for bays and sandy beaches. This is the other one, winding
B2 round a series of coves and inlets with offshore skerries and a treeless rocky
hinterland – the classic Hebridean landscape esp Finsbay. Tweed is woven in this
area; you can visit the crofts but it would be impolite to leave without buying
something.

852 SLEAT PENINSULA, SKYE: The unclassified rd off the A851 (main Sleat rd) esp
MAP 2 coming from S, i.e. take rd for Tokavaig beside Clan Donald Centre; it meets
B4 coast after 9km. Affords rare views of the Cuillins from a craggy coast. Follow
with afternoon tea at Ord House before returning to 'main' rd S of Isleornsay.

853 LOCHINVER-ACHILTIBUIE: Achiltibuie is 40km from Ullapool; this is the route
MAP 2 from the N; 28km of winding rd/unwinding Highland scenery; partly coastal.
C2 Known locally as the 'wee mad road' (it is maddening if you're in a hurry)
Passes Achin's Bookshop (1259/CRAFTS), the path to Kincraig Falls and the
mighty Suilven.

854 LOCHINVER-DRUMBEG: The coast rd N from Lochinver (20km) is also
MAP 2 marvellous; essential Assynt. Actually best travelled N-S so that you leave the
C2 splendid vista of Eddrachillis Bay and pass through lochan, moor and even
woodland, touching the coast again by sandy beaches (at Stoer a rd leads 7km to
the lighthouse and a fabulous coast walk of 3km to the Point and the Old Man
of Stoer) and approach Lochinver with one of the classic long views of Suilven.

855 LEADERFOOT-CLINTMAINS, nr ST BOSWELLS: The B6356 betw the A68 and the
MAP 8 B6404 Kelso-St Boswells rd. This small rd, busy in summer, links Scott's View
C3 and Dryburgh Abbey (best found by following Abbey signs) and Smailholm
Tower and passes through classic Border/Tweedside scenery. 869/VIEWS;
974/ABBEYS. Don't miss Irvine's View.

856 BRAEMAR-LINN OF DEE: 12km of renowned Highland river scenery along the
MAP 3 upper valley of the (Royal) Dee. The Linn (rapids) is at the end of the rd but
A4 there are river walks and the start of the great Glen Tilt walk to Blair Atholl
(1078/SERIOUS WALKS). Deer abound.

857 FORT AUGUSTUS-DORES nr INVERNESS: The B862 often single-track rd that
MAP 2 follows and for much of its length skirts L Ness. Much quieter and more
D4 interesting than the main W bank A82. Starts off in rugged country and follows
the extraordinary straight rd built by Wade to tame the Highlands. Reaches the
lochside at Foyers (837/FALLS) and all the way to Dores (15km from Inverness).
There are paths to the shore of the Loch. 35km total; worth taking slowly.

THE DUKE'S PASS, ABERFOYLE-BRIG O' TURK: Of the many roads through the Trossachs, this one is well kent and busy, but has numerous possibilities for stopping, exploration and great views. Good viewpt 4km from L Achray Hotel, above rd and lay-by. One-way Forest Rd goes round L Achray. Good hillwalking starts (1092/HILLWALKS) and L Katrine Ferry (2km) 3 times a day Apr-Sept (355 5333). Bike hire in Aberfoyle (08772 614) and Callander (0877 31100). 858
MAP 6
B3

GLENFINNAN-MALLAIG: The A830, Road to the Isles. Through some of the most impressive and romantic landscapes in the Highlands, splendid in any weather (it does rain rather a lot) to the coast at the Sands of Morar (813/BEACHES). This is deepest Bonnie Prince Charlie country (1017/MARY, CHARLIE and BOB) and demonstrates what a misty eye he had for magnificent settings. The rd is shadowed for much of the way by the West Highland Railway which is an even better way to enjoy the scenery (1400/JOURNEYS). 859
MAP 2
C4

Loch Eilt, West Highland Line

AMULREE-KENMORE: The unclassified single track and often v narrow rd that leads from the hill-country hamlet of Amulree to cosy Kenmore. Past L Freuchie, a steep climb takes you to a plateau ringed by magnificent (distant) mountains and by the time you descend to L Tay you may be completely intoxicated with the scenery. But don't forget to close the gates. 860
MAP 4
B3

THE CLASSIC VIEWS

For views of and around Edinburgh and Glasgow, see pages 36 and 70. No views from hill or mountain tops are included here.

THE QUIRANG, SKYE: Best approach is from Uig direction taking the right-hand unclassified rd off the hairpin of the A855 above and 2km from town (more usual approach from Staffin side is less of a revelation). View (and walk) from carpark, the massive rock formations of a towering, contorted ridge. Solidified lava heaved and eroded into fantastic pinnacles. Fine views also across Staffin Bay to Wester Ross. 1370/ISLAND WALKS. 861
MAP 2
B3

THE VIEWS OF AN TEALLACH and LIATHACH: An Teallach, that great favourite of Scottish hillwalkers, 40km S of Ullapool by the A835/A832, is best viewed from the side of little Loch Broom on the A832 nr the Dundonald Hotel. 862
MAP 2
C2

The classic view of the other great Torridon mountains (Bienn Eighe and Liathach together, 100km S by rd from Ullapool), for those who can't imagine how (or why) you would attempt to go up them, is from the track around L Clair which is reached from the entrance to the Coulin estate off the A896, Glen Torridon rd (be aware of stalking). These mountains have to be seen to be believed. 863
MAP 2
C3

864 FROM RAASAY: There are a number of fabulous views looking over to
MAP 2 Skye from Raasay, the small island reached by ferry from Sconser (1341/
B3 MAGIC ISLANDS). The panorama from Dun Caan, the hill in the centre of the island
(444m) is of Munro proportions, producing an elation quite incommensurate with
the small effort required to get there. Start from the rd to the 'North End'. 2-B-2

865 THE REST AND BE THANKFUL: On A83 L Lomond-Inveraray rd where
MAP 1 it's met by the B828 from Lochgoilhead. In summer the rest may be
C2 from driving stress and you may not be thankful for the camera-toting masses
but this was always one of the most accessible, rewarding viewpts in the land.
Surprisingly, none of the encompassing hills are Munros but they are
nonetheless dramatic; there are mercifully few carpets of conifer to smother the
grandeur of the crags as you look down the valley.

866 ELGOL, SKYE: End of the rd on the A881, 22km from Broadford. The classic
MAP 2 view of the Cuillins from across L Scavaig (and Soay and Rum). Crossing
B4 can be made in summer to the famous corrie of L Coruisk, painted by Turner,
romanticised by Walter Scott.

867 CAMAS NAN GEALL, ARDNAMURCHAN: 12km Salen on B8007. 4km from
MAP 2 Ardnamurchan's Natural History Centre; 65km Ft William. Coming especially
C4 from the Kilchoan direction, a magnificent bay appears below you, where the
road first meets the sea. Almost symmetrical with high cliffs and a perfect field
(still cultivated) in the bowl fringed by a shingle beach. Carpark viewpt and
there is a path down. Deer graze around here.

868 GLENGARRY: 3km after Tomdoun turnoff on A87, Invergarry-Kyle of Lochalsh
MAP 2 rd. Lay-by with viewfinder. An uncluttered vista up and down loch and glen
C4 with not a house in sight (pity about the salmon cages). Distant peaks of
Knoydart are identified but not L Quoich nestling spookily and full of fish in
the wilderness at the head of the glen. Bonnie Prince Charlie passed this way.

869 SCOTT'S VIEW, ST BOSWELLS: Off A68 at Leaderfoot Bridge nr St Boswells,
MAP 8 signed Gattonside. 'The View', old Walter's favourite (the horses still stopped
C3 there long after he'd gone), is 4km along the rd (Dryburgh Abbey 3km further;
974/ABBEYS). Magnificent sweep of his beloved Border country, but only in one
direction. If you cross the gate and head up the hill towards
the jagged standing stone, you reach. . .
IRVINE'S VIEW: The full panorama from the Cheviots to the Lammermuirs. This,
the finest view in S Scotland, is only a furlong further.

870 THE LAW, DUNDEE: Few cities have such a single good viewpt. To N of the
MAP 4 centre, it reveals the panoramic perspective of the city on the estuary of the
D3 silvery Tay. Best to walk from town; the one-way system is a nightmare. Get
your chips at Luigi's (1202/FISH 'N' CHIPS) on the way up; you've got Dundee in
a poke.

871 QUEEN'S VIEW, LOCH TUMMEL nr PITLOCHRY: 8km on B8019 to Kinloch
MAP 4 Rannoch. Carpark/Fr Comm Centre and 100m walk to rocky knoll where
B2 pioneers of tourism, Queen Victoria and Albert, were 'transported into ecstasies'
by the view of L Tummell and Schiehallion.

872 CALIFER, nr FORRES: 7km from Forres on A96 to Elgin, turn rt for 'Pluscarden',
MAP 3 follow narrow rd for 5km. Viewpt is on rd and looks down across Findhorn Bay
B2 and the wide vista of the Moray Firth to the Black Isle and Ben Wyvis. Fantastic
light.

872a THE MALCOLM MEMORIAL, LANGHOLM: 3km from Langholm and signed from
MAP 8 main A7, a single-track rd leads to a path to this obelisk raised to celebrate the
C4 military and masonic achievements of one John Malcolm. The eulogy is fulsome
esp compared with that for Hugh MacDiarmid on the cairn by the stunning
sculpture at the start of the path (970A/MEMORIALS). Views from the obelisk,
however, are among the finest in the south, encompassing a vista from the
Lakeland Fells and the Solway Firth to the wild Border hills. Path 1km.

872b DUNCRYNE HILL, GARTOCHARN, nr BALLOCH: Gartocharn is betw Balloch and
MAP 1 Drymen on the A811, and this view suggested to me by a Mr William Steven is
D2 recommended by writer and outdoorsman Tom Weir as 'the finest viewpoint of
any small hill in Scotland'. Turn up the rd at the E end of village and park 1km
on left by a small wood (a sign reads 'Watch out for teddy bears'). The hill is
only 463ft high and 'easy', but the view of L Lomond and the Kilpatrick Hills is
apparently superb. I'll see it one of these days.

WHERE BEST TO WATCH BIRDS

See p. 137 for wildlfe reserves, all of which are bird reserves too.

✝ ✝ **HANDA ISLAND, nr SCOURIE, SUTHERLAND:** Take the boat from Tarbet 873
Beach 6km off A894 5km N of Scourie and land on a beautiful island MAP 2
run by the Scottish Wildlife Trust as a seabird reserve. Boats (Apr-mid Sept C1
though fewer birds after Aug) are continuous depending on demand (Willie
Macrae 0971 2156/2148). Crossing 15min. Small reception hut and 2.5km walk
over island to cliffs which rise 350m and are layered in colonies from fulmars to
shags. Allow 3 to 4 hrs. Perhaps you can persuade Willie to take you round in
his boat to see the cliffs and the formidable stack from below. Though you must
take care not to disturb the birds, you'll be eye to eye with seals and bill to bill
with razorbills. No boats on Sun.

✝ ✝ **CAERLAVEROCK, nr DUMFRIES:** 15km S on B725, signed from rd. Park at 874
'The Wildlife and Wetlands Centre'. Admission to observation towers MAP 9
and walkways betw embankments into which hides have been built at intervals D3
allowing fine views of the surrounding wetlands. Large assemblies of numerous
species; sightings posted. Great success story for Barnacle Geese now wintering
from Spitzbergen in many thousands. A well-managed site where it is possible to
get so close to the birds, that it's hard to imagine that they don't know you're
there. Oct-April.

Caerlaverock Castle (922)

✝ ✝ **LUNGA AND THE TRESHNISH ISLANDS:** Off Mull. Sail from Iona, or 875
Fionnphort or Ulva ferry on Mull to these uninhabited islands on a 5 or MAP 1
6 hr excursion which probably takes in Staffa and Fingal's Cave. Best months are A1
May-July when birds are breeding. Some trips allow 3hrs on Lunga. Razorbills,
guillemots and a carpet of puffins oblivious to your presence. This will be a
memorable day. Boat trips 06884 242 or check Tobermory TO 0688 2182, who
will advise of other boatmen. All trips dependent on sea conditions.

✝ ✝ **ISLE OF MAY, FIRTH OF FORTH:** Island at mouth of Forth off Crail/ 876
Anstruther reached by daily boat trip from Anstruther Harbour (0333 MAP 5
310103), May-Sept 9am-2.30pm depending on tides. Boats hold 40/50; trip 45mins E3
allows 3hrs ashore. Island (incl isthmus to Rona) 1.5km x 0.5km. Info centre and
resident wardens. See guillemots, razorbills and kittiwakes on cliffs and shags, terns
and thousands of puffins. Most popns increasing. On a clear day, this is bliss.

✝ **FOWLSHEUGH, nr STONEHAVEN:** 8km S of Stonehaven and signed from A92 877
with path from Crawton. Seabird city on spectacular cliffs where you can MAP 3
lie on your front and look over. The cliffs are 75m high; take great care. 80,000 D4
pairs of 6 species esp guillemots, kittiwakes, razorbills and also fulmar, shag,
puffins. Poss to view the birds without disturbing them and see the 'layers' they
occupy on the cliff face. Best seen May-July.

878 LOCH OF THE LOWES, DUNKELD: 4km NE Dunkeld on A923 to Blairgowrie. ✝
MAP 4 Properly managed (SWT) site with double-floored hide and permanent
C3 binocs. Main attractions are the captivating ospreys (from early Apr-Aug/Sept).
Nest 100m over loch and clearly visible. Their revival is well documented incl
diary of movements, breeding history etc; sighting charts of other species.

879 LOCH GARTEN, BOAT OF GARTEN: 3km village off B970 into Abernethy ✝
MAP 2 Forest. Famous for the ospreys and so popular that access may be restricted
D4 until after the eggs have hatched. 2 carparks: the first has nature trails through
Scots Pine woods and around loch; other has the main hide 300m away. Contrary
to expectations the nest isn't near the loch and the birds don't even fish there –
fishfarms are easier. But they are magnificent.

880 ISLAY, LOCH GRUINART, LOCH INDAAL: RSPB reserve. Take A847 at Bridgend ✝
MAP 1 then B8017 turning north and right for Gruinart. The mudflats and fields at
A3 the head of the loch provide winter grazing for huge flocks of Barnacle and
Greenland geese. They arrive as do flocks of fellow birdwatchers in late Oct.
Hides and good vantage-points near rd. The Rhinns and in S, The Oa sustain a
huge variety of birdlife.

881 MARWICK HEAD, ORKNEY MAINLAND: 40km NW of Kirkwall, via Finstown ✝
MAP 10 and Dounby; take left at Birsay after Loch of Isbister cross the B9056 and
park at Cumlaquoy. Spectacular seabird breeding colony on 100m cliffs and
nearby at the Loons Reserve, wet meadowland, 8 species of duck and many
waders. Orkney sites incl the Noup cliffs on Westray, North Hill on Papa
Westray and Copinsay, 3km E of the mainland. The remoter, the merrier.

882 BARONSHAUGH, MOTHERWELL: nr Strathclyde Park. From Motherwell Civic
MAP 1 Centre, take rd for Hamilton then left (1km) up Leven St, bearing rt to end (there
E3 are signs). RSPB reserve of woodland, marsh and scrub by R Clyde; a sanctuary
in a heavily built-up area. Furthest of 4 hides is 1.5km walk. Surprising range of
species esp in winter. Dalzell Country Park adj, has trails.

883 THE LAGOON, MUSSELBURGH: On E edge of town behind the racecourse (follow
MAP 7 rd round), at the estuarine mouth of the R Esk. Waders, seabirds, ducks aplenty
C1 and often interesting migrants on the mudflats and wide littoral. The 'lagoon'
itself is a man-made pond behind and attracts big populations (both birds and
binocs). This is the nearest diverse-species area to Edinburgh (15km).

884 THE BASS ROCK, off NORTH BERWICK: The 'temple of gannets' that sits 2km from
MAP 7 shore, reached May-Sept in large open boat, a tourist trip leaving daily (1.5hr
D1 round trip) from N Berwick harbour. Thousands of gannets comparable with
Ailsa Craig and St Kilda and rather easier to get to. Smaller numbers of other
species. Landings poss. Same boat also to Fidra nearby. Mr Marr, 0620 2838.

885 LOCH OF KINNORDY, KIRRIEMUIR: 4km W of town on B951, an easily accessible
MAP 4 site with 2 hides o/looking loch and wetland area managed by RSPB. Geese in
D3 winter, gulls aplenty; always tickworthy.

886 STRATHBEG, nr FRASERBURGH: 12km S off main Fraserburgh-Peterhead rd, the
MAP 3 A952 and signed by RSPB. Wide shallow loch v close to coastline a 'magnet for
E2 migrating wildfowl' and from the (unmanned) reception centre at lochside it's
poss to get a v good view of them. Marsh/fen, dune and meadow habitats. In
winter there are 30,000 geese/widgeon/mallard/swans and occ rarities like cranes
and egrets. Binoculars in centre and 2 other hides, but access limited to set route.

INTERESTING WILDLIFE RESERVES

*These wildlife reserves are not merely birdwatching places. Most of them are easy
to get to from major centres; none require permits.*

887 ST ABBS HEAD, nr BERWICK: 22km N Berwick, 9km N Eyemouth and ✝ ✝
MAP 8 only 10km E of main A1. Spectacular cliff scenery (1071/COASTAL
E1 WALKS), a huge seabird colony, rich marine life and a varied flora make this a
place of fascination and diverse interest. Good view from top of stacks, geos and
cliff face full of serried ranks of guillemot, kittiwake, razorbill etc. Hanging
gardens of grasses and campion. Behind cliffs, grassland rolls down to the Mire
Loch and its varied habitat of bird, insect and butterfly life and vegn. Superb.

888 SANDS OF FORVIE and THE YTHAN ESTUARY, NEWBURGH: 25km N of ✝
MAP 3 Aberdeen. Cross bridge outside Newburgh on A975 to Cruden Bay and
E3 park. Path follows Ythan estuary and, bearing N, enters the largest dune system
in the UK undisturbed by man. Dunes in every aspect of formation. Collieston, a
17/18th-century fishing village arranged in terraces on the cliffs, is 5km away.
The various coastal habitats support the largest popn of eiders in UK (esp June)
and huge numbers of terns. Plenty to see even from main rd lay-bys; also hides.

JOHN MUIR COUNTRY PARK, DUNBAR: The vast park betw Dunbar and N Berwick 889 named after the naturalist/explorer who was born in Dunbar and who, in MAP 7 founding Yellowstone National Park in the US, is regarded as the father of the E1 Conservation movement. Incorporating the estuary of the Tyne (park is known locally as Tyninghame), cliffs, sand spits and woodland, it covers a wide range of habitats. Innumerable bird species incl at least 30 waders, 7 kinds of crab, huge variety of lichens, sea and marsh plants. Enter at E extremity of Dunbar at Belhaven, off the B6370 from A1; or off A198 to N Berwick 3km from A1.

LOCHWINNOCH: 30km SW of Glasgow via M8 jnct 29 then A737 and A760 past 890 Johnstone. Also from Largs 20km via A760. Reserve is just outside village on MAP 1 lochside and comprises wetland and woodland habitats. A 'nature centre' C3 incorporates an observation tower and there are other hides and marked trails. Centre 10am-5.15pm.

RSPB

INSH MARSHES, KINGUSSIE: 4km from town along B970 (after Ruthven Barracks, 891 931/RUINS), a reserve run by RSPB but with much more than just birds to see. MAP 2 Trail (3km) marked out through meadow and marshland and a note of species to D4 look out for (incl 6 types of orchid). Also 2 hides (250m and 450m) high above marshes, fine vantage-points to see waterfowl, birds of prey, otters and deer.

TENTSMUIR, betw NEWPORT and LEUCHARS: The northern tip of Fife at the 892 mouth of the Firth of Tay, reached from Tayport or Leuchars via the B945. MAP 5 Follow signs for Kinshaldy Beach taking rd that winds for 4km over flat and then D2 forested land. Park amongst Corsican Pine plantation and walk across dunes to a broad strand which many consider to be a better beach than the West Sands at St Andrews. Walks in either direction: W back to Tayport, E towards Eden Bird Sanctuary. Also 4km circ walk of beach and forest. Hide 2km away at Ice House Pond. Seals often watch from waves. Lots of butterflies. Waders aplenty and, to E, one of UK's most significant populations of eider. Most wildfowl offshore on Abertay Sands (white with gulls). Geese in winter.

VANE FARM: RSPB reserve on S shore of L Leven, beside and bisected by B9097 893 off jnct 5 of M90. Easily reached and v busy visitor centre with observation MAP 5 lounge and education/orientation facs. Hide nearer lochside reached by tunnel B3 under rd. Nature Trail on hill behind through heath and birchwood (2km circ). Good place to introduce kids to the important business of nature watching. ADM

WHERE TO SEE DOLPHINS, PORPOISES AND MINKE WHALES

MORAY FIRTH, nr INVERNESS and CROMARTY: From numerous sites on the Moray Firth, and Black Isle coasts, Dolphins most active on a rising tide can often be seen even from the Kessock Bridge at Inverness. Other sites with helpful marker boards at **FOULIS FERRY,** W end of carpark; **BALINTORE,** opp Seaboard Memorial Hall; **TARBERT NESS,** end of path thro reserve; esp **CHANONRY POINT,** E end of pt beyond lighthouse.

MOUSA SOUND, SHETLAND: 20km S of Lerwick. See 950/PREHISTORIC SITES.

CARRADALE, MULL OF KYNTYRE: Take B879 from B842 the E coast rd S to Campbeltown. Carradale Point looks over the Kilbrannan Sound to Arran.

ARDNAMURCHAN, THE POINT: The most westerly pt (and lighthouse) on this wildly beautiful peninsula. Go to end of rd or park nr Sanna Beach and walk round.

STORNOWAY, ISLE OF LEWIS: Heading out of town for Eye Peninsula, at Holm nr Sandwick S of A866 or from Bayble Bay (all within easy walking distance).

FOR BOAT TRIPS: **DOLPHIN ECOSSE, CROMARTY:** 03817 323.

SEA-LIFE CRUISES, MULL: 06884 223.

. . . AND OTTERS

Otters can be seen all over the NW Highlands in sheltered inlets, esp early morning and late evening. Isle of Skye good; and organised, **OTTER WATCH AT KYLERHEA:** 3km from ferry (from Glenelg), signposted. Also – **SKYE ENVIRONMENTS CENTRE BROADFORD:** 06884 223. Wildlife walks, hols, w/ends.

RIVER PICNICS AND GREAT
SWIMMING HOLES

Lest it needs to be said: great care should be taken when swimming in rivers; don't take them for granted. Kids should be watched. Most of these places are traditional local swimming and picnic spots where people have swum for years, but rivers continuously change their course and their nature. Wearing sandals or old sports shoes is a good idea.

894 **NEIDPATH, PEEBLES:** 2km from town on A72, Biggar rd; sign for castle. Park
MAP 8 on road in lay-by 100m further on, or down track by castle (gates shut at
B2 5pm and they get shirty if you're still parked). Idyllic setting of a broad meander of the Tweed, with medieval Neidpath Castle, a sentinel above (open to public Apr- Sept). Two 'pools' (3m deep in av summer) linked by shallow rapids which the adventurous chute down on their backs. Usually a rope-swing at upper pool. TAKE CARE.

895 **DULSIE BRIDGE nr NAIRN:** 16km S of Nairn on the A939 to Grantown, this
MAP 2 locally revered beauty spot is fabulous for swimming in summer. The ancient
D3 arched bridge (1794) spans the rocky gorge of the Findhorn and there are ledges and even sandy beaches for picnics and from which to launch or paddle into the peaty waters.

896 **FALLS OF BRUAR nr BLAIR ATHOLL:** Just off A9, 12km N of Blair Atholl. 250m
MAP 4 walk from carpark to lower fall (825/FALLS) where there is an accessible large
B2 deep pool by the bridge. Cold, fresh mountain water in a woodland gorge. Birds flit around you. And probably water sprites.

897 **THE OTTER'S POOL, NEW GALLOWAY FOREST:** A clearing in the forest reached by a
MAP 9 track, 'The Raider's Road', running from 8km N of Laurieston on the A762, for
C3 16km to Clatteringshaws Loch. The track which is only open Apr-Oct has a toll of £1.50 and gets busy. It follows the Water of Dee and halfway down the rd you come to the Otter's Pool. It's hardly secret; a bronze otter marks the spot and it's a place mainly for kids and paddling but 50m downstream is another pool, deep enough to swim. 1057/WOODLAND WALKS.

898 **ANCRUM:** A secret place on the quiet Ale Water (out of village towards Lilliesleaf)
MAP 8 3km a recessed gate on the rt on a bend). A meadow, a Border burn, a surprising
D3 3m pool to swim. Arcadia!

899 **THE COBBY, KELSO:** A stretch of the Tweed with wide grassy banks, a traditional
MAP 8 picnic/swimming spot with Floors Castle in the background. Road to Floors and
D3 left to river. Fairly deep and wide at this point; good swimmers only.

900 **'THE PIER', DOUNE:** Where the tiny Ardoch flows into the Teith (a river which
MAP 6 makes a more prominent appearance at Callander), a swimming place on a river
D3 meadow known for no obvious reason as 'The Pier'. Walk downhill from Doune Castle past the sewage works (no, really!) and on for 100m.

901 **PARADISE, SHERIFFMUIR nr DUNBLANE:** A pool at the foot of an unexpected leafy
MAP 6 gorge on the moor betw the Ochils and Strathallan. Here the Wharry Burn is
D3 known locally as 'Paradise' and for good reason. Take road from 'behind' Dunblane or Bridge of Allan to the Sheriffmuir Inn; head downhill (back) towards Br of Allan and park nr the humped bridge. Walk downsteam for 1km. It can be midgy and it can be perfect. The inn, built in the same yr as the battle (1715), has ales, food (6-9pm) and a warm welcome.

902 **CAMBUS O'MAY nr BALLATER:** A stretch rather than pool of the R Dee in
MAP 3 Aberdeenshire. Walk down river from Ballater (6km), stopping perhaps at The
C4 Willows for tea, or park by the river. Locals swim, picnic on rocks, etc, and there are forest walks on the other side of rd (and an orienteering course).

STRATHCARRON nr BONAR BRIDGE: Dream river. 816/GLENS.

902a **INVERMORISTON:** On main L Ness rd A82 betw Inverness and Ft Augustus, this
MAP 2 is the best bit. R Moriston tumbles under an ancient bridge. Perfectly Highland.
D4 Ledges for picnics, invigorating pools, ozone-friendly. Behind Linda Usher's.

902b **STRATHMASHIE nr NEWTONMORE:** On A86 Newtonmore on A9 (25km) to Ft
MAP 2 William rd 5km from end of L Laggan, watch for Strathmashie Forest sign and
D4 lay-by. River follows rd. Falls follow you – you will always want to get back here.

902c **THE FAIRY POOLS, GLEN BRITTLE, SKYE:** Below level of heather (invisible 20m),
MAP 2 these deep, crystal-clear pools one with an underwater stone arch you can swim
B3 under, are a perfect prospect after walking the Cuillins. Betw Bruach na Frith and Sgurr a Mhadaith, you'll have to consult map or ask at campsite.

SECTION 7
Historical Places

THE BEST CASTLES

NTS: Under the care of the National Trust for Scotland. Hours vary. HS: Under the care of Historic Scotland. Standard hours are: Apr-end Sept Mon-Sat 9.30am-6.30pm; Sun 2-6pm. Oct-Mar Mon-Sat 9.30am-4.30pm; Sun 2-4.30pm.

903 CULZEAN CASTLE, MAYBOLE: 24km S of Ayr on A719. Imposs to
MAP 1 convey here the scale and the scope of the house and the country
C4 park. Allow the best part of a day. From the 12th century, but rebuilt by Robert Adam in 1775, a time of soaring ambition, its grandeur is almost out of place in this exposed clifftop position. Wartime associations as well as the Kennedys (not those Kennedys) across the warp of Scottish history. 560 acres of grounds incl clifftop walk, formal gardens, walled garden, Swan Pond (a must) and Happy Valley. Harmonious home farm is Vis Centre with café, exhibits and shop etc. Open Apr-Oct 10am-5pm. Culzean is pron 'Cullane'. NTS

Culzean Castle (903)

904 STIRLING CASTLE: Some would say that Stirling is 'better' than
MAP 6 Edinburgh; perched on its rock above the town it is instantly
D4 comparable. And like Edinburgh, it's a timeless attraction that can withstand waves of tourism as it survived the centuries of warfare for which it was built. Despite this primary function, it does seem a v civilised billet, with peaceful gardens and rampart walks from which the views are excellent (esp the aerial view of the Royal Gardens, 'the cup and saucer' as they're known locally). The tableau in the barracks of Orrey's Regiment is well done. But it's the renovation of the Great Hall which will recreate the jewel in Stirling's crown. Interesting even as a building site, when it's finished it will demonstrate how magnificent the banquets must have been in the Court of James V. What a place for the 1999 party. HS

905 EDINBURGH CASTLE: Edin city centre. Impressive from any angle and
MAP A all the more so from inside. Despite the tides of tourists and time, it
C3 still enthralls. Superb perspectives of the city and of Scottish history. New café and restau (superb views) with efficient catering operation; open only castle hrs and to castle visitors. Full report: 198/EDIN ATTRACTIONS; 1031/SPOOKY PLACES. HS

906 BRODIE CASTLE nr NAIRN: 12km E of Nairn off main A96. More a (Z plan)
MAP 2 tower house than a castle, dating from 1567 and still lived in by the
D3 *Godfather*-sounding 'Brodie of Brodie'. With a minimum of historical hocum, this mainly Victorian/Edwardian country house is furnished from rugs to moulded ceilings in the most excellent taste. Every picture (v few gloomies) bears examination. The nursery and nannies room, the guest rooms, indeed all the rooms, are eminently habitable. I could live in the library. There are regular musical evenings in the drawing-room (03094 371 for event programme). Tea-room and informal walks in grounds. An avenue leads to a lake; in spring the daffodils are famous. Apr-Sept 11am-6pm; Sun 2-6pm. Grounds open all year till sunset. NTS

† † **FALKLAND PALACE, FALKLAND:** Middle of farming Fife, 15km from M90 at jnct 8. Not a castle at all, but the hunting palace of the Stewart dynasty. Despite its recreational, rather than political role, it's one of the landmark buildings in Scottish history and in the 16th century was the finest Renaissance building in Britain. They all came here for archery, falconry and hunting boar and deer on the Lomonds; and for Royal Tennis which is displayed and explained. Still occupied by the Crichton-Stewarts, the house is dark and rich and redolent of those days of 'dancin and deray at Falkland on the Grene'. Apr-Sept 10am-6pm, Sun 2-6pm. Oct Cl at 5pm.
907 MAP 5 C3
NTS

† **EARLSHALL nr LEUCHARS/ST ANDREWS:** A 16th-century Laird's house discovered and meticulously renovated by Robert Lorimer and considered by him and many others to be his finest work. The painted Long Gallery from 1620 is outstanding and Mary Q of Scots' bedroom (yes she spent the night here too) is v quaint. His over-the-top topiary is widely celebrated. Informative guides. May-Sept 2-6pm.
908 MAP 5 D2

† **TOROSAY CASTLE, MULL:** 3km from Craignure and the ferry. A Victorian arriviste in this strategic corner where Duart Castle has ruled for centuries. Not many apartments open but who could blame them – this is a family home, endearing and eccentric esp their more recent history – like Dad's Loch Ness Monster fixation. The heirlooms are valuable because they have been cherished and there's a charming disarray which visitors are welcome to rake through. The gardens, attributed to Lorimer, are fabulous, esp the Italianate Statue Walk and are open all year. Try arriving by the Mull Light Railway from Craignure. Tea-room. Apr-Oct 10.30am-5.30pm.
909 MAP 1 B1

DUART CASTLE, MULL: A better tea-room than Torosay and an imposing seaboard situation, but Duart's history (despite continuous occupancy, a curious preoccupation with the recent Royals and its importance as the stronghold of the Clan Maclean) seems remote. Rather gloomy chambers, but above them the battlement view is to die for; presumably they did. May-Sept 10.30am-6pm.
910 MAP 1 B1

BRODICK CASTLE, ARRAN: 4km from town (bike hire 2272/2460). Impressive, well-maintained castle, exotic formal gardens and extensive grounds. Goat Fell in the background and the sea through the trees. Dating from 13th century and until recently the home of the Dukes of Hamilton. An over-antlered hall leads to liveable rooms with portraits and heirlooms, an atmosphere of long-ago afternoons. Tangible sense of relief in the kitchens now the banquet is over. Robert the Bruce's cell is not so convincing. Apr & Oct: Mon/Wed/Sat 1-5pm. Mid Apr-Sept, 7days 1-5pm. Grounds open all year.
911 MAP 1 B3
NTS

DUNVEGAN CASTLE, SKYE: 3km Dunvegan village. Romantic history and setting, though more baronial than castellate, the result of mid-19th-century restoration that incorporated the disparate parts. Necessary crowd management leads you through a series of rooms where the Fairy Flag, displayed above a table of exquisite marquetry, has pride of place. Gardens down to the loch, where boats leave the jetty 'to see the seals'. Busy café and gift-shop at gateside carpark.
912 MAP 2 C3

EILEAN DONAN, DORNIE: On A87, 13km before Kyle of Lochalsh. A calendar favourite, often depicted illuminated, but with the airport runway lights on the new bridge behind, it's even more like Coney Eilean. Inside it's a v decent slice of history for £1. The Banqueting Hall with its Pipers' Gallery must make for splendid dinner parties for the Macraes. Much military regalia amongst the bric-à-brac, but also the impressive Raasay Punchbowl partaken of by Johnson and Boswell. Mystical views from ramparts.
913 MAP 2 C3

GLAMIS, FORFAR: 8km from Forfar via A94 or off main A929, Dundee-Aberdeen rd (turnoff 10km N of Dundee, a picturesque approach). Fairytale castle in majestic setting known chiefly for Queen Mum connection. From 1372, remodelled 17th cent. Guided tours (cont/50mins duration) of richly furnished chambers. Restau/gallery shop. Grounds relieve any claustrophobia. Mid Apr-mid Oct, noon-5.30pm.
914 MAP 4 D3

BLAIR CASTLE, BLAIR ATHOLL: Impressively visible from the A9, the castle and the landscape of the Dukes of Atholl; 10km N of Pitlochry. Hugely popular with almost a holiday camp atmos. Numbered rooms chock-full of 'collections': costumes, toys, plates, weapons, stag skulls, walking sticks – so many things! Upstairs, the more usual stuffed apartments including the Jacobite bits. Walks in the policies. Restaus. Apr-Oct 10am-6pm.
915 MAP 4 B2

916 **CASTLE MENZIES, WEEM nr ABERFELDY:** In Tay valley with spectacular ridge
MAP 4 behind (there are walks here in the Weem Forest, part of the Tummel Valley
B3 Forest Park; separate carpark). On B846, 7km W of Aberfeldy, through Weem.
The 16th-century stronghold of the Menzies (pron Ming-iss), one of Scotland's
oldest Clans, only recently and still being restored. Sparsely furnished with odd
clan memorabilia, the house nevertheless conveys more of a sense of Jacobite
times than many more brimful of bric-à-brac. Charlie stopped here on the way
to Culloden. Open farmland situation, so manured rather than manicured
grounds. Apr-Oct 10.30am-5pm, Sun 2-5pm.

917 **CRAGIEVAR nr BANCHORY:** 15km N of main A93 Aberdeen-Braemar rd betw
MAP 3 Banchory and Aboyne. A classic tower-house, perfect like a porcelain miniature;
C3 all random windows, turrets and balustrades set amongst sloping lawns and
beautiful tall trees. Inside, there may be a deal of shuffling and squeezing to be
done and looking over heads to see round 'Danzig Willie's' pile. In 1994
Cragievar may have restricted visiting hrs. Phone 0330 22000 to check. May-Sept
2-6pm.   NTS

918 **DRUM CASTLE nr BANCHORY:** 1km off main A93 Aberdeen-Braemar rd betw
MAP 3 Banchory and Peterculter and 20km from Aberdeen centre. For 24 generations
D4 this has been the seat of the Irvines. Yes, my place! Gifted to one William De
Irwin by Robert the Bruce for services rendered at Bannockburn, it combines
the original keep, a Jacobean mansion and Victorian expansionism. I duly signed
the book in the Irvine Room and wandered through the accumulated history
hopeful of identifying with something. Hugh Irvine, the family 'artist' whose
extravagant self-portrait as the Angel Gabriel raised more than a few eyebrows
in 1810, sounded more interesting than most of my soldiering forebears.
Grounds have a peaceful walled rose garden. The house has the best-looking
guide in the NTS. May-Sept 2-6pm.

919 **BALMORAL nr BALLATER:** On main A93 betw Ballater and Braemar. Grounds
MAP 3 open May-July and limited access to the house i.e. only the ballroom. Public
B4 functions are held here when *they're* in residence. For royalty rooters only and if
you like Landseers . . . Crathie Church along the main rd has a good rose
window, an altar of Iona Marble and the grave where that John Brown lies
a-mouldering.

920 **DUNROBIN CASTLE, GOLSPIE:** The largest house in the Highlands, the home of
MAP 2 the Dukes of Sutherland who once owned more land than anyone else in the
D2 British Empire. It's the first Duke who occupies an accursed place in Scots
history for his inhumane replacement, in these vast tracts, of people with sheep.
His statue stands on Ben Bhraggie above the town (968/MONUMENTS). Living
the life of English grandees, the Sutherlands transformed the castle into a
château and filled it with their obscene wealth. Once there were 100 servants for
a houseparty of 20 and it had 30 gardeners. Now it's all just history. The gardens
are still fabulous. The castle and separate museum are open May-mid Oct.
Check 0408 633177 for times.

920a **CAWDOR CASTLE, CAWDOR, nr NAIRN (12km) and INVERNESS (20km):**
MAP 2 Inexcusable that I missed out Cawdor in the first edition, because it is first rate.
D3 The family clear off for the summer and leave their romantic yet eminently
habitable castle, sylvan grounds and gurgling Cawdor Burn to you. Pictures
from Claude to Conroy, a modern kitchen as fascinating (in its recent
occupancy) as the enormous one of yore. The burn is the colour of tea. An easy
drive (25km) to Brodie (see 906/CASTLES) means you can see two of Scotland's
most appealing castles in one day. May-early Oct, 10-5.30pm, 7 days, 9 hole
golf, tearoom.

CRATHES nr BANCHORY: 761/GARDENS; 946/COUNTRY HOUSES.

FYVIE, ABERDEENSHIRE: 944/COUNTRY HOUSES.

FASQUE nr STONEHAVEN: 937/COUNTRY HOUSES.

FLOORS CASTLE, KELSO: 940/COUNTRY HOUSES.

TRAQUAIR, INNERLEITHEN: 939/COUNTRY HOUSES.

THIRLESTANE, LAUDER: 942/COUNTRY HOUSES.

THE MOST INTERESTING RUINS

HS: Under the care of Historic Scotland. Standard hours are: Apr-end Sept Mon-Sat 9.30am-6pm; Sun 2-6pm. Oct-Mar Mon-Sat 9.30am-4.30pm, Sun 2-4.30pm. 'Friends of Historic Scotland' membership: 031 244 3099 *or any of the manned sites (annual charge but then free admission).*

✝✝✝ **LINLITHGOW PALACE:** Impossible to miss, but don't confuse the magnificent Renaissance edifice with St Michael's Church next door, topped with its controversial crown and spear spire (commissioned when David Steele's dad was the minister). From the richly carved fountain in the courtyard, to the Great Hall with its adj huge kitchens, you get a real impression of the lavish lifestyle of the Court. It's still a great place for a party. 921 MAP 7 B1 HS

✝✝ **CAERLAVEROCK nr DUMFRIES:** 17km S by B725. Follow signs for Wetlands Reserve (874/BIRDWATCHING), but go past road end. Fairytale fortress within double moat and manicured lawns, the daunting frontage being the apex of an uncommon triangular shape. Since 1270, the bastion of the Maxwells, the Wardens of the W Marches. Destroyed by Bruce, beseiged in 1640; now only waiting to be turned into a movie. 922 MAP 9 D3 HS

✝ **DUNNOTTAR CASTLE nr STONEHAVEN:** 3km S of Stonehaven on the coast rd just off the A92. Like Slains further N, the ruins are impressively and precariously perched on a clifftop. Historical links with Wallace, Mary Q of S (the odd night) and even Oliver Cromwell whose Roundheads beseiged it in 1650. 400m walk from carpark. Also possible to walk along cliff from bend in rd above Stonehaven Harbour (2km). Mar-Oct 9am-6pm, Sun 2-5pm. 923 MAP 3 D4

BOTHWELL CASTLE: Uddingston, Glasgow. 15km E of city via M74, Uddingston turn-off into main st and follow signs. Hugely impressive 13th-century ruin, the home of the Black Douglases, o/looking Clyde (along which there are fine walks). Remarkable considering proximity to city that there is hardly any 20th-century intrusion except yourself. 1km from carpark. ADM to go inside. 924 MAP 1 D3 HS

FORT GEORGE nr INVERNESS: On promontory of Moray Firth 18km NE via A96 by village of Ardersier. A vast site and 'one of the most outstanding artillery fortifications in Europe'. Planned after Culloden as a base for George II's army and completed 1769, it has remained unaltered ever since and allows a v complete picture. May provoke palpitations in the Nationalist heart, but it's heaven for militarists and altogether impressive. 925 MAP 2 D3 HS

DUNOLLIE CASTLE: Oban. Just outside town via Corran Esplanade towards Ganavan. Best to walk to or park on Esplanade and then walk 1km. (No safe parking on main rd below castle.) Bit of a scramble up and a slither down, but the views are superb. More atmospheric than Dunstaffnage and not commercialised. You can climb one flight up, but the ruin is only a remnant of the great stronghold of the Lorn Kings that it was. The Macdougals who took it over in the 12th century still live in the house below. Do not disturb. 926 MAP 1 B1

TARBERT CASTLE: Tarbert, Argyll. Strategically and dramatically overlooks the sheltered harbour of this epitome of a West Highland port. Unsafe to clamber over, it's for the timeless view rather than an evocation of tangible history that it's worth finding the way up. Robert the Bruce extended it in the 14th century and though it's always had a royal status, it's now pleasingly tumbledown. Unmarked steps by the café next to the craft shop/gallery on Harbour Rd are the best approach. 927 MAP 1 B3

SKIPNESS CASTLE: Claonaig, Kintyre, 26km S of Tarbert. Skipness lies at the very end of the B8001, off the A83 to Campbeltown. A fortress overlooking the seaways of Kilbrannan Sound and the Sound of Bute, since the late 13th century. Pleasant open grassed courtyard. There's a ruined chapel on the foreshore 700m away if you feel like an amble. A seafood 'cabin' sells nice *al fresco* snacks (Easter-Sept). 928 MAP 1 B3 HS

CRICHTON CASTLE nr PATHHEAD: 6km W of A68 at Pathhead and 28km S Edinburgh; can also app via A7 turning E, 3km S of Gorebridge, heading for Borthwick Castle (a hotel, 36/EDIN: HOTELS OUTSIDE TOWN). Massive Border keep dominating the Tyne valley on knoll with church ruin nearby. Spectacular 'range' built late 16th century. 500m walk from Crichton village or 3km from hotel (though this path is not obvious all the way). ADM. 929 MAP 7 C2 HS

Manderston, Duns (938)

930 TANTALLON CASTLE, NORTH BERWICK: 5km E of town by coast rd; 500m to
MAP 7 dramatic clifftop setting with views to Bass Rock. Dates from 1350 with massive
D1 'curtain wall' to see it through stormy weather and stormy history. The Red
Douglases and their friends kept the world at bay. ADM.   HS

931 RUTHVEN BARRACKS, KINGUSSIE: 2km along B970 and visible from A9 esp at
MAP 2 night when it's illuminated, these former barracks built by the English Redcoats
D4 as part of the campaign to tame the Highlands after the first Jacobite rising in
1715, were actually destroyed by the Jacobites in 1746 after Culloden. It was
here that Bonnie Prince Charlie sent his final order, 'let every man seek his own
safety', signalling the absolute end of the doomed cause. Life for the soldiers is
well described and visualised. Open all year.   HS

932 URQUHART CASTLE, DRUMNADROCHIT, LOCH NESS: 28km S of Inverness on A82.
MAP 2 The classic Highland fortress on a promontory o/looking L Ness visited every
D4 year by busloads and boatloads of tourists. Photo opportunities galore amongst
the well-kept lawns and extensive ruins of the once formidable stronghold of the
Picts and their scions, finally abandoned in the 18th century. ADM.   HS

933 DOUNE CASTLE, DOUNE: Follow signs from centre of village which is just off A84
MAP 6 Callander-Dunblane rd. O/looking the R Teith, the well-preserved ruin of a late
C3 14th-century courtyard castle with a Great Hall and another draughty room
where Mary Queen of Scots slept. ADM.   HS

934 SLAINS CASTLE, betw NEWBURGH and CRUDEN BAY: 32km N of Aberdeen off
MAP 3 the A975 perched on the cliffs. Obviously because of its location but also
E3 because there's no reception centre/postcard shop and guided tour, this is a ruin
that whispers to you. Your imagination, like Bram Stoker's (whom it is said was
inspired after staying here to write *Dracula*), can be cast to the winds. The seat
of the Earls of Errol, it has been gradually disintegrating since the roof was
removed in 1925. Once, it had the finest dining-room in Scotland. The waves
crash below, as always. Careful!

935 ELGIN CATHEDRAL, ELGIN: Follow signs in town centre. Set in a meadow by the
MAP 3 river, a tranquil corner of this busy market town, the scattered ruins and
B2 surrounding graveyard of what was once Scotland's finest cathedral. The nasty
Wolf of Badenoch burned it down in 1390, but there's some 13th-century and
medieval renewals. The octagonal chapterhouse is esp revered. ADM.   HS

936 ST ANDREWS CATHEDRAL: The ruins of the largest church in Scotland before the
MAP 5 Reformation, a place of great influence and pilgrimage. St Rule's Tower and the
D2 jagged fragment of the huge West Front in their striking position at the
convergence of the main streets and o/looking the sea, are remnants of its great
glory.

GREAT COUNTRY HOUSES

✝ ✝ **FASQUE, betw STONEHAVEN and MONTROSE:** W of A92 at Laurencekirk 937 and through Victorian Fettercairn to Fasque, one of the most fascinating MAP 3 old houses you'll ever be permitted to wander through on your own. Home of C4 Gladstone (4 times Prime Minister) whose descendants still live in the west wing. Shut down in 1939 till the 1970s, the world before and betw the wars was preserved and is still there for faded-grandeur connoisseurs to savour and all of us to sense. There's a mountain of furniture that indefatigable curator Jo Smith wants to restore. Go and support a worthy cause and take a trip back in time that leaves most 'heritage museums' stuck in the 1980s. No souvenirs, plenty memories. May-Sept, 1.30-5.30pm. Cl Fri.

✝ **MANDERSTON, DUNS:** Off A6105, 2km down Duns-Berwick rd. Described 938 as the swan-song of the Great Classical House, one of the finest examples of MAP 8 Edwardian opulence in UK. A silver staircase and marble stables are amongst D2 staggering but not distasteful ostentation. Below stairs as fascinating as up; sublime gardens. Open May-Sept, Thu/Sun and some Mon afternoons.

✝ **TRAQUAIR, INNERLEITHEN:** 0896 830323. 2km from A72 Peebles-Gala rd. 939 Archetypal romantic Border retreat steeped in Jacobite history. Human MAP 8 proportions, liveability and lots of atmosphere; an enchanting house. Traquair B2 ale still brewed. Major crafts and music fair held in grounds in early Aug. Apr-Sept.

FLOORS CASTLE, KELSO: 0573 23333. More a vast country mansion than a castle, the 940 ancestral home of the Duke of Roxburgh, o/looking with imposing grandeur the MAP 8 town and the Tweed. 18th-century with later additions. Visitors are led round D3 lofty public rooms past the family collections of fine furniture, tapestries and porcelain. Priceless and spectacularly impractical. Massed pipe bands in Aug. Interesting garden centre (1299/GARDEN CENTRES). Open seasonally, but usually Sun-Thu, May-Sept.

MELLERSTAIN nr GORDON/KELSO: 057381 225. Home of the Earl of Haddington, 941 signed from B6089 (Kelso-Gordon) or A6105 (Earlston-Greenlaw). One of MAP 8 Scotland's great Georgian houses, begun by William Adam in 1725, completed D3 by Robert. Outstanding decorative interiors esp the library. Some important paintings. Thatched cottage in grounds, tea-room etc. May-Sept 12.30-5pm.

THIRLESTANE, LAUDER: 05782 430. 2km off A68. A castellate/baronial seat of the 942 Earls and Duke of Lauderdale and family home of the Maitlands; it must take MAP 8 some upkeeping. Extraordinary state-rooms, esp plasterwork; the ceilings must C2 be seen to be believed. In contrast, the nurseries (with toy collection), kitchens and laundry are more approachable. May-Sept 2-5pm, Cl Sat.

ABBOTSFORD nr MELROSE: Home of Walter Scott (1027/LITERARY PLACES).

BOWHILL, SELKIRK: 6km W of town on A708 to Moffat. House and renowned 943 art collection open July only, but the grounds with some wonderful walks are MAP 8 open May-Sept. Also riding school and extraordinary theatre (1321/THEATRES). C3 Walks should incl ruin of Newark Castle on a bluff above the Yarrow and the loch nr the house. Good adventure playground in trees is best for older kids.

FYVIE, ABERDEENSHIRE: Not near any major towns but 42km NW Aberdeen and 944 firmly on the 'Castle Trail' whereby you trundle from one NT House to the MAP 3 next quickly becoming satiated and less impressed by it all. In tree-lined acres D2 with lochside walks, one of the crowning glories of Scottish Baronial. Fantastic roofscape and ceilings to match. Grand design/Edwardian atmos. NTS

HADDO HOUSE: About 15km away by aforementioned 'Trail' over back roads, 945 the Palladian-style Adam mansion well known for its musical evenings. Rather MAP 3 austere, but the basements are a place to ponder. You can see all the castles of D2 Scotland in watercolour. The window by Burne Jones in the chapel is glorious. Well worth checking the event programme of the NT to find out what's on at Haddo. Tickets avail in Aberdeen 0224 641122.

CRATHES nr BANCHORY: 25km W of Aberdeen on A93. Amidst superb gardens 946 (761/GARDENS) a tower house which is also one of the most interesting of these MAP 3 'fairytale castles' to visit. Up and down spiral staircases and into small but D4 liveable rooms. The notable painted ceilings and the Long Gallery at the top are all worth lingering over. 350 yrs of the Burnett family are ingrained in this oak. Proper tea-room; adventure playground. Apr-Oct 11am-6pm. NTS

THE BEST PREHISTORIC SITES

947 SKARA BRAE, ORKNEY MAINLAND: 32km Kirkwall by A965/966 via
MAP 10 Finstown and Dounby. Can be a windy walk to this remarkable
shoreline site, the subterranean remains of a compact village 5,000 yrs old. It was
engulfed by a sandstorm 600yrs later and lay perfectly preserved until uncovered
by another storm in 1850. Now it permits one of the most evocative glimpses of
truly ancient times in the UK. ADM.   HS

948 THE STANDING STONES OF STENNESS, ORKNEY MAINLAND: Together
MAP 10 with the Ring of Brodgar and the great chambered tomb of Maes Howe,
all within walking dist of the A965, 18km from Kirkwall, this is as impressive a
ceremonial site as you'll find anywhere. From same period as Skara Brae. The
individual stones and the scale of the Ring are v impressive and deeply
mysterious. The burial cairn is the finest megalithic tomb in the UK. Seen
together they will stimulate even the most jaded sense of wonder.   HS

Ring of Brodgar, Orkney (948)

949 THE CALLANISH STONES, ISLE OF LEWIS: 24km from Stornoway. Take
MAP 2 Tarbert rd and go rt at Leurbost. The best preserved and most unusual
B2 combination of standing stones in a ring around a tomb, with radiating arms in
cross shape. Dating from 4000BC, they were unearthed from the peat in the mid-
19th cent and have become the major historical attraction of the Hebrides. Other
configurations nearby. At dawn there's nobody else there. Free.   HS

950 THE MOUSA BROCH, SHETLAND: On small island of Mousa, off Shetland
MAP 10 mainland 20km S of Lerwick, visible from main A970 but to be seen
properly, take boat from Sandwick (Tom Jamieson 09505 367). Isolated in its
island fastness, this is the best preserved broch in Scotland. Walls are 13m high
(orig 15m) and galleries run up the middle, in one case to the top. Solid as a rock,
this example of a uniquely Scottish phenomenon would have been a very des res
at the turn of the millennium. JARLSHOF in the far S next to Sumburgh airport
has remnants and ruins from Neolithic to Viking times to the 18th century, with
esp impressive 'wheelhouses'. ADM.   HS

951 THE BROCHS, GLENELG: 110km from Ft William. Glenelg is 14km from the A87
MAP 2 at Shiel Br (849/SCENIC ROUTES). 5km from Glenelg village in beautiful Glen
C4 Beag. The two brochs, Dun Trodden and Dun Telve, are the best preserved
examples on the mainland of these mysterious 1st-century homesteads. Easy
here to distinguish the twin stone walls that kept out the cold and the more
disagreeable neighbours. Free.   HS

952 BARPA LANYASS, NORTH UIST: 8km S Lochmaddy, visible from main A867 rd. A
MAP 2 'squashed' beehive burial cairn dating from 1000BC, the tomb of a chieftain. It's
A3 largely intact and you can explore inside, crawling thro the short entrance tunnel
and down through the years. A bit spooky.

TOMB OF THE EAGLES, ORKNEY MAINLAND: 33km S of Kirkwall at the foot of S 953 Ronaldsay and signed from Burwick. A 'recent' discovery, the excavation of this MAP 10 cliff cave is on private land. You should call in at the house first and they'll tell you the whole story! Then there's a 2km walk. Allow a bit of time; it's . . . justified and ancient. ADM.

CAIRNPAPPLE HILL nr LINLITHGOW, WEST LOTHIAN: App from the 'Beecraigs' rd 954 off W end of Linlithgow main st. Go past the Beecraigs turn-off and cont for MAP 7 3km. Cairnpapple is signed. Cairn and remnants of various rings of stones evince A1 the long sequence of ceremonial activities that took place on this high, windy hill betw 2800 and 500BC. Atmosphere even more strange by the very 20th-century communications mast that Mercury have been able to erect next door. Go into the tomb; there are standing stones inside. ADM.
HS

BAR HILL nr KIRKINTILLOCH: 431/GLASGOW: VIEWS. A fine example of the low 955 ruins of a Roman fort on the Antonine Wall which ran across Scotland for MAP 1 200yrs early AD. Great place for an out-of-town walk. D3

CAIRNHOLY, betw NEWTON STEWART/GATEHOUSE: 1km off main A75. Signed 956 from rd, a pleasant walk up the glenside. A mini Callanish of standing stones MAP 9 around a burial cairn on v human scale and in a serene setting with views of B4 Wigtown Bay, the S Uplands behind.

EAST AQUHORTHIES STONE CIRCLE, nr INVERURIE nr ABERDEEN: Signed from 957 B993 from Inverurie to Monymusk. A circle of pinkish stones with 2 grey MAP 3 sentinels flanking a huge recumbent stone set in the rolling countryside of the D3 Don Valley with Bennachie in the background. (1045/FAVOURITE HILLS).

LOANHEAD OF DAVIOT STONE CIRCLE, nr INVERURIE/ABERDEEN: Head for the 958 village of Daviot on B9001 from Inverurie; or Loanhead, signed off A920 rd betw MAP 3 Old Meldrum and Insch. The site is 500m from top of village. Impressive and D3 spooky circle of 11 stones and one recumbent from 4000/5000BC. Unusual second circle adj encloses a cremation cemetery from 1500BC. Remains of 32 people were found here. Obviously, an important place for God-knows-what rituals.

THE GREY CAIRNS OF CANSTER nr WICK: 20km S of Wick, a very straight rd 959 (signed for Cairns) heads W from the A9 for 8km. The cairns are instantly MAP 2 identifiable nr the rd and impressively complete. The 'horned cairn' is the best in E2 the UK. In 2500BC these stone-piled structures were used for the disposal of the dead. You can crawl inside them if you're agile. Nearby, also signed from A9 is:
HILL O' MANY STANES: Aptly named place with extraordinary number of small 960 standing stones; 200 in 22 rows. If fan shape was complete there would be 600. MAP 2 Their v purposeful layout is enigmatic and strangely stirring. E2

THE WHITHORN DIG: Recent ongoing excavations of medieval priory, the shrine of 960a St Ninian and home of the earliest church in Scotland. Not much to see but a MAP 9 serene spot behind main st of a forgotten town. Go further (799A/COASTAL VILLS). B4

GREAT MONUMENTS, MEMORIALS AND FOLLIES

These sites are open at all times and free unless o/wise stated.

THE AMERICAN MONUMENT, ISLAY: On the SW peninsula of the island, 961 known as the Oa (pron 'O'), 13km from Port Ellen. A monument to MAP 1 commemorate the shipwrecks in nearby waters, of 2 American ships, the A3 *Tuscania* and the *Ontranto*, both of which sank in 1918 at the end of the war. The obelisk overlooks this sea – which is often beset by storms – from a spectacular headland, the sort of disquieting place where you could imagine looking round and finding the person you're with – gone. Take rd from Port Ellen past Maltings marked Mull of Oa for 9km, through gate and left at broken sign. Park and walk 1.5km steadily uphill to monument. Birdlife good in Oa area.
1-A-2

WALLACE MONUMENT, STIRLING: Visible for miles and with great views 962 though not as dramatic as Stirling Castle. Approach from A91 or Br of MAP 6 Allan rd. 150m walk from carpark and 246 steps up. Victorian gothic spire marking D3 the place where Scotland's great patriot swooped down upon the English at the Battle of Stirling Bridge. Hall of Heroes (no heroines) is 'educational'. The famous sword is very big. Clifftop walk through Abbey Craig woods is worth detour. Monument open Apr-Oct 10am-5pm (9am-6pm July/Aug)
ADM

963 THE GRAVE OF FLORA MACDONALD, SKYE: Kilmuir on A855, Uig-Staffin rd,
MAP 2 40km N of Portree. A 10ft-high Celtic cross supported against the wind, high on
B3 the ridge overlooking the Uists from whence she came. Long after the legendary
journey, her funeral in 1790 attracted the biggest crowd since Culloden. The
present memorial replaced the original, which was chipped away by souvenir
hunters. Dubious though the whole business may have been, she still helped to
shape the folklore of the Highlands.

964 CARFIN GROTTO, MOTHERWELL: A723 just outside Motherwell 4km from M8, on
MAP 1 left after 2nd garage. A homage to Lourdes, built largely by striking miners in
E3 1921. (God's) acre of gardens and pathways with reliquaries, shrines, a glass
pavilion and chapel; Ravenscraig is always in the background. Spiritual
sustenance despite the throngs, for the true believers; something of a curiosity
for the rest of us. Open at all times.

965 HAMILTON MAUSOLEUM, STRATHCLYDE PARK: Off (and visible from) M74 at junc
MAP 1 5/6, 15km from Glasgow. 774/COUNTRY PARKS. Huge, over-the-top/over-the-
D3 tomb (though removed 1921) stone memorial to the 10th Duke of Hamilton.
Guided tours daily (Easter-Sept at 3pm and even better, evenings in June-Aug at
7pm; winter Sat/Sun at 2pm). Eerie and chilling and with remarkable acoustics –
the 'longest echo in Europe'. Give it a shout or take your violin.

966 PENIEL HEUGH, nr ANCRUM/JEDBURGH: (pron 'Pinal-hue'.) An obelisk visible for
MAP 8 miles and on a rise which offers some of the most exhilarating views of the
D3 Borders. Also known as the Waterloo Monument, it was built on the Marquis of
Lothian's estate to commemorate the battle. It's said that the woodland on the
surrounding slopes represents the positions of Wellington's troops. From A68
opp Ancrum turn-off, on B6400, go 1km past 'Woodland Centre' up steep,
unmarked rd to left for 150m. Park, walk up through woods.

967 THE PINEAPPLE, AIRTH: From Airth N of Grangemouth, take A905 to Stirling
MAP 6 and after 1km the B9124 for Cowie. It sits on the edge of a walled garden at the
D4 end of the drive. 45ft high, it was built in 1761 as a garden retreat by an
unknown architect and remained 'undiscovered' until 1963. How exotic the fruit
must have seemed in the 18th century, never mind this extraordinary folly.
Open all year.

968 THE MONUMENT ON BEN BHRAGGIE, GOLSPIE: Atop the hill (pron 'Brachee') that
MAP 2 dominates the town, the domineering statue and plinth (over 35m) of the
D2 dreaded first Duke of Sutherland. Surprising that nobody ever tried to blow it
up, since his callous policy of Highland Clearance made him an enemy of
Gaeldom for evermore (920/CASTLES; 1313/MUSEUMS). Climb from the town
fountain on marked path. The hill race go up in 10mins but allow 2hrs return.
His private view along the NE coast is superb.

969 McCAIG'S TOWER OR FOLLY, OBAN: Oban's great landmark built in 1897 by
MAP 1 McCaig, a local banker, to give 'work to the unemployed' and as a memorial to
B1 his family. It's like a temple or coliseum and time has mellowed whatever
incongruous effect it may have had originally. The views of the town and the
bay are magnificent and it's easy to get up from several points in town centre.
See OBAN, p 234.

970 THE PROP OF YTHSIE nr ABERDEEN: 35km NW city nr Ellon to W of A92, or
MAP 3 pass on the 'Castle Trail' since this monument commemorates one George
D2 Gordon of Haddo House nearby, who was prime minister 1852-55 (the good-
looking guy in the first portrait you come to in the house). Tower visible from
all of rolling Aberdeenshire around and there are reciprocal views should you
take the easy but unclear route up. On B999 Aberdeen-Tarves rd and 2km from
entrance to house. Take rd for the Ythsie (pron 'icy') farms, 100m.

970a THE MONUMENT TO HUGH MacDIARMID, LANGHOLM: Brilliant piece of modern
MAP 8 sculpture by Jake Harvey on the hill above Langholm 3km from A7 at beginning
C4 of path to the Malcolm obelisk from where there are great views (869A/VIEWS).
MacDiarmid, our national poet, was born in Langholm in 1872 and though they
never liked him much after he left, the monument was commissioned and a cairn
beside it raised in 1992. The bare hills surround you. The motifs of the sculpture
have been used by Runrig on the cover of their 1993 album, *Amazing Things*.

SCOTT MONUMENT, EDINBURGH: 215/EDINBURGH VIEWS.

THE GREAT ABBEYS

✠ ✠ ✠ **PLUSCARDEN ABBEY betw FORRES and ELGIN:** A fully working 971
monastic community (694/RETREATS) in one of the most spiritual of MAP 3
places. Founded by Alexander II in 1250 and being restored since 1948. *B2*
Benedictine services (starting with Matins at 5am through Prime-Terce-Sext-None-
Vespers at 6pm and Compline at 8.05) open to public. The ancient honey-coloured
walls, the brilliant stained glass, the monks' Gregorian chant; the whole effect is a
truly uplifting experience. The bell rings down the valley. Open at all times.

✠ ✠ **PAISLEY ABBEY:** Town centre. An abbey founded in 1163, razed (by the 972
English) in 1307 and with successive deteriorations and renovations ever MAP 1
since. Major restoration in the 1920s brought it to present-day cathedral-like *D3*
magnificence. Exceptional stained glass (the recent window complementing the
formidable Strachan East Window), an impressive choir and an edifying sense of
space. Sunday Services (11am/6.30pm) are superb esp full-dress communion and
there are open days (about one Sat a month, 041 889 0711) with coffee in the
cloisters, organ music and the tower open for climbing. Otherwise Abbey open
Mon-Sat 10am-3.30pm. Café/shop.

✠ ✠ **JEDBURGH ABBEY:** The classic abbey ruin, certainly the one which 973
conveys the most complete impression of those early abbeys built under MAP 8
the patronage of David I in the 12th century. Occupied 1138 (Augustinian *D3*
Canons from Beauvais) and ransacked many times, its tower and remarkable
rose window are still intact. Recent excavations have extended grounds. Best
perspective is from across the Jed in the 'Glebe'. HS

✠ **DRYBURGH ABBEY, nr ST BOSWELLS:** One of the most evocative of ruins, an 974
aesthetic attraction since the late 18th century. Sustained innumerable MAP 8
attacks from the English since its inauguration by Premonstratensian Canons in *C3*
1150. Celebrated by Sir Walter Scott, buried here in 1832 (with his biographer
Lockhart at his feet), its setting, amongst trees on the banks of the Tweed is one
of pure historical romance. 3km A68. 869/VIEWS HS

CROSSRAGUEL ABBEY, MAYBOLE: 24km S of Ayr on A77. Built 1244, one of first 975
Cluniac settlements in Scotland, an influential and rich order, stripped in the MAP 1
Reformation. Now an extensive ruin of architectural distinction, the ground *C4*
plan v well preserved and obvious. Open daily. HS

SWEETHEART, NEW ABBEY nr DUMFRIES: 12km S by A710. The endearing and 976
enduring warm red sandstone abbey in the shadow of Criffel, so named because MAP 9
Devorguilla de Balliol, devoted to her husband (he of the Oxford College), *D3*
founded the abbey for Cistercian monks and kept his heart in a casket which is
buried with her here. The ruin is unroofed but the tower is intact. 981/SW
HOTELS.

MELROSE ABBEY: Another romantic setting, the abbey seems to give an atmos to 977
the whole town. Built by David I (what a guy!) for Cistercian monks from MAP 8
Rievaulx from 1136, there wasn't much left, spiritually or architecturally, by the *C3*
Reformation. Once, however, it sustained a huge community as evinced by the
widespread excavations. There's a museum of Abbey, church and Roman relics.
Open daily, but best to 'visit it by pale moonlight'. HS

ARBROATH ABBEY: 25km N of Dundee. Founded in 1178 and endowed on an 978
unparalleled scale, this is an important place in Scots history. It's where the MAP 4
Declaration was signed in 1320 to appeal to the Pope to release the Scots from *E3*
the yoke of the English (you can buy facsimiles of the yellow parchment, the
original is in Charter House in Edin). It was to Arbroath that the Stone of
Destiny (on which the Kings of Scotland were traditionally crowned) was
returned after being stolen from Westminster Abbey in the 1950s. HS

IONA ABBEY: Oh Lord, how could I have omitted Iona Abbey from the first 978a
edition – anyway I did! This hugely significant place of pilgrimage for new age MAP 1
and old age pilgrims and tourists alike is reached from Fionnphort, SW Mull by *A1*
frequent Calmac Ferry (5min crossing). Walk 1km. Here in 563BC St Columba
began his mission for a Celtic Church that changed the face of Europe. Cloisters,
graveyard of Scottish kings, regular services. Good shop (1261/CRAFTSHOPS).
Residential courses and retreats (MacLeod Centre adj) 06817 404. See 1346/
ISLANDS.

THE MOST INTERESTING CHURCHES

*All 'generally open' unless o/wise stated; * have public services.*

979 *ST CONAN'S KIRK, LOCH AWE: A85 33km E of Oban. Perched amongst
MAP 1 trees on the side of Loch Awe, this small but spacious church seems to
C1 incorporate every ecclesiastical architectural style. Its building was a labour of
love for one Walter Campbell who was perhaps striving for beauty rather than
consistency. Though modern (begun by him in 1881 and finished by his sister
and a board of trustees in 1930), the result is a place of ethereal light and
atmosphere, enhanced by and befitting the inherent spirituality of the setting.
There's a spooky carved effigy of Robert the Bruce, a cosy cloister and the most
amazing flying buttresses. A place to wander and reflect.

980 *THE ITALIAN CHAPEL, ORKNEY MAINLAND: 8km S of Kirkwall at Lamb
MAP 10 Holm and the first causeway on the way to St Margaret's Hope. In
1943, Italian PoWs brought to work on the Churchill Barriers transformed a
Nissen hut using the most meagre materials into this remarkable ornate chapel.
The meticulous *trompe l'oeil* and wrought-iron work are a touching affirmation
of faith. At the other end of the architectural scale, St Magnus Cathedral in
Kirkwall is an edifice, but also filled with spirituality.

The Italian Chapel, Orkney (980)

981 QUEEN'S CROSS CHURCH, GLASGOW: 870 Garscube Rd where it becomes
MAP B Maryhill Rd at Springbank St. The church was built by Charles Rennie
xB1 Mackintosh in 1899 and, like all his work, is harmonious in every detail. Dark
wood, typical stained glass, serenity and simplicity. Tue/Thu/Fri noon-5.30pm;
Sun 2.30-5pm. No services. 435/MACKINTOSH.

982 *ROSSLYN CHAPEL, ROSLIN nr EDINBURGH: 12km S of city centre. Take
MAP 7 A702, then A703 from ring-route rd, marked 'Penicuik'. Roslin village 1km
C2 from main rd and chapel 500m from village crossroads above Roslin Glen
(223/WALKS OUTSIDE CITY). Very fine example of 15th-century ecclesiastical
architecture and decoration, though a grander church had originally been
planned. Outstanding stonemasonry and carving; deeply spiritual atmos. The
delicate 'Prentice Pillar' in the Lady Chapel has a sad and moving story. Vital
evidence at Rosslyn that Columbus did not discover America – follow the story.
The vaults are spooky and cold. Open Apr-Oct 10am-5pm, Sun till Evensong at
4.45pm, earlier in winter (a beautiful service). Episc.

983 *CATHEDRAL OF THE ISLES, MILLPORT ON THE ISLAND OF CUMBRAE:
MAP 1 Frequent ferry service from Largs is met by bus for 6km journey to
C3 Millport. Lane from main st by Newton pub, 250m then through gate. The
smallest 'cathedral' in Europe, one of Butterfield's great works (other is Keble
Coll, Oxford). Here, small is outstandingly beautiful. 696/RETREATS.

✠ **ST CLEMENTS, RODEL, SOUTH HARRIS:** Tarbert 40km. Classic island kirk in 984 Hebridean landscape (as long as the Super Quarry hasn't arrived by the MAP 2 time you do). Simple cruciform structure with tower which the adventurous can B3 climb. Probably influenced by Iona. Now an empty but atmospheric shell, with blackened effigies and important monumental sculpture. Goats in the churchyard graze amongst headstones of all the young Harris lads lost at sea in the Great War. There are other fallen angels on the outside of the tower.

*ST MICHAEL'S CHAPEL, ERISKAY nr S UIST/BARRA: That rare example of an 985 ordinary modern church without history or grand architecture, which has charm MAP 2 and serenity and imbues the sense of well-being that a religious centre should. A4 The focal point of a relatively devout Catholic community who obviously care about it. Alabaster angels abound. O/looks Sound of Barra.

*ST FILLAN'S CHURCH, ABERDOUR: Behind the ruined Castle in this pleasant 986 seaside village (796/COASTAL VILLAGES), a more agreeable old kirk would be MAP 5 hard to find. Restored from a 12th-century ruin in 1926, the warm stonework B4 and stained glass create a v soothing atmos.

*ST ATHERNASE, LEUCHARS: The parish church on a corner of of what is 987 essentially an Air Force base spans centuries of warfare and architecture. The MAP 5 Norman bell tower is remarkable. D2

*DUNBLANE CATHEDRAL: A huge nave of a church built around a Norman tower 988 (from David I) on the Allen Water and restored 1892. The wondrously bright MAP 6 stained glass is mostly 20th-century. The poisoned sisters buried under the altar D3 helped change the course of Scottish history, their elimination allowing James IV to marry Margaret Tudor, a union that led to Mary Queen of Scots. HS

*ST MACHAR'S CATHEDRAL, ABERDEEN: The Chanonry in 'Old Aberdeen' off St 989 Machar's Dr about 2km from centre. Best seen as part of a walk round the old MAP C 'village within the city' occupied mainly by the university's old and modern xC1 buildings. Cathedral's fine granite nave and twin-spired West Front date from 15th century, on site of 6th-century Celtic church. Noted for heraldic ceiling and 19/20th-century stained glass. Seaton Park adj has pleasant Don-side walks, adventure playground etc. Church open daily 9am-5pm.

THE EAST LOTHIAN CHURCHES at **ABERLADY, WHITEKIRK, ATHELSTANEFORD:** 3 989a historic, charming churches in bucolic settings; quiet corners to explore and MAP 7 reflect. D1

CROICK CHURCH nr BONAR BRIDGE: 16km W of Ardgay which is just over the 990 river from Bonar Bridge and through the splendid glen of Strathcarron MAP 2 (816/GLENS). This humble and charming church is chiefly remembered for its D2 place in the history of the Highland clearances. In May 1845 90 folk took shelter in the graveyard around the church after they had been cleared from their homes in nearby Glencalvie. Not allowed even in the kirk, their plight did not go unnoticed and was reported in *The Times*. The harrowing account is there to read, and the messages they scratched on the windows. Sheep graze all around. AYR.

*THOMAS COATES MEMORIAL CHURCH, PAISLEY: Built by Coates of thread fame, 990a an imposing edifice, one of the grandest Baptist churches in the UK. A MAP 1 monument to God, prosperity and the Industrial Revolution. Caretaker 041 889 D3 9980 to visit.

ST GILES CATHEDRAL, EDINBURGH: 210/EDINBURGH LESS OBVIOUS ATTRACTIONS.

GLASGOW CATHEDRAL/UNIVERSITY CHAPEL: 417/419/GLASGOW MAIN ATTRACTIONS.

THE MOST INTERESTING GRAVEYARDS

These graveyards are open at all times.

✠ ✠ **GLASGOW NECROPOLIS:** The vast burial ground behind the Cathedral in 991 the oldest part of the city. Currently closed due to storm damage and MAP B general deterioration, it's sometimes possible to get thro the railings and have E2 one of Glasgow's spookiest experiences to yourself. Dominated by the obelisk of John Knox, you share his magnificent (but stern) view of the city esp the Cathedral, the Infirmary and the Brewery all so very appropiately in the foreground. Many ostentatious graves and mausoleums.

Glasgow Necropolis (991)

EDINBURGH: In a city with many very old and atmospheric graveyards, these 3 stand out. They're best seen on wet or 'dreich' days or when there's a mist or 'haar' off the Forth.

CANONGATE: On left of Royal Mile going down to Palace. Adam Smith and the tragic poet Robert Fergusson revered by Robbie Burns (who raised the memorial stone in 1787 over his pauper's grave) are buried here in the heart of Auld Reekie. The tourist tide rarely seeps in from the street.

992
MAP A
E2

GREYFRIARS: A place of ancient mystery, famous for the wee dog who guarded his master's grave for 14yrs, for the plundering of graves in the early 18th century for the Anatomy School and for the graves of Allan Ramsay (prominent poet and burgher), James Hutton (the father of geology), William McGonagall (the 'world's worst poet') and sundry serious Highlanders. The annals of a great city are written on these stones.

993
MAP A
D3

WARRISTON: Warriston Rd by B&Q or end of cul-de-sac at Warriston Cres (Canonmills), up bank and along railway line. Overgrown, peaceful, steeped in atmosphere. Gothic horrorland.

994
MAP A
xD1

ISLE OF JURA: Killchianaig graveyard in the north. Follow rd as far as it goes to Inverlussa, graveyard is on right, just before hamlet. Mairi Ribeach apparently lived until she was 128. In the south at Keils (2km from rd N out of Craighouse, bearing left past Keils houses and through the deer-fence), her father is buried and he was 180! Both sites are beautiful, isolated and redolent of island history, with much to reflect on, not least the mysterious longevity of the inhabitants.

995
MAP 1
B2/B3

CAMPBELTOWN CEMETERY: Campbeltown. Odd, but one of the nicest things about this end-of-the-line town is the cemetery. It's at the end of a row of fascinating posh houses, the original merchant and mariner owners of which will be interred in the leafy plots next door. Still very much in use after centuries of commerce and seafaring disasters, it has crept up the terraces of a steep and lush overhanging bank. Palm trees preside over this civilised resting place. Guess you could do worse than see Campbeltown and die.

996
MAP 1
B4

ARDCHATTAN PRIORY: 20km from Oban, via Connel/N Connel. An ancient graveyard in the ruins of the Priory founded in the 13th century and occupied by the rigorous Valliscaulian order until the 17th century. Ruins lie behind what is one of the oldest inhabited houses in Scotland and beside a working farm which gives the whole site a pleasing continuity. Many late medieval tombstones incl the Red Fox, victim of the notorious Appin murder. Open Easter-Oct. Tea-room in an outbuilding.

997
MAP 1
C1

ANCRUM GRAVEYARD, nr JEDBURGH: The quintessential country churchyard; away from the village (2km along B6400), by a lazy river (the Ale Water) crossed to a farm by a hump-backed bridge and a chapel in ruins. Elegiac and deeply peaceful.

998
MAP 8
D3

BALQUHIDDER CHURCHYARD: Chiefly notable as the last resting place of one Rob Roy Macgregor who was buried in 1734 after causing a heap of trouble hereabouts and then raised to immortality by Sir Walter Scott. Picturesque Highland graveyard around kirk which hosts Sunday night concerts in summer; a great idea.

999
MAP 6
C2

LOGIE OLD KIRK nr STIRLING: A crumbling chapel and an ancient graveyard at the foot of the Ochils. The wall is round to keep out the demons, a burn gurgles beside and there are some fine and very old stones going back to the 16th century. Take rd for Wallace Monument off A91, 2km from Stirling, then first right.

1000
MAP 6
D3

TUTNAGUAIL, DUNBEATH: A cemetery in an enchanted place 5km from Dunbeath, Neil Gunn's birthplace and found by walking up the 'Strath' he describes in his book *Highland River* (1025/LIT PLACES). With a white wall around it, this graveyard which before the clearances once served a valley community of 400 souls, can be seen for miles. Despite isolation, it's still tended and used.

1001
MAP 2
E2

THE GREAT BATTLEGROUNDS

Chosen for accessibility and sense of history as well as historical significance.

1002 CULLODEN, INVERNESS: Signed from A9 and A96 into Inverness and about 8km
MAP 2 from town. Extensive battlefield on either side of the rd before you even get to
D3 the Visitor Centre. Positions of the clans and the troops marked out across the
moor; flags enable you to get a real sense of scale. If you go in spring you see
how wet and miserable the Moor can be (the battle took place on 16 April 1746).
No matter how many other folk are there, wandering down the lines, a visit to
this most infamous of battlefields can still leave a pain in the heart. Open at all
times for more solitary reflections.   NTS

1003 BATTLE OF THE BRAES, SKYE: 10km Portree. Take main A850 rd S for 3km then
MAP 2 left, marked 'Braes' for 7km. Monument is on a rise on rt. The last battle fought
B3 on British soil and a significant place in Scots history. When the clearances,
uninterrupted by any organised opposition, were virtually complete and vast
tracts of Scotland had been depopulated for sheep, the Skye crofters finally
stood up in 1882 to the Govt troops and said, enough is enough. A cairn has
been erected nr the spot where they fought on behalf of 'all the crofters of
Gaeldom', a battle which led eventually to the Crofters Act which has
guaranteed their rights ever since. At the end of this rd at Peinchorran, there are
fine views of Raasay (which was devastated by clearances) and Glamaig, the
conical Cuillin, across L Sligachan.

1004 GLENCOE: Not much of a battle, of course, but one of the most infamous
MAP 2 massacres in British history. Much has been written (John Prebble's *Glencoe* and
C5 many recent interpretations) and the Visitor Centre provides the audio-visual
scenario. There's the Macdonald monument nr Glencoe village and the walk to
the more evocative Signal Rock where the bonfire was lit, now a happy
woodland trail in this doom-laden landscape. About 4km ret from Centre. Also
1029/SPOOKY PLACES.

1005 SCAPA FLOW, ORKNEY MAINLAND AND HOY: Scapa Flow surrounded by various
MAP 10 of the southern Orkney islands is one of the most sheltered anchorages in
Europe. Hence the huge presence in Orkney of ships and personnel during both
wars. The Germans scuttled 54 of their warships here in 1919 and many still lie
in the bay. The *Royal Oak* was torpedoed in 1939 with the loss of 833 men.
Much still remains of the war years (esp if you're a diver): the rusting hulks, the
shore fortifications, the Churchill Barriers and the ghosts of a long-gone army at
Scapa and Lyness on Hoy.

1006 PHILIPSHAUGH, SELKIRK: 5km from town on A708 Moffat rd, before turn for
MAP 8 Bowhill (943/COUNTRY HOUSES) on other side of rd a driveway signed for
C3 Philipshaugh. 1km on, an unusual conical cairn in memory of the Covenanters
who put an end here, in 1645, to the brilliant campaign of the royalist Earl of
Montrose, but were crushed by Cromwell a year later. Now a quiet woodland
spot with somebody's private tennis court adj, tempting you to play.

1007 LILLIARD'S EDGE, nr ST BOSWELLS: On main A68, look for Lilliard's Edge
MAP 8 Caravan Park 5km S of St Boswells; park and walk back towards St Boswells to
C3 the brim of the hill (about 500m), then cross rough ground on rt along ridge,
following whin hedge. Marvellous view attests to strategic location. 200m along
a cairn marks the grave of Lilliard who, in 1545, joined the Battle of Ancrum
Moor against the English 'loons' under the Earl of Angus. 'And when her legs
were cuttit off, she fought upon her stumps'. An ancient poem etched on the
stone records her legendary . . . feet.

1008 KILLIECRANKIE, nr PITLOCHRY: The first battle of the Jacobite Risings where, in
MAP 4 July 1689, the Highlanders lost their leader Viscount (aka Bonnie) Dundee, but
C2 won the battle, using the narrow Pass of Killiecrankie. One escaping soldier
made a famous leap. Well-depicted scenario in Visitor Centre; short walk to
'The Leap'. Battle viewpt and cairn is further along rd to Blair Atholl, turning rt
and doubling back at Little Chef and on, almost to A9 underpass (3km from Vis
Centre). You get the lie of the land from here. Many good walks in this area.

1009 BANNOCKBURN, nr STIRLING: 4km town centre via Burghmuir Rd and Glasgow
MAP 6 rd (it's well signposted) or jnct 9 of M9 (3km). Some visitors might be perplexed
D4 as to why 24 June 1314 was such a big deal for the Scots and apart from the 50m
walk to the flag-pole and the huge statue, there's not a lot doing. But the Visitor

Centre does bring the scale of it to life, the horror and the glory. The battlefield itself is thought to lie around the orange building of the High School some distance away and the best place to see the famous wee burn is from below the magnificent Telford Br. Ask at Centre for directions (5km by road).

SHERIFFMUIR, nr DUNBLANE: Rd over moor from Dunblane or Br of Allan 1010 signed Sheriffmuir and meeting A9 S of Auchterarder. The battle site where on MAP 6 13 Nov 1715 the Highland army under the Earl of Mar (aka Bobbin John) met D3 the Hanoverian troops under the Duke of Argyll, in a skirmish in the Jacobite campaign with huge casualities on both sides and no decisive victory. A cairn by the roadside commemorates the Clan Macrae who fell almost to a man defending the House of Stuart. Site, mainly covered by forest, stretches up to the Sheriffmuir Inn, open only a few months when the battle took place. It is still open for your refreshment. 901/SWIM HOLES.

MARY, CHARLIE AND BOB

Mary Queen of Scots 1542-87

LINLITHGOW PALACE: Where she was born (921/RUINS).

HOLYROOD PALACE, EDINBURGH: And lived (199/EDIN MAIN ATTRACTIONS).

INCHMAHOME PRIORY, PORT OF MENTEITH: The ruins of the Priory on the island 1011 in Scotland's only lake, where the infant Queen spent her early years in the safe MAP 6 keeping of the Augustinian monks. Short journey by boat from quay nr Lake B3 hotel. Signal the ferryman by turning the board to the island, much as she did. 7days 9.30am-6pm. Delights of the Trossachs surround you.   HS

MARY QUEEN OF SCOTS' HOUSE, JEDBURGH: In gardens via Smiths Wynd off 1012 main st. Historians quibble but this long-standing museum claims to be 'the' MAP 8 house where she became ill in 1566, but somehow made it over to visit the D3 injured Bothwell at Hermitage Castle 50km away. Tower-house in good condition; displays well-told saga.

LOCH LEVEN CASTLE nr KINROSS: The ultimate in romantic penitentiaries; on the 1013 island in the middle of the loch and clearly visible from the M90. Not much left MAP 4 of the ruin to fill out the fantasy, but this is where Mary spent 10 months in 1568 C4 before her famous escape and her final attempt to get back the throne. Sailings Apr-Sept, 9.30am-6pm in wee launch. 7 min trip, return as you like.

DUNDRENNAN ABBEY nr AUCHENCAIRN and KIRKCUDBRIGHT: Mary Queen of 1014 Scots got around and there are innumerable places, castles and abbeys where she MAP 9 spent the night. This, however, was where she spent her last one on Scottish soil. C4 She left next day from Port Mary (nothing much to see there except a beach – it's 2km along the rd that skirts the sinister MOD range – the pier's long gone and . . . well, there's no plaque). The Cistercian abbey of Whitemonks (est 1142), which harboured her on her last night, is now a tranquil ruin.   HS

'In my end is my beginning,' she said, facing her execution which came 19 years later. Her 'death mask' is displayed at **LENNOXLOVE HOUSE nr HADDINGTON**; it does seem on the small side for someone who was six feet tall!

Bonnie Prince Charlie 1720-88

PRINCE CHARLIE'S BAY, ERISKAY: The uncelebrated, unmarked and beautiful 1015 beach where Charlie first landed in Scotland to begin the Jacobite Rebellion. MAP 2 Nothing much has changed and this crescent of sand with soft machair and a A4 turquoise sea is still a secret place. 1km from township heading south. 1349/ISLANDS.

LOCH NAN UAMH nr ARISAIG, THE PRINCE'S CAIRN: 7km from Lochailort on 1016 A830, 48km Ft William. Signed from the rd, a path leads down to the left. This is MAP 2 the 'traditional' spot (pron 'Loch Na Nuan') where Charlie embarked for France C4 in Sept 1746, having lost the battle and the cause. The rocky headland also o/looks the bay and its skerries where he had landed in July the year before to begin the campaign. So this place was the beginning and the end and it has all the airy romance necessary to be utterly convincing. Is that a French ship out there in the mist?

1017 **GLENFINNAN:** The place where he 'raised his standard' to rally the clans to the
MAP 2 Jacobite cause. For a while on that August day in 1745 it had looked as if only a
C4 handful were coming. Then they heard the pipes and 600 Camerons came
marching from the valley (where the viaduct now spans). That must have been
one helluva' moment. Though it's thought that he actually stood on the higher
ground, there is a powerful sense of place and history here. The Vis Centre has
an excl map of Charlie's path/flight through Scotland – somehow he touched all
the most alluring places! Tower can be climbed.   NTS

CULLODEN nr INVERNESS: 1002/BATTLEGROUNDS.

Robert the Bruce 1274-1329

1018 **BRUCE'S STONE, GLEN TROOL nr NEWTON STEWART:** 26km N by A714 via
MAP 9 Bargrennan which is on the S Upland Way (1080/LONG WALKS). The fair Glen
B3 Trool is a celebrated spot in the Galloway Forest Park (821/GLENS). The stone is
signed and marks the area where Bruce's guerrilla band rained boulders down on
the pursuing English after they had routed the main army at Solway Moss.

1019 **BANNOCKBURN nr STIRLING:** The climactic battle in June 1314, when Bruce
MAP 6 decisively whipped the English and got himself the kingdom (though Scotland
D3 was not recognised as independent until 1328 just before his death). The scale of
the skirmish can be visualised at the Visitor Centre, but not so readily 'in the
field'. 1009/BATTLEGROUNDS.

1020 **ARBROATH ABBEY:** Not much of the Bruce trail here, but this is where the
MAP 4 famous Declaration was signed that was the attempt of the Scots nobility united
E3 behind him to gain international recognition of the independence they had won
on the battlefield. What it says is stirring stuff; the original is in Edinburgh.
978/ABBEYS.   HS

1021 **DUNFERMLINE ABBEY CHURCH:** Here at last, some tangible evidence, his tomb.
MAP 5 Buried in 1329, his remains were discovered wrapped in gold cloth, when the site
B4 was being cleared for the new church in 1818. Many of the other great kings, the
Alexanders I and III, were not so readily identifiable (Bruce's ribcage had been
cut to remove his heart). With great national emotion he was reinterred under-
neath the pulpit. The church (don't confuse with the Abbey ruins or the Norman
Nave next door) is open Apr-Sept 9.30am-5pm.

1022 **MELROSE ABBEY:** Bruce, like others before (and since), wanted to be buried in
MAP 8 Jerusalem and so his heart was removed and taken on a Crusade. However, after
C3 the casket had been waved a bit at the Infidels, it was brought back and buried at
Melrose Abbey. With sackings over the centuries it's impossible to know what
happened to it, but perhaps it is here somewhere. 977/ABBEYS.   HS

THE IMPORTANT LITERARY PLACES

1023 **RABBIE BURNS (1759-96), ALLOWAY nr AYR, AYR AND DUMFRIES:** Black and
MAP 1 white signs showing the bard's nut mark a heritage trail through his life and
D4 haunts in Ayrshire and Dumfriesshire. Best is at **ALLOWAY:** The Auld Brig o'
Doon and the Auld Kirk where Tam o' Shanter saw the witches dance are more
evocative than the Monument and surrounding gardens or, 1km up the rd, the
cottage (his birthplace; with little atmosphere) and the modern Burns Centre
betw them (mainly a shop and AV display, nice café/engaging bird table). **AYR:**
The Auld Kirk off main st by river; graveyard with diagram of where his friends
are buried; open at all times. **DUMFRIES:** House where he spent his last yrs and
mausoleum 250m away at back of a kirkyard stuffed with extravagant masonry.
10km N of Dumfries on A76 at **ELLISLAND FARM** is the most interesting of all the
sites. The farmhouse with genuine memorabilia e.g. his mirror, fishing rod, a
poem scratched on glass, orig manuscripts. There's his favourite walk by the
river where he composed 'Tam o' Shanter' and a strong atmosphere about the
place. The Irvings let you in 'at all reasonable hrs'. At the **BROW WELL nr
RUTHWELL** on the B725 20km S Dumfries and nr Caerlaverock (874/BIRD-
WATCHING), in a quiet place, there's a well with curative properties where he'd go
in the latter stages of his illness. Not many folk find this one.

LEWIS GRASSIC GIBBON (1901-34), ARBUTHNOT nr STONEHAVEN: Although James 1024 Leslie Mitchell left the area in 1917, this is where he was born and spent his ^{MAP 3} formative years. A Vis Centre at the end of the village (via B967, 16km S of *D5* Stonehaven off main A92) has details of his life and can point you in the direction of the places he writes about in his trilogy *The Scots Quair. Sunset Song*, the first part, is generally considered to be one of the great Scots novels and this area, the HOWE OF THE MEARNS, is the place he so effectively evokes. Arbuthnot was 'Kinraddie' and the churchyard 1km away on the other side of rd still has the atmosphere of that time of innocence before the war which pervades the book. His ashes are here in a grave in a corner. From 1928 to when he died 6 yrs later at the age of only 33, he wrote an incredible 17 books.

NEIL GUNN (1891-1973) DUNBEATH nr WICK: Scotland's foremost writer on 1025 Highland life, only now receiving the recognition he deserves, was brought up in ^{MAP 2} this NE fishing village and based 3 of his greatest yarns here, particularly *E2 Highland River* which must stand in any literature as a brilliant evocation of place. The STRATH in which it is set is below the house (a nondescript terraced house next to the Stores) and makes for a great walk (1056/GLEN WALKS). There's a commemorative statue by the harbour, not quite the harbour you imagine from the books. Gunn also lived for many years nr DINGWALL and there is a memorial on the back rd to Strathpeffer and a wonderful view in a place he often walked (on A834, 4km from Dingwall).

JAMES HOGG (1770-1835), ST MARY'S LOCH, ETTRICK: 'The Ettrick Shepherd' 1026 who wrote one of the great works of Scottish literature, *The Confessions of a* ^{MAP 8} *Justified Sinner,* was born, lived and died in the valleys of the YARROW and the *B3* ETTRICK, some of the most starkly beautiful landscapes in Scotland. ST MARY'S LOCH on the A708, 28km W of Selkirk: there's a commemorative statue looking over the loch and the adj and the supernatural seeming Loch of the Lowes. On the strip of land betw is TIBBIE SHIELS pub (and hotel) once a gathering place for the writer and his friends (e.g. Sir Walter Scott) and still a notable hostelry. Across the valley divide (11km on foot, part of the S. Upland Way – 1080/LONG WALKS, or 25km by rd past the Gordon Arms Hotel – 489/BORDERS BEST HOTELS) is the remote village of ETTRICK, another monument and his grave (and Tibbie Shiels') in the churchyard. He was born, lived, died and was buried within this one acre.

SIR WALTER SCOTT (1771-1832), ABBOTSFORD, MELROSE: No other place in 1027 Scotland (and few anywhere) contains so much of a writer's life and work. This ^{MAP 8} was the house he rebuilt from the farmhouse he moved to in 1812 in the *C3* countryside which he did so much to popularise. The house is still lived in by his descendants and the library and study are pretty much as he left them, incl 9,000 rare books, antiquarian even in his day. There are pleasant grounds and topiary and a walk by the Tweed which the house o/looks. His grave is at DRYBURGH ABBEY (974/ABBEYS). House open Apr-Oct 10am-5pm; Sun 2-5pm.

ROBERT LOUIS STEVENSON (1850-94), EDINBURGH: Though Stevenson travelled 1028 widely – lived in France, emigrated to America and died and was buried in Samoa ^{MAP A} – he spent the first 30 years of his short life in Edinburgh. He was born and ^{MAP 7} brought up in the New Town, living at 17 HERIOT ROW from 1857-80 in a *B1/C2* fashionable townhouse which is still lived in (not open to the public). Most of his youth was spent in this newly built and expanding part of the city in an area bounded then by parkland and farms. Both the BOTANICS (206/EDIN ATTRACTIONS) and WARRISTON CEMETERY (994/GRAVEYARDS) are part of the landscape of his childhood. However, his fondest recollections were of the PENTLAND HILLS and, virtually unchanged as they are, it's here that one is following most poignantly in his footsteps. The 'cottage' at SWANSTON (a delightful village with some remarkable thatched cottages reached via the City Bypass/Colinton t/off or from Oxgangs Rd and a bridge over the bypass; the village nestles in a grove of trees below the hills and is a good place to walk from), the ruins of GLENCORSE CHURCH (ruins even then and where he later asked that a prayer be said for him) and COLINTON MANSE can all be seen, but not visited. The fact is, Edinburgh has no Stevenson Museum (though his lifetime was relatively recent and his acclaim international). You can always stay at the HAWES INN in South Queensferry and dream of *Kidnapped.*

THE REALLY SPOOKY PLACES

1029 HIDDEN VALLEY, GLENCOE: The secret glen where the ill-fated Macdonalds hid
MAP 2 the cattle they'd stolen from the Lowlands and which became (with politics and
C5 power struggles) their undoing. A narrow wooded cleft takes you betw the
imposing and gnarled '3 Sisters' Hills and over the threshold (God knows how
the cattle got there) and into the huge bowl of Coire Gabhail. The place envelops
you in its tragic history, more redolent perhaps than any of the massacre sites.
Park on the A82 5km from the Visitor Centre 200m to the E of 2 white
buildings on either side of the rd (Alt-na-reigh). Cross rd and follow clear path
down to and across the R Coe. Ascend keeping burn to left; 1.5km further up,
it's best to ford it. Allow 3hrs. 1004/BATTLEGROUNDS.   2-B-2

1030 MARY KING'S CLOSE, EDINBURGH: The medieval street under the Royal Mile,
MAP A generally not open to the public though 'groups' are permitted access by
D3 arrangement (phone Bob Morton 664 4525). Going down steps below the City
Chambers, you enter a 60m section of a street that was closed up in 1670. It can
be steep and slippery down there and full of ancient ghosts.

1031 NATIONAL WAR MEMORIAL, EDINBURGH CASTLE: Citadel at the heart of the
MAP A Castle and actually the most modern part. This shrine to commemorate the dead
C3 of the Great War was designed by Lorimer and opened in 1927. In the dark
subdued interior lit by excellent stained glass, insignia from all the Scottish
regiments are displayed with roll books of the dead. The Scots have always made
soldiers and there's something chilling here about this sombre glorification and
their vast numbers.

1032 THE YESNABY STACKS, ORKNEY MAINLAND: A clifftop viewpt that's so wild, so
MAP 10 dramatic and, if you walk nr the edge, so precarious that its supernaturalism
verges on the uneasy. Shells of lookout posts from the war echo the melancholy
spirit of the place. ('The bloody town's a bloody cuss – No bloody trains, no
bloody bus – And no one cares for bloody us – In bloody Orkney.' – first lines
of a poem written then, a soldier's lament.) Nr Skara Brae, it's about 30km from
Kirkwall and way out west.

1033 THE FAIRY GLEN, SKYE: A place so strange, it's hard to believe that it's merely a
MAP 2 geological phenomenon. Entering Uig on the A855 from Portree, there's a turret
B3 on the left (Macrae's Folly) and, shortly after, a bus shelter on the right with a rd
beside it. Take this rd for 2km and you enter an area of extraordinary conical
hills which in certain conditions of light and weather seems to entirely justify its
legendary provenance. Your mood may determine whether you believe they
were good or bad fairies, but there's supposed to be an incredible 365 of these
grassy hillocks, some 35m high – how else could they be there?

1033a CLOVA CAIRNS, nr CULLODEN, INVERNESS: This is a place I haven't visited but
MAP 2 Fiona Dempster wrote to say that she couldn't get back on her bike quick
D3 enough, even on a warm sunny day. There are chambered cairns and a ring cairn
in a grove of trees nr the river. Perhaps ask at the visitor centre (1002/BATTLE-
GROUNDS) for directions.

1033b THE BURN O' VAT, nr BALLATER: Recommended by David Gartside and others,
MAP 3 this impressive and rather spooky glacial curiousity on Royal Deeside is well
C4 worth the short walk. 8km from Ballater towards Aberdeen on main A93, take
A97 for Hunty for 2km to a roadside info kiosk at the Muir of Dinnet nature
reserve. Some scrambling to reach the huge cavern from which the burn flows to
L Kinord.

THE NECROPOLIS, GLASGOW: 991/GRAVEYARDS.

HAMILTON MAUSOLEUM, STRATHCLYDE PARK: 965/MONUMENTS.

LOANHEAD OF DAVIOT nr OLD MELDRUM, ABERDEENSHIRE: 958/PREHISTORIC
SITES.

*Any ideas or suggestions for other spooky places gratefully received, for possible
inclusion in future editions. See page 11.*

SECTION 8
Strolls, Walks and Hikes

FAVOURITE HILLS

Popular and notable hills in the various regions of Scotland but not including Munros or difficult climbs. Always best to remember that the weather can change very quickly. Take an OS map on higher tops. See p. 9 for walk codes.

1034 **SUILVEN, LOCHINVER:** From close or far away, this is one of Scotland's
MAP 2 most awe-inspiring mountains. The 'sugar loaf' can seem almost
C2 insurmountable, but in good weather it's not so difficult. Route from
Inverkirkaig 5km S of Lochinver on rd to Achiltibuie, turns up track by Achin's
Bookshop (1259/ CRAFTS) on the path for the Kirkaig Falls (1093/WALKING
CENTRES); once at the loch, you head for the Bealach, the central waistline
through an unexpected dyke and follow track to the top. The slightly quicker
route from the N (Glencanisp) following a stalkers' track that eventually leads to
Elphin, also heads for the central breach in the mountain's defences. Either way
it's a long walk-in; 8km before the climb. Allow 8hrs ret. From the top –
amazing Assynt. 731m. Take OS map.   2·C·3

Suilven, Lochinver (1034)

1035 **STAC POLLAIDH/POLLY nr ULLAPOOL:** The hill which is descibed
MAP 2 variously as 'perfect', 'preposterous' and 'great fun', certainly has
C2 character and rising out of the Sutherland moors on the rd to Achiltibuie off the
A835 N from Ullapool, demands to be climbed. The route everyone takes is
from the carpark by L Lurgainn 8km from main rd. Head for the central ridge
which for many folk is enough; the path to the pinnacles is exposed and can be
off-putting. Allow 3-4hrs return. 613m.   2·B·3

1036 **CRIFFEL, NEW ABBEY nr DUMFRIES:** 12km S by A710 to New Abbey which
MAP 9 Criffel dominates. It's only 569m, but seems higher. Exceptional views from top
D3 as far as English lakes and across to Borders. Granite lump with brilliant
outcrops of quartzite. The annual race gets up and back to the Abbey Arms in
under an hour; you can take it easier. Start 2km S of village, turn-off A710 by a
curious painted bus shelter signed for Ardwell Mains Farm. Park before the farm
buildings and get on up.   2·A·2

1037 **GOAT FELL, ARRAN:** Starting from the carpark at Cladach before Brodick
MAP 1 Castle grounds 3km from town, or from Corrie further up the coast
C3 (12km). Worn path, a steady climb, rarely much of a scramble but a rewarding
afternoon's exertion. Some scree and some view! 874m. Allow 5hrs.   2·B·2

THE COBBLER (BEN ARTHUR), ARROCHAR: Perennial favourite of the Glasgow 1038 hillwalker and, for sheer exhilaration, the most popular of 'the Arrochar Alps'. MAP 1 A motorway path ascends from the A83 on the other side of L Long from C2 Arrochar (park in lay-bys nr Succoth rd end; there's always loads of cars) and takes 2.5-3 hrs to traverse the up 'n' down route to the top. Just short of a Munro at 881m, it has 3 tops of which the Central is the simplest scramble. Way isn't marked; consult map or other walkers. 2·B·3

BEN VENUE and BEN A'AN, THE TROSSACHS: Two celebrated hills in the 1039 Highland microcosm of the Trossachs around L Achray, 15km W of Callander; MAP 6 strenuous but not difficult and with superb views. Ben Venue (727m) is the more B3 serious; allow 4 to 5 hrs ret. Start from Kinlochard side at Ledard or more usually from behind L Achray Hotel: 100m along 'Forest Path' go left and then it's waymarked. Ben A'An (415m) starts with a steep climb from the main A821 along from the old Trossachs Hotel. Scramble at top. Allow 2 to 3 hrs. 2·B·3

NORTH BERWICK LAW: The conical volcanic hill, a beacon in the E Lothian 1040 landscape. TRAPRAIN LAW nearby, is higher, tends to be frequented by rock MAP 7 climbers, but has prehistorical significance and a definite aura. At 187m NBL is D1 easy and rewarding. Leave town by Law Rd, path marked beyond houses. Views as far as Cairngorms and way along the Forth. Both I·A·I

RUBERSLAW, DENHOLM nr HAWICK: The smooth hummock that sits above the 1041 Teviot valley and affords views of 7 counties incl Northumberland. At 424m, it's MAP 8 a gentle climb taking about 1 hr from the usual start at Denholm Hill Farm C3 (private land, be aware of livestock). Leave Denholm at corner of Green by shop and go past GPO. Take left after 3km to farm.

TINTO HILL, nr BIGGAR and LANARK: A favourite climb in S/Central Scotland 1042 with easy access to start from A73 nr Symington, 10km S of Lanark. Park 100m MAP 1 behind Tinto Hills Farm Shop, after stocking up with rolls and juice. Good E4 track, though it has its ups and downs before you get there. Allow 3 hrs (707m). Braw views.

CONIC HILL, BALMAHA, LOCH LOMOND: An easier climb than the Ben up the road 1043 and a good place to view it from, Conic, on the Highland fault line, is one of the MAP 6 first Highland hills you reach from Glasgow. Stunning views also of L Lomond B4 from its 358m peak. Ascend thro woodland from the corner of Balmaha carpark. 1.5hrs up.

KINNOUL HILL, PERTH: Various starts from town (the path from beyond 1044 Branklyn Gardens on the Dundee Rd is less frequented) to the wooded ridge MAP 4 above the Tay with its tower and incredible views to S from the precipitous C4 cliffs. Surprisingly extensive area of hillside common and it's not difficult to get lost. The leaflet/map from Perth TO helps. I·A·I

BENNACHIE nr ABERDEEN: The pilgrimage hill, an easy 528m often busy at 1045 weekends but never a let-down. Various trails take in 'the Taps'. Trad route MAP 3 from Rowan Tree nr Chapel of Garioch (pron 'Geery') signed Pittodrie off A96 C3 nr Pitcaple. Also from Essons carpark on rd from Chapel-Monymusk, which is steeper. Or from other side the Lord's Throat rd, a longer more forested approach from banks of the Don. All carparks have trailfinders. From the fortified top you see what Aberdeenshire's about. 2hrs. 2·B·2

MORVEN, BERRIEDALE nr WICK: The great hill of Caithness from which you can 1046 see the whole county and from Orkney to the Moray Firth. 3 routes, but main MAP 2 ones are (**1**) The Braemore rd from Dunbeath (Wick 32km) on the coast, to E2 Braemore Lodge (9km), park and walk; about 5km ret and a 2hr climb. The adj hill, the Maiden's Pap, really does look like a tit from this angle. (**2**) From further down coast take the rd from Berriedale (Helmsdale 15km) to the cottage at the Wag (15km). Less steep but longer route; depends how far you can get a car up the track. In either case check with the keepers esp Aug-Oct. (05933 371/05935 214).706m. 2·C·3

HILL WALKS

Apart from the mainly isolated hilltops mentioned previously, the following ranges of hills offer walks in various directions and more than one summit. They are all accessible and fairly easy. See p. 9 for walk codes.

1047 LOMOND HILLS, FIFE nr FALKLAND: The conservation village lies below a
MAP 5 prominent ridge easily reached from the main st esp via Back Wynd (off which
C3 there's a carpark) – just head on up. More usual approach to both E and W
Lomond, the main tops, is from Craigmead carpark 3km from village towards
Leslie where there is a trailfinder board. The celebrated Lomonds (aka the Paps of
Fife), aren't that high (West is 522m), but they can see and be seen for miles.
Marked walks also from Freuchie and Glenrothes.   3-10KM   CIRC   XBIKES   2-A-2
An easy rewarding single climb is Bishop's Hill. Start opp the church in
Scotlandwell. A steep path veers left and then there are several ways up. Allow 2
hrs. Gr view of L Leven, Fife and a good swathe of Central Scotland.

1048 THE EILDONS, MELROSE: The 3 much-loved hills or paps visible from most of the
MAP 8 Central Borders and easily climbed from the town of Melrose which nestles at
C3 their foot. Leave main sq by rd to station (the Dingleton rd), after 100m a path
begins betw 2 pebble-dash houses on the left. You climb the smaller first, then
the highest central one (422m). You can make a circular route of it by returning
to the golf course. Allow 1.5 hrs.   3KM   CIRC   XBIKES   1-A-2

1049 THE OCHILS: Most usual approach from the 'hillfoot towns' at the foot of the
MAP 6 glens that cut into their S-facing slopes, along the A91 Stirling-St Andrews rd.
D3 Alva, Tillicoultry and Dollar all have impressive glen walks easily found from
the main streets and, from there, there are tracks marked (1053/GLEN/RIVER
WALKS). Good start nr Stirling from the Sheriffmuir rd uphill from Bridge of
Allan. Fine graveyard nearby (1000/GRAVEYARDS) and place to swim in the
summer (901/SWIMMING HOLES). From last houses about 3km, there's a lay-by
on the rt and a reservoir just visible on the left. There are usually other cars here.
A stile leads to the hills which stretch away to the east for 40km and afford great
views for little effort. Highest pt is Ben Cleugh, 721m.
                                    2-40KM   SOME CIRC   XBIKES   1/2-B-2

1050 THE LAMMERMUIRS: The hills SE of Edinburgh that form a divide betw the rich
MAP 7 farmlands of E Lothian and the valley of the Tweed in the Borders. Mostly a
E2 high wide moorland but there's wooded gentle hill country in the watersheds of
the southern rivers and spectacular coastal scenery betw Cockburnspath and St
Abb's Head. (887/WILDLIFE RESERVES; 1071/COASTAL WALKS.) The eastern part
of the S Upland Way follows the Lammermuirs to the coast (1080/LONG
WALKS). Many moorland walks begin at the carpark at the head of Whiteadder
Reservoir (A1 to Haddington, B6369 towards Humbie, then E on B6355 thro
Gifford), a mysterious loch in the bowl of the hills. Excl walks also centre on
Abbey St Bathans to the S Head off A1 at Cockburnspath. Through village
(1178/TEA-ROOMS) to Toot Corner (signed 1km) and off to left, foll path above
valley of Whiteadder to Edinshall Broch (2km). Further on, along river (1km) is
a swing bridge and a fine place to swim. Circ walks possible, ask in village.
                                    5-15KM   SOME CIRC   MT BIKES   1/2-B-2

1050a THE CHEVIOTS: Not strictly in Scotland of course, but they straddle the border
MAP 8 and Border history. There are many fine walks starting from Kirk Yetholm (incl
D3 the Pennine Way which stretches 400km S to the Peak district) incl an 8km circ
route of typical Cheviot foothill terrain that follows the actual border for half its
route (leaflet avail in the pub). Most forays start at Wooler 20km from
Coldstream and the border. Cheviot itself (2676ft) has wide boggy plateau,
Hedgehope via the Harthope Burn usually more fun.

THE CAMPSIE FELLS, nr GLASGOW: 445/GLASGOW WALKS.

THE KILPATRICK HILLS nr GLASGOW: 449/GLASGOW WALKS.

THE PENTLAND HILLS nr EDINBURGH: 222/EDINBURGH WALKS.

GLEN AND RIVER WALKS

See also GREAT GLENS, *p.127. Walk codes are on p. 9.*

GLEN TILT, BLAIR ATHOLL: A walk of variable length in this classic Highland 1051
glen, easily accessible from the caravan park off the main A9 in Blair Atholl. MAP 4
Trail leaflet from park office and local TOs. Fine walking and unspoiled scenery C2
begins only a short distance into the deeply wooded gorge of the R Tilt, but to
cover the circular route it's necessary to walk to 'Gilbert's Bridge' (9km return)
or the longer trail to Gow's Bridge (17km ret). Begin here also the great route
into the Cairngorms leading to the Linn of Dee and Braemar, joining the track
from Speyside which starts at Feshiebridge or Glenmore Forest (1078/SERIOUS
WALKS). I'd recommend Dolina MacLennan's celebrated B&B if I thought you'd
have any chance of getting in. UP TO 17KM CIRC XBIKE 1-B-2

GLEN AFFRIC, CANNICH nr DRUMNADROCHIT: Easy short walks are marked and 1052
hugely rewarding in this magnificent glen well known as the first stretch in the MAP 2
great E-W route to Kintail (1077/SERIOUS WALKS) and the Falls of Glomach C3
(823/WATERFALLS). The starting pt of this track into the wilds is at the end of the
rd at L Affric and there are many short and circular trails indicated here.
Carpark is beyond metal rd 2km along forest track towards Affric Lodge (cars
not allowed to Lodge itself). Track not open in stalking season. Other easier
walks amongst the famous Affric Pine (and birch) Forest from carpark at Dog
Falls, 7km from Cannich. Waterfalls and spookily tame birds. Good idea to hire
bikes at Drumnadrochit or Cannich (Caravan Park). But don't miss Glen Affric
(814/ GLENS). 5/8KM CIRC BIKE 1-B-2

DOLLAR GLEN, DOLLAR nr STIRLING: The classic fairy glen in Central Scotland, 1053
positively hoaching with water spirits, reeking of ozone and euphoric after rain. MAP 6
20km from Stirling by A91, or 18km from M90 at Kinross jnct 6. Start from top E3
of tree-lined av on either side of burn or from further up rd signed Castle
Campbell where there's a carpark and a path down into glen. The Castle at head
of glen is open 7 days till 6pm (Oct-Mar till 4pm), and has boggling views.
There's a circ walk back or take off for the Ochil Tops, the hills that surround
the glen. Possibly forever. There are also first-class walks (less frequented) up
the glens of the other hillfoot towns, Alva and Tillicoultry; they also lead to the
hills (1049/HILL WALKS). 3KM + TOPS CIRC XBIKE 1-A-2

RUMBLING BRIDGE: Nr Dollar and formed by another burn running off the same 1054
hills, an easier short walk in an Ochil Glen with something of the chasmic MAP 4
experience and the added delight of the unique double bridge (built 1713). C4
There's a point here at the end of one of the walkways under the bridge where
you are looking into a Scottish jungle landscape just like the Romantics
imagined. Near Powmill on the A977 from Kinross (jnct 6, M90) then 2km.
The POWMILL MILKBAR: has been serving excl home-made food for 35yrs – real
Scottish baking. It's 5km W on the A977. Open 7 days till 5.30pm (8.30pm in
summer). Go after your walk! **The GARTWHINZEAN HOTEL** 1km further-on is a
roadhouse with superior barfood all day.

THE BIG BURN WALK, GOLSPIE: A non-taxing, perfect little glen walk through 1055
lush diverse woodland. Variations possible, but start just beyond Sutherland MAP 2
Arms (573/HIGHLAND INX HOTELS) in the garage yard which is just off the A9 D2
before Dunrobin Castle. Go past derelict mill and under aquaduct following
river. A real supernature trail unfolds with ancient tangled trees, meadows,
waterfalls, cliffs and much wildlife. 3km to falls, ret via route to castle woods for
best all-round intoxication. 6KM CIRC XBIKE 1-B-1

THE STRATH at DUNBEATH: The glen or strath so eloquently evoked in Neil 1056
Gunn's *Highland River* (1025/LITERARY PLACES), a book which is as much about MAP 2
the geography as the history of his childhood. A path follows the river for many E2
miles. A leaflet from the Dunbeath Heritage Centre points out places on the
way. It's a spate river and in summer becomes a trickle; hard to imagine Gunn's
salmon odyssey. It's only 500m to the broch, but it's worth going into the
hinterland where it becomes quite mystical (1001/GRAVEYARDS).

WOODLAND WALKS

1057 THE NEW GALLOWAY FOREST: Huge area of forest and hill country with
MAP 9 every type and length of trail incl section of S Upland Way from
B3 Bargrennan to Dalry (1080/LONG WALKS). Vis Centres at Kirroughtree (5km
Newton Stewart) and Clatteringshaws Loch on the 'Queen's Way' (9km New
Galloway) with easy routes around them. Glen and Loch Trool are v fine
(821/GLENS); the 'Retreat Oakwood' nr Laurieston has 5km trails. The Smithy in
New Galloway has walk books and walk food (1179/COFFEE SHOPS). There's a
river pool on the Raiders' Rd (897/SWIMMING HOLES). One could ramble on . . .

1058 ROTHIEMURCHUS FOREST, nr AVIEMORE: One of the best places to
MAP 2 experience the magic and the majesty of the great Caledonian Forest and
D4 the beauty of Scots Pine. Approach from B970 the rd that parallels the A9 from
Coylumbridge to Kincraig/Kingussie. 2km from Inverdruie nr Coylumbridge
follow sign for Loch an Eilean; one of the most perfect lochans in these, or any
woods. Loch circuit is 5km (840/LOCHS).

1059 LOCHAWESIDE: Unclassified rd on N side of loch betw Kilchrenan and Ford,
MAP 1 centred on Dalavich. Illustrated brochure avail from Inverinan craft centre (6km
C2 Kilchrenan), describes 6 walks in the mixed, mature forest all starting from
carparking places on the rd. 3 starting from the Barnaline carpark are trail-
marked and could be followed without brochure. Avich Falls route crosses R
Avich after 2km with falls on return route. Inverinan Glen starting from the
Christmas tree nursery (4km) is superb.   2-8KM   CIRC   XBIKE   2-A-2

1060 ARIUNDLE OAKWOODS: Strontian. 35km Ft William via Corran Ferry. Good
MAP 2 Forestry Comm Guide avail from Tourist Office in Strontian. Many walks
C4 around L Sunart and Ariundle: rare oak and other native species (esp on the
wetter ground). You see how very different was the landscape of Scotland before
the Industrial Revolution used up the wood. Start over town bridge, turning rt
for Polloch. Go on past Cosy Knits with its excellent home baking and park
1km further on. 2 walks; well marked. River walk can be wet.
                                                       5KM   CIRC   (MT)BIKE   1-A-2

1061 BALMACARRA: 5km S Kyle of Lochalsh on A87. A woodland walk around the
MAP 2 shore of Loch Alsh, centred on Lochalsh House. Mixed woodland in fairly
C3 formal garden setting where you are confined to paths. Views over to Skye. A
fragrant and verdant amble.   3KM   CIRC   XBIKE   1-A-1

1062 THE BIRKS O' ABERFELDY: Circ walk thro oak, beech and the birch (or birk)
MAP 4 woods of the title, easily reached and signed from town main st (1km). Steep-
B3 sided wooded glen of the Moness Burn with attractive falls esp the higher one
spanned by bridge where the 2 marked walks converge. This is where Burns
'spread the lightsome days' in his eponymous poem.   3KM   CIRC   XBIKE   1-A-2

1063 THE HERMITAGE, DUNKELD: On A9 2km N of Dunkeld. Popular, easy accessible
MAP 4 walks along the glen and gorge of R Braan with pavilion o/looking the Falls and,
C3 further on, 'Ossian's Cave'.   2KM   CIRC   XBIKE   1-A-1

1064 GLENMORE FOREST PARK, nr AVIEMORE: Along from Coylumbridge (and adj
MAP 2 Rothiemurchus) on rd to ski resort, the forest trail area centred on L Morlich
D4 (sandy beaches, good swimming, watersports). Vis Centre has maps of walk and
bike trails (680/CAMP/CARAVAN SITES).

1065 ABOVE THE PASS OF LENY, CALLANDER: A walk thro mixed forest (beech, oak,
MAP 6 birch, pine) with great Trossachs views. Start from carpark on A84 4km N of
C3 Callander (the Falls of Leny are on opp side of rd, 100m away) on path at back,
the one on the left which has a burn to the rt. Way-marked and boarded where
marshy, the path divides after 1km to head further up to crest (4km ret) or back
down (2km).   2 OR 4KM   CIRC   XBIKE   1-A-2

THE BEST WOODLAND WALKS NEAR EDINBURGH

DALKEITH HOUSE GROUNDS: 15km SE by A68. Enter via end of Main St.

VOGRIE COUNTRY PARK: 25km S by A7 then B6372 6km from Gorebridge.

ROSLIN GLEN: 18km S by A702/703. 223/EDIN: WALKS OUTSIDE TOWN.

CARDRONA FOREST/ GLENTRESS nr PEEBLES: 40km S to Peebles, 8km E on A72.

DAWYCK GARDENS nr STOBO: 10km W of Peebles. 764/GARDENS. Follow glen.

✝ WOODHALL DENE nr DUNBAR: A1 Dunbar bypass, E to Spott then 5 km.

THE BEST WOODLAND WALKS NEAR GLASGOW

CHATELHERAULT nr HAMILTON: M74 jnct 6, 3km from town. (446/GLAS WALKS.)

FORMAKIN ESTATE: 35km W via M8, jnct 31. (775/COUNTRY PARKS.)

MUGDOCK COUNTRY PARK: 25km NW via Milngavie (3km). (444/GLASGOW WALKS.)

WHERE TO FIND SCOTS PINE

Scots pine, along with oak and birch etc, formed the great Caledonian Forest which once covered most of Scotland. Native Scots Pine is very different from the regimented rows of pine trees that we associate with forestry plantations and which now drape much of the countryside. It is more like a deciduous tree with reddish bark and irregular foliage; no two ever look the same. The remnants of the great stands of pine that are left are beautiful to see, mystical and majestic, a joy to walk among and no less worthy of conservation than a castle or a bird of prey. Here's where to find them:

ROTHIEMURCHUS FOREST: See 1058/WOODLAND WALKS.

GLENTANAR, ROYAL DEESIDE: Nr Ballater, 10-15km SW of Aboyne.

Around BRAEMAR and GRANTOWN-on-SPEY.

STRATHYRE, nr CALLANDER: S of village on rt of main rd after L Lubnaig.

ACHRAY FOREST, nr ABERFOYLE: Some pine nr the Duke's Pass rd, the A821 to L Katrine, and amongst the mixed woodland in the 'forest drive' to L Achray.

BLACKWOOD OF RANNOCH: S of L Rannoch, 30km W of Pitlochry via Kinloch Rannoch. Start from Carie, fair walk-in. 250yr-old pines; an important site.

ROWARDENNAN, L LOMOND: End of the rd along E side of loch nr Ben Lomond. Easily accessible pines nr the lochside, picnic sites etc.

GLEN AFFRIC, nr DRUMNADROCHIT: See 814/GLENS.

Native pinewoods aren't found south of Pethshire, but there are fine plantation examples in southern Scotland at:

GLENTRESS, nr PEEBLES: 7km on A72 to Innerleithen. Mature forest up the burnside, though surrounded by commercial forest.

SHAMBELLIE ESTATE, nr DUMFRIES: 1km from New Abbey beside A710 at the Shambellie House, 100yds sign. Ancient stands of pine over the wall amongst other glorious trees; this is like virgin woodland. Planted 1775-1780. Magnificent.

COASTAL WALKS

1066 KINTRA, ISLAY: From the end of the rd from Pt Ellen (9km) there's a good
MAP 1 restau/bar with accommodation, a place to camp (684/CAMPING), a
A3 fabulous beach (805/BEACHES) which runs in opposite direction and a notable golf
course behind it (1113/GOLF). This walk leads along N coast of the Mull of Oa, an
area of diverse beauty, sometimes pastoral, sometimes wild, with a wonderful
shoreline. In the café, a detailed route map has been annotated with pics.

ANY KM   XCIRC   XBIKE   2-B-2

1067 THE BULLERS OF BUCHAN nr PETERHEAD: 8km S of Peterhead on A975
MAP 3 rd to/from Cruden Bay. Park and walk 100m to cottages. To right is
E2 precarious and spectacular clifftop walk to Cruden Bay (3km), to left the walk to
Longhaven Nature Reserve, a continuation of the dramatic cliffs and more
seabird city. The Bullers is at start of walk, a sheer-sided 'hole' 75m deep with an
outlet to the sea thro a natural arch. Walk round the edge of it, looking down on
layers of birds (who might try to dive-bomb you away from their nests); it's a
wonder of nature on an awesome coast. Take great care.

1068 CAPE WRATH AND THE CLIFFS OF CLO MOR: Britain's most NW point reached by
MAP 2 ferry from 1km off the A838 4km S of Durness by Cape Wrath Hotel; a 10min
C1 crossing then 30min minibus ride to Cape. Ferry holds 14 and runs May-Sept,
9.30am-4.30pm. 0971 511376. At 280m Clo Mor are the highest cliffs in UK; 5km
round trip from Cape. MOD range – access may be restricted. In other
direction, the 28km to Kinlochbervie is one of Britain's most wild and
wonderful coastal walks. Beaches incl Sandwood (803/BEACHES). While in this
NW area: **SMOO CAVE** 2km E of Durness is worth seeing. 200m down from main
A838.

1069 PLOCKTON: Plockton is a v special wee place and best seen on foot (788/COASTAL
MAP 2 VILLAGES). There's a great view to start, from Frithard Hill up from the end of
C3 the street, about 1km and taking path to rt just before the new houses. The
shore/beach walk starts beyond the airstrip; follow rd round High School
playing fields at top of village and then shore path.

8KM RET OR 5 FROM SCHOOL   1-A-2

1070 ROCKCLIFFE TO KIPPFORD: A stroll along the 'Scottish Riviera', an easy
MAP 9 clifftop/shore walk of about 4km past the 'Mote of Mark' a Dark Age hill fort
C4 and views to Rough Island. Kippford is HQ for Solway Yacht Club. The
Anchor has food and ale. 793/COASTAL VILLAGES.

1071 ST ABBS HEAD: The most dramatic coastal scenery in S Scotland, scary in a wind,
MAP 8 rhapsodic on a blue summer's day. Extensive wildlife reserve and trails thro
E1 coastal hills and vales to cliffs. Cars can go as far as lighthouse, but best to park
at Vis Centre nr farm on St Abbs village rd 3km from A1107 to Eyemouth and
follow route. 887/WILDLIFE RESERVES.

5-10KM   CIRC   XBIKE   1-B-2

1072 CROMARTY, THE SOUTH SOUTARS: The walk that takes you from Cromarty
MAP 2 village (790/COASTAL VILLAGES; 1185/TEA-ROOMS; 566/HIGHL RESTAUS) round
D3 the tip of the S promontory at the narrow entrance to the Cromarty Firth.
Starting at Miller St (foot of Church St), follow the shoreline then gradually
climb thro woods of Scots Pine over the headland. From deserted wartime ruins
you can head back by rd. Oil platforms and Nigg Bay are left behind and there
are airy views across to the cave-pocked cliffs of opp headland and out to sea.

5KM   CIRC   XBIKE   1-A-1

1073 CRAIL-ANSTRUTHER/PITTENWEEM: The breezy cliff and rocky foreshore walk
MAP 5 from the best harbour in the East Neuk of Fife to the 'main' town (or in
E3 reverse). Only fields betw path and coast road, but a much more civilised way to
go. Not circ, but regular buses back. Path starts from bottom of West Braes, a
cul-de-sac off main rd just before the last new houses towards Anstruther. In
either direction, head for last house in village to start.

6/8KM   XCIRC   XBIKE   1-A-1

1073a THE CHAIN WALK, ELIE: A unique and adventurous way to get round this headland
MAP 5 at the W end of Elie (and Earlferry), this walk (and clamber) is exhilarating and
D3 great fun but not for anyone with vertigo, a dog, young kids, inagility. You walk
along beach/around golf course and across a boulder field, then start around the
cliff following path and using hand- and footholds carved into rock and chains to
haul yourself up. Watch the tide and don't go alone. If you're careful, it's a (sea)
breeze. Allow 2 hrs.

SERIOUS WALKS

None of these should be attempted without OS maps, proper equipment and preparation. Hill or ridge walking experience may be essential.

THE CUILLINS, SKYE: Much scrambling and, if you want it, serious climbing over these famously unforgiving peaks. The Red ones are easier and many walks start at the Sligachan Hotel on the main Portree-Broadford rd. Glamaig, the conical one which overlooks the hotel, has been climbed in 37mins. Most of the Black Cuillins incl the highest, Sgurr Alasdair (993m), and Sgurr Dearg, 'the inaccessible pinnacle' (978m), can be attacked from the campsite or the youth hostel in Glen Brittle. A good guide is *Introductory Scrambles from Glen Brittle* by Charles Rhodes, available locally, but you will need something. (737/ ATTRACTIONS; 677/CAMPSITES; 829/WATERFALLS; 1088/MUNROS.) 1074 MAP 2 B3 3-C-3

AONACH EAGACH, GLENCOE: One of several possible major expeditions in the Glencoe area and one of the world's classic ridge walks. Not for the faint-hearted or the ill-prepared. It's the ridge on your right for almost the whole length of the glen from Altnafeadh to the Visitor Centre (where you might consult over the route). Start from the main rd and once you're up and have hopped across, do resist the descent from the last summit (Sgorr nam Fiannaidh) to the welcoming bar of the Clachaig Hotel. On your way, you'll have come close to heaven, seen Lochaber in its immense glory and reconnoitred some fairly exposed edges and pinnacles. Go with somebody good. 848/SCENIC ROUTES; 704/PUBS; 669/HOSTELS; 1004/BATTLEGROUNDS. 1075 MAP 2 C5 3-C-3

BEN NEVIS: Start on Glen Nevis rd 3km Ft William town centre by bridge opp youth hostel or take car along Claggan Ind Estate Rd to the end at Achintee Farm (4km town). These starts lead to the same 'tourist' path which continues to the top. Allow the best part of a day and I do mean the best – the weather can turn quickly here. Many people are killed every yr, even experienced climbers. It is the biggest, though not the best; you can see 100 Munros on a clear day (ie. about once a yr.) You climb it because . . . well because you have to. Go prepared. 1076 MAP 2 C4 2-B-3

THE FIVE SISTERS OF KINTAIL: Generally started from A87 along from Cluanie Inn (702/GREAT PUBS) and walked east to west. An uncomplicated but inspiring ridge walk, a classic which can be done on a single clear day, taking in 2 Munros and 2 tops. Not as strenuous as it looks, tho it's a hard pull up and you descend to a pt 8km further up the rd (so arrange transport). Many side spurs to vantage pts and wild views. 670/HOSTELS. 1077 MAP 2 C4 3-C-3

From the Morvich Outdoor Centre off A87 nr Shiel Bridge another long distance walk starts to Glen Affric (1082/LONG WALKS).

GRAMPIAN WALKS: The mainly E-W routes thro the mountains linking R Dee at Braemar via the Linn of Dee (856/SCENIC ROUTES) with the great central Highland river systems (the Spey). Approach from W and A9: 1078 MAP 3 A4

(1) GLEN TILT: starting at Blair Atholl (1051/GLEN WALKS); about 35km of superb Highland scenery. Converges with routes below. MAP 4 C2

(2) GLEN FESHIE: from Feshiebridge (starting at the bridge); 40km. MAP 2 D4

(3) GLEN MORE FOREST PARK: from Coylumbridge and L Morlich; 32km. 2 joins 3 beyond L Morlich and both go thro the Rothiemurchus Forest (1058/WOODLAND WALKS) and the famous LAIRIG GHRU, the ancient Right of Way thro the Cairngorms which passes betw Ben Macdui and Braeriach. Ascent is over 700m and going can be rough. This is one of the great Scottish trails. At end of June, the Lairig Ghru Race completes this course E-W in 3.5 hrs, but generally this is a full-day trip. The famous shelter, Corrour Bothy betw 'Devil's Point' and Carn A Mhaim, can be a halfway house. Nr Linn of Dee, routes 1 and 2/3 converge and pass through the ancient Caledonian Forest of Mar. Going E-W is less gruelling and there's Aviemore to look forward to! MAP 2 E4

GLEN AFFRIC: Or rather beyond Glen Affric and L Affric (1052/GLEN WALKS; 814/GLENS), the serious walking begins – 1082/LONG WALKS.

LONG WALKS

Once again these walks require preparation, route maps, very good boots etc. But don't carry too much. Sections are always possible. See p. 9 for walk codes.

1079 **THE WEST HIGHLAND WAY:** The 150km walk which starts at Milngavie 12km
MAP 1/2 outside Glasgow and goes via some of Scotland's most celebrated scenery to
D3/C4 emerge in Glen Nevis before the Ben. The route goes via Mugdock Moor-Drymen-L Lomond-Rowardennan-Inversnaid-Inverarnan-Crianlarich-Tyndrum-Bridge of Orchy-Rannoch Moor-Kingshouse Hotel-Glencoe-The Devil's Staircase-Kinlochleven. The latter part from Bridge of Orchy is the most dramatic. The Inveroran Hotel, B of Orchy (08384 220), and Kingshouse (08556 259), both historic staging posts, are recomm, as is the Drover's Inn, Inverarnan (498/CENTRAL: BEST HOTELS). It's a good idea to pre-book accom (allowing time for muscle fatigue) and don't take too much stuff. Info leaflet/pack from shops or Scottish Natural Heritage. 0738 27921.
START: Officially at Milngavie (pron 'Mull-guy') Railway Stn (reg service from Glasgow Central, also buses from Buchanan St Bus Stn), but actually from Milngavie shopping precinct (Douglas St) 500m away; an inauspicious ramp down to Allander River by the side of Victoria Wine and then behind Presto Supermkt. However, the countryside is close. Start from other end 1km down Glen Nevis rd from r/bout on A82 N from Ft William. Way is well marked, but you must have a route map. 2·B·3

1080 **SOUTHERN UPLAND WAY:** 350km walk from Portpatrick S of Stranraer across the
MAP 8/9 Rhinns of Galloway, muckle moorland, the Galloway Forest Park, the wild
A4 heartland of Southern Scotland, then thro James Hogg country (1026/LITERARY PLACES) to the gentler East Borders and the sea at Pease Bay (official end, Cockburnspath). Route is Stranraer-N Luce-Dalry-Sanquhar-Wanlockhead-Beattock-St Mary's Loch-Melrose-Lauder-Abbey St Bathans. The first and latter sections are the most obviously picturesque but highlights incl Loch Trool, the Lowther Hills, St Mary's Loch, R Tweed. Usually walked W to E, the SU Way is a formidable undertaking . . . think about it! Info SNH as above.
START: Portpatrick by the harbour and up along the cliffs past the lighthouse. Or Cockburnspath, map is on side of shop at Cross. 2·B·3

1081 **SPEYSIDE WAY:** The walk that follows R Spey from the coast at Speybay betw
MAP 3 Buckie and Lossiemouth to Ballindalloch (there are plans to extend much
B1/B3 further south to Boat of Garten) with side spurs to Dufftown from Craigellachie up Glenfiddich (5km) and to Tomintoul foll the R Avon (pron 'A'rn') regarded currently as the end of the walk (24km). Main section from coast to Ballindalloch thro Fochabers and Craigellachie is about 50km and closely follows the river. Much less strenuous than SU or WH Ways. Tomintoul spur has more hillwalking character and a great viewpt at 600m. Throughout walk you are in whisky country with opportunities to visit Tamdhu, Knockando, Glenlivet and other distilleries nearby. Trail criss-crosses river.
START: Usual start is from coast end. Speybay is 8km N of Fochabers; the first marker is by the banks of shingle at the river mouth. I·A·3

1082 **GLEN AFFRIC:** In enchanting Glen Affric and L Affric beyond (1052/GLEN
MAP 2 WALKS; 814/GLENS), some serious walking begins on the 32km Kintail trail.
C3 Done either W-E starting at the Morvich Outdoor Centre 2km from A87 nr Shiel Bridge, or E-W starting at the Affric Lodge 15km W of Cannich. Route can include one of the approaches to the Falls of Glomach (823/FALLS). In mid-June, this strenuous walk is the first part of an Iron Man type race called the Highland Cross where 600 self-confessed crazies complete the trail W-E with a 50km cycle dash to Beauly in 3.5hrs. Possible stopover at one of Scotland's remotest YH, 'Alt Beithe'. 671/HOSTELS. O/wise allow 10hrs. 2·C·3

Glencoe

SOME GREAT MUNROS

There are almost 300 hills in Scotland over 3,000ft as tabled by Sir Hugh Munro in 1891. Recently Munro-bagging has become popularised by numerous books and Muriel Gray's TV programme. The Munros selected here have been chosen for their ease of access both to the bottom and (thence) to the top. They all offer rewarding climbs, but none should be attempted without proper clothing (esp boots) and sustenance for the journey. You may also need an OS map. Always remember that the weather can change quickly in the Scottish mountains.

1083 **BEN LOMOND, ROWARDENNAN, LOCH LOMOND:** Many folk's first Munro, given
MAP 6 proximity to Glasgow (soul and city). It's not too taxing a climb and has
A3 rewarding views (in good weather). 2 main ascents: 'tourist route' is easier, from
toilet block at Rowardennan carpark (end of rd from Drymen), well-trodden all
the way; or 500m up past Youth Hostel, a path follows burn – the 'Ptarmigan
Route'. Circ walk possible. 3hrs up.

1084 **SCHIEHALLION, KINLOCH RANNOCH:** The faerie hill of the Caledonians, forgiving,
MAP 4 not too exerting and possessing what the Munro mystic might call Earth Vibes.
B3 It was the first mountain drawn up in contour lines and was used by other
pioneers of physics. 2 routes up both from Schiehallion rd betw Kinloch
Rannoch and Aberfeldy. Usual route from carpark on obvious path takes 2.5-3
hrs up. Bit of a slog over slabs and boulders at top.

1085 **BEN MORE, MULL:** The 'cool, high ben' sits in isolated splendour, the only
MAP 1 Munro, bar the Cuillins, across water. Has a sea-level start from a lay-by on the
B1 coast rd B8073 that skirts the southern coast of Loch Na Keal, then a fairly clear
path thro the bleak landscape. Can be slightly tricky nr the top (don't think
about it without good boots), but there are fabulous views across the islands, as
far as Ireland. 966m.

1086 **BEN WYVIS nr GARVE:** Standing apart from its northern neighbours, you can feel
MAP 2 the presence of this mountain from a long way off. Just to N of main A835 rd
D3 from Inverness-Ullapool and v accessible from it, park 6km N of Garve (48km
from Inverness) and follow marked path by stream and thro the forest. Vast
plantations all around but you leave them behind and the approach to the
summit is by a soft and mossy ridge. Magnificent 1046m.

1087 **LOCHNAGAR nr BALLATER:** Described as a fine, complex mountain, its nobility
MAP 3 and mystique apparent from afar, not least Balmoral Castle. Approach via Glen
B4 Muick (pron 'Mick') rd from Ballater to carpark at Loch Miuck (844/LOCHS).
Path to mountain well-signed and well-trodden. 18km ret, allow 6hrs. Steep at
top. Apparently on a clear day you can see the Forth Bridge. 1155m.

1088 **BLA BHEINN, SKYE:** The magnificent massif, isolated from the other Cuillins, has
MAP 2 a sea-level start and seems much higher than it is. The Munro Guide describes it
B4 as 'exceptionally accessible'. It has an eerie jagged beauty and – though some
scrambling is involved and it helps to have a head for exposed situations – there
are no serious dangers. Take A881 from Broadford to Elgol through Torrin and
park 1km S of the head of L Slapin, walking W at Allt na Dunaiche along N
bank of stream. Bla Bheinn (pron 'Blahven') is an enormously rewarding climb
and permits rapid descent for scree runners to shorten the usual time of 7 to
8hrs. 928m.

1089 **BEN LAWERS betw KILLIN and ABERFELDY, PERTHSHIRE:** The massif of 7
MAP 4 summits incl 6 Munros that dominates the N side of L Tay. They are linked by a
B3 twisting ridge 12km long that only once falls below 800m and if you're v fit it's
possible to do the lot in a single day starting from the N or Glen Lyon side.
However, much as Muriel may have an aversion to visitor centres, the Munro
beginner or non-bagger should start and plan route at the centre 5km off the
A827 nr Lawers.
MEALL NAN PTARMIGAN: The part of the ridge to the W, which takes in a Munro
and several tops, is not arduous and is immensely impressive. In 3 hrs you can
get up, along some of it and back, and feel great for the rest of the week. Start
1km further on from Vis Centre down 100m track and thro gate. Head up to
saddle, paths indistinct but just climb. At the top the path becomes clear, as does
your reason for being here.

GREAT WALKING AREAS AND CENTRES

Loch Duich/Shiel Bridge/Glenelg

100km Ft William by A82/A87; 120km Inverness by A82/A887/A87.

ACCOMMODATION: Cluanie Inn (702/PUBS) 0320 40238, MED.INX; Glenelg 1090
Inn (a great pub) 059982 273, MED.INX; Loch Duich Hotel 0599 85213, INX; Kintail MAP 2
Lodge 059981 275, MED.EX; Ratagan YH (670/HOSTELS) 059981 243. C4

FOOD: As above esp L Duich, Cluanie and Glenelg. Also pub food at the Clachan Inn at Dornie.

WALKS: Falls of Glomach (823/WATERFALLS); 5 Sisters of Kintail (1077/SERIOUS WALKS); Kintail South Ridge: 7 Munros in a 13km, 7 hour excursion from nr Cluanie Inn (3-C-3); The Saddle also from A87, 7hrs 3-C-3; Easy-moderate walks around Glenelg (951/PREHIST SITES), Glen More and Tor Beag 1-A-1/1-B-2; Stroll in Balmacarra and the Lochalsh Woodlands (1061/WOODLAND WALKS). 1-A-1

Torridon/Shieldaig/Loch Maree

85km Inverness by A835(N)/A832; 100km Ullapool by A835(S)/A832.

ACCOMMODATION: Tigh-an-Eilean, Shieldaig (571/HIGHLAND HOTELS) 1091
05205 251, MED.INX; Loch Maree Hotel (569/HIGHLAND HOTELS) 044584 288, INX; MAP 2
The Old Mill by L Maree 044584 271, MED.INX; Torridon YH 044587 284. C3

FOOD: As above esp Tigh-an-Eilean, Loch Maree.

WALKS: Liathach and Beinn Eighe (v serious, Beinn Alligin easier); Coire Mhic Fhearchair, the 'secret' loch betw the buttresses of Beinn Eighe only visible from the other side of Glen Torridon. (Start from carpark at head of glen, Kinlochewe 8km.) 2-C-3; Loch Clair in Glen Torridon A896, entrance rd to Coulin Estate for the classic views of Liathach and Bienn Eighe (862/VIEWS) 1-A-2; Marked trails around L Maree from carpark 5km from Kinlochewe: in old Caledonian Forest (3km) and Bienn Eighe foothills (7km) 1-A-2 Also Slioch, the great Munro that overlooks the loch. Start from SE above Gleann Bianasdail, 5km from Incheril. N top has best views. 980m. 2-C-3

The Trossachs/Callander/ Aberfoyle/Brig O' Turk

Callander: 28km Stirling by A84; Aberfoyle: 45km Glasgow by A81.

ACCOMMODATION: 1394/HOLIDAY CENTRES: CALLANDER; Covenanter's 1092
Inn, Aberfoyle 0877 2347 MED.INX; Old Coach Inn, Aberfoyle 0877 2822, CHP; MAP 6
Dundarroch Co House 0877 6200, MED.INX. Lochard YH 0877 7256. B3

FOOD: Callander as above. Also 499/CENTRAL/BEST RESTAUS for Braeval Old Mill, 734/PUB FOOD for The Byre. Tea-room/restau at Brig O' Turk who didn't want mentioned in this book – they had 'enough customers already'; by main rd with hanging baskets outside (1195/CAFES).

WALKS: Ben Venue and Ben A'An (1039/HILLS); many walks in Queen Eliz Forest and L Achray Forest, see Forestry Comm leaflets from Vis Centre on Duke's Pass Rd (858/SCENIC ROUTES) 3km N Aberfoyle. Walks on Menteith Hills, esp ridge to N of the Lake of Menteith – easy from A81. Walks from Callander include: the Pass of Leny (1065/WOODLAND WALKS); the Bracklinn Falls; Ben Ledi (a stiff walk C-3-C requiring OS maps etc); the walk from the boathouse on L Venachar. None of this walking is esp arduous, but all are rewarding and amongst exceptional scenery. Mainly A-2-B.

Assynt/Lochinver

Lochinver is 60km NW of Ullapool by A837, 150km Inverness.

ACCOMMODATION: The Inver Lodge Hotel 05714 496, MED.EX; the 1093
Albannach, Baddidarroch 2km vill, 05714 407. CHP; Inchnadamph Hotel 05712 MAP 2
C2

171

202 20km E on A837, MED.INX; Eddrachilles Hotel nr Scourie 0971 502080 MED.EX 572/HIGHLANDS: INEXP HOTELS; Achmelvich YH 05714 480 and Achinver YH at Achiltibuie (no phone).

FOOD: Riverside Bistro, Main St, 05714 356 (585/HIGHLS: INX RESTAUS); Summer Isles Hotel, Achiltibuie, 085482 282 (560/HIGHLS: BEST RESTAUS) Achin's Bookshop, Inverkirkaig, café open 10am-5pm (1259/CRAFTS).

WALKS: Suilven (1034/HILLS) and Kirkaig Falls (5km ret, allow 2hrs) both of which start from Inverkirkaig 5km from Lochinver. On falls walk, it's worth-while walking on main track for another 15mins to the lochside (1-A-2). Stac Polly (1035/HILLS). Ben More Assynt, a serious Munro at 998m/Quinag (pron 'Koon yack') another stiff walk of 5 separate peaks (both 3-C-3). Coast walks from Lochinver to Achmelvich and/or Old Man of Stoer cliffs (854/SCENIC ROUTES).

SECTION 9
Sports

THE GREAT GOLF COURSES

Those listed are open to non-members and are available to visitors (incl women) at most times, unless otherwise stated. Always phone. Handicap certs may be required.

Ayrshire (MAP 1)

1094 **GLASGOW GAILES/WESTERN GAILES:** Superb links courses next to one another
C4 5km S of Irvine off A78. 0294 311347/311649.

1095 **TROON: ROYAL OLD COURSE:** V difficult to get on. No ladies. Staying at Marine
C4 Highland Hotel (0292 314444) helps. Easier is **THE PORTLAND COURSE:** Across
1096 rd from Royal. Both 0292 311555. And 470/SW BEST HOTELS for the adj Piersland
C4 House Hotel.

1097 **OLD PRESTWICK:** Original home of the Open and 'every challenge you'd wish to
D4 meet'. Mon-Fri (not Thu). 0292 77404. Hotels opp (The Old Course 78316 and
the Golf View 671234) cost less than a round.

1098 **TURNBERRY:** Ailsa (championship) and Arran. Sometimes poss by application.
C4 Otherwise you must stay at hotel. 467/SW BEST HOTELS.

1099 **BELLEISLE, AYR:** Good parkland course. Easy on. 0292 41258.
MAP 2
D4

East Lothian (MAP 7)

1100 **GULLANE NO.1:** One of 3 courses surrounding charming village on links and
D1 within driving dist (35km) of Edin. Muirfield is nearby, but you need intro or to
stay at Greywalls (504/LOTHIANS BEST HOTELS). Gullane is OK most days except
Sat. 0620 842255. 1 and 2 are easy on. New visitor centre.

1101 **NORTH BERWICK EAST AND WEST LINKS:** East has stunning views, a superb
D1 clifftop course. West is taxing (esp the classic 'Redan') used for Open qualifying;
a fine links course. 0620 2726 (E)/2135.

1102 **MUSSELBURGH:** The original home of golf, the 9-hole links are now sadly
C1 neglected and enclosed by Musselburgh Racecourse. Nostalgia still appeals and
Royal Musselburgh compensates. 0875 810276.

North-East

1103 **CARNOUSTIE:** 3 good links courses; even poss (with handicap cert) to get on the
MAP 4 championship course (though w/ends diff). Every hole has character. Buddon
E3 Links is cheaper and often quiet. Combination tickets avail. A well-managed and
accessible golfing must. 0241 53789.

1104 **MURCAR, ABERDEEN:** Getting on Royal Aberdeen Course is difficult for most
MAP 3 people; Murcar is a testing alternative; a seaside course 6km N of centre off
D3 Peterhead rd signed at r/bout after Exhibition Centre. 0224 704370. Municipal
courses esp Hazlehead/Links aren't bad.

1105 **CRUDEN BAY nr PETERHEAD:** On A975 40km N Aberdeen. Designed by Tom
MAP 3 Simpson and ranked in UK top 50, a spectacular links course with 'the intangible
E2 aura of bygone days'. Quirky holes epitomise old-fashioned style. Weekends
difficult. 0779 812414.

1106 **NAIRN:** Traditional seaside links course and one of the easiest championship
MAP 2 courses to get on. Good clubhouse, friendly folk. Nairn Dunbar on other side of
D3 town also has good links. 0667 52787.

1107 **ROYAL DORNOCH:** Sutherland championship course laid out by Tom Morris in
MAP 2 1877. Amongst top 10 courses in UK, but not busy or incessantly pounded. No
D2 poor holes. Stimulating sequences. Where else in the world could you get on
such a course so easily? 0862 810219.

Fife (MAP 5)

ST ANDREWS: The home and Mecca of golf, v much part of the town (HOLIDAY 1108
CENTRES, p. 241). Old Course most central, celebrated and difficult to get on – D2
but not imposs. Normal club handicaps OK. Visitors must apply the day before
for the daily ballot (0334 73393). For New Course (1896, less subtle) and Jubilee
(1897, best holes at the turn), just turn up to play. For Eden (1914, laid out by
Harry S. Holt paying homage to the Old with large, sloping greens), apply 24
hrs in advance (0334 74296). All 4 courses contiguous and 'in town'.

ELIE: Splendid links maintained in top condition; open and can be windswept. 1109
The starter has his famous periscope and may be watching you. Book 0333 D3
330955. Adj 9-hole course, often busy with kids, is fun.

CRAIL: Originally designed by the legendary Tom Morris, links and park; all 1110
holes in sight of sea. Not expensive; easy on. 0333 50960. E3

LUNDIN LINKS: Challenging seaside course often used as Open qualifier. Some 1111
devious contourings. Separate ladies course. 0333 320202. D3

LADYBANK: Best inland course in Fife; Tom Morris again. V well kept and 1112
organised. Good facilities. Tree-lined and picturesque. 0337 30814. C3

GOOD GOLF COURSES IN GREAT PLACES

All these courses are open to women, non-members and inexpert players.

✝ ✝ **MACHRIE:** 0496 2310. Isle of Islay. 7km Pt Ellen. Worth going to Islay 1113
(Loganair's airstrip adj course or Calmac ferry from Oban) just for the MAP 1
golf. The Machrie (Golf) Hotel does deals. Old-fashioned course to be played A3
by feel and instinct. Splendid, sometimes windy isolation with a warm bar and a
decent restau at the end of it. The notorious 17th, 'Iffrin' (it means Hell), a
vortex shaped from the up-down dune system of marram and beautiful close-
cropped grass, is one of many great holes. 18.

✝ **MACHRIHANISH:** 0586 81213. By Campbeltown (10km). Amongst the dunes 1114
and links of the glorious 8km stretch of the Machrihanish Beach MAP 1
(801/BEACHES). The Atlantic provides thunderous applause for your triumphs B4
over a challenging course. 9/18.

✝ **SOUTHERNESS, SOLWAY FIRTH:** 0387 88677. 25km S of Dumfries by A710. A 1115
championship course on links on the silt flats of the Firth. Despite its MAP 9
prestige, it's not difficult to get on. Under the wide Solway sky, it's not just the D4
name of a place – southerness is what you feel. 18.

✝ **ROSEMOUNT, BLAIRGOWRIE:** 0250 2622. An excellent, pampered and well- 1116
managed course in the middle of green Perthshire, an alternative perhaps to MAP 4
Gleneagles, being much easier to get on (most days, esp Mon, Tue, Thu) and C3
rather cheaper. Off A93, S of Blairgowrie. 18.

GLENCRUITTEN, OBAN: 0631 62868. Picturesque course on the edge of town. Take 1117
direction S (A816) from Argyll Sq, bearing left at church. Course is signed. MAP 1
Quite tricky with many blind holes. Can get busy, phone first. 18. B1

GAIRLOCH: 0445 2407. Just as you come into town from the south on A832, it looks 1118
over the bay and down to a perfect, pink, sandy beach. Small clubhouse with MAP 2
honesty box. Not the world's most agonising course; in fact, on a clear day with C3
views to Skye, you can forget agonising over anything. 9/18.

NEW GALLOWAY: 0556 2794. Local course on S edge of this fine wee toon. Almost 1119
all on slope but affording great views of Loch Ken in the valley; and the MAP 9
Galloway Forest behind. No bunkers and only 9 short holes, but exhilarating C3
play. Easy on, except Sun.

TAYMOUTH CASTLE, KENMORE: 0887 830228. Spacious green acres around the 1120
enigmatic empty hulk of the castle. Well-tended and organised course betw MAP 4
A827 to Aberfeldy and the river. Inexp and guests at Kenmore Hotel B3
(527/TAYSIDE HOTELS) get special rate. 18.

1121 **MINTO, DENHOLM:** 0450 72180. 9km E Hawick. Spacious parkland in Teviot valley.
MAP 8 **VERTISH HILL, HAWICK:** 0450 72293, is a more challenging hill course. Both amongst
C3 best in Borders. 18.

1122 **GIFFORD:** 0620 81267. Dinky (9/11 tees) inland course on the edge of a dinky
MAP 7 village, bypassed by the queue for the big E Lothian courses and a guarded
D2 secret amongst the regulars. Inexp. Easy on.

1123 **STRATHPEFFER:** 0997 21219. V hilly (and we do mean hilly) course full of character
MAP 2 and with exhilarating Highland views. Small-town friendliness. You are playing
D3 up there with the gods. 18.

1124 **ELGIN:** 0343 542338. 1km from town on A941 Perth rd. Many memorable holes
MAP 2 (incl 1 and 2) on moorland/parkland course in area where links may lure you to
B2 the coast (Nairn, Lossiemouth). 18.

1125 **DURNESS:** 0971 511364. The most northerly golf course on mainland UK, in the
MAP 2 wild and wonderful headland by Balnakeil Bay, looking over to Faraid Head.
D1 The last hole is 'over the sea'. Only est 1988, it's already got cult status. 2km W
Durness village. 9.

1125a **BOAT OF GARTEN:** 047983 282. Challenging, picturesque course in the town where
MAP 2 ospreys have been known to wheel overhead. Has been called the 'Gleneagles of
D4 the North', certainly the best round around, though not for novices. 18.

1125b **ROTHESAY:** 0700 502244. Sloping course with breathtaking views of Clyde. Visitors
MAP 1 welcome. What could be finer than taking the train from Glasgow to Wemyss
C3 Bay for the ferry over (1396/JOURNEYS) and 18 holes. Finish up with fish 'n'
chips at The West End (1206/FISH 'N' CHIPS) on the way home.

THE BEST SLEDGING PLACES

*No, it doesn't snow in Scotland all winter, but when it does (and it seems to less
frequently) we might head for the hills. Many towns are surrounded by slopes, so
you can take your pick. The following are some grown-up suggestions for the
main centres only:*

Edinburgh

THE BRAID HILLS: The connoisseur's choice where, in a range of anoraks and just
possibly Barbours and Christmas scarves, you sledge down friendly and not-
too-challenging slopes in a crowded L. S. Lowry landscape that you will
remember long after the thaw. Off Braid Hills Drive at the golf course. Can
walk in via Blackford Glen Rd. **CORSTORPHINE HILL:** Gentle broad slope with
woodland at top and trails (219/CITY WALKS) and a busy rd at the bottom. App
via Clermiston Rd off Queensferry Rd. **QUEEN'S PARK:** The lesser slopes that
skirt Arthur's Seat, and further in around Hunter's Bog for the more
adventurous or less sociable sledger.

Glasgow

KELVINGROVE PARK: At Park Terr side. No long runs but a winter wonderland
when the rime's in the trees. **GARTNAVEL HOSPITAL GROUNDS:** In W end
(Hyndland) off Gt Western Rd. You can play safe sledging into the playing field,
or more adventurously thro the woodlands. **QUEEN'S VIEW:** On A809 N of
Bearsden 20km from centre. One of Glasgow's most popular walks (429/VIEWS)
is also a great place to sledge. Variable slopes off the main path. The Highlands
can be seen on a clear day. **RUCHILL PARK:** In N of city (430/VIEWS) and **QUEEN'S
PARK** in south.

Dundee

LOCHEE PARK: Ancrum Rd end. Clump of trees at top. Steep in places. **BAXTER
PARK:** 'Daisy Hill' off Arbroath Rd. Can get mogully, but lots of fun.

Aberdeen

KAIM HILL: At Bridge of Dee off Garthdee Rd, nr main rd into town from
Stonehaven. There's a dry ski slope and a hill adjacent. **BROAD HILL:** When it
snows, head for the beach. This popular sledging run is behind the Beach Leisure
Centre. Go from town via Beach Boulevard. **ROYAL INFIRMARY GROUNDS:**
Westburn Rd side. Injuries instantly dealt with.

Jedburgh

ALLERLY WELL PARK: My childhood; the sledge my brother made; happy days.

BEST OF THE SKIING

In a good year the Scottish ski season can extend from December (or even November) till the 'lambing snow' of late April. And on a good day it can be as exhilarating as anywhere in Europe. Here's a summary (distances in km):

	GLEN-SHEE	CAIRN-GORM	AONACH MOR	GLEN-COE	THE LECHT
DIST/EDIN	130	215	215	165	200
GLASGOW	170	235	200	150	160
NR CENTRE	PERTH 65	INVERN 45	FT WILL 8	FT WILL 40	ABERDEEN
NR TOWN	BRAEMAR 20	AVIEM 15	FT WILL 8	BALLACHU-LISH 20	TOMINTOUL 11
NO OF RUNS	38	28	18	15	17
BEGINNERS	10	11	5	3	6
INTERMED	26	15	12	11	10
BLACKS	2	2	1	1	1
NO OF TOWS	26	17	9	6	11
CAFES	3	3	2	1	1
GOOD FOR	Size Access from rd Views Glas Maol 2 distinct areas	Size Non-skiing Views Beginners	Uplift Access Views/Sunsets Ski School Café	Less crowds Nr road Views Most alpine	Less crowds Nr road Families Near NE

Glenshee

BASE STATION: 03397 41320. **SCHOOL:** 03397 41331 or 025085 216.

1126
MAP 4
C2

WHERE TO STAY

BRIDGE OF CALLY HOTEL: 025086 231. 32km S. Great value, pleasant spot on the way. 683A/ROADSIDE INNS. INX

DALMUNZIE HOUSE: 025085 224. 9km S. Country House. Golf. Family run. MED.EX

SPITTAL OF GLENSHEE: 025085 215. 8km S. Package hols. Cheap and cheerful. MED.INX

COMPASS CHRISTIAN CENTRE: 0250 885209. 12km S. Recomm hostel not only for Jesus freaks. CHP

WHERE TO EAT

BRIDGE OF CALLY HOTEL/DALMUNZIE as above. No others. Recommended. INX

APRES SKI

BLACKWATER INN: 17km S on main rd. A good all-round pub. Occasional live music, pub meals and 8 rooms which are v cheap.

SKI HIRE

BRIDGE OF CALLY SKI HIRE: 025086 350. Opp hotel. Convenient.

BLACKWATER SKI HIRE: 025082 234. As above, on main rd to slopes.

Cairngorm

BASE STATION: 0479 86261. **SCHOOL:** 0479 810336 or 0479 810310.

1127
MAP 2
D4

WHERE TO STAY

CORROUR HOUSE: 0479 810220. 11km W. 654/COUNTRY-HOUSE HOTELS. INX

ARD-NA-COILLE: 0540 673214. 36 km S. 565A/BEST HIGHLAND HOTELS. MED.EX

COYLUMBRIDGE: 0479 810661. 10km W. Nearest and best of modern Aviemore hotels. 2 pools/sauna. Ski hire. Acceptable restau. Comfort when you need it. MED.EX

COLUMBA HOUSE: 0540 661402. In Kingussie 32km S. Small country house in village. INX

THE OSPREY: 0540 661510. Also Kingussie, also good value.

WHERE TO EAT
THE CROSS, KINGUSSIE: 0540 661166. 567/HIGHLS/BEST RESTAUS.

THE BOATHOUSE, KINCRAIG: 0540 4272. 581/HIGHL/BEST RESTAUS.

ARD-NA-COILLE: See above.

APRES SKI
THE WINKING OWL, AVIEMORE: At end of main st. Owl's Nest.

THE OLDE BRIDGE, AVIEMORE: Small, welcoming, good atmos and cooking.

ROYAL HOTEL, KINGUSSIE: Real ales (8) and malts. 721/REAL ALE PUBS.

SKI HIRE
COYLUMBRIDGE HOTEL: 0479 810661. Behind hotel, run by Caird Sport (major operators) and nearest to slopes. Open AM and 4-6.30pm.

Aonach Mor/The Nevis Range

1128 **BASE STATION:** 0397 705825. **SCHOOL:** 0397 705825.

MAP 2
C4 ## WHERE TO STAY
See **FORT WILLIAM**, page 231.

WHERE TO EAT
See **FORT WILLIAM**, page 231.

APRES SKI
No pub in immediate vicinity. Nearest all-in ski centre:

NEVIS SPORT, FORT WILLIAM: 0397 704921. Bar (side entrance) till 11pm. Self/S cafe all day till 5pm. Bookshop and extensive ski/outdoor shop on ground floor. Also ski hire.

SKI HIRE
As above (0397 704921) and at base station 0397 705825.

Glencoe

1129 **BASE STATION:** 08552 303. **SCHOOL:** 08552 350.

MAP 2
C5 ## WHERE TO STAY
See **FORT WILLIAM**, p. 231, and also:

ISLES OF GLENCOE HOTEL: 08552 603. Ballachulish. Modern development Leisure Centre incl pool. Not exp. 660/HOTELS THAT WELCOME KIDS.

CLACHAIG INN, GLENCOE: 08552 252. Famous 'outdoor inn' for walkers, climbers etc with pub (704/GREAT PUBS), pub food and inexp accomm.

KINGSHOUSE HOTEL: 08556 250. The classic travellers inn 1km from A82 through Glen and nr slopes (8km). Pub with food/whisky. Inexp rooms.

WHERE TO EAT
As above.

APRES SKI
As above, esp Clachaig Inn and Kingshouse.

SKI HIRE
At base station or check ticket office 08556 226.

The Lecht

1130 **BASE STATION:** 09756 51440. **SCHOOL:** 09756 51440.

MAP 3
B3 ## WHERE TO STAY
Nearest town (28km S) with choice of hotels is Ballater.

DARROCH LEARG, BALLATER: 03397 55443. 1395/HOL CENTRES. MED.INX

GLENAVON HOTEL, TOMINTOUL: 08074 218. On sq in nearest town. CHP

RICHMOND ARMS, TOMINTOUL: 08074 209. Also on sq. Traditional hotel, log fires.
MED.INX

WHERE TO EAT
GREEN INN, BALLATER: 03397 55701. 1395/HOLIDAY CENTRES. MED

THE WHITE COTTAGE nr ABOYNE: 03398 86265. 1395/HOLIDAY CENTRES. MED

THE CLOCKHOUSE, TOMINTOUL: 08074 474. Bistro/café, open till 9pm. INX

APRES SKI
GLENAVON HOTEL, TOMINTOUL: Good large bar for skiers, walkers (S end of Speyside Way is here) and locals.

ALLARGUE HOTEL, COCKBRIDGE: On rd S to Ballater 5km from slopes and o/looking Corgarff Castle and the trickle of the R Don. Rooms also.

SKI HIRE
From ski school 09756 51440.

Weather and Road Reports

0898 654 then: 654 CAIRNGORM
                  656 GLENSHEE
                  658 GLENCOE
                  660 NEVIS RANGE

OTHER SKI HOTLINES (ALL AREAS) ARE: 0891 654654 or 0839 202030.

THE BEST WATERSPORTS CENTRES

CROFT-NA-CABER nr KENMORE, LOCH TAY: 0887 830 588. S side of loch, 2km from village. Purpose-built watersports centre with instruction and hire of windsurfers, canoes, kayaks, dinghies, motor boats as well as waterskiing, river rafting (down the Tay through Taymouth Castle grounds to white water at Grandtully: pure exhilaration), parascending, archery and clay shooting. A v good all-round activities centre in a great setting. Chalet accom and restau. 1131
MAP 4
B3

LINNHE MARINE: 063173 227. Lettershuna, Port Appin. 32km N of Oban on A828 nr Portnacroish. Established, personally run biz in a field of rapid openers and closers. A fine sheltered spot for learning and ploutering. They almost guarantee to get you windsurfing over to the island in 2hrs. Individual or group instruction. Waterskiing, Wayfarers, Luggers and fishing boats for hire. Castle Stalker and Lismore are just round the corner, and the joy of sailing. 1132
MAP 1
C1

PORT EDGAR, SOUTH QUEENSFERRY: 031 331 3330. At end of village, under and beyond the Forth Road Bridge. Major marina and watersports centre specialising in dinghy sailing, hire and instruction. Wayfarers, Wanderers, Mirrors and Toppers. Also canoes and windsurfers. Run by Local Authority with high-quality instruction and vast range of courses at all levels. Open Easter-Oct. 1133
MAP 7
B1

STRATHCLYDE PARK: 0698 66155. Major watersports centre 15km SE of Glasgow and easily reached from most of Central Scotland via M8 or M74 (jnct 5 or 6). 200-acre loch and centre with instruction on sailing, canoeing, windsurfing, rowing, waterskiing and hire facilities for canoes, Mirrors and Wayfarers, windsurfers and trimarans. Sessions: summer 9.30am-8.30pm; winter 9.30am-3.30pm. 1134
MAP 1
E3

LOCHEARNHEAD WATERSPORTS: 056 73367. On A85 nr jnct with A84 a watersports centre where they suggest you'll never be out of your depth. Certainly the loch is wide open and (usually) gently lapping. Instruction and hire of windsurfers, dinghies and canoes. Waterskiing, jet-biking and mt bike hire. Café. 1135
MAP 6
C2

GREAT GLEN WATER PARK: 089093 381. 3km S Invergarry on A82. On shores of tiny Loch Oich and Loch Lochy in the Great Glen. Wonderful spot, with many other notable lochs nearby. Day visitors welcome with windsurfers, Wayfarers, kayaks, Toppers, canoes and also mt bikes and fishing rods for hire. Mainly, however, a chalet park with all the usual condo/timeshare facilities (you can rent by wk). 1136
MAP 2
C4

1137 **CASTLE SEMPLE COUNTRY PARK, LOCHWINNOCH:** 0505 842882. 30km SW Glasgow
MAP 1 M8 jnct 29, A737 then A760 past Johnstone. Also 25km from Largs via A760.
C3 Loch (nr village) is 3km x 1km and at the Rangers' Centre you can hire
windsurfers, dinghies, canoes etc. Bird Reserve on opp bank (890/RESERVES).
Peaceful place to learn.

1138 **KIP MARINA, INVERKIP:** 0475 521485. Major sailing centre on Clyde coast 50km W
MAP 1 of Glasgow via M8, A8 and A78 from Port Glasgow heading S for Largs. A
C3 yacht heaven as well as haven and recently elevated to Grand Prix status. Sales,
charters, pub/restau, chandlers and a myriad of boats. Diving and jet-ski hires.

1139 **LOCHINSH WATERSPORTS, KINCRAIG:** 0540 4272. On B970, 2km from Kincraig
MAP 2 towards Kingussie and the A9. Marvellous lochside site launching from gently
D4 sloping dinky beach into forgiving waters of Loch Inch. Hire of canoes, dinghies
(Mirrors, Toppers, Lasers, Wayfarers) and windsurfers as well as rowing boats;
river trips. An idyllic place to learn. Watch the others and the sunset from the
balcony restau above (581/HIGHLANDS BEST RESTAUS). Sports 8.30am-5.30pm.

1140 **LOCHORE nr LOCHGELLY:** 0592 860086. From Dunfermline-Kirkcaldy m/way take
MAP 5 Lochgelly turn-off, into town and follow signs for Lochore Country Park. Small
B4 safe loch for learning and perfecting. Canoes, dinghies and esp windsurfing.
Instruction and hire. Other distractions in park include a good adventure
playground. Windsurfing: 0592 860264.

THE BEST WINDSURFING

1141 *For Beginners and Instruction*

See WATERSPORTS *on previous page for those centres which give courses in boardsailing along with many other activities. Especially:*

STRATHCLYDE PARK nr MOTHERWELL and GLASGOW: 0698 66155.

PORT EDGAR, SOUTH QUEENSFERRY nr EDINBURGH: 031 331 3330.

CROFT-NA-CABER, KENMORE, LOCH TAY: 0887 830588.

LINNHE MARINE nr OBAN: 0631 73227.

LOCH WINNOCH, betw PAISLEY and LARGS: 0505 842882.

LOCHEARNHEAD WATERSPORTS: 05673 330.

LOCHORE MEADOWS, LOCHGELLY, FIFE: 0592 860264.

1142 *Windsurfing Places*

WHERE THERE ARE OTHER THINGS TO DO ESPECIALLY IF YOU'RE WITH PEOPLE WHO DON'T SHARE YOUR ENTHUSIASM

ELIE, EAST NEUK OF FIFE: Small, friendly windsurfing (sailing and canoeing)
operation more or less on the beach (beyond the Ship Inn). Sheltered lagoon and
open sea. Elie is an attractive, genteel sort of place (729/PUB FOOD; 521/FIFE BEST
RESTAUS; 810/BEACHES; 1109/GOLF). 0333 310366 or 031 228 1707.

STRATHCLYDE PARK nr MOTHERWELL and GLASGOW: 774/COUNTRY PARKS.

PORT EDGAR, SOUTH QUEENSFERRY: 20km W of Edinburgh underneath Road
Bridge. Many other watersports and yachty things. Interesting marina, coffee
shop. Hopetoun House nearby (1293/GARDEN CENTRES).

Windsurfers also converge on the following beaches where there's a good chance
of clean waves and steady winds:

West Coast

MACHRIHANISH: Wave sailing, fabulous long beach (801/BEACHES). Mainly at Air
Force base end.

PRESTWICK/TROON: Town beaches.

East Coast

FRASERBURGH: Town beach.

LUNAN BAY: 12km N of Arbroath.

CARNOUSTIE: Town beach.

ST ANDREWS: West Sands.

LONGNIDDRY/GULLANE: 25/35km E of Edinburgh via A1 and A198.

PEASE BAY: 14km S of Dunbar, 60km S of Edinburgh via A1.

North Coast

THURSO: Many beaches nr town and further W to choose from (812/BEACHES).

For Enthusiasts

ISLAND OF TIREE: The windsurfing capital of Scotland. 40km W of Mull. Innumerable clean, gently sloping beaches all round island (and small inland loch) allowing surfing in all wind directions.'Wave Classic', a major windsurfing event held in October. Tiree Lodge Hotel (08792 368), Kirkapol Guest House (08792 729) or self-catering (Oban TO 0631 63122). Loganair fly every day except Sunday (041 889 3181) and Calmac run ferries from Oban 3 or 4 times a week (0475 34531).

INFORMATION/BOARD HIRE:

GLASGOW: 7th WAVE, 30 St Georges Rd. 041 331 1432.

EDINBURGH: MACH, Lady Lawson St. 031 229 5887.

ABERDEEN: SUB SEA SERVICES, 631 George St. 0224 638588.

THE BEST WHITEWATER RAFTING

In recent years whitewater rafting (or paddling down a river with a group of people in a large inflatable rubber raft and shooting the rapids) has become increasingly popular worldwide. For summer-long use the river needs to be large and remain reasonably full. In Scotland, rafting has tended to centre on the Tay though it may yet develop on the Spey or the Tweed. The following operators are professional and friendly. Almost anyone can do it – and should.

WHITEWATER ADVENTURES, ABERFELDY: 0241 828940 (24hrs). Martin Lowther's team operate out of Friockheim in Angus but the stretch of the Tay they use is from Aberfeldy to Grantully (14km). Meet at the café in Grantully, then they drive you to Aberfeldy, 2-3hrs on a beautiful river in bonniest Scotland. Most thrills at the end. Rafts take 8 plus guide. June-Sept (booking advisable but not essential) or by arrangement outwith season.

CROFT-NA-CABER, nr KENMORE: 0887 830588. Rafting is just one of the watersports and other activities organised by this excl facility on L Tay 2km from Kenmore (1131/WATERSPORTS). Alistair Leitch says he found the Grantully section of the Tay first and it's definitely the most exhilarating of the various runs offered by Croft-na-Caber. The half-day trip starts as above from Aberfeldy (minibus from Centre, morning and afternoon), a whole-day trip starts in the loch. A 1hr sampler through Taymouth Castle grounds is scenic rather than rapid.

SPLASH, nr PERTH: 0738 87430. Also on the Tay, in summer further downriver where it's likely to be fuller, but also from Aberfeldy in winter. Meet at carpark just before Stanley (4km from A9, 8km N of Perth, signed Stanley/Lincarty). 3 dinghies (modern/self-baling), all gear provided. 8km verdant stretch of river with easy whitewater of Stanley Weir. Splash also use the Orchy and the Findhorn by arrangement – both gnarlier and more fun.

BIGFOOT ADVENTURES, BANCHORY, nr ABERDEEN: 09756 51312. Mostly winter-only when the Dee is in spate. Phone day before for river conditions. Dinghies take minimum of 4, max of 6 (you pay per raft, £100 plus VAT). Meet at pub in Potarch betw Kincardine O'Neil and Banchory on A93. 15km stretch of delightful Dee to Banchory. Bigfoot do other watery things in summer.

THE BETTER SWIMMING POOLS AND GYMS

For Edinburgh, see p. 39; for Glasgow, see p. 74. Also see leisure centres, p. 118.

1144 **PORT SETON POOL, nr EDINBURGH:** 0875 811709. On coast rd from
MAP 7 Musselburgh and about 20km from city centre. Only open in June, July,
C1 Aug (weather permitting). Built on the rocks by the sea, this open-air pool is
pure joy on a warm day. You could be in southern Oz. There are other even
bigger open-air baths at N Berwick 22km down the coast, but at Port Seton
summer memories are made.

1145 **GOUROCK BATHING POND:** 0475 315611. On coast rd S of town centre 45km
MAP 1 from Glasgow centre (train Central Station, bus No 500, Buchanan Street
C3 Station). Another 1950s' style open-air pool, the only one on the W coast.
Heated, so it doesn't need to be a scorcher (blissful, but crowded when it is).
Open May-Sept. Mon-Fri 10am-7.30pm, Sat/Sun closes 4pm.

1146 **CARNEGIE CENTRE, DUNFERMLINE:** 0383 723211. Pilmuir St. Excellent all-round
MAP 5 sports centre with many courses and classes. 2 pools (ozone treated) 25yds
B4 and 25m and kids' pool. Lane swimming lunchtime and evenings. Authentic
Turkish and Aeretone Suite with men's, women's and mixed sessions. Large
gym with Powersport stations etc. Badminton, squash, aerobic classes. Usually
open till 9pm (incl pool), but check.

1147 **BISHOPBRIGGS SPORTS CENTRE, GLASGOW:** 041 772 6391. 147 Balmuildy Rd. At the
MAP B v N edge of Glasgow, best reached by car or 1km walk from stn; adj Forth and
xE1 Clyde Canal walkway (442/GLASGOW WALKS). Large, modern, efficient with
33.3m pool, gym, sauna/sun complex, bar, café etc. Open 9am-10pm (pool
varies).

1148 **THE TRYST CENTRE, CUMBERNAULD:** 0236 728138. In Cumbernauld Centre and
MAP 1 easily reached from M8/M80 and most of Central Scotland. 3 pools (kids,
E3 improvers and 25m), so main pool usually good for lengths. Only pool in
Central Scotland that's open in evenings at w/ends (till 9pm). Also gym, saunas
etc. Has convenience rather than character.

1149 **BATHGATE POOL:** 0506 52783. The town pool in this central belt, suburban area,
MAP 7 friendly and neighbourly and pre-metric (25yds, not metres). Bright at night,
A2 light during the day. A touch over-chlorinated at times, but a happy atmosphere.
Signed from A89, the road through town. Phone for openings.

1150 **GALASHIELS POOL:** 0896 4274. A new pool in the Central Borders on the edge of
MAP 8 parkland with picture windows bringing the outside in. No leisurama nonsense,
C3 just a good deck-level pool (25m). Various hours, usually open till 8.30pm but
check. Pool in Hawick also good.

1151 **INVERNESS POOL:** 0463 233799. Newish pool of brick and bright lights nr riverside
MAP 2 via Bank St or Academy St. 25m ozone treated. Kids' pool, saunas etc and
D3 poolside gym with Universal stations. Poss to hire towels and swimsuits, which
is v civilised. Hours vary.

1152 **ABERDEEN BATHS:** 0224 587920. City well served with swimming pools. 3 in
MAP c suburbs are not esp easy to find, though Hazlehead (0224 310062) is signed from
inner ring rd to W of centre. Bon Accord Baths are a fine example of a municipal
pool. Recently refurbished, they're centrally situated behind the W end of
Union St. Open till 7.45pm weekdays, 4.30pm Sat/Sun. Annie Lennox learned to
swim here.

1153 **PORTSOY OPEN AIR POOL:** One of the great wee coastal villages on this N
MAP 3 Aberdeenshire coast 7km W of Banff with a pool flushed by the sea in an idyllic
C1 setting to W of last houses. Run by local swimming club with changing facilities
and tea-room, it's only open Jun-Aug but take advantage of it on any sunny day.
Brill...iant!

1154 **GOLSPIE SWIMMING POOL:** 0408 633437. A neat little pool (20m) next to the High
MAP 2 School. Nothing too high tech, but a friendly atmos and a friendly mural at one
D2 end. Times vary

SECTION 10
Good Food and Drink

THE BEST VEGETARIAN RESTAURANTS

For vegetarian restaurants in EDINBURGH, see p.24; for GLASGOW, see p.57.

1155 **HIGHLAND DESIGNWORKS, KYLE OF LOCHALSH:** 0599 4388. On edge of town, rd to
MAP 2 Plockton. Open end of Mar-Oct. In a former hostel 2km from ferry (to Skye)
C3 terminal, a high quality 'wholefood' restau and a real find in this neck of the
Highlands. Imaginative variations. Always some vegan. Fish but no meat. No
Smk. Jul-Aug: 7 days 11am-9pm; o/wise: 11am-7pm. Cl Sun/Mon.

1156 **THE MOUNTAIN RESTAURANT, GAIRLOCH:** 0445 2316. Not wholly, but mainly,
MAP 2 vegetarian, with v good range of salads and hot dishes and esp home baking in a
C3 modern restau with good views over bay and Torridon mountains. Craft shop
adj and v reasonable accom above with the same great view. You get the
impression there's a guru in there somewhere, but it's not clear which one. All
day. LO 9.45pm summer, 8.30/9pm winter. Licensed. Not exclusively vegn.

1157 **CULLODEN POTTERY AND RESTAURANT, GOLLANFIELD nr NAIRN:** On main A96 rd
MAP 2 betw Inverness and Nairn (about mid-way). A pottery and craft shop and,
D3 upstairs, a self/s vegan and vegetarian restau. Organic wines, free range eggs.
Hot dishes or coffee and cakes (dairy-free). Open 7days 10am-5.30pm; Fri/Sat
till 9.30pm. A roadside diner with uncompromising attitude to roadside food.

1158 **THE NUTSHELL, CUPAR:** 0334 54147. 17 Bonnygate, the main st of this bonny North
MAP 5 Fife market town. Café by day with wholefoodish menu and good selection of
D2 pies; dinner menu at night (Thu-Sat). Some fish, some vegan. Mon-Sat, 9am-
5.30pm.

1159 **CARLIN MAGGIE'S, KINROSS:** 0577 63652. 191 High St nr the end of the main st
MAP 4 through but only 4km from M90 jnct 6. Rare outpost of careful, cordon-bleu
C4 (mainly) vegn home-cooking. VG vino, No smk. Wed-Sat lunch/dinner.

1159a **CAFE INNEAN (THE ANVIL CAFÉ), PORTREE, SKYE:** 0478 613306. Off Dunvegan rd (at
MAP 2 the Co-op). Kate Tetley (of once-famed Skye vegn restau, the Greenhouse)
B3 returns with fab new art gallery restau (some meat). Food with care and flair.

OTHER GOOD RESTAURANTS THAT DO WELL BY VEGETARIANS:

1160 **GORDON ARMS HOTEL, KINCARDINE O'NEIL, ROYAL DEESIDE:** 033398 84236. Halfway
betw Ballater and Aberdeen Hotel with pub food. Lunch/dinner.   CHP

1161 **CUILFAIL HOTEL nr OBAN:** 08522 274. At Kimelford 25km S on A816. A busy hotel
bar good for family fare and always has a vegn choice.   INX

DUNNET HEAD TEAROOM nr THURSO: 084785 774 (587/HIGHLAND RESTAUS).   CHP

BIADH MATH CAFE, KYLE OF LOCHALSH: Railway Station, nr Skye Ferry. Great
baking and atmos. (581/HIGHLAND RESTAUS.) Mon-Sat 9.30am-5pm and
evenings too in summer.   CHP

THISTLES, CROMARTY: 0381 7471 (566/HIGHLAND RESTAUS).   MED

LEMON TREE, ABERDEEN: 0224 642230 (601/ABERDEEN RESTAUS).   CHP

OWLIE'S, ABERDEEN: 0224 649267 (609/ABERDEEN RESTAUS).   INX

PARROT CAFE, DUNDEE: 0382 24813 (635/DUNDEE RESTAUS) daytime only.   CHP

KILLIECRANKIE HOTEL BAR, KILLIECRANKIE: 0796 473220 (528/TAYSIDE HOTELS). INX

ATKIN'S BISTRO nr ABERFELDY: 0887 820332 (523/TAYSIDE HOTELS).   MED

OSTLER'S CLOSE, CUPAR: 0334 55574 (519/FIFE RESTAUS).   MED

WATERSIDE BISTRO, HADDINGTON: 0620 825674 (510/LOTHIAN RESTAUS).   INX

DROVER'S INN, EAST LINTON: 0620 860298 (181/PUBS WITH GREAT FOOD).   INX

PHILIPBURN HOUSE HOTEL, SELKIRK: 0750 20747 (483/BORDER HOTELS).   INX

MARMION'S, MELROSE: 089682 2245 (490/BORDER RESTAUS).   INX

OLD FORGE, HAWICK: 0450 852981 (491/BORDER RESTAUS).   MED

OLD SCHOOL, KINLOCHBERVIE: 0971 82383 (584/HIGHLAND RESTAUS).   INX

RIVERSIDE BISTRO, LOCHINVER: 05714 356 (585/HIGHLAND RESTAUS).   INX

THE CEILIDH PLACE, ULLAPOOL: 0854 612103 (568/HIGHLAND HOTELS).   CHP/MED

ARISAIG HOUSE HOTEL, ARISAIG: 06875 622 (652/COUNTRY-HOUSE HOTELS).   EXP

THE BEST SEAFOOD RESTAURANTS

LOCK 16, CRINAN HOTEL, CRINAN: 054683 261. 8km off A816. On coast, 60km S of Oban (Lochgilphead 12km) at head of the Crinan Canal which joins Loch Fyne with the sea. Rather ordinary third-floor room, but eating fish here prompts a revelation about the word 'fresh'. Dinner is landed daily outside the hotel and served against the awesome seascape from which it was caught – the Sound of Jura and the dreaded Gulf of Corryvreckan. Ground-floor restau serves similar fare but not only seafood. Here I had the best Dover sole I'd ever tasted. Wander around the canalside after supper and wish that life could always be like this. 1166 / MAP 1 / B2 / EXP

LOCHBAY INN, SKYE: 047083 235. 14km N Dunvegan off A850 to Portree on the Waternish Peninsula. V small cottage café/restau at the end of the row in lochside village which also has a nice pub. Locally caught lobster, shark, skate and shellfish. Main dishes served unfussily with chips or baked potato. Puds include Clootie Dumpling. Open fire. Simply very good – the place and the plaice are perfectly *simpatico*. Book. Cl Sat. 1167 / MAP 2 / B3 / INX

LOCH FYNE SEAFOOD AND SMOKERY: 04996 346. On A83 the L Lomond-Inveraray rd, 20km Inveraray/11km Rest and Be Thankful. Roadside smokery which is not merely a net across the end of the loch to catch tourists. In summer you may well have to book or wait; people come from afar for the oysters and the smokery fare esp the kippers. Spacious, though the booths can seem cramped. House white (and others incl whisky) well chosen. Same menu all day, no 'meal times'. Also shop selling every conceivable packaging of salmon etc 9am-9pm. All in all, a great idea. 1168 / MAP 1 / C2 / INX

CREELERS, BRODICK, ARRAN: 0770 2810. Just outside Brodick on rd N to Brodick Castle and Corrie, in a modern tourist plaza-plex. Local oysters, langoustines, monkfish etc in cafeteria surroundings that allow the food to make the main impression. The puddings can be persuasive. Wines appropriate and inexp. LO 10pm. 1169 / MAP 1 / C4 / MED

MOREFIELD HOTEL, ULLAPOOL: 0854 612161. Unlikely location for a great seafood supper (a hotel in a housing estate at the back of beyond), but that's what you get. They have their own trawler and you get what they got – the same day! Bar food too. 1170 / MAP 2 / C2 / MED

CRANNOG, FORT WILLIAM: 0397 705589. The jetty in the centre of town. Simple, modern and light. A la carte menu with langoustines caught from their own boat, salmon from their own smokery etc (they mail-order seafood too). Blackboard specials (incl vegetarian) according to season. All main courses with baked potato and salad. Small wine-list is ok, e.g. Sauvignon is en Bris, the Muscadet is Sur Lie. Nice puds. There's also a city branch in GLASGOW at 28 Cheapside (221 1727), which is betw the m/way and the *Daily Record* building at the top of the street. Similar in every respect, just a little further from the sea. 1171 / MAP 2 / C4 / MED

TWO FAT LADIES, GLASGOW: 339 1944. 88 Dumbarton Rd. Two not so broad dining-rooms in the hallway behind a small frontage where the kitchen is literally in the window. Daily starters, half-a-dozen imaginative fish dishes (and a meaty alternative), oozy puds; a handleable, original menu though not as cheap as you'd like. Tue-Sat evenings only, LO 10.30pm. 1172 / MAP B / A1 / MED

THE ANCHORAGE, TARBERT: 0880 820 881. Perfect location on busy quay of quintessential Highland port. Locally caught means locally caught. Fish, seafood and Black Angus (the steak alternative). Crisp whites. 5pm-10pm. Cl Mon. 1172a / MAP 1 / B3 / MED

NO 33, PERTH: 0738 33771. Kinnoull St nr art gallery. Seafood longue and prob the best meal in town, with bar area for oysters and other morsels (incl after-theatre supper). Restau lunch and LO 9.30pm, bar 10.30pm+. Cl Sun/Mon. 1172b / MAP 4 / C4 / MED

SILVER DARLINGS, ABERDEEN: 0224 576229. Down by the harbour, probably the best restau in the city. Exquisite char-grilled seafood. 597/ABERDEEN RESTAUS. 1173 / MAP 5 / E3 / MED

THE CELLAR, ANSTRUTHER: 0333 310378. Behind Fisheries Museum in busy East Neuk of Fife town. Fish and shellfish from hereabouts, some meat options. Great French bistro atmos. 520/FIFE RESTAUS. 1174 / MED

GINGERHILL, MILNGAVIE, GLASGOW: 041 956 6515. 297/GLAS BEST RESTAUS. INX

MARINETTE, EDINBURGH: 031 555 0922. 53A/EDIN BEST RESTAUS. INX

THE BEST TEA-ROOMS AND COFFEE SHOPS

For Edinburgh see page 26, Glasgow page 60.

1175 **THE TUDOR RESTAURANT, AYR:** 8 Beresford Terr nr Odeon and Burns ✝
MAP 1 Monument Sq. For over 25 yrs a tea-room and restau, a classic of its type;
D4 roomy, well-used, full of life. Bakery counter at front (sausage rolls and 'fly cemeteries' as they're supposed to be) and waitress service in the body of the kirk. B/fast 9-11am, high tea 3.15-8pm and lunch(eon) in betw. Traditional without being tacky.

1176 **THE SUNFLOWER, PEEBLES:** 4 Bridgegate off main st and behind Veitch's. A ✝
MAP 8 wee deli out front (excl cheese board) and a celebrated and individual coffee
B2 shop/bistro spread around small (well, poky) rooms full of chatting Peeblesiders and crazy paintings. Excl hot dishes like stew with garlic and dijon mustard, snacks and baking. Dinner Thu, Fri and Sat (or Tue-Sat in summer) 7.30-9pm. Owner Elizabeth Waddell should have written this book.

1177 **KAILZIE GARDENS TEAROOMS, PEEBLES:** There's something about Peebles ✝
MAP 8 which makes it big on the afternoon tea circuit (there's also Gino's in the main
B2 st, 1192/CAFÉS). Kailzie is just out of town towards Traquair (769/GARDENS) and has a v civilised courtyard coffee shop nr the Garden entrance. The superior sort of home baking you get from the right cook books and courses. Open 7 days, till 4pm Mon-Fri and 5pm at w/ends (5.30pm in summer). Apr-Oct.

1178 **THE RIVERSIDE, ABBEY ST BATHANS:** By the trout farm, nr the R Whiteadder ✝
MAP 8 in the middle of this scattered and rustic village on the Southern Upland
D1 Way. Dream home baking with a hint of extravagance e.g. wild boar and pheasant pie (certainly plenty of the latter about; rather fewer of the former) and some damaging desserts. There are occasional 'musical evenings'. Signposted from A1 at Cockburnspath. Tue-Sun 11am-5/6pm.

1179 **THE SMITHY, NEW GALLOWAY:** Nr end of main st a bookshop/coffee shop/ ✝
MAP 9 general centre for the village and walkers/wanderers in this neck of the
C3 Galloway woods. Home baking with esp good pastry and oatcakes and meals all day till 6pm, 9pm in summer. Licensed.

1180 **THE WHITEHOUSE OLD SCHOOL TEA-ROOM, by KENNACRAIG:** Nr the ferry
MAP 1 terminal to Islay, 14km S of Tarbert; 100m off the main A83 rd to Campbel-
B3 town. A small schoolhouse in a neat cottage garden serving home-baked goodies and light snacks like salmon mousse. The malt whisky ice-cream makes a good carry-oot.

1181 **THE CLIFTON COFFEE SHOP, TYNDRUM:** On A82, a strategically-placed pit stop
MAP 6 on the drive to Oban or Ft William (just before the road divides), with a Scottish
A2 produce shop and the 'Green Welly Shop' selling outdoor gear. Fast (Scottish) food to an unusually good standard (let's face it, they don't have to: bus parties seldom come back) and some welcome variations on the wholefood theme. Seats outside on warm days. 8.30am-5.30pm, 7 days.

1182 **THE CHATTERBOX, NEWTON STEWART:** Main st nr corner on A75. Cringeworthy
MAP 9 name but the twee cakes are v good. Old teatime faves (Border Tart for a start)
B3 and newer ones, described as 'wicked', like pavlova and banoffie pie. Also snacks. Mon-Sat, 9am-5pm.

1183 **COFFEE PARLOUR, GRANTOWN-ON-SPEY:** 35 High St. Surprisingly authentic
MAP 2 Italian caff with genuine Italian cakes, ice-cream and expresso. They do stew as
E3 well as a pretty good pasta. This place would hold its own in Soho, but here it is on the very Northern Line.

1184 **THE COFFEE SHOPPE, FRASERBURGH:** 30 Cross St. Small front-room-of-
MAP 3 somebody's-hoose-type place. Scottish and imported cakes (e.g. carrot cake/
D1 pavlova) all home-made. Mum's soup. Mon-Sat, 9am-4.30pm.

1185 **FLORENCE'S TEAROOM, CROMARTY:** In great wee village in Black Isle 30km NE of
MAP 2 Inverness (790/COASTAL VILLAGES) on corner of Church St. Home baking à la
D3 Townswomen's Guild with some excl cakes and shortbread. Verandah on main st. Open Thu, Sat, Sun and Mon till 5pm. Another tea-room opposite, Binnie's, is open on alternate days.

KIND KYTTOCK'S KITCHEN, FALKLAND: Folk come to Falkland (907/CASTLES; 1307/GALLERIES; 1047/HILL WALKS) for many reasons, but this is most certainly one of them. Omelettes, toasties, baked potatoes but mainly superior home baking and service. No smk room upstairs. 10.30am-5.30pm. Cl Mon.

1186
MAP 5
C3

MERCHANT'S HOUSE, ST ANDREWS: South St in the middle. Self/S restau-cum-coffee shop with urbane, relaxed yet busy atmos reminds you of a coffee shop in an old university town! Read the papers, discuss the news, gradually miss your tutorial. 7 days, 10am-5.30pm. Also **BRAMBLES:** 5 College St.

1187
MAP 5
D2

DUN WHINNY'S, CALLANDER: Off main st at Glasgow rd, a welcoming wee but not twee, tea-room; you will need one in Callander. They have cinammon toast, they have toffee apple pecan pie, they have attitude. 10am-6pm. No smk.

1188
MAP 6
C3

THE GRANARY, COMRIE: On main st parlour room with gr home-bakes arrangd on an old-fashoned counter – you go up and choose though it ain't easy. Nice bread with soup; baked pots etc. Jams/chutneys. No smk. Mar-Oct 10-5pm. Cl Mon.

1188.1
MAP 4
B4

THE DUNNET HEAD TEA-ROOM, DUNNET HEAD nr THURSO: 15km N on the coast rd via Castletown. 587/HIGHLANDS: GOOD INEX RESTAUS.

VISOCCHI'S, BROUGHTY FERRY and KIRRIEMUIR: Gray St in the Ferry and downtown Kirriemuir (the original). 1222/ICE-CREAM; 633/DUNDEE: RESTAUS.

GREAT CAFES

For Cafés in Edinburgh, see p.25, Glasgow p. 58.

✝ ✝ **NARDINI'S, LARGS:** 0475 674555. The Esplanade, Glasgow side. An institution. The epitome of the seaside cafeteria and all the nostalgia of Doon the Watter days. An airy brasserie with cake, ice-cream and chocolate counters and in the back a trad tratt with full Italian à la carte and ok wines; a timeless formula which works as well today as it ever did and creates an ambience which designer café bars can only aim for. The slight shabbiness and cardboardy ice-cream are indivisible parts of the appeal. And those light fittings . . . Summer till 10.30pm/winter 8pm. High teas till 7.30pm.

1189
MAP 1
C3

MELBOURNE CAFE, SALTCOATS: 72 Hamilton St opp Safeways along from main st. Unchanged for years, all the 1950s' nostalgia you could want. A very good sandwich roll is served and milky coffee you could bathe in. 9am-5.30pm.

1190
MAP 1
C3

THE MERCAT CAFE, JEDBURGH: On the main square, a family-run café that's served snacks and meals to weary travellers (the town bus stand used to be outside) for ages and now the legions of tourists that descend on Jedburgh Abbey (973/ABBEYS). The famous Jethart Snails (incredibly good minty sweets) are on sale here. Till 6pm winter, 10pm summer. 7days.

1191
MAP 8
D3

GINO'S CAFE DE LUXE, PEEBLES: On the main st nr the bridge. Gino's, even though it's been there for generations, has a v contemporary feel. The café's through the back past the rows of sweetie jars and there's a proper restau upstairs. Gets seriously busy in summer. In winter you just hang out. LO 9.30pm, Cl Wed pm.

1192
MAP 8
B2

THE MARKET BAR AND RESTAURANT, LANARK MARKET: Hyndford Rd. Betw the auction rings and only on auction days (e.g. Mon), a café from a bygone era. Farmers' sons of farmers' sons still cram the tables and the seats by the counter for the canteen cooking that's always hit the spot. Jam roly-poly, jelly, apples and custard after your mince and chips. The walls creak. The waitresses josh with the regulars; there's a cake-stand on every table. Till 6 or 8pm.

1193
MAP 1
E3

THE BIRKS, ABERFELDY: Main st nr square (14 Dunkeld St). A gr small town café, family-run, Perfect chips with everything. Home-made pies, soups and excl Scottish cakes. Frothy coffee, shortbread and the complete range of Buchanans, the best sweeties you can get in jars. 7 days till 5.30pm (Cl Sun in Jan/Feb).

1194
MAP 4
B3

THE CAFE IN BRIG O'TURK IN THE TROSSACHS: Hanging baskets of flowers outside this shack are what you notice from the road (the A821 12km W of Callander) in the heart of the afternoon-tea belt of the Trossachs. But more substantial high teas are served: Highland stew, herring in oatmeal and great chips. A place not to be advertised – keep mum! Open till 8pm, cl Tue.

1195
MAP 6
B3

THE BEST FISH AND CHIP SHOPS

1196 **THE ASHVALE, ABERDEEN:** 46 Gt Western Rd nr Union St. Set up in 1985, ✝ ✝
MAP C to take advantage of the city's famed supply of fresh fish, this take-away ✝
xA4 and restau complex (seats 300) is first class. Various sizes of haddock, turbot, sole, plaice and some (frozen) fish from New Zealand. Home-made stovies etc, all served fresh and fast. Open 7 days, 12-1am; restau: 12-11pm Sun-Thu; till midnight Fri/Sat. There are many, however, who swear by

THE NEW DOLPHIN, Chapel St. Few tables, superb take-away. 11.45am-1/2am.

1196a **VALENTE'S, KIRKCALDY:** 73 Overton Rd. Ask directions to this excl. ✝ ✝
chippy (missed last edition), worth the queue. Cl Wed. Till 11pm. ✝

1197 **THE UNIQUE, GLASGOW:** 223 Allison St. Not exactly central, but if you're ✝
MAP B mobile or on the South Side this is where you'll find the best fish and chips in ✝
xD4 town (look for the clock, it still tells the right time). Through the curtain in the café, they serve lunches and battered fish teas etc. As well as impeccable haddock, there's the nostalgic delight of the spam fritter. Veg oil used. Old-fashioned hours viz 8.15am-1.15pm, 3.45-9pm. That's right, 9pm – closed.

1198 **HARRY RAMSDEN'S, GLASGOW and EDINBURGH:** Paisley Rd West, and ✝
MAP B/A Newhaven Rd. Both are best reached by car. In Glasgow beside the m/way ✝
B3/xC1 flyover on the S side. In Edin (the latest addition to the franchised family), at Newhaven Harbour in the converted fishmarket, an attractive site. Big, bright, tacky-decor restau and take-away with constant queue due to fresh fry policy. Both 7 days till 11pm. But in Edinburgh locals prefer

YE OLDE PEACOCK INN across the rd which has been serving up *fresh* Scottish fish for yrs. Lunch/high tea and LO 9pm. Sit-in only.

1199 **L'ALBA D'ORO, EDINBURGH:** Henderson Row, nr corner with Dundas St. Large
MAP A selection of deep-fried goodies incl many vegn savouries. Inexpensive proper
C1/D1 pasta and real pizzas. Even the wine's ok. A lot more than your usual fry-up and has won several accolades over the years. Open midnight, 1am w/ends. **THE RAPIDO:** 77 Broughton St, is also very popular with late-night ravers stumbling back down the hill to the New Town. 2am and 3am. Fri/Sat.

1200 **THE DEEP SEA, EDINBURGH:** Leith Walk opp Playhouse. Open late and often has
MAP A queues but these are quickly dispatched. The haddock has to be of 'a certain size'.
D2 Traditional menu. A recent refurb has cooled the famously bright lights, still one of the best fish suppers you'll ever feed a hangover with. 2am and 4.30 Fri/Sat.

1201 **DEEP SEA, DUNDEE:** 81 Nethergate at bottom end of Perth Rd v central. The
MAP D Sterpaio family have been serving the Dundonians excellent fish 'n' chips since
B4 1939. Café with aproned-waitress service is a classic. Vegt oil. Mon-Sat, 11.30am-8.15pm.

1202 **LUIGI'S, DUNDEE:** 17 Strathmartine Rd nr Dundee Law (870/VIEWS). Chip shop
MAP D with newer pizza shop next door, both with dinettes. Lard used; no two chips are
xB1 ever alike. Take them up the hill to eat. 10am-8pm (Fri till 10pm). Cl Sun.

1203 **PEPPO'S, ARBROATH:** 51 Ladybridge St next to the Harbour where those fish
MAP 4 come in. Fresh as that and chips to match in dripping, of course. Peppo has been
E3 here for over 40yrs and should be given the keys to the harbour if not the town. Sun-Thu 4-11pm, Fri 4-9pm and, amazingly, closed on Sat.

1204 **HOLDGATES, PERTH:** 146 South St. Owned by the same family (the Hills, not the
MAP 4 Holdgates) from time immemorial, a trad chip shop serving fish teas thro the
C4 back. Lard used and best haddock from Aberdeen. Noon-8.30pm. Cl Sun.

1205 **THE ANSTRUTHER FISH BAR:** On the front in Fife seaside town (795/COASTAL
MAP 5 VILLAGES); just look for the queue. Lard used. Get a great fish supper and walk
E3 round the Harbour. 7days till 11pm.

1206 **WEST END, ROTHESAY:** 1 Gallowgate. One of the best things about Rothesay and
MAP 9 winner of the Seafish Best Fish 'n' Chip-shop award for 1992. Only haddock, but
D3 wide range of other fries and fresh pizza. Only place we found that uses groundnut oil, the best though not the cheapest. Summer: noon-midnight (Sun 4-11pm), winter noon-2pm and 4-midnight. Café in summer only till 8pm.

1207 **BRUNO'S, DUMFRIES:** Balmoral Rd. Seems as old and essential as the Bard himself.
MAP 1 The best chip in the South. Cl Tue.
C3

1207a **ONORIO'S, OBAN:** George St. Legendary but modernised. 'Anyone who says that
MAP 1 you can fry good chips in veg oil is having you on.' Lunch/4-11.30pm.
B2

THE BEST SCOTCH BAKERS

BLACK'S OF DUNOON: aka Cowal Cottage Bakery at 144 Argyll St, the main st of Dunoon. Constant queues are quickly and cheerfully despatched. The American legacy can be detected in the multifarious donuts amidst the cupcakes, but v solid on the fundamentals like potato scones and shortbread. Piles of pies. 1208
MAP 1
C3

BRADFORD'S: 245 Sauchiehall St, Glasgow, and suburban branches in selected areas i.e. they have not over-expanded; for a bakery 'chain', some lines seem almost home-made. Certainly better than all the industrial 'home' bakers around. Individual fruit pies, for example, are uniquely yummy and the all-important Scotch pie pastry is exemplary. 357/GLASGOW COFFEE SHOPS. 1209
MAP B
C2

McINTYRE'S, PERTH: Main branch at 2 Main St on corner of Perth Br (over Tay) and main A93. Home of the best morning rolls in Scotland and also estimable for their Black Bun (the trad Scots bannock, a necessary component of Hogmanay celebrations) and that staple of respectable afternoon tea, the Battenburg cake. 1210
MAP 4
C4

FISHER AND DONALDSON, DUNDEE/ST ANDREWS/CUPAR: Main branches (3) in Dundee which is v well served with decent bakers shops, e.g. Goodfellow and Steven (several branches incl coffee shops) and Wallaces, famous for their pies and massive bridies. But F and D are out in front in my book. Good on those sickly wee cakes, bread and posh Gat-O; they even do muffins, for God's sake. Whitehall St, 300 Perth Rd, Lochee. 1211
MAP 5
D2

THE BAKERY IN GULLANE: On corner in centre of main st. Supplying the douce denizens of Gullane with their well-baked daily bread and pies. The cakes are not prizewinners, but then the ones made by the wifies of Gullane probably are. 1212
MAP 7
D1

HOUSTON'S OF HAWICK: Nothing too mould-breaking about old Houston's; just honest Border baking. They're at 16 Bourtree Pl as you come into Hawick from the Jedburgh rd just as they've always been. It's where I came in too, to go to school, and I have incl the place where I found an alternative to school dinners, for purely nostalgic reasons. They do make the best Selkirk bannocks. 1213
MAP 8
C3

BREADALBANE BAKERY, ABERFELDY: 37 Dunkeld St. On rd out of town to Grandtully opp petrol stn. Home of Aberfeldy Whisky Cake (a rich fruit job with single malt flavour) and Holyrood Tarts (no, not Hollywood) and brill home-made biscuits etc. Half-day, Wed. 1214
MAP 4
B3

COUNTRY BAKERY, DUNKELD: In main st. Chiefly notable for their variations on the Scotch pie. Odd that more places don't fill the distinctive pastry cases with other things apart from soggy grey mince. They do here. 1215
MAP 4
C3

ASHER'S, NAIRN: 2 branches at either end of Main St and also in Inverness (Church St) and Forres. Baking on the Moray Firth for 100 yrs esp good bread and rolls. Coffee shops attached; the one upstairs at the E end of Nairn is pure '50s (go with your mum). 1216
MAP 2
D3

PILLANS AND SONS, KIRKCALDY: 2 branches at either end of High St. Main shop and bakery at 59, where for 100 yrs or so they've been turning out their Scottish rolls and cakes and unconventional Scotch pies. These, the old clock and the neat trios of cakes in the window, are part of a tasty vignette for anyone with an appetite for nostalgia along with carbohydrate. 1217
MAP 5
C4

SCOTCH OVEN, CALLANDER: Opp Royal Hotel in busy touristy main st and one of the best things about it. Good bread, rolls (incl Ayrshire rolls, whatever they are), cakes, the biggest tattie scones and sublime donuts. This is where to stock up for your walk on the Braes, the other great thing about Callander. Open 7 days. 1218
MAP 6
C3

THE BEST ICE-CREAM

1219 LUCA'S, MUSSELBURGH nr EDINBURGH: 32 High St. Always queues in
MAP 7 the narrow doorway of this famous ice-cream shop, which still mainly
C1 makes the 3 classics (vanilla, chocolate, strawberry). People come from
Edinburgh (14km) though there is a branch in the nearby suburb of Craigmillar.
Olympia café through the back has basic snacks and the ice-cream in its sundae
best, but you might wait a wee while, it gets busy. Every day, 10am-10pm.

1220 MANCINI'S, THE ROYAL CAFE, AYR: 11 New Rd, the rd to Prestwick. Ice-
MAP 1 cream that's taken seriously, entered for competitions and usually wins
D4 one category or another. Family biz for aeons. Countless flavours incl the new
killer, Teddy's Honeypot, which may take over the world. Folk come from
Glasgow just to bask in their Knickerbocker Glory. 9.30am-11.30pm; Cl Thu in
winter.

1220a CASA MARCHINI, ABERDEEN: 333 King St, heading out of town for A92 N but
MAP 6 only 500m from end of E end of Union St. It's true what they say – this is the
C2 home of the classic Italian ice-cream and has been since 1910. Natural flavours,
some exotic concoctions (like egg yolk and marsalla, apricots in brandy), excl
cakes, bombes and zuccottos. It's a long way to roam from Roma, but Aberdeen
is definitely the better for this long-ago migration. 10.30am-8.30pm. Cl Mon.

1221 CALDWELL'S, INNERLEITHEN: On the High St in this ribbon of a town betw
MAP 8 Peebles and Gala, they've been making ice-cream since 1911. Purists will
B2 approve of the fact that they still make only vanilla. The shop sells everything
from Blue Nun to bicycles. The ice-cream is plain white brilliant. Mon-Fri till
8.30pm, Sat/Sun 7.30pm.

1222 VISOCCHI'S, BROUGHTY FERRY/KIRRIEMUIR: Orig from St Andrews ice-cream
MAP 4 makers for 30 yrs and still with the café they opened in Kirriemuir in 1953. On
D3 the main drag of the Angus town (818/GLENS), it's a hang-out for everybody.
Broughty Ferry (Dundee's seaside suburb) more middle-class, with more of a
contemporary menu; home-made pasta as well as the peach melba. But whatever
comes and goes, the ice-cream will go on for ever. 7 days (633/DUNDEE
RESTAUS).

1223 JANETTA'S, ST ANDREWS: 31 South St. Family firm since 1908. There is an
MAP 5 offshoot impostor down the street, but the pure line and the pure ice-cream is
D2 opp Byre Theatre. Once only vanilla, Americans up for the Open asked for
other flavours. Now there are 52 incl the favourites, ginger, hokey pokey and
the famous irn-bru sorbet. Long after you've graduated, you'll remember these
halcyon days and the hokey pokey. 7 days 9am-6pm.

1223a THE ALLAN WATER CAFE, BRIDGE OF ALLAN: Just as you imagine an old-fashioned
MAP 6 café in an old-fashioned town, nr the eponymous bridge in the main st. Since
D3 1902, fish 'n' chips and ice-cream. The former now dispensed from a modernised
shop next door and v good they are too. For the ice-cream (only vanilla) you
still stand in line in the old wood-lined café. Mon-Sat, 8am-10pm (9pm Sun).

1223b COLPI, MILNGAVIE, GLASGOW: Opp Black Bull Hotel in Milngavie centre (pron
MAP B 'Mullguy') and there since 1928 though I didn't hear about it till Eddie Mair's
xC1 programme on Radio Scotland asked people to nominate their fave ice-cream.
Only vanilla at the cone counter but strawb/amaretto/honeycomb to take home.
Other branches in Newton Mearns and Clydebank. Till 9pm, 7 days.

1223c NARDINI'S, LARGS: On the Esplanade. OK OK I said it was cardboardy and
MAP 1 almost everyone disagreed. Nardini's is so celebrated, so nostalgic, so indispens-
C3 able that its ice-cream is practically beyond reproach – I'd have to admit that a
peach sundae here beats a Sunday at home anyday. (1189/CAFES.)

1223d DRUMUIR FARM, COLLIN, nr DUMFRIES: 5km off A75 (Carlisle/Annan) rd E of
MAP 9 Dumfries at Collin (signed for Clarencefield). A real farm where Marion
D3 Kirkwood turns Daisy's finest into marvellous ice-cream. It's an outing from
Dumfries but the stuff's also available at Calmac Georgetown, Callander's
Moniave, Thornhill etc. A dozen flavours though 'the original' still the most
popular (it's creamier than vanilla). Easter-Sept noon-5.30pm. Cl Mon.

1223e KATIE ROGERS' HOME-MADE ICE-CREAM: They told me about Katie Rogers ice-
MAP 1 cream at Gingerhill, Milngavie, and if it's good enough for them . . . She supplies
the Spar shop in Killearn, A la Carte in Bearsden, Aberfoyle Caravan Park and
Glen Turret Distillery. If you are lucky to be near any of these, stock up and
have a melon and ginger dream ice-cream for me.

THE REALLY GOOD DELIS

VALVONA AND CROLLA, EDINBURGH: 19 Elm Row, part of Leith Walk nr
the top. Since 1934, an Edinburgh institution, the shop you show to
visitors. Full of smells, genial, knowledgeable staff and a floor-to-ceiling range of
cheese (Ital/Scot etc), meats, oils and the hand-picked produce of Italy. You
could do all your Christmas shopping here. Demos, tastings, even a show during
the Festival! This isn't a shop, it's an affirmation of the good things in life. Mon-
Sat 8.30am-6pm.

1224
MAP A
E1

GOURMET PASTA, EDINBURGH: 52 Morningside Rd. As the name suggests,
this shop/pasta kitchen in a busy part of Morningside sells mainly freshly
made pasta and various sauces, as good or better than you can make yourself.
Time spent going there will be saved with your quickly cooked delicious,
nutritious supper, esp if it's a dinner party (they do trays of lasagne etc and your
guests need never know). Also tortes, tarts and roulades sweet or savoury and by
the slice. Cl Sun.

1225
MAP A
xC4

PECKHAM'S, CENTRAL STATION, GLASGOW: The best of several branches,
most remarkable for its location on the concourse of Glasgow's main
station. From early train times to late (usually 11pm, midnight on Fri/Sat and
10pm on Sun), they've got everything you need to take home, from staples to
fine wines and cheeses and a good range of up-market nibbles and quick meals.

1226
MAP B
D3

FAZZI'S, GLASGOW: Main branch at 232 Clyde St and also 67 Cambridge St
where there's a great café (315/GLASGOW: ITALIAN RESTAUS). The Glasgow
Italian connection that Valvona's is to Edinburgh. The recession brought
problems (and anxiety to their legions of loyal supporters). Now the uncertainty
is resolved and though 'taken over', Fazzi's looks like going on forever.

1227
MAP B
D3

ELLERY'S, PERTH: 2 Mill St behind Marks & Spencer. Every county town
should have a place like Ellery's, an antidote to the monotony of the
modern High St. This is full of good things – not only the usual foody delights,
but many home-cooked meats, pies, tortes, cakes, excl vegn selection and great
range of cheeses esp Scottish. Leave the motorway and come to Perth just for
this. Mon-Sat 9am-5.30pm.

1228
MAP 4
C4

GORDON AND MACPHAIL, ELGIN: South St. Purveyors of fine wines, cheeses,
meats, Mediterranean goodies, unusual breads and other epicurean delights to
the good burghers of Elgin for nigh on a century. Traditional shopkeeping, in
the style of the 'family grocer', which will surely make a comeback as we weary
of supermarkets. G and M are widely known as bottlers of lesser-known high-
quality malts ('Connoisseurs' range) – on sale here. Mon-Sat 9am-5.15pm.

1229
MAP 3
B2

NUMBER 20, OBAN: Argyll Sq. Attractive shop serving a wide area of the SW
Highlands and Islands with delicatessen and locally produced fare incl smoked
meats and fish and Scottish hand-made cheeses. The speciality breads are warm
from the oven and this is where to go in Oban for your vinegars and extra
virgins. Cl Sun.

1230
MAP 1
B1

SCOTTISH CHEESES

MULL OR TOBERMORY CHEDDAR: From Sgriob-Ruadh Farm (pron 'Skibrua').
Comes in big 50lb cheeses and 1lb truckles. Good, strong cheddar, one of the v
best in the UK. The Ingle Smokehouse in Perth make a fine oak-smoked cheddar
and Loch Arthur from Beeswing in Dumfries is a tangy organic cheddar which
deserves wider recognition.

DUNSYRE BLUE/LANARK BLUE: Made by Humphry Errington at Carnwath. Next
to Stilton, Dunsyre made from the unpasteurised milk of Ayrshire cows is the
best blue in the UK. It is soft rather like Dolcelatte. Lanark, the original, is
Scotland's Roquefort and made from ewe's milk. Both are excellent.

BONCHESTER/TEVIOTDALE: From John Curtis at E. Weems Farm in the Borders.
Bonchester, a Camembert-style cheese hand-made from Jersey milk and creamy-
rich with an orange tang. Teviotdale, firmer and fuller flavour.

STICHILL/KELSAE: Hand-made hard cheeses from Brenda Leddie nr Kelso. Rich,
hard and crumbly cheeses, found only on the more informed cheeseboards. My
own favourites of the new Scottish cheeses.

CABOC/CROWDIE/GRUTH DHU: Widely available and established soft cheeses from
Highland Fine Cheeses in Tain. Crowdie is traditional cottage or crofters cheese,
v basic; others made from double cream rolled in oatmeal/pepper.
Rich/delicious; usually avail in wee 'logs'.

And where to find them

All the delis above will have a selection (esp Valvona's). Also:

PECKHAMS, GLASGOW: The other branches, which are at 100 Byres Rd and 43 Clarence Drive.

IAIN MELLIS, EDINBURGH: 30A Victoria St. A real cheesemonger!

JENNERS DEPARTMENT STORE, EDINBURGH: Princes St.

HERBIE, EDINBURGH: 66 Raeburn Pl.

THE FARMHOUSE, ABERDEEN: 11 Chapel St.

COMRIE CHEESE AND SMOKEHOUSE, COMRIE: Main St.

PETER MACLENNAN, FORT WILLIAM: 28 High St.

SCOTTISH SPECIALITY FOOD SHOP, NORTH BALLACHULISH: By Loch Leven Hotel.

KIRKTON MANOR, CADEMUIR, PEEBLES: 0721 740 210. Not retail but can supply.

THE SUNFLOWER, PEEBLES: 4 Bridgegate.

THE OLIVE TREE, PEEBLES: 7 High St.

OUTSTANDING WINE-LISTS

1231 **THE UBIQUITOUS CHIP, GLASGOW:** 041 334 5007. Ashton Lane. Wine bar, off-licence
MAP B and notable restau (294/GLAS: BEST RESTAUS). Great range/good attitude; house
xA1 wines inexp. 2 pages of malts.

1232 **LA POTINIERE, GULLANE nr EDINBURGH:** 0620 843214. Main St. Recipient of
MAP 7 innumerable awards and accolades for wine-list esp French. Amazing choice and
D1 range. Wine-list a discussion document. David Brown always there to discreetly
advise. 46/EDIN BEST RESTAUS.

1233 **CHAMPANY INN, LINLITHGOW nr EDINBURGH:** 0506 834532. Impressive but no
MAP 7 bargains wine-list chosen to go with their mainly steak/seafood menu.
B1 53/LOTHIAN BEST RESTAUS.

1234 **CELLAR ·NO I, EDINBURGH:** 220 4298. Bistro and wine bar with unpretentious and
MAP A well chosen selection. Informal quaffing. 58/EDIN BISTROS.
D3

1235 **THE WATERFRONT, EDINBURGH:** 554 7427. 1c Dock Pl. A popular wine bar/restau
MAP A in Leith with conservatory and wee rooms. Wines on blackboard for informal
xE1 drinking with or without meal. 55/EDIN BISTROS.

1236 **HARDING'S, NORTH BERWICK:** 0620 4737. 2 Station Rd. Almost solely Australian
MAP 7 wines and prob the best choice of them in Scotland. Chris Harding will take you
D1 thro the wineries. 509/LOTHIAN BEST RESTAUS.

PHILIPBURN HOUSE, SELKIRK: 0750 20747. On edge of town and in Central
Borders, a hotel that has everything, not least an extensive and inexpensive wine-
list. 483/BORDERS HOTELS.

1237 **SUNLAWS HOUSE HOTEL nr KELSO:** 05735 331. 5km from Kelso on the A698
MAP 7 towards Jedburgh. A non-encyclopeadic carte of classic wines. 484/BORDERS
B1 HOTELS.

1238 **THE CELLAR, ANSTRUTHER:** 0333 310378. Behind the Fisheries Museum, a bistro for
MAP 5 seafood and v fine wine-list esp New World. 520/FIFE.
E3

1239 **THE PEAT INN nr CUPAR:** 0334 84206. The gastronomic crossroads of Fife and a
MAP 5 wine-list to swither over. There are more Aloxe-Corton's than one would know
D3 what to do with. 518/FIFE BEST RESTAUS.

1240 **THE CROSS, KINGUSSIE:** 0540 661166. Off main st. Esp clarets, Californian,
MAP 2 Australasian, half-bottles and dessert wines. 567/HIGHL BEST RESTAUS.
D4

1241 **ARD-NA-COILLE, KINGUSSIE.** 0540 673214. Surprising range, great value. 'Some wines
MAP 2 seem to have little or no mark-up' Excl retau (565A/HIGHL BEST RESTAUS).
D4

WHISKY
The Best Distillery Tours

The process is basically the same in every distillery, but some are more atmospheric and some have more interesting tours, like these:

THE ISLAY MALTS: On one day you can visit several of Scotland's most impressive distilleries and sample some famous malts. The distilleries here look like distilleries ought to. **LAGAVULIN** (with daily tours 0496 2400) and **LAPHROAIG** are in the south, nr Port Ellen, **BUNNAHABHAINN** is in the north nr Port Ascaig and **BRUICHLADDICH** is on the rd to Port Charlotte. Most will show you round by arrangement, but the most organised and frequent tour is **BOWMORE** in Bowmore itself. Morning and afternoon, lasting 1hr, it includes a video and the usual dram at the end – the tour is fascinating, friendly and authentic. All these distilleries are in settings that entirely justify the romantic hyperbole of their advertising. Worth seeing from the outside as well as the floor.

1242
MAP 1
A3

Lagavulin Distillery, Islay (1242)

TALISKER, CARBOST, ISLE OF SKYE: From Sligachan-Dunvegan rd (A863) take B8009 for Carbost and Glen Brittle along the S side of L Harport for 5km. The only distillery on Skye. Since 1830, they've been making this classic island after-dinner malt from barley and the burn that runs off Hawkhill behind the buildings. A friendly welcome awaits (you get your dram before the tour) and an informative 25mins. No coach tours. Apr-Mar 9am-4.30pm (winter 2-4.30pm).

1243
MAP 2
B3

GLENKINCHIE, PENCAITLAND nr EDINBURGH: 0875340 333. Only 25km from city centre (via A68 and A6093 before Pathhead) so it gets busy; up to 8 guides taking continuous tours all day (Mon-Fri 9.30am-4pm). Founded in 1837 and a peaceful, pastoral place (it's 3km from the village) with its own bowling green; this is a trip to the country as well as a tour of the plant. They have 'silent seasons', so best to check since all you'd see then is a video. Museum.

1244
MAP 7
D2

1245 EDRADOUR, nr PITLOCHRY: Claims to be the smallest distillery in Scotland,
producing single malts for blends since 1825 and limited quantities of the
Edradour (since 1986) as well as the House of Lords' own brand. Guided tour of
charming cottage complex, every 20mins. 4km from Pitlochry off Kirkmichael rd,
A924; signed after Moulin vill. 7 days, till 5pm. Cl Sun.
MAP 4 / C2

1246 GLENTURRET nr CRIEFF: 2km from town off A85 to Comrie. A village has almost
been built around this quaint distillery, the oldest in Scotland (1775) with award-
winning visitor centre. Continuous tours, restau and shop with extensive range
of branded products. The whisky itself has a smoky roasted aroma; it's superb in
its older bottlings e.g. 1967-72. Open Mar-Dec, Mon-Sat 9.30am-4.30pm, and
Sun from noon. Jan-Feb, Mon-Fri 11.30am-2.30pm.
MAP 4 / B4

1247 HIGHLAND PARK, KIRKWALL, ORKNEY: 2km from town on main A961 rd S to S
Ronaldsay. The whisky is great and the tour one of the best. The most northerly
whisky in a class and a bottle of its own. You walk through the floor maltings
and you get to touch the warm barley and smell the peat. Good combination of
the industrial and the traditional aspect. Open AYR (2-3.30pm only in winter).
MAP 10

THE BEST OF THE SPEYSIDE WHISKY TRAIL: Well signposted but bewildering
number of tours, though by no means at every distillery. Many are in rather
featureless industrial complexes and settings. Notable are:

1248 THE GLENLIVET, MINMORE: Starting as an illicit dram celebrated as far S as
Edinburgh, George Smith licensed the brand in 1824 and founded this distillery
in 1858, registering the already mighty name so that anyone else had to use a
prefix. After various successions and mergers, the long history of independence
was lost in 1978 when Seagrams took over. The famous Josie's Well, from which
the water springs, is underground and not shown, but small parties and a walk-
through which is not on a gantry, make the tour as satisfying and as popular, esp
with Americans, as the product. Large bar, shop and reception centre. Apr-Oct,
10am-4pm; till 7pm July/Aug.
MAP 3 / B3

1249 GLENFIDDICH, DUFFTOWN: Outside town on the A941 to Craigellachie by the
ruins of Balvenie castle. Well-oiled tourist operation and the only distillery
where you can see the whisky bottled on the premises; indeed the whole process
from barley to bar. AYR 9.30am-4.30pm incl Sat/Sun, Apr-Oct. On the same rd
there's a chance to see a whisky-related industry/craft that hasn't changed in
decades. The SPEYSIDE COOPERAGE is 1km from Craigellachie. Watch a
fascinating process, 9.30am-4.30pm.
MAP 3 / B2

1250 CARDHU and TAMDHU, CARRON: On either side of the B9102 from Craigellachie
to Grantown through deepest Speyside, two smallish distilleries easily viewed
together. Cardhu (United Distillers) has more charm; a small community, a
millpond, picnic tables etc. Tamdhu (Highland Distilleries) has its visitor centre
in the old railway stn. Both offer tours on a more intimate basis than the biggies
and drams of their sound after-dinner malts. Cardhu AYR, 9.30am-4.30pm;
Tamdhu Apr-Oct 10am-4pm. Sat, June-Sept.
MAP 3 / B2

1251 STRATHISLA, KEITH: The oldest working distillery in the Highlands, literally on
the Strath of the Isla river and with probably the most evocative atmosphere of
all the Speyside distilleries. Used as the 'heart' of Chivas Regal, the malt is not
commonly available but it's a fine dram. May-Sept, 9am- 4.30pm.
MAP 3 / C2

1252 DALLAS DHU nr FORRES: Not really nr the Spey (3km S of Forres on B9010) and
no longer a working distillery (ceased 1983), but instant history provided by
Historic Scotland and you don't have to go round on a tour. The wax workers
are a bit spooky; the product itself is more lifelike and rather good.   AYR.
MAP 3 / A2

Where to Find the Best Selection of Malts

GLASGOW:	THE POT STILL: 154 Hope St.
	THE BON ACCORD: 153 North St.
EDINBURGH:	BENNETS: 8 Leven St by Kings Theatre.
	KAYS BAR: 39 Jamaica St.
	THE BOW BAR: West Bow.
	CADENHEADS: 172 Canongate. The shop with the lot.
	SCOTCH MALT WHISKY SOCIETY: The Vaults, 87 Giles St, Leith. Your search will end here. More a club (with membership) but visitors welcome.

THE BORESTONE BAR, STIRLING: St Ninians on the Bannockburn rd 2km from centre. Over 400 including the almost complete Gordon and Macphail's Connoisseur's collection. The fullest range in Scotland?

ARISAIG HOTEL, ARISAIG nr MALLAIG: On the seafront. Small, civilised lounge and busy local. 100 malts move between the bars.

CROWN AND ANCHOR, FINDHORN: O/looking jetty. Over 100.

OBAN INN, OBAN: Good mix of customers, whisky and ale.

FERRYHILL HOUSE HOTEL, ABERDEEN: Bon Accord St. Many ales and good family pub. 612/ABERDEEN PUBS. Over 150 malts.

FISHERMAN'S TAVERN, BROUGHTY FERRY: Many whiskies/ales. 637/DUNDEE.

CAWDOR TAVERN, CAWDOR nr NAIRN: Over 100. 711/PUBS.

CLACHAIG INN, GLENCOE: Over 100 malts to go with the range of ales and the range of folk that come here to drink after the hills. 704/PUBS.

THE DROVER'S INN, INVERARNAN: Same as above, with over 100 to choose from and the right atmosphere to drink them in. 701/PUBS.

DUNAIN PARK HOTEL, INVERNESS: After dinner in one of the best places to eat hereabouts, there's a serious malts list to mull over. 559/HIGHLAND HOTELS.

ROYAL HOTEL, KINGUSSIE: Main st of small town S of Aviemore. Great local (721/PUBS) and astonishing range of whiskies.

HOTEL EILEAN IARMAIN, SKYE: Also known as the Isle Ornsay Hotel (1357/ SKYE); not the biggest range but one of the best places to drink (it).

LOCHSIDE HOTEL, BOWMORE, ISLAY: More Islay malts than you ever imagined in friendly local nr the distillery. Malt whisky weekends.

The Best Malts and When to Drink Them

Obviously, opinions vary. The following list is compiled from the consensus of various whisky buffs and 'authorities' and Billy Mac at the Borestone Bar who knows them all. Vintages can make a very discernible difference to the connoisseur; the whiskies here are excellent in any of their readily available forms.

BEFORE DINNER

Bruichladdich	ISLAY	(pron 'Brew ich laddie')
Caol Ila	ISLAY	(pron 'Coal eela')
Glenmorangie	SPEYSIDE	
Tomintoul-Glenlivet	SPEYSIDE	

AFTER DINNER

Aberlour	SPEYSIDE	
Ardbeg	ISLAY	
Bowmore	ISLAY	
Bunnahabhain	ISLAY	(pron 'Bun a havan')
Glenfarclas	SPEYSIDE	
Highland Park	ORKNEY	
Lagavulin	ISLAY	(pron 'Laga voolin')
Laphroaig	ISLAY	(pron 'La froig')
Talisker	SKYE	
Tamdhu	SPEYSIDE	(pron 'Tam do')

ANYTIME

Balvenie	SPEYSIDE
Cragganmore	SPEYSIDE
Glenfiddich	SPEYSIDE
Glenkinchie	LOWLAND
Glenlivet	SPEYSIDE
Linkwood	SPEYSIDE
Macallan	SPEYSIDE
Springbank	CAMPBELTOWN

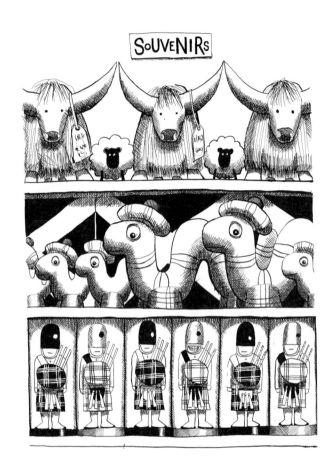

SECTION 11
Shopping

THE BEST CRAFT SHOPS

See also 1310/INEXPENSIVE ART AND CERAMICS.

1253 **SKYEBATIKS, ARMADALE, SKYE:** 400m from Mallaig ferry. Mainly hand-made
MAP 2 clothing; colourful cotton batik which is truly original and wearable;
B4 contemporary design. Some interesting, locally made jewellery. This is not really
souvenir-land, but people will ask where you got that shirt. Then you'll think of
Skye.

1254 **CRAIL POTTERY, CRAIL, FIFE:** At the foot of Rose Wynd, signposted from
MAP 5 main st (best to walk). In a tree-shaded Mediterranean courtyard and upstairs
E3 attic. a cornucopia of brilliant, useful, irresistible things. Open 9-5pm (Sun 2-5pm)
Don't miss the Harbour nearby, one of the most romantic neuks in the Neuk.

1254a **EDINBANE POTTERY, EDINBANE, SKYE:** 500m off A850 Portree (22km) –
MAP 2 Dunvegan rd. Long-established and reputable working pottery where all the
B3 various processes are often in progress. High-quality stonewear, tablewear and
things from clocks to lamps to take back home. AYR. 9am-6pm. 7 days in
summer.

1255 **THE STUDIO CRAFT SHOP, PLOCKTON:** 8km over hill from Kyle at the corner of
MAP 2 the two 'main' streets in this picturesque and much-loved village (788/COASTAL
C3 VILLAGES). Well-chosen knicknacks and smallish, affordable pictures by Scottish
artists. The prints by Anthony Cain will bring back memories.

1256 **HIGHLAND STONEWARE, ULLAPOOL:** Mill St on way north beyond centre (also in
MAP 2 Lochinver). A modern and fairly large-scale pottery business: a shop/warehouse
C2 and studios that you can walk round. Similar to the 'ceramica' places you find in
the Med, but not terracotta; painted, patterned stoneware in set styles. Useful,
attractive and robust. Mail-order service if you can't carry it home.

1257 **KILN ROOM POTTERY AND COFFEE SHOP, LAGGAN:** On main A86 rd (off A9 betw
MAP 2 Pitlochry and Inverness), E-W route to Ft William and Skye. Simple, usable
D4 pottery made by the long wood-fired kiln method, with distinctive warm
colouration. Selected knitwear and other stuff. Home-made cakes. 9am-6pm, 7
days.

1258 **BALNAKEIL, DURNESS, SUTHERLAND:** From Durness and the main A836, take
MAP 2 Balnakeil and Faraid Head rd for 2km W. This craft village really is a village,
D1 occupying the prefab huts of a former early-warning station. The community
has been there since 1964 and it's a bit like going back in time; dropping in from
the rat race from which they've dropped out (though hardly any of the original
members are still here). Standard-wise it's a bit hit or miss, but there's great
choice and some genuinely unique, creative stuff. Lotte Glob's pottery, the
wood picture shop and the candle and home-made wine emporium stand out.
There are 2 cafés and even a hotel, the Far North (0971 511221), cheap, cheerful
and different, in the former officers' mess. Village open Apr-Oct 10am-6pm.

1259 **ACHIN'S BOOKSHOP, LOCHINVER:** At Inverkirkaig 5km from Lochinver on the
MAP 2 'wee mad road' to Achiltibuie (853/SCENIC ROUTES). This celebrated 'remotest
C2 bookshop in Britain', a real bookshop with an eclectic range, also sells sensible
and selected crafty things, esp the sort you can wear or use in the great outdoors
which are just over the threshold. Indeed the path to the Kirkaig Falls and
Suilven begins at the gate. Open Mon-Sat till 6pm, café 10am-5pm.

1260 **KNOCKAN GALLERY AND CRAFTS, ELPHIN nr ULLAPOOL:** A converted barn by the
MAP 2 A835 Ullapool-Lairg rd 22km N of Ullapool nr the Knockan Outdoor Centre.
C2 Mainly Sally Phillips' prize-winning knitwear and Paul Phillips' photographs,
drawings etc of landscape amongst the most inspirational in the UK. You may
well want a reminder of Assynt, Sutherland, or Stac Pollaidh, and there are many
ideas here though no tea-towels. Apr-Oct, 9am-6pm 7days.

1261 **IONA ABBEY SHOP:** Iona via Calmac ferry from Fionnphort on Mull. Crafts and
MAP 1 souvenirs in a room off the Abbey cloisters, the proceeds from which support a
A2 worthy, committed organisation. Christian literature, tapes etc, but mostly
artefacts from nearby and around Scotland. Celtic crosses much in evidence, but
then this is where they came from! Mar-Oct 9.30am-5pm.

1262 **SIMPLY SCOTLAND, KINGUSSIE:** In main st, a superior selection of Scottish-only
MAP 2 crafts: knitwear, jewellery, plaids, good present potential. Also in **ST ANDREWS** at
D4 158 South St.

BRODIE COUNTRY FARE: Not a souvenir shoppie in the traditional sense, more a drive-in one-stop shopping experience. By main A96 betw Nairn and Forres. It's nr Brodie Castle (906/CASTLES). Quality deli food, a fairly upmarket boutique and lots of pressie ideas, as well as self/s restau which gets as busy as a motorway café. 7 days. 1263 MAP 3 A2

DRUMLANRIG CASTLE, nr THORNHILL nr DUMFRIES: A whole day-out of things to do (772/CO PARKS) incl the Craft Centre in the old stable/courtyard to the side of the house. Studio-type shops with leatherwork, jewellery, dried flowers and t-shirts. David Ayres' watercolours are pretty nice. Hire a bike and go for a ride while you decide. 1264 MAP 9 C2

JENNY'S POTTERY, DRUMNADROCHIT: 1km S of Drumnadrochit on main A82, signed from bend in the road (even in Japanese!) to Bunloit. 6km into Highland timewarp, leaving the mainstream behind. Bring back a shard. All reasonable hrs. 1264a MAP 2 D3

CRAFTS AND THINGS, nr GLENCOE VILLAGE: Just out of the glen after Glencoe vill and before Ballachulish on old part of A82. Cottagey craft and coffee-shop with wide and superior selection of Scottish bits, baubles and books; also woollen shop with surprising range of inexpensive knitwear. Apr-Oct 9am-6pm (or later). 1264b MAP 5 C5

WHERE TO BUY GOOD WOOLLIES

JUDITH GLUE, EDINBURGH and ORKNEY: Next to Scandic Crown Hotel in Royal Mile and opp the Cathedral in Kirkwall. Same range of distinctive hand-made jumpers and woolly wearables – the runic designs are a real winner. Some gluesome prices but this stuff will last and be admired when you're in New York. Jewellery, potions and lotions, crafty stuff esp local Orkney things. 1265 MAP A D3

NUMBER TWO, EDINBURGH: St Stephen Pl. They were here on the corner of St Stephen St in the first 1960s flush of alternative culture long before their trail-blazing range of Scottish machine and handmade knitwear could be called 'designer'. Still innovative, still filling the shop with wonderful wearable wool. 1266 MAP A C1

ST ANDREWS WOOLLEN MILL, ST ANDREWS: At the bottom end of North St nr the Old Course, a vast emporium/indoor market of every conceivable woolly from heavy knits to mitts. All the big names, hand-mades, cashmere and also tweeds, kilts etc. Mon-Sat 9am-5pm (cl 1-2pm) and Sun in season. AUCHTERLONIES next door has everything anyone would ever need on a golf course incl those awful bonnets. 1266a MAP 5 D2

INVERALLEN, ST ANDREWS: 121 Market St. Hand-made knits 'to last a lifetime', perhaps not cheap but they'll keep on keeping you warm. Many Arrans. Cl Sun. 1266b MAP 5 D2

PETER ANDERSON, GALASHIELS: If you're in Gala (or Hawick), which grew up around their woollen mills, you might expect to find a good selection of woollens you can't get everywhere else; and bargains. Well, tough! There's no stand-out place, but Anderson's has built itself into a tourist attraction with mill tours (Apr-Oct, 4 times a day) and exhibits and an ok mill shop. 1267 MAP 8 C2

CHAS N. WHILLANS, HAWICK (and GALA, PEEBLES and elsewhere): Their main shop is in Hawick (Teviotdale Mills, over the bridge at S end of main st; instead of cont on A7, turn rt and they're on the rt). They stock all the local big names incl a good range of Pringle, Lyle and Scott and Braemar. Best to stick to the classic cuts; the 'fashion' versions are not too warm and not too cool. 1268 MAP 8 C3

THE MILL SHOP, ELGIN: Sub-titled 'The Cashmere Visitor Centre' (no comment) and enticingly located nr the Cathedral ruins. It's only the rugs and scarves that are made here (the knitwear is made in Hawick), but there is a wide range in a vast shop and Johnston's of Elgin are one of the 'quality' names in Scottish knitwear. Mon-Sat, 9am-5.30pm. 1269 MAP 3 B2

LYNDA USHER KNITWEAR STUDIO, INVERMORISTON: The studio/shop is postcard pitched o/looking the Falls of the R Moriston by the Telford Bridge, just off the new bridge over the A82 from Inverness (45km) to Ft Augustus. Purely woollies and textiles incl hand knits and Fair Isles, designer collections of machine knits and yarns incl hard-to-find Shetland wool and hand dyes. Apr- Oct 10am-6pm. 1270 MAP 2 D4

RAGAMUFFIN, SKYE: On Armadale Pier, so one of the first or last things you can do on Skye is rummage through the Ragamuffin store and get some nice knits. Every kind of jumper (mostly machine-made) and crafts as well incl tweedy things. 7 days. Also in Skye: 1271 MAP 2 B4

OVER THE RAINBOW: Quay St, Portree (rd down to Harbour). Expensive but excellent.

THE BEST OUTFITTERS

These, the kind of shops where you can buy everything from tweeds to walking boots and often Scottish traditional wear, tend to be old-fashioned emporiums established for generations which are interesting just to browse through. I haven't incl the chains of 'mill shops' or 'outdoor shops' that are everywhere.

1271a **MACNAUGHTON'S, PITLOCHRY:** Station Rd on corner of main st and opp Hunter's
MAP 4 (same firm) who sell the outdoor/non-Scottish end of their incredible range. A
C3 vast old-fashioned outfitter with acres of tartan attire, though I could find no pyjamas (which are, of course, a must). Ties they have. Make their own cloth; and kilts to order (6-8 wks). Och, it is the real McCoy. 7 days till 6pm.

1271b **KINLOCH ANDERSON, EDINBURGH:** Commercial St, Leith. A bit of a trek from
MAP A uptown, but firmly on the tourist trail and rightly so. Experts in Highland dress
xE1 and all things tartan; they've supplied *everybody*. Gr cashmeres and other woollies. Taxi fares refunded if you spend more than £35 (and you will). Mon-Sat 9am-5.30pm.

1271c **STEWART, CHRISTIE AND CO, EDINBURGH:** 63 Queen St. Est 1792 and still selling
MAP A breeches! Menswear only – but ladies, you'd love those tartan waistcoats and
C2 Harris Tweed jackets; maybe not the sporrans. 9am-5.30pm. Sat till 12.30pm. Cl Sun.

NOTE: Rather than buy an expensive new kilt or wait to have one made, there are 2 places in Edinburgh where you can buy gr second-hand stuff. **ARMSTRONGS:** 2 shops in the Cowgate, Mon-Sat; and **ST STEPHENS ST:** 3 good second-hand shops where you'll probably find jackets, kilts, tweeds etc. Mon-Sat.

1271d **SLATER MENSWEAR, GLASGOW:** 165 Howard St in E end nr river. Not much in the
MAP B way of outdoor clothes or Scottish stuff (or anything for women except getting
D3 him into a new shirt), but remarkable for the 2 vast floors of menswear and, esp. cheap suits. They claim to be the world's biggest (perhaps they haven't been to Singapore). Stock up and marvel at how Armani costs 20 times as much. Cl Sun.

1271e **GREEN WELLY SHOP, TYNDRUM:** On main A82 rd W to Oban/Ft William. Adj
MAP 1 Clifton Coffee-shop (1181/TEA-ROOMS). Outdoorwear emporium in strategic
C1 position, with racks of Goretex and other membranes. Musto, Barbour and the all-important midge-helmet (now there's a great souvenir!). 7 days, till 5.30pm.

1271f **NANCY BLACK, OBAN:** 3 shops around Argyll Sq in centre of Oban, a 'chandlery',
MAP 1 an outdoor shop (all the big names in breathable linings) on the corner and a
B1 fashion-for-fogeys shop in the middle. From Scottish knits to Swiss army knives. Cl Sun.

1271g **MORTIMER'S and RITCHIE'S, GRANTOWN-ON-SPEY:** 2 shops on the main st in this
MAP 2 county town, selling country clothes and (esp Ritchie's) fishing 'gear'. On
E3 Speyside not only your Barbour will waxen lyrical. Go sit on the bank!

1271h **WALKING AND RIDING and COUNTRY WEAR, BALLATER:** 2 shops, once with the
MAP 3 same owner, on opp sides of the main st into Ballater, and the best place on Royal
B4 Deeside for all the hunting, shooting and fishing accoutrements you might need when you're out on the hills with the Royals.

1271j **KERR & CO, CRIEFF:** James Sq in town centre. Of 3 generations of outfitters, this is
MAP 4 the last branch. Old-fashioned feel/stock (except for Drizabone and the odd wild
B4 tie)/and probably clientele. Ladies to the left. Mon-Sat 10am-5pm.

1271k **D. CROCKART AND SON, STIRLING:** Outdoor clothing secondary to the serious
MAP 6 selection of H/S/F equipment, esp fishing (shop can supply permits), but if you
D4 need something waterproof....

1271l **CALEDONIAN COUNTRYWEAR, CALLANDER:** Main st (next to Crown Hotel), a sliver
MAP 6 of a shop in a long strip of mill shops and big names catering for busloads of
C3 souvenir-hunters. Real hunters might be happier here and plenty outdoor gear for excursions into the hills, 7 days till 5.30pm.

1271m **TWEEDSIDE TACKLE, KELSO:** 36 Bridge St nr the Abbey. Much ado about fishing
MAP 8 and everything to wear in and out of the water. Surprising range of socks as well
D3 as flys. Fascinating shop even for non-fishie persons. Mon-Sat 9am-5.30pm.

MARKETS AND ANTIQUE MARKETS

✝ ✝ **THE BARROWS, GLASGOW:** A market spread out around the streets and 1272 alleys in the East End, approached via the Tron at the end of Argyle St MAP B and then Gallowgate. Acres of cheap stuff old and new in shops, doorways, E3 stalls, sheds and round the back. As with all great markets it's full of character and characters and it's still poss to find bargains and collectibles. Wander and rummage all over, but look esp for the 'Square Yard' and the Cartwheel opp in Stevenson St West (parallel to Gallowgate) and also for the Upstairs Market in Gibson St at the side of Barrowlands (457/GLASGOW NIGHTLIFE) where you'll find the Barras as it always was and everything from clairvoyants to the latest scam (e.g. computer games). Open Sat and Sun only 10am-5pm.

PADDY'S MARKET, GLASGOW: In the same area as the Barrows but distinctly 1273 different; open Mon-Sat 9am-4pm, mostly for clothes and v basic junk. In the MAP B alleys behind Bridgegate, this is a unique and traditional free-for-all, with some E3 bits and bobs just laid out on the pavement. This is no upmarket market, but a slice of life you won't find anywhere else.

DENS ROAD, DUNDEE: A kind of mini Barrowland in the Hilltown i.e. on the hill 1274 N of town centre area of Dundee. By car you have to negotiate the bewildering MAP D and irritating one-way system. The market, which sells all kinds of junk, cheap D1 essentials and nonsense, is all undercover in sheds and has a particular atmos.

LANARK MARKET: Principally a cattle auction, and apart from the spectacle and 1275 sawdust of the ring, of interest to those us who ain't farmers or butchers, mainly MAP 1 for the café (1193/CAFES) but also for the incredible fruit market in one of the big E3 sheds. There's nothing quite like it in Scotland (except on Thu at Stirling Cattle Market where the same McKechnies purvey similar high-quality and vast-quantity stuff). Mondays 8am-3 or 4pm.

GRETNA GREEN: Sunday market in carpark area at Dumfries end of town, by 1276 Gables Hotel. Traders from all over, selling cheap goods rather than goodies, but MAP 9 worth a wander round. V few class acts. E3

DUMFRIES: Sat/Sun mkt in vacant lots on the river. Back of a van/car boot sale 1277 type stuff. Some essentials like fish and fruit, but mostly as above. MAP 9

INGLISTON outside EDINBURGH on A8 nr Airport/**EAST FORTUNE nr EDINBURGH** 1278 off A1 E of Haddington/**KINROSS** jnct 5/6 of the M90. All tacky markets on unattractive sites nr Edinburgh, massively popular and mightily depressing. They're all on Sundays. I mention them just in case you wonder what the traffic's all about, but best avoid.

EDINBURGH MARKETS: One remarkable thing about Edinburgh and all its 1279 aspirations to be seen as a major European city, is that, unlike all the others, it doesn't have a street market. All attempts to actuate one are met with huge popular support e.g. the Grassmarket Fair (w/ends during the Festival only), the 'Car Boot Sale' in the University carpark, Teviot Row, which at time of going to press had just stopped, but nothing seems to withstand the inevitable opposition. Trains to Glasgow leave every half hour.

FALKIRK MARKET: In ice-rink carpark nr technical college on Grangemouth rd, a 1279a market on Wed and Sat which I'm reliably informed is a cut above the rest and MAP 6 may be the best open-air regular market in Scotland. 2-4pm. D4

BYZANTIUM, EDINBURGH: Top of Victoria St. Not a market in the streetmarket 1280 sense, but a converted church full of interesting stalls selling bric-à-brac, books, MAP A pictures, ethnic clothes etc and crafts. Like a true bazaar, it's good for browsing D3 and there's a mezzanine café open all day. Not Sun.

THE VICTORIAN VILLAGE, GLASGOW: 53 W Regent St. Another indoor market of 1281 stalls selling Victoriana, bric-à-brac, clothes and pictures. More selective and MAP B interesting than most and good for presents. D2

AUCTIONS AND JUNKYARDS

1282 **R. McTEAR and J. A. CATHCART, GLASGOW:** Two auctioneers in opp lanes off St
MAP B Vincent Pl nr George Sq. McTear's at 4 N Court have sales every Fri (view Thu)
D2 and Cathcart's at 20 Anchor Lane on Wed. Both am. See *Herald* on Mon for
details.

1283 **BURNTHILLS DEMOLITION, QUARRELTON, JOHNSTON nr GLASGOW:** 0505 29644. Jnct
MAP 1 29 off M8 then A740 to r/bout (2km), A761 to T-jnct (1.5km), turn rt onto
D3 A737, the Beith Rd, for 4km turning rt up Quarrelton Rd just before a park and
rt after 200m into Floorsburn Cres which leads to Floors St . . . and this amazing
yard. Outside there's everything from flooring to chimney pots but the shed is
an Aladdin's Cave of fascinating and useful junk. It would be v hard not to find
something that would look great back home. Open Mon-Fri 9am-5pm; Sat 9am-
noon. Alas cl Sun. About 12km from airport.

1284 **THE LANE SALES, EDINBURGH:** Organised by Lyon and Turnbull in the lane
MAP A behind their showrooms which face out to George St. At the back they are far
C2 from elegant. It's possibly why these Tue, Wed and Fri morning sales are still
popular with Edinburgh's army of antique dealers, many of whom got the bug
here. All kinds of junk, furniture and bric-à-brac is on view for an hour, then
auctioned at 11am. Once 'somebody got an original William Blake'; similar sagas
keep the cowboys going. Great atmosphere. Afterwards, go for a coffee at the
Laigh in Hanover St (119/EDIN COFFEE SHOPS). The 'lane' is off Thistle St at
Hanover. Other furn/antique sales on Wed/Sat (225 4627) and Philips along
George St at 67 have good Thu morning sales (225 2266).

1285 **SAM BURNS' YARD, PRESTONPANS, nr EDINBURGH:** On the coast rd out of
MAP 7 Musselburgh; if you get to Prestonpans, you've missed it. By a gate in the wall
C1 you'll see cars on the kerbs of a long straight stretch. The 'yard' is jam-packed
with junk, some mouldering, some freshly piled. Furniture is mostly in sheds.
You can find almost anything here amongst acres of 20th-century trash and
you'll be rummaging with home-makers, antique exporters, artists, and all the
folk who've come here for years and never bought anything. 7 days till 5pm.

1286 **EASY, EDINBURGH ARCHITECTURAL SALVAGE YARD:** 554 7077. Couper St off Coburg
MAP A St (at N end of Gt Junction St nr mini r/bout). Warehouseful of original house-
xE1 fittings and where to go for baths, sinks, radiators, fireplaces, doors (there are
rows of them) and all the other bits of Old Edinburgh that used to be thrown
out, but are now worth lots. Similar set-ups at Craighall, Rattray nr Blairgowrie
(phone Lochie Rattray first, 0250 874749) and Angus Architectural Antiques,
Arbroath 0674 74291, Hill St in Harbour area.

1287 **LADYBANK AUCTION:** 0337 30488. Kinloch St along from railway stn in flat village in
MAP 5 middle of farming Fife. Weekly sale of all kinds of household stuff from
C3 Victoriana through nifty '50s to '70s collectibles. Eminently worth a gander.
Every Fri 6pm. Viewing Thu till 9pm, Fri from 10am.

1288 **KINBUCK AUCTION:** 0786 822603. 6km N of Dunblane on B8033 2nd Sat every
MAP 6 month at 11am. Viewing: Fri 10am-3pm. Also shed opp.
D3

1289 **COMRIE AUCTION:** 0764 70613. In old church on main st. Occ Tue at 10.30am.
MAP 4 Viewing: Sat 10am-2pm, Mon 10am-6pm.
B4

1290 **CRIEFF AUCTION:** 0764 3276. Galvelmore St off rd in from S. Once or twice a month
MAP 4 on Wed. Viewing Tue 8.30am-6pm. These 3 salerooms in Perthshire are like
B4 'country sales'; general goods and antiques. Gr for furniture and bric-à-brac.
Much of it finds it's way into antique shops. These sales are addictive.

1291 **TAYLOR'S AUCTIONS, MONTROSE:** 0674 72775. Panmure Row. Auction Rooms for
MAP 4 regular sales of household furniture and effects (on Thu evens, view Wed 6-8pm
E2 and Thu from 2pm) and Sat sales of more interesting antique and quality stuff of
all kinds incl bric-à-brac, jewellery, garden furniture (view Fri 2-5pm and 6-
9pm; Sat 9-10.30am). Also occ specific sales on Fridays of e.g. pictures, jewellery
and books. Often fascinating just to wander round; you'll want something.

THE BEST GARDEN CENTRES

✝ **KINLOCHLAICH HOUSE, PORT APPIN:** On main A28 Oban-Ft William rd just N of Pt Appin turn-off, the West Highlands' largest nursery/garden centre, a place amongst great scenery where horticulture is taken seriously. The centre is worth visiting just for the walled gardens and for inspiration. Still a family home and business (which incl charming cottages for let. 063173 342), determination and the Gulf Stream have produced a dear green place. 7 days, 10am-5.30pm. Cl Sun in winter. *1292 MAP 2 C5*

✝ **DOUGAL PHILIP'S WALLED GARDEN CENTRE nr SOUTH QUEENSFERRY:** 031 319 1122. Only 18km from Edinburgh centre and a pleasant excursion. It's exactly what it says it is – an old walled garden in the grounds of Hopetoun House (the impressive stately home begun by William Bruce in 1699, but mainly an important work of the Adam family, o/looking the Forth, open Easter-Oct 10am-5.30pm) and with Dougal usually on hand for advice. Centre seems to spread like vine, but this is where Edinburgh's discerning gardeners come for theirs. Discounts on Wed. Open AYR 10am-5.30pm. *1293 MAP 7 B1*

✝ **INSHRIACH nr KINCRAIG nr AVIEMORE:** On B970 betw Kincraig and Inverdruie (which is on the Coylumbridge ski rd out of Aviemore), a garden centre that puts most others in the shade. Specialising in alpines and bog plants, but with neat beds of all sorts in the grounds of the house by the Spey and frames full of perfect specimens, this is a potterer's paradise. Mon-Fri 9am-5pm, Sat 9am-4pm. Cl Sun. *1294 MAP 2 D4*

✝ **FINDLAY CLARK, MILNGAVIE, GLASGOW:** In Campsie countryside N of city, 20km from centre via A81 or A807 (Milngavie or Kirkintilloch rds) or heading for Milngavie (pron 'Mullguy'), turn rt on Boclair Rd. Vast garden complex and all-round visitor experience; an institution. 'Famous' coffee shop (waitresses and cakes), Saddlery with everything except horses; labels from Crabtree and Evelyn to Fisons, plus books, clothes and piles of plants. 9am-9pm (till 7pm wint). *1295 MAP 1 D3*

BEN LOMOND NURSERY, BALMAHA, LOCH LOMOND: Nearer Conic Hill than Ben Lomond, on the B837 just before Balmaha. A family-run nursery supplying the trade and gardeners in the know, as well as passing motorists, particularly with bedding plants grown in their long greenhouses on the side of the loch. 9.30am-6pm, 7 days. *1296 MAP 6 B4*

DOCHFOUR, LOCH NESS: On A82 Inverness to Ft William rd 12km S of Inverness. 20 acres of terraced Victorian garden in the grounds of Dochfour House. Yew hedges with not a leaf out of place enclose formal gardens for ambling about in. Largish shrubs are esp cheap. Raspberry-picking in dreaming walled gardens. Open 7 days 10am-5pm (Sat/Sun 2-5pm). *1297 MAP 2 D3*

BRIN SCHOOL FIELDS, FLICHITY nr INVERNESS: Off A9 S of Daviot, 12km S of Inverness, then 10km W along rd to Farr. An old school and playground dedicated to herbs, plants and all the potions and lotions that come from them. 8.30am-7pm, Sun 2-5pm, Cl Thu. *1298 MAP 2 D3*

FLOORS CASTLE, KELSO: 3km outside town off B6397 St Boswells rd (garden centre has separate entrance to main visitors' gate in town). Set amongst lovely old greenhouses within walled gardens some distance from house, it has a showpiece herbaceous border all round. Centre is open all year. 10am-5pm. 940/COUNTRY HOUSES. *1299 MAP 8 D3*

CHRISTIE'S NURSERY, KIRRIEMUIR: 0575 72977. On long straight stretch of A926 to Blairgowrie in the vill of Westmuir, 4km from Kirriemuir. Looking towards the Sidlaw Hills, a family-run nursery specialising in Alpines and other hardy plants. Suppliers to the trade and well kent at all the right shows, this is where to go for gentians and primulas and reassurance about your rock garden. Mar-Oct 10am-6pm; outwith these times phone first. *1300 MAP 4 D3*

GLENDOICK, GLENCARSE nr PERTH: On A85, 10km from Perth, in the fertile Carse of the Tay. A large garden centre notable esp for rhododendrons and azaleas, a riot of which can be viewed in the nursery behind (in month of May only). 7 days till 6pm. *1301 MAP 4 D4*

CHRISTIE'S, FOCHABERS: On A98 going into town from Buckie side. Huge garden centre and forest nursery, the centre of a family empire which has florists, hotels and a golf course. Good for shrubs, indoor plants etc and a great place for keen and not so keen gardeners to browse around. Famous floral clock and aviary. 9am-5.30pm, 7 days.

SECTION 12
Galleries, Museums, Theatres and Music

THE MOST INTERESTING GALLERIES

For Edinburgh, see pages 34, 35 and 40; Glasgow, 67, 68 and 75.

1304 ABERDEEN ART GALLERY: Schoolhill. Major gallery with temp exhibits and eclectic
MAP C permanent collection from Impressionists to Bellany. Large bequest from local
B2 granite merchant Alex Macdonald in 1900 contributes fascinating collection of his
contemporaries: Bloomsburys, Scottish, Pre-Raphaelites. Excellent watercolour
room. An easy and rewarding gallery to visit. Open 10am-5pm (Sun 2-5pm).

1305 THE PIER ART GALLERY, STROMNESS, ORKNEY MAINLAND: On main st
MAP 10 (789/COASTAL VILLAGES), a gallery on a small quay which could have come lock,
stock and canvases from Cornwall. Permanent St Ives-style collection of Barbara
Hepworth, Ben Nicholson, Paolozzi and others shown in a *simpatico*
environment with the sea outside. Temp exhibitions downstairs. A breath of art.
Cl Mon.

1306 PAISLEY ART GALLERY AND MUSEUM: High St. One of several impressive
MAP 1 municipal buildings in Paisley, this, in the Greek Ionic style, provides a light and
D3 lofty setting for the town's eclectic collection, notably the world-famous Paisley
shawls. Mon-Sat 10am-5pm.

1307 THE FERGUSSON GALLERY, PERTH: Marshall Pl corner of Tay St in distinctive
MAP 4 round tower (former Water Works). The assembled works on two floors of
C4 J. D. Fergusson 1874-1961. Though he spent much of his life in France, he had an
influence on Scottish art and was pre-eminent amongst those now called the
Colourists. It's a long way from Perth to Antibes 1913 but these pictures are a
draught of the warm south. Mon-Sat 10-5pm. Museum of the Year 1992.

1308 ANCRUM GALLERY: A small, surprising upstairs/downstairs gallery in this village
MAP 8 just off the A68 nr Jedburgh. It seems entirely right that there should be a village
D3 gallery along with a pub (which is adj) and a shop. Surprising, informed gallery
showing serious work by new and established artists. Noon-5pm. Cl Tue.
Wander in the graveyard afterwards (998/GRAVEYARDS).

1309 TOLQUHON GALLERY, nr ABERDEEN: Betw Ellon and Oldmeldrum and nr Haddo
MAP 3 House (945/COUNTRY HOUSES) and Pitmeddon (770/GARDENS), a farmhouse
D3 gallery in the countryside with selected Scottish contemporary paintings,
sculpture and ceramics. Real art at realistic prices. (Pron T'hon.) 11am-5pm, Sun
2-5pm. Cl Thu.

1309a HORNEL GALLERY, KIRKCUDBRIGHT: Broughton House where he lived, now a
MAP 9 fabulous evocation with collection of his work and atelier as was. 'Even the
C4 Queen was amazed'. Beautiful gardens to river. April-Oct. 11am-5pm (Cl 1-
2pm/Tue), Sun 2-5pm.

MACLAURIN GALLERY, AYR: In Rozelle Park. Mon-Sat 10am-5pm, Sun 2-5pm.

WHERE TO BUY INEXPENSIVE ART
AND CERAMICS

1310 PRINTMAKERS' WORKSHOPS: 239/EDINBURGH; 453/GLASGOW. Inverness: 20 Bank
St.

THE DEGREE SHOWS, EDINBURGH/GLASGOW ART SCHOOLS: Work from final yr
students. Discover the Bellanys/Howsons of the future. 2 wk exhib after manic
first night (June/July).

ROWAN GALLERY, DRYMEN: Main St opp Salmon Leap Inn. Contemp Scottish
painting and ceramics personally selected.

CORNERSTONE GALLERY/SHOP, DUNBLANE: Close to front of the Cathedral, a
gallery with changing exhibs and stock Scottish contemporaries. Inexp art.

STABLES GALLERY, FALKLAND: Converted stables in Back Wynd off main st in
conservation vill. Mainly Scottish watercolours. Fri-Sun in summer.

GAILEIRIDH ASAINTE nr LOCHINVER: On coast rd N of Lochinver to Drumbeg and
Scourie. Roadside gallery at Stoer with paintings, photographs and maps.

McIAN GALLERY, OBAN: 10 Argyll Sq. 19/20th-century work by Scottish artists.
Some notable names ('Glasgow School'). Pottery, prints. Mon-Sat, 9am-5pm.

THE STUDIOS, PORT APPIN: By pier and behind café, Dorinda Johnston and John
Harley's innovative, inexp paintings and sculpture. Both exhibit.

ST ANDREWS FINE ART: Huge assemblage of Scottish art from early 18th century
and incl some v good work from kent contemporaries. Exhibitions. Cl Sun.

THE MOST INTERESTING MUSEUMS

For Edinburgh museums, see pages 34, 35; Glasgow, see pages 67, 68.

✚ **EASDALE ISLAND FOLK MUSEUM:** On Easdale, an island/township reached by
a 5min (cont) boat service from Seil 'island' at the end of the B844 (off the
A816, 18km S of Oban). Something special about this grassy hamlet of
whitewashed houses on a rocky outcrop with a pub, a tea-room and a craft shop,
and this museum across the green. The history of the place (a thriving slate
industry erased one stormy night in 1881, when the sea drowned the quarry)
brought to life in displays from local contributions. Easter-Sept 11am-5pm.
1311
MAP 1
B2

✚ **THE BLACK HOUSE AT ARNOL, LEWIS:** 0851 71501. The A857 Barvas rd from
Stornoway, left at junction for 7km, then rt through township for 2km. The
traditional thatched dwelling of the Hebrides with earth floor, bed boxes and
central peat fire (no chimney hole), occupied by the family and their animals
alike. Remarkably, this house was lived in until the 1960s. When you leave, it's
not only the peat smoke in your clothes that lingers.
1312
MAP 2
B1
HS

STRATHNAVER MUSEUM, BETTYHILL: On N coast 70km W of Thurso in a
converted church which is v much part of the whole appalling saga: a graphic
account of the Highland clearances told through the social history of this fishing
village and the Strath that lies behind it from whence its dispossessed population
came. 2,500 folk were driven from their homes and it's worth going up the valley
(from 2km W along the main A836) to see, esp at Auchenlochy, the beautiful
land they had to leave in 1812, for sheep. Easter-Oct, 10am-1pm, 2-5pm.
1313
MAP 2
D1

SUMMERLEE, COATBRIDGE: West Canal St. Not easy to find but head for town
centre (from M8) and follow signs. Here in the Iron Town, this is a tribute to the
industry, ingenuity and graft that powered the Industrial Revolution and made
Glasgow great. Anyone with a mechanical bent or an interest in the social
history of the working class will find plenty here; smaller kids and bored
teenagers may not. Tea-room. Open 10am-5pm. Free.
1314
MAP 1
D3

DOUNE MOTOR MUSEUM, DOUNE: 0786 841203. Great example of how a particular
personal interest can develop into something to interest everybody – or at least
everyone who likes beautiful things. You don't need to be a car nut to drool
over these. Not the range of Glasgow's Transport Museum (420/GLAS LESS OBV
ATTRACTIONS), but many exquisite classics from 1905-68. Apr-Oct, 10am-
5/5.30pm. Café. Occ events.
1315
MAP 6
C3

SKYE MUSEUM OF ISLAND LIFE: Kilmuir on Uig-Staffin rd, the A855, 32km N of
Portree. The most authentic, or at least official, of several converted cottages on
Skye where the poor crofter's life is recreated for the enrichment of ours. The
small thatched township includes agricultural implements as well as domestic
artefacts, many of which illustrate an improbable fascination with the Royal
Family. Flora Macdonald's grave is nearby (963/MONUMENTS).
1316
MAP 2
B3

INVERARAY JAIL: 'The story of Scottish Crime and Punishment' (*sic*) told in
'award-winning' reconstruction of courtroom with cells below, where the
waxwork miscreants and their taped voices bring local history to life. Makes you
think that guided tours of Peterhead can't be far off. AYR, 10am-5pm.
1317
MAP 1
C2

AUCHENDRAIN, INVERARAY: 8km W of town on A83. A whole township
reconstructed to give a v fair impression of both the historical and spatial
relationship betw the cottages and their various occupants. Longhouses and byre
dwellings; their furniture and their ghosts and no forcing of the imagination.
Apr, May, Sept 10am-4.30pm (not Sat); June, July, Aug, 7 days 10am-5pm.
1318
MAP 1
C2

SHAMBELLIE HOUSE MUSEUM OF COSTUME, NEW ABBEY, nr DUMFRIES: Another
obsession that became a museum. On 2 floors of this country house set among
spectacular woodlands. Fab frocks etc from every 'period'. May-Sept 10-5.30, Cl
Tue/Wed.
1318a
MAP 9
D3

ROBERT SMAIL'S PRINTING WORKS, INNERLEITHEN: Main st. A trad printing
works till 1986 and still in use. Fascinating vignettes/instant history. Apr-Oct.
1318b
MAP 8
B2

SCOTTISH FISHERIES MUSEUM, ANSTRUTHER: 0333 310628. In and around a cobbled
courtyard o/looking the old fishing harbour in this busy East Neuk town. Excl
evocation of traditional industry still alive (if not kicking). Impressive collection
of models and actual vessels incl those moored at adj quay. Crail Harbour 9km
up the coast, for the full picture (and fresh crab/lobster). AYR 10am-5pm, Sun
11am-5pm (Cl 4.30pm in winter, and Sun afternoons only).
1318c
MAP 5
E3

INTERESTING THEATRES AND CINEMAS

For Edinburgh, see p. 41; and Glasgow, see p. 76.

1319 **MULL LITTLE THEATRE, DERVAIG, MULL:** 06884 245/234. 'The smallest theatre in
MAP 1 Britain' is still there after more than 25yrs. On edge of nice wee village, 10km
B1 from Tobermory. Bar and good restau adjacent at the Druimard Country House
Hotel. Tiny auditorium so that you're almost on top of the actors. Never
predictable repertoire, often unusual plays that would be worth seeing
anywhere. On a summer's evening it can be more *engagé* than Stratford. Easter-
Oct. Curtain up 8.30pm. Cosy seats; cosy intervals.

1320 **CUMBERNAULD THEATRE:** 0236 732887. Near old part of New Town on a rise
MAP 1 o/looking the ubiquitous dual carriageway (to Stirling). Follow signs for
E3 Cumbernauld House. Bar/café-restau and 300-seat theatre (in the round) with a
mixed programme of one-nighters and short runs of mainly Scottish touring
companies. Also concerts, drama w/shops and kids' progs. A community-based
and vital theatre, and one of the better reasons to 'relocate in Cumbernauld'.

1321 **BOWHILL LITTLE THEATRE, BOWHILL HOUSE, nr SELKIRK:** 0750 20732. Tiny theatre
MAP 8 off the courtyard below Bowhill House (943/COUNTRY HOUSES) with inter-
C3 mittent mixed prog (must phone), but always delightful esp with supper after-
wards (also phone to book).

1322 **PITLOCHRY THEATRE:** 0796 472680. Modern rep theatre across river from Main St
MAP 4 performing usually 6 plays on different and varying nights of the week. With a
C3 well-chosen prog of classics and popular works, the 500+-seat theatre is often
full. V mixed Sunday concerts and foyer fringe events. Coffee bar open at all
times. Best place to eat after show is East Haugh House on rd S (2km town
centre). Phone to book 0796 473121.

1323 **EDEN COURT THEATRE, INVERNESS:** 0463 221718. With the estimable Catherine
MAP 2 Robins at the helm, this theatre complex makes waves on the national arts scene
D3 and an absolutely vital contribution to life, never mind cultural life, in the
Highlands. Diverse prog of theatre, dance, variety, all kinds of music, opera,
tradn; and occasional coups. Easy to book by credit card; lots do sell out. Self/S
restau and bar o/look R Ness (1385/CENTRES: INVERNESS). Cinema prog of
selected art-house/first-run movies. What would Inverness watch without it?

1324 **BYRES THEATRE, ST ANDREWS:** 0334 76288. Abbey St or enter down lane from
MAP 5 South St. Serious theatre with new work, established faves and an altogether
D2 imaginative and well-balanced programme. 174 seats only, so often need to
book. Bar, café, theatre folk.

1325 **CAMPBELTOWN PICTURE HOUSE:** 0586 53657. Campbeltown, Argyll. Cinema
MAP 1 Paradiso on the Kintyre peninsula. Lovingly preserved art deco gem; a shrine to
B4 the movies. Opened 1913, closed 1983, but such was the tide of nostalgic
affection that it was refurbished and reopened resplendent in 1989. Shows
mainly first-run films. To see a film here and emerge onto the esplanade of
Campbeltown Loch is to experience the lost magic of a night at the pictures.

1326 **THE NEW PICTURE HOUSE, ST ANDREWS:** 0334 73509. On North St. 'New' means
MAP 5 1931 and apart from adding another screen, the small Cinema 2, it hasn't
D2 changed much, as generations of students will remember with fondness. Mainly
first-run flicks and Oct-May, there's a programme of late night cult/art movies.
And you can still smoke!

1327 **THE ROXY, KELSO:** 0573 224609. Horsemarket. A cinema from my youth, still
MAP 8 remarkably here and unchanged; still the smell of hot celluloid. Few better
D3 places to watch their 'alternative' prog of arthouse flicks on Tue. Kids' club Sat.
Usually one performance only. Bingo on Mon and Fri. Don't ever close!

THE MOST HAPPENING NIGHTCLUBS

For EDINBURGH, see pages 41; for GLASGOW page 77; and for ABERDEEN, see page 100.

Clubs in Dundee

All the clubs operate on w/end nights and occ others and are packed Fri and Sat.   1328

DEHSTIL: 0382 200066. S Ward Rd. Going for 5yrs and still ok for slightly older,   MAP D
smarter crowd. Thu-Sun 10pm-2/3am. No jeans on Fri/Sat.   B3

FAT SAM'S: 0382 26836. 31 S Ward Rd. Street/student/music cred. Occ live bands
on national tour circuit. 2 dance areas; diner (smell of burger pervades). No dress
code, no hassles. Thu-Sun, 10pm-3am.

THE VENUE: Camperdown Leisure Complex off Harefield Rd in Lochee N of
centre. A vast punterland of disco in a plaza along with a megabowl, bingo
palace and supermarket. Elitist it is not, more a '90s version of the Town
Dancehall. 2 areas and great sound system. This is where Studio 54 and the
Mudd were bound to end up. On the site of a former jute mill, this plaza with its
mosaic motif makes it a 'mecca' for social
historians. Fri-Sun 10pm-2.30am. Hey, be smart but casual!

THE EDGE: 0382 22367. 85 Commercial St. High-tech subterrania, smoke and sweat,
this space is for dancing. Thu, Fri (gay) and Sat (raverama).

Clubs elsewhere

METROPOLIS, SALTCOATS: 0294 60221. Hamilton St in centre of small town N of   1329
Ayr, 45km from Glasgow. Unlikely toon for a nightspot perhaps, but clubbers   MAP 1
have been known to converge from miles around (there are all-dayers once a   C3
month). Roomy main area is very *Saturday Night Fever*; a serious dance floor.
Over-25s Thu, and Fri/Sat 10pm-2am. At time of writing, Sat were raverama.

FLICKS, BRECHIN: Another unlikely setting for a disco, the main st of a sleepy   1330
town off A94 Dundee-Aberdeen rd (45km N of Dundee) esp when licensing   MAP 4
laws don't allow admission after 11pm. At least that's what they told me when   E2
they knocked me back at the door; either that or I was too old or wrongly
dressed or too uncool. From what I could see (folk eating fish 'n' chips in the
foyer), it's not exactly the A-team that they do admit, but remarkably, they
think of themselves as a serious club. They buy soap stars, hasbeens and disco
dross for occasional PAs. Thu-Sun 10pm-11pm. You may detect my sour grapes
(most unlike me).

JACKIE O'S, KIRKCALDY: 0592 264496. On the Esplanade. Any place still called after   1331
this now elderly lady who epitomised jet-setting nightclub glamour at the time   MAP 5
when the élitist fashionable discos were on another planet to Kirkcaldy and   C4
whose clientele can probably barely remember her, has to have something going
for it. And it does. It's an unpretentious, non-stressful *palais de danse*. Wed-Sun
9pm-2am. No jeans or trainers on Fri/Sat. There's another place in Kirkcaldy, so
it's theoretically possible to 'go clubbing it'.

THE LIDO, KIRKCALDY: 0592 200417. Victoria Rd, 1km from Esplanade. More recent   1332
refurb, but nothing too Balearic. Sensible 'cocktail'/chill out bar separate from
music. Some Sunday raving. O/wise Thu-Sat 9pm-2am.   C4

AYR PAVILION and other clubs in Ayr: Remarkable number of clubs in Ayr (well,   1332a
it is a long way from Glasgow). At time of writing, **HANGER 13** (Sats only) at   MAP 1
Ayr Pavilion (0292 265489) was the place to be on this coast for dance/rave music.   D4
On Thu the **Pavilion** has 'grab a memory' (or granny) nights with 60/70s music,
and Fri are 'rock nights', demonstrating the abiding attraction of heavy metal in
the hinterland. Other clubs are **THE POWERHOUSE**, 0292 267898 in Nile Court off
the High St – rockish, indie on Fri, heavier on Sat; **BOBBY JONES**, 0292 282356.
Burns' Statue Sq, non-raver territory Wed (older crowd)/Fri/Sat; **CLUB DE MAR**,
0292 611136.

*As with most places, the good clubs are short-lived, one-night-a-week scenes that
you just 'hear about' (or see flyposted). The List magazine, on sale at most city
centre newsagents, will tell you what is on in Edinburgh and Glasgow. For
elsewhere, ask someone like yourself. And write and tell me if you know of
somewhere good.*

WHERE TO FIND GOOD FOLK MUSIC

1333
MAP A
Edinburgh

See p. 32 and Festivals opposite.

Particularly good bars to frequent, some with regular and some with occasional live music, include:

D3 BANNERMANS: Cowgate. 163/EDIN REAL ALE; 136/SUNDAY BREAKFAST. Also, through the back, occ live bands (not just folk, but it has a folky atmos) and try Sunday night.

D3 SANDY BELL'S aka THE FORREST HILL BAR: Famous and forever. Sometimes you could look in and wonder why; other times you know you're in exactly the right place. Try Fri/Sat night, Sun pm.

C3 FIDDLERS ARMS: Grassmarket. 153/EDIN OLD PUBS. And fiddle they do on Monday nights. Good crack and blether at all times.

D3 THE TRON CEILIDH HOUSE: 220 1550. Hunter Square. One of Edinburgh's major live venues; up and downstairs. Busy, friendly, folky.

B3 WEST END HOTEL BAR: 225 3656. Palmerston Place. 17/EDIN INX HOTELS. A good place to stay or just to hang out with the Highlanders. Some trad folk live at w/ends and whenever.

1334
MAP B
Glasgow

See also p. 66.

E3 BABBITY BOWSTERS: Blackfriars St nr George Sq. 392/GLAS REAL ALE; 402/PUB FOOD. Occ music above the hum, esp Sunday nights.

B1 HALT BAR: Woodlands Rd. Amongst a mixed music prog, always some folk for the kind of folk who inhabit the bar. Wed. 378/GREAT PUBS.

D3 RIVERSIDE: Fox St off Clyde St. The Fri and Sat Ceilidh Dance with a proper band and the full works. Doors open 8pm, band 9pm and often full by 10pm. Just as you imagined it.

D3 SCOTIA BAR: 112 Stockwell St. 372/GREAT PUBS. The folk club and writers' retreat and all things non-high cultural. Club meets Wed night and Sat pm. Always the 'right folk' here.

B2 STAR FOLK CLUB, GLASGOW SOCIETY OF MUSICIANS: 73 Berkeley St. Every Thu, the real McCoy and many other Macs.

E3 VICTORIA BAR: Bridgegate. Nr the Scotia and similar set-up. Fri and Sat night sessions of Irish/Scottish tradn.

1335
Rest of Scotland

GALLEY OF LORNE HOTEL, ARDFERN: Hotel changing hands at time of going to press and will depend on incoming owners, but great atmos.

THISTLE TAVERN, BALDRIDGE, DUNFERMLINE: Where the Dunfermline Folk Club meet on alternate Wed.

ANDY'S PLACE, LAMLASH, ARRAN.

BLACK BITCH TAVERN, LINLITHGOW: High St. Esp Mondays.

BEACH BAR, LOSSIEMOUTH: Commerce St. Esp Tuesdays.

TIGH A CLACHAN, MALLAIG: esp Tuesdays and Saturdays.

LOCHINDAAL HOTEL, PORT CHARLOTTE, ISLAY.

MACDONALD ARMS and MISHNISH HOTEL, TOBERMORY, MULL.

CEILIDH PLACE, ULLAPOOL: 568/HIGHLAND: INEXP HOTELS.

EDINBURGH: MID-APRIL lasts a week. The biggest. 031 220 0464.

INVERNESS: MID-APRIL long weekend. 0463 231823.

SHETLAND: END-APRIL/MAY long (and they mean long) weekend. 0595 4757.

GIRVAN: EARLY MAY long weekend. 0563 29902.

ORKNEY: MID TO END OF MAY 3 days. 0856 850773.

ISLAY: END OF MAY over 2 weeks, till June. 0496 2413.

GLASGOW: MID-JUNE lasts a week, at Tron Theatre. 041 552 4267.

BLAIRGOWRIE: EARLY JULY long weekend, long running. 0250 2960.

ISLE OF BUTE: END JULY long weekend, traditional. 0700 83614.

AUCHTERMUCHTY: MID-AUGUST weekend. 0337 27052.

MELROSE: EARLY SEPT long weekend. 0835 23592.

TARBERT: MID-SEPT long weekend. 0880 820429.

THE BEST OF ROCK AND POP MUSIC

Concerts

The best ways to find out what's going on are to consult:

THE LIST MAGAZINE: Twice-monthly listings mag similar to *Time Out* in London; comprehensive day-by-day guide to all concerts, clubs etc (plus all other entertainment). Covers mainly Central Scotland and is avail from most uptown newsagents.

THE SUNDAY MAIL: Scotland's mostly widely-read tabloid; most promoters will advertise major upcoming concerts here.

TLN (TENNENTS LIVE NEWS): A free magazine produced for Tennents Lager and with wide-ranging coverage of the live music scene. Avail bi-monthly in fashionable and muso bars in Central Scotland.

The major venues used are as follows:

EDINBURGH 1337

INGLISTON EXHIBITION CENTRE: Rarely used, outside town, biggies only.

PLAYHOUSE THEATRE: Major theatre in Scotland, most regular programme, holds 3,000. From teen frenzy to heavy metal hocum. 031 557 2590.

USHER HALL: Great auditorium, but mainly classical. 031 228 1155.

THE QUEEN'S HALL: Most diverse (choral, jazz, art pop), seated at tables or standing. Good atmos. In use every night; your best bet if you just want to go somewhere for decent music. 031 668 2019.

GLASGOW 1338

SCOTTISH EXHIBITION AND CONFERENCE CENTRE: Scotland's major venue for arena rock 'n' roll (or Pavarotti). Used occas. 041 248 3000.

ROYAL CONCERT HALL: Full programme of mainly classical music, but also a civilised theatre for more thoughtful pop. 041 227 5511.

BARROWLANDS: The world-famous ballroom; pure rock 'n' roll. More in use in winter months, but go whatever's on. 456/GLASGOW NIGHTS. Doesn't have its own box office. Ticket info 031 557 6969.

THE PAVILION THEATRE: Intimate, tiered music hall with very mixed prog incl hypnotism and hip and hyped pop. 041 332 1846.

ABERDEEN

ABERDEEN EXHIBITION HALL: Similar to SECC above, but in use for concerts even less. Only a few major acts go this distance. 0224 824824.

THE CAPITOL THEATRE: Old theatre/cinema in main st. Holds 2,000. Occasional concerts from country to Big Country. 0224 583141.

THE MUSIC HALL: Medium-range civic (seated/standing). 0224 632080.

ELSEWHERE
The only other place where concerts are held on anything like a regular basis is THE EDÉN COURT THEATRE, INVERNESS. 1323/THEATRES.

Clubs

Information as above, especially *The List*. Main club venue listed on other pages: **GLASGOW,** p.77; **EDINBURGH,** p.41; **ABERDEEN,** p.100; **DUNDEE,** p.209; **GAY CLUBS,** p.244.

THE BEST CEILIDHS

One element of Scottish culture enjoying a revival is the Ceilidh. This is not just an excuse to purchase large amounts of alcohol (there's one held most Saturdays in the Walpole Hall, Chesser Av, Edinburgh, with BYOB and no smk), but is a friendly get-together easy to join in. Trad dances like the Gay Gordons and eightsome reels are usually 'called' and most of them are easy to pick up. You might come across a ceilidh anywhere, but the following are regular events.

THE RENFREW FERRY, GLASGOW: Enter by Clyde Pl via Jamaica St Bridge from N of river or Bridge St. The real Renfrew ferry moored on the Clyde, a brilliant ambiance for ceilidhs an gigs of all kinds. Every Fri 9pm-2am. Tickets at quay or in adv from Ticket Centre, Candleriggs (227 5511), usually sold out by 10pm. Visitors and locals. Dances are called. Great bands.

THE RIVERSIDE, GLASGOW: 248 3144. Fox St off Clyde St. The place that started the ceilidh revival in Glasgow. Upstairs in quiet st, the joint is jumping. Fri/Sat from 8pm, fills up quickly. Good band. Good, mixed crowd.

THE ASSEMBLY ROOMS, EDINBURGH: George St. Municipal halls but grand, the venue for all kinds of culture (esp during the Festival), and though a long way from the draughty village hall kind of jig, they've been positively reeling every Fri night in recent months as the ceilidh captures a new audience. Pay at door.

ZETLAND HALLS, EDINBURGH: Leith Walk. Occ legendary local ceilidh. Check TO for details.

WEST END HOTEL, EDINBURGH: 225 3656. 35 Palmerston Pl, Edinburgh's Heilan' hame hotel has occ sessions of music/singing and story-telling (more like a traditional ceilidh) but no dancing. This is where to come (or phone) to find out where the others are (occ ceilidhs held in the church hall nearby).

CUMMINGS HOTEL, INVERNESS: Ceilidhs there are aplenty in Inverness and thereabouts – make enquiries – but this nightly show at Cummings Hotel in Church St though non-participatory is a real enough slice of over-the-top Scottishness to be included here. Tacky tartan and yet . . . This show will confirm all your expectations and all our worst hang-ups; I guess it's how we are. Sample and sing-a-long if you must. Mon-Sat, early June-mid Sept. 0468 232531.

VICTORIA HALL, BALLATER: Real ceilidh in village hall in tourist centre on Royal Deeside. The Victoria Hall is where many local events are held so it's reasonably authentic as opposed to a hotel function created purely for visitors. More like the village Friday night dance, and licensed till midnight. Every Fri, late June-Sept. Info on 03397 55865, but just turn up.

ISLE OF SKYE: In this most Highland of islands 3 hoolies are worth mentioning, all welcoming to visitors, usually a grand melee if not a riot: **EDINBANE LODGE HOTEL:** 22km from Portree, 12km Dunvegan just off A850. Wed/Sat, June-Sept and New Year's Eve. Gets hot but don't chill out without midge cream. **FLODIGARRY COUNTRY HOUSE HOTEL:** 32km N Portree. V north, v Staffin and the stuff of a damned good shindig. Every Sat, plus other nights. Backpackers from adj hostel (671/HOSTELS), locals and hotel guests happily get down. Till 11.30pm officially. **THE GATHERING HALL, PORTREE:** Not a ceilidh, but the full-on Friday-night-on Skye experience. Don't go if you don't drink or don't like people. Pay at door.

SECTION 13
The Islands

THE MAGICAL ISLANDS

1341 **RAASAY:** A small car ferry (car useful but bikes best) from Sconser betw
MAP 2 Portree and Broadford on Skye takes you to this, the best of places. The
B3 distinctive flat top of Dun Caan presides over an island whose history and
natural history is Highland Scotland in microcosm. The village with MED. INX
hotel and bar (not open every night) and rows of mining-type cottages, is 3km
from jetty. The Outdoor Centre in the big hoose (once the home of the
notorious Dr No who, like many others before him, allowed Raasay to go to rack and
ruin) has courses galore. They'll put you up if they've got room (mostly
bunkrooms). The views from the lawn, or the viewpoint above the house, or
better still from Dun Caan with the Cuillins on one side and Torridon on the
other, are *sans pareil*. There's a ruined castle, a secret rhododendron-lined loch
for swimming, seals, otters and eagles. Much to explore. Go quietly.
Calmac ferry from Sconser, 4/5 times a day, not Sun. Last return 4.45pm.

1342 **ISLE OF GIGHA:** Privately owned small island in Argyll 20 mins from
MAP 1 mainland, so day visits poss. The recent troubled ownership and uncertain
B3 future for the islanders is hopefully resolved and all services will have been
restored by the time you read this. This should include the hotel (1353/ISLAND
HOTELS), the quayside bistro, the famous Achamore gardens (763/GARDENS) and
the 9-hole golf course. There are easy walks and bike hire from the post office
(you can cycle the entire length in an hour).
Best Walk: Left after golf course, thro gate and follow track past Mill Loch to
Mill and shore; views to Jura.   1-B-2
See: Double Beach, where the the Queen once swam off the Royal Yacht; two
crescents of sand on either side of the north end of the isthmus of Eilean Garbh
(seen from rd but path poorly marked).
*Calmac ferry from Tayinloan on A83, 27km S of Tarbert (Glasgow 165km). One
an hour in summer (last back 5.30pm, or 4.30pm Sun), fewer in winter. Cars
expensive and unnecessary. Calmac 0475 33755.*

1343 **LUING:** (Pron 'Ling') An island which can be seen in an afternoon. 25km S of
MAP 1 Oban via A816, then B844 across Seil 'island' to ferry. One rd across island to
B2 Toberonochy and a sidetrack to Cullipool: the island shop, the grassy strand
with its view of the skerries and the Isles of the Sea tea-room, open noon-5pm
Apr-Sept and in evening (dinner by arrangmt 08524 230). A gentle land of low
hills, easy walking (and cycling) and docile, handsome Luing cattle.
Strathclyde Region cont ferry. Only some take cars. 08523 252.

1344 **LISMORE:** Sail from Oban (car ferry) or better from Port Appin, where bikes can
MAP 1 be hired at the store (063173 553) and where there's a tea-room/pub and an
B1 interesting studio/gallery (1310/GALLERIES). A road goes down the centre of the
island, but there are many hill and cliff walks and even the near end round Port
Ramsay feels away from it all. History, natural history and air.
*Calmac service from Oban, 4/5 times a day (not Sun). From Port Appin (32km N
of Oban) several per day. 5mins. Last back 7pm (6pm winter).*

1345 **ULVA:** Off W coast of Mull. A boat leaves Ulva Ferry on the B8073 26km S
MAP 1 of Dervaig. Idyllic wee island with 5 well-marked walks incl to the curious
A1 basalt columns similar to Staffa, or by causeway to the smaller island of Gometra;
plan routes at boathouse 'interpretive centre' and tea-room. No accommodation.
A charming Telford church has services 4 times a year. Get ulva there.
Cont 5min service during day in summer. Ferryman: 06885 226.

1346 **IONA:** Needs little commendation from me; some think there are far
MAP 1 too many people there already. It is packed with daytrippers, not so
A2 much a pilgrimage, more an invasion, but Iona still enchants esp if you can get
away to the Bay at the Back of the Ocean or watch the cavalcade from the hill
above the Abbey. Or stay: Argyll Hotel best (06817 334) or B&B. Abbey shop isn't
bad. 1261/CRAFTS. *Reg 5min Calmac service from Fionnphort till 6/7pm (earlier in
winter).*

1347 **COLONSAY:** Ferry 3 times a week, so daytrips not poss. Very congenial hotel
MAP 1 (1352/ISLAND HOTELS) and self-catering units nearby. Some holiday cottages
A2 (0786 62355 or 09512 312), but camping discouraged. Coffee shop by pier and by hotel
(with bookshop) and civilised pub. A wild 18-hole golf course, a big hoose with
almost botanical gardens and fine walks, esp to Oronsay (1368/ISLAND WALKS).
Hotel has free bikes. You can't get lost. Also 800/FANTASTIC BEACHES.
Calmac from Oban (or Islay) Mon, Wed, Fri. Crossing 2hrs 10mins.

† † † **JURA:** Small regular car ferry from Port Askaig on Islay takes you 1348
into a different world. Jura is remote, unpopulated and has an MAP 1
ineffable grandeur indifferent to the demands of tourism. Great little hotel and B2
pub (1351/ISLAND HOTELS) in the only village (Craighouse) 15km from ferry at
Feolin; shop and tea-room. Walking guides avail at hotel and essential esp for the
Paps, the hills that maintain such a powerful hold over the island. Easiest climb
is from Three Arch Bridge; allow 6hrs. In May they run up all of them and back
to the distillery in 3.5hrs. The Corrievreckan whirlpool is another lure, but
you'll prob need a ride in a jeep to get close enough to walk and it can be a v
distant anti-climax. Orwell's house, Barnhill, is not open to visitors, but there
are many other fascinating sidetracks: the wild west coast and around L Tarbert
and the long littoral betw Craighouse and Lagg. 807/BEACHES; 995/GRAVEYARDS.
Western Ferries (049684 681) *reg 7 days, 5 min service from Pt Ascaig.*

† **ERISKAY:** Made famous by the sinking nearby of the SS *Politician* in 1941 1349
and the salvaging of its cargo of whisky, immortalised by Compton MAP 2
Mackenzie in *Whisky Galore*, this Hebridean gem has all the 'idyllic island' A4
ingredients: perfect beaches (1015/MARY, CHARLIE AND BOB), a hill to climb, a
pub (called the Politician and telling the story round its walls; it sells decent pub
food all day in summer), and a small, frequent ferry. There's only limited B and
B and no hotel, but camping is OK if you're discreet. Eriskay and Barra together
– the pure island experience. Also 985/CHURCHES.
Car ferry (08786 216) *from Ludaig, S Uist (10km S Lochboisdale) 6 per day in*
summer (3 in wint). Passenger boat (08786 233) *at least twice per day, depending on*
tides. This also serves Barra.

† **BARRA:** The last large island in the Hebridean chain, now joined to Vatersay
by a causeway. Main town is Castlebay with 3 hotels (best is Castlebay and
709/PUBS) and dramatic Kismul Castle 100m offshore (visit Wed, Fri and Sat at
2pm from beach or phone 228). Many easy walks and Heaval to climb (383m);
bike hire nr ferry (or phone 284; good Raleigh Pioneers). Visit airstrip, where
planes land on a wide beach or, better still, arrive in one (1402/GREAT JOURNEYS).
See Seal Bay and Vatersay (808/809/BEACHES). No hostels, but camping poss;
people here are easygoing. It's a long way to come, but you won't want to leave.
Calmac car ferry from Oban: Mon, Wed, Thur and Sat in summer. From
Lochboisdale, S Uist. Tues, Thur, Fri and Sun and from Ludaig (S Uist), see
above.

† † **RUM:** The large island in the group S of Skye, off the coast at Mallaig. 1350
The Calmac ferry plies betw Canna, Eigg, Muck and Rum but not MAP 2
conveniently and it's not easy to island hop and make a decent visit. Rum is the B4
most wild and dramatic. It has an extraordinary time-warp hotel in Kinloch
Castle and bunk accom as an alternative to its antique opulence. Bistro below
stairs, house party above (1360/ISLAND HOTELS). Rum is run by Scottish Natural
Hertitage and there are fine trails, climbs, bird-watching spots. One of the many
inaccessible coves is where the royal family disembark from *Britannia* for their
favourite picnic. The doric temple mausoleum to George Bullough, the
industrialist whose Highland fantasy the Castle was, is a 12km walk across the
island to Harris Bay. And sighting the sea eagles may be one of the best things
that ever happens to you.
Calmac ferry from Mallaig Mon, Wed, Fri via Eigg (3.5hrs) and Fri/Sat via
Canna at an ungodly hr. Also from Arisaig Tues and Thur in summer, with 3hrs
ashore (Murdo Grant 06875 224*); a more civilised journey.*

THE BEST ISLAND HOTELS

**1351 JURA HOTEL: 0496 82243. Craighouse 15km from Islay ferry at Feolin. Basic, friendly hotel o/looking Small Isles Bay; will oblige with all walking/exploring requirements. Pub is social hub of island. Rooms at front may be small, but have the views.
MAP 1
B3

18RMS JAN-DEC X/X PETS CC KIDS INX

1352 ISLE OF COLONSAY HOTEL: 09512 316. Indivisible from the delights of this fine island, since there's no other accom and daytrips aren't on. 400m from ferry (they collect you) and free bikes. Fixed menu, but diets OK. Smart lounge bar (with food) and good pub. Coffee shop also sells books! A good port in a storm.
MAP 1
A2

11RMS MAR-OCT X/X PETS CC KIDS MED.EX

1353 THE GIGHA HOTEL, ISLE OF GIGHA: 05835 254. Closed during the 'troubles' (the island, the hotel, everything, was repossessed by a bank) but will hopefully be open by the time you read this. A short walk from the ferry on an island perfectly proportioned for a short visit; easy walking and cycling. Hotel (was) modernised to simple, fairly tasteful standard. Island life without remoteness.
MAP 1
B3

13RMS JAN-DEC X/X XPETS CC KIDS MED.EX

1354 WESTERN ISLES HOTEL, TOBERMORY, MULL: 0688 2012. Victorian edifice more reminiscent of a station hotel in town – till you see the view from your bedroom. Great atmosphere, individual rooms and lounges. Conservatory also looks over the harbour and the bay.
MAP 1
B1

28RMS MAR-OCT T/T PETS CC KIDS TOS MED.EX

1355 DRUIMARD COUNTRY HOUSE, DERVAIG, MULL: 06884 345. 10km Tobermory beside (and assoc with) Mull Little Theatre on edge of handsome village. The whiff of greasepaint is just enough; bookish but not thespian. Theatre-goers use conservatory bar. Good restau. Comfy.
MAP 1
B1

5RMS JAN-DEC T/T PETS CC KIDS TOS MED.EX

1356 LAGG HOTEL, ARRAN: 0770 87255. 25km S of Brodick by scenic coast rd. A coaching inn on a woody bend of the road with gardens terraced down to river. Restau and roadside coffee shop. A conservatory and other compact public rooms. Some bedrooms small.
MAP 1
C4

15RMS JAN-DEC T/X PETS XCC KIDS MED.EX

1357 EILEAN IARMAIN, SKYE: 04713 332. Isleornsay, Sleat. 60km S of Portree. A Highland inn by a tiny harbour with an island in the bay. V Gaelic in character which may not suit the tourist seeking finger-snapping service, but this is a special and individual retreat.
MAP 2
C4

9RMS JAN-DEC T/X PETS CC KIDS TOS MED.INX

1357a VIEWFIELD HOUSE, PORTREE, SKYE: 0478 612217. One of the first hotels you come to in Portree on the rd from S (driveway opp gas station) and you need look no further. Individual, grand but comfortable, full of antiques and *objets* though not at all precious, this is also one of the best-value hotels on the island. Log fires, communal dinner; you have the run of a remarkable country house.
MAP 2
B3

9RMS APR-OCT X/X PETS CC KIDS MED.INX

FLODIGARRY, SKYE: 047052 203. Staffin, 32km N of Portree. Excellent value, stunning setting; a real find. 653/COUNTRY-HOUSE HOTELS.

16RMS JAN-DEC X/X PETS CC KIDS TOS MED.INX

1358 BAILE-NA CILLE, TIMSGARRY, UIG, HARRIS: 085175 242. 58km W of Stornoway via Garynahine and Leurbost. A far away and much loved refuge which takes you in and restores you. O/looks sea. Easygoing; you're one of the family and they welcome yours. 656/HOTELS THAT WELCOME KIDS.
MAP 2
B2

12RMS APR-OCT X/X PETS XCC KIDS MED.INX

1359 SCARISTA HOUSE, SOUTH HARRIS: 085985 238. 21km Tarbert, 78km Stornoway. On the W coast famous for its beaches and o/looking one of the best. Once the subject of a book about setting up a country-house hotel in a remote spot, it's been celebrated since.
MAP 2
B2

7RMS APR-OCT X/X PETS XCC KIDS TOS MED.EX

1360 KINLOCH CASTLE, RUM: 0687 2037. George Bullough, an eccentric industrialist was once king of this Edwardian castle and filled it with extravagant tack from around the world. It has changed little and staying here is a unique experience. The food and the bathrooms and the walks are all remarkable. Bunk accom also avail with bistro.
MAP 2
B4

9RMS+HOSTEL MAR-OCT X/X XPETS XCC XKIDS TOS EXP/CHP

Jura (1348)

THE BEST RESTAURANTS IN THE ISLANDS

✦ **KINLOCH LODGE, SKYE:** 04713 214. In south on Sleat Peninsula, 55km S of
Portree signed off the 'main' Sleat rd and over a moor, but this food is
worth coming over the water for (e.g. the Atlantic). Lady Claire Macdonald
creates a mouthwatering (fixed) menu from the first-rate ingredients she
advocates in her cookbooks. Veg are probably organic, the bread etc home-
baked. Despite the cholesterol-loaded desserts (her *pièce de résistance*), the
perfect cheeses on the sideboard are practically irresistible. Pity that this feast is
outside the range of most visitors to Skye; there are few Scots voices amongst the
post-prandial chat in the lounge and fewer still amongst the mueslis. But if you
can, treat yourself! 1361 MAP 2 C4 EXP

✦ **THE THREE CHIMNEYS, SKYE:** 047081 258. Calbost. 7km W Dunvegan on B884
to Glendale. Though off the well-beaten track to Dunvegan Castle, this
cottage restau is most certainly on the food map of Scotland. Shirley Spear
somehow finds the best and freshest ingredients locally and combines them with
effortless ease and conviction into a delightful and unpretentious meal. When it's
raining in Skye (and it does) the Three Chimneys will cheer you up. Seafood
especially fine, and vegn. Apr-Oct Lunch (not Sun) and dinner LO 9pm. 1362 MAP 2 B2 EXP

✦ **STRONGARBH HOUSE, TOBERMORY, MULL:** 0688 2328. Dining-room of
mansion-house hotel high above town, where Ian McAdam continues to
justify the 2 rosettes conferred on the hotel by the AA. Lobster and steak are
specialities (and, of course, sticky toffee pudding), but the menu reflects the excl
produce available locally, esp from the dock of the bay. Open AYR, 7-9pm.
Book w/ends. 1363 MAP 1 B1 MED

CALGARY FARMHOUSE AND DOVECOTE RESTAU, MULL: 06884 256. 7km from
Dervaig on B8073 nr Mull's famous beach. Roadside farm setting with inexp
light piney bedrooms and a bistro/wine bar restau using v local produce. Also a
gallery/coffee shop in summer. 1364 MAP 1 A1 INX

KILCHOMAN HOUSE, ISLAY: 049685 382. Off A847 nr Machir behind church, 16km
Bridgend. Small, whispering dining-room in island farmhouse/mansion; passable
local food – prawns, venison etc. Sensible prices. Cl Sun and Mon. Book (and get
directions). 1365 MAP 1 A3 INX

LOCHBAY INN, SKYE: 047083 235. 14km N Dunvegan. (1167/SEAFOOD RESTAUS.) INX

CREELERS, ARRAN: 0770 2810. Edge of Brodick. (1169/SEAFOOD RESTAUS.) MED

TIRORAN HOUSE, MULL: 06815 232. (643/COUNTRY-HOUSE HOTELS.) EXP

BUSTA HOUSE, SHETLAND: 0806 22506. 35km N of Lerwick at Brae. MED

FANTASTIC WALKS IN THE ISLANDS

For walk codes, see p.9.

1366 THE LOST GLEN, HARRIS: Take B887 W from Tarbert almost to the end
MAP 2 (where at Hushinish there's a good beach and maybe a sunset), but go
B2 right before Amhuinnsuidhe House to power station. Park here and walk up to
dam (1km). Take rt track round reservoir and the left around the upper loch.
Over the brim you arrive in a wide, wild glen; an overhang 2km ahead is said to
have the steepest angle in Europe. Go quietly; if you don't see deer and eagles
here, you're making too much noise on the gneiss. 10KM RET XCIRC XBIKE 2-B-2

1367 CARSAIG, MULL: In south of island, 7km from A849 Fionnphort-Craignure
MAP 1 rd nr Pennyghael. 2 walks start at pier: going left towards Lochbuie for a
B1 spectacular coastal/woodland walk past Adnunan Stack (7km); or rt towards the
imposing headland where, under the cliffs, the Nuns' Cave was a shelter for nuns
evicted from Iona during the Reformation. Nearby is a quarry used to build Iona
Abbey and much further on (9km Carsaig), at Malcolm's Point, the extraordinary
Carsaig Arches carved by wind and sea. 15/20KM XCIRC XBIKE 2-B-2

1368 COLONSAY: (1347/MAGIC ISLANDS). From the hotel or the quay, walk to
MAP 1 Colonsay House and its lush, overgrown intermingling of native plants and
A2 exotics (8km round trip); or to the priory on Oronsay, the smaller island. 6km to
'the Strand' (you might get a lift with the postman) then cross at low tide, with
enough time (at least 2hrs) to walk to the ruins. Allow longer if you want to
climb the easy peak of Ben Oronsay. Tide tables at shop or hotel.
12+6KM XCIRC BIKE 1-A-2

1369 THE OLD MAN OF STORR, SKYE: The enigmatic basalt finger visible from
MAP 2 the Portree-Staffin rd (A855). Start from carpark on left, 12km from
B3 Portree. There's a well-defined path through or around the clump of woodland
towards the cliffs and a steep climb up the grassy slope to the pinnacle which
towers 165ft tall. Great views over Raasay to the mainland. Lots of space and
rabbits and birds who make the most of it. 5KM XCIRC XBIKE 2-B-2

1370 THE QUIRANG, SKYE: 861/CLASSIC VIEWS for directions to start point.
MAP 2 The strange formations have names (e.g. the Table, the Needle, the
B3 Prison) and it's poss to walk round all of them. Start of the path from the
carpark is easy. At the first saddle, take the second scree slope to the Table,
rather than the first. When you get to the Needle, the path to the rt betw two
giant pinnacles is the easiest of the 3 options. From the top you can see the
Hebrides. This place is supernatural; whole parties of schoolgirls could
disappear here. So might you if you're not careful. 6KM XCIRC XBIKE 2-B-2

1371 HOY, ORKNEY: There are innumerable walks on the scattered Orkney Islands and
1AP 10 on Hoy itself and on a good day you can get round the north part of the island
and see some of the most dramatic coastal scenery you'll find anywhere. A
passenger ferry leaves Stromness 2 or 3 times a day and takes 30mins. Make
tracks N or S from junction nr pier and use free Hoy brochure from TO so as
not to miss the landmarks, the bird sanctuaries and the Old Man himself.
20/25KM CIRC MTBIKE 2-B-2

1372 CORRYVRECKAN, JURA: The whirlpool in the Gulf of Corryvreckan is notorious
MAP 1 and classified by the Royal Navy as un-navigable. It's betw Jura and Scarba and
B2 to see it you must get to the far N of the island. From the end of the road at
Ardlussa (25km Craighouse, the main village), there's a rough track to Lealt then
a walk (or a jeep ride) of 12km to Kinuachdrach, then a further walk of 3km.
The phenomenon is best seen at certain states of tide. Consult at hotel (1351/
ISLAND HOTELS) and get the walk guide. 1348/MAGIC ISLANDS.
6/24KM XCIRC XBIKE 2-C-2

THE BEST OF ARRAN

FERRY: Ardrossan-Brodick, 55mins. 6 per day Mon-Sat, 4 on Sun. Ardrossan-Glasgow, train or road via A77/A71 1.5hr. Claonaig-Lochranza, 30mins. 10 per day (summer only).

WHERE TO STAY

AUCHRANNIE HOUSE, Brodick: 0770 302234. Old house enlarged but not altogether enhanced by the very mod cons. Some rooms look into 'the country'. Good pool, gym. This is Arran's upmarket hotel.

27RMS   JAN-DEC   T/T   XPETS   CC   KIDS   TOS   MED.EX

THE LAGG HOTEL, Kilmory: 0770 870255. Cosy coaching inn with terraced gardens on river. Smallish rooms; good restau. Far south. (1356/ISLAND HOTELS.)

ROSEBURN LODGE, Brodick: 0770 302383. On edge of Brodick, the main rd to Corrie and Brodick Castle. Welcoming family house. Book!

3RMS   JAN-DEC   X/X   PETS   XCC   KIDS   CHP

KILMICHAEL HOUSE, Brodick: 0770 302219. 3km from the main rd through town down a lane in real country. Attention to detail and guests. STB de luxe rating.

9RMS   APR-OCT   X/X   PETS   XCC   KIDS   CHP

S.Y. HOSTELS: at Lochranza (0770 830631) and Whiting Bay (0770700 339). Both busy Grade 2s in picturesque areas but 25 and 15km from Brodick.

CAMPING AND CARAVAN PARKS: at Glen Rosa nr Brodick (4km) 077030 2380, also Lamlash 0770870 241, Lochranza (by golf course) 0770830 273. All friendly sites. Good for tenting it.

WHERE TO EAT

CREELERS, Brodick: 077030 2810. Very good seafood and puddings in unlikely 'shed' – not masses of atmos, but no pretension 12-2pm, 7-11pm.   MED

LAGG HOTEL: as above. May be a fair drive to go for a meal but poss the best all-round restau on the island. Coffee shop for snacks.   MED

WHAT TO SEE

BRODICK CASTLE: 5km walk or cycle from Brodick. Impressive museum and gardens. Tea-room. Flagship NT property. 911/CASTLES.

GOATFELL: 6km/5hr walk starting from the carpark at Cladach or sea start at Corrie. Free route leaflet at TO. 1037/HILLS.   2-A-2

GLENASHDALE FALLS: 5km/2hr forest walk from Glenashdale Bridge at Whiting Bay. Steady, easy climb, lovely forest walk. 828/FALLS.   1-B-1

ARRAN HERITAGE MUSEUM: Good folk museum on edge of Brodick.

CORRIE: No other village on Arran has quite the same composure. 9km N of Brodick and an easy shoreline bike ride from there. Hotel for refreshment.

MACHRIE MOOR STANDING STONES: Off main coast rd 7km N of Blackwater Foot. On bleak Machrie Moor various collections of Stones, some squat, some tall, all part of an ancient hidden landscape. Spooky spot.

GLEN SANNOX: A fine glen in hilly NE, 11km N Brodick. App via small house opp phone box in Sannox Vill; go past cemetery. 4hrs ret.   1-B-2

WHAT TO DO

GOLF: Lots of golf courses. Brodick 0770 302513; Lochranza 0770 830273; Lamlash 0770 600296; Whiting Bay 0770 700487 to name but a few. All 18 holes. Corrie and Machrie (9).

TENNIS: Brodick, Lamlash, Blackwaterfoot, Machrie.

FISHING: On Machrie (enqs 0770 840241) and Iorsa (0770 840259) – no fishing on Sundays. Also loch fishing on Loch Garbad (stocked).

CYCLE HIRE: Brodick 2272/2460 (opp Vill Hall); Whiting Bay 0770 700382.

TOURIST INFO: 0770 302140. **CALMAC:** 0475 33755.

THE BEST OF ISLAY AND JURA

A3 **FERRY:** Kennacraig-Port Askaig: 2hrs. 1 per day (not Sun in winter). Kennacraig-Port Ellen: over 2hrs. 2 per day excl Wed (1 in wint, 1 on Sun). Port Askaig-Feolin, Jura: 5 mins. Many per day (enqs: 0496 84681).

BY AIR: Twice daily from Glasgow (once Sat). Airport 8km Pt Ellen in S of island. Loganair 041 889 3181; (local) 0496 2022.

WHERE TO STAY

THE MACHRIE, Port Ellen: 0496 2310. 7km N on A846. Excl golfing hotel, rooms w/o bathrooms are good value; decent restau and esp bar meals in clubhouse atmos. Nr airport. 27RMS JAN-DEC X/T PETS CC KIDS MED.EX/INX

JURA HOTEL, Craighouse: 0496 82243. Ferry at Foelin 15km. The only one, but happily a v good island inn (1351/ISLAND HOTELS). Front rooms best. Bar is social hub of the island. 18RMS JAN-DEC X/X PETS CC KIDS INX

BRIDGEND HOTEL, Bridgend: 0496 81212. 5km Bowmore. Roadside hotel centrally situated nr Islay House; some rooms small. Good lounge bar. 10RMS JAN-DEC T/T PETS CC KIDS MED.INX

PORT ASKAIG HOTEL, Port Askaig: 0496 84245. Port-side hostelry (by Jura and mainland ferries) with lawn terrace and often busy bar. Traditional hospitality and busy atmosphere. 9RMS JAN-DEC X/T PETS XCC KIDS MED.EX

LOCHSIDE HOTEL, Bowmore: 049681 244. Central, good ambience (and whisky). INX

TIGHCARGMAN, Port Ellen: 0496 2345. Edge of town nr unsightly maltings but views over bay. B&B/3 cottages. Pottery out back. 4RMS JAN-DEC X/T XPETS XCC KIDS CHP

CAMPING (and limited) **CARAVAN SITE** at Kintra Farm. 0496 2051. Rd to Oa at Pt Ellen Malting, follow Kintra signs. Halcyon grassy strand. Restau, gr walks.

WHERE TO EAT

KILCHOMAN HOUSE: 0496 85382. 20 mins Bruichladdich off A847 towards Machir and behind church. Local produce; v personal. Must book. MED

THE OLD GRANARY: Kintra Beach (as Camping, above). Open Apr-Oct. Fairly basic menu in 'barn' setting. Perfect post-prandial walks. CHP

MACHRIE HOTEL as above; **CROFT KITCHEN,** Port Charlotte. Decent roadside and shoreside coffee/bookshop.

BALLYGRANT INN: 049684 277. S of Pt Askaig. Prob best pub food on island.

WHAT TO SEE

ISLAY: THE DISTILLERIES esp Laphroaig and Lagavulin (classic settings) both on rd to Ardbeg from Port Ellen and with guided tours and visitor centres. Bowmore in Bowmore itself, with regular well-planned tour (1242/WHISKY TRAIL). **THE AMERICAN MONUMENT:** 961/MONUMENTS; **OA and LOCH GRUINART:** 819/BIRDWATCHING; **PORT CHARLOTTE:** 792/COASTAL VILLAGES; **KINTRA:** 1066/COASTAL WALKS. **BOWMORE POOL:** Swimming pool. **LOCHSIDE HOTEL,** p. 195 WHISKY. **FINLAGGAN:** The romantic, but sparse ruin, on an 'island' in L Finlaggan, the last home of the Lord of the Isles. Off A846 5km S of Port Askaig. Cross the fen by a wee bridge or boat. Visitor Centre.

JURA: THE ISLAND ITSELF 1348/MAGIC ISLANDS; **THE PAPS OF JURA;** **CORRYVRECKAN** 1372/ISLAND WALKS; **KILLCHIANAIG and KEILS** 995/GRAVEYARDS; **BARNHILL** 1372/ISLAND WALKS; **LOWLANDMAN'S BAY** 807/BEACHES.

WHAT TO DO

GOLF at Machrie (1113/GOLF IN GREAT PLACES); **PONY TREKKING** at Rockside Farm. 0496 85231; **SWIMMING** at Bowmore. 0496 81767; **BIKE HIRE** From R. Murphy. 049685 397.

TOURIST INFO: 049681 254. **CALMAC:** 0475 33755.

THE BEST OF LEWIS AND HARRIS

FERRY: Ullapool-Stornaway, 3hrs 30mins, 1 or 2 per day (not Sun). Uig (Skye)-
Tarbert (Harris), 1hr 45 mins, 1 or 2 per day (not Sun in winter).

BY AIR: BA 3 times daily (2 Sat, not Sun). Morning flight through Inverness.
Local 0851 702340 or Linkline 0345 222111. Loganair 2 daily (not Sun). Local 0851
703067 or 041 889 3181.

WHERE TO STAY
BAILE-NA-CILLE, TIMSGARRY: 0851 75242. Nr Uig, 55km W Stornoway off A858.
Welcoming old manse in the far west. 1358/ISLAND HOTELS.

SCARISTA HOUSE, HARRIS: 0859 85238. 20km S of Tarbert. Nr famous but often
deserted beach; celebrated country house retreat. 1359/ISLAND HOTELS.

ARDVOURLIE CASTLE, ARDVOURLIE: 0859 2307. 16km N of Tarbert on shore of L
Seaforth in hills of N Harris. Victorian hunting lodge. I haven't stayed.
                        4RMS   JAN-DEC   X/T   PETS   XCC   KIDS   TOS   MED.EX

ROYAL, STORNOWAY: 0851 2109. The best value and most central of the 3 main
hotels in town. All usual comforts. Coffee shop.
                        26RMS   JAN-DEC   T/T   PETS   CC   KIDS   MED.INX

LEACHIN HOUSE, TARBERT: 085950 2157. 2km N on A859. Small, Victorian family
house. The personal touch in furnishings, food and your excursions.
                        3RMS   JAN-DEC   T/T   XPETS   XCC   KIDS   INX

PARK GUEST HOUSE, STORNOWAY: 0851 2485. James St. Refurbished townhouse
with surprisingly good menu and comfy rooms. A superior guest house.
                        7RMS   JAN-DEC   X/T   XPETS   XCC   XKIDS   CHP

S.Y. HOSTELS: At Garenin, Rhenigdale (v basic; the farflung alternative). Best is
Stockinish on 'the Golden Rd'. Grade 3. Tarbert 11km. No phone.

WHERE TO EAT
TIMSGARRY and **SCARISTA HOUSE:** (see above). Dinner possible for non-residents.
Both a long way from Stornoway (and anywhere). Must book.

TIGH MEALROS at **GARYNAHINE:** 0851 92333. On A858 22km from Stornoway. End
of township on way to Callanish. Unpretentious fare, seafood.

COFFEE SHOPS at **AN LANNTAIR GALLERY, STORNOWAY** and also in a converted
'barn' at **18 CALLANAIS,** by the Callanish Stones. Daytime hours.

WHAT TO SEE
THE CALLANISH STONES: 24km W of Stornoway, A859 rt at Leurbost. Scotland's
most famous ring of standing stones. 949/PREHISTORIC SITES.

THE BLACK HOUSE at **ARNOL:** 24km N of Stornoway A857, then A858.
Compelling evocation of surprisingly recent history. 1312/MUSEUMS.

THE GOLDEN ROAD: The east coast road in S Harris. Harris tweed in the cottages
and the wild Hebridean coast. 851/SCENIC ROUTES.

THE CHURCH at **RODEL:** 984/CHURCHES; **THE RODEL BAR:** the pub at the end of
the universe (it's an experience!). **THE LOST GLEN:** 1366/ISLAND WALKS; **THE
HARRIS BEACHES:** Hushinish, Scarista (and others W coast).

WHAT TO DO
GOLF at Stornoway 0851 702240 and Scarista in Harris (check at hotel).

SWIMMING (Sports Centre) in Stornoway. 0851 702603.

FISHING for brown trout in innumerable lochs. Some estate fishing for
salmon/sea trout by the day. Sea angling info: 0851 703244

CYCLE HIRE Alex Dan Campbell, Kenneth Street, Stornoway 0851 704025.

TOURIST INFO: 0851 703088. **CALMAC:** 0475 33755.

THE BEST OF MULL

FERRY: Oban-Craignure, 40mins. 6 a day. (2-4 in winter). Lochaline-Fishnish, 15mins. 9-15 a day. Kilchoan-Tobermory, 35mins. 4 a day (summer only).

WHERE TO STAY
Also see ISLAND HOTELS AND RESTAUS, p. 216-7.

WESTERN ISLES, TOBERMORY: 0688 2012. High above town, excellent views over bay; real individuality, fire in foyer, conservatory. Good suites and restau.

28RMS MAR-OCT T/T PETS CC KIDS TOS MED.EX

STRONGARBH, TOBERMORY: 0688 2142. Behind Western Isles Hotel, a bit back of beyond, but well worth finding. Splendid rooms. Personal. Excl food.

4RMS JAN-DEC X/T PETS CC KIDS MED.INX

TOBERMORY HOTEL: 0688 2091. On waterfront, cheapish/cheerful. Gr location.

17RMS JAN-DEC X/X PETS CC KIDS MED.INX

CALGARY FARMHOUSE, CALGARY: 06884 256. Nr Dervaig On B8073 nr Mull's famous beach. Gallery/coffee-shop and good bistro/restau.

9RMS MAR-DEC X/X PETS CC KIDS INX

DRUIMARD COUNTRY HOUSE, DERVAIG: 06884 345. Small, comfortable haven beside Mull Little Theatre; conservatory bar, books, informal. A touch overpriced.

5RMS JAN-DEC T/T PETS CC KID MED.EX

S.Y.HOSTEL: In Tobermory main street on bay. See 668/BEST HOSTELS.

CARAVAN PARKS: At Fishnish (all facs, nr Ferry, 0631 62285), Craignure and Fionnphort. **CAMPING:** Calgary Beach, Fishnish and at Loch Na Keal shore. 686/CAMPING.

WHERE TO EAT
TIRORAN HOUSE: 0681 5232. 2km off B8035, Calgary-Fionnphort rd. Book first and arrive in good time with best manners and good appetite. 643/HOTELS. EXP

STRONGARBH HOUSE: 0688 2142. See above. Hotelish dining-room but the hot chef in town. 2 AA rosettes. After dinner it's downhill from here. Must book. MED

WESTERN ISLES: 0688 2012. See above. Careful cuisine *dans la salle* (or bar). MED

CALGARY FARMHOUSE: As above. The Dovecote Restaurant. Local produce in wine-bar setting. 1364/ISLAND RESTAUS. INX

THE PUFFER AGROUND, SALEN: 0680 300389. Popl roadside café/restau. INX

WHAT TO SEE
TOROSAY CASTLE: Walk or train (!) from Craignure. Fabulous gardens and fascinating insight into an endearing family's life. 909/CASTLES.

DUART CASTLE: 5km Craignure. Seat of Clan Maclean. Impressive from a distance, good view of clan history and from battlements. Teashop. 910/CASTLES.

EAS FORS: Waterfall on Dervaig to Fionnphort rd. Very accessible series of cataracts tumbling into the sea. 827/WATERFALLS.

Excursions to IONA (from Fionnphort) and ULVA (from Ulva Ferry). 1346/1345/MAGIC ISLANDS. STAFFA: (from Fionnphort or Iona) and THE TRESHNISH ISLES (Ulva Ferry or Fionnphort). Marvellous trips in summer. 875/BIRDS.

Walks from CARSAIG PIER, 1367/ISLAND WALKS; or up BEN MORE, 1085/MUNROS;

CROIG and QUINISH in N, nr Dervaig and LOCHBUIE off the A849 at Strathcoil 9km S of Craignure, for serene shorelines to explore.

AROS PARK forest walk, from Tobermory, about 7km round trip.

WHAT TO DO
GOLF: Tobermory Golf Course 0688 2020. Craignure Golf Course 0680 2372. Both 9 holes. **FISHING:** Information: 'Tackle and Books', 0688 2336. **BIKE HIRE:** 0688 2226.

TOURIST INFORMATION: 0688 2182. **CALMAC:** 0475 33755

THE BEST OF SKYE

FERRY: Kyle of Lochalsh-Kyleakin, 10mins. Continuous (incl Sun) Mallaig-Armadale, 30mins. 4/5 per day (not Sun; 2/3 in winter) Glenelg-Kylerhea, 10mins. Continuous (not Suns). Easter-Sept. Tarbert (Harris)-Uig, 1hr 45mins. 1/2 per day (not Sun in winter).

WHERE TO STAY
See also ISLAND HOTELS, p. 216.

✝✝ **FLODIGARRY:** 0470 52203. 30km N. Portree on A855. Excellent value smartly run baronial/country house with stunning views, ambitious cuisine, a funky local bar and a bit of Flora Macdonald. (653/COUNTRY-HOUSE HOTELS.)

16RMS   APR-OCT   X/X   PETS   CC   KIDS   TOS   MED.INX

✝✝ **ISLE ORNSAY:** 0471 3332. 15km S of Broadford on A851. Traditional and v Gaelic inn on mystic shore. All rms incl annex, homely. (1357/ISLAND HOTELS.)

12RMS   JAN-DEC   T/X   PETS   CC   KIDS   MED.INX

VIEWFIELD HOUSE, PORTREE: 0478 612217. Gr atmos in co house nr town centre. Unique; gr value (1357A/ISLAND HOTS). 9RMS   APR-OCT   X/X   PETS   CC   KIDS   MED.EX

ROSEDALE, PORTREE: 0478 3131. Waterfront/harbour location; but a well-appointed way to be at the centre of Portree things.

23RMS   MAY-SEPT   T/T   PETS   CC   KIDS   MED.EX

SKEABOST: 0470 32202. 11km W of Portree on A850. Golfing (9 holes) and fishing (12km of R Snizort) country house, centre for touring. Famous Sunday buffet lunch (before you take to the hills). 26RMS   APR-OCT   T/T   PETS   XCC   KIDS   MED.EX

UIG HOTEL, UIG: 047042 205. In far N of island nr ferry to Hebrides; grand position o/looking township and bay. An inn on the rd. Good facs; friendly.

17RMS   APR-OCT   T/T   PETS   CC   KIDS   MED.EX

S.Y. HOSTELS: At Kyleakin (biggest, nearest mainland), Armadale (interesting area in south), Broadford, Glen Brittle (for all things Cuillin), Uig (for N Skye, ferry to Hebrides). **INDEPENDENT HOSTELS** at Kyleakin and Staffin (671/BEST HOSTELS).

CAMPING AND CARAVAN PARKS: At Glen Brittle (0478 42232). 677/CAMPSITES and Loch Greshernish at Edinbane, 18km Portree (0470 82230) – grassy terrace overlooking loch; best for facilities but exposed.

WHERE TO EAT
THREE CHIMNEYS: 0470 81258. 7km W of Dunvegan on B884. Guide books agree the best on Skye. Cottage ambience. 1362/ISLAND RESTAUS.   MED

KINLOCH LODGE: 0471 3214. 13km S Broadford off A851. Superb food if you're in the mood, in the south and in the black. Lady Claire Macdonald's Café. 1361/ISLAND RESTAUS.   EXP

LOCHBAY INN: 0470 83235. 12km N Dunvegan off A850. Small; simple fresh seafood in lochside setting. 1167/BEST SEAFOOD RESTAUS.   INX

CAFE INNEAN (ANVIL CAFE): 0478 616606. Not only vegn, but see 1159A/VEGN RESTAUS.

HARLOSH HOTEL: (047022 367 by Dunvegan); **ARDVASAR HOTEL:** (04714 223 in Sleat in the south) and **THE OLD SCHOOLHOUSE:** (Dunvegan) are all recomm.

WHAT TO SEE
THE CUILLINS: 737/ATTRACTIONS; **RAASAY:** 1341/MAGIC ISLANDS; **THE QUIRANG:** 861/CLASSIC VIEWS; 1370/ISLAND WALKS; **DUNVEGAN:** 912/CASTLES; **EAS MOR:** 829/WATERFALLS; **ELGOL:** 866/CLASSIC VIEWS; **SKYEBATIKS:** 1253/CRAFTSHOPS; **SKYE MUSEUM OF ISLAND LIFE:** 1316/MUSEUMS; **FLORA MACDONALD'S GRAVE:** 963/MONUMENTS; **EDINBANE POTTERY:** 11254A/CRAFTSHOPS; **SKYE CEILIDHS:** p.212.

WHAT TO DO
GOLF at Skeabost (see above) and Sconsor (04786 12277). **FISHING:** ask at hotels, Skeabost, Isle Ornsay (see above) and Greshhornish House (0470 82266). **SWIMMING** at Portree Pool (047861 2655). **BIKE HIRE:** Island Cycles (0470 72284).

TOURIST INFO: Main no 047861 2137 **CALMAC:** 0475 33755.

THE BEST OF ORKNEY

FERRY: P&O (0856 850655) Aberdeen-Stromness, 8hrs. Tues, Wed, Fri and Sat. Scrabster-Stromness, 2hrs. 2/3 per day (1 Sun, 1 wint/not Sun). T&B (0955 81353) John O' Groats-Burwick, 45mins, 4 a day summer.

BY AIR: BA (0856 2233) from Aberdeen, 3 a day (2 Sat); from Inverness, 1 a day. Loganair (2420) from Edinburgh, 1 a day; from Wick, 5 (1 on Sat). No Sunday flights on either airline.

WHERE TO STAY

MERKISTER, HARRAY: 0856 77366. Old fisherman's hotel on shore of L Harray, 15km Kirkwall. Brown trout, bird-watching and quiet.

15RMS   MAR-NOV   T/T   PETS   CC   KIDS   MED.INX

STROMNESS HOTEL, STROMNESS: 0856 850298. Traditional, 'commercial' type hotel by harbour and at the heart of the old part of town.

38RMS   JAN-DEC   T/T   PETS   CC   KIDS   MED.INX

Stromness

AYRE HOTEL, KIRKWALL: 085687 3001. Probably the best appointed of the hotels in 'town'. Some rooms have sea views. Busy bar.

34RMS   JAN-DEC   T/T   PETS   CC   KIDS   MED.INX

BARONY, BIRSAY: 0856 72327. 40km from Kirkwall but a peaceful place for fishing (free on L Birsay), walking and whiling away.

10RMS   APR-OCT   X/X   PETS   XCC   KIDS   INX

S.Y. HOSTELS: At Stromness (excellent location, Gr 2), Kirkwall (the largest), Hoy, Rackwick, Eday and the wonderful Papa Westray.

CAMPING/CARAVAN: At Kirkwall and Stromness (both 085687 3535).

WHERE TO EAT

THE CREEL, ST MARGARET'S HOPE: 0856 83311. On S Ronaldsay, 20km S of Kirkwall. Menu/wine-list not ambitious, but good for fish. Dinner only. INX

HAMNAVOE, STROMNESS: 0856 850606. Unpretentious à la carte in friendly back-street bistro. Mar-Oct; dinner only, LO 10pm. INX

TORMISTON MILL, STENNESS: 0856 76372. 16km Kirkwall. I haven't been able to try this place, but it 'looked OK'. Reports please. INX

WHAT TO SEE

SKARA BRAE: 25km W Kirkwall. Amazingly well-preserved underground labyrinth, a 5,000-yr-old village. 947/PREHISTORIC SITES.

THE OLD MAN OF HOY: on Hoy; 30 min ferry 2 or 3 times a day from Stromness. 3hr walk along spectacular coast. 1371/ISLAND WALKS.

STANDING STONES OF STENNESS, THE RING OF BRODGAR, MAES HOWE: Around 18km W of Kirkwall on A965. Strong vibrations. 948/PREHISTORIC SITES.

THE YESNABY SEA STACKS: 24km W of Kirkwall. A precarious cliff top at the end of the world. 1032/SPOOKY (or spiritual) PLACES.

THE ITALIAN CHAPEL: 8km S of Kirkwall at first causeway. Enduring and enchanting memorial to piety; and the war. 980/CHURCHES.

ST MAGNUS CATHEDRAL: 980/CHURCHES; **STROMNESS** itself, 789/COASTAL VILLAGES; **THE PIER ART GALLERY,** 1305/INTERESTING GALLERIES; **TOMB OF THE EAGLES,** 953/PREHISTORIC SITES; **MARWICK HEAD** (and many of the smaller islands), 881/BIRDWATCHING; **SCAPA FLOW,** 1005/BATTLEGROUNDS; **HIGHLAND PARK,** 1247/WHISKY TRAIL.

WHAT TO DO
GOLF: Golf courses open to public at Kirkwall and Stromness. **SWIMMING:** Pools at Kirkwall, Stromness and Hoy. **FISHING:** Permits not required, though permission needed to fish Loch of Skile. **BIKE HIRE:** Paterson Cycles, 0856 3097.

TOURIST INFO: 0856 872856 or 0856 850716.

THE BEST OF SHETLAND

FERRY: P&O (0224 572615) Aberdeen-Lerwick 14hrs (leaves 6pm arr 8am) Mon-Fri (not Tue Jun-Aug). Also via Orkney (leaves Aberdeen on Sat at noon and Stromness at noon on Sun; also Tue Jun-Aug).

BY AIR: BA (linkline 0345 222111, Shetland 0950 60345) from Aberdeen (4 a day, 3 Sat, 2 Sun. From Inverness (2 a day, 1 Sat). From Glasgow (2 a day, 1 Sat). From Edinburgh (1 Mon-Fri at 1105).

LOGANAIR: (041 889 3181, Shetland 0595 84 246) from Glasgow (1 a day Mon-Sat at 1120). From Edinburgh (1 a day Mon-Sat 1140).

WHERE TO STAY
BUSTA HOUSE, BRAE: 0806 22506. Former laird's house (18th century) in remote setting o/looking sea with own harbour and views of Busta Voe. Some style, good service, best restau on island, huge malt selection. 35km N Lerwick by A970 to Brae. Peat/wood fire, library. 20RMS JAN-DEC T/T PETS CC KIDS MED.EX

QUEEN'S HOTEL, LERWICK: 0595 2826. In the centre of Lerwick on waterfront and next to harbour. Old-fashioned and the better for it, all rooms different, some with real character and sea views. 26RMS JAN-DEC T/T PETS CC KIDS MED.INX

BURRASTOW HOUSE, WALLS: 0595 71307. On far west of mainland about 35km from Lerwick, a small Georgian house with views across to Island of Vaila. Remote and amazingly peaceful, private pier and safe sandy beach. Peat fires, tasteful well-worn furnishings. Excl healthy food, everything home-made incl bread; organic wines. Kids welcome.

5RMS MAY-OCT X/X PETS XCC KIDS MED.INX

SUMBURGH HOTEL, SUMBURGH: 0950 60201. Recently refurbished manor house in very S of mainland 42km from Lerwick. Next to airport and Jarlshof excavations. Seaviews as far as Fair Isle (50km S). Beaches and birds!

24RMS JAN-DEC T/T PETS CC KIDS MED.INX

S.Y. HOSTEL in Lerwick, Isleburgh House: 0595 2114. Recently upgraded and v central. Also camping bods (fishermen's barns) available, esp **THE BOD OF NESBISTER** on a small promontory on Whiteness Voe (12km NW of Lerwick) and the **SAIL LOFT** at Voe (25km N of Lerwick). Cheap sleep in wonderful seashore settings. Phone Tourist Information for details.

CAMPING/CARAVAN: CLICKIMIN, LERWICK 0595 4555. **LEVENWICK** 0950 2207.

WHERE TO EAT

BUSTA HOUSE, BRAE: See above. Probably the best meal in the islands.

DA PEERIE FISK: 0806 22679. Means 'the small fish' and specialises in seafood esp halibut, turbot, sole. Nr Busta House 35km N of Lerwick, but worth the 30min drive. Open Apr-Oct lunch and dinner.

SHETLAND HOTEL: 0595 5515, **LERWICK HOTEL:** 0595 2166 and the **KVELDSRO HOTEL:** (pron 'Kelro') 0595 2195 all have fairly reliable dining-rooms (the Kveldsro has recently gone upmarket and is exp) and pub food.

Pub food also recommended at the following:

THE MID BRAE INN, BRAE: 32km N of Lerwick, 0806 22634. Lunch and supper till 9pm, 7 days. All home-made, superb fish 'n' chips. Bar till 1 am.

HERRISLEA HOUSE, TINGWALL: 7km NW of Lerwick. 0595 84208. Lunch and supper till 9pm, 7 days. Basic, good home-cooking.

NORSEMAN'S INN, WEISDALE: 18km NW of Lerwick. 0595 72304. Apr-Oct lunch and dinner till 9.30pm, 7 days. Esp steaks, but consult daily menu.

WHAT TO SEE

MOUSA BROCH and JARLSHOF: 950/PREHISTORIC SITES.

ST NINIAN'S ISLE, BIGTON: 8km N of Sumburgh on W Coast. An island linked by exquisite tombolo of shell-sand. Hoard of Pictish silver found in 1958 (now in Edinburgh). Beautiful, serene spot.

SCALLOWAY: 7km W of Lerwick, a township once the ancient capital of Shetland, dominated by the atmospheric ruins of Scalloway Castle. **SHETLAND WOOLLEN COMPANY** is worth a rummage.

NOUP OF NOSS, ISLE OF NOSS off BRESSAY: 8km W of Lerwick by frequent ferry and then boat (also direct from Lerwick 0595 2577), May-Aug only. Excellent seabird watching and airy walks. Also Fair Isle, Fetlar, Sumburgh Head (far S) and Hermaness (far N).

UP HELLY AA: Festival held in Lerwick on the last Tuesday in January. Ritual with hundreds of torch-bearers and much fire and firewater. Norse, northern and pagan. A wild time.

TOURIST INFORMATION: 0595 3434.

SECTION 14
Local Centres and Odds and Sods
Where to eat and stay, what to do and see

THE BEST OF AYR

WHERE TO STAY

NORTHPARK HOUSE: 0292 42336. 3km fom centre on rd to Alloway and Burns Country Trail. Sympathetic conversion of Ayrshire mansion, o/looking the course/park of Belleisle (1099/ GOLF). 6RMS JAN-DEC T/T PETS CC KIDS MED.EX

LOCHGREEN HOUSE: 0292 313343. Monktonhall Rd, Troon 12km N on way in from Ayr. White seaside mansion with red pan-tiled roof o/looking the famous golf courses of Troon (1095/GOLF). Civilised decor and dining. 7RMS JAN-DEC T/T PETS CC KIDS MED.EX

PIERSLAND, TROON: 0292 314747. 12km N of Ayr. 470/STRATHCLYDE S: HOTELS.

BURNS MONUMENT, ALLOWAY: 0292 42466. 5km S of Ayr. 471/STRATH HOTELS.

KYLESTROME: 0292 262474. 11 Miller Rd. Recent refurbishment à la mode. Residential st nr centre. Not a lot of character but sound. 12RMS JAN-DEC T/T PETS CC KIDS TOS MED.EX

OLD RACECOURSE: 0292 262873. 2 Victoria Park. On corner of Old Racecourse (arterial) Rd, 2km from centre. 'Modernised', good value. 12RMS JAN-DEC T/T PETS CC KIDS INX

THE RICHMOND: 0292 265153. 38 Park Circus. Good old-fashioned terraced house in quiet st nr the two hotels above. Quite the best place in town for the price. Honesty is also in a vase in the hall. 6RMS JAN-DEC X/T PETS XCC KIDS CHP

S.Y. HOSTEL: 0292 262322. Craigwiel Rd, off Racecourse Rd close to seafront, 10min walk to centre. Rms for 4 to 14. Booking reqd in June, July, Aug.

CARAVAN SITE: Cragie Park nr centre. 0292 264909. 90 pitches, no tents. Good location is at Heads of Ayr, 9km S on A719 rd to Dunure and Culzean 0292 42269. Most facilities at Sundrum Castle, 10km E off A70; 'a holiday camp atmos', 0292 570057. Skeldon nr Dalrymple, 14km S by A713 on the banks of Doon. 0292 56202.

WHERE TO EAT

FOUTERS: 0292 261391. 2A Academy St. 472/STRATHCLYDE SOUTH: BEST RESTAUS.

THE BOATHOUSE: 0292 280212. 4 S Harbour St. Quayside bar/restau with barmeals/real ale etc one end, dinner the other. River views superb. MED

PIERRE VICTOIRE: 0292 282087. Auld Brig. Gr address, gr setting, Pierre's pops up again (72/EDIN FRENCH and others). Same reliable formula, better puds. INX

FAUSTO'S: 0292 268204. 16 Cathcart St. Credible Italian restau with Fausto Volpi's pasta, steaks etc, Helen Volpi's scrummy desserts. LO 10pm (Fri, Sat 10.30pm). Cl Sun. INX

BONFANTI: 0292 266577. 64 Sandgate. Excl value, Italian. 5-10pm (Sun from 1pm).

THE TUDOR RESTAURANT: 8 Beresford St. 1175/COFFEE SHOPS.

THE STABLES: Queen's Court, behind the tourist office. Coffee shop/bistro with ambience, courtyard seating, imaginative Scottish menu, enlightened attitude. Always improving. 7 days, till 5pm.

THE HUNNY POT: 37 Bereford Terr nr Odeon, next Safeway. Popular coffee bar with snacks, real home baking, chatty atmos. Mon-Sat 10am-10pm, Sun 1-5pm.

WHAT TO SEE

CULZEAN (903/CASTLES); DUNURE VILLAGE (799/COASTAL VILLS) and nearby (3km S on the A719) the ELECTRIC BRAE; BURNS HERITAGE TRAIL (1023/LITERARY PLACES); TROON/PRESTWICK/BELLEISLE/TURNBERRY/GALES (see p.174/GOLF); IRVINE LEISURE CENTRE (752/LEISURE CENTRES).

WHAT TO DO

SWIMMING: V good pool complex at South Beach Rd, 0292 269793, and at Prestwick (off road-in from Ayr), 0292 74015.

RIDING: High Mains Farm, Wallacetown, Maybole 20km S. 046581 504.

TENNIS: Good all-weather courts at Citadel Pl nr TO and Craigie Av nr Craigie Park. Just turn up.

CLUBS: 1332A.

TOURIST OFFICE: 39 Sandgate. 0292 284196. Jan-Dec.

THE BEST OF DUNFERMLINE AND KIRKCALDY

WHERE TO STAY

KEAVIL HOUSE HOTEL, CROSSFORD, DUNFERMLINE: 0383 736258. 3km W of Dunfermline on A994 towards Culross (794/COASTAL VILLAGES) and Kincardine. Rambling mansion house in grounds within a suburban area of town, converted into modern business-type hotel with all facilities incl separate leisure club (not bad pool).

36RMS JAN-DEC T/T PETS CC KIDS MED.EX

PIBLAUCHIE HOUSE HOTEL, DUNFERMLINE: 0383 722282. Aberdour Rd which is off main rd S to Rosyth and Forth Rd Bridge, the A823. House in own grounds just off rd and about 2km from town centre. Rooms in old part or annex. Fairly serviceable accommodation.

40RMS JAN-DEC T/T PETS CC KIDS MED.EX

THE BELVEDERE, WEST WEMYSS nr KIRKCALDY: 0592 54167. 8km E of centre via A955 coast rd at beginning of attractive village, a curious mixture of dereliction and conservation. Views of bay and Kirkcaldy from comfortable rooms within white house with red-tiled roof sitting rather splendidly above harbour. Restau also has views – and decent menu.

22RMS JAN-DEC T/T PETS CC KIDS MED.INX

STRATHEARN HOTEL, KIRKCALDY: 0592 52210. 2 Wishart Pl opp Ravenscraig Park on coast rd and main rd E from town, about 3km from centre. Victorian merchant's house sitting above rd with lawn. Some art nouveau glass and effects. The large park across the rd offers interesting coastal walks with access to coves and beaches. Reasonable facilities.

21RMS JAN-DEC T/T PETS CC KIDS MED.INX

There are no hostels (nearest SYH is at Falkland, 25/40km away) and no campsites in vicinity to recommend. Further along the coast from Kirkcaldy, in the 'East Neuk' and starting at Lundin Links (15km E), there are numerous camp/caravan parks.

WHERE TO EAT IN DUNFERMLINE

KHANS: 0383 739478. 33 Carnegie Dr opp Fire Stn, along from Bus Stn. Central, serviceable Indian restau with herbs in jars and in the sauces (a good sign) and European food on menu (not such a good sign). INX

IL· PESCATORE, LIMEKILNS: 0383 872999. 7km from town via B9156 or to Rosyth, then Charlestown. An Italian restaurateur who moved out of the centre to the coast and does a roaring trade (esp in 'celebrations'). The music tends towards tenors and the food's full of surprises e.g. fresh tomatoes in the Neapolitana (but skip the cheese). The tacky Italian atmos is absolutely spot-on. INX

WHERE TO EAT IN KIRKCALDY

MAXIN: 0592 263406. 5 High St at the W end opp Prestos. Modern and reasonably stylish Chinese. From dim sum to some din at w/ends. Cl Tue. INX

HOFFMAN'S: 0592 204584. Just beyond High St on main rd E out of town, a pub with v decent home-made food. Lunch and 'supper' Sun, Mon, Tues (6-8pm) and dinner Wed-Sat 6-9.30pm. Book at w/ends. CHP

VALENTE'S: 05922 651991. Not sit-in, but *the best* (1196A/FISH 'N' CHIPS).

WHAT TO SEE

PITTENCRIEFF PARK, DUNFERMLINE: (781/TOWN PARKS) and **BEVERIDGE PARK, KIRKCALDY:** 782/TOWN PARKS. **CARNEGIE CENTRE, DUNFERMLINE:** 1146/POOLS. **DUNFERMLINE ABBEY:** 1021/MARY, CHARLIE AND BOB. **PILLANS, KIRKCALDY:** 1217/BAKERS. **JACKIE O'S, KIRKCALDY:** 1331/CLUBS.

WHAT TO DO

SWIMMING/INDOOR SPORTS: As above. **GOLF:** Kirkcaldy is within reach of some of the best in Scotland. See p.174/GOLF. **TENNIS:** Both towns have municipal and private courts. Check TO. **SNOOKER:** Loads of it (Stephen Hendry lives over the water). Check TO.

TOURIST OFFICES
DUNFERMLINE: Abbot House, Maygate. 0383 720999. Easter-Sept.
KIRKCALDY: 19 White's Causeway. 0592 267775. Jan-Dec.

THE BEST OF DUMFRIES

WHERE TO STAY

COMLONGON CASTLE, CLARENCEFIELD: 0387 87283. 14km S via A75 t/off at Collin on B724. Turn rt at Clarencefield, signed for hotel and up 2km avenue of trees to privately owned Castle and hotel in adj manor house. Castle open to public (guests get guided tour before dinner) and seems v much the genuine article. Hotel similarly atmospheric: suits of armour, oak-panelled dining-room; authenticity deriving from genuine family interest rather than contrived decoration. Excl value.
                                                    11RMS   MAR-DEC   T/T   PETS   CC   KIDS   MED.EX

STATION HOTEL: 0387 54316. 49 Lovers' Walk. The best all-round business/tourist hotel in town with decent upgrading of the traditional station-hotel elegance and ambience (from 1896), though not as dead central as similar types. 'Bistro' as well as dining-room.
                                                    32RMS   JAN-DEC   T/T   PETS   CC   KIDS   TOS   MED.EX

CRIFFEL INN, NEW ABBEY: 038785 244. The Square in New Abbey, the village famous for Sweetheart Abbey (976/ABBEYS), nestling below Criffel (1036/ FAVOURITE HILLS), 12km S of Dumfries on A710. A fine wee village pub with rooms above. Snug bar with ales: Broughton Bitter/Oatmeal Stout. Great bar meals.
                                                    5RMS   JAN-DEC   X/T   PETS   CC   KIDS   INX

EDENBANK/LAURELBANK: 2 reasonably-priced places on Laurieknowe, a main rd leading S from centre. Edenbank (0387 52759) is small townhouse hotel with bar. Lauriebank (69388) more a guest house, privately owned, more intimate.
                                  10/4RMS   JAN-DEC/FEB-NOV   T/T   X/T   PETS   CC/XCC   KIDS   INX/CHP

MABIE HOUSE: Interesting, individual hotel 7km S on A710 New Abbey rd. An inx country house adj the very walkable Mabie Woods. Jazz on Sundays. Mt bike hire. Good for kids.
                                                    10RMS   JAN-DEC   X/T   PETS   CC   KIDS   INX

No SYH or other hostel accommodation.

No camping and caravan parks recommended in immediate area. Nearest: SANDYHILLS: 0387 78257. 34km S by A710. Well-managed and equipped site in prominent beach location. 30 pitches on grass/sand. Apr-Oct.

WHERE TO EAT

PIZZERIA IL FIUME: 0387 65154. An unmarked restau (always a good sign), just inside Dock Park by St Michael's Bridge. From corner of carpark, go 50m up Octocentenary Walk, restau is underneath Riverside Bar. Usual Italian menu but great pizzas and cosy tratt atmos. 6-10pm. Cl Tue.   INX

BENVENUTO: 0387 59890. 42 Eastfield Rd. Off Brooms Rd extn of St Michael's Bridge Rd in a suburban shopping mall consisting of Piero's chip shop/ice-cream place and this, his Italian restau. 6-10pm, 7 days.   INX

BRUNO'S: 0387 55757. 3 Balmoral Rd. Off Annan Rd, the A75. Here for years; perhaps inconsistent, but it would be inconceivable to be without Bruno's in Dumfries (1207/CHIPSHOPS). 6-10pm, Cl Tue.   INX

LUCKY STAR: 0387 53655. 43 English St. Pedestrian part of town centre. It's not Italian; they say it's the best Chinese. Lunch/till midnight.   INX

WHAT TO SEE

ROCKCLIFFE 793/COASTAL VILLAGES; ROCKCLIFFE TO KIPPFORD 1070/COASTAL WALKS; SOUTHERNESS 1115/GOLF IN GREAT PLACES; SWEETHEART ABBEY 976/ABBEYS; CRIFFEL 1036/FAVOURITE HILLS; CAERLAVEROCK 874/BIRD WATCHING PLACES; CAERLAVEROCK CASTLE 922/CASTLE RUINS; DUMFRIES MARKET 1277/MARKETS; ELLISLAND FARM 1023/LITERARY PLACES.

WHAT TO DO

SWIMMING: Modern pool on riverside nr Buccleugh St Bridge. 0387 52908.
GOLF: Southerness 25km S on A710 or Powfoot, 20km SW on B724. 04617327.
RIDING: Barend at Sandyhills on 34km S on A710. 0387 78663.

TOURIST OFFICE: Whitesands. 0387 53862. Jan-Dec.

THE BEST OF FORT WILLIAM

WHERE TO STAY

INVERLOCHY CASTLE: 0397 702177. 5km out on A82 Inverness rd. One of Scotland's major hotels. If you're even thinking of asking the price you shouldn't be there. 553/HIGHLANDS: BEST HOTELS. 16RMS MAR-NOV T/T XPETS CC KIDS LOTS

THE MOORINGS: 0397 772797. At Banavie, 5km out on A830 Corpach/Mallaig rd. O/looks the Caledonian canal by Neptune's Staircase, but approached thro' a housing estate. 'Modern' refurbishings, no particular atmosphere and music piped even into the loo, but a competent chef makes the interior dining-room one of the best restaus in the area. Always one vegn option (and it's well done). 24RMS JAN-DEC T/T PETS CC KIDS TOS MED.EX

HIGHLAND HOTEL: 0397 702291. Union Rd. Fairly high above the town which is probably the best place to be, with great views esp when you walk out the front door to the terraced lawns. Rooms basic but foyer has character. This hotel is on the conveyor belt to the Highlands, but its old-fashioned tackiness can be charming. 112RMS MAR-NOV X/X PETS CC KIDS MED.INEX

LODGE ON THE LOCH: Onich, 15km S on A82 08553 237. 562/HIGHLAND HOTELS.

S.Y. HOSTEL at GLEN NEVIS: 5km from town by picturesque but busy Glen Nevis rd. The Ben is above. Grade 1. Fax poss. 0397 2336.

CAMPING/CARAVAN SITE also GLEN NEVIS: Nr hostel. Well-run site, mainly caravans (also for rent). 678/CARAVAN SITES. 0397 2191.

WHERE TO EAT

CRANNOG: 0397 705589. On lochfront. Seafood. 1171/SEAFOOD RESTAUS.

THE MOORINGS: 0397 772797. 5km by A830. See above.

THE FACTOR'S HOUSE: 0397 705767. At the exit gate of Inverlochy Castle and on main A82 Inverness rd, 5km from town. Modern/Mediterranean style decor. Fixed menu; vegn/diets advise. Those that know go, so booking w/ends essential. Also accom: 6 MED.EX rooms. Mar-Nov. MED

LA CREME: A tea-room open during daytime, on the small park at the end of the main st by Wm Low. Shares a doorway with a motor insurer and it's a bit like that inside. But the soup and home baking are fully comprehensive; the cakes need no further endorsement.

WHAT TO SEE

Most of the good things about Fort William are outside the town, but these include some very big items, such as the following:

GLENCOE: 30km S. 848/SCENIC ROUTES; 1075/SERIOUS WALKS; 1004/BATTLE-GROUNDS. **BEN NEVIS:** 6km E on Glen Nevis Rd, 1076/SERIOUS WALKS; **WEST HIGHLAND WAY,** 1079/LONG WALKS. **STEALL FALLS,** Glen Nevis, 830/WATER-FALLS. **GLENCOE,** 1129; **AONACH MOR,** 1128/SKIING.

NEVIS RANGE GONDOLA: Aonach Mor (see below) is open all year and is now a major attraction. Go up for the incredible view and the air and the Ben over there.

WHAT TO DO

GOLF: Fort William Golf Club, 0397 4644. 5km to Inverness on A82.

SWIMMING/SPORTS: Lochaber Centre, 0397 704 359. Beyond main st and Alexandra Hotel. Squash, sauna, gym, climbing wall, swimming.

TENNIS: One court at Lochaber Centre, free of charge.

SKIING: Aonach Mor. 0397 705825. 12km via A82. Scotland's most modern ski resort (1128/SKIING). Gondola goes up in summer for the view.

BIKE HIRE: At Ski Base Station. Phone as above. Forest trails.

TOURIST OFFICE: Cameron Square. 0397 703781. Jan-Dec.

THE BEST OF HAWICK AND GALASHIELS

Hawick and Galashiels are the largest centres in the region, but distances betw towns aren't great. This page includes Selkirk, Melrose and Jedburgh, all within 20km. See also: BORDERS/BEST HOTELS AND RESTAUS, p.85.

WHERE TO STAY

PHILIPBURN HOUSE, SELKIRK: 0750 20747. 650/COUNTRY-HOUSE HOTELS.   EXP

BURTS, MELROSE: 089682 2285. 485/BORDERS: BEST HOTELS.   MED.EX

WOODLANDS, GALA: 0896 4722. Windyknowe Rd off A7 in Edin direction, A72 to Peebles. Substantial mansion above town centre with elegant hall, spacious public rooms and growing reputation for food and service.

10RMS   JAN-DEC   T/T   PETS   CC   KIDS   TOS   MED.INX

GLEN HOTEL and HEATHERLIE HOTEL, SELKIRK: 0750 20259/21200. Both inexpensive family-run hotels in manor houses with views over town. Well-run, dependable. Selkirk makes a good touring centre.

9/7RMS   JAN-DEC   T/T   X/T   PETS/XPETS   CC   KIDS   INX

HUNDALEE HOUSE, JEDBURGH: 0835 63011. Guest house in beautiful country S of Jedburgh 5km off A68, signed to 'Hundalee'. High above Jed and the ancient Capon Tree, a large family house in nice gardens.

4RMS   MAR-OCT   X/T   XPETS   CC   KIDS   CHP

WHITCHESTER, HAWICK: 0450 77477. On Roberton Rd off A7, 4km S of Hawick. They call it a 'Christian Guest House' and they're a bit too on your case though there's no actual bible-thumping. However, it is the most reasonable accom in the area and the house is tastefully done. Dinner has vegn option.

8RMS   JAN-DEC   X/X   PETS   XCC   KIDS   TOS   CHP

S.Y. HOSTELS: V good in this area. 664/BEST HOSTELS.

CAMPING/CARAVAN PARK: at Jedwater, Camptown 11km S Jedburgh. 08354 219.

Jedburgh Abbey (973)

WHERE TO EAT

MARMIONS, MELROSE: 089682 2245. 490/BORDERS: BEST RESTAUS.

OLD MELROSE STATION: 0896 822546. In station waiting-room. Good reports!

THE OLD FORGE, nr HAWICK: 0450 85298. 491/BORDERS: BEST RESTAUS.

SANDERS, GALASHIELS: 0896 56055. 94a High St. In the northward section towards A7 (and down alley) of main st. **LAIRD'S TABLE:** High St. Both café-restaus that suffice. Cl in evenings.

WHAT TO SEE

THIRLESTANE CASTLE/BOWHILL: 942/COUNTRY HOUSES; **TWEED FISHING:** *see below;* **PENIEL HEUGH:** 966/MONUMENTS; **MERCAT CAFE:** 1191/CAFÉS; **MARY**

QUEEN OF SCOTS' HOUSE: 1012/MARY, CHARLIE AND BOB; ANCRUM: 998/GRAVEYARDS; 898/SWIMMING HOLES; 1308/GALLERIES; ABBEYS at 973/JEDBURGH; 974/DRYBURGH; 977/MELROSE; PRIORWOOD: 768/GARDENS; ABBOTSFORD: 1027/LITERARY PLACES; EILDON HILLS: 1048/HILL WALKS; RUBERSLAW: 1041/FAVOURITE HILLS; SCOTT'S VIEW: 869/VIEWS; LILLIARDS EDGE: 1007/BATTLEGROUNDS; ANDERSONS and CHAS WHILLANS: 1267/1268/WOOLLENS.

WHAT TO DO

SWIMMING: Very good leisure facilities both in and around Hawick and Gala. Galashiels Pool 0896 2154 (1150/SWIMMING POOLS) at Livingston Pl up the hill from the one way main st is excl. Hawick's Teviotdale Leisure Centre 0450 74440 has squash courts, a gym (Universal) and a pool with fun stuff as well as length swimming. Pools also Jed/Selkirk.

GOLF: Good courses at Minto nr Denholm 0450 72180 (18); Selkirk 0750 20427 (9); Melrose 0896 822391 (9); Hawick 0450 72293 (18); Jedburgh 0835 64175 (9). All picturesque, in fair condition, avail to visitors.

RIDING: Bowhill, 0750 20192 (943/COUNTRY HOUSES); Hazeldean, Hassendean Burn 0450 87373. Off A7.

TENNIS: Gala, Abbotsford Terr; Hawick, Wilton Lodge Park; also Melrose.

CYCLE HIRE: Gala, 58 High St 0896 57587; Hawick, 45 N Bridge St 73352.

FISHING: There can be last-minute vacancies even on the famous Tweed. Tweed Foundation: 0898 666 412; Mr J. Leeming's indp agency: 0573 7280. Tackle: Angler's Choice, Melrose, 0896 3070; Tweedside Tackle, Kelso, 0573 24687.

TOURIST INFORMATION

HAWICK: Common Ground. 0450 72547. Apr-Oct.
GALASHIELS: 0896 55551. Apr-Oct.
JEDBURGH: Murray's Green. 0835 63435. Jan-Dec.

THE BEST OF INVERNESS

WHERE TO STAY

BUNCHREW HOUSE: 0463 234917. 5km W on A862. 556/HIGHLS: BEST HOTELS. EXP

CULLODEN HOUSE: 0463 790461. 5km E. 557/HIGHLS: BEST HOTELS. LOTS

DUNAIN PARK: 0463 230512. 6km SW on A82. 559/HIGHLS: BEST HOTELS. EXP

KINGSMILLS HOTEL: 0463 237166. Culcabock Rd. In suburban area S of centre nr A9. Modern, v well-appointed hotel with high standards; excl bedrooms.

84RMS JAN-DEC T/T PETS CC KIDS EXP

STATION HOTEL: 0463 231926. Academy St. Bang in centre, above stn; app by Inverness's fearful one-way system. Good foyer to meet in; grand staircase leads to variable rooms. Rather gloomy dining-room. V trad.

67RMS JAN-DEC T/T PETS CC KIDS EXP

WHINPARK: 0463 232549. 17 Ardross St. Small family hotel across main bridge over R Ness nr Eden Court Theatre. Restau well regarded.

9RMS JAN-DEC X/T PETS CC KIDS TOS CHP

GLENDRUIDH HOUSE: 0463 226499. Old Edinburgh Rd, the edge of town (centre 3km) with great outlook and welcome. Fresh food, fine malts, comfy and friendly. No smk. 7RMS JAN-DEC T/T XPETS CC KIDS MED.INX

ARDMUIR/BRAENESS/FELSTEAD: 0463 231151/712266/231634. 3 hotels on Ness Bank, along the river opp Eden Court and v central. Felstead more a guest house and cheaper. All family-run, basic. Many other hotels in this st. These ones are decent value. 11/10/7RMS VARIES X/T PETS CC KIDS CHP

S.Y. HOSTEL: 0463 231771. 1 Edinburgh Rd; nr Castle and quite central.

STUDENT HOTEL: 8 Culduthel Rd (opp SYH above). 665/BEST HOSTELS.

CAMPING AND CARAVAN PARKS: Most central (2km) at BUGHT PARK, 0463 237802. Well-equipped and large-scale municipal site on flat river meadow. Many facilities. App via A82 Ft William rd. More picturesque at SCANIPORT, 0463 75351. 8km SW on B862 the scenic route to Ft Augustus. Rural meadow site surrounded by gorse and mature trees. Small, basic.

233

WHERE TO EAT

DUNAIN PARK HOTEL: As above. 3 adj dining-rooms and drawing-room for *avant* and *après*. Where the great and the good burghers come to pay homage to Ann Nicholl's honest-to-goodness cookery and wish they'd left more room for the sideboard full of sweets. Fair wines, excl malts.   MED

THE WHITE CROSS: 0463 240386. 2km off Beauly rd at canal. Paul Whitecross's irresistible menu, the best food in town. Cl Sun/Mon.   MED

PIERRE VICTOIRE: 0463 225662. 75 Castle St. Restaus have been on-off at this site nr the Castle. PV has moved in (again) from the Edinburgh base and their unfussy French cuisine is here at its best. Till 11pm. (72/FRENCH RESTAUS.)   INX

LA RIVIERA at the GLEN MORISTON HOTEL: 0463 223777. Ness Bank. On rd along river with dining-room (kind of) o/looking. Italian cuisine, but hotel atmos; you wouldn't drop in for a quick spag. They do try.   MED

ROSE OF BENGAL: 0463 233831. Ness Walk just over main bridge on busy riverside rd to Eden Court Theatre. Unprepossessing, but more than adequate Indian nosh. In the Curry Guide. Till 11.45pm 7 days. Also **RAJA:** 237190, behind Post Office.   INX

EDEN COURT THEATRE: 0463 221718. Bishop's Rd. Self/S restau in this important theatre complex (1323/THEATRES) with large windows o/looking river. Roasts, vegn, salads. Lunch and 5.45-7.45pm on show nights.   CHP

WHAT TO SEE

CULLODEN (1002/BATTLEGROUNDS); **LOCH NESS** (739/MAIN ATTRACTIONS); **THE PHOENIX** (710/GREAT PUBS); **EDEN COURT THEATRE** (1323/THEATRES). **SOUTH BANK, LOCH NESS** (857/SCENIC ROUTES); **GLEN AFFRIC** (814/GREAT GLENS).

THE NESS ISLANDS: Islands in the stream of R Ness joined by iron bridges and to both banks; a fine place to stroll of an evening. App via Bught Park or from Ness Walk (by Eden Court) and from Dores Rd.

HEBRIDEAN LOUNGE: Closed at press-time after one too many Invernusian shindigs. For teuchterism at its best/worst try **SHOWTIME at CUMMINGS HOTEL,** 1339/CEILIDHS.

WHAT TO DO

GOLF: Inverness Club. 0463 239882; Torvean (on A82) 0463 237543. Championship course at Nairn, 25km E (1106/GREAT GOLF). 066752787.

SWIMMING: Inverness Baths. 0463 233799 (1151/SWIMMING POOLS).

RIDING: Loch Ness Equicentre. 0463 75251. Dores 16km SE along L Ness.

TENNIS: Inverness Tennis and Squash Club. Bishop's Rd. 0463 230751. Also Municipal Courts at Bellfield Park (just turn up, 7 days).

CYCLE HIRE: Sharp Cycles, 0463 236684; Pedalway, 0463 233456.

TOURIST OFFICE: Castle Wynd. 0463 234353. Jan-Dec.

THE BEST OF OBAN

WHERE TO STAY

MANOR HOUSE: 0631 62087. Gallanach Rd. On southern coast rd out of town towards Kerrera ferry, o/looking bay. Quite elegant in contemporary style and a restau that serves, in an intimate dining-room, probably the best meal in town.
11RMS JAN-DEC T/T PETS CC KIDS TOS EXP

BARRIEMORE HOTEL: 0631 66356. Corran Esplanade. The last hotel on a long sweep of hotels to N of centre and though I'd have to admit that I haven't tried all of them, I'd say this was streets above the rest. 464/STRATHCLYDE NORTH HOTELS.
11RMS MAR-JAN X/T PETS XCC KIDS INX

CALEDONIAN HOTEL: 0631 63133. Station Sq. There are several Victorian/municipal gothic edifices in Oban from the days when, as now, there were many visitors. It's hard to know what to recommend since rooms vary enormously as does service etc. However, at least here you are quite definitely at the centre of things – I mean the port. Try and get a room at the front; and eat out.
70RMS JAN-DEC T/T PETS CC KIDS MED.EX

FOXHOLES: 0631 64982. Lerags 6km S, off A816. Set amongst low hills, a modern hotel with mod cons and peaceful surroundings. Home-grown food and fairly

234

ambitious menu. Good value. 7RMS MAY-OCT X/T PETS XCC KIDS INX

S.Y. HOSTEL: 0631 62025. On Esplanade i.e. on the front. Grade 1.

CAMPING/CARAVAN SITES: Gallanochmore Farm and Ganavan Sands, along Esplanade and coast rd (3km); an attractive grassy site adj to the v popular beach/leisure area (so not quiet, but plenty to do). 80 pitches, no tents. 0631 66479. Book.

WHERE TO EAT

THE MANOR HOUSE: See above. Seafood plus. Booking essential.

AIRDS HOTEL: 0631 73236. Port Appin. 40km N by A828. A wee way to go for dinner, but if in the area you might want to eat at one of the best restaus in Scotland. 459/STRATHCLYDE N: BEST RESTAUS.

GALLERY RESTAURANT: 0631 64641. Argyll Sq. Unpretentious, all-purpose restau from snacks to high teas, and dinner till 10pm. CHP

SALMON CENTRE: 08526 263. 12km S at Kilninver on L Feochan. Seafood with a view.

THE BARN BAR: 0631 64501. 6km S at Lerags nr Foxholes Hotel (see above). Both these places just outside town to south enjoy good local reputations.

THE STUDIO: 0631 62030. Craigard Rd. Simple fare/solid rep. Book. 5-10pm. INX

WHAT TO SEE

DUNOLLIE CASTLE: On rd to Ganavan. 926/RUINS.

GLEN LONAN: Great wee glen starting 8km out of town. 820/GLENS.

SEA LIFE CENTRE: 16km N on A28. 748/PLACES TO TAKE KIDS.

RARE BREEDS FARM: 4km S from Argyll Sq. 747/PLACES TO TAKE KIDS

McIAN GALLERY: 1310/GALLERIES; **OBAN INN:** See MALTS, p.195.

McCAIG'S TOWER or FOLLY: You can't miss it, dominating the skyline. A circular granite coliseum. Superb views of the bay. Many ways up, but a good place to start is via Stevenson St, opposite Cally Hotel. Free, open all year. 969/MONUMENTS.

KERRERA: The island in the Sound reached by regular ferry from coast rd to Gallanach (4km town). Mon-Sat 8am-6pm, Sun 10.30am-5pm, but turn the board round if ferry not obviously running. 0631 63122 (T.O.). A fine wee island for walking, but pack your lunch.

LISMORE: The other, larger island. Ferry from Oban (Calmac) or Port Appin (passengers only). 1344/MAGICAL ISLANDS.

DUNSTAFFNAGE CASTLE: Signed and visible off A85 betw Oban and Connel (7km). 13th-century and still occupied! Impressive setting and in good repair. Chapel in the woods. Cl Thu and Fri. HS

ARDCHATTAN: 20km N via Connel. Along N shore of L Etive, a place to wander amongst ruins and gardens. Tea-room. (997/GRAVEYARDS.) If you're along that way, go to the end of the rd at Bonawe where the famous granite that cobbled the world was (and still is) quarried. Bonawe Ironworks is open as a museum. HS

WHAT TO DO

GOLF: Glencruitten, 0631 62868. (1117/GOLF IN GREAT PLACES).

SWIMMING: Oban Swimming Pool at Dalriach Rd. 0631 65013.

PONY TREKKING: Achnalarig Farm, Glencruitten, 0631 62745.

WINDSURFING: Oban Windsurfing, Ganavan. 0631 64380. Also at Linnhe Marine, 063173 227. 32km N via A828. Incl waterski and sailing. (1132/ WATERSPORTS.)

FISHING: Plenty possible on lochs and Rivers Awe and Avich. Check Tourist Office for availabilities and permits.

BIKE HIRE: Oban Cycles, 0631 66996.

TOURIST INFORMATION: Argyll Sq. 0631 63122. Jan-Dec.

THE BEST OF PERTH

WHERE TO STAY

BALLATHIE HOUSE, KINCLAVEN: 025083 268. 20km N of Perth via Blairgowrie rd A93/left follow signs after 16km just before the famous beech hedge; or A9 and 4km N, take B9000 thro Stanley. A comfy, welcoming baronial shooting- lodge with lawns down to Tay. Relaxing, civilised.

38RMS   JAN-DEC   T/T   PETS   CC   KIDS   TOS   LOTS

HUNTINGTOWER HOTEL: 0738 83771. Crieff Rd (1km off the A85, 3km W of ring route A9 and signed). Elegant, modernised mansion house in landscaped gardens just outside town. Subdued, wood-panelled restau with decent menu and wine-list. Good service.

28RMS   JAN-DEC   T/T   PETS   CC   KIDS   TOS   MED.EX

ROYAL GEORGE: 0738 24455. Tay St by the Perth Bridge over the Tay to the A93 rd to Blairgowrie and relatively close to Dundee rd and motorway system. Bridge is illuminated at night. A THF town-centre hotel with Georgian proportion and elegance. Queen Victoria came by in 1842.

43RMS   JAN-DEC   T/T   PETS   CC   KIDS   MED.EX

WATERYBUTTS LODGE, nr ERROL: 0821 642894. 22km E of Perth towards Dundee via A85; turn rt for Errol Station (no need to go into Errol), cross railway, left at T junct, thro Grange and rt to cross line again then immed rt for 1km. Hunting, shooting, fishing country house amidst herb gardens (*sic*). Everyone round same table for dinner. Great value.

7RMS   JAN-DEC   X/X   PETS   CC   XKIDS   INX

SUNBANK HOUSE: 0738 24882. 50 Dundee Rd. On main rd out of town over river but removed from traffic and with good views of town and Tay. Friendly and decent value. Nr Branklyn Gardens/Kinnoul Hill (see below).

11RMS   JAN-DEC   X/T   XPETS   CC   KIDS   INX

S.Y. HOSTEL: 107 Glasgow Rd in suburban area off main rd 1km centre. Grade 1 hostel, mostly larger dorms. No café. 0738 23658.

CAMPING AND CARAVAN PARKS: SCONE RACECOURSE, 0738 52323. 4km NE centre via A93 to Blairgowrie and left after Scone Palace. Grassy, flat site amongst whispering pines. 150 pitches. Also **CLEEVE,** 0738 39521. off Glasgow Rd nr ring route (2km) and 3km from centre. Narrow tree-ringed site nr road. Sheltered, but some traffic noise. 100 pitches.

WHERE TO EAT

PIERRE VICTOIRE: 0738 444222. 38 South St. Perth was perfect territory for the invasion of PV, which is taking over Scotland (72/EDINBURGH FRENCH), and this one has quickly become *de rigueur*. Cheap and v cheerful bistro. Cl Sun.

INX

NEWTON HOUSE HOTEL, GLENCARSE: 0738 86250. Visible from main Dundee rd A85 in bypassed vill 9km from Perth. Family hotel with restau and lighter bar meals; a secret waiting for wider recognition (but book w/ends).

MED

TIMOTHY'S: 0738 26641. 24 St John's St. For ages the only restau in the area that ever featured in guidebooks. The formula of open sandwiches (starters are called snitters, mains are smorrebrod) with baked potatoes and fondues still packs 'em in. Morning coffee/lunch and 7-10pm. Cl Sun and Mon.

INX

ALMONDBANK INN: 0738 83242. Main st, Almondbank. Old pub looking down to R Almond in village 4km along Crieff rd W of ring route and A9. Pub lunches/suppers (6.30-8.30pm). People come from all over. Book w/ends.

INX

MARCELLO'S: 143 South St. Not a restau, but for those craving Italian food, this is the best pizza in town. Takeaway only. 12-11pm (midnight Fri/Sat).

NO 33: 0738 33771. Kinnoull St. Bar with bar meals and *à la carte* restau serving v credible and v edible seafood (1172B/SEAFOOD RESTAUS). Queenies from Knoydart, excl bouillabaisse, fish as is. Complementary puds like elderflower ice-cream and the best selection of white wine in town. LO 9pm.

INX(BAR)/MED

BETTY'S: 67 George St. An old-world parlour tea-room with excl home baking and toastie type snacks, opp the Art Gallery. 10am-5.30pm (Sun noon-6pm summer only).

STRANGEWAYS: 24 George St. A modern/modish bar, pale wood and lighting *circa* 1990. Long list of designer lagers. Typical bar/café food served noon-6/7pm incl Sun (breakfast's a good idea).

WHAT TO SEE
KINNOULL HILL 1044/FAVOURITE HILLS; THE FERGUSSON GALLERY
1307/GALLERIES; McINTYRE'S 1210/BAKERS; GLENDOICK 1301/GARDEN CENTRES;
ELLERY'S 1228/DELIS.

CHERRYBANK GARDENS/BRANKLYN GARDENS: Cherrybank is off Glasgow Rd, 18
acres of formal gardens around the offices of United Distillers, notable esp for
heathers (open May-Oct 9am-5pm). Branklyn is signed off Dundee Rd beyond
Queen's Bridge; park and walk 100m. A tightly packed cornucopia of typical
garden flowers and shrubs. Open 7 days 9.30am-dusk.

PERTH THEATRE: 0738 21031. Long est (1935) and Scotland's most successful
repertory theatre with wide-ranging mixed prog and bar/coffee bar and restau.
Essential all-round centre even for non-theatregoers.

WHAT TO DO
SWIMMING: Large leisure centre with flumes pool and 'training' pool for lengths.
Part is outdoors. Best app via Glasgow Rd. 0738 30535.

SPORTS CENTRE: The Gannochy or 'Bells' Complex for multigym (Universal),
squash (5 courts), badminton etc. Hay St off Barrack St. 0738 22301.

GOLF: Interesting course on Moncrieffe Island in the middle of the Tay, 0738
25170. Good course at Murrayshall, New Scone (see RESTAUS, above); excellent
course at Blairgowrie (1116/GOLF IN GREAT PLACES), 0250 2622.

TENNIS: Robert Douglas Park, Scone. Info (office hrs) 0738 39911 x3167.

TOURIST INFORMATION: 45 High St. 0783 38353. Jan-Dec.

THE BEST OF STIRLING

1388

MAP 6

D4

WHERE TO STAY
THE GEAN HOUSE, ALLOA: 0259 219275. 12km E. 492/CENTRAL: BEST HOTELS.

STIRLING HIGHLAND: 0786 475444. 494/CENTRAL: BEST HOTELS.

BLAIRLOGIE HOUSE: 0259 61441. 7km E on A91. 495/CENTRAL: BEST HOTELS.

PARK LODGE: 0786 474862. 32 Park Terrace off main Kings Park Rd, 500m from
centre. Rather posh hotel in town house nr the park and golf course. Full of
pictures and fabrics and *objets*; summer lawn at the back. Dinner taken (and
recommended) at the Heritage, below. 9RMS JAN-DEC T/T PETS CC KIDS MED.EX

THE HERITAGE: 0786 473660. 16 Allen Park, a quiet suburban st v close to centre,
tourist office and main Bannockburn Rd. Owned by same folk as above; cheery
French chef. An inexp and welcoming Georgian townhouse.

4RMS JAN-DEC T/T PETS CC KIDS MED.INX

CASTLE HOTEL: 0786 472290. Castle Wynd, which is no more than a cannon-ball's
throw from the Castle itself and one of the best locations in town. Rooms above
the pub in this historic building are basic, but all face the front and have views of
the meandering Forth far below. Great value, if short on service. Ghost Walks
start from here (see below). 5RMS JAN-DEC X/T PETS CC KIDS CHP

STIRLING MANAGEMENT CENTRE: 0786 451666. Here's a place that not a lot of
people have in their filofax: a fully serviced 'budget' hotel on the univ campus
(7km from centre in Bridge of Allan). Usually not full. Many sports/entertain-
ment facilities nearby. Better than you might think – i.e. not just 'college' accom.
74RMS JAN-DEC T/T XPETS CC KIDS INX

S.Y. HOSTEL: On rd up to Castle in recently renovated jail is a new-style hostel,
more like a budget hotel. 0786 473442. 666/BEST HOSTELS.

CAMPING AND CARAVAN PARK: WITCHES CRAIG at BLAIRLOGIE, 5km E on A91, St
Andrews rd. A smallish park conveniently located and in meadow below the
wonderful Ochils. Wallace Monument shows you the way home. 60 pitches.
Apr-Oct. 0786 474947.

WHERE TO EAT

KIPLINGS, BRIDGE OF ALLAN: 0786 833617. **8km N. 503**/CENTRAL: BEST RESTAUS.

HARVIESTON INN, TILLICOULTRY: 0259 52522. **18km E. 502**/CENTRAL: BEST RESTAUS.

39: 0786 473929. 39 Broad St, on rd up to castle. Not tried. Cl Sun/Mon.

RIZZIOS: 0786 473052. Though this book recomms few walk-in-off-the street hotel restaus, this one is v well done. On ground floor of Stirling Highland (494/CENTRAL: BEST HOTELS) in converted school, this Italian Ristorante is good for pasta/pizza lunch or more elaborate dinner. INX

THE EAST INDIA COMPANY: 0786 471330. 7 Viewfield Pl. Some say it's not as good as it was, some say it's the best Indian north of the border. I'll stick my neck out and say it's the best Indian in town. Certainly a good atmosphere in woody basement room. Open 7 days till 11pm. INX

THE REGENT; 0786 472513. 30 Upper Craigs. The most reliable and genuine Chinese restau. Good service. Canton/Peking. 7 days. INX

ITALIA NOSTRA: 0786 473208. 25 Baker St. Great name. Usual Italian tratt paraphernalia: orange lighting, crazy decor, good service and the waiters wear neckerchiefs. Not bad grub and busy atmos. 7 days. 11pm/midnight. CHP

WHAT TO SEE

STIRLING CASTLE 904/CASTLES; **WALLACE MONUMENT/THE PINEAPPLE** 962/967/ MONUMENTS; **BANNOCKBURN/SHERIFFMUIR** 1009/1010/BATTLEGROUNDS; **THE OCHILS** 1049/HILL WALKS; 1053/GLEN AND RIVER WALKS; **LOGIE OLD KIRK** 1000/GRAVEYARDS; **PARADISE** 901/SWIMMING HOLES; **DUNBLANE CATHEDRAL** 988/CHURCHES.

THE GHOST WALK: A nightly walk through the old part of the town nr the Castle: 'a world of restless spirits and lost souls' (sound familiar?). Promenade theatre that's rather well done. Starts from Castle Hotel or Whistlebinkies pub nightly June-Sept at 9.30, with an earlier 'family' walk at 7pm. Book (not essential) on 0786 450945.

RAINBOW SLIDES: Nr Railway Stn. A leisure centre with good 25m pool and gym (Pulsestar) and for kids 3 water slides of varying thrill factors. Open 7 days (Sat and Sun till 4pm). Check times: 0786 462521.

WHAT TO DO

SWIMMING/SPORTS: See above. There's also a pool at the University Sports Centre and at the Stirling Highland Hotel (with squash).

GOLF: Stirling Golf Course v central at Queens Rd. Quite testing and one of best in area. 0786 464098.

BIKE HIRE: 0786 450809. Stewart Wilson Cycles, 49 Barnton St.

TOURIST INFORMATION: Dumbarton Rd. 0786 475019. Jan-Dec.

THE BEST OF ULLAPOOL

WHERE TO STAY

ALTNAHARRIE INN: 085483 230. 2km Ullapool on other side of L Broom (by private boat). One of the very best (640/COUNTRY-HOUSE HOTELS).

7RMS   APR-OCT   X/X   PETS   XCC   KIDS   LOTS

THE CEILIDH PLACE: 0854 2103. 14 W Argyle St. An all-round great place to stay, eat and hang out. (568/HIGHLAND HOTELS).

24RMS   JAN-DEC   X/X   PETS   CC   KIDS   MED.INX

MOREFIELD MOTEL: 0854 612161. Edge of town A835 heading N. An odd set-up: a proper drive-in motel in a housing estate. Real 'cabins' are small, interior and round the back, but there's something funky about it and the seafood is a revelation (1170/BEST SEAFOOD RESTAUS). 12RMS   APR-OCT   X/T   PETS   CC   KIDS   CHP

TIR ALUINN: 0854 612074. Leckmelm 5km S on A835. Stay in a country-house hotel on the cheap. Own grounds, great views over L Broom. The rooms may not be colour co-ordinated or the hallways groaning with antiques, but it's not so much run down, as just not run up – and this applies to your bill.

16RMS   MAY-SEPT   X/X   PETS   XCC   KIDS   CHP

S.Y. HOSTEL: 0854 2254. On Shore St (the Front) converted from cottages. Grade 2. Fax booking poss. Also hostel at Acininver, Achiltibuie 40km by rd but 22km by footpath – a good base for this scenic area; best to book in summer through Head Office 041 226 3976.
CAMPING/CARAVAN SITE: Ardmair Point. 6km N on A835. 0854 2054.

WHERE TO EAT

THE CEILIDH PLACE: as above (568/HIGHLANDS: INEXP HOTELS).

THE MOREFIELD HOTEL: as above (and 1170/SEAFOOD RESTAUS).

THE FERRY BOAT INN: 0854 612366. On Shore St. Bar meals at lunch, hotel dining at night. Has been recommended, I haven't tried it.

WHAT TO SEE

Nothing too vital in town comes rushing to mind, but nearby:
THE CORRIESHALLOCH GORGE: 20km S (831/WATERFALLS); **AN TEALLACH** 40km S by road (862/VIEWS); **ACHILTIBUIE** 40km NW (853/SCENIC ROUTES). **STAC POLLAIDH** (pron 'Polly', 1035/HILLS); **KNOCKAN GALLERY** (1260/CRAFTS).

TOURIST INFORMATION: Shore St. 0854 612135. Easter-Nov.

THE BEST OF WICK AND THURSO

WHERE TO STAY

FORSS HOUSE HOTEL nr THURSO: 0847 86202. 8km W on main A836. A v reasonably priced country-house hotel on the main rd along the N coast. Light, relaxing public rooms; breakfast in the conservatory. 2 chalets in grounds as well as bedrooms. I'd say quite definitely the best hotel in these parts. Fishing and superb walks in grounds. 7RMS   JAN-DEC   T/T   PETS   CC   KIDS   MED.EX

ROYAL HOTEL, THURSO: 0847 63191. Trail St in town centre. Pleasantly old-fashioned hotel with atmosphere of commercial hotel in days gone by. Spreads along st with vast number of rooms, some of which are rather fine; bus parties do alight and fill them up. 105RMS   JAN-DEC   T/T   PETS   CC   KIDS   MED.INX

PORTLAND ARMS, LYBSTER: 05932 208. On main A9 20km S of Wick and 45km S of Thurso by A895. Old coaching-inn in coastal village though A9 is not nr coast or harbour. Owned until recently by Lord Thurso; a previous owner has taken it back and may develop the restau. Spacious residents' lounge and popular bar/lounge with meals and malts. Loyal clientele.

20RMS   JAN-DEC   T/T   PETS   CC   KIDS   TOS   MED.INX

MELVICH HOTEL, MELVICH: 06412 206. Roadside inn 28km W of Thurso and 10km W of Dounreay on main coast rd, the A836. Friendly, family-run place over-looking Melvich Bay and estuary of Halladale River. Rooms in modern annexe.

Bar meals and dining-room with some local produce.

14RMS JAN-DEC T/T PETS CC KIDS MEDJNX

S.Y. HOSTEL: 095581 424. At Canisbay, John O'Groats (7km). Wick 25km. Reg bus service. The furthest flung YH on the mainland.

CAMPING AND CARAVAN PARK, DUNNET BAY: 084782 319. On grassy strand nr wonderful crescent of beach; a nature reserve. 14km N of Thurso.

THURSO, SCRABSTER RD: 0847 64631. Exposed clifftop site to W of town.

WHERE TO EAT

LA MIRAGE, HELMSDALE: 04312 615. 60km S. 582/HIGHLANDS: INX RESTAUS. INX

THE BOWER INN: 095586 292. In the middle of the nowhere betw Wick and Thurso; off coast rd at Castletown on B876. Old coaching inn with dining-room and bar meals. Timber beams, open fires, a real country pub. LO 9.30pm. Good Sunday lunch. May have to book for dining-room. INX

SINCLAIR BAY HOTEL, KEISS: (pron 'kees'). 095583 233. 15km N of Wick on A9 to John O'Groats. Good local rep for fresh seafood etc. INX

THE UPPER DECK, SCRABSTER: 0847 62814. 3km W of Thurso in busy port area o/looking ferry terminal for Orkney. Fifties kind of room above pub with great port view; not big on seafood despite proximity. Mainly noted for steaks, haddock and chips etc. Lunch and 7-11pm, 7 days. INX

DUNNET TEAROOM by DUNNET HEAD: 0847 85774. 15km N of Thurso by coast rd. Tea-room with extensive menu. LO 9pm. 587/HIGHLANDS: INX RESTAUS. CHP

WHAT TO SEE

DUNBEATH: 32km S of Wick (1025/LITERARY PLACES/GLENS); **THE CAIRNS OF CAMSTER:** 15km S of Wick (959/PREHISTORIC SITES); **THE BETTYHILL MUSEUM:** 50km W of Thurso (1313/MUSEUMS); **THE NORTH COAST BEACHES:** 812/BEACHES.

THE TRINKIE: A walk along the rocky coast E of Wick. Foll signs for Old Wick Castle. Flat rocks and open-air pool. 2km further for the Brig O'Trams.

WHAT TO DO

SWIMMING: Thurso Pool. Sessions: Usually till 8pm, Sat and Sun 4pm. 0847 63260.

GOLF: Wick 0955 2726. Thurso 0847 63807. Reay 0847 81288.

SURFING AND WINDSURFING: Esp round Thurso. TO have leaflet about beaches.

RIDING: Dunnet Trekking. Glorious trekking on Dunnet Beach. 0847 85689.

BIKE HIRE: From Bike and Camping Shop. 0847 66124.

TOURIST INFORMATION

WICK: Whitechapel Rd. 0955 2596. Jan-Dec.

THURSO: Riverside. 0847 62371. Apr-Oct.

HOLIDAY CENTRES
Pitlochry

WHERE TO STAY
KILLIECRANKIE HOTEL: 0796 473220 (**528**/TAYSIDE HOTELS). MED.EX

PINE TREES: 0796 472121. Off Main St (**562A**/TAYSIDE HOTS). MED.EX

DUNFALLANDY HOUSE: 0796 472648. Quiet, family country house. MED.INX

WHERE TO EAT
KILLIECRANKIE HOTEL: As above. Restau/excl bar meals. INX

THE OLD SMITHY: 0796 472356. Main St. Coffee shop/restau. LO 8.30pm. INX

MILL POND COFFEE SHOP: At Burnside 'continental' apartment block, 500m main st up Braemar Rd. Excl home-baking (med.inx suites to rent). LO 6.30pm. MED

THE LOFT, BLAIR ATHOLL: 0796 481377. 12km N (**533C**/TAYSIDE RESTAUS).

WHAT TO SEE
THE SALMON LADDER: From Main St and across dam to see 34-pool fish ladder (salmon leaping May-Oct) and Hydro Board displays (if you like that sort of thing).

BEN Y VRACKIE: Local fave with fab Trossachs views climbed from Moulin (2km from town). Rd behind Moulin Inn. Carpark. 734m. Scree at top; and goats.

FASKALLY WOODS/LINN OF TUMMEL WALKS: Well-marked woodland walks around L Faskally and Garry River; can incl the Linn (rapids) and Pass of Killiecrankie (**1008**/BATTLEGROUNDS). Start: Town/Garry Br/Visitor Centre.

WOOLLEN SHOPS: Many major chains and local shops in one small area/the main street. **PITLOCHRY THEATRE:** (**1322**/THEATRES). **QUEEN'S VIEW:** (**871**/VIEWS). **EDRADOUR DISTILLERY:** (**1245**/WHISKY TRAIL); **MACNAUGHTONS** (**1271A**/OUTFITTERS).

Inveraray

WHERE TO STAY
THE GREAT INN: 0499 2466. Old estate inn still owned by Duke of Argyll nr Castle and o/looking loch and main road. MED.INX

LOCH FYNE HOTEL: 0499 2148. On A83 rd out of town towards west, overlooks loch. Personally run. Good bar meals. MED.INX

WHERE TO EAT
GREAT INN/LOCH FYNE: Bar meals espec. See above. CHP

LOCH FYNE OYSTER BAR: 04996 217. 14km E on A83 (**1168**/SEAFOOD RESTAUS). INX

CREGGANS INN: 036986 279. 32km E and S via A83/A815. On opp bank of L Fyne, but 35mins by rd. Bar meals/restau (**465**/STRATHCLYDE NORTH: RESTAUS). MED

WHAT TO SEE
INVERARAY CASTLE: Home of the Duke of Argyll and clan seat of the Campbells. Spectacular entrance hall; chronicle of Highland shenanigans unfurls in the gilded apartments. Fine walks in grounds espec to the prominent hill and folly (45mins up). Apr-Oct. ADM

CRARAE: 15km S on A83; **STRONE WOODLAND:** 17km E on A83 (**766**/GARDENS). **AUCHINDRAIN:** 8km S on A83; **INVERARAY JAIL:** **1317**/MUSEUMS; **ARGYLL WILDLIFE PARK:** 4km S on A83 (**744**/PLACES TO TAKE KIDS).

St Andrews

WHERE TO STAY
OLD COURSE HOTEL: 0334 74371 (**513**/FIFE: BEST HOTELS). LOTS

RUFFLETS: 0334 72594 (**514**/FIFE: BEST HOTELS). EXP

RUSACKS: 0334 74321. A Forte hotel, rather exp (but most hotels in St Andrews seem over-exp). Nr all courses and o/looking the 18th of the Old. Nice sun lounge but dining-room very interior. LOTS

ASHLEIGH HOUSE: 0334 75429. 37 St Mary's St. On Crail rd (A917) and towards E Sands Leisure Centre 1km from centre. Good value, recent (and curious) conversion; some 'attic' rooms. Golfy, on a budget. INX

ARGYLE HOUSE: 0334 73387. 127 North St. On corner of Murray Park with numerous guest house alternatives. This one is central and adequate. INX

THE SPORTING LAIRD: 0334 75906. Playfair Terr. Central; fine. MED.INX

WHERE TO EAT
THE PEAT INN: 033484 206. 15km SW (518/FIFE: BEST RESTAUS). EXP

THE GRANGE INN: 0334 72670. 4km E off Anstruther rd A917. 726A/BEST PUBFOOD.

BABUR: 0334 77778. 89 South St. A fine Indian restau as good as any in Edin/Glas foodwise, though not cheap. T/away deals for students. MED

THE MERCHANT'S HOUSE: 1187/COFFEE SHOPS. Also **BRAMBLES,** 5 College St, another favourite with superb home-baking. Mon-Sat 10am-5pm (Sun 2-5pm).

WHAT TO SEE
THE TOWN ITSELF: The lanes, cloisters, gardens and the University Halls and Colleges. The Harbour and the Botanic Gardens.

THE CASTLE RUINS: Founded in the 13th century on promontory; good for clambering over. There's an 'escape tunnel' to explore if you're not tall.

BRITISH GOLF MUSEUM: Sophisticated A/V exhibn illustrating history and allure of the game. Even non-players will enjoy. Also and nearby, nr the beach: **THE HIMALAYAS:** Putting that's just piles of fun. Apr-Oct till 8pm, 7 days.

MANY GOLF COURSES (1108/GREAT GOLF); **WEST SANDS/KINSHALDY BEACH** (810/BEACHES); **LEUCHARS CHURCH:** 9km by A91 N (987/CHURCHES); **TENTSMUIR:** 20km by A91/A919 N (892/WILDLIFE RESERVES); **EARLSHALL CASTLE:** 11km N by A91 (908/CASTLES); **NEW PICTURE HOUSE** (1326/CINEMAS); **JANETTAS** (1223/ICE-CREAM); **ST ANDREWS FINE ART** (1310/GALLERIES); **THE CATHEDRAL** (936/RUINS); **SEA-LIFE CENTRE** (748/KIDS).

Callander

1394
MAP 6 C3 ## WHERE TO STAY
ROMAN CAMP: 0877 30003. 493/CENTRAL: BEST HOTELS. LOTS

LUBNAIG HOTEL: 0877 30376 Leny Feus (as below). They say excl! INX

BROOK LINN: 0877 30103. Leny Feus off main A84 just beyond High St, uphill 500m; one of the highest houses in the town and with stunning views. Stream runs through garden. V friendly and excl value. CHP

POPPIES: 0877 30329 At quieter end of main st, small mansion. Great value. INX

BRIDGEND: 0877 30130. 100m main st on A81 to Glasgow. Roadside inn, oddly tudoresque. Pub d/stairs, beer garden. Rooms have character. INX

DUNDARROCH, BRIG O'TURK: 08776 200. 12km W via A821 in heart of Trossachs, a small country house at the end of L Achray. Good base for walks. No evening meal, but adj pub provides (734/PUB FOOD). MED.INX

WHERE TO EAT
BRAEVAL, ABERFOYLE: 0877 2711 (499/CENTRAL: BEST RESTAUS). EXP

ROMAN CAMP: As above (493/CENTRAL: BEST RESTAUS). EXP

CREAGAN HOUSE, STRATHYRE: 0877 4638 (501/CENTRAL: BEST RESTAUS). INX/MED

DUN WHINNY: 1188/COFFEE SHOPS.

MYRTLE INN: 0877 30919. Stirling Rd, the main A84; one of first/last houses. Old roadsde inn, fireplace and low ceilings. Decent pub food mostly home-made. Good vegn. 7 days, lunch and 5.30-9pm. INX

LADE INN: 0877 30152. Kilmahog 2km from town, on corner of main A84 and A821 to Trossachs. Trad road/riverside inn and good all-round busy place. Food a bit freezed, but some home-made e.g. Cullen Skink. 2 rms above. LO 9pm. CHP

CROWN HOTEL: 0877 30040. Upstairs restau that locals like, esp the lady in that gr bookshop over the road! 7 days till 10pm+.

WHAT TO SEE

The scenery of THE TROSSACHS (1092/WALKING AREAS; 858/SCENIC ROUTES); also DOUNE CASTLE: (933/RUINS; 900/SWIMMING HOLES);

DOUNE MOTOR MUSEUM (1315/INTERESTING MUSEUMS).

CYCLING: For Trossach trails, enquire at TO.

GOLF: See GOLF/GREAT PLACES, P. 175-6.

BRACKLINN FALLS: Take rd to golf course from main st heading up-hill and foll signs 1km to carpark. Clear path to Falls (1km) and some interesting river/glen perspectives if you explore around. Also 2 good W/Falls – FALLS OF LENY: 2 carparks on main A84 NW to Crianlarich, 5km from town. From first carpark Falls are on other side of rd 200m. From 2nd, walk downstream for riverside stroll (2km).

Aviemore

For Aviemore Hotels etc, see BEST OF THE SKIING, p. 177-80.

Royal Deeside: Ballater and Banchory

1395
MAP 3
B4/D4

WHERE TO STAY

INVERY HOUSE, BANCHORY: 03302 4782. 534/GRAMPIANS: BEST HOTELS.   LOTS

BANCHORY LODGE, BANCHORY: 03302 2625. 538/GRAMPIANS: BEST HOTELS.   EXP

RAEMOIR, BANCHORY: 03302 4884. Large mansion in secluded grounds 3km town by Raemoir Rd off A93. Relaxed/discreet. 9-hole golf/tennis.   LOTS

TOR-NA-COILLE: 03302 2242. Town mansion above/just off main A93 on way in from Ballater. Nr golf. Antiques in tasteful/individual rooms.   EXP

DARROCH LEARG, BALLATER: 03397 55443. Town mansion above/off (at tight bend) A93 on way in from Braemar. Reasonably priced/friendly.   MED.INX

WHERE TO EAT

THE OAKS, BALLATER: 03397 55858. 539/GRAMPIANS: BEST RESTAUS.   EXP

INVERY HOUSE/BANCHORY LODGE/RAEMOIR, BANCHORY: as above.   EXP/MED

THE GREEN INN, BALLATER: 03397 55701. In main sq. Small restau (with 3 inx rms above), Scottish fresh prod, home cooking. Lunch/7-9pm.   MED

THE WHITE COTTAGE nr ABOYNE: 03398 86265. On main A93 4km towards Banchory. Cottage dining and conservatory. Good home cooking/atmos   MED

WHAT TO SEE

CRAIGIEVAR/DRUM/FASQUE: see CASTLES, p. 142; LOCHNAGAR: 1087/MUNROS.

GLEN MUICK: GLEN WALKS, p. 163; CAMBUS O'MAY: 902/SWIMMING HOLES.

GOLF: Well managed/picturesque courses, open to visitors at both Ballater: 0338 55567. and Banchory: 03397 2447. Both 18.

FISHING: Difficult, not imposs, on Dee (try 03398 86891 or 0738 21121) or on R Feugh (north bank only) – permits Feughside Inn 033045 225.

WALKS: Walks down both sides of Dee esp Ballater-Cambus O'May 7km.

VIEWPTS: Up Craigendarroch, the Hill of the Oaks, Ballater, from Braemar Rd (45mins). Scolty Hill and Monument, Banchory. Ask directions.

GAY SCOTLAND THE BEST!

Edinburgh

BARS AND CLUBS

NEW TOWN BAR: 556 3971. 26 Dublin St. Newest bar in residential st of New Town. Civilised and still cruisy. D/stairs lounge more lovable and snooker room where the boys only occasinally get a look-in, and diesels dominate, 7 days till 12.30am. **THE LAUGHING DUCK:** 225 6711. 24 Howe St. The duck's had its feathers ruffled by the New Town (above); will it just drift gracelessly downmarket? Probably not – despite OTT karaoke (T/W/Sun), it'll go on forever. Disco Fri/Sat. Till 2am. **CHAPPS:** 558 1270. 22 Greenside Pl. Part of frontage of Playhouse Theatre. Discreet on outside (and recently revamped), basic clone-zone inside; many eyes on your entrance. Leather queens welcome. Not many girls! Dance-floor upstairs. Convenient for the 'Gardens of Fun'! 7 days, 9.30pm-4am.
STAR TAVERN: 439 8070. 1 Northumberland Pl. Corner of the New Town nr Drummond Sq. Mixed at lunchtime (so you can't hold hands over your sausage roll), more cosy knit in the evenings, 7 days till 12.30am.
FRENCH CONNECTION: 225 7651. Rose St Lane North nr Castle St (and beside the burned-out remnants of the Blue Oyster Club, once a hot gay bar that got too hot). Somewhere betw Amsterdam and the Damned. You may have to ring to get in.
CITY CAFE: Blair St; **LEITH OYSTER BAR:** The Shore, Leith. Both v mixed but viable.

No separate clubs that are on every night – Chapps and the Duck have dance-floors. In addition, there are likely to be clubs at 12 Shandwick Pl on Sundays and at **THE STORE,** Niddry St, off the High St, on Wed 10pm-3am.

OTHER PLACES

BLUE MOON CAFE: 556 2788. 60 Broughton St. Friendly, neighbourhood café with wholefoody menu and whole kinds of folk dropping in. 7 days till 11pm.

WEST & WILDE BOOKSHOP: 556 0079. 25A Dundas St. Great small bookshop specialising in gay and lesbian literature; release from the straight jackets! 7 days.

HOTELS

MANSFIELD HOUSE: 556 7980. 25A 57 Dublin St. Desirable New Town address and prob the best gay stay in town, the service can be, well . . . whimsical. Candelabra in the hall, various other camperie. No public rooms – you'll have to leave your door open to meet anybody. New Town Bar (see above) up the street.
6RMS JAN-DEC X/X XPETS XCC XKIDS MED.INX

LINDEN HOTEL: 557 4344. 9 Nelson St. Also in New Town halfway betw Duck and the New Town Bar. A real hotel; not exclusively gay. Thai restau (v good) and bar (not gay).
20RMS JAN-DEC T/T PETS CC KIDS INX

ARMADILLO GUEST HOUSE: 229 4669. 5 Upper Gilmore Pl (off 95 Gilmore Pl) 200m from King's Theatre. Small back street but quite central. Discreet lodgings. Book!
5RMS JAN-DEC X/X PETS XCC XKIDS CHP

Glasgow

BARS AND CLUBS

DELMONICA'S: 552 4803. 68 Virginia St. Rel stylish pub with long bar and booths in quiet lane in Merchant City. Pally, youngish crowd. The room thro the back has gr cabaret atmos though mainly for Glasgow karaoke/cairry-on – most nights. Regular Sun aft. Tues is 'the lassies night'. 7 days till 11.45pm.
AUSTINS: 332 2707. 183A Hope St. Downstairs bar in busy central st. Young crowd, more mixed in daytime; seems renty, be choosy. 7 days till midnight.
WATERLOO BAR: 221 7539. 306 Argyle St. Old-established bar and clientele. You might not fancy anybody but they're a friendly old bunch. Occ cabaret (i.e. a good sing-song). 7 days till midnight (1am Fri, 11pm Sun).
SQUIRE'S LOUNGE: 221 9184. 106 W Campbell St. Below street level, not exactly a dive bar but small and can be cruisy. Mixed ages. DJs most nights too loud and too chatty. 7 days till midnight.
COURT BAR: 552 2463. 69 Hutcheson St. In revamped and fashionable bit of

Merchant city, a pub that ain't. Older crowd, sombre mood of quiet desperation that comes to us all sometimes. Till midnight. Cl Sun.

CLUB XCHANGE: 204 4599. Royal Exchange Sq. Gr club whatever your persuasion but stymied at time of going to press by the City Council curfew whereby you have to be in by midnight and leave by 2am (see p.77). 2 small dry-ice dancefloors for looking at (and, with mirrors, at yourself). Frenetic bar. All ages who like to party. Tue-Sun till 2am, but times will change, so check.

BENNETS: 552 5761. 80 Glassford St. Established disco-disco, where everybody goes in the beginning – and in the end. Saturday Night and Sunday Morning most nights (depending on who you leave with). Dissolve! Wed, Fri-Sun hrs as above.

THE TUNNEL: 204 1000. 84 Mitchell St. Mondays only in this techno, designery disco that for several months in the 1990s was where to be seen. Crowd young and tanned and probably not to be trusted. It's all good to look at. 10pm-2am.

PARISIAN CLUB: 552 7411. 17 King St nr Trongate, E end. Coffee-shop and restau opening after going to press. Musical evenings promised. Mon-Sat 7-10.30pm.

THE GUEST HOUSE: 427 0129. 56 Drumbeck Rd. No reports and, amazingly, it's the only one. (Self-catering flatlet on 770 5213.)

Aberdeen

FLANNIES BAR: 0224 571266. Stirling St nr the station. Small bar and room thro' the back. Mixed Aberdonia. Karaoke, bright lights. Does suffice. 7 days till midnight.

THE CABERFEIDH: (pron 'caberfay'): 0224 212181. Hadden St. Nr the above. Gr club which can really buzz; it's a long way from Barcelona but . . . . Thu-Sun, 10pm-2am.

EXCHANGE CLUB: 0224 213009. Carmelite St. V close to both above. Pals and locals kind of bar/club. Women welcome. 7 days, till 2am (midnight Mon/Tue, 1am Sun).

Dundee

THE GAUGER: (pron 'gay-ger') 0382 26840. 75 Seagate nr Canon Cinema. OK pub, small-city scene, but if you're in Dundee for the night, you might. 7 days till 11/12.

THE EDGE: 0382 22367. 85 Commercial St. Friday night discorama in tech-y basement club (p.209). You won't see who you're going home with until it's too late.

Elsewhere

Not surprisingly, *not* a lot. The following are not gay hotels, but no eyebrows will be raised if you arrive *à deux* and quite like the pictures.

AUCHENDEAN LODGE, DULNAIN BRIDGE, nr GRANTOWN-ON-SPEY: 047985 347. A Highland retreat and a real treat for anybody. Nice gardens, innovative cooking, lots of interesting 'things'. Near skiing and gr scenery, walks etc. 570/HIGHL HOTELS.
7RMS JAN-DEC X/T PETS CC KIDS TOS INX

RAVENSCOURT HOUSE, GRANTOWN-ON-SPEY: 0479 2286. Near Auchendean above but not related. Former manse. Thespian overtones. Conservatory restau. Grantown's a tasteful but conservative town; Freddy and Sammy will make you welcome.
9RMS JAN-DEC X/X XPETS XCC XKIDS INX

NICO'S, GLENMOHR HOTEL, NESS BANK, INVERNESS: The bar Wed only; occ stray gays on other nights. This is not a gay hotel.

Beaches/Outdoors

This ain't the Mediterranean; what do you expect? Choice?

ABERLADY NATURE RESERVE: 1km E of town across wooden bridge; head for dunes and beach. Naturism sometimes poss amongst the nature. Note: be sensible – some of those guys really are birdwatchers (or Nigel Tranter).

And outdoor-enthusiasts might find others in the park or down by the river in the following towns:

GLASGOW: (3 places); **EDINBURGH:** (same); **INVERNESS; DUNDEE; ABERDEEN; KIRKALDY; DUNFERMLINE; AYR, HELENSBURGH:** (Helensburgh); All AYR.

GREAT SCOTTISH JOURNEYS

A miscellany of memorable journeys by trains, boats and planes.

1396 **WEMYSS BAY-ROTHESAY FERRY:** The glass-roofed station at Wemyss Bay is the railhead from Glasgow (60km by road on the A78), and has the atmosphere and vitality of an age-old terminus. The frequent ferry (Calmac) has all the Scottish traits and sausage rolls you can handle and Rothesay (with its Winter Garden and Castle and period seaside mansions) appears out of blood-smeared sunsets and rain-sodden mornings alike, a gentle watercolour from summer holidays past. Calmac 0475 520521.

1397 **LOCH ETIVE CRUISES:** From Taynuilt (Oban 20km) through the long narrow waters of one of Scotland's most atmospheric lochs, a 3hr journey in a small cruiser with indoor and outdoor seating. Pier is 2km from main Taynuilt crossroads on A85. Leaves 2pm (and 10.30am in summer). Travel into the heart of the Highlands, the lochsides inaccessible by car; deer and golden eagles may attend your journey. 08662 430, though booking not essential.

1398 **CORRAN FERRY:** From Ardgour on A861-Nether Lochaber on the A82 across the narrows of L Linnhe. A convenient 5-minute crossing which can save time to points south of Mallaig and takes you to the wildernesses of Moidart and Ardnamurchan and which is a charming and fondly regarded journey in its own right. Runs continuously until 8.50pm summer, 6.20pm winter.

1399 **THE MAID OF THE FORTH CRUISE TO INCHCOLM ISLAND:** The wee boat (though they say it holds 200 people) that leaves every day from Hawes Pier in S Queensferry (15km Central Edinburgh via A90) opp the Hawes Inn and just under the famous Railway Bridge (205/EDIN: ATTRACTIONS). 30min trips under the bridge and on to Inchcolm, an attractive island with walks and an impressive ruined abbey. Much birdlife and also seals. 1.5hrs ashore. Tickets at pier. 031 331 4857.

1400 **THE WEST HIGHLAND LINE:** One of the most picturesque railway journeys in Europe and quite the best way to get to Skye from the south. Travel to Ft William from Glasgow, then relax and watch the stunning scenery, the Bonnie Prince Charlie country (MARY, CHARLIE AND BOB, pp. 155-6) and much that is close to a railwayman's heart, go past the window. Viaducts and tunnels over loch and down dale. Also poss to make the same journey (from Ft William to Mallaig and/or return), by steam train on certain days. Journey time 1hr 45mins. Check 0397 3791/0687 2227. For anyone interested in trains, there's a museum in the restored stn at Glenfinnan. Trains for Mallaig leave from Glasgow Queen St about 3 times a day and takes about 5hrs (INFO: 041 204 2844).

1401 **FROM INVERNESS:** Two less-celebrated, but mesmerising rail journeys start from Inverness. The journey to Kyle of Lochalsh has an Observation Car in the summer months with a courier commentary; the last section thro Glen Carron and around the coast at Loch Carron is esp fine. There are 4 trains a day and it takes 2.5hrs. Inverness to Wick is a 3.5hr journey. The section skirting the E coast from Lairg-Helmsdale is full of drama and is then followed by the transfixing monotony of the Flow Country (it's the best way to see it). There are 4 trains a day in summer. INFO 0463 238924

1402 **THE PLANE TO BARRA:** Most of the island plane journeys pass over many smaller islands (e.g. Glasgow-Tiree, Glasgow-Stornoway, Wick-Orkney) and are fascinating on a clear day, but Loganair's daily flight to Barra is doubly special because the island doesn't have an airport and you land on the beach in the N of the island (11 km from Castlebay) after a splendid approach. The twin otter plane holds 17 passengers and leaves (tide permitting) at around 12.50pm (not Sun in winter). 041 889 3181.

THE ESSENTIAL SCOTTISH BOOKS

FICTION

Iain Banks, *The Wasp Factory/The Bridge* (Little Brown).

George Douglas Brown, *The House with the Green Shutters* (Penguin).

George Mackay Brown, *Greenvoe/The Masked Fisherman* (Penguin).

John Buchan, *The 39 Steps/Short Stories* (Penguin).

Lewis Grassic Gibbon, *Sunset Song* (Canongate).

Neil Gunn, *Highland River/The Silver Darlings* (Canongate/Faber).

Alasdair Gray, *Lanark* (Picador).

Archie Hind, *The Dear Green Place* (Corgi).

James Hogg, *Confessions of a Justified Sinner* (Canongate).

Robin Jenkins, *The Cone Gatherers* (Penguin).

William McIlvanney, *Docherty* (Sceptre).

Bess Ross, *A Bit of Crack and Car Culture* (Balmain).

Sir Walter Scott, *The Heart of Midlothian/The Two Droves and Other Stories/Old Mortality* (Penguin).

Robert Louis Stevenson, *Kidnapped/Master of Ballantrae/Catriona/Short Stories* (Oxford Univ Press).

Muriel Spark, *The Prime of Miss Jean Brodie* (Penguin).

Alexander, Trocthi, *Young Adam* (John Colder).

Irvine Welsh, *Trainspotting* (Serter and Warburg).

NON-FICTION

Boswell and Johnson, *Journey to the Western Islands* (Penguin).

Jim Crumley, *A High And Lonely Place* (Cape).

Raymond Eagle, *Seton Gordon, A Highland Gentleman* (Lochar).

Antonia Fraser, *Mary Queen of Scots* (Methuen).

Elizabeth Grant of Rothimurchus, *Memoirs of a Highland Lady* (Canongate).

Muriel Gray, *The First Fifty: Munro-Bagging Without a Beard* (Mainstream).

Osgood Mackenzie, *100 Years in the Highlands* (Out of print but still available at Inverewe Gardens).

Gavin Maxwell, *Ring of Bright Water* (Penguin).

William Poucher, *The Magic of Skye* (Constable).

John Prebble, *1000 Years of Scotland's History/The Lion in the North/The Highland Clearances/Culloden/Glencoe* (Penguin).

T. C. Smout, *A History of the Scottish People* (Fontana).

Nigel Tranter, *The Story of Scotland* (Lochar).

POETRY

Robert Burns, *The Collected Songs and Poems* (Oxford University Press).

Norman MacCaig, *Collected Poems* (Chatto).

Sorley MacLean, *From Wood to Ridge* (Vintage).

SEVEN THINGS TO DO BEFORE YOU DIE

WALK THE AONACH EAGACH, GLENCOE: The ridge on the right as you travel W through the glen is one of the world's classic high-ridge walks. Do it before you're too doddery as you'll need to be agile and a bit fearless; take a map, a flask of good whisky (be careful!) and somebody who's done it before, and don't attempt if the vertigo gets you. (1075/SERIOUS WALKS.)

SEE THE PUFFINS ON LUNGA IN THE TRESHNISH ISLANDS, OR THE ISLE OF MAY: The latter is more accessible (from Anstruther), but the trip to the Treshnish (from Ulva Ferry on Mull) on a summer's day is a voyage of discovery (incl Staffa). Go in July, walk amongst these enchanting creatures before they disappear back into the Atlantic. Purify the soul. (875/876/BIRDWATCHING.)

SAIL TO ST KILDA: The most W islands in the UK, 110 miles into the Atlantic. Remote, symbolic, superlative in every way, ingrained deep in the spiritual heart of the Scots. The community evacuated in 1930 represented the last in an age of innocence and freedom now gone forever; life was hard but perfectly attuned to this dramatically beautiful place. Highest seacliffs in UK, premier seabird breeding station. Village of Hirta conserved. NTS (031 226 5922) arrange 'working parties' (May-Aug, 14day trips from Oban) or boat charter from Oban 3 times a yr (0254 826591) 10day cruises.

GO FOR DINNER WITH GOOD FRIENDS TO:
The Peat Inn nr Cupar (518/FIFE RESTAUS); Airds Hotel, Port Appin, Argyle (565/HIGHLAND RESTAUS); Braeval Old Mill, Aberfoyle (499/CENTRAL RESTAUS); Kinnaird House nr Dunkeld (641/CO HOUSE HOTELS).

STAY THE WEEKEND WITH SOMEONE YOU LOVE AT:
Suite 27 of One Devonshire Gardens, Glasgow (253/GLASGOW/BEST HOTELS); Altnaharrie Inn, Ullapool (640/COUNTRY HOUSE HOTELS); Auchterarder House, Gleneagles (incl a game on the Queen's Course) (646/COUNTRY HOUSE HOTELS); Kinnaird House (see above).

SEE DAWN ON THE LONGEST DAY FROM THE TOP OF LOCHNAGAR: Nr Ballater via L Muick. Leave evening before and camp/keep vigil. 4hrs to get up. Take map, good boots, food, dram etc. From first light across the Cairngorm Plateau, the Dee Valley, Morvern, Bennachie appear; and God. (1087/MUNROS.)

SAIL THE HEBRIDES on the *Malcolm Miller*: a tall ship where you join in as one of the crew and see the islands from the top of the crow's nest. If you just want to be pampered, try the ***Hebridean Princess*** (0756 701338), which sails once a wk from Oban (Mar-Oct); the lap of the Minch in the lap of luxury (£900-£3,000 per person).

A FEW THINGS THE SCOTS GAVE THE WORLD

Population of Scotland has never exceeded 5 million.

The decimal point	The thermos flask
Documentary films	Anaesthesia
Colour photographs	Antiseptics
Golf clubs	The 18-hole golf course
Encyclopedia Britannica	The bowling green
The hypodermic syringe	The thermometer
Postcards	The gravitating compass
The gas mask	The threshing machine
The advertising film	Insulin
Tennis courts	Penicillin
The motor bus	Interferon
The steam engine	The pneumatic tyre
The fax machine	The modern road surface
The photocopier	Television
Video	Radar
The telephone	The telegraph
The Mackintosh	The kaleidoscope
The lawnmower	Marmalade
Continuous electric light	The self-acting fountain pen
The alpha chip	Gardenias

MAPS

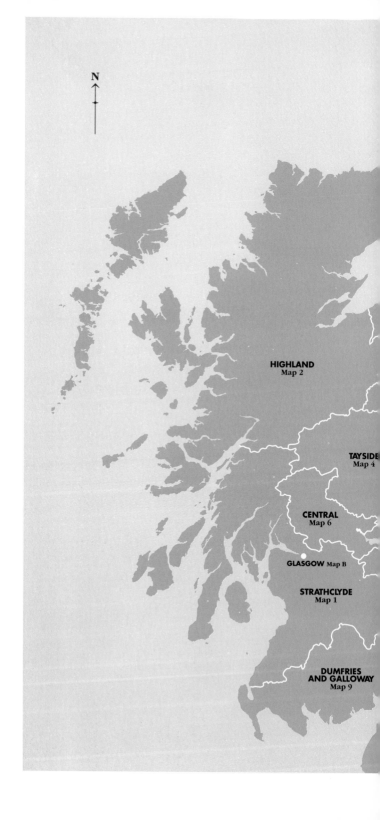

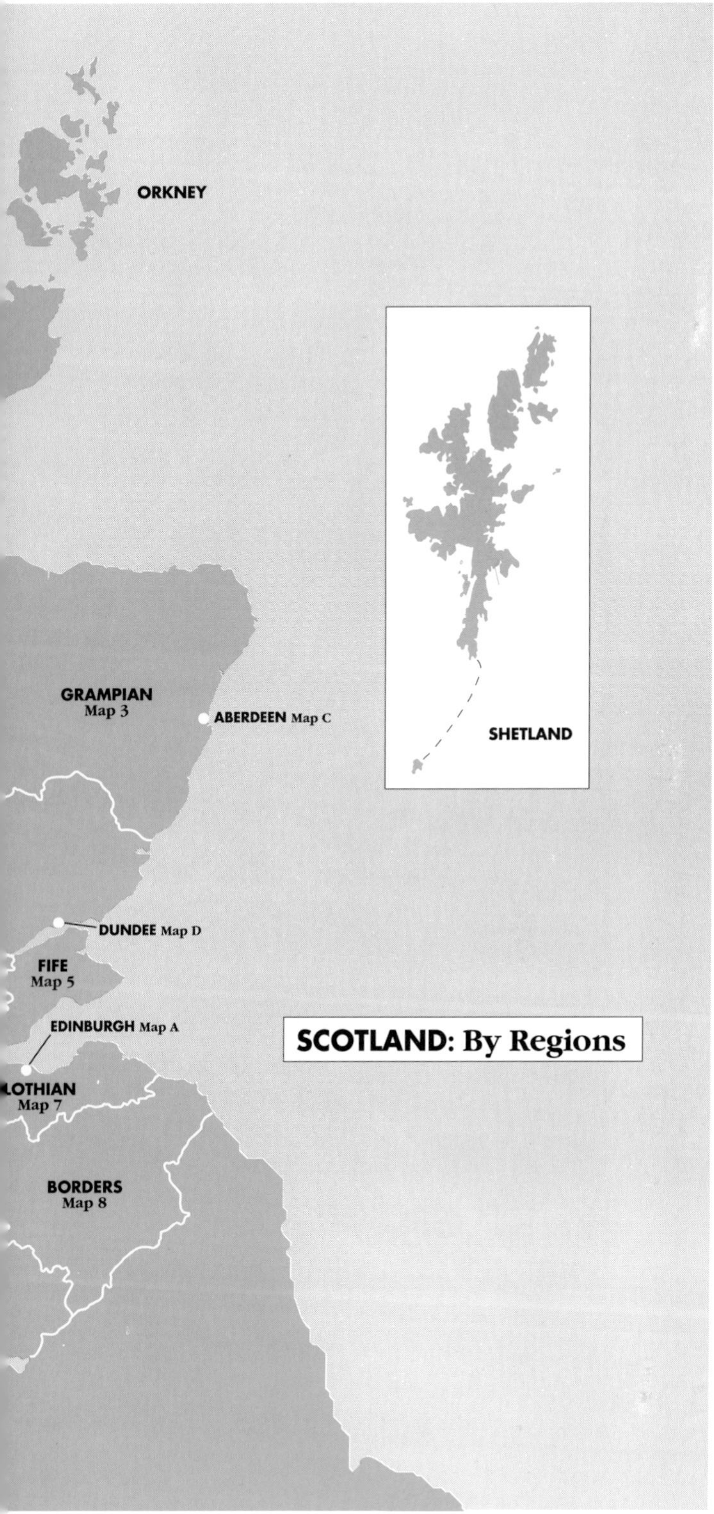

ORKNEY

GRAMPIAN
Map 3

●ABERDEEN Map C

SHETLAND

○DUNDEE Map D

FIFE
Map 5

EDINBURGH Map A

LOTHIAN
Map 7

SCOTLAND: By Regions

BORDERS
Map 8

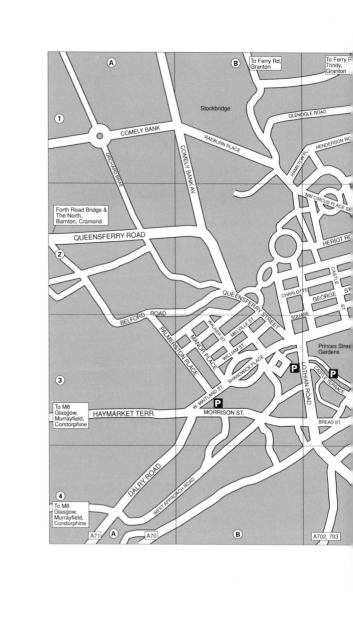

MAP A: Edinburgh City Centre

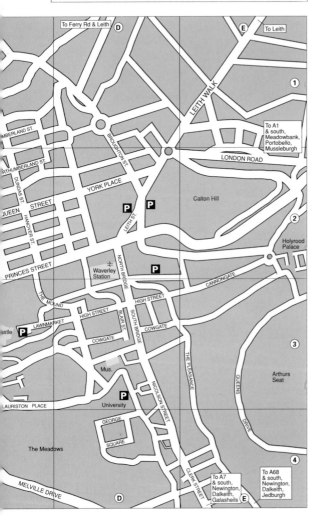

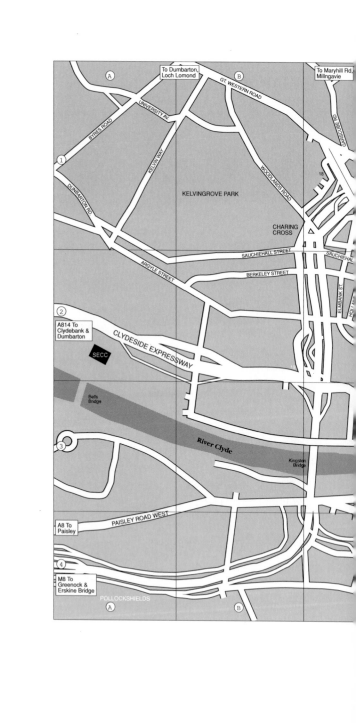

Map B: Glasgow City Centre

Map C: Aberdeen City Centre

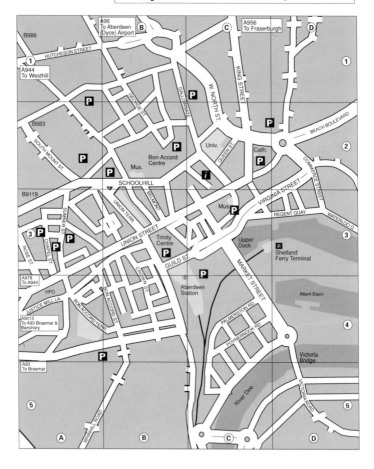

MAP D: Dundee City Centre

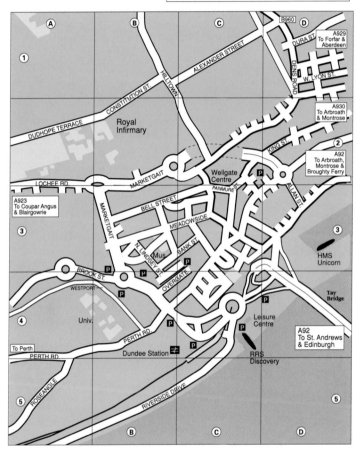

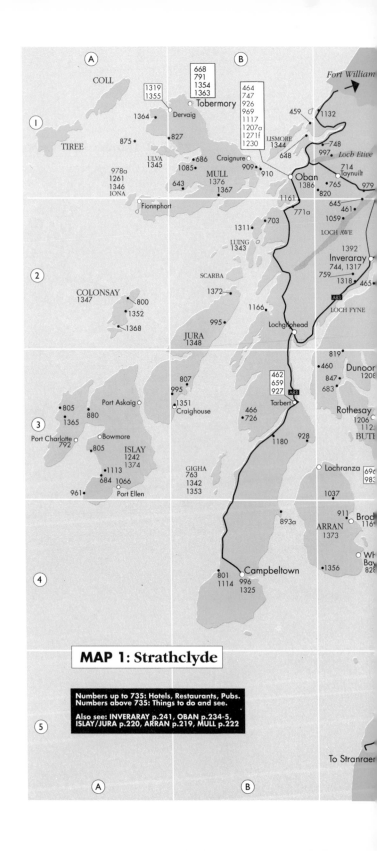

COLL

1319
1355

TIREE

TOBERMORY
668
791
1354
1363

464
747
926
969
1117
1207a
1271f
1230

1364 Dervaig

● Tobermory

827

875

ULVA
1345

686
1085●

MULL
1376
1367

643

978a
1261
1346
IONA

Fionnphort

459 ○
LISMORE
1344

648

Craignure

909
910

Oban
1386

1161

703

1311●

LUING
1343

SCARBA

1372

1166●

995●

JURA
1348

COLONSAY
1347

● 800

●1352

●1368

807
995

1351
Craighouse

Port Askaig ○

805
1365

880

Port Charlotte
792

○ Bowmore

● 805

ISLAY
1242
1374

1113
684 1066
961
Port Ellen

GIGHA
763
1342
1353

466
726

Lochgilphead

462
659
927

Tarbert

1180

928

801
1114

Campbeltown

996
1325

893a

Fort William

1132

748
997 Loch Etive

714
Taynuilt

765
820

979

645
461
1059

LOCH AWE

1392

Inveraray
744, 1317
759
1318

465

LOCH FYNE

771a

A83

819
● 460
847●
683●

Dunoon
1208

Rothesay
1206
112
BUTE

○ Lochranza

696
983

1037

911
● Brod
116

ARRAN
1373

● Wh
Bay
828

●1356

MAP 1: Strathclyde

Numbers up to 735: Hotels, Restaurants, Pubs.
Numbers above 735: Things to do and see.

Also see: INVERARAY p.241, OBAN p.234-5,
ISLAY/JURA p.220, ARRAN p.219, MULL p.222

To Stranraer

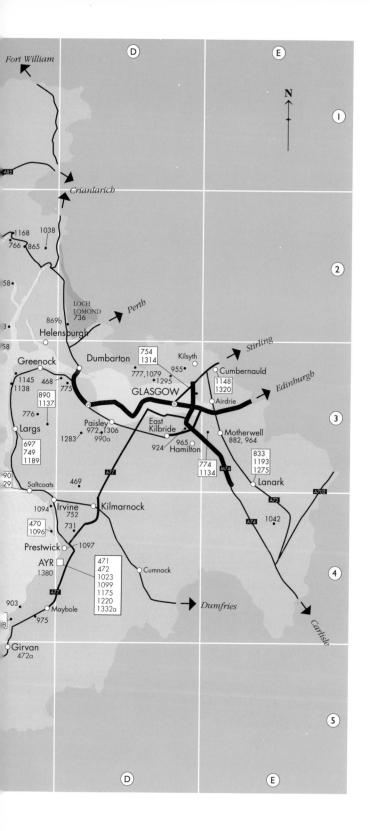

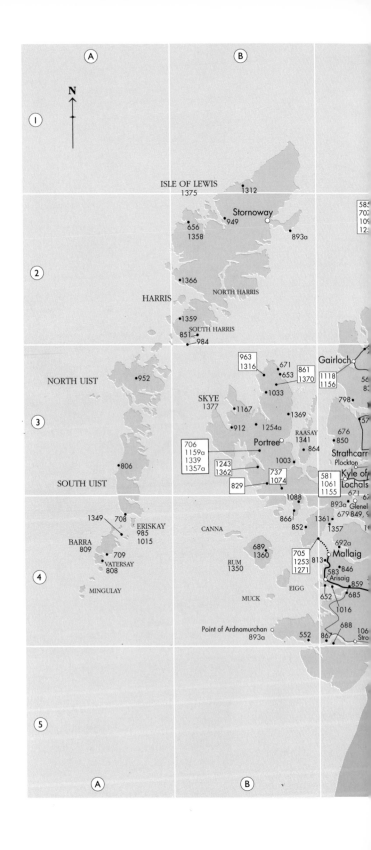

A
B

N

1

ISLE OF LEWIS
1375 •1312

Stornoway
•949

656
1358 •893a

585
707
109
12

2

•1366
NORTH HARRIS

HARRIS

•1359
851•SOUTH HARRIS
•984

963
1316 •671 861
•653 1370
1118
1156

Gairloch

56
83

NORTH UIST •952
SKYE
1377 •1167 •1033
•1369
798•

•912 •1254a
RAASAY
1341 676
•850
57

Portree
706
1159a
1339
1357a
1243
1362
829

1003 •864
Strathcarr
Plockton
581
1061
1155
Kyle of
Lochals

3

•806
SOUTH UIST
737
1074

1088

671
67
893a Glenel
679 849, 9

1349 •708
708
ERISKAY
985
1015
866
852
•1361
1357

692a
705
1253
1271
813•
Mallaig

4

BARRA
809 •709
VATERSAY
808
CANNA
689
1360
RUM
1350
EIGG
583 846
Arisaig
859
652 •685

MINGULAY
MUCK
1016

Point of Ardnamurchan
893a •552 •867
688
106
Stro

5

A
B

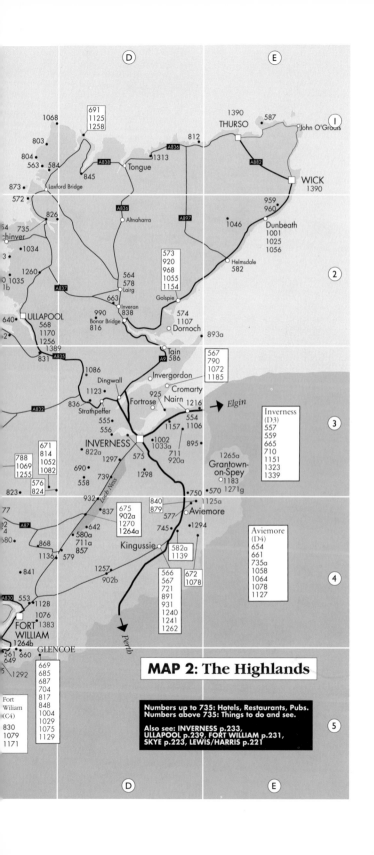

1068

803

804
563   584

873

572

54 735
chinver

3 •1034

0 1035
1b

1260

640•

2•

691
1125
1258

845

A838   Tongue

Laxford Bridge

826

Altnaharra

A837

ULLAPOOL
568
1170
1256
1389

831   A835

1086

Dingwall
1123

A832   836
Strathpeffer

671
814
1052
1082

788
1069
1255

576
824

823•

77

2• A87
4•

680•   868
711a
1136 857

•841

A830 553
•1128

FORT 1076
WILLIAM 1383

1264b   GLENCOE

561 660
649

5 1292

Fort
William
(C4)

830
1079
1171

669
685
687
704
817
848
1004
1029
1075
1129

564
578
Lairg

663
Inveran
838

990
Bonar Bridge
816

1313

A836

A836

A897

573
920
968
1055
1154

Golspie

574
1107
Dornoch

893a

THURSO   587

812

1390   587

John O'Groats

A882

WICK
1390

959
960

1046   Dunbeath
1001
1025
1056

Helmsdale
582

Tain
586

A9

Invergordon

Cromarty
925   Nairn
Fortrose

555•
556

INVERNESS
822a

690•
558

739

932•

•837

580a
642
579

Kingussie

1257
902b

1216   → Elgin

554
1157 1106

•1002
1033a
711
920a   895•

575

1297

1298

Loch Ness

675
902a
1270
1264a

840
879

577

745•

582a
1139

566
567
721
891
931
1240
1241
1262

•750

1125a

Aviemore

•1294

672
1078

Perth

567
790
1072
1185

Inverness
(D3)
557
559
665
710
1151
1323
1339

1265a

Grantown-
on-Spey
1183

570 1271g

Aviemore
(D4)
654
661
735a
1058
1064
1078
1127

MAP 2: The Highlands

Numbers up to 735: Hotels, Restaurants, Pubs.
Numbers above 735: Things to do and see.

Also see: INVERNESS p.233,
ULLAPOOL p.239, FORT WILLIAM p.231,
SKYE p.223, LEWIS/HARRIS p.221

1390

D   E   1

2

3

4

5

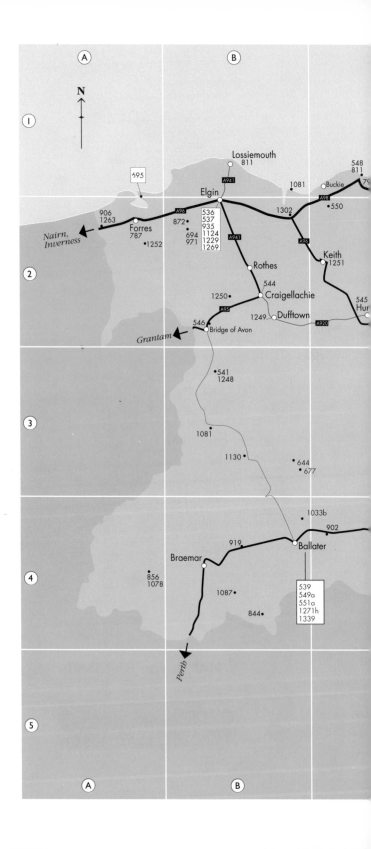

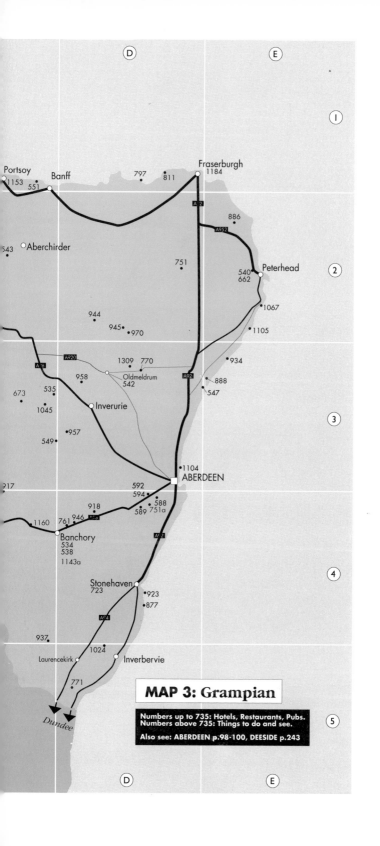

I

Portsoy
1153
Banff
551
797
811
Fraserburgh
1184

A 2

886

A952

543
Aberchirder
751

540
662
Peterhead

2

1067

944
945 970

1105

A920
1309 770
934

A 6
958
Oldmeldrum
542
A92
888

673
535
547

1045
Inverurie

3

549
957

1104
ABERDEEN

917
592
594
918
588
589 751a
761 946
A58
1160
A 2

Banchory
534
538
1143a

4

Stonehaven
723
923
877

A94

937
1024

771
Laurencekirk
Inverbervie

MAP 3: Grampian

Numbers up to 735: Hotels, Restaurants, Pubs.
Numbers above 735: Things to do and see.

Also see: ABERDEEN p.98-100, DEESIDE p.243

5

Dundee

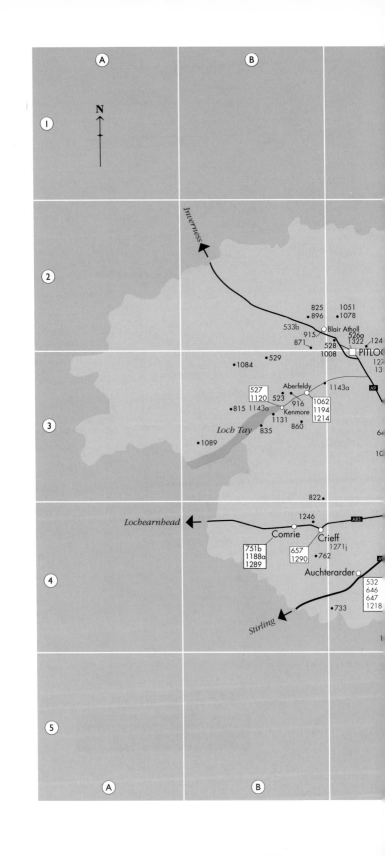

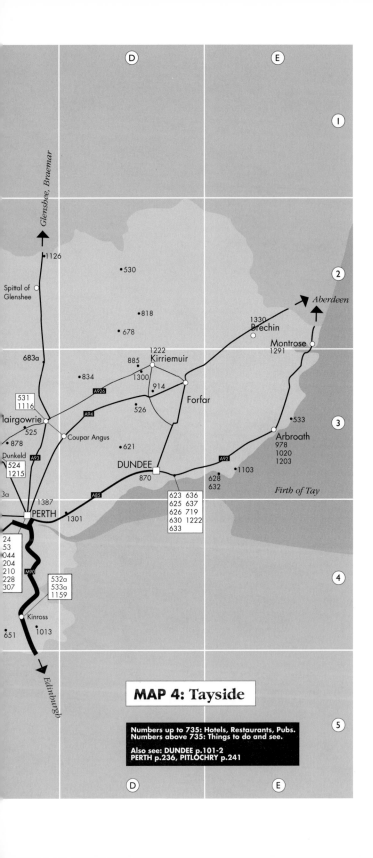

MAP 4: Tayside

Numbers up to 735: Hotels, Restaurants, Pubs.
Numbers above 735: Things to do and see.

Also see: DUNDEE p.101-2
PERTH p.236, PITLOCHRY p.241

N

Ⓐ Ⓑ

①

②

③

A9

907
1186
Falkla

•1047

Glenrothes

Leslie

893•

•1140

④

KIRKCALD
782
1217
1331
1332

781
1021
1146

DUNFERMLINE

M90

794•

Aberdour

516
517
796
986

Firth of Fo

522

Forth Road Bridge   Forth Rail Bridge 205

→ To Edinburgh

⑤

Ⓐ Ⓑ

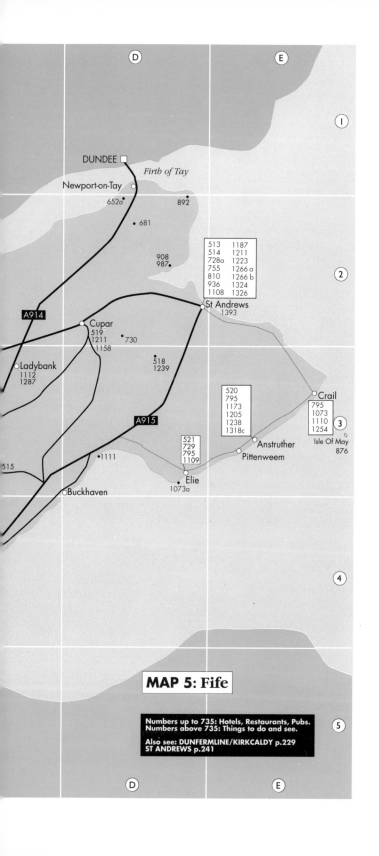

DUNDEE

Firth of Tay

Newport-on-Tay

652a

892

681

908
987

513   1187
514   1211
728a   1223
755   1266 a
810   1266 b
936   1324
1108   1326

St Andrews
1393

A914

Cupar
519
1211
1158

730

Ladybank
1112
1287

518
1239

520
795
1173
1205
1238
1318c

Crail
795
1073
1110
1254

A915

Anstruther
Pittenweem

Isle Of May
876

521
729
795
1109

1111

Elie
1073a

515

Buckhaven

MAP 5: Fife

Numbers up to 735: Hotels, Restaurants, Pubs.
Numbers above 735: Things to do and see.

Also see: DUNFERMLINE/KIRKCALDY p.229
ST ANDREWS p.241

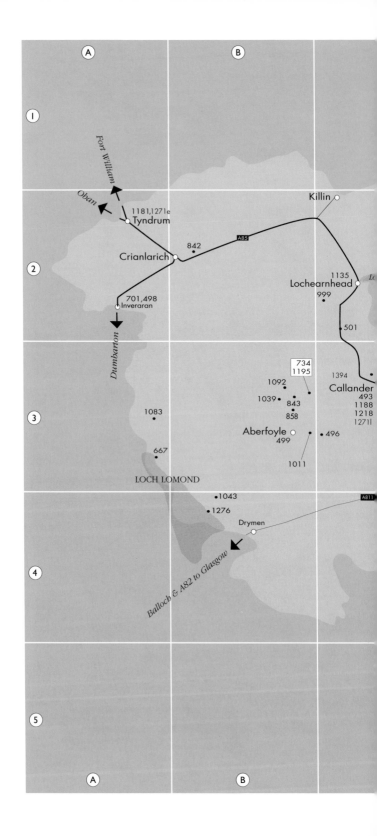

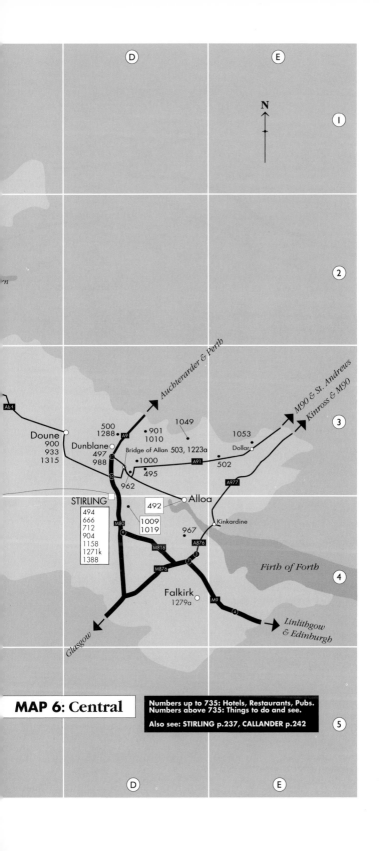

N

Ab1

Auchterarder & Perth

M90 & St. Andrews

Kinross & M90

Doune
900
933
1315

500
1288

A9

901
1010

1049

1053

Dunblane
497
988

Bridge of Allan 503, 1223a

Dollar

1000

495

A91

502

962

A977

STIRLING

492

Alloa

494
666
712
904
1158
1271k
1388

M80

1009
1019

967

Kinkardine

A876

M816

Firth of Forth

M876

Falkirk
1279a

M9

Glasgow

Linlithgow
& Edinburgh

MAP 6: Central

Numbers up to 735: Hotels, Restaurants, Pubs.
Numbers above 735: Things to do and see.

Also see: STIRLING p.237, CALLANDER p.242

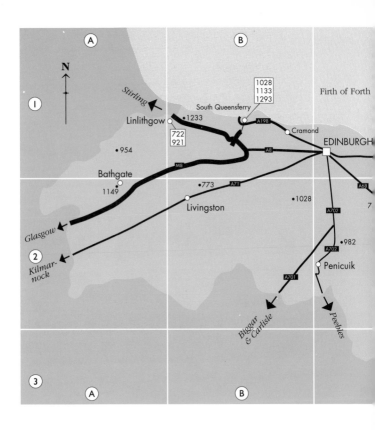

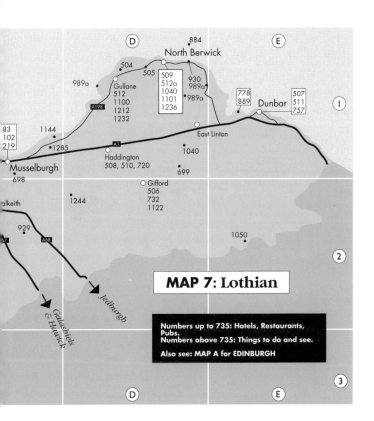

MAP 7: Lothian

Numbers up to 735: Hotels, Restaurants, Pubs.
Numbers above 735: Things to do and see.

Also see: MAP A for EDINBURGH

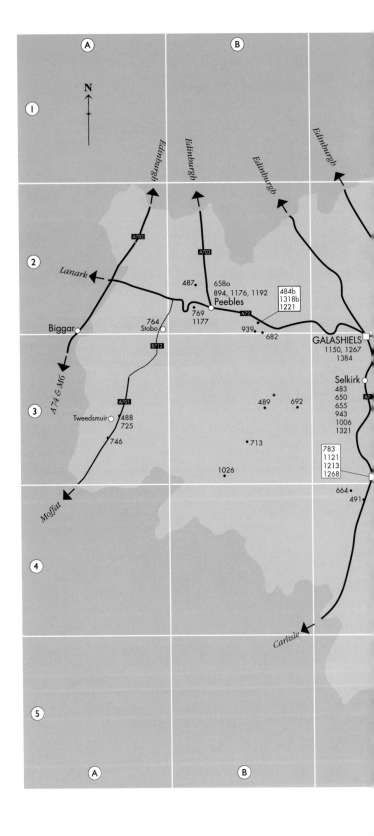

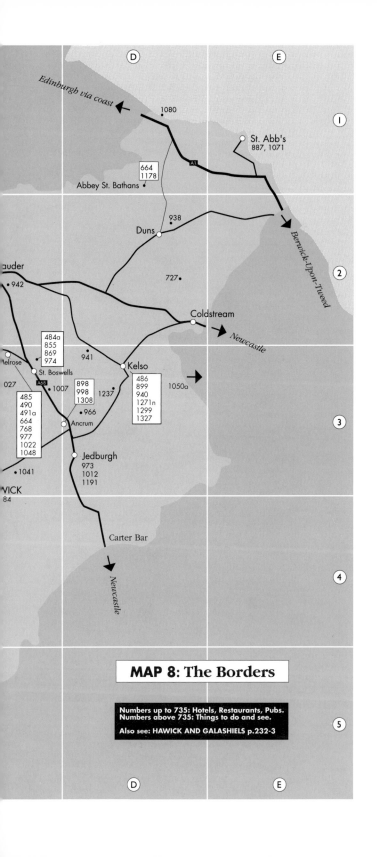

Edinburgh *via coast*

1080

St. Abb's
887, 1071

A1

664
1178

Abbey St. Bathans

938

Duns

Berwick-Upon-Tweed

727

Lauder

942

Coldstream

Newcastle

484a
855
869
974

941

Kelso

486
899
940
1271n
1299
1327

1050a

Melrose

St. Boswells

A68

027   1007

898
998
1308   1237

485
490
491a
664
768
977
1022
1048

966

Ancrum

Jedburgh
973
1012
1191

1041

VICK
84

Carter Bar

Newcastle

MAP 8: The Borders

Numbers up to 735: Hotels, Restaurants, Pubs.
Numbers above 735: Things to do and see.

Also see: HAWICK AND GALASHIELS p.232-3

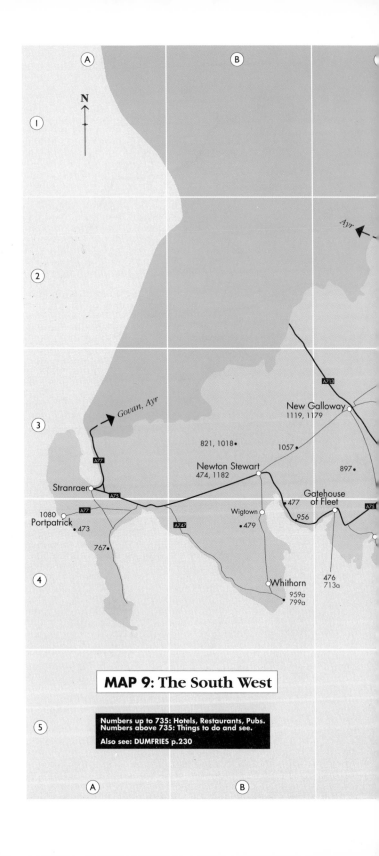

Ⓐ   Ⓑ

N

① ②

Ayr

A713

New Galloway
1119, 1179

③ *Govan, Ayr*

821, 1018•   •1057

A77   Newton Stewart
474, 1182   897•

Stranraer   •477   Gatehouse
A75   of Fleet   A75

1080 Portpatrick   A77   Wigtown•   956
•473   A747   •479

767•   476
713a

④   •Whithorn
959a
799a

MAP 9: The South West

⑤   Numbers up to 735: Hotels, Restaurants, Pubs.
Numbers above 735: Things to do and see.
Also see: DUMFRIES p.230

Ⓐ   Ⓑ

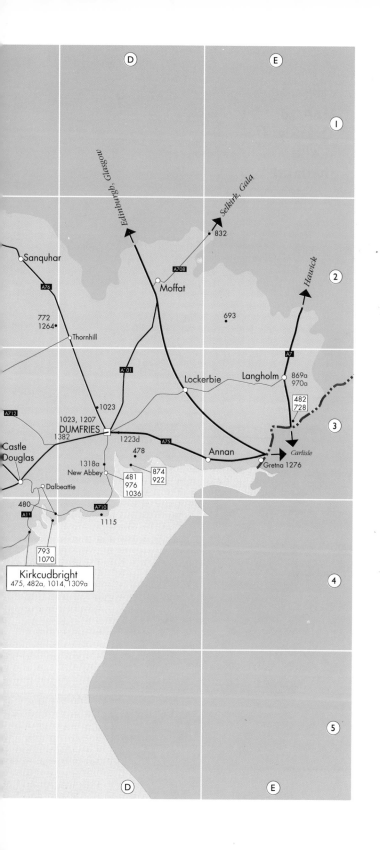

MAP 10:
Orkney
And
Shetland

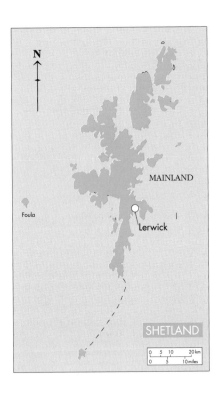

N

MAINLAND

Foula

Lerwick

SHETLAND

0	5	10	20 km
0	5		10 miles

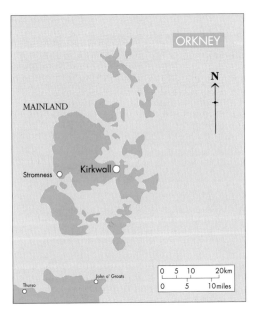

ORKNEY

N

MAINLAND

Stromness

Kirkwall

Thurso

John o' Groats

0	5	10	20km
0	5		10 miles

INDEX

284

286